Rebecca M. Pauly

The Transparent Illusion

Image and Ideology
in French Text and Film

PETER LANG
New York • Washington, D.C./Baltimore • Bern
Frankfurt am Main • Berlin • Brussels • Vienna • Oxford

Library of Congress Cataloging-in-Publication Data

Pauly, Rebecca M.
The transparent illusion : image and ideology in French text and film /
by Rebecca M. Pauly.
p. cm. — (Ars interpretandi=The Art of Interpretation ; vol. 3)
Includes bibliographical references.
1. Motion pictures—France. 2. Motion pictures and literature—France.
3.French literature: film and video adaptations. 4. Intertextuality.
5. Historical films—France—History and criticism. 1. Title. II. Series:
Ars interpretandi (New York, NY); vol. 3.
PN1993.5.F7P35   791.43'0944—dc20   92-16539
ISBN 0-8204-1930-3
ISSN 1043-5778

Die Deutsche Bibliothek-CIP-Einheitsaufnahme

Pauly, Rebecca M.:
The transparent illusion : image and ideology in French text and film /
Rebecca M. Pauly. —New York; Washington, D.C./Baltimore; Bern;
Frankfurt am Main; Berlin; Brussels; Vienna; Oxford: Lang, 1993
(Ars interpretandi ; Vol. 3)
ISBN 0-8204-1930-3
NE: GT

Cover design by George Lallas

The paper in this book meets the guidelines for permanence and
durability of the Committee on Production Guidelines for
Book Longevity of the Council on Library Resources.

© 2003, 1993 Peter Lang Publishing, Inc., New York
275 Seventh Avenue, 28th Floor, New York, NY 10001
www.peterlangusa.com

Printed in the United States of America

for Glenn and Jeff

Table of Contents

A Note on the Films:
The above selections are available for rent or purchase on video or in most cases DVD, all but *Le Retour* with subtitles. *Un Amour de Swann*, *Baisers volés* and *La Nuit américaine* are now available in the original French with subtitles. There are of course hundreds of other French films available on video or DVD or on film. The films studied here can also be presented in chronological order of their production as a study of film history, or the films adapted from literary texts in the order of the literary production. Or these films can be presented chronologically by subject matter to offer a collective mythology of images of French history and civilization, an order which however necessarily acknowledges the double diegesis of portrayed and portrayal. In addition, there are sufficient materials for complete courses on two individual filmmakers, Renoir and Truffaut. A note on the organization of this book: *La Règle du jeu* could be included in the section on original filmscripts of course, just as *Vivement dimanche* could be considered an adaptation from novel to film. It is in fact the originality of certain films, which defies easy generic classification, that brings the critics back to them again and again.

Commercial suppliers of the videos/DVDs presented include: Facets Multimedia (800) 331–6197, Movies Unlimited (888) 331–9850, Films for the Humanities (800) 257–5126, FACSEA (French Cultural Services) (800) 937–3624, Interama (212) 977–4830, Insight Media (212) 721–6316, Vedette Visuals (253) 564–4960, and numerous websites like amazon.com.

Introduction:
The Transparent Illusion

The central paradox of the cinematic experience lies in the intense illusion of reality created on and behind the screen by the projection of two abstract functions: sound and light. Their interrelationship and the relationship between film and time, film and space, film and movement, film and narrative (intrigue, character, description), film as/and writing have been addressed by myriad critical voices. Following the seminal work of Christian Metz, semiotic analysis of the signs proffered by the cinema was almost endless in its own projected scope. More recently, study of cinematic signs has been extended to their relationship to text and context in the light of comparative poetics and cultural pluralism. Concurrently, the relationship between image and identity has undergone a progressive decentering and deconstruction, continuing the chain of evolving constructs whereby "Structuralists identified existentialists as Cartesian, even though existentialists took their position by attacking neo-Kantians as Cartesians. From Sartre contra Brunschvicg to Lévi-Strauss contra Sartre to Derrida contra Lacan, the rush continues to the position of the decentered self."[1]

The significance of film and film criticism has at times been deconstructed to the point of nihilism. In the 1985 *Diacritics* special issue (15:1) on film, Raymond Bellour quotes in "Analysis in Flames" his 1975 article "Le Texte introuvable" included in *Ça: Cinéma* in honor of Christian Metz, an article which appeared again in Bellour's 1979 *L'Analyse du film*. His primary contention is the impossibility of analyzing something as evanescent and evasive as film sound and image. He feels that because film is a moving sound-image, there is no way to attach semiotic textual analysis to a filmic text. This diffusion of meaning stands in somewhat ironic contrast to semiotic structuring of sense in an homage to Metz. As Bellour contends that film cannot even be equated thus to a painting, he fails to address either the painterly aspects of cinematography or the portrait effect of final freeze frames like that of *Les Quatre Cents Coups* (*The 400 Blows*) which leave a lasting "effet-personnage" (effect of character) to coalesce in the spectator's memory/imagination, not unlike the closure of character at the end of a literary text.

Bellour's extreme deconstruction of cinema to a "degré zéro de l'écriture fil-mique" (degree zero of film writing) reflects the ongoing frustration of critics who have for centuries sought a linguistic equivalent of pictorial depiction, the appropriate discourse of images. Lessing, Diderot, Baudelaire and virtually all art critics attempt to narrate the visual experience of the observer, just as Roland Barthes in his 1980 *La Chambre claire* (*Camera Lucida*) sought with the help of earlier Sartrian dialectic an appropriate phenomenology of the photographic image. Much like Barthes anguishing before the *punctum* or the reification, the deadly objectification, of the photo, Bellour feels most acutely the absence at the center of the film image:

> The image is indeed located, with respect to the echo it might receive from language, halfway between the semi-transparency of written titles and dialogue and the more or less complete opacity of music and noise.[2]

Theoretical questions of the relationship between sound, image, text and meaning are undeniably central to film study, but the problem of transparency and opacity in film can be confronted in a different fashion, through consideration of the gamut of diegetic paradigms both depicted and depicting, similar to the narratological opposition of *énoncé* and *énonciation* (enunciated and enunciating), starting with transparent historically authentic documentary or documentary-style filmmaking, passing through realistic historic tales or legends and transpositions to the screen of literary realism, of theater, of fable, to the intertextuality of the self-reflexive, self-conscious New Wave auteur filmmakers, and ending with process as product, with narcissistic reflections of the work of filmmaking.

Without attempting a taxonomy of classic film genres—horror film, comedy, film noir, all stereotypical canons within film criticism—I would like to explore the relationship between the various diegetic thematics presented in the films I treat and the filmmakers' use of narrative voice, characterization (people, animals, objects), presentation of image as memory or imagination, metaphor or metonymy, temporalization through linear or fragmented chronology, structuring of meaning or ideological representation through editing, direction and set decoration. I hope to demonstrate how certain aspects of filmmaking constitute a tradition of the illusion of reality on the screen in both historic and fictional diegeses and how other techniques comprise the movement that unmasked that illusion with its self-reflexive mirrors. Of prime interest are the underlying ideological constructs driving film production and their manifestations in these representations of history, fiction and self in filmmaking. In terms of the broader cultural, historic or sociological significance of the cinema, I propose to explore the implications of Claude Chabrol's quote of Oscar Wilde challenged by Theodore Zeldin in *The French*:

> He [Chabrol] believes that 'writers and artists [including filmmakers] do more than hold up mirrors in which people can recognize with delight their ideology, their rites and their hidden thoughts'; they also provide a model of conduct, they create a way of talking which may at first appear outrageous but is eventually copied almost religiously. He [Chabrol] thinks this imitation is particularly practiced by the bourgeoisie 'which has no personality of its own'; from time to time its mirror gets broken and it seeks out a new model.[3]

Thus is raised the problem of class structure and the question of influence and dominance in the cinema, in a Bourdieu-like inclusion or exclusion from broader sets or paradigms, as well as the importance of prior models for its attitudes, both its reflections of and construction of cultural history. In all the subsequent considerations of film's transparency and opacity, its narrative strategies of focalization, its various modes of discourse, its writing in sound and light, my primary goal is not to establish a hierarchy of film genres with respect to any truthful or accurate recreation of external reality (at best a philosophical problematic), but rather to examine the ensemble of strategies, priorities and even obsessions of the filmmakers in question and their relationship to their subject, whether historic, literary, or a thematic of process. The uncertain sense of self is not exclusively modernist, either, for all filmmaking, whether documentary or historic, treatment of individual or collective fables and myths, or subjective symbology in signs and images, results from the filmmaker questioning simultaneously the process and the product, doubly deconstructing filmic discourse, reflecting in the seventh art the fundamental paradox of modernism in the twentieth century, the seemingly incompatible opposition of technological positivism and the image in crisis. The studies of individual films offered here are intended for all critics of French text and film, and moreover for use in presenting films in a variety of contexts. Variations in the focus of the filmnotes result from the fact that particular films lend themselves to specific critical considerations. As stated in the note appended to the table of contents, these films can be arranged in several formats of presentation for film series or courses. Above all, it is hoped that the following work will provide a research tool, of notes, bibliography and glossary, for all interested readers and spectators.

Notes

Bibliographical note: From semiotics and reader/spectator response theory through deconstruction and postmodernism to the new historicism and cultural studies of all persuasions (feminism, pluralism, etc.) can be found a lasting interest in the comparative poetics of text and image and the ideological implications of such juxtapositions. Jean-Louis Shefer in *Scénographie d'un tableau* and *L'Homme ordinaire du cinéma* addresses the problems of equation between text and image and the self. Pascal Bonitzer, Noël Burch, or Jean-Louis Leutrat in *Kaléidoscope: analyses de film*, and Jean-Louis Baudry with *L'Effet cinéma* also pursue experiential analyses. Other valuable works on the ontology of image include Henri Focillon's *Vie des Formes* and Tom Conley's *Film Hieroglyphs*. François Jost generates a cinematic narratology in *L'Oeil-caméra* and *Le Récit cinématographique*, as does Seymour Chatman in *Story and Discourse*. Gilles Deleuze's seminal *L'Image-mouvement* and *L'Image- temps* explore the phenomenology of the cinematic experience, while Peter Brunette and David Wills offer a comparative study of Derrida and film theory in *Screen/Play*. Marie-Claire Ropars-Wuilleumier's studies *De la littérature au cinéma*, *L'Ecran de la mémoire*, *Le Texte divisé*, *Ecraniques* and *L'Idée d'image* address fundamental theoretical considerations of filmic and literary text and writing and constructs of identity and ideology. Two valuable recent works on French text and film are Susan Hayward and Ginette Vincendeau's *French Film: Texts and Contexts* and Jeff Kline's *Screening the Text*. The relationship between film and history is essentially another critical field, with analyses like John O'Connor's *Image as Artifact*, Paul Virilio's or Joseph Daniel's *Guerre et cinéma*, or K. R. M. Short's *Feature Films as History*. Studies of the history of cinema includes Georges Sadoul's *Le Cinéma français*, Jean-Pierre Jeancolas's *15 ans d'années trente*, *Générique des années*

4   Introduction

trente by Michèle Lagny, Marie-Claire Ropars and Pierre Sorlin, works by René Prédal or Henri Agel. Bill Nichols's works *Ideology and the Image* and *Representing Reality* are especially relevant to this study. Theoretical studies of documentary also include works by Alan Rosenthal and William Guynn. Retrospective studies on French film with theoretical focus include Allen Thiher's *The Cinematic Muse* and the essays edited by Mary Lea Bandy in *Rediscovering French Film*, as well as studies by Richard Abel and Dudley Andrew, whose *Concepts in Film Theory* relies on comparative studies with French literary theory. Works of feminist film theory by Laura Mulvey and David Rodowick among many others naturally address central questions of image, ideology and gender identity. Among valuable studies of more specifically filmic questions are the works of Réda Bensmaïa, Maureen Turim (*Flashbacks in Film*) and Dana Polan. A French introductory text, Philippe Rouyer's 1990 *Initiation au cinéma*, offers extensive technical terminology in French and an overall perspective on cinema genres and production. Numerous interview texts like Anne Gillain's *Le Cinéma de François Truffaut* or François Thomas's *L'Atelier d'Alain Resnais* offer a closer perspective on the collaborative process of film creation. The relationship between film and evolving constructs in art is elucidated by works like *Modernité dans le cinéma* by Youssef Ishaghpour, Michel Fabien and Michel de Certeau. The relationship between sound, image and ideology is addressed in Michel Chion's *La Voix au cinéma* or Colin MacCabe's *Godard: Images, Sounds, Politics*. French series or collections such as Nathan's *Synopsis*, *L'Interdisciplinaire (Films)*, or Hatier's *Images par images* offer studies of individual films. Other studies on individual filmmakers, screenwriters or literary authors will be listed at the end of each chapter. A general bibliography of film theory and French film history follows at the end of this book.

1. Mark Poster, *Critical Theory and Poststructuralism: In Search of a Context* (Ithaca: Cornell University Press, 1989) 52.
2. Raymond Bellour, "Analysis in Flames," *Diacritics* 15:1 (1985) 55.
3. Theodore Zeldin, *The French* (New York: Vintage Books, 1984) 320.

I

History on Film

Historic Realism:
From Documentary to Myth

In his 1940 work *L 'Imaginaire*, Jean-Paul Sartre referred to the photographic image as "le néant de l'être" (the nothingness of being/of the self). Roland Barthes used this concept as a basic tenet of his 1980 essay on photography, *La Chambre claire (Camera Lucida)*, in which he dwells on the dispossession of the subject before the camera. This primitive phobia constitutes a dilemma at the center of documentary filmmaking, a complex genre which has received of late a great deal of critical attention. Several concepts are operative in classifying documentary as such. Paramount is the pact or intent of the filmmaker, which is closely linked to his or her relationship to the subject(s), contemporary or historic. A primary paradox in documentary filmmaking is what the anthropologist Lévi-Strauss referred to in *Tristes Tropiques (Sad Tropics)* as the imprint of the foot on the beach, the intrusion of man and machine into the subject's territory. In spite of the technological marvels of telephoto lenses, hidden remote-controlled cameras and microphones, the documentarist is inevitably guilty of altering or staging the material. The camera lens alone frames reality; editing truncates and abstracts it in surrealistic fashion. It is this self-conscious cubist element of the process of filming itself that has created a link in France and elsewhere between documentary and modernist filmmaking.

The generic variants of documentary filmmaking include actual footage of events, interviews with participants, witnesses or primary subjects, archival texts or artifacts which bear witness, the testimony of the filmmaker, either as voice-over or as participant in the filmmaking process. Perhaps the most "transparent" footage is that which is unwittingly taken by an amateur participant or witness to a historic event, where the camera is turning by chance while the event occurs. A private amateur film becomes public evidence and a record of history, sometimes the only record. The news photographer, whose handheld video camcorder is often jostled, accosted or even destroyed, claims to be the authentic on-the-spot witness of events. Yet recently, dramatizations and accounts of photojournalists' actions indicate that they are just as vulnerable to staging history as the most modernist arcane play-wright. There has been considerable debate over the moral justification for news photographers allowing tragedies to occur in order to film them, or playing into terrorists' hands by giving them media exposure. Of particular controversy of late have been the dramatized reenactment of news which was not covered by the media, the media circus generated by the Gulf War, the plethora of TV vérité exposé shows, and the Rodney King tape.

To document simply means to make a permanent record of an event, to transpose live actions of real people to some other medium for posterity. The objective passivity of the classic image of the documentary filmmaker is perhaps one of the greatest illusions of the genre. Only an automatic eye camera impassively recording mechanically all events within the field of its lens, such as a bank security unit, could be said to be merely documenting the world before it. Once a journalist or cinematographer holds the camera, a truly objective documentary is no longer possible, in spite of the fact that the word for lens in French, similar to that in other Romance languages, is *objectif*. The documentary offers rather a different sort of objective: a goal, an artistic achievement, a moral message, a warning. Propaganda is most often produced in the purest documentary style, to confirm its authenticity. The extreme example of this technique would be Frank Capra's and Luis Buñuel's work during World War II, wherein they simply framed Hitler's own promotional films and let him horrify the free world audiences firsthand.

The cinematographer like the director is necessarily subjective; he or she frames, chooses, starts and stops shooting, uses particular shots and angles or film for special effects, develops and helps edit the film. Even the plural perspectives of the collaborative effort of a film crew cannot guarantee objectivity, accuracy and authenticity, primarily because of the bonding phenomenon which usually unites such a group.

In between documentation of events as they occur and dramatic recreation of events for documentary purposes lies another form of documentary: the staging of natural phenomena. In this type of film, cameras are hidden in dens or burrows or in blinds, even under water, to permit documentation of events that would never occur in the presence of a human being. Baiting or feeding is sometimes involved to set up the subject/object; sometimes only luck or chance create the photo opportunity, as in George Page's rare footage of the snow leopard for which his crew waited three years.

Thus there are many modes or styles of documentary: expository, observational, interactive, reflexive, as Bill Nichols characterizes them. Most if not all documentaries combine one or more of these approaches in collage. Hybrids abound; not only documentary but fiction films incorporate historic archival footage to enhance the illusion of authenticity and immediacy on the screen. Docudrama lies in between, exploiting documentary tradition to give an aura of real history to staged events, whether with documentary intent, propagandistic motives or in search of a cinéma vérité equation between art and reality. In this section I will treat just two expository/observational documentaries often packaged together: *Nuit et brouillard* (*Night and Fog*) and *Le Retour* (*The Return*). Although space does not permit treating them in this study, interactive French documentaries of prime interest include Marcel Ophüls's four-and-a-half-hour 1969 *Le Chagrin et la pitié* (*The Sorrow and the Pity*) and 1988 *Hôtel Terminus*, Claude Lanzmann's nine-and-a-half-hour *Shoah* (1985), and Pierre Sauvage's 1987 *Weapons of the Spirit*, all interview format film retrospectives on events during World War II. In a sense, certain techniques of reflexive documentary filmmaking are represented here by Resnais's *Hiroshima mon amour* and François Truffaut's *La Nuit américaine* (*Day for night*), although both films are declared experimental fictions.

Docudrama, the dramatic restaging of historic events, is represented by Gillo Pontecorvo's 1965 *La Bataille d'Alger* (*The Battle of Algiers*), a work that recreates with documentary-style immediacy the events, especially the terrorist incidents, in Algiers from 1954 to 1957 (which resulted in the popular mandate for independence, granted in 1962), a work that stands in striking contrast to the overtly propagandistic French newsreels from the years of the Algerian crisis as seen in *Sartre par lui-même* (*Sartre by Himself*). In spite of the technical generic distinction between documentary and docudrama in Resnais's and Pontecorvo's films, they are linked by many aspects, not the least of which is Resnais's own assertion that he was thinking of Algeria and the growing horrors there when he made *Nuit et brouillard*.

Recreating retrospectively the events of a significant point in time and space in the form of a docudrama is the type of historic realism closest to documentary and is often used in the latter, although acknowledged. However sincere, all eyewitness oral or written accounts of events which were not originally filmed constitute distortions of lived experience, which becomes thus a construct of memory and imagination. Once the opportunity for recording events *in situ* and *in media res* is lost, all past events are equally vulnerable topics for the documentarist's portrayal, which must be called a film art, and is recognized as such by the Academy. Thus with proper investigation and archival research, the filmmaker who longs to "incarnate" "reality" in the illusory and elusive images on the silver screen can recreate past events in the evanescent present of film, i.e. re-present them. If there is no archival footage, there is thus no qualitative or generic distinction between a docudrama of something that happened the week before, ten years earlier or half a millennium ago. There are only distinctions in the challenge of bridging greater cul-tural gaps, materially, politically, economically, morally, in representing successfully that which has gone before, of bringing history and the past to life.

This lack of distinction leads to temptation, just as in the artificial ingenuousness of the narrative voice in autobiographic fiction. The difference between a "real" historic documentary film and a dramatic adaptation of historic events is not one of results or even process, but rather one of intent, a moral rather than esthetic pact the filmmaker strikes with the spectator, such as the disclaimer at the end of the extremely realistic *La Bataille d'Alger* that it has not one foot of documentary newsreel in it. Political affiliations lead filmmakers to present history if not from a particular perspective then certainly to a partisan purpose. Moreover, because "le vrai n'est pas toujours vraisemblable" (reality is not always realistic), most docudramatists are drawn inevitably to transform historic events, to falsify proportions, perspectives and causalities in the interest of literary models and stereotypes, or fictional cinematic codes, in short, to heighten the dramatic effect of the events and characters they are portraying.

The subsequent selections in the section on historic realism are films which possess apparent historic authenticity, particularly in their meticulous material culture documentation, but which in reality present something quite different: a vision of history filtered by *written* texts, by literary accounts of historic events, by a preliminary transposition of experience into the symbolic system of language on the printed page. Daniel Vigne's 1982 *Le Retour de Martin Guerre* and Ettore Scola's 1982 *La Nuit de Varennes* both contain the metaphoric elaboration of a historic paradigm, a symbolic dialectic of identity.

The line between authentic historic recreation and historic exploitation is easily crossed. The pretense of historic realism is especially evident in a film like *Le Retour de Martin Guerre*, where the thematic of the film, imposture, announces its own generic cinematic appurtenance. Scola goes one step further in *La Nuit de Varennes* by arbitrarily (and successfully) combining à la Doctorow documented historic events, well-known literary texts and figures, and a large dose of artistic inventiveness to create the fictional or marginal version of those events, thus tantalizing the audience by using imaginative artifice to blend historically plausible scenes with theatrical sequences of pure fantasy.

The most deceptive and mystifying of the historic films treated in this section use apparently accurate historic figures and events as a metaphor for contemporary political and artistic conditions, fictionalizing the past to symbolize the filmmaker's present, creating a double historic reading similar in intent to Resnais's *Nuit et brouillard*, but lacking its authenticity, conscripting a primary historic text to serve as a pretext for another message. The contemporary context constitutes an extended referential intertext in all these films: *Napoléon*, *La Marseillaise*, *Danton*, and *La Grande Illusion*.

Abel Gance's 1927 silent epic *Napoléon* (of which he completed only the first two parts) is at once a display of modernist cinematic art and experimentation, a portrayal of 1920s postwar politics, and a saga of the conquests of Napleon Bonaparte. The episodes of the Reign of Terror, of the Convention, are presented first as populist madness and fervor, then as spectres of the past, ghosts which would haunt France far beyond the era of Napoleon and which were ironically apt images for the consequences of World War I. Jean Renoir's 1938 *La Marseillaise*, attempting like Gance's sweeping drama to involve the audience intimately and intensely in historic events, focuses on the early years of the Revolution and on one battalion from Marseilles, on their formation, their march to Paris, their assault on the Tuileries and of course their marching song, declared the French National Hymn in 1879. The regionalism and populism, the *gaillarde camaraderie* of the southern peasants, dominate the costumes, sets and historic battle scenes of the film. Renoir involves his audience (the film was released just after the collapse of the Front Populaire) through identification with the people—simple, earnest, loyal. Andrzej Wadja's 1982 *Danton* is another close-focus, apparently accurate portrayal of historic events (with academic historic consultants like those for *Le Retour de Martin Guerre* and *La Nuit de Varennes*): the last days of Danton in 1794 including his condemnation by Robespierre, his trial and death on the guillotine. Yet in spite of extremely realistic sets, costumes and incarnations of the historic rival figures, the film is marked by its Polish origins. Like the Czech film *Amadeus*, which is as much a defense of the individual against mass mediocrity and repression as it is a historic depiction of the life and genius of Mozart, *Danton* is a transposed portrayal of the battle for control of a nation between two very different styles of leadership, two contrasting political ideologies. In the scenes of *Danton* are inscribed the struggles of the Polish people to achieve freedom and national identity over two centuries. Jean Renoir's classic *La Grande Illusion* uses a realistic historic wartime phenomenon, POW camps, to formulate a portrait of class, racial and national stereotypes, in a miniature model of society, a microcosm like that in *La Nuit de Varennes*. Bill Nichols takes Christian Metz's primary distinction of metaphor and metonymy in film and attributes the former to fiction and the latter to documentary or factual film. However, all the films in this section have a metaphoric function which gives them ultimately a dimension of legend, symbol or fable, built on their historic recreations.

The reflexive style of documentary filmmaking is a key aspect of the paradoxical connection between numerous New Wave French filmmakers' mature works of art and their early apprenticeship as documentarists. The auteur apolitical modernist style of the *Nouvelle Vague* is, on the surface at least, the antithesis of documentary filmmaking. Indeed, the New Wave films as such constitute the other end of this study, the most self-reflexive, subjective productions in the gamut from transparent to opaque. As we will see later in detail, the paradox of the transition of Alain Resnais's work from *Nuit et brouillard* to *Hiroshima mon amour* and *L'Année dernière à Marienbad* (*Last Year at Marienbad*) is resolved on two levels. A closer look at *Nuit et brouillard* reveals it to be in fact a sort of cinematic fugue, alternating historic black and white footage of Nazi concentration camps in operation, particularly Auschwitz/Birkenau, with later color footage of the empty remains of these human abattoirs.

Not just structural but also ideological similarities, as we shall see, link the New Wave modernist works to their documentary origins, in a sense closing the circle of this study, buckling the end to the beginning. It is in the spiral evolution of ideological paradigms over time that the dance of documentary and fiction interweaves its motifs and motives. *Nuit et brouillard* projects a sense of the hopelessness of the task of the documentary filmmaker and the despair of ever transposing to the screen, even with captured archival footage, the tragic realities which occurred in these places, while emphasizing the lasting relevance of those events, whose magnitude seems to defy imagining if not imaging. It is this dilemma—artistic, cultural and moral—that confronts the documentarist: how can the filmmaker impose graphically, sensorially, viscerally an awareness, awaken political vigilance in the 1950s Cold War spectator, seated comfortably in a theater, ten years and worlds away from the cataclysmic moments of World War II, how use these images to alert this spectator to hidden present dangers.

Other documentaries from New Wave filmmakers include Jean-Luc Godard's banned *Le Petit Soldat* (1960), his *La Chinoise* (1967), *Vent d'est* (1970), *Numéro deux* (1975), Chris Marker's *Lettre de Sibérie* (1957), *Le Joli Mai* (1962), *Sans Soleil* (1982), Georges Franju's *Le Sang des bêtes* (1949) and *Hôtel des Invalides* (1951). Like Godard, Marker and Franju, Resnais articulated powerful ideological statements in his documentary work, including the overtly anticolonial film *Les Statues meurent aussi* (1950–1954) (statues also die).

If the camera "freezes" reality on film and reifies life in a death-image, then the ability of the succession of "moving pictures" to duplicate real-life action is an intrinsic illusion. If films are but Platonic reflections of our deepest desires (as Bertolucci, Deleuze, Nichols all demonstrate), then documentary as a socially responsible discourse is an idealization of an art which is eminently vulnerable to subversion. The equation between image and reality, like that between the two sides of the linguistic sign, is established within a closed system of self-referentiality that generates as much as it reflects the ideology of the culture that produces it. Bill Nichols suggests that "Documentary films, though, are part and parcel of the discursive formations, the language games, and rhetorical stratagems by and through which pleasure and power, ideologies and utopias, subjects and subjectives receive tangible representation."[1] If, as Nichols affirms, "Historic reality is under siege," then the social discourse of documentary has indeed a daunting charge, not only to reflect but to construct a coherent ideology.

The distinction, moral if not artistic, between documentary and fiction, is problematic at best, much like that between autobiography and fictional autobiographic narrative which I addressed in *Le Berceau et la bibliothèque*. Nichols claims a privileged access to the id for fiction that is denied to the sober discourse of documentary, domain of the ego and superego. But if film by its very nature is an oneiric experience, then the images in both fiction and documentary film belong more appropriately to the Lacanian *imaginaire* as phantasmal constructs of a society's collective phobias and desires. And the use of language in film, whether as voice-over narrative, didactic or observational, or in dialogical exchange, witnessing past real experience or generating the cinematic illusion of historic reality, is necessarily the province of the Lacanian symbolic, at once the socialization and the depersonalization of the speaker in the public domain of mass communication. Hence the ontological impossibility of transparent filmmaking, whatever the moral or ideological intent of the filmmaker. And yet clearcut distinctions remain between documentary, historic realism and myth or parable. It is intriguing to look at the gamut of films in this section on historic realism in the light of these concepts.

Thus I propose to study films which achieve and exploit historic transparent effects, beginning with two documentaries, then a docudrama which offers documentary-style images of past events, using techniques inherited from Italian neorealism, to illustrate a political position. I will then look at two films which appear to be historically accurate through effective use of music, sets, costumes, inclusion of documented historic events, but which actually exploit the referential illusion or fallacy in offering us something quite different. Finally I will treat four historic films which not only transpose history to legend and myth but exploit historic figures and events as symbols of contemporary situations, something literature has been doing successfully for centuries in metaphoric satire.

Note

1. Bill Nichols, *Representing Reality* (Bloomington: Indiana University Press, 1991) 10.

Bibliography

Anderegg, Michael. "A Documentary Fantasy: Jean-Luc Godard's *La Chinoise.*" *North Dakota Quarterly* 50:2 (1982) 31–40.
Avisar, Ilan. *Screening the Holocaust: Cinema's Images of the Unimaginable.* Bloomington: Indiana University Press, 1988.
Barnouw, Erik. *Documentary: a History of the Non-fiction Film.* New York: Oxford University Press, 1974.
Barsam, Richard. *Nonfiction Film: a Critical History.* New York: Dutton, 1973.
Barthes, Roland. *La Chambre claire.* Paris: Seuil, Cahiers Cinéma, 1980.
Baudrillard, Jean. *The Evil Demon of Images.* Sydney: Power Institute Publications, 1988.
Bazin, André. *What is Cinema?* Berkeley: University of California Press, 1967.
Benjamin, Walter. *Illuminations.* New York: Schocken Books, 1969.
Bordwell, David and Kristin Thompson. *Film Art: An Introduction.* New York: McGraw-Hill, 1990.
Conley, Tom. "Documentary Surrealism: On *Land without Bread.*" *Dada/Surrealism* 15 (1986) 176–198.
Daniel, Joseph. *Guerre et cinéma: grandes illusions et petits soldats, 1895–1971.* Paris: Armand Colin, 1972.
Deshpande, Shekhar. "Semiotics and Realism: Toward a Theory of Documentary Film." 129–135. In Deely, John, ed. *Semiotics 1984.* Lanham, MD: University Press of America, 1985.
Feldman, Seth. "Footnote to Fact: The Docudrama." In Grant, Barry, ed. *Film Genre Reader.* Austin: University of Texas Press, 1986.
Ferro, Marc. *Cinema and History.* Detroit: Wayne State University Press, 1988.
Guynn, William. *A Cinema of Nonfiction.* Rutherford: Fairleigh Dickinson University Press, 1990.
Hall, Jeanne, ed. *Twelfth Annual Ohio University Film Conference: Documentary. Wide Angle* 13:2 (1991). Entire issue.
Icart, Roger. *La Révolution française à l'écran.* Toulouse: Milan, 1988.
Insdorf, Annette. *Indelible Shadows.* New York: Cambridge, 1989.
Jacobs, Lewis, ed. *The Documentary Tradition.* New York: W. W. Norton, 1979.
James, Carol Plyley. "Documentary and Allegory: History Moralized in *Le Chagrin et la pitié.*" *French Review* 59:1 (1985) 84–89.
Jeancolas, Jean-Pierre. *15 ans d'années trente.* Paris: Stock Cinéma, 1983.
Lagny, Michèle, Marie-Claire Ropars, Pierre Sorlin. *Générique des années trente.* St. Denis: Presses Universitaires de Vincennes, 1986.

Lefèvre, Raymond. *Cinéma et Révolution*. Paris: Edilig, 1988.

Linder, Ann. "Great War Narratives into Film: Transformation, Reception, and Reaction." *International Fiction Review* 28:1–2 (2001) 1–12.

Lovell, Terry. *Pictures of Reality*. London: British Film Institute, 1980.

MacBean, James Roy. *Film and Revolution*. Bloomington: Indiana University Press, 1975.

Minh-Ha, Trinh. "Mechanical Eye, Electronic Ear and the Lure of Authenticity." *Wide Angle* 6:2 (1984) 58–63.

Nichols, Bill. *Ideology and the Image*. Bloomington: Indiana University Press, 1981.

————, ed. *Movies and Methods* I, II. Berkeley: University of California Press, 1976, 1985.

————. *Representing Reality*. Bloomington: Indiana University Press, 1991.

O'Connor, John. *The Image as Artifact*. Malabar, FL: Krieger Publishing, 1990.

Plantinga, Carl. "The Mirror Framed: A Case for Expression in Documentary." *Wide Angle* 13:2 (1991) 40–53.

Radcliff-Umstead, Douglas, ed. *National Traditions in Motion Pictures*. Kent, OH: Kent State University, 1985.

Renov, Michael. "Re-thinking Documentary: Toward a Taxonomy of Mediation." *Wide Angle* 8:3–4 (1986) 71–77.

————. *Documentary Film*. New York: Routledge, 1992.

Rosen, Miriam. "The Architecture of Documentary Filmmaking." *Cinéaste* 17:3 (1990) 48–50.

Rosenthal, Alan. *New Challenges for Documentary*. Berkeley: University of California Press, 1988.

————. *Writing, Directing and Producing Documentary Films*. Carbondale: Southern Illinois University Press, 1990.

Siegel, Marc. "Clichés of Unity: History and Memory in Postwar French Film." *Paroles Gelées* 16:2 (1998) 57–64.

Sherzer, Dina, ed. *Cinema, Colonialism, Postcolonialism: Perspectives from the French and Francophone World*. Austin: University of Texas Press, 1996.

Short, K.R.M., ed. *Feature Films as History*. London: Helm, 1981.

Sorlin, Pierre. *The Film in History*. Oxford: Blackwell, 1980.

Vincendeau, Ginette. "Unsettling Memories." *Sight and Sound* 5:7 (July 1995) 30–32.

Virilio, Paul. *Guerre et cinéma I: logistique de la perception*. Paris: Editions de l'Etoile, 1984.

Williams, Christopher, ed. *Realism and the Cinema*. London: Routledge and Kegan Paul, 1980.

Youdelman, Jeffrey. "Narration, Invention, and History: A Documentary Dilemma." *Cinéaste* 12:2 (1982) 9–15.

Nuit et brouillard
(Night and Fog)

directed by Alain Resnais (1955)
written by Jean Cayrol

This documentary depiction of the horrors of the Shoah is a maximum exercise in restraint, both didactically and cinematically. Resnais acknow-ledges through camerawork, editing, narration and musical score the illusion of transparent objectivity, the inevitability of distance and distortion. At the same time, he reaffirms his deeply sincere desire to tell the truth, to record events for posterity, to leave a lasting collage of revelation that will not only stand as a memorial to suffering and loss but remind us eternally that, as the narrative by Jean Cayrol states at the end, the inhuman dragon monster of war sleeps lightly just below the surface in all of us, with one eye open.

Throughout *Nuit et brouillard*, Resnais exercises his frustration and somber disbelief through the contrast between the captured footage and stills, the album of Auschwitz/Birkenau documenting Nazi horrors and prisoners' agony, and the passivity and indifference of the empty camp ten years later. The difficulties of portraying such surrealistic images and the battle between memory and oblivion have been addressed by Annette Insdorf in *Indelible Shadows* and by Ilan Avisar in *Screening the Holocaust*. Other critics like John Moses in his 1987 article in *Literature/Film Quarterly* on "Vision Denied in *Night and Fog* and *Hiroshima mon amour*" also address the paradox at the center of such cinema, a problem I treat further in the study on *Hiroshima mon amour* in the final section of this book.

Resnais's *Nuit et brouillard* stands as a lasting image of the devastation and absurdity of World War II, depicting its greatest horror: the hatred, humiliation, slow suffering, terrible loneliness and confusion, death without meaning, dehumanized dog's death suffered by the millions of prisoners in detainment and extermination camps from the 1930s (especially after the Kristallnacht in November 1938) until 1945. Images comparable to those of *Nuit et brouillard* would include footage and stills of the Japanese nuclear holocausts or the frantic charred remains of the citizens of Pompeii preserved in the Naples Museum, entombed alive by the poisonous gas and hot ash of Vesuvius, contorted in their pathetic anguish, overwhelmed by a killer force that reduced to nothingness their daily ambitions, hopes and dreams. The power of Hitler's Third Reich and the unbelievable machinations of his prized SS left an impact equatable to the cataclysmic unleashing of natural forces, although the calculated program of genocide stands apart from other holocausts.

A number of talented filmmakers collaborated with Resnais on this project, emphasizing its universal importance. The opening credits list a dozen or more international organizations which sponsored the film, primarily the Comité d'Histoire de la Seconde Guerre Mondiale. Sacha Vierny's work on the frame sequences is a tracking, contemplating camera which attempts to absorb the irony of the empty landscapes that tell no tale today. Resnais was assisted by Chris Marker, another talented documentarist who also went on to become a New Wave filmmaker. Henri Colpi, whose crosscutting and flashback editing would fully develop in *Hiroshima mon amour* and *L'Année dernière à Marienbad*, skillfully combined the historic black and white footage with the color sequences framing it. And Georges Delerue, beginning a forty-year career, including the later waltz theme of *Hiroshima mon amour*, presented a haunting musical score by Hanns Eisler, himself driven from his homeland by Hitler.

Nuit et brouillard opens with Sacha Vierny's contemporary (1955) color shots of the sites of various concentration camps and Michel Bouquet's voice-over remarking on the indifference of the surrounding landscape, on nature's ability to forget and cover up the evidence of past atrocities, on the apparently innocent function of the fields, fences, towers and buildings. The first integrated archival historic footage in black and white depicts the early days of Hitler's irresistible rise to power. The shots of the masses of fervid adherents to his racist domination theories and Arian destiny dreams compare ironically to the final image of the masses of cadavers left behind to rot by the fleeing SS wardens of the concentration camps.

The initial frame color sequence of the camera panning across the serene green grass covering the killing fields of Auschwitz and the black humor parodic analysis of the various architectural styles of the guard towers can be seen as a mitigating of the intensity of the horrors depicted in the ensuing archival footage. However, this framing, distancing and depersonalizing of the events being memorialized has the opposite effect for some. Resnais's "formal experimentation" in creating contemporary color framing for historic black and white footage brings some spectators closer to the impact of the archival segments and highlights the ironies of time and space, as it depicts the empty chambers of horror where tourists now have their pictures taken, a simultaneous desecration and memorialization that is repeated in the atomic bomb bus tours of Hiroshima.

The wandering eye of the camera exploring the empty ovens, houses of incarceration and gas chambers in a sense duplicates the stunned disbelief of the occupant victims who first entered these spaces, at the same time that it expresses the filmmaker's frustration in attempting to return to the past, to affirm, like Proust and Barthes before the photo of the dead, the *ça a été* (this once was) of lived and felt experience. The use of stills accentuates the freeze-frame phenomenon of the death of the self in the image, the Sartrian *néant de l'être* (nothingness of being/of the self). In existential fashion, this distance and this absence make it difficult for later generations to achieve a just focus on those events. The Cayrol narrative emphasizes the affective chasm between the faint present traces of human clawing at the ceilings of the gas chambers and the past agony of the dying, between the remaining rows of sterile bunks or holes and the former filth and suffering of the occupants. The furor over the attempt to establish a Carmel nunnery on this site reflects the ambiguity of our relationship to the past: one can accuse the Catholic church of callous disregard for Jewish hallowed ground or one can interpret the vow of silence and loving devotion of the nuns as a memorial tribute to the spirit of those who suffered there.

Footage of the construction of the death camps sets the stage for the horrific drama about to unfold. Scenes of the ferreting out and deporting of Jewish and other targeted civilians from all over Europe follow, as they are closed into sealed box cars, treated worse than cattle, like the lifeless heaps they will become, bodies devoid of all spirit. Stripped of their belongings (especially their gold, which would be used to finance the Nazi war machine), marched in humiliating nudity, then clothed in the now legendary striped pyjamas and slippers, they carry numbers and tatoos, including for some seven thousand resistance fighters the logo N & N on their backs: *Nacht und Nebel, Nuit et Brouillard*, Night and Fog. The decree of 7 December 1941 (ironic date) ordered that they be made to vanish into the fog of the night.

While this symbol was intended to dramatize the fate of the millions of deported Jews who would never be seen again, Resnais has been criticized for misrepresentation and for muddying the distinction between political detainment and racial extermination and the functions of the various camps by both Robert Michael in *Cinéaste* in 1984 in "A Second Look: *Night and Fog*" and Charles Krantz in "Alain Resnais' *Nuit et brouillard*: A Historical and Cultural Analysis" (included in the 1985 Holocaust Studies Annual, *Literature, the Arts, and the Holocaust*, edited by Sanford Pinsker and Jack Fischel). Although there have been over two hundred very different films made about the holocaust, including numerous dramatizations like Andrzej Wadja's *Landscape after Battle* and documentaries such as Claude Lanzmann's *Shoah*, *Nuit et brouillard* stands as one of the most chillingly shocking depictions of genocide of all time. Resnais's film also has a complex political history of its own, as it indicted attitudes and values of 1950s Cold War France.

The fact that the thousands of faces and bodies portrayed—humiliated, tortured and desecrated—are not specifically designated as Jews and that the title refers to the disappearance of few thousand resistance fighters can be seen not as a refusal to properly designate the victims, but as a rewriting of the historic signifi-cance of the Shoah in the light of French 1950s political and racial problems. François Truffaut called *Nuit et brouillard* an important history lesson, and Resnais admitted that it was intended as an extended metaphor opposing the atrocities being committed in Algeria and warning against the dangers facing France there. In this light, the film can be compared with Resnais's 1954 anticolonial film *Les Statues meurent aussi* or the 1965 docudrama on the same 1950s conflicts in Algeria, *La Bataille d'Alger* by Gillo Pontecorvo (who also made in 1960 a dramatic film, *Kapo*, on heroism and betrayal at Auschwitz). In *Nuit et brouillard*, the tone of the narrative in voice-over, described by Truffaut as having "une douceur terrifiante" (a terrifying gentleness) created a new journalistic style of antirhetorical understatement which contrasted markedly the official hyperbole of French newsreels of the day and which influenced certain later documentary and docudrama filmmakers. It is this restraint that gives the film greater power than so many other attempts to find the equation in sound and image of the experience of the death camps.

The fundamental inability of film, or even personal memory, to memorialize the enormity of the Shoah, led a group of relatives of the victims to recreate the experience of the deportations in which eighty thousand French Jews were sent to the death camps, from which only 2,500 returned. A fourteen-car train marked "Drancy-Auschwitz 1942–1992. The Memory Train" traveled from Paris to Poland overnight 5–6 April 1992, creating an oral library of suffering, the ultimate and only pilgrimage of its kind, yet another attempt to reach into the oneiric surrealistic realm of those historic horrors.

In 1987, Richard Raskin and Sacha Vierny interviewed Resnais and published a retrospective study of the making of *Nuit et brouillard*. In their book they offer some intriguing observations regarding the meaning of the title of Resnais's film. The *Nacht und Nebel* designation NN also abbreviates the Latin logo *Nomen Nescio* (name unknown). The term *Nacht und Nebel* comes appropriately from a work Hitler idolized, Wagner's *Rhinegold*, wherein the dwarf Alberich dives into the Rhine into *Nacht und Nebel*, taking his helmet, and directs the accumulation of the treasure with his magic ring. It was Jean Cayrol, who was interned at Mauthausen, who first used the term when he published *Poèmes de la nuit et du brouillard* with Seghers in 1946 and who provided the film's title. Other prior attempts to record the atrocities of the Shoah include the 1954 *Tragédie de la déportation*, with stations like those of the cross, by Henri Michel and Olga Wormser, consultants on this film.

Because of its contemporary implications as well as its primary indictment, *Nuit et brouillard* elicited censorship reactions from both the French (who doctored a shot of a French prison guard) and the Germans, who requested that it be withdrawn from the Cannes Film Festival. It was in fact, like the later *Hiroshima mon amour*, shown outside the competition, ironically to placate the objections of the officials whose repressive actions it implicitly condemned. There were other postwar echoes that year, including the first version of the Australian epic, *A Town like Alice*, released in 1956. And ironically, the German film *Ciel sans étoile* (sky without stars) was withdrawn from the same Cannes festival because of the Russian objection to the tale of a love affair between a West German police agent and an East German girl (remarkably similar to Elle's tale from *Hiroshima mon amour*). Resnais's reference to the Algerian conflict was not only to the colony; there were in fact internment "regroupment" camps in France for Algerian Arabs at the time. The film's retrospective relevance has only grown with the passage of time, as it warns against racist abuses of human rights anywhere in the world in any era.

One of the most heart-rending aspects of *Nuit et brouillard* is its portrayal of the dogged attempts on the part of the prisoners to continue a structured social order, a situation which created for those placed in charge of other prisoners a horrible dilemma. In the midst of their suffering, the prisoners manage a society, converse, write, play music (not only traditional classical pieces, but works composed *in situ*, such as the late Olivier Messiaen's searingly lyric *Quattuor pour la fin du temps—Quartet for the End of Time*). Hierarchies emerge in the camp communities as well, specializations of cruelty: whorehouses, prisons, hospitals and surgeries where unspeakable treatment and experiments occur. And the prisoners are forced while starving, diseased and dying to construct their own instruments of torture: gas chambers, crematoria. When the rate of extermination exceeds the disposal capacities of the camps, the victims' bodies are simply burned on open pyres. Legends of the smell on the wind are based on fact.

Other legendary horrors are documented as well: rolls of cloth made of human hair, bones converted to fertilizer, bodies to soap, skin to artwork and lampshades. Like an abattoir, the slaughterhouses of the deathcamps manufacture by-products from the bodies they process. It has defied the world's imagination ever since the end of the madness, as people struggle to understand how the German camp operators, male and female, could have committed such horrors. After the fall of the Reich, they all disavowed responsibility. The trials at Nuremberg and later of Eichmann, Barbie and other butchers stand more as a testimony to people's ability to forget, to bury deep in the subconscious zones of one's being the parts of oneself one cannot acknowledge, than as an exemplary indictment or punishment. The sentence of capital punishment of a civil penal system seems sane and clean compared to the slow torture suffered at their hands by millions of innocent, confused, law-abiding citizens. Films like Michael Verhoeven's 1991 *The Nasty Girl* in fact treat the long-lasting echoes of the Reich and the question of repressed sadomasochistic guilt.

The last sequences of Resnais's film depict the arrival of the Allied invasion forces liberating the camps, which had been abandoned to their fate by fleeing Nazis. Confronted with acres of corpses and thousands of prisoners near death, the Allies in one of the great ironies of history were obliged to take over the administration and management of the camps, to bulldoze the dead into trenches, to try to feed and revive the hollow-eyed zombies who could not comprehend that it was over, to attempt to rekindle in them the necessary spark of life, the spirit needed to survive. It is also one of history's profound ironies that it was in fact the Russians who liberated Auschwitz, troops from a nation under Stalin, whose repressive purges and exterminations, although more political than racist, far exceeded those of Hitler.

The power of Resnais's film has endured through all the evolving critical interpretation and polemic. Spectators familiar with numerous documentary and dramatized accounts of the Shoah still react to *Nuit et brouillard* with visceral revulsion, shock and tears of anguish. I think that it is the lack of specificity regarding the victims in the film that complements its documentary veracity and gives it the oneiric power that penetrates time and space to the core of the spectator's being. It transcends didactic remonstrance, admonition or warning, in piercing through the protective layers of socialization in all of us, in signalling the danger of the ensnaring logic of unbroken realist narrative, as it focuses on the vaporization of being into nothingness, a message most apt for the 1950s Cold War phobia of Resnais's next subject: the Bomb.

This chapter appeared as part of an article on Resnais in *French Cultural Studies* 3 (October 1992) published in England by Alpha Academic.

Bibliography

Armes, Roy. *The Cinema of Alain Resnais.* New York: A. S. Barnes, 1968.

Avisar, Ilan. *Screening the Holocaust: Cinema's Images of the Unimaginable.* Bloomington: Indiana University Press, 1988.

Cantor, Jay. "Death and the Image." In Warren, Charles, and Stanley Cavell, eds. *Beyond Document: Essays on Nonfiction Film.* Hanover: University Press of New England, 1996.

Casebier, Allan. "Idealist and Realist Theories of the Documentary." *Post-Script* 6:1 (1986) 66–75.

Cayrol, Jean. *Night and Fog* (filmscript). In Robert Hughes, ed. *Film: Book 2: Films of Peace and War.* New York: Grove, 1962. 234–255.

———. *Poèmes de la nuit et du brouillard.* Paris: Seghers, 1946.

Flitterman-Lewis, Sandy. "Documenting the Ineffable: Terror and Memory in Alain Resnais's *Night and Fog.*" In Grant, Sloniowski, and Nichols, eds. *Documenting the Documentary: Close Readings of Documentary Film and Video.* Detroit: Wayne State University Press, 1998.

Hebard, Andrew. "Disruptive Histories: Toward a Radical Politics of Remembrance in Alain Resnais's *Night and Fog.*" *New German Critique* 71 (Spring-Summer 1997) 87–113.

Insdorf, Annette. *Indelible Shadows: Film and the Holocaust.* New York: Cambridge University Press, 1989.

LaCapra, Dominick. *History and Memory after Auschwitz.* Ithaca, NY: Cornell University Press, 1998.

MacLeay, Daniel. "Vision and Re-vision: The Restoration of Films by Jean Cocteau and Alain Resnais." *Publications of the Missouri Philological Association* 25 (2000) 107–112.

Michael, Robert. "A Second Look: *Night and Fog.*" *Cinéaste* 13:4 (1984) 36–37

———. "The Terrible Flaw of *Night and Fog.*" *Martyrdom and Resistance* (Sept–Oct 1981) 11–15.

Michel, Henri, et Olga Wormser. *Tragédie de la déportation.* Paris, 1954.

Monaco, James. *Alain Resnais: The Role of Imagination.* New York: Oxford University Press, 1978.

Moses, John. "Vision Denied in *Night and Fog* and *Hiroshima mon amour.*" *Literature/Film Quarterly* 15:3 (1987) 159–163.

Pautrot, Jean-Louis. "Music and Memory in Film and Fiction: Listening to *Nuit et brouillard* (1955), *Lacombe Lucien* (1973) and *La Ronde de nuit* (1969). *Dalhousie French Studies* 55 (Summer 2001) 168–182.

Pinsker, Sanford, and Jack Fischel, eds. *Literature, the Arts, and the Holocaust.* Greenwood, FL: Penkeville Press, 1987.

Raskin, Richard, and Sacha Vierny. *Nuit et brouillard by Alain Resnais: On the Making, Reception and Functions of a Major Documentary Film.* Aarhus, Denmark: Aarhus University Press, 1987.

Robbins, Jill. "The Writing of the Holocaust: Claude Lanzmann's *Shoah.*" *Prooftexts* 7:3 (1987) 249–258.

Sweet, Freddy. *The Film Narratives of Alain Resnais.* Ann Arbor: UMI Research Press, 1981.

Le Retour
(The Return)

directed by Henri Cartier-Bresson (1945)
written by Claude Roy

This brief but powerful documentary chronicles events at the time of the liberation of the POW, internment and death camps in 1945, witnessing firsthand an unusually poignant and ironic period in history. It is often combined with Alain Resnais's *Nuit et brouillard*, which it in a sense complements and continues, although the two films are very different in tone, technique, and their spatio-temporal relationship to their subject. Like Roberto Rossellini's *Paisà* made the following year, *Le Retour* is infused with the melodramatic emotions expressed in the immediacy of liberation.

As noted in the chapter on *Nuit et brouillard*, the liberation of the camps involved assuming the tasks abandoned by the Nazis and then attempting to reverse the tide of displacement, dispossession and degradation. Convincing the victims of the war that they were still alive and actually free was only the beginning of the enormous challenge facing the liberators. Once the prisoners were freed from the horrors of internment, getting home constituted another trial: arduous journeys in incredibly weakened physical condition, through many political zones and delays due to bureaucratic entanglements.

Under the auspices of the American Information Service and the American Army, still photographer Henri Cartier-Bresson, who had begun working in cine-matography before the war, and writer Claude Roy worked together to document the massive refugee problem at the end of World War II in *Le Retour*. They both did time in Stalags, German prisoner-of-war camps; their footage and narrative is a firsthand documenting of the events following the defeat of the Third Reich, covering the spring and summer of 1945. Initial sequences depict the joyful yet incredulous liberated prisoners of war who must begin the long trek home on foot. In contrast to the relatively positive state of the POWs, sick and weak interned Jews are loaded onto trucks and trains to reverse the deadly deportation journeys they made, in some cases many years earlier. Their will to survive in the face of complete physical deprivation gives them the last strength to deal with the demands of freedom. Spontaneous roadside camps spring up as refugees fall by the wayside; official centers are opened to receive and reorient thousands. All are screened to trap the Nazis trying to escape undetected. At the points of encounter of the Allied and Russian troops along the Elbe and the Moldau, millions of displaced soldiers and civilians begin a massive exchange, an almost biblical repatriation of populations: in one direction 2,400,000 Russians, 1,500,000 Poles, 330,000 Czechs, 1,750,000 citizens of the Baltic nations, 600,000 Central Europeans, even 292,000 French liberated by the Russians who would have a reverse journey later. In the other direction moved 2,100,000 French, 570,000 Belgians, 400,000 Dutch, 420,000 Italians.

The danger of epidemics in unsanitary refugee conditions was so great that extreme measures had to be taken to protect both refugees and liberators. From our perspective of ecological awareness, we cannot help but cringe when we see the refugees dusted white with DDT, as the film boasts that this miracle chemical prevented typhoid and other epidemics.

The last two sequences of *Le Retour* have a special drama of their own that is more intense than any staged scenario. The massive airlift from 10 April to 10 May 1945, by the American Air Transport Command and the Royal Air Force, of 168,000 French, combined the thrilling experience of flying, a first for most of the passengers, the exhilaration of liberty and the emotion of reunion with loved ones. These last scenes of embraces and tears—of disbelief and at the prospect of the long struggle to reestablish a normal life—move the spectator like no historic fiction ever could, for they are real. We have the knowledge that this happened, if we trust the sources presenting us this film. Many so-called documentaries are of course just the opposite, pure propaganda designed to manipulate the spectator, but this one serves another purpose; it simply desires to tell a heart-rending story after the tragedy and the suffering are over. Or does it? No mention is made other than in passing of the tremendous tragedies facing repatriated POWs and Jews, of survival guilt or nightmares, of all the symptoms of postwar stress and trauma which are much better understood half a century later than they were at the time. In a sense, some of the memorial pilgrimages that have been made to traumatic sites have been as much a journey in search of the self as an attempt to relocate a lost past.

In this film, the emphasis on the strong sense of heroism, the worship of the liberators, the generous nourishing of the returning refugees by total strangers along the way masks the pain and suffering. The charge is clear, though: those who lived through the decade of agony must forget in order to find the strength and the will to go on, to return to a normal productive life. The final implicit message, like that of *Nuit et brouillard*, is equally eloquent: those of us who look back from our comfortable peacetime perspective have the responsibility to remember, to confront the echoes and images of the nightmare of the Shoah, lest we forget and allow the Hitlers of the world to take control once again.

In the fall of 1988, the speaker of the West German parliament, Philipp Jenninger, was forced to resign his post because of a conciliatory, almost pro-Nazi speech that he made on the fiftieth anniversary of the November 1938 Kristallnacht, the first incident of mass arrest of the Jews by the Nazis. Days later, Michael Furst, the deputy leader of West Germany's thirty-thousand-member Jewish community, was forced to resign for refusing to condemn Jenninger. Both the chief defense witness and the defense lawyer for the man thought to be Nazi war criminal John Demjanjuk attempted suicide during his 1988 trial in Jerusalem; the lawyer, Israeli Dov Eitan, succeeded. Perhaps it is thus the Germans and the Jews themselves who have the greatest task in dealing daily with this part of their past, and therefore of their identity, which is for many of them an intolerable memory in the context of modern pluralism and democratic freedom.

Events since 1989 which have rewritten the maps and history of Europe have not, in spite of their will to freedom, eliminated beliefs and behavior similar to that of the Nazis and the Fascists. They thrive today, by one name or another, in political organizations all over the world and in nations where repression and torture are commonplace. Perhaps the most lasting evidence of the specter of the Third Reich is the anxiety regarding the ultimate character of the Fourth, as some have called the reunited Germany, an irrational fear among those who cannot forget, even through they realize that the majority of the population of this new nation was not even born when the war ended. The most recent postscript to retrospective treatment of Nazi atrocities is the number of neoNazi organizations active around the world a half century later, often gangs and youth groups, proving that the forces of hatred and of repression are still available to be marshalled into mass action.

Bibliography

Cartier-Bresson, Henri. *Henri Cartier-Bresson*. New York: Aperture Foundation, 1987.
Daniel, Joseph. *Guerre et cinéma: grandes illusions et petits soldats, 1895–1971*. Paris: A. Colin, 1972.

La Bataille d'Alger
(The Battle of Algiers)

directed by Gillo Pontecorvo (1965)
written by Franco Solinas

This 1965 dramatized black and white documentary-style film was banned in France until 1970–1971 (when it was shown and then quickly withdrawn from theaters after numerous right-wing terrorist attacks), even though it had won many awards, including the Grand Prize at the Venice Film Festival in 1966. It convincingly traces the actions of the Arab nationalist terrorists in Algiers from 1954 to 1957, in a flashback from the final scene of the arrest of their leader, Ali La Pointe, by the French army colonel Mathieu and his paratroopers, in the Arab casbah of Algiers. A lengthy postscript with voice-over shows the masses of the Algerian people rebelling in 1960 and 1961, the final wave of popular protest against the French colonial presence which led to Algeria's independence on 2 July 1962. France still feels the effects of these traumatic events; more recently, Algeria has been torn apart by internal factional struggles for control.

Three major groups battled for control of this North African nation: the FLN, the Arab leftist (although not Communist) *Front de la Libération Nationale,* de Gaulle's centrist party, and the OAS, the *Organisation de l'Armée Secrète,* a rightist military faction wanting to retain total control of Algeria similar to right-wing ambitions in South Africa. De Gaulle won in 1962, the centrist Arab government he helped establish did not last, and the corruption of successive leftist Arab governments incited bloody conflicts in 1988 and 1989. In 1992, a conservative army-backed regime battled for control of Algeria against the fundamentalist Moslem faction. Virtually the entire 1990s were marked by butchery and bloodshed.

The French colonial presence in Algeria (1831–1962) had devastating effects: one million Arabs died at their hands and twenty thousand French lost their lives. Not only did the thousands of French *pieds noirs* (black feet) repatriated during the last years of the struggle lose most of their holdings to nationalization, the war rent the very fabric of the French nation, particularly during 1961 and 1962 when sporadic terrorist bombings and mass demonstrations rocked Paris.

France has developed new patterns of trade in the EU to supplant its prior exchanges with its colony, as it has attempted to repress the painful memory and images of its former involvement in Africa as in Indochina. And the immigration of thousands of Arabs into France has established an Arab subculture, especially in the major cities, creating new conflicts within the Hexagon itself.

La Bataille d'Alger has both a diachronic and synchronic generic appurtenance. It belongs to the group of political films regarding France's involvement in Algeria, many of which were banned, including Jean-Luc Godard's *Le Petit Soldat* (1960) and the anonymous works *J'ai huit ans* and *Octobre à Paris*. Other more commercial films reflected the separation, loss or confusion generated by the war among the French: Agnès Varda's 1962 *Cléo de 5 à 7*, Jacques Demy's 1964 *Les Parapluies de Cherbourg* (entirely sung as an opera) or grimmer renditions like Daniel Anselme's *La Permission*, Robert Enrico's *La Belle Vie*, or Alain Resnais's *Muriel*. More leftist films, still distant from internal events in Algeria, included Jacques Doniol-Valcroze's *La Dénonciation* and Alain Cavalier's *Combat dans l'île* in 1962 or Chris Marker's *Le Joli Mai*. Yet no French films portrayed internally the Arab-French experience. Crowded refugee ghettos and internment camps (alluded to by Resnais in *Nuit et brouillard*) remained a shadowy intertext of filmmaking about the Algerian conflict. Reacting like the Americans repressing their humiliating defeat in Vietnam (similar to that suffered earlier by the French), France struggled throughout the 1960s with the reality of its history and the cultural reflections of its self-image on the screen. Only in 1972 did the film of Yves Courrière's 1969 book *La Guerre d'Algérie* appear.

The other genealogical connection of the film is its place as a docudrama in the world-wide historical tradition of the genre. Because its pretext and its diegetic reality are fundamentally at odds, docudrama is ever vulnerable to criticism, imitation or subversion into fictional modes masquerading as historic events. The modus and morality propelling docudrama is rarely as dispassionate or objective an account of historic events as true documentary. The drive to recreate an eminently veracious and believable diegesis is inherently suspect; the filmmaker may be attempting to witness injustices, as in many contemporary Latin American films, or there may be a political dialectic driving the production.

The leftist pro-Arab nature of *La Bataille d'Alger* led to its use by the PLO (Palestine Liberation Organization) as a training film for its soldiers and terrorists and to its popularity with the Black Panthers as an example of urban guerrilla warfare. For these groups, the film has both the strong fervor of African nationalism and a lot of technical information about the organization of a terrorist movement: its pyramidal structure, ways of carrying out attacks, of avoiding detection. It is such a historic irony that the leader of the PLO, Yasser Arafat, should have received the Nobel Peace Prize in 1994, ostensibly for his efforts to put an end to sporadic extremism.

Although the film was made by an Italian director in conjunction with Yacef Saadi's Casbah film company, the actors speak French or Arabic. In fact the two languages could be said to war with each other, just as the two national and racial groups fight to dominate Algeria. The contrapuntal play of these opposing tonalities and voices is lost in other language versions. It is interesting that the original version of the film, like Roberto Rossellini's neorealist classic *Roma città aperta* (*Open City*), was postsynchronized, due to the amateur status of most of the participating actors and the contingencies of filming in the streets of Algiers.

Gillo Pontecorvo was working in Paris as a journalist right after World War II when he happened to see another great Rossellini film, *Paisà* (1946). Pontecorvo was so moved by the experience that he quit his job, bought a camera, and began making documentaries. It is this combined affinity for neorealism and documentary-style filmmaking that makes *La Bataille d'Alger* so effective; its illusion of historic reality is perhaps as great as any ever achieved on the screen, and its black and white format and handheld cameras give it a journalistic realism. Even though ten years elapsed between the events depicted and the making of this film three years after the end of the war, its sense of immediacy is intense. The producer of the film, Yacef Saadi, who also has a role, was himself the FLN commander in Algiers. Pontecorvo once said that a film should be three-quarters Rossellini and one-quarter Eisenstein (combining the close focus of personal drama and the epic sweep of collective destiny). Sequences of impoverished families in crowded ghetto flats evoke images of the former's early work, especially *Open City*. And the camera angles and crowd scenes certainly show their debt to the latter, particularly the cutting of *The Battleship Potemkin*.

In Pontecorvo's film, he follows both Rossellini and Eisenstein in setting off both the battle between the protagonists, Ali La Pointe and the paratrooper commander Colonel Mathieu and their followers, and the contrast between their very different vision and logic, against the backdrop of the Arab and French populace. The fate of the innocent victims of terrorism on both sides is a raw portrayal of human suffering whose dramatic irony and moral ambivalence leave the decision to history. Pontecorvo also follows Rossellini and Eisenstein in involving women and children in the battle for control of their city and nation.

The distinctions between documentary and docudrama are many. First of all, the absence of authentic newsreel or photojournalist footage of key events in this story of national self-determination forced Pontecorvo to recreate, using nonprofessional actors and even real terrorists of the Arab casbah of Algiers, the series of terrorist acts which led to the French Army's intervention. Closed meetings between terrorists, clandestine encounters passing weapons and bombs, meetings of the police and army involving strategy responses and screening classified footage (the film within the film), even torturing of captured terrorists—all were recreated dramatically. The main evidence of dramatization is in the sequences which anticipate key incidents, building tension and suspense: closeups of faces of innocent civilians just before bombs explode, social scenes masking vicious acts, confrontations both verbal and physical between French and Arabs, intimate camera angles depicting actions of women and children involved in the FLN. Concomitantly, the crowd scenes, the haunting ululation (also used in mourning) of the women, here crying freedom, the demonstrators displaying the new Algerian flag in the crowded streets, even the long shots of the cityscape at dawn or dusk, are all carefully staged with unbelievable precision. Particularly ironic was the filming of the scenes where masses of Algerian and French extras (or tourists from other countries) followed marks on the pavement, while the camera focused only on the foreground and the protagonists.

The film shows the hand of the master naturalist narrator-filmmaker who accomplishes a historically believable *mise en scène* without intruding a melodramatic presence. Although not accurate, the film makes a powerful and convincing statement about the historic impact of the events it portrays. In her study guide to the film, Joan Mellen, to whom I am indebted for much of the factual information in this chapter, summarizes the achievement of Pontecorvo thusly:

> What is so noteworthy about *The Battle of Algiers* is not only that we feel that we are watching a film of events as they occurred, but that Pontecorvo has achieved a supreme fiction, capturing the inner truth of the history he transforms.[1]

Pontecorvo created thus a distorted view of history with an ulterior moral purpose not unlike Resnais's goal in making *Nuit et brouillard.*

In this respect, the film was so successful in creating an ambiance of authenticity that as mentioned earlier it carries a printed disclaimer, a political as well as artistic affirmation, assuring the spectator that it is a staged recreation of events. In the video version, the disclaimer is saved for the end, thus permitting the uninformed spectator the experience of the film's illusion of historic immediacy, and creating a special *coup de théâtre* of its own. It is interesting to compare this leftist film with the newsreel footage of the same events incorporated into *Sartre par lui-même,* footage which as already noted constitutes patent right-wing propaganda of the day.

The resemblance between *La Bataille d'Alger* and Rossellini's work is more than just homage. Pontecorvo had trouble financing his project, and wound up shooting the film for just $800,000, with only nine Italians in the crew and cast. The rest came from the streets of Algeria, including the tourists who also served as journalists and as Mathieu's paratroopers (whose authentic appearance was the result of recreated uniforms and the use of Algerian Army equipment). Mathieu himself has generated a lot of controversy, as a composite of several renowned commanders. According to Pontecorvo, he is modeled more on Bigeard than the infamous Massu. Turned down by Paul Newman and Warren Beatty, the role is interpreted by Jean Martin, who makes an imposing and almost impassive leader under pressure. When he chooses "Champagne" for the name of his counter-insurgency plan, it elicits images of French sophistication (as well as colonial domination and economic exploitation for some) rather than of the bottle blowing its cork. The collaboration of Yacef Saadi was pervasive; as former commander of the FLN in Algiers, he was well equipped to play Djafar, the leader arrested at the end with Zohra Drif, his real-life lover with whom he had in fact been arrested in intimate circumstances. Ali La Pointe was played by Brahim Aggiag, who had no previous acting experience but who went on to play a role in Luchino Visconti's film of *L'Etranger* (*The Stranger*), also produced by Casbah Films. The thirteen-year-old Omar was played by one of Saadi's nephews.

One of the major historic inaccuracies in the film involves the character of Ali La Pointe, who rather than the hapless illiterate con artist portrayed was really a seasoned hit man. Yet his vulnerability on screen stands for that of his people, like that of the luckless Arab caught in the white neighborhood who is beaten up (in a scene which elicits associations with racial strife in the streets in any time and place). One of the real ironies of the film was that the house they constructed as a set for the scene wherein the paratroopers close in on Ali and blow up his hiding place (killing him, Omar, and the bride and groom from the Moslem wedding ceremony, Mamoud and Hassiba ben Bouali) had to be built on the open space where the real house had stood in the Casbah. In reality, also, it was Ali's own cache of dynamite that exploded and destroyed the building.

Several scenes from the film represent central beliefs of the Moslem religion. Ali is first tested by being sent to assassinate a police officer with an unloaded gun, then put into service fully armed to eliminate Hacene Le Blidea, a drug dealer. That sequence and the scene where the children drag the old drunk down the stairs and beat him indicate the Moslem determination to rid the revolution of the weakening influence of drugs and alcohol.

Mellen discusses at length the use of sound and silence, in point and counter-point, in the film. Pontecorvo composed the music for the film himself and had his friend Ennio Morricone score it. The authentic Arab elements in the score, Arab music and the frequent ululating of the women, as well as the insistent drums and even heartbeats used, all contribute to the dramatic tension of the film as it builds to its climax. Because the film opens with its final scene and flashes back three years, the audience is held enthralled even while party to the outcome. The extension of the film to the mass demonstrations at the end is prepared by the various themes throughout. Mellen points out that Pontecorvo also eliminated much of the dialogue surrounding the scenes of the bombings, leaving the tension of taut faces and drumbeats to build. Similarly, the absence of lengthy explicative narrative one would expect in a documentary heightens the drama and adds a dimension of testimonial immediacy to the images.

The three bombing sequences—the milk bar, the cafeteria and the Air France Terminal—are emblematic of the hundreds of terrorist bombings of Algiers in 1956 (eighty-five in September alone). The film telescopes the three to intensify the effect, just as it creates a collage of the day of assassinations of the police officers. Other effects which heighten the realism of the film are the datelines, hourly reports, loudspeakers and megaphones addressing the populace or sequestered terrorists. The one point where Pontecorvo backs down from realism is in his use of the musical soundtrack to cover up the victims' screams of agony when they are being tortured.

During the news conference Mathieu gives (another documentary-style effect), he presents the recently arrested leader of the FLN in Algeria, Larbi Ben M'Hidi, depicted in the film as a middle-class intellectual in a business suit. While Ben M'Hidi's presence represents the extent of the rebellion throughout the country, Pontecorvo has been criticized for portraying such a narrow segment of the total picture in Algeria. Historians take umbrage over the omission of reference to the MNA, the rival Arab nationalist organization led by Messali Hadj. They also point out that the dancing flag-waving woman at the end would surely have been gunned down by the French. And of course the film omits a prime historic irony, that the Arabs had been fighting with the Free French against the Nazis in North Africa only ten years earlier, a situation similar to that of Ho Chi Minh in Vietnam. Nonetheless, the film stands as one of the most powerful depictions of conflict of all time, which explains the intense reactions it elicited at its release, reactions which often mingled anger with praise for its undeniable effectiveness as a work of art as well as a testimony to historic events of lasting importance. Inevitably viewer response to this film has been greatly affected during the last decade by the events caused by Islamic fundamentalist extremist terrorist groups such as the Front Islamique du Salut and Al Qaeda.

Note

1. Joan Mellen, *Filmguide to 'The Battle of Algiers'* (Bloomington: Indiana University Press, 1973) 57.

Bibliography

Bignardi, Irene. "The Making of *The Battle of Algiers*." *Cinéaste* 25:2 (2000) 14–22.
Bromberger, Serge. *Les Rebelles algériens*. Paris: Plon, 1958.
Castelli, Luisa. "La Battaglia di Algeri." *Occhio Critico* 3 (1967) 5–23.
Clark, M. J. *Politics and the Media: Film and Television for the Political Scientist and Historian*. New York: Pergamon Press, 1979.
Conley, Tom. "Algerian Off-Map." *Parallax* 4:2:7 (Apr–Jun 1998) 99–112.
Courrière, Yves. *La Guerre d'Algérie*. Paris: Fayard, 1969.
Daniel, Joseph. *Guerre et cinéma: grandes illusions et petits soldats, 1895–1971*. Paris: A.Colin, 1972.
Davidson, Naomi. "Naming la Guerre sans nom: Memory, Nation and Identity in French Representations of the Algerian War, 1963–1992." *Paroles Gelées* 16:2 (1998) 65–90.
Davis, Natalie Zemon. *Slaves on Screen: Film and Historical Vision*. Cambridge, MA: Harvard University Press, 2000.
Dine, Philippe. "French Culture and the Algerian War: Mobilizing Icons." *Journal of European Studies* 28:1–2: 109–110 (Mar-Jun 1998) 51–68.
Fanon, Frantz. *A Dying Colonialism*. New York: Grove Press, 1966.
Feldman, Seth. "Footnote to Fact: The Docudrama." In Grant, Barry, ed. *Film Genre Reader*. Austin: University of Texas Press, 1986.
Furhammer, Leif, and Isaksson, Folke. *Politics and Film*. New York: Praeger, 1971.
Heggoy, Alf. *Insurgency and Counterinsurgency in Algeria*. Bloomington: Indiana University

Press, 1972.

Hennebelle, Guy. "Une Si Jeune Paix." *Cinéma 65* 101 (1965) 20–29.

Mellen, Joan. *Filmguide to 'The Battle of Algiers'*. Bloomington: Indiana University Press, 1973.

Michalczyk, John. *Italian Political Filmmakers.*Cranbury, NJ: Associated University Presses, 1986.

Morgenstern, Joseph. "The Terror." *Newsweek* (23 October 1967) 102.

Orlando, Valerie. "Historiographic Metafiction in Gillo Pontecorvo's *La Bataille d'Alger*: Remembering the 'Forgotten War'." *Quarterly Review of Film and Video* 17:3 (Oct 2000) 261–271.

Pontecorvo, Gillo. *"The Battle of Algiers*: An Adventure in Filmmaking." *American Cinematographer* (1967) 266–269.

Saadi, Yacef. *Souvenirs de la Bataille d'Alger*. Paris: Julliard, 1962.

Said, Edward. "The Dictatorship of Truth: An Interview with Gillo Pontecorvo. *Cinéaste* 25:2 (2000) 14–22.

Sainsbury, Peter. "Battle of Algiers." *Afterimage* 3 (1971) 5–7.

Le Retour de Martin Guerre
(The Return of Martin Guerre)

directed by Daniel Vigne (1982)
written by Jean-Claude Carrière and Daniel Vigne

The time is August, 1560. The place is Artigat, in Foix, near the Pyrénées Mountains in southwestern France. The reign of François Premier ended in 1547, but through his influence, his conquests of Italy and support of letters and arts at his court, France has entered the Renaissance. It is also the time of religious conflict, forty-three years after Martin Luther's proclamations and only twenty-six years after Henry the Eighth's break with Rome and Catholicism. The reign of Henri II (1547–1559) has been a time of war as well; the soldiers in the film have been fighting in Picardy in northern France and in Spain. In 1560, François II has ended the wars; the new peace is important to the outcome of this tale.

In the village peasant existence depicted in this film, the setting still seems medieval; time moves more slowly in remote provincial communities, where tradition also works against change. It is the Renaissance, however; the judges in the film represent the parliamentary regional court in Toulouse, and they demonstrate, especially Jean de Coras, a remarkably tolerant humanism, a new paradigm of the individual and the ingredients of his identity.

In her 1989 article in *South Atlantic Quarterly*, "Securing the Fictional Narrative as a Tale of the Historical Real," Janet Staiger proposes to deconstruct the text and intertexts of *Le Retour de Martin Guerre* with a leftist Freudian reading of film as satisfying a need to reconcile *eros* and *thanatos*, desire and death, in narrative closure. She deconstructs the historic pretext of the film as a manifestation of an ideological power struggle, an extrapolation, as we shall later see, of Natalie Zemon Davis's contention that it is a tale of two conflicting historic models of the self and its integration into, or segregation from, society. I would like to take another look at the historicity of *Le Retour de Martin Guerre* to resituate its fundamental duplicity in a broader historic intertextuality than that proposed by Staiger.

In fact, not one but two modern books about the subject of Daniel Vigne's 1982 film of double identity and triple indemnity treat the question of authenticity in the story of Martin Guerre, first inscribed in 1560 by the judicial counsellor Jean de Coras of Toulouse and published the following year in Lyons as *Arrest Memorable*.

And these works, Janet Lewis's 1941 *The Wife of Martin Guerre* and Natalie Zemon Davis's 1983 *The Return of Martin Guerre*, are but the latest in a long list of written accounts of this legendary trial of an impostor. Natalie Davis had been working on a film about Martin Guerre (having unsuccessfully approached René Allio and Bertrand Tavernier) for several years when she found out about Jean-Claude Carrière and Daniel Vigne's project. Their collaboration was extensive, as Davis provided much historic information and documentation for the film. The many alterations and discrepancies between her findings and the film indicate a funda-mental impossibility of exact reconstruction of a historical event which has belonged to literature for four centuries. More practically, they stemmed from problems of the cost of changing the script, from differences of male and female perspectives (as do Jean de Coras's and Bertrande's accounts), and from conscious choices to rewrite history for the sake of drama. Davis reiterates, in her interview with Pringle and Prior, her frustration over Carrière and Vigne's persistent characterization of Bertrande as a docile romanticized nineteenth-century heroine. Thus the power and suspense of the film are generated not only in conflicting narratives and their accompanying images, but finally at the expense of certain historic ironies and subtleties that did not serve cinematic art. Likewise, the ontological question of identity, as it was understood in the sixteenth century, is interwoven with a modern teleology of mask and resemblance, of seeming and being. Davis talks of "invent-ing" Bertrande and Martin (all three) from archival information, piecing together reasonable facsimiles of their Renaissance peasant identities and contexts. Moreo-ver, the story from its origins belongs to a great tradition of imposture and substitu-tion, from Plautus's Amphitryon and Sosius through centuries of disguises and travesties to other modern works which have been filmed, such as Pirandello's 1904 *The Late Matthew Pascal* (films by L'Herbier, Chenal and Pirandello's son Stefano) or 1921 *Henry IV* (film by Bellocchio in 1985) or Antonioni's 1975 *The Passenger*. Interestingly, Davis compares the substitution of the new father-husband figure to the main construct of Marcel Pagnol's *Marius* trilogy. Davis also cites Leonardo Sciascia's *Teatro della memoria* (Turin: Einaudi, 1981) as another source of tales of invented identity and imposture.

Vigne's film appeared in a wave of "historic realism" productions, including *La Nuit de Varennes* and *Danton*. And numerous elements of the cinematic diegesis of *Le Retour de Martin Guerre* engage the spectator in its 1550s *mise en scène*: the costumes, the villages and fields, the interiors shot by candlelight and firelight, the carmine-garbed judges in their courtroom, the striking musical score. The ending credits of the film acknowledge the assistance of the conservators of Toulouse and the villages of the region, which were substituted for Artigat in Foix, Rieux and Toulouse. The film offers innumerable validations of its own authenticity, of its capacity to document, so much so that John O'Connor opens his video project on teaching history through feature film, *Image as Artifact*, with an analysis of the film and Natalie Zemon Davis's documentation.

Yet a close study of *Le Retour de Martin Guerre* reveals that it is only apparently an objective historic film documenting the story of Arnauld du Tilh, that it is a mirror of itself as well as a window on the past, that the subterfuge, collusion and imposture depicted on the screen invade and infuse the film, that it is at once a surreal, existential image of identity, a deconstruction of its characters' attempts to document their reality. It offers an image of the individual as hero against the mob, a mockery of adjudication, a tale of a soldier missing in action with all its modern echoes, and a collage of fables and myths, local contemporary and ancient, with allusions to the Bible and to classical mythology and wayfaring literature like the *Odyssey*, the *Iliad* and the *Aeneid*. It is essentially a demonstration of the seductive power of language, of narrative, in an intriguing counterpoint between the male and female accounts of shared experiences.

It constitutes ultimately a textual and metatextual process of doubling, as its principal sequences prefigure and echo one another in perfect symmetry, and as it displays systematically its own self-reflexive duplicity, undermining the process of revelation of truth which it pretends to unfold. This process of doubling in fact pervades the film; the title is itself a trap, duplicitous and twofold, as the real "return of Martin Guerre" is of course the *coup de théâtre* of the final trial scene. It goes without saying that in a film, no one is the "real" Martin Guerre, as all three roles are interpreted by actors exploiting the power of mask, of imitation, central to cinematic interpretive art, an art which by definition reduces any ambition to recreate reality to a succession of present images and sounds ordered by the recombinant collage of editing the illusory sequences registered and reregistered during filming.

The opening shot of the film behind the credits announces the nature of its narrative, as the magistrate on a white mule (an equine impostor) wends his way along the path to the village, the cinematic equivalent of the entry into the text, *chemin faisant*, making a path, prefiguring the struggle of the individual against the collective, in this case the "mob" of sheep blocking his path, declaring the developmental *devenir* of becoming, the process of the creation of identity which will dominate the film, working in dynamic opposition to its surface structuring of identity through memory. In his 1983 work *The French*, Theodore Zeldin, analyzing the phenomenon of identity through identification, sums up the paradox at the center of this film: "Local identity is not just a memory, it is a process of evolution and creation, and its shape is constantly altering."[1] In fact, the power and seduction of nomination are at the center of this film, which thus declares itself an onomastic adventure.

The initial sequences of the 1540s rites of marriage uniting the young Martin Guerre and Bertrande de Rols and her dowry agreement (not only historically authentic but reinforced with intercut shots of domestic activities) are followed by the first dialogical exchange between Jean de Coras (Roger Planchon) and the mature Bertrande (Nathalie Baye), who is reflecting on these past events in her ultimate deposition more than a decade later. Thus we are offered a fragmented, achronological narrative, a framed tale whose retrospective format already distances us from the events depicted and recounted; the film reveals itself as a re-presentative art, a tale of "fiction" fabricated and woven together like the treasured cloth distributed in tribute to the women of the household by the impostor Martin Guerre on his "return."

The impotence of the young Martin Guerre, passively bedded down with his bride, surrounded and dominated by the strong patriarchal family structure of his world, is finally exorcised by the village priest. Thus the original Martin Guerre is thought to be possessed by demons, just as the impostor Arnauld (Gérard Depardieu) is later accused of diabolic powers during the trial scene. The young Martin's impotence marks him as a village outcast, and he is pursued and mocked by costumed spirits (just as Arnauld will be) in a *masque* or play within the play, a *mise-en-abyme* wherein garbed in a bearskin he is symbolically castrated by the villagers in the primitive *charivari* ritual of Candlemas. This sequence was perhaps generated by the fact that the name "Martin" then meant "ass" or "bear." Just as this humiliating experience prefigures Martin's later second symbolic castration in the loss of his leg, Arnauld will suffer a similarly symbolic castration at the end when he is hung before the crowd. Yet Martin Guerre's genealogical authenticity and procreative capability is demonstrated unequivocally by the creation of a son, Sanxi, while the impostor's first-born child was actually stillborn.

In the film, the first Martin Guerre is cruel and irresponsible, betraying his family as he steals the grain (fertility, heritage) and deserts his wife and son, going off to war (although historically that may not have been his original intent; it was because he joined the household of a Spanish nobleman that he wound up fighting for Philip II *against* the French. Arnauld du Tilh also ran off, to join the forces of Henri II in Picardy, and thus fought for his own king *against* Martin Guerre. Historically, it is most doubtful that the two ever met; it was rather because he was taken for Martin Guerre by two villagers from Artigat that Arnauld decided to pump them for information and then return to southern France to usurp his place, his wife and his fortune). In the film, the first Martin Guerre though not guilty of treason was however indirectly guilty of parricide, as we are told that his parents died of grief over his disappearance (historically they died by accident). The limping stranger guilty of parricide who returns home conjures images of primal myths like Oedipus, as does the arrival of Arnauld to take another man's marriage bed and transform it to the site of an illicit sexual relationship. It is perhaps this primordial mythical intertextuality that gives the film its power, even more effective than its "authentic" sets and costumes.

The doubling is pervasive; Arnauld du Tilh committed virtually the same original crime that Martin Guerre did: he abandoned his family, village and fields, ran off to seek adventure and left his uncle Carbon Barrau of Sajas (who later identified him as Pansette, his nickname) to manage his affairs. This generates the fundamental moral ambiguity of the tale that haunts the spectator at the end; it is very difficult in a twenty-first-century context to affirm the superiority of the old hierarchical value system. Existentialism and modern humanism have since then redefined both ontological and moral being.

If we consider Bertrande's moral status, we are forced to acknowledge the extenuating circumstances surrounding her *crime passionnel* of abandoning her long-standing chastity and devotion in receiving Arnauld into her bed. In the film, this plunge into the realm of the godless is symbolized by her removing the crucifix from the pillow of her bed before her first union with Arnauld. It also prefigures his martyrdom at the end. Both Natalie Davis and Janet Lewis (as sympathetic female voices) emphasize Bertrande's plight: in Catholic France of that era, remarriage for her was impossible; she was inexorably trapped by her family situation, unable to inherit, unable to have her own life, imprisoned by the civil code of the day just as historically she was later imprisoned along with Arnauld. In the film, the final verdict of her innocence leaves her free to accept her first husband and raise her two children (Sanxi and Bernarde, her daughter by Arnauld). But by modern (read Protestant) moral standards, Martin Guerre's final reclaiming of his heritage seems somehow as great a betrayal as the imposture of Arnauld. As Davis speculates, perhaps it was Jean de Coras's own heretical Protestantism (which would later cost him his life) and his undying devotion to his own second spouse, who mothered his son so well and was also a Protestant, which led him to feel such unusual sympathy and fascination for the situation of Bertrande de Rols Guerre. Davis further assumes that for similar reasons he must have identified as well with Arnauld du Tilh, clever, charming and verbal, who was shaping a new identity for himself with his own wits.

Identity and all its moral and civil accoutrements are put to the supreme test in this legendary tale. Davis was the first to posit, and I think rightly so, that the story is a struggle between two historic religious paradigms, between the Catholic and Protestant concepts of spiritual identity and the individual, of new against old. In any event, it is above all a tale of the hazards of identification. Predication, attribution and nomination, essential elements of identity as outlined by Peter Strawsen in *Individuals*,[2] are all in play in this tale.

The initial "return" of Martin Guerre is shadowed in doubt by the queries of the first villagers he encounters: "You aren't really the son of Mathurin Guerre?...Is it really you?" (All translations of the film dialogue are mine.) His imposture and unlawful possession of Bertrande are perfectly prefigured by the *crapaud* toad she finds in her bed not long before his appearance. The narrative declares itself a fable, a fairy tale, redolent of the narratives circulating throughout Germany, France and Italy in the sixteenth century, of the frog become a prince through the sexual benediction of the ideal woman, a tale which could be retraced to the power of the Virgin Mary in the Middle Ages.

An obvious biblical allusion is announced during the sequence of the vagabonds, as recounted by Bertrande to Jean de Coras. The vagabonds identify Arnauld as Pansette of Tilh, just as Nicolas calls him "the Prodigal Son." It is however in this case the uncle, Pierre Guerre, and not the father, now dead, who has received the returning Martin after an absence of "eight or nine winters." This episode supposedly marked Bertrande's first doubts, although earlier additional clues for the astute spectator, such as Arnauld not recognizing Nicolas, his boot size differing from Martin's (ironic considering Martin would lose a leg), his not remembering the location of the candles, his having the power to read and write, virtually prove that she knew the truth from the beginning and was a willing accessory to the crime. Arnauld's literacy and oratorical powers are doubly significant, as they emphasize and reflect the transforming and seductive power of narrative, of language, while offering yet another biblical allusion: the interdiction of eating of the fruit of the tree of the knowledge of good and evil.

The film redoubles the ambiguity for the spectator by substituting different actors for the first Martin and Bertrande, creating thus three images of Martin. Time has changed the identities and the bodies of the pair; Baye and Depardieu have no resemblance to the actors who played the young couple at the beginning. We are just as uncertain, as incapable of swearing the authenticity of their identity as are half of the villagers, family and servants. In the end, we are frustrated in our need to project our own desires on Arnauld and empower him with the authenticity he lacks. Our initial choice like Bertrande's is sexual rather than moral, present rather than absent, material rather than abstract.

Le Retour de Martin Guerre demonstrates that film by its very nature deconstructs its own discourse, transforms images of reality into sound and light, projects literally its own illusion in the place of experiential memory. Whereas in traditional mythology Mnemosyne, the goddess of memory, is the mother of the Muses, here the uncertainty of memory collaborates with the creative acts to construct multiple images, as the three successive incarnations of Martin Guerre constitute a palimpsest of identity.

Historically, the sensational tale of the imposture and unmasking of Arnauld as Martin Guerre captivated all who encountered it, from the first judges and spectators (including Michel de Montaigne and other nobles of the region), to a number of storytellers who published the tale throughout the later sixteenth century and beyond. Specifically, Montaigne referred to it in his 1588 essay *Des Boyteux* (*Of the Lame*). It has descended the ages as legend, as a morality tale drawn from life. Natalie Zemon Davis's account and the screenplay by Jean-Claude Carrière and Daniel Vigne are not the first resurrection of the tale in our time. As noted, Janet Lewis published in 1941 a lyric novella of *The Wife of Martin Guerre*, in response to her discovery of the story in a volume called *Famous Cases of Circumstantial Evidence*, which led her in turn to the account of the trial in Estienne Pasquier's *Les Recherches de la France*. Pasquier (1529–1615) had unearthed the tale by Maître Jean Corras [sic]. Lewis's novella is like its title sympathetic to Bertrande's experience, depicting her suffering from her young husband's sexual neglect and physical abuse, then portraying her loneliness and her fantasizing a miraculous return of her long absent husband. After reading the passages describing Bertrande's long lyric deprivation, her bewilderment at the return of the impostor, her growing doubts, her sense of suffocation at the time of the trials, her final anguish, one cannot help but wonder if this first modern revival of the now famous tale, which went virtually unnoticed at its release (just before America's entry into war), would not have made just as interesting a film as the version actually produced.

The latest version of the recurrent return of Martin Guerre, resurrected from the archives of Toulouse, takes place in the movie, with the spectators as the newest victims of the illusion of his historic authenticity. Yet the initiated moviegoer doubts the narrative capacity of film to portray historic reality. And the very subject matter of the film warns against the willing suspension of disbelief, emphasizes the inherent opacity of film at the center of its apparent transparence, its fundamental existential lack of essence, its moving illusory becoming, its non-being.

The impostor's downfall is his attempt to extract a payment of silver from his uncle Pierre Guerre. In a gesture worthy of Judas, he sells his own soul, his own credibility, for the sum of six thousand pounds. In the ensuing sequence of the murder attempt in the granary, Arnauld is flailed and nearly impaled by Pierre, saved symbolically for the first time by the heroic intervention of the loving and loyal Bertrande. Davis questions Pierre's position, wondering if he would have been that murderously vengeful if he had been in collusion with Arnauld from the beginning. To me, his rage is even more logical if it comes from the anger of betrayal, of having been set up by Arnauld.

Bertrande's silence at critical moments (as when Arnauld, restored to her bed, is again accosted by Pierre and dragged off by the soldiers) creates a second narrative ambiguity in the film, which is constructed retrospectively from her tale as related to Jean de Coras. It is unlikely that Bertrande ever doubted the identity of Arnauld; rather she vacillated about her own fate. Thus her oscillating between acceptance and rejection, thrice depicted, is due to the central moral ambiguity of her position: if she rejects Arnauld, having taken him to bed in a madly spontaneous *acte désinvolte*, she condemns herself to a state of sin, becoming the adulterous Mary Magdalene she symbolizes as she washes Arnauld's feet. In existential fashion, she is forced to take responsibility for her act, to live out the consequent identity it has created in her, and at the end she bows before her first husband only at the behest of Arnauld, in whose pleading glance she reads: "All is lost, save yourself for the sake of the children."

A further biblical allusion pervades the sequence where the judge comes to Artigat and asks the families and the villagers to declare themselves in favor of or against the validity of the impostor Martin Guerre by grouping themselves on his right hand or his left hand, a dramatized scene of the last judgment. It is in this scene that the village priest sides with those against Arnauld. This is the same village priest who earlier washed his hands of the moral responsibility for the fate of Arnauld, in a Pontius Pilate gesture, and who represents the old moral order. It is obvious why Vigne didn't include in his film a real historic substitution, that of a new priest in the village: his denial of the impostor would thus have been rendered meaningless, as he would have had no memory of the original Martin Guerre.

Thus this stranger, who has profited from the chance fate of being taken for Martin Guerre and fled the horrors of war in his place (having lost his leg, Martin would be confined in Picardy until the end of the war with the death of Henri II in 1559), this opportunist, twice a deserter, uses his prodigious memory and seductive storytelling capacities to create an identity attractive enough if not believable enough to convince the family to accept him. In her book, Davis mentions that the surname "Guerre" was originally "Daguerre" (which elicits ironic associations with photography), but the shortened name meaning war is only too apt, as the two Martins wage war against each other, first on the battlefield, then in the village and lastly in the courtroom. In fact, the impostor wages throughout the film a war of wills and words for his survival, regaling the family with tales of Paris ("I got lost") and the tribal Indians from Brazil who go around nude and whose women are in control, a description which elicits from Pierre the modern day assertion: "Here the day women will command will be the end of the world." Although Davis tried unsuccessfully to strengthen the character portrayal and voice of Bertrande in the film, the operative irony is that Bertrande is in fact controlling the narrative, filtering the entire story, asserting her ultimate oratorical power in telling her tale to Coras, just as she undermines Pierre's second attempt to convict Arnauld by writing her name, a new image of identity she has learned from him, thus negating the collaborative X mark she supposedly placed on the condemning document. Moreover, since in the film the entire story is reconstructed through flashbacks and the narrative is a function of Bertrande's memory, it is inevitably altered by the concomitant functions of the imagination and its powers of spatial and temporal reordering.

The third trial sequence elicits another biblical subtext, the betrayal of Christ by Peter, who denies him three times as the cock crows. During his defense, Arnauld states, "I have no reason to fear the condemnation of Arnauld du Tilh as a demonic perpetrator of evil deception, for I am not that man." His adept sophistry marks all his arguments in his defense, such as "If I were the Devil with all his powers, would I be here standing trial for my life?" One of the things that condemns the impostor though is the fact that he cannot produce Arnauld du Tilh to prove they are not one and the same.

At the very end of the trial, Bertrande reveals before the open courtroom: "I accepted him into my bed because he knew what gave me satisfaction; he knew the words I wanted to hear, before, during and after." Thus Arnauld demonstrates the seductive power of narrative, of language. Bertrande's *jouissance* is accomplished through the fantasy of her imagination, through the associations elicited by the signs Arnauld offers her. The spectator identifies with this confession through the realization of the seductive power of the film narrative to entice and satisfy by demanding collaboration and conspiracy in maintaining the illusion of identity, which is ultimately unmasked; the play ends, the truth prevails, the real Martin Guerre, boring and ungrateful, returns. In the final moments of the trial, Arnauld is trapped by his own silver tongue as he in turn questions Martin Guerre, undone by losing his control of the persona of Martin, whom he now faces in the flesh.

The closing sequences of the film leave us with an image of the martyrdom of Arnauld, as he publicly apologizes and walks hands bound in a white shirt to his death on the scaffold by hanging. His verbal repentance is as convincing as his earlier role-playing. It is as difficult for the spectator as it was for Bertrande to deny this engaging, seductive man. Even Davis expresses a *malaise* about making a final judgment or construct of Arnauld, sensing that Pansette will always elude our grasp of his identity, vacillating as Carrière stated between "songe" and "mensonge" (dream and lie).

Yet exonerating Arnauld creates even more difficulties: although he was a better husband than Martin Guerre, who abused and deserted his young wife, he too stole from his family and abandoned them. Finally it was Arnauld's willful conspiracy in adultery that condemned him by the code of the sixteenth century. In the end, it is not a Christlike martyr who dies before us, but one of the men on Christ's left or his right: a common criminal who got caught. The sentence from the Catholic judges that he be hanged and burned would repeat itself in the fate of Jean de Coras in 1572 (a story of persecution which served D. W. Griffith as the final sequence of his 1916 *Intolerance*). In the age of the Reformation and Counter Reformation, the sentencing of Arnauld was not only a condemnation of adultery and theft by impersonation but moreover an attempt to suppress the creative individual's right to his own self-determination, to forge his own destiny, a right which would assert itself two hundred years later in the violent overthrow of the power structure of both church and state, and would result in the definitive dominance of this new paradigm of identity.

Notes

1. Theodore Zeldin, *The French* (New York: Vintage Books, 1984) 30.
2. Peter Strawsen, *Individuals* (London: Methuen, 1959) passim.

Bibliography

Benson, E. "Martin Guerre, the Historian and the Filmmakers: an interview with Natalie Zemon Davis." *Film & History* XIII, 3 (Sep 1983), 49–65.

Coras, Jean de. *Arrest Mémorable, du Parlement de Tolose, contenant une histoire prodigieuse, de nostre temps*. Lyons: Antoine Vincent, 1561.

Davis, Natalie Zemon. *The Return of Martin Guerre*. Princeton: Princeton University Press, 1983.

———. *Society and Culture in Early Modern France*. Stanford: Stanford University Press, 1975.

Duvigneau, M. "Daniel Vigne: d'Inventaire des campagnes au *Retour de Martin Guerre*." *CinémAction* 36 (Jan 1986) 91–95.

Fotheringham, Richard. "Theorising the Individual Body on Stage and Screen; or, the Jizz of Martin Guerre." *Journal of Dramatic Theory and Criticism* 15:2 (Spring 2001) 17–32.

Guild, Elizabeth. "Adultery on Trial: Martin Guerre and His Wife, from Judge's Tale to the Screen." In White, Nicholas and Naomi Segal, eds. *Scarlet Letters: Fictions of Adultery from*

Antiquity to the 1990s. New York, NY: Macmillan, 1997.

Humbert, Brigitte E. "Remaking History and Cultural Identity: from *The Return of Martin Guerre* to *Sommersby*." *Film Criticism* XXVI, 1 (Fall 2001) 2–24.

Isaac, Rhys. "Pictures of Peasantry." *The Age* (1984).

Lewis, Janet. *The Wife of Martin Guerre*. Athens, OH: Swallow Press, 1941.

O'Connor, John. *Image as Artifact*. Video and Study Guide. Washington, D.C.: American Historical Association.

————. *Image as Artifact: The Historical Analysis of Film and Television*. Malabar, FL: Krieger Publishing, 1990.

————. *Teaching History with Film and Television*. Washington, D.C.: American Historical Association, 1987.

Pringle, Helen, and Elizabeth Prior. "Inventing Martin Guerre: An Interview with Natalie Zemon Davis." *Southern Review: Literary and Interdisciplinary Essays* 19:3 (1986) 231–241.

Sciascia, Leonardo. *Teatro della memoria*. Turin: Einaudi, 1981.

Serceau, Daniel. "Entretien avec Daniel Vigne." *Image et Son* 378 (Dec 1982) 121–123.

Staiger, Janet. "Securing the Fictional Narrative as a Tale of the Historical Real." *South Atlantic Quarterly* 88:2 (1989) 393–413.

La Nuit de Varennes

directed by Ettore Scola (1982)
written by Sergio Amidei and Ettore Scola

As already noted, from photojournalism and documentary to docudrama there is primarily a distinction based on experiential authenticity rather than considerations of formal difference. The example just presented of historic realism, *Le Retour de Martin Guerre*, moves yet another step away from the recording of history and the re-creating of history to the paradigmatic interpretation of a historic event already filtered by four centuries of text. Ettore Scola's 1982 *La Nuit de Varennes* adds yet another element of artifice, in the manner of E. L. Doctorow. It carefully researches a historic event and the authentic texts depicting that occurrence or contemporary to that time and place, and then it arbitrarily mixes characters together, some of whom actually knew each other, in a marginal setting, giving a deconstructed optic to the whole. Scola's film in fact goes even farther: it becomes a double catalogue, of authors, composers, philosophers, and of the topics of the day, presenting a thematic gamut, political, economic, social, sexual, a sort of cinematic *encyclopédie*, a taxonomy of the Revolution.

There was another production entitled *La Nuit de Varennes* for French television by Stellio Lorenzi in 1958. This 1981 French-Italian television co-production, published as a novel in 1982 by Catherine Rihoit, presents history as theater, combining in collage historic events, texts, and intertexts—fact, fiction, and fantasy. The attempted escape of Louis XVI and his family in June 1791, the political figures involved in the surrounding events, and the fictional encounter of three key historical figures who represent three distinct perspectives—Restif de la Bretonne (Jean-Louis Barrault), Thomas Paine (Harvey Keitel), and Giacomo Casanova (Marcello Mastroianni)—are interwoven in an arabesque of dialogic exchanges with other social stereotypes that highlight critical considerations of genre, libertinage, censorship, politics, and economics.

The texts depicted in the film were chosen to illustrate the liberating and revolutionary potential of the printed text in its many forms. Among these texts are: the books seized at the beginning of the film, where the libertine calendar of amorous acts is read by the censor (Vernon Dobtcheff) and the camera; Restif's newspaper article (which he reads in the first metatextual vignette of the film) predicting a violent revolution; the arrest decree from the Assemblée dictated at the *relais* of Meaux by the Commandant Bayon (Patrick Osmond), the messenger of the people; Leporello's "Aria del Catalogo" from Mozart's 1787 *Don Giovanni,* whose lyrics Casanova supposedly helped to write in Da Ponte's absence; the carefully guarded map of France on which Paine and Restif study the various possible routes of the king's flight; the bills of credit signed by Count Waldstein and Casanova that are read by the innkeeper; the newspaper article by Marat read to the mob by torchlight; the actual decree from La Fayette that Jean-Louis Romeuf (Hugues Quester) brings to the king; the passage at the end that Restif recites from his *Nuits révolutionnaires* anticipating the reception of the text in 1992.

The film also presents a virtual catalogue of literary citations, ranging from Restif's *Le Paysan perverti, Le Pornographe, Le Pied de Fanchette, La Fille naturelle, Le Ménage parisien,* and *Les Contemporaines* to the *philosophes* (specifically Diderot) to Beaumarchais to the *Mémoires* of Casanova, who also quotes Dante. Near the end, the film also alludes to the life and writings of Carlo Goldoni, who, having lost his government pension, was living in poverty in Paris at the time of the flight to Varennes, and who, as a Venetian writing his memoirs in French, becomes a mirror of Casanova. Furthermore, the very title of the film accentuates its balance between historic and literary perspective, wherein the *fuite de Varennes* is filtered through Restif's *Nuits révolutionnaires* (specifically the Fifth). By way of further inter- and intratextual citation, Casanova compares Leporello to Sancho Panza, confirming the earlier Don Quixotic parodic allusion by Restif on and off horseback. That Casanova himself is fleeing house arrest as servant-librarian and object of ridicule makes him a *sosie* double of the king in flight.

The choice of the three writers featured is intriguing. They represent three nationalities, as do the three women in the coach. In some respects, they represent three classes as well: Thomas Paine is the obvious populist rebel. Restif, in spite of his noble-sounding name, having been a farmboy from Auxerre and a printer by trade, has a plebeian perspective on events. Casanova, although a legendary figure in court circles, is no longer the powerful Chevalier de Seingalt. In fact, all three are impoverished exiles of a sort. And they complement one another in offering their aristocratic, intellectual, and populist political points of view.

The film's narrative structure is also citational and self-reflexive, incorporating numerous mimetic *mise-en-abyme* scenarios. In the opening sequence of the New World puppet show, *Il Mondo Nuovo* (the Italian title of the film), the barker (Enzo Jannacci) announces the generic appurtenance of the film, hawking historical events as fantasy and fantasy as history. The *diligence* (stage of state) symbolically rearranges and even inverts vertical social structures. The numerous sequences in inns—especially the catalogue of sins depicted in the deconsecrated church—call up endless literary antecedents from Dante to Diderot. These narrative frames and techniques also serve as extratextual historical critical commentary, as they were all popular in eighteenth-century literature, when they were novel if not revolutionary. I would like to explore in closer perspective a number of the elements enumerated above, to illustrate in more detail the film's liberated and contemporary deconstructed discourse of uncertainty in its special blending of fantasy and history. The opening credits of the film are accompanied by stately music and a sustained long shot, upward from the lower quay along the Seine, of Notre Dame Cathedral, where the kings of France were traditionally crowned. Beginning as an engraving in *camaïeu*, the shot then dissolves to the live frame of the same setting. The subsequent shots of the traveling puppet show depict in graphic miniature the events preceding the flight to Varennes, particularly the storming of the Bastille and the October march on Versailles, when ten thousand women (including men disguised as women) demanded the king and queen's return to Paris. Marie-Antoinette, terrified, appears on the balcony in the company of the Marquis de La Fayette, already hero of one revolution and head of the Garde Nationale.

The film cuts to the basement printing press of Restif de la Bretonne, where 1,230 copies of his libertine calendar of amorous acts and the entire French edition of Thomas Paine's *The Rights of Man* are seized for insolvency. In fact, Restif did not print Paine. *Mon Kalendrier* was first published in *Monsieur Nicolas* in 1796 and 1797, and Restif's only seized work was *Les Posthumes*, taken in 1802. This scene shows the new power structure suppressing simultaneously what it deemed the excesses of libertinage and the excesses of Paine's treatise on civil liberties, of the political theories of a man already in exile from the United States and England for extreme radicalism. Thus, although not historically accurate, this event however symbolically establishes the equation between sexual and political freedom.

The film's next shot introduces Restif on one of his nightly prowls, observing with penetrating acuity the ingredients of an era. He documents in his *Nuits révolutionnaires* (which was made into a European TV miniseries in 1989) the constituent elements of a society undergoing serial political upheaval and the phenomenon of an epistemological rift that would create a new paradigm of freedom and the individual. The imaging of the writing of *Les Nuits de Paris* also reinforces the thesis of history as theater, performance or fantasy and links Restif to the cinema audience through the subtitle of the work: *Le Spectateur nocturne*.

The subsequent sequence blends sex and politics as Restif accepts the offer from Madame Faustine (Caterina Boratto) of a beautiful girl but neglects her in favor of some juicy royal gossip. Then, hunting like the owl he is called, he smells a rat and becomes involved in events surrounding the royal family's clandestine flight from Paris on the night of 20 June 1791. His brief encounter with the royal lady-in-waiting, the Comtesse Sophie de la Borde (Hanna Schygulla), inspires a further adventure that, after numerous *péripéties*, finally reunites Restif and Paine in the *diligence de l'état*, ship of state become stagecoach. As this classic cliché narrative frame pursues the royal *berline* across France, it becomes a stagecoach citation emblematic in its second-hand flight of the textual citations offered by its occupants.

The seating on the stage is vertically symbolic of revolution, of the various elements of French society in upheaval. As the travelers inside the coach, eager for a new experience, join the "outsiders" (driver, postilions, servants, student) from time to time, the latter—formerly excluded from power—suddenly seem to surround and control the mixed society of bourgeois, aristocrats, artists, and intellectuals within. In one sequence, the stage crosses a fertile plain of hay being harvested by peasants while the countess's black servant Marie-Madeleine (Aline Messe) and the student Emile Delage (Pierre Malet) embrace in full view of the countryside, demonstrating an interracial, rebellious, populist sexuality that offers a new mode of libertinage contrasting Restif's and Casanova's.

Restif's attempt to catch up with the stagecoach on horseback and his failure as a chevalier unites him with an aged Casanova, like the carnival barker a heavily made up caricature, whose senility and impotence prefigure the coming catastrophes. This encounter offers Casanova the occasion to list Restif's major libertine works and to add a historic and fantastic dimension to their meeting by quoting from Dante the passage in which he meets Hugues Capet in purgatory. The aging libertines Restif and Casanova reminisce on this first of several occasions over their lost capacities, their physical decay a decadence symbolic of the decline and fall of the aristocracy and the monarchy and of the castrating decapitation of the guillotine, the moment in which a nation literally and figuratively loses its head.

After the ensuing sequence of the impromptu chariot race with the state stagecoach, Casanova's *désobligeante* (a small, inhospitable carriage) lives up to its name doubly as it breaks down. This inconvenience results in a redistribution of the occupants of the stage, when it stops to offer assistance. The countess's effete homosexual *perruquier*, Monsieur Jacob (Jean-Claude Brialy), is left behind under his parasol to serve a new master; the lowering of his box of wigs (symbolic heads) from the stage anticipates like his name the Jacobins' later acts of terror. The stage resumes its journey to the east with its now complete cargo of literary, political, artistic, economic, and social ingredients: Marie-Antoinette's lady-in-waiting the Comtesse de la Borde; the elegant fortyish bourgeois widow (a character inspired by the champagne Veuve Clicquot) of a champagne vintner, Adélaïde Gagnon (Andréa Férréol); the crude, self-parodying Italian soprano Virginia Capacelli (Laura Betti); her paramour, the hypocritical magistrate de Florange (Michel Vitold); Monsieur Wendel, the symbolically named iron foundry owner from Alsace-Lorraine (Daniel Gélin); Thomas Paine, Casanova, and Restif. The geometrics of staging the stagecoach as theater dictate that two of the men be relegated to the roof. Wendel volunteers and, having had his condemning say of libertinage, both sexual and political, the magistrate is kicked upstairs as well, leaving the remaining six players in sexual symmetry.

The stagecoach as stage set is next replaced on the first of several occasions by the *relais* or inn, an eighteenth-century literary convention. At the *relais* of Meaux, Casanova does his toilette, literally, facing the sad reality of his debility while he tries to repair the fading mask of the seductive aristocrat that covers his carnal self. Even the name of this legendary nomadic figure was a mask, a pseudonym. Casanova, child of actors, had in fact lived his entire life as a stage role. This initial stop depicts the radical pursuit of the monarchy as an exhausted Bayon dictates the arrest order of the Assemblée. This first interlude also prepares the later complex sequence at the church *relais* which, as we shall see, is central and crucial to the thesis of the film.

The film is scattered not only with images of loss and aristocratic decay but also with those of the raw power of the populace. The first confrontation occurs when this miniature society is dumped by the stage to ascend on foot an appropriately steep hill in the forest; with such a heavy burden to carry, the stage of state cannot surmount the natural obstacle in its path. The revolutions of the wheels of the stage pushed by the people offer us the image in time and space of the coming turn of events.

Setting off up the hill, Casanova comments to the soprano Virginia that he collaborated on the libretto of *Don Giovanni*, a partial historic truth, as it wasn't on Leporello's "Aria del Catalogo" but rather the end of Act II. Scola substitutes this aria for its symbolic significance in equating Casanova and Don Juan as well as alluding to his present status as servant librarian to the German Count Waldstein. The aria itself is another textual *mise-en-abyme*; Leporello sings it from Don Giovanni's little black book, which he kisses at the end. Casanova comments on the discontented Leporello's refusal to serve just anybody, affirming the luxury of serving the ideal master. In an intriguing intratextual double allusion, Casanova compares Leporello to Sancho Panza, already imaged by Restif's quixotic horsemanship. And this Dantesque setting of the steep forested hill recalls Casanova's long quotation from the *Commedia* when he first meets Restif. It is as though the film's editors have created in sound and image the equivalent of a Mozartian thematic. Scola's film is in fact a *catalogo* of the forces intertwined and at play in the eighteenth century. The film's particular originality lies in the way it combines historic realism, expository sequences, theatrics, mask, and fantasy.

The Leporello sequence leads Casanova to a confrontation with the student Emile Delage, wherein the harsh rhetoric of popular militancy, with its insults, accusations, and offenses, confirms the aristocrats' convictions that the potential rule of the people is a vision of hell. At the end of this sequence in the forest, the travelers come upon a setting which sends a coded message: the picnic is over. Hastily abandoned by the not-so-royal family in flight, the wine bottle from the royal cellar lies empty, and the king's discarded white handkerchief sits as a token of surrender in this rugged natural setting which in eighteenth-century ethic and esthetic carries an additional message of its own.

The next sequence of a *relais* is at Sainte-Menehould in the converted deconsecrated church, where all manner of sins are acted out—gluttony, greed, lust, pride—and where it is apparent that now nothing is sacred. With the adoring widow at his side, Casanova devours singlehandedly a Rabelaisian banquet, an implicit if not overt symbol of the man who consumed women. He has in fact won the heart of all three of the women on the stagecoach: the Austrian *aristocrate*, the French *bourgeoise*, the Italian *artiste déclassée*, thus illustrating the power of language to stimulate memory and imagination, making it his present tool of seduction. As he explains to us in the third didactic expository vignette of the film (metacinematic discourses from the viewpoint of history), he is to write his memoirs before his death in 1798, thus extending his verbal power of seduction to the narrative voice and the written text, in a work finally published only in 1820. Historically, the aging Casanova was still virile and impetuous, only sixty-six years old in 1791, but this decaying figure serves Scola better as an emblem of nostalgia for a lost world, and of the collapse of a social and cultural paradigm.

In this second interval at a *relais*, the countess is grossly accosted by a peasant, another image of the crude, rapacious power of the people and another foreshadowing of the Reign of Terror. The way the film nostalgically registers the loss of esthetic sensibilities, of grace and dignity, doesn't advocate a conservative return to the old order but offers rather a commentary on the terrifying anarchy of uneducated power that leads to a sort of cultural treason rather than to political utopia. The angry power of the people, whom the king once saw as his children, now surrounds and threatens to overwhelm these nobles and their aristocratic emblems of excessive finery and refinement.

When Thomas Paine rescues the countess, he is rewarded with a slap in the face, her response to his harsh populism advocating abolition of the monarchy and aristocracy and freedom of the people. Her slap is the desperate gesture of a wounded, confused animal confronting for the first time the certainty of its own vulnerability, the unavoidable truth of the end in sight. In his tirade against the monarchy, Paine has not just attacked monarchy but insulted her king, referring to him as an ass in the place of a lion, "un âne à la place d'un lion." Later in the film, the cry goes out among the people to "chercher le poulailler et le ramener à l'étable" (find the family of chickens and bring it back to the stable). Both of these expressions allude to popular satiric cartoons of the day, particularly one depicting the royal family as "La Famille des cochons ramenée dans l'étable" (the family of pigs brought back into the stable). These cartoons were hung framed or unframed on the walls of inns and taverns where they, along with newspapers, elicited political debate and discussion.

The countess represents historic conservative reaction to Paine's radicalism as spokesman for the people in two revolutions. *Common Sense*, the now apocryphal pamphlets of *The Crisis*, *The Rights of Man*, and *The Age of Reason* were clarion calls for democratic equality, heresy in the era in which such supporters of equal privileges for Americans as Edmund Burke could not accept religious and social extremism or the idea of popular rule. Paine's opposition to Burke's *Reflections on the Revolution in France* led to his expulsion from England by William Pitt. He returned to France, where he was made a citizen in August 1792. Paine was not alone in his attraction to revolutionary France; both William Wordsworth and the Scottish poet John Oswald were curious and sympathetic observers of the events in Paris in 1791, along with numerous other political and literary figures. Ironically, Paine's later opposition to the excesses of the Convention lost him his own citizen's rights, and he served ten months in prison before James Monroe effected his release. Thus this uneducated, eternally poor *enfant terrible* lived as a vagabond, like Jean-

Jacques Rousseau an uncompromising idealist, ever a citizen of somewhere else. Originally buried in America, his body was returned to England and vanished. The study of power that pervades this film focuses repeatedly on that of language. It is no coincidence that the three literary figures united by fictitious circumstances in the stagecoach are all masters of language. The power of the word both oral and written, seductive and seditious, parodied by the carnival barker in the opening and closing narrative frame, reaches its dominance not in the dialogical dialectic in the stagecoach but in the mouth of the revolutionary extremist standing atop a carriage at Varennes. He reads to a volcanic mob from a Paris newspaper Marat's exhortations to convict the Marquis de La Fayette for loyalty to the king and to try him at a military tribunal.

Concomitant with the power of the word is that of the person, the mask, the figure. The heavy cake makeup and elaborate wigs and attire of the aristocrats are the trappings of power and refinement for the old order. Yet this order has fallen, as evident in the final scene at the inn at Varennes, when the king's regal finery is unwrapped from the mysterious packages carried earlier by Restif and assembled on a wooden valet. The countess in her ruffles and lace defers to this empty shell of royal power, the sign deprived of its referent, anticipating the political vacuum to come. The costume mounted on the inanimate valet contrasts with the expository vignette depicting the king's power and glory in the same outfit at the inauguration of the Cherbourg harbor five years earlier to the day. The power of the body filling this costume at a ceremonial beginning has degenerated to a hollow mockery in this ceremonious ending.

The marginal roles throughout the film of the three literary voyeurs and even of the countess are symbolized by the camera angle at the home of a candlemaker and seller of colonial products, the bourgeois entrepreneur Monsieur Sauce (Jean-Louis Trintignant). As Romeuf gives La Fayette's arrest proclamation to the king and queen, the travelers and the audience see their bodies only from the shoulders down; their heads are already missing. The king utters, "En France il n'y a plus de roi" (In France there is no longer a king). The Dauphin is lying motionless on the bed, creating an image of his future imprisonment and death.

Outside, the mob overwhelms the countess with cries and torches, and she loses her head, emitting a long scream of terror. Like the candles illuminating the miniature stage of the puppet theater and the candles sold by Monsieur Sauce, the torches illuminate the historic ascent to the stage of a new cast of characters, the people, singing "The Carmagnole." Their flickering torches constitute distorted echoes of the illuminating ideals of the enlightenment, their uneducated anger a betrayal of the rationalism of the *philosophes*, their torching of France an ironic ending to the *siècle des lumières*.

The final sequences of Scola's film achieve an open ending cutting through time and space. The film returns to the puppet theater, where the miniature scenes depict events after the king's flight and capture, including his execution. The camera then follows a thoughtful Restif reciting an incredibly prophetic passage from the

Seventeenth Night of his *Nuits révolutionnaires* as he climbs the steps to the street above:

> Ces idées me fatiguaient horriblement!...Pour me soulager, je m'enfonçai dans la suite des siècles: je vis les hommes de 1992, lire notre histoire; je m'efforçai de les entendre, et je les entendis. La sévérité de leur jugement m'effraya! Il me sembla que les uns nous reprochaient d'avoir manqué d'humanité, tandis que les extrêmes, tels qu'il en est aujourd'hui, nous approuvaient. Je crus voir que toute l'Europe avait pris un gouvernement nouveau; mais je voyais sur les pages de l'histoire, les horribles secousses qu'elle avait éprouvées! Il me semblait entendre les lecteurs, se dire entre eux: "Que nous sommes heureux, de n'avoir pas vécu dans ces temps horribles, où la vie des hommes était comptée pour rien!" Un de leurs philosophes s'écriait: "Il faut de temps en temps de ces secousses, pour faire sentir aux hommes le prix de la tranquillité, comme il faut une maladie pour sentir le prix de la santé. . . Le mal passé, quand on n'en est pas mort, est une jouissance...—Ha! les beaux raisonneurs! s'écria un songe-creux, tapi dans un coin; vous l'avez été. Vous étiez les hommes d'il y a 200 ans. Vous êtes composés de leurs molécules organiques: et vous êtes en paix, parce que ces molécules sont lasses d'avoir été en guerre. Vous y reviendrez après un long repos....."[1]

This passage connecting past and present adds the perspective of the centuries to the film's thesis of the power of text and language, which has encompassed sexual politics, social structure, and revolution in the triple strata of *aristocratie, bourgeoisie, peuple*, foregrounding in many modes the dialectic of the master and the slave.

By way of epilogue, the film offers a telescoping superimposition of a vertical image of history, like that of the stagecoach, as Restif climbs up to the street above into the twentieth century. The final narrative frame integrates the opening shot of Notre Dame into a complex contemporary context (the busy traffic and people of Paris of the 1980s), compressing time and space and suggesting that the revolutionary creature beneath the surface can rise again any time from the *pavés* so often used as weapons by the people.

There are two intriguing comments on the relationship between film and history, film and freedom, film and reality, film and revolution in Maurice Mourier's 1985 book *Le Parfum de la salle en noir*, written under the pseu-donym of Michel Mesnil, in which he affirms the intrinsic liberating and revolutionary nature of film. The first seems almost willfully optimistic: "Le cinéma, c'est la liberté. Son message est, par essence, libérateur, on ne peut l'utiliser pour l'asservissement des peuples."[2] Although it could certainly be said that many have tried to repress people with propagandistic film, the liberating functions of the cinema are undeniable, in film's oneiric quality, its ability to cut through time and space in the eternal present of its sound and light, and, finally, film's lack of certainty, its nature as an open discourse. As Mourier also says: "Il constitue donc, comme l'amour, la liberté ou l'art avec qui il entretient des rapports équivoques, l'entreprise la plus subversive qui soit" (128).

Thus Mourier attests to film's ability to overthrow existing orders. Scola's film depicts historic upheaval by subverting history and cinematic historic realism with its polyvalent ambiguous discourse.

As Restif climbs to the streets of Paris today, the *coup de théâtre* blends past and present, destroying the distancing of traditional chronology as the past rises literally from the *pavés*, a haunting image of the ghost of revolutions, past, present, and future. Thus the question of historic truth and authenticity in film can be reconsidered in the light of a truth larger than the appearance of fidelity to fact. Film's achievement is its ability to confront us with a mirror of ourselves, wherein we can examine the greater truths of human nature as they reappear in the cycles of events and in the collective cultural mythology of the artistic history of a people.

Restif and Casanova sum up the question of the relative importance of fact, fiction, and fantasy in their mutual confession in the coach after the sequence with the female innkeeper. At the inn, in the course of their seductive imaginings, they fashion a history for her and her daughter, and for themselves, which gives them a family relationship. The subsequent demystification of their fantasy destroys the illusion, which they created to please the innkeeper, *l'art de plaire* being a paramount virtue in the canon of the eighteenth century. At the same time, the collusion of confession creates a new relationship for the two aging libertines, a relationship founded on their understanding of the need for mask, theater, drama, and persona, and of a primary truth of theater and performance, that the mask can be more real than reality itself.

Notes

1. Restif de la Bretonne, *Les Nuits révolutionnaires* (Paris: Livre de Poche, 1978) 293–294. The following is the text of the English subtitles, which varies slightly from the more exact translation of the 1964 Random House edition of *Les Nuits de Paris*, 313. "All those ideas exhausted me. For relief I plunged into the centuries that followed. I saw the people of 1992 reading our history. I strained to hear them and I heard. The harshness of their judgments terrified me! Some claimed we lacked humanity, whereas those with extreme views, as in my day, approved. All Europe, apparently, had a new government, unified and at peace. But I saw in the pages of History the terrible jolts it had endured. I thought I heard the readers saying: we're glad we didn't live through those terrible times, when human life was worthless! Pain, once it's over, and if you survive it, becomes pleasure. You need those jolts now and again, so men appreciate peace and quiet, just as one needs sickness to value good health. What deep thinkers you are, such a dreamer, from this corner. But you're the same as you were 200 years ago, formed of the same organic molecules. Today you're at peace, because those molecules are weary of war. But beware, after a period of rest, you'll feel strong and then, I fear, you'll start it all over again."
2. Michel Mesnil (Maurice Mourier), *Le Parfum de la salle en noir* (Paris: Presses Universitaires de France, 1985) 121. The subsequent reference to this work is included in parentheses after the quote. ("Cinema is freedom. Its message is in essence liberating, it cannot be used to repress whole peoples," and the second passage: "It thus constitutes, like love, freedom or art, with which it has equivocal connections, the most subversive enterprise there is." My translation.)

An earlier version of this chapter appeared as an article in *Eighteenth-Century Life* 14:3 (November 1990) 99–107.

Bibliography

Baker, Keith. *Inventing the Revolution: essays on French Political Culture in the Eighteenth Century.* New York: Cambridge University Press, 1989.

Bernier, Olivier. *Words of Fire, Deeds of Blood: the Mob, the Monarchy, and the French Revolution.* Boston: Little, Brown, 1989.

Blanchot, Maurice. *Sade et Restif de la Bretonne.* Paris: Editions Complexe, 1986.

Casanova de Seingalt, Jacques. *Histoire de ma vie.* Paris: Gallimard, 1986.

————. *History of my Life.* New York: Harcourt, Brace & World, 1966–1971.

Chadourne, Marc. *Restif de la Bretonne: ou Le Siècle prophétique.* Paris: Hachette, 1958.

Chartier, Roger. *The Cultural Origins of the French Revolution.* Durham: Duke University Press, 1991.

Coward, David. *The Philosophy of Restif de la Bretonne. Studies in Voltaire and the Eighteenth Century* 283. Oxford: Voltaire Foundation, 1991.

Doyle, William. *Origins of the French Revolution.* New York: Oxford University Press, 1988.

Hedges, Inez. *Breaking the Frame: Film Language and the Experience of Limits.* Bloomington: Indiana University Press, 1991.

Jackson, Giovanna. "Casanova's Heirs: Fellini and Scola." In Radcliff-Umstead, Douglas, ed. *National Traditions in Motion Pictures.* Kent, OH: Kent State University, 1985.

Karmel, Alex. *My Revolution: Promenades in Paris, 1789–1794, being the diary of Restif de la Bretonne.* New York: McGraw-Hill, 1970.

Lefèvre, Raymond. *Cinéma et Révolution.* Paris: Edilig, 1988.

Merrick, Jeffrey. *The Desacralization of the French Monarchy in the Eighteenth Century.* Baton Rouge: Louisiana State University Press, 1990.

Mimoso-Ruiz, Duarte, and Jacques Rustin. "Casanova à Londres: de *L'Histoire de ma vie* au Fellini-Casanova." *Europe* 697 (May 1987) 86–92.

Paine, Thomas. *Droits de l'homme, ou Réponse à l'ouvrage de Monsieur Burke contre la Révolution française.* Hamburg: Chez les frères Herold, 1791.

————. *The Rights of Man.* London: H. D. Symonds, 1792.

Poster, Mark. *The Utopian Thought of Restif de la Bretonne.* New York: New York University Press, 1971.

Restif de la Bretonne, Nicolas Edmé. *Les Nuits de Paris.* New York: Random House, 1964.

————. *Les Nuits révolutionnaires.* Paris: Librairie Générale Française, 1978.

Reynaud, Patricia. "De la nuit de Varennes à la terreur: le voyage de la mystification. *Canadian Journal of Italian Studies* 20:55–56 (1997) 221–234.

Schlafly, Shannon. "A Modern Echo of the French Revolution: Ettore Scola's *La Nuit de Varennes.*" *Studies in Voltaire and the Eighteenth Century* 264 (1989) 360–364.

La Marseillaise
(The Marseillaise)

written and directed by Jean Renoir (1938)

André Gain, writing in *La Petite Tribune* in Paris on 10 June 1927, rhapsodized that "As a glorification of France on the screen, Abel Gance's *Napoléon* is the most wonderful hymn to France. It's the Marseillaise of the image."[1] A decade later, Jean Renoir would invert that concept in filming the image of "The Marseillaise." The song and the film constitute a dual close focus on the populist fervor leading to the First Republic and its echoes in the France of the Front Populaire, echoes that, while certainly as patriotic as those of Gance's work, assume a very different significance in the context of the growing might of the Nazis and Fascists in the late 1930s.

The origins of the song and the circumstances of its composition have long been debated. Some say it was an old Protestant hymn with popular slogans for lyrics, others that it was written in one night at a banquet in Strasbourg given by Mayor Dietrich for Republican Army volunteers. The incendiary nature of its lyrics has come under recent criticism in a bicentennial attempt to mollify European compatriots with a new version converting swords into plowshares to turn under the bloody furrows. It is generally accepted that a young captain of the engineers named Claude Joseph Rouget de Lisle 1760–1836) composed the stirring patriotic song and lyrics which became the French National Hymn in 1879 (when the town of its origin was again hostage of the Germans). Its original title was the "Chant de Guerre pour l'Armée du Rhin" and it was written 25–26 April 1792, five days after war was declared against Bohemia and Hungary, but it was first heard in Paris that summer when the *Marseillais* regiment marched into town, hence the final title.

Renoir may have been partially inspired to make this film by the 1936 centennial of the death of Rouget de Lisle. Above all, the film uses the fervid lyrics of the song to affirm populist sentiment of the era, to elicit a sympathetic response to the passing of power to the people as the Marseilles regiment marches to Paris to join other revolutionary battalions in taking the Tuileries and then defeating the Prussians at Valmy. Renoir's attraction to the song as a central "character" in the film is more than historic and political, though; it is explained in part by his lasting fascination with music hall vaudeville entertainment and his use of such *divertimenti* vignettes in all his movies.

"The Marseillaise" as a song is also the French national counterpart to "The Internationale" of Renoir's 1936 film made for the Communist Party, *La Vie est à nous*. The national hymn had in fact been substituted for "The Internationale" at political rallies since 1934. Renoir partially completed his project of financing a national film through a two-franc-per-person subscription, redeemable as a ticket, acquiring ten million francs through the Compagnie Générale du Travail, as well as the extras for several military scenes that the Daladier government had refused him. Sponsored thus, the film constituted such a declaration of support for the leftist Popular Front and such a call for solidarity in the face of growing right-wing totalitarian regimes in Germany, Italy, Spain, and even France that it was eventually banned by the Pétain government.[2]

Because of the peasant Mediterranean origins of the soldiers and their participation in what was essentially a civil war, the film can also be seen as a gesture of support for the Spanish Republican Army in its battle against Franco in the Spanish Civil War (1936–1939) when Daladier's government had declared a policy of nonintervention. The film's lasting message, like that of *La Grande Illusion* made the year before, is in its portraits of individuals caught up in war. Among all his characters, Renoir's depictions of the common man, influenced by Charlie Chaplin and Abel Gance's and René Clair's characters, are the most endearing and enduring. Renoir researched the background and occupation of the soldiers, eager to disprove the right-wing image of revolutionaries as rabble, proving that indeed they were family men, responsible, capable workers, and solvent.

Although Renoir used the singing of "The Marseillaise" as a political act of defiance in *La Grande Illusion*, it here becomes the title character and unifying thematic of the film, extending the national anthem to the level of the mythical. Renoir participated in a long tradition in using the song on film. In *Napoléon*, Gance not only incorporated "The Marseillaise" in the scenes from the Cordeliers Club and the Convention, but it is used extensively in all accompanying musical scores. Four years later during World War II, Michael Curtiz paid homage to his predecessors in *Casablanca* by having the pro-French and French *pieds noirs* in Rick's café in Morocco sing the national anthem in defiance of occupying German soldiers and their "Deutschland Uber Alles" (which had its lyrics rewritten after the war).

Organized as a series of historic vignettes from 14 July 1789 to 20 September 1792, Renoir's film opens appropriately with the theater and mask of royalty and aristocracy, as the credits and subtitle, "Chronicle of some facts contributing to the fall of the Monarchy," are accompanied by scenes and music of the Ancien Régime (although Renoir wrote the script with Carl Koch, they enlisted the Martel-Dreyfus as technical historical consultants). The film is in fact an admixture of fact and invention, a national myth. A demystified Louis XVI, homey, clumsy and naive, a stupid self-indulgent man of appetites, is played by Renoir's brother Pierre, whose likeness to the king in profile is almost haunting. The upheaval of the old order and the marginalizing of their power and role is effectively conveyed in the opening scene at Versailles with a symbolic changing of the guard. Like the moving camera invading the halls, the Duke de la Rochefoucauld-Liancourt (William Aguet) comes to report the fall of the Bastille. The king, resting after the hunt, eats reclining in bed, prefiguring his coming downfall and demise. When he asks the duke if it is a revolt, the duke replies, "No Sire, a revolution."

The "neorealist" focus of Renoir's film next foregrounds peasants as individuals, filtering the abstract events of history at the level of the people. In Provence the following year, a peasant, Anatole Roux, called Cabri (Edouard Delmont), is tried before Giraud (Jean Acquistapace), the village mayor, for killing pigeons on the land of the village aristocrat (Maurice Escande). The peasant poaching on a noble's land represents the popular revolt against feudal rights and the divine right of the aristocracy, and calls up a serious historic matter of the peasants not being allowed to feed themselves by hunting the local land. In fact, these restrictions and the hated *capitaineries* were abolished on 4 August 1789. Renoir may have taken the dialogue of his film from historic texts, but he rearranges chronology to serve his own didactic and artistic ends. In another allusion to the changing power structure, the peasant escapes while the mayor, the lawyer and the aristocratic landowner all argue.

Cabri heads for the hills, where he meets Bomier (Edmond Ardisson), Honoré Arnaud (Andrex) from Marseilles, and a priest (Edmond Beauchamp) sympathetic to the cause of the people. The peasants as hunters are the popular counterpart to the king's pastime. The three men hiding high in the rugged countryside talk of bringing the revolution down into the towns to get rid of the aristocrats. The priest represents another aspect of the problem of poverty and starvation, complaining that even the church is corrupt; the bishop is living in a palace with mistresses, while he has no windows and no possibility of advancement. Cabri has lost his wife and children to poverty, commenting that there is no future for the people under the aristocracy. Renoir repeatedly blames the aristocrats as well as the monarchy for France's ills. In 1938 they again controlled France and elicited his original screenplay for the 1939 *La Règle du jeu* comparing their corruption and decadence to that of their eighteenth-century ancestors. The sight of two châteaux ablaze leads the peasants to defend revolutionary acts of terrorism and violence, commenting that the cruelty of the people in revolt is simply an imitation of the abuses of the aristocrats. In this sequence, we see the virtues of the Rights of Man extolled, in the liberty, equality and fraternity between these four men in the mountains.

The scene shifts to the streets of Marseilles in October 1790 where civil officials are checking personal papers, as in *Danton* imaging military controls and restrictions. At the revolutionary club, the Société des Amis de la Constitution, a member calls for order in the streets. The dockworkers declare that they are against violence, troublemakers, the black market, the reactionary army faction, as Renoir decries corruption and extremism on both ends of the spectrum.

The next sequence is the taking of the main fort of Saint Nicolas held by the Royalist army faction, delayed several months beyond its historic April 1790 occurrence to telescope it dramatically with subsequent vignettes. Renoir's mastery of popular and provincial realism comes through with verve and humor, as he offers popular entertainment as much as an intellectual consideration of events. But he does not shy away from classical symbolism and allusions, as evidenced by the character of the allegorical painter Javel (Paul Dullac) and his discourse on all the ancients, Greeks and Romans. In this context, the rebels' introduction of Bomier hidden in a wine barrel into the fort recalls the ploy of the Trojan horse. Focused on overthrowing a corrupt aristocracy, the rebels liberate their friend and the twenty-one other political prisoners, finding sympathy among the guards. This whole sequence is a provincial echo of the taking of the Bastille and a prefiguration of the coming assault on the Tuileries. The commander of the fort, the Marquis de Saint-Laurent (Aimé Clariond), the archetypal blue blood, is shocked to find that his formulas of courtesy are no longer effective and that he will be deported to Germany (establishing a link to the later sequence of the expatriots in Coblenz). Saint-Laurent will repeat there the new definition of the nation as the sum of its citizens that he learns as the new flag is hoisted.

The sequence of the expatriot aristocrats in Coblenz (down the Rhine from Strasbourg) is set in 1792, portraying the frustrated isolation they experienced (like the American Tories who returned to England, displaced). The song of nostalgia they sing, actually written by Chateaubriand, is a counterpart to "The Marseillaise." As the aristocrats are planning to take Paris, with the help of the Prussians and the Duke of Brunswick, the victor in the French and Indian War (Seven Years War), there are more references to ancient Greek heroes. The nation is characterized as a reunion of rabble against the aristocracy, eliciting from Saint-Laurent the new version, of the solidarity of honest citizens. Renoir parodies the frivolity of the old life at Versailles with a gavotte whose figures the dancers have already forgotten. There is an explicit reference in these German sequences to the sympathies of the French right wing with Hitler's Third Reich.

Shifting to April 1792 at Valenciennes, Renoir depicts the low morale of La Fayette's army at war with the Austrians and the anomaly of General Rochambeau's army supported by Marat and Robespierre and the Assemblée Nationale while its officers are still aristocrats. The Hussar mercenaries are now defecting to join the Austrians, who have money to pay them.

In the ensuing scene in Marseilles, Renoir introduces a very different image of woman from the aristocrats and Marie-Antoinette, as the *citoyenne* Louise Vauclair (Jenny Hélia) speaks out at an assembly against the betrayal of the French nation by the king and queen and accuses the bourgeoisie of wanting revolution for profit. The women in this film are all strong and brave personalities, but still depicted in their family roles, as mother, sister, lover, wife, widow. At another meeting of the Club of Friends of the Constitution (which declares itself a Jacobin tribunal), it is clear that the Revolution is a three-way economic and moral class struggle between the aristocracy, the bourgeoisie and the people, and that the regional regiments are being formed in response to the will of the nation to eliminate from the government speculators, reactionaries, and ministers siding with the king.

Renoir now combines the story of "The Marseillaise," written for conscription of volunteers, and the Marseilles origins of the regiment. At the beginning of the film, they were singing other battle songs of the day, like "Ça ira." Another irony of history: it will be primarily southern France that will mount the Resistance against the German Occupation of France during World War II, just two years after the release of this film. The next sequence integrates Bomier into his family situation and the women in his life, as he complains that he cannot join up because he has debts (debtors were considered criminals in the eighteenth century), incurred by non repayment of a loan to a girlfriend. Renoir cuts to Javel the artist who is now working on a painting depicting Brutus killing Caesar, foreshadowing the death of the king. "The Marseillaise" is introduced obliquely as the film and theater audiences hear through a doorway the singer Mireur from Montpellier performing the "Song of the Army of the Rhine." The following day, as the fishermen comment on the story, the melody and the lyrics of the song, Bomier rejects its alien sounds, in true populist regional mind, but appreciates its message, hoping that the Revolution will pass to the poor from the rich. Renoir invented a wandering Jew to bring the song from Strasbourg to the South, creating another historic irony, as so many Jews would take refuge from the Nazis in free France.

Renoir uses editing to create a perfect dramatic irony, as the film shifts from the comment that everyone will have forgotten the song in two weeks to the mass of soldiers readying to march and their families bidding them farewell, all singing "The Marseillaise." One man sings the second verse (that typically no one knows). Bomier's mother in black (Marthe Marty) is a symbol of the grieving country that will lose so many children in the war, and a modern echo of World War I when so many millions died. She also maintains the focus on the individual human element in a collective setting. Renoir's scenes of the army regiment crossing France from south to north have historic echoes of Garibaldi leading the peasants of Italy to reunification in 1859. As already seen in the mountain sequence, there is talk that all the Church is not on the side of the king. (However, after the September massacre in 1792, all Catholic priests had to go underground.) The next scene depicts a soldier training the recruits while "The Marseillaise" is sung in the background. The journey to Paris is endless; the roads are in deplorable condition, created deliberately by the aristocrats to prove that revolution disrupts the nation (or to keep people from marching to Paris). Renoir demonstrates the power of "The Marseillaise" in uniting the people against the king and queen, the value of song in general for arousing patriotic fervor, the force and unity of the people. It has acquired the same function as "The Internationale," as the unification of disparate elements of the populace with their regional accents and dialects is signaled by the sign stating "Here one is honored to speak French." Renoir emphasized the French nationality of these troops in response to rightist xenophobic accusations that the populist troops were recruited from Italy.

The next sequence brings us finally to Paris, where the people are celebrating in the street, partying on the ruins of the Bastille. A tumultuous populace greets a Breton regiment, then applauds the arrival of the Marseilles regiment singing their song, in a rousing reception. This historic encounter gave its name to the island of

Réunion, now an overseas *département*. As the crowd proceeds to a banquet on the Champs-Elysées, they are derided by a group of aristocrats. The "rabble" easily overwhelm the contemptuous aristocrats, and the regiments get into the mêlée, emblematic of numerous conflicts all over France between the people and the aristocracy, of the bloody civil war to come. Twice as many people died in conflicts like this as died on the guillotine. Ironically, the aristocrats seek protection at the Tuileries. The stormy weather is a political mimesis (not always intentional as Renoir had more bad weather than any filmmaker in history). Inside the Tuileries Louis XVI is reading the proclamation from the Prussians stating that he is now allied with foreign countries against his own people and that any Frenchman opposing him is a traitor. The Prussians have since then been the enemy of France on four different occasions; "The Marseillaise" became the anthem just eight years after their humiliation of France in 1871. As the Austrian Marie-Antoinette (Lise Delamare) points out, the French aristocrats have more in common with the nobility in other countries than with their own countrymen, as in *La Grande Illusion* (where Renoir and Eric von Stroheim collaborated to create the scenes between Boeldieu and von Rauffenstein). Louis proves this as he is more interested in hunting and his wife than in the French people.

Thus the King makes a fatal error in announcing Brunswick's Manifesto to the nation. Popular sentiment is aroused by reaction in the press: newspapers, pamphlets, inflammatory declarations by Marat like the one read at the end of *La Nuit de Varennes*. Robespierre is said to be working to unite the various quarters of Paris and army regiments for unified action, in a model for government by representation which will soon come. The soldiers running out of food with only potatoes to eat decide to attack the palace in one week. Bills of protest and republican activism are posted on the walls all over Paris. (Newspapers weren't printed for private consumption or home delivery, but for the public, in clubs, taverns, and squares.) Renoir shows a Chinese shadow theater performance, of puppets in silhouettes, a comic opera of contemporary events. There is a stage show of some sort in every Renoir movie. The theater of history is emphasized throughout the film when Marie-Antoinette and Louis talk of the "tragedy," the "comedy," the "drama" of their downfall. Here the *canard* (marked by the ducks under the broken bridge) is the Manifesto by Brunswick. Constituting another audience within the film, the soldiers enjoy a romantic interlude with their Parisian lovers, Bomier with Louison (Nadia Sibirskaïa); Louison was a nickname for the guillotine.

The various regiments organize plans to appeal to the popular sympathies of some of the palace guards. The popular image of Marie-Antoinette is that of a domineering bitch, *l'Autri-chienne*. Louis XVI is appropriately eating tomatoes (blood red fruit from the new world) brought by the *Marseillais*. Scenes of food consumption form a unifying thematic in the film. Louis's wig is askew, again symbolic of what will happen to his head, like the insecure wigs in *La Nuit de Varennes* and *Danton*. As Louis goes to review his troops, his courtiers sing their loyalty in "O Richard, O Mon Roi" (actually an aria that everyone knew from a contemporary opera by Grétry) in another counterpart to "The Marseillaise." Louis ventures outdoors into a group of French troops who begin to shout Republican slogans. The excessive luxury of the court finery seems out of place amid the popular rebellion. Urged to seek the protection of the Assemblée Nationale, the royal family is escorted by Roederer (Louis Jouvet) out through the formal *allées* of the Tuileries Gardens (today a public park). The leaves are falling early, placing the fall of the monarchy in the natural cycle of things.

As the Republican forces invade the Tuileries, and the Marseilles regiment storms the Royal Palace, the palace guard does not resist. This scenario has repeated itself throughout the world many times with populist army overthrows of dictators. The mercenaries join the French regiments, but when the palace guards and the aristocrats make a last bloody stand, Bomier and Arnaud are both shot by the Swiss Guards. There ensues a massacre of all the troops in the courtyard and a chaotic retreat. Bomier dies under a sign which says "Here, one is honored by the title of Citizen." This battle taken up by the people brought down the French monarchy and began the final and bloodiest stage of the French Revolution. The representatives of the national regions and of the districts of Paris are depicted battling in the street grouped in the way they will be representing the people in the legislative assembly. Seven years before Roberto Rossellini's *Roma città aperta* (*Open City*), Renoir finds the balance of neorealism, the passion of the individual love story against the backdrop of troops fighting in the street, both the close focus and the epic sweep of civil war. And he achieves the French equivalent of Eisenstein's *The Battleship Potemkin* when intercutting shots of the troops clashing and Bomier dying. In 1965, Gillo Pontecorvo amalgamated as mentioned the heritage of the above influences in *La Bataille d'Alger*.

The male courtiers are executed, the women taken away, their valuables confiscated, but no looting is allowed, demonstrating a discipline superior to the previous exploitation of the people by the nobility. Representatives of the Commune of Paris from the Assemblée declare the king deposed and announce the forthcoming election of a National Convention by all the people regardless of class (except for women, who did not get the vote until 1945). The fall of the monarchy and the dissolving of the Assemblée mark the beginning of the real people's revolution that changed the world. The last words of the film go to Javel at the battle of Valmy: *Vive la liberté!*

The French Republican Army miraculously defeated the Prussians at Valmy on 20 September 1792, and made possible the creation of the Republic, but their struggles and uncertain fortunes continued for years. Beset by Royalist counter-revolts from within and by attacks from enemies loyal to the monarchy, they were finally united by Napoleon's military genius under the Directory government (1795–1799). As a postscript to the film, Renoir leaves us the reaction of the German writer Goethe who watched the battle of Valmy: "In that place and on that day began a new era in the history of the world."

Notes

1. Norman King, *Abel Gance* (London: British Film Institute, 1984) 20, 220.
2. Leo Braudy, *Jean Renoir: The World of his Films* (New York: Columbia University Press, 1989) 207–208. See also the chapter on *La Marseillaise* in Alexander Sesonske's *Jean Renoir: The French Films 1924–1939* (Cambridge: Harvard University Press, 1980).

Bibliography

Amy-de-la-Breteque, François. "Voyages au long du Rhône revisités par le cinéma: De *Vende-miaire* à *La Marseillaise.*" In Fardy, Philippe. *Mistral et Lou Pouemo dou Rose.* Bordes, France: CELO, 1997.

Aragon, Louis. *"La Marseillaise." CICIM* 39–40 (June 1994) 175–177.

Bazin, André. *Jean Renoir.* New York: Simon & Schuster, 1973.

Bergan, Ronald. *Jean Renoir: Projections of Paradise.*

Berteuil, B. "D'Albert Mathiez à Jean Renoir: Inspirations et interprétations historiques autour de *La Marseillaise." Cahiers de la Cinémathèque* 53 (Dec 1989) 87–98.

Bertin, Célia. *Jean Renoir: a Life in Pictures.* Baltimore: Johns Hopkins University Press, 1991.

Braudy, Leo. *Jean Renoir: The World of his Films.* New York: Columbia University Press, 1989.

————."Renoir at Home: an Interview with Jean Renoir."*Film Quarterly* 50:1 (Fall 1996) 2–8.

Comolli, Jean-Louis. "Historical Fiction: A body too much." *Screen* XIX, 2 (Summer 1978) 41–53.

Dallet, Sylvie. *La Révolution française et le cinéma.* Paris: Lherminier, 1988.

Durgnat, Raymond. *Jean Renoir.* Berkeley: University of California Press, 1974.

Faulkner, Christopher. *Jean Renoir, a Guide to References and Resources.* Boston: G. K. Hall, 1979.

————. *The Social Cinema of Jean Renoir.* Princeton: Princeton University Press, 1986.

Gauteur, Claude. "Jean Renoir." *Image et Son* 315 (Mar 1977) 19–48.

Gilliatt, Penelope. *Jean Renoir: Essays, Conversations, Reviews.* New York: McGraw-Hill, 1975.

Grindon, Leger. "History and the Historians in *La Marseillaise." Film History* IV, 3 (1990), 227–235.

King, Norman."Patrie et nation: Fictions populistes dans le *Napoléon* d'Abel Ganz et *La Marseillaise* de Jean Renoir." in *Europe: Revue Littéraire Mensuelle* 715–716 (Nov–Dec 1988) 68–75.

Koch, Carl. *"La Marseillaise." CICIM* 39–40 (June 1994) 177–178.

"La Marseillaise." Avant-Scène Cinéma. Special Issue 383–384 (Jul–Aug 1989) 2–168.

Lebovics, Herman. "Open the Gates, Break Down the Barriers: the French Revolution, the Popular Front, and Jean Renoir." *Persistence of Vision* 12–13 (1996) 9–28.

Lefèvre, Raymond. *Cinéma et Révolution.* Paris: Edilig, 1988.

Leprohon, Pierre. *Jean Renoir.* New York: Crown Publishers, 1971.

Lesses, Glenn. "Renoir, Bazin and Film Realism." Purdue University Seventh Annual Conference on Film. West Lafayette, Indiana: Purdue University, 1983.

Liebman, Stuart. "Dossier on *La Marseillaise." Persistence of Vision* 12–13 (1996) 144–169.

Michelson, Annette."*La Marseillaise*, a Jacobin text?" *Persistence of Vision* 12–13 (1996) 49–63.

O'Shaughnessy, Martin. *Jean Renoir.* Manchester, England: Manchester University Press, 2000.

Reader, Keith. "Jean Renoir." In *The Oxford Guide to Film Studies*. New York, NY: Oxford University Press, 1998.

Renoir, Jean. *Ma Vie et mes films*. Paris: Flammarion, 1974.

————. *My Life and My Films*. New York: Atheneum, 1974.

Serceau, Daniel. *Jean Renoir*. Paris: Edilig, 1985.

Sesonske, Alexander. *Jean Renoir: The French Films 1924–1939*.Cambridge: Harvard University Press, 1980.

Simon, John. "To See is to Believe: The Life and Films of Jean Renoir." *The New Criterion* 13:2 (1994) 33–41.

Smith, Gavin."A Man of Excess: Paul Schrader on Jean Renoir." *Sight and Sound* 5:1 (1995) 24–29.

Sorlin, Pierre. *The Film in History*. Oxford: Blackwell, 1980.

Strebel, Elizabeth. "Jean Renoir and the Popular Front." In Short, K.R.M., ed. *Feature Films as History*. London: Helm, 1981.

————. *French Social Cinema of the Nineteen-Thirties: A Cinematic Expression of Popular Front Consciousness*. New York: Arno, 1980.

Vincendeau, Ginette, and Keith Reader. *'La Vie est à nous', French Cinema of the Popular Front, 1935–1938*. London: British Film Institute, 1986.

Danton

directed by Andrzej Wadja (1982)
adapted from the Polish play by Jean-Claude Carrière

In contrast to Renoir's populist focus on the collective purpose of the Marseilles battalion, in a film which deliberately avoided heroic imaging of individual leaders, this Polish-French film depicts the battle to the death for control of France between the two most charismatic figures of the French Revolution: Danton and Robespierre. For such arch rivals of starkly contrasting temperaments, historically their lives had many striking similarities. Georges Jacques Danton was born in Arcis-sur-Aube of middle-class parents in 1759, just five years after the birth of Louis XVI, the king he would imprison on 10 August 1792 and execute on 21 January 1793. In 1789, at age thirty, Danton was a successful lawyer living in Paris, in 1790 one of the founders of the Cordeliers Club. Until 1791, he was actually a legal counsellor to the king. With the end of the monarchy, Danton and the other Republican leaders, including Camille Desmoulins, Maximilien Robespierre, Jean-Paul Marat and Antoine Saint-Just, established the Convention and the Revolutionary Tribunal, which ruled France until 1795 and which earned its lasting reputation as one of the most brutal radical revolutionary governments in history.

Officially, seventeen thousand aristocrats, including the king and queen of France, died on the guillotine during those years. But unofficial estimates, including provincial executions, reach two or three times that number. Of the major figures in the French Revolution, ironically the journalist Desmoulins enjoys the least renown as a historic figure today. But Danton, Robespierre, Condorcet, La Fayette, Mirabeau and Saint-Just still elicit a response in two-thirds or more of the French people (more or less favorable depending on their political leanings). Marat, assassinated in his bathtub by Charlotte Corday, the Girondiste guillotined soon after in 1793, is regarded with the least sympathy. All of these popular image reactions have been inevitably as influenced by the depictions of these figures in art, literature, film and the media as by the implications of their actual historic roles. It is clear, though, that Danton and Robespierre have become over two centuries synonymous with these extreme factions of the Revolution and especially the Reign of Terror.

Over the years, they have continued to be rivals for popular sentiment just as they fought each other for control of the Convention. In 1889, Danton was lionized as a hero during the Centennial of the French Revolution. And Robespierre was always the favorite figure of the Communists. Historically, of the two, Danton was the more moderate idealist, wanting to curb the executions and establish a working constitution. His denunciation of his fellow Tribunal members and the popular power of his bold oratory frightened them, and they executed him on 5 April 1794. Robespierre controlled France from then until his own death on 28 July 1794, the official end date of the Reign of Terror and some would say of the Revolution.

Maximilien François Marie Isidore de Robespierre has been characterized as the "incorruptible straight line" of the Revolution, fanatically obsessed with it and with power. He consolidated that power with each passing year (he too was a lawyer in Paris in 1789, having been elected representative to the States-General by the people of Arras, where he was born into the petty aristocracy in 1758). Robespierre's rise to power and his final tyrannical control of the Revolution came from his brilliance distorted by paranoia. Driven by the will to purify the government of its moderate and to him therefore corrupt elements, he was elected to the Paris Commune, the Convention, the Committees of Public Safety and General Security, helped set up the Revolutionary Tribunal, was a leader of the Jacobins, and moved farther and farther away from constitutional democracy into the uncharted waters of revolutionary extremism, whose other face is totalitarian tyranny. Robespierre's demagogical ambitions culminated in the *Fête de L'Être Suprême* (whose three circumflex accents form a temple to his monomania), an extravagant parade in Paris on 8 June 1794 to worship the Supreme Being in a new revolutionary deistic cult. What began as a drive to purge France of its immorality ended by suppressing all freedom. Robespierre finally terrorized his cohorts in a speech on 26 July 1794, and they voted to arrest him. In his escape attempt, his jaw was broken, so the last great orator of the French Revolution went to his death symbolically silenced by his own violence.

There have been at least three plays and six films treating Danton, and a television production, *La Mort de Danton*, by Claude Barma, in 1970. Three of the films, D. W. Griffith's 1921 *Orphans of the Storm*, Hans Behrendt's 1931 *Danton*, and André Roubaud's 1932 *Danton*, were original filmscripts. Two of the films constitute adaptations of the three plays: Buchowetzki's 1921 German *Danton* from Georg Büchner's *Dantons Tod* and Romain Rolland's *La Mort de Danton*, and Wadja's 1982 Polish-French production of *Danton* from the 1935 work by Stanislawa Przybyszewka, *The Danton Affair*, staged from 1975 to 1979 and in 1981 by Wadja. Wadja chose both his leading actors, Gérard Depardieu (Danton) and Wojciech Pszoniak (Robespierre), on stage. Pszoniak had in fact to perform his role in Polish in the French film because he had so internalized it in his native language in his live theater performances.

The film is a triple parable for its Polish audiences, of Tadeusz Kosciuszko's role in fighting the Russians in 1794, of conditions in Poland during the 1930s when the play appeared, and lastly of Poland's situation in 1981, when Lech Walesa and Solidarity were struggling to free the nation from dominance by a stale Soviet bureaucracy and its secret police. Interestingly, history has belied the most recent situation most of all in the decade since the film's release.

There are four films in this book depicting the French Revolution. *La Nuit de Varennes* portrays 1789 to 1793, but especially 1791, *La Marseillaise* 1789 to 1792, *Danton* 1794, and *Napoléon* treats events throughout the Revolution and the Directory up to his conquest of Italy in 1796. These four films are all historic in purpose, decor, characterization and scope. And yet all four offer very different points of view on the events of the Revolution because they have four different motives behind the production of the film. Like *Le Retour de Martin Guerre*, *La Nuit de Varennes* stages history as mask, as theater, mixing fact and fantasy on various levels. And *Napoléon*, *La Marseillaise* and *Danton* use historic events and figures didactically, as parable, fable, myth or allegory for movements, moods and events of the twentieth century, in France and in Poland, including Russian war crimes, censorship of the press, and the civil rights abuses of the government which finally fell in 1990.

In *Cinéma et Révolution*, Raymond Lefèvre offers a succinct analysis of the historic intertexts of the plays and films about Danton. And in his 1990 book *The Kiss of Lamourette*, Robert Darnton elucidates at length the historical and political complexities in both Poland and France which are reflected in the film, as well as its very different reception in the two countries. Both emphasize the importance of the play by Przybyszewska and the ways her work served as a rallying point for the Polish Left in the 1930s, generating an obvious equation with the 1936 French Front Populaire and Renoir's work.

The first instinctive political equation one makes between *Danton* and Polish history is erroneous, that of Danton as Lech Walesa and the striking Gdànsk shipyard Solidarity workers and Robespierre as the hardline autocratic proSoviet regime of General Jaruzelski. Wadja emphatically denied this parallel, possibly to protect himself, foregrounding instead as does the play the historic contextual allusion to Polish struggles for national identity and freedom from Russian invasion in the 1790s. Works like Paul Coates's *The Story of the Lost Reflection* comparing Western and Polish cinema and Wadja's own previous documentary films offer additional insights into the contextual constructs represented by Polish cinema.

As equally intriguing as the Polish political house of mirrors is the reaction to the film in France after its first screening in 1983. The persona of Danton created by the immensely popular Gérard Depardieu, like that of Emil Jannings in the 1921 film, elicited a conservative bourgeois hedonist image in France, was even labeled Gaullist. Thus the implications of the film in Poland and France were reversed. The pro-western materialism and drunken gourmandise of Danton that undermined and tainted his identification with Solidarity in Poland came across in Depardieu's homeland as stubborn individualism and the mandate for personal freedom that characterizes French national identity. Conversely, Robespierre's sickly stiff egomaniacal character was well received in Poland as a damning of reactionary tyranny, but came across postsynched in France as an indictment of the hardline Left, struggling to maintain its identity after the stunning 1981 victory of the Socialists led by Mitterrand. Government support for the film, including millions of francs which were contributed by Minister of Culture Jack Lang, generated a political battle. The battle revived with the 1989 Bicentennial when the Communists erected a statue in Arras in Robespierre's honor, in spite of official protests.

The music of Jean Prodromides with the opening credits of Wadja's film is somber and foreboding. The talented scriptwriter Jean-Claude Carrière (*Le Retour de Martin Guerre, Le Charme discret de la bourgeoisie, Milou en mai*) adapted *L'Affaire Danton* to the screen. The film used historic consultants, as did *La Marseillaise, Le Retour de Martin Guerre* and *La Nuit de Varennes*, including here two professors: Jan Baszkiewicz and Stefan Meller. The judge in the trial of Danton, Fouquier-Tinville, is played by Roger Planchon, who played the judge in *Le Retour de Martin Guerre*. Depardieu and Planchon thus faced each other twice in one year in similarly opposing roles.

The opening scene of identity checks at the entrance to Paris alludes to military control in eastern Europe of the day as well as memories of the horrors the Poles suffered at the hands of the Nazis, or in the Stalinist purges. Danton's carriage symbolically circles the guillotine draped in black, known as *la veuve*, the widow. A viewer familiar with Paris might note the narrative inconsistency of the guillotine placed in the Place Vendôme rather than in its historic but now extremely congested location of the Place de la Concorde.

In the next scene, the nude young son of Robespierre's landlord is standing in the bathtub trying to recite from memory *The Declaration of the Rights of Man*. Slapped repeatedly by his older sister, he offers a poignant personification of the young Republic which has forgotten its original purpose from 1789, just as Robespierre lying in bed ill represents the moral and spiritual decadence of the Terror. The following sequence depicts citizens as they are still today in the former Eastern Block countries, without heat and bread, lined up in the streets, tired of their suffering and, at the time of the film, of government brutality and senseless executions, imaged by the guillotine. Danton in the carriage touches the unstable wig on his head, analogous to his perilous position. He is received with acclaim and enthusiasm by the people as the sick Robespierre looks on from behind his window, the frame of death and barrier between them that returns in the film's closing scenes.

In a subsequent scene reminiscent of *La Nuit de Varennes*, the printing press for Desmoulins's and Danton's *Le Vieux Cordelier* is sacked by Robespierre's henchmen to suppress criticism of his policies, the Committees and their excesses. The comment about lack of freedom of the press in Moscow applies to both 1794 and 1982. Sheets of the confiscated paper are scattered down the street on the wind, as someone comments that Camille Desmoulins (Patrice Chéreau) has not yet been arrested. In the first of numerous implications of homosexuality among Robespierre's faction, he receives a visit from Saint-Just (Boguslaw Linda) acting like a young lover.

When Saint-Just reports that Danton is encouraging the people against the Committees, Robespierre queries ironically, "Has Danton lost his head?" In further images of food shortages, there is bread but no sugar for Robespierre's breakfast.

The great distance between the people and the government is apparent. Wadja uses a meeting of the Committee of Public Safety as a narrative ploy to review Danton's historic rise, his founding of the Cordeliers Club and role as a leader at the Champs de Mars. With *Le Vieux Cordelier* eliminated, the committee fears that his faction will replace it with *Le Jeune Jacobin*, acknowledging the power of the media as a political weapon. Although Mirabeau, Amar and others are loyal to the committee, Robespierre defends Danton, knowing that he is his alter ego, and that to eliminate him would be suicide. The fact that Danton founded the Tribunal and is Minister of Justice is later rendered ironic when he is tried with Fabre d'Eglantine and Desmoulins along with common criminals in a mockery of justice. (It would be possible to see Danton's return to Paris from the country, his political trial and execution as a parable of the last days of Christ. Christian or not, he is certainly depicted as a martyr. Another intertext is the assassination attempt on the Pole Karol Wojtyla, Pope since 1978.)

In the committee meeting, Robespierre equates the use of terror to an admission of despair, alluding to weaknesses in the contemporary Polish regime. Some committee members recommend amnesty for Danton to avoid a counterrevolution by the bourgeoisie. (Danton is connected to them by implication by his riches, arrogance and overconfidence.) The importance of the role of women historically in periods of political upheaval is embodied in the portrait of Lucile Desmoulins (Angela Winkler), intensely loyal and articulate, also a martyr figure swooning with babe in arms, prefiguring her coming death on the guillotine. The scenes at the Convention portray the machinations of the parliamentary body, as the moderate Philippeaux (Serge Merlin) offers Danton his support but accuses him of enriching himself at the expense of the people. The political moderates are increasingly terrified by the decrees of the Committee of Public Safety and the activities of Héron (Alain Mace), the head of Robespierre's secret police, hated and feared by the people like the KGB for generating suspicion and betrayal.

The scene of the private meeting between Robespierre and Danton is central to the film. Danton displays his excessive self-indulgent vulgar taste, serving a suite of elaborate dishes. The dessert has sauce Varennes—an allusion to the king's failed attempt to escape if not to Scola's film. Danton now carries his head in his hand in the form of his wig. Someone else will hold up his head at the end of the film. The two leaders are left alone, like the old battle of the two knights representing their factions, or a summit meeting, of the kind portrayed in Giraudoux's *La Guerre de Troie n'aura pas lieu.*

Their encounter takes place in a club, where corruption and libertinage are continued under the guise of revolutionary ardor. As Danton preempts the normal activities, card players, mystics, exotic dancers, prostitutes and customers are evicted. Danton, elaborately attired in red silk, confronts Robespierre garbed in blue satin, a metaphoric distortion of the tricolor motif of rebellion. Late as usual (a privilege of power), Robespierre refuses the food which Danton offers, perhaps fearing poison, certainly feeling sick and having no stomach for the event. In contrast, the healthy robust man of appetites (he was fat) and extravagant gestures, Danton drinks to inebriation and clears the table with the back of his hand, a gratuitous gesture of desperation and reckless defiance. Here the two men seem more personal rivals than political enemies. Danton fills Robespierre's wine glass to the brim as a challenge, *la goutte qui fait déborder le vase* (the last straw, the straw that breaks the camel's back), determined to unnerve his opponent.

Although at this point Danton and Robespierre are both above the people, Robespierre has committed the greater excesses, created poverty in the name of equality, "frozen" the Revolution. Danton has the support of the people in the street, whereas Robespierre behaves as an effete aristocrat who is unshakable. Danton tells Robespierre that he will have to guillotine him to get rid of him, thus becoming equally intransigent in his own way. Faced with this impasse, Robespierre turns to his old friend Desmoulins for help, to no avail, as the chasm between the two sides is now too great to cross on personal ground. The idealists Desmoulins and Danton are effectively declaring their willingness to die to stop the abuses of the Terror, a stance which Robespierre interprets as a counterrevolution.

Robespierre asks Desmoulins to retract his attacks, stating that suppression of freedom of the press is now essential to the Revolution, which has betrayed itself. Then, tightening his grip even as he is losing it, Robespierre plays the role of a king with his ministers at the committee. With the approval of the Committee of Public Safety, the Committee of General Security (which sent all political enemies to the guillotine) decides to arrest Lacroix, Philippeaux, Desmoulins and Danton (historically Fabre d'Eglantine was also executed with them). This schism in the revolutionary forces compares to the battle between the KGB and the Politburo, to purges of political rivals in the Eastern Block (and of course has uncanny resemblance to twentieth-century events in the breakup of the Soviet Union). Danton offers the most obvious parallel to the figure of Lech Walesa, who was arrested many times before the liberation and his final ascendancy to the presidency of Poland. Although Darnton faults the film for using first names in direct address, the revolutionaries do authentically use the familiar *tu* form, a practice which was revived by the Left in 1968, in another period of social revolution.

For the trial of its enemies, the committee can find only seven jurors it is sure of, thus violating the law of twelve. A group of renegades are also arrested as a cover for the purge of Danton and Desmoulins. Instead of taking flight, Danton waits for his captors, lets himself be arrested as an act of defiance, knowing his death will demonstrate Robespierre's corruption if not end the Terror. The implication is that the sick, criminal, crippled, and homosexual are supporting the Terror, and that the Convention no longer has any real power. Robespierre tries to speak out to defend his actions, and the entire Convention sings "The Marseillaise," a scene which also figures in *Napoléon*, invented by Gance. Darnton also criticizes Saint-Just's earring and manner as inauthentic, but they can be traced to the character generated on screen by Gance, the epitome of sinister decadence, and thus offer a cinematic historic citation.

Danton's trial, a miscarriage of justice, raises the question of human rights and the right to live. Danton, overly sure of his charismatic oratorical power, thinks they will be saved, but the four have been set up to be executed out of personal malice and spite by their jealous paranoid rivals. The economic woes of the nation are furthered emphasized in accusations lodged against them of black market graft and cheating the Compagnie des Indes. Danton speaks to the people against the government, calling on them as witnesses to this abuse of human rights and betrayal of the principles of the Revolution. The intensity of the confrontation prefigures the chaos to follow and the collapse of the Terror.

The film offers a mirror of its own function of documenting historical events through artistic images in the scene depicting the painter Jacques-Louis David working on the neoclassic allegorical mural of the Tennis Court Oath, from the early days of the Revolution (20 June 1789). Robespierre is draped in classic garb for the coming *Fête de l'Être Suprême*, in ironic contrast to his abuse of the high ideals implied by the symbolism of the work. Furthermore, in an allusion to Polish authorities' revisionist abuses of the nation's history, he asks David to remove Fabre d'Eglantine from the painting, as he is about to remove him from the political scene forever, commenting that he wasn't there and calling him a traitor. Darnton points out, as does Robespierre, in the chapter on *Danton*, that David's depiction of Fabre was itself a rewriting, as he was not yet a member of the Estates General at the time of the Tennis Court Oath.

Justice and law have been abandoned to eliminate enemies of the Republic, and the genocide of the Revolution is compared to the mythological Saturn devouring its own children. The real enemy of the people has become the government, as far from its founding principles as the Eastern Block regimes from the Russian Revolution intended to free the people from aristocratic oppression. Danton and Robespierre are both trapped and destroyed by the very system they created. The end of the Terror can almost be characterized as a mass suicide of extremism. The implications of *Danton* for subsequent events in Eastern Block countries are quite startlingly prophetic, and its influence cannot be discounted.

The editor's wife Lucie Desmoulins, who will be made a *veuve* by the other *veuve*, is accused of plotting to rescue the four, and as no one is above suspicion or immune, she will also soon die. The end of the Revolution that Danton predicts would come in less than four months, although the official end date is not until 1799 (akin to the rhythm of contemporary events in Poland of an entire decade to freedom).

David sits in a window sketching as the carts carry the prisoners to their death, supposedly seeking a last image of these famous men to use in his painting depicting the first solidarity of the Revolution. In fact, these sketches of the condemned survive, along with other artists' documenting "snapshots" of these historic events. The last sign of the Revolution is Robespierre lying in bed in despair, covering his head with the sheet like the corpse he will soon become, as Saint-Just urges him to assume the role of dictator with the failure of democracy. The boy we saw at the beginning now recites flawlessly to Robespierre *La Déclaration des Droits de l'Homme* in an ironic postscript in counterpoint to the tyrannical blood bath of the Terror. The film's structure is perfectly circular: Robespierre being shaved and coiffed at the beginning is echoed in Danton's cropping before his death; Robespierre is again lying ill in his room at the end; the boy is again reciting his history; the blade of the guillotine whose reflection glinted on Danton's neck inside the carriage at the beginning has fallen there. This is not only flawless plot structure but a metaphoric comment on the cyclical nature of history, like so many other cautionary films discussed in this study.

During the early 1980s, Wadja suffered extensive government repression; his Studio X film production group was dissolved and he was forced to resign as head of the national filmmakers' association. Since the collapse of the proSoviet regime, history has vindicated the people of Poland and other Eastern Block communist countries which have finally freed themselves from the oppression of totalitarianism. But as in France in the 1790s, they are undergoing extended deprivation caused by the years of prior abuses and economic breakdown due to political upheaval. *Danton* will stand in the longer perspective as a captivating portrait of conflicting personalities at the crossroads of destiny, and a condemnation of the betrayal of the ideals of the people's revolution, in whatever century or setting it occurs.

Bibliography

Barbur, Eli. "An Interview with Andrzej Wajda." *Tel-Aviv Review* 2 (Fall–Winter 1989–1990) 104–119.

Barthélemy. "Andrzej Wajda metteur en scène." *La Quinzaine Littéraire* 319 (Feb 1980) 27–28.

Büchner, Georg. *Dantons Tod*. Manchester: Manchester University Press, 1954.

Coates, Paul. *The Story of the Lost Reflection: the Alienation of the Image in Western and Polish Cinema*. London: Verso, 1985.

Cozic, Alain. "Danton face à Robespierre dans *Dantons Tod* de Büchner." *Littératures* 20 (1989) 25–37.

Darnton, Robert. *The Kiss of Lamourette*. New York: Norton, 1990.

Dowell, Pat. "The Man who put Poland on the Postwar Map of Cinema: An Interview with Andrzej Wajda." *Cinéaste* 19:4 (1993) 51–53.

Eagle, Herbert. "Wadja's *Danton*." *Cross Currents* 3 (1984) 361–373.

Falkowska, Janina. *The Political Films of Andrzej Wajda: Dialogism in 'Man of Marble', 'Man of Iron', and 'Danton'*. Providence, RI: Berghahn, 1996.

————. "'The Political' in the Films of Andrzej Wajda and Krzysztof Kieslowski." *Cinema Journal* 34:2 (Winter 1995) 37–50.

Friedman, Regine Mihal. "Violence du Sacrifice et Scarifice de la Violence dans *Danton* de A. Wajda." *Athanor* 2 (1991) 126–136.

Garrity, Henry. "The French Revolution and the Seventh Art." *The French Review* 62 (1989) 1041–1051.

Godechot, Jacques. *La Révolution française: chronologie commentée, 1787–1799*. Paris:Librairie Académique Perrin, 1988.

Hampson, Norman. *Danton*. New York: Holmes & Meier, 1978.

Lefèvre, Raymond. *Cinéma et Révolution*. Paris: Edilig, 1988.

McAllister, Elaine. "Film as Historical Text: *Danton*." In Simons, John D. *Literature and Film in the Historical Dimension*. Gainesville: University Press of Florida, 1994.

Michalek, Boleslaw. *The Cinema of Andrzej Wadja*. New York: A. S. Barnes, 1973.

Michnik, Adam. "The Wadja Question." *Salmagundi* 128–129 (Fall–Winter 2000–2001) 137–179.

Parker, Noel. *Portrayals of Revolution: Images, Debates and Patterns of Thought on the French Revolution*. Carbondale: Southern Illinois University Press, 1990.

Prendowska, Krystyna. "Artist as Politician: An Interview with Polish Director Andrzej Wajda." *Literature/Film Quarterly* 22:4 (1994) 246–252.

Rolland, Romain. *Le 14 juillet: Danton: Les loups*. Paris: A. Michel, 1926.

Todorov, Tzvetan; Robert Julian, tr. "The Wajda Problem." *Salmagundi* 92 (Fall 1991) 29–35.

Napoléon

written and directed by Abel Gance (1927)

Of all the films which exploit the "pre-text" of history in order to illustrate a mythological construct, Abel Gance's *Napoléon* has the advantage, in featuring a figure of legendary status, of Bonaparte's inventive genius in shaping his own historic role and destiny and of the breadth of his impact on the face of Europe. Napoleon's rise to power embodied complex positive and negative values and offered to France of the 1920s the image of a Janus-like persona, a survivor of prior trials (the Revolution equating World War I) looking ahead with epic optimism. In Gance's film, the ironies of this dual diegesis are foregrounded in the contradictions in the protagonist and the vagaries of fate awaiting him.

This dimension of historic ambiguity and irony made *Napoléon* a controversial film at its original release in 1927 and has contributed to the critical response in the context of its numerous showings since its first reconstructed screening in 1973 at the Kennedy Center in Washington, D.C. In between the original and revival releases, Gance himself pursued the elusive equation between the image of Napoleon, his own philosophy and artistry as a filmmaker and the contexts of contemporary France in numerous projects, the first a postsynchronized sound version in 1934. (Lupu Pick had used the final portion of Gance's lengthy screenplay in filming *Napoléon à Sainte-Hélène* in 1929). Two more attempts by Gance to further embody the legend enlisted the help of other directors, Nelly Kaplan on *Austerlitz* in 1959, and Claude Lelouch for the 1972 *Bonaparte et la Révolution*, an admixture of new footage and documentary perspective with a narrower focus on Napoleon as heir to the Revolution, a frame which destroyed more than it added.

Literally hundreds of critical voices have responded to Gance and his work since he began his acting, writing and film career before World War I. The disparities in their responses are due not just to the wide range of their personal, artistic, political or historical perspectives, but even more to the kaleidoscopic nature of Gance's own ideology and creativity. Early contemporary critics called Gance everything from a fascist to a paranoid Jew. The one thing they could not dismiss, however, politics aside, was his inventive genius. Unshackled by conventional constraints in an era of experimental cinema, Gance combined the best of the two sides of modernism: unbridled enthusiasm for technological innovation (close-ups, Polyvision, first sound film, Stereophonic Perspective Sound, Pictographe, Magirama) and a troubled and often contradictory poetic vision of the self. Drawn to the Nietzschean suffering hero, Gance made films on war (two versions of *J'accuse*), on artists (*Un grand amour de Beethoven*), on the apocalypse (*La Fin du monde*), and transposed classical mythology (his early play *La Victoire de Samothrace* and the 1921 film *La Roue*, whose hero Sisif is not just a contemporization of Sisyphus but also a tragic Oedipal figure transposed to the industrial revolution).

Born in 1889, Gance was part of the generation caught between the theories of Nietzsche or Hegel, and Schopenhauer or Bergson. He assiduously avoided conscription into World War I, only to be drafted into a Cinematographic Unit in 1917. By the time Gance produced *Napoléon*, he had developed his own personal world view, an anthropomorphic mysticism blending epic idealism and impressionistic lyricism, calling for a spiritual and esthetic revolution and the development of a new national identity through cinema for France.

Gance's inspiration for his film on Napoleon was Elie Faure's biography, but his choice of topic was informed if not destined by traumatic events in his own life. As stated, he was dragged into war and conceived of Napoleon's military achievements as a destiny that took possession of the man rather than the reverse. When the love of Gance's life died tragically in 1921, he went off to America, only to return under the spell of D. W. Griffith. In his journals published as *Prisme* in 1930, Gance expounded a mystical theory of a theosophy of light which bridged the widening gap between essentialism and phenomenology, a theory of light redolent of the inspiration of the cathedral builders of the Middle Ages. Like the Proustian metaphor for the novel, cinema is accorded supernatural powers, joining personal lyricism with technological innovation. Viewing *Napoléon* through the filter of these ideological constructs gives the film an additional focus not unlike the double images superimposed of Josephine and Napoleon on screen. In fact the final Polyvision contrapuntal sequences seem to embody the conflicting dynamics of both Gance's thought and the era around him, much as the figure of Napoleon incarnates a similar dichotomy between his mastery of technology and strategy and his vulnerability to his instincts.

Recent critical response to Gance has varied as much as the initial reviews in April 1927. Georges Sadoul in *French Film* criticized *Napoléon* for its caricatures and Gance for abhorring the Revolution. Other works characterize Gance as a cubist, a fascist, a madman, a populist, a genius. Most critics are drawn to him repeatedly. Robert Icart published studies of *Abel Gance* in 1960 and 1984. Nelly Kaplan, assistant director of *Austerlitz*, wrote a journal of the 1960 film and produced the documentary *Abel Gance: hier et demain* in 1963. Kevin Brownlow has evinced a long-term fascination with Gance and his work, from his 1968 book *The Parade's Gone By* and documentary film *The Charm of Dynamite* to the 1983 *Napoléon, Abel Gance's Classic Film*. Brownlow's projects of reconstruction were shown first in Washington, then at Telluride in 1979, London in 1980, Rome in 1981, and finally after Gance's death, France in 1982 and 1983. Pursuant to Gance's attempt to reduce his own original in 1972, Brownlow created a reconstruction of virtually exactly the length (but not the same scenes) which Gance had cut to in 1927 from extensive footage. The Harris/Coppola/Universal version released in the United States cuts about half of the original Apollo version, as well as substituting for Honegger's strange original score—which had incorporated themes from "The Marseillaise," "The Carmagnole" (named after the short jacket worn with trousers by the *sansculottes*) and "Ça ira"—a new score by Carmine Coppola, performed appropriately by the Milan Symphony Orchestra. In spite of its stirring original thematic elements and reprises of "The Marseillaise," it has generated considerable criticism.

Both Norman King, in his 1984 book on Gance, and James Welsh, in his 1978 Twayne study with Steven Kramer and his current book on Gance, emphasize the series of transformations the original *Napoléon* has experienced. They and other critics are drawn to particular sequences in the film which have become classics in their own right. I would like to look at these and other scenes as emblematic, much like Napoleon's infamous eagle, of the subject, the filmmaker and the era, to examine whether *Napoléon* glorifies France in the rising fascist mode, attempts to compensate the void left by the Great War, or turns away from the present to historical fantasy, to what extent it is shaped by social and sexual images of the 1920s, to what extent it is dominated by a modern(ist) ethic and esthetic. I think the film is a rare blend of the two apparently conflicting definitions of modernism: faith in technological progress and philosophical positivism versus the surrealistic, leftist, fragmented experimental movement in the arts of postwar Europe. It is in Gance's exuberant exploitation of the myriad expressions possible in film art as well as his elegiacal portrayal of the quirky charismatic self-made hero who was Napoleon I that the two currents of modernism converge.

The film's special effects mark Gance's work as that of the same kind of visionary genius as the man he is lionizing. Particularly memorable are the overlapping shots of Josephine and the globe (Napoleon's two primary ambitions of conquest superimposed), the crosscutting and the dancing camera of the erotic sequence of the ball scene, the ghosts of the Convention leaders, and the grand finale of the triple screen in red, white and blue with the sweeping battle sequences in counterpoint to overlapping portrait shots of Italy, the globe, Napoleon and Josephine. The film is full of portraits, signs, texts, maps; even Napoleon's eye is equated to the camera on more than one occasion, just as he is to the eagle, especially in the final visionary dream sequence. The film is a landmark of experimental cinema, a self-revealing myth of the glorious rise to power of cinematic art, as well as an engrossing portrayal of the Napoleonic legend enmeshed with events and figures of the 1780s and 1790s, uniting the revolutionary in form and thematic.

Perhaps because Gance never filmed all five parts of this silent epic biography of Napoleon that he wrote and because of the inconsistencies of his and others' reworkings of the screenplay, it is tantalizing to project in one's imagination versions of the later sections on Bonaparte's rise and fall, especially because his political triumphs, coronation, major victories and defeats, and dual exiles are so well prepared and metaphorically prefigured by the first two parts. The snowball fight at the military school at Brienne-le-Château, the pet eagle, the escape by boat from Corsica, the victory at Toulon and the republican enthusiasm of the Jacobins in Part One, the merciless days of the Reign of Terror, Napoleon as political prisoner, then his elevation to heir of the Revolution, conqueror of Josephine and commander of the Army of Italy in Part Two develop the principal thematic of Gance's *Napoléon* project, whose epic stature is heralded in the Polyvision sequences.

Gance's imagery not only of Napoleon but of populist heroism and the various stages of the Revolution left its mark on all subsequent cinematic interpretations of the era and its protagonists, in such films as Renoir's *La Marseillaise* and Wadja's *Danton*. Jean-Claude Bonnet and Philippe Roger have compiled an interesting book on *La Légende de la Révolution au XXe siècle. De Gance à Renoir* for Flammarion, one of numerous Bicentennial retrospective studies, but of special relevance due to its double historic focus. Although it is regrettable that Gance never finished his portrait of Napoleon, somehow in retrospect the saga of the young, impetuous, energetic, idealistic, visionary Napoleon is more appropriate to the mood of the 1920s than the exploits and conquests of the later ruler, who has been compared so often to the megalomaniac who would dominate Europe in the years after this film.

One of the strengths of Gance's first *Napoléon* that dominates all later efforts is the casting of Albert Dieudonné as Napoleon, Antonin Artaud (talented surrealist poet and playwright) as Marat, Gance himself as Saint-Just, Alexandre Koubitzky as Danton, Edmond Van Daële as Robespierre, and Gina Manès as Josephine. And the great L. H. Burel, whose later career included such classics as Robert Bresson's *Journal d'un curé de campagne*, was one of the cinematographers on this film.

Gance's making of the Napoleonic legend begins with the military instinctual genius the boy displays in the now classic snowball fight at Brienne Military College, wherein the slight, fierce child holds off all the other boys in a prefiguration of his future brilliant victories when outnumbered. Subsequent scenes of an isolated Napoleon with his pet eagle serve as metaphor of his identity and destiny, offering the first of many symbolic images creating a leitmotiv throughout the film.

The historic significance implied in the initial sequences of Napoleon's provincial schooling is reinforced by a cut telescoping ten years to a meeting of the Club des Cordeliers in Paris, where the leaders of the Revolution are introduced: Danton, Marat, Robspierre, Saint-Just, as the above cast is also credited. This historic cast of characters returns to the screen in *Danton*, including Camille Desmoulins, Danton's secretary, guillotined with him on 5 April 1794, and his wife Lucile, executed soon after. The club meeting is in a former church, where the radicals are preaching revolution from the pulpit. This deconsecration sequence resembles that of the populist fervor in the church *relais* of *La Nuit de Varennes*. Gance has the composer Rouget de Lisle sing "The Marseillaise" to the club and lead the members in a choral rendition, whereas he exists only as a narrative character in Renoir's eponymous film. There are numerous other popular comic characters that inevitably served as models for later Renoir films, which like Gance's work reify the abstract events of history in prosaic encounters between populist, often vaudeville-style figures. The Cordeliers sequence marks the beginning of the historic rivalry of Danton and the people with Robespierre and Saint-Just for control of the Revolution. Projected in a 1920s film, these events can also be seen as transposed depictions of the stages of the revolution which had just occurred in Russia and which fascinated many French artists and writers of the era.

The attack on the Tuileries on 10 August 1792, with Paris exploding and people driven by hunger, for food and freedom, was to become the climactic sequence of Jean Renoir's 1938 *La Marseillaise*. The figure of Napoleon embodies the popular fear of anarchy when the captured king and queen are taken to the National Assembly. Gance resorts to another populist metaphor when he depicts Danton with a farrier, symbolically forging the Republic. The extensive use of superimposed images and quick crosscutting throughout Gance's film creates many dreamlike sequences in collage, often with dramatic irony as well, as in the crosscut shots of the Declaration of the Rights of Man and acts of brutality. There is another implicit reference in these scenes, shot two years after the death of Lenin, to the extreme factions of the Russian Revolution. Gance also crosscuts the humiliating dethroning of Louis XVI and portrait shots of Napoleon as his heir, an element he expanded greatly in the 1972 film. Into this revolutionary turmoil is introduced another upheaval, as Napoleon first glimpses Josephine in the street with her lover Barras, on her way to a fortune teller who predicts that she will become queen of France.

Gance's mythologizing and mystification of Napoleon's life is patent in the sequence in his native Corsica (sold to the French the year before his birth there on 15 August 1769) wherein he finds himself in conflict in 1794 with the Corsican independence movement leader Paoli. As Gance depicts Napoleon escaping Corsica under threat of death in a small boat, symbolically using a French flag as a sail, he establishes an extended metaphor by crosscutting the fledgling ship of state tossed on stormy seas with the stormy sessions of the Convention, where Marat confronts Danton and all the leaders of the Revolution are drawn into the Terror, expressed by the frightened faces of the members of the Convention overlaid with shots of the guillotine. The equation is intensified by the camera swaying in the hall of the Convention as though on board ship. Coppola adds a few slightly discordant strains of "The Marseillaise" here in ironic echo of the rousing patriotic idealism of the Cordeliers Club's earlier rendition.

When Napoleon is rescued by his brothers in the large sailing ship *Le Hasard*, Gance creates another historic irony, as he has Nelson observe and dismiss them. Atop the mast, ensigns of the future glory of the Napoleonic Empire, ride the tricolor flag and eagle. The ensuing sequences of the siege of Toulon (held by the English) by the French Army convey Napoleon's military genius and his magic power over his commanding officers. In contrast, political rivals like Salicetti (Philippe Hériat), the Corsican deputy to the Convention, threaten his power. The portrayal of the artillery in total disarray (soldiers are growing vegetables in unused cannons and lying about idle) prefigures Napoleon's later triumph in Italy as much as it sets up his brash midnight attack in fierce weather and his subsequent promotion as reward for the victory. Gance characterizes the chaos of the opposition alliance during this battle with signs on the screen, like Godard's graffiti, saying in many languages, "I do not understand you," transforming their lack of communication, the linguistic and political barrier to their concerted resistance, not only into a preview of the later alliances against Napoleon but into a strikingly modernist exploitation of the screen surface and its coded discourse.

There are numerous varied images of women in this work, ranging from the quixotic narcissistic Josephine to the single-minded assassin Charlotte Corday (Madame Abel Gance). Both these heroines however could be characterized as castrating women, to be simultaneously feared and admired. Corday, the Mata Hari femme fatale Girondiste, comes from Caen to Paris to kill Marat, the powerful rival Jacobin leader, suffering and confined to a bathtub because of his severe skin disease. Under the pretext of listing suspects, Corday enters Marat's quarters and stabs him with a dagger (behind a closed curtain, respecting the prudery of classic theater, but also denying the audience access to this intimate act of violence). As Corday is apprehended and taken away to be guillotined, the camera lingers on Antonin Artaud as the mortally wounded Marat slumping exactly as in Jacques-Louis David's memorial painting to this martyr.

Bonaparte at this period is tossed by conflicting forces just as his boat was earlier, caught between his rival Salicetti who wants to put him on trial and Robespierre who now needs him to command the Paris garrison. It is March 1794 and Robespierre, Saint-Just and Couthon (Viguier), at the pinnacle of their power, reveal their decadent, self-indulgent excesses, in scenes which would seem to confirm Gance's abhorrence of the Revolution. Critics have often speculated as to why the heterosexual Gance chose to portray Saint-Just: as a prophetic frame for the triumph of Napoleon, as the complementary opposite, as an acting challenge. The sexual and social decadence of the leaders is parodied as much as signified by their garb (including earrings), their music (the *vielle*, which turns like a movie camera), their play with a pet rabbit (dual symbol of sexuality and vulnerability). Danton in contrast is the popular martyr, arrested and condemned to death, in a sequence which lingers in palimpsest in Wadja's film. Gance frames Robespierre again behind the window, classic cinematic symbol of separation and death, and in the Coppola version "The Marseillaise" is heard again, in a minor key. As the populace calls for Danton's release, Gance has Robespierre reading the life of the Puritan rebel Oliver Cromwell (regicide of Charles I of England in 1649), creating a historic intertextual analogy: one tyrant replaces another.

The scene in which Bonaparte refuses the command of the Army under the Terror and is put in prison by Robespierre, to be guillotined, demonstrates his patriotism and designates him a hero destined to suffer. It also demonstrates Gance's license, as Napoleon was in fact put in prison after the fall of Robespierre. Subsequent cinematic accounts have unwittingly paid tribute to Gance's influence by perpetuating this error. In Gance's film Josephine is also denounced (her husband was in fact guillotined and she narrowly escaped death), martyred at Fort Carré, Antibes, separated from her children and imprisoned at Carmes. The imprisoned General Hoche (Pierre Batcheff) who comforts her is here introduced to prepare for the chess game sequence during the ball. Gance affirms Napoleon's military, engineering, and architectural genius by depicting him working while in prison on plans to construct the Suez Canal (in fact an anachronism, as although Napoleon completed several canals in France, his idea for the Suez came during his conquest of Egypt in 1799; the actual canal was designed by Ferdinand de Lesseps in 1854 and built from 1859 to 1869).

Gance has the Vicomte de Beauharnais (G. Cahuzac), Josephine's husband, sacrifice himself to save his wife's life, while the peasants deride him, whereas historically he was not moral master of his destiny. Gance also portrays famous figures like Lavoisier and the poet André Chénier (Vonelly) as further victims of the Terror, generating historic melodrama. He counterbalances these scenes with the subsequent farcical sequence of the bureaucrats in the surrealistic records office, where the victims of the Terror are piling up and a sympathetic clerk eats the paper bearing Josephine's death order. His colleague, a supposed school chum of Napoleon's, tries to consume his death warrant, which proves hard to swallow.

In the final critical scene of the Terror (July 1794), Gance depicts Barras (Maxudian) speaking out at the Convention, demanding that they guillotine Robespierre, Saint-Just and the members of the Committee of Public Safety, as they are taken prisoner by the guards. The end of the Terror is a crucial point in Gance's film. Like the pendulum on the clock in the assembly hall, imaging the Hegelian dialectic of historic forces which characterized the Terror as an aberration, the balance swings back to normality, as the prisoners, including Josephine and Napoleon, are finally free.

Emphasizing a leitmotiv of loyalty and patriotism, Gance shows the Corsican Napoleon refusing a commission in the infantry in the Vendée (against a Royalist uprising) and declaring that he prefers to fight foreigners. These sequences prepare the coming events, as Napoleon gets another look at Josephine as Barras's mistress, and General Schérer (Mathillon) reviews Napoleon's plans for the conquest of Italy, deeming them the schemes of a madman, challenging, "Let him come and carry them out." (This is the map that covers a broken window in Napoleon's cold flat, blocking his view of Paris and awaiting a change in the winds of history.)

With the Revolution weakened by the starvation and suffering of the French people (echoed in Wajda's *Danton*) and forty thousand Royalist troops preparing to take Paris and occupy the Convention, Bonaparte finally accepts the commission on the 12th Vendémiaire to defend the city, and insists that the Convention members be armed. Standing below the Declaration of the Rights of Man, Napoleon now in sync with their idealism orders Murat (Genica Missirio) to rescue the Sablon cannons.

In a sequence demonstrating Napoleon's supposed generosity toward his previous enemies, he frees Salicetti, displaying the largesse appropriate to greatness and power that will attract Josephine to him. As he is applauded by the Convention for successfully defending Paris, Napoleon affirms the equation Gance used as the basis for his final film on this subject: "From now on, I am the Revolution." This blending of self, image and power could be seen as an extrapolation of Gance's own artistic ambitions, just as some have seen in *Napoléon* a filmic autobiography of Gance.

The Harris/Coppola version of Gance's work maintains throughout the counterpoint between military or political incidents and social or personal sequences. These elements are united in the ball scene, from the period of popular partying to celebrate the liberation of the French people, akin to recent events in the Paris of the twenties. Gance's film, standing as it does between two wars, looks forward in fear and back in horror as it indulges the fantasy gaiety distancing the population from reality, focusing instead on beauties like Madame Tallien (J. Gaudray), Madame Récamier (Suzy Vernon) and Madame de Beauharnais, the stars of the hour in 1795. In a brilliant series of quick flashbacks, Napoleon remembers the previous moments he has glimpsed Josephine. Gance also connects past and present events in the same setting, as the ball takes place in a former prison, giving rise to nostalgic flashbacks of the victims' shared fate.

The ensuing decisive encounter between Napoleon and Josephine occurs in counterpoint to the setting of orgiastic celebration wherein the camera registers a dance-hall display of bare legs and flash shots of girls on a swing, then jostled about, dances itself. Napoleon's obsessive ego enables him to conquer Hoche at chess while Josephine watches. After he takes Hoche's queen, in both senses, Napoleon engages her in a seated dance of discourse, in a tightly cut sequence of shot/countershot. Against the backdrop of an erotic rococo dance of spinning nude women comparable to the show at the Folies Bergères, Napoleon focuses in the midst of this orgy of postwar sexual liberation on the political reality of Barras's control of Josephine and the fact that he will have to liberate her from him.

Napoleon's relationship with Josephine advances in the celebrated anecdote after his decree seizing all citizens' arms, when Eugène de Beauharnais (Henin) comes to request that he be allowed to keep his father's sword, a request that Napoleon of course grants. His largesse is reflected henceforth in his regal, theatrical costume with sequins on the lapels and coattails, flashing his brilliance and signifying his promotion. In contrast to this demonstrable military and political strength, Napoleon is comically vulnerable, awkward and self-conscious when Josephine appears the next day to thank him. His position is doubly weakened by her in fact, as although Barras arranges for her to marry Napoleon, he gives him command of the Army of Italy to get him out of France.

Napoleon's continuing courtship of Josephine further demonstrates his vulnerability in a scene with her children where he kisses her daughter Hortense (Janine Pen) and appropriately plays blind man's bluff. When Napoleon embraces Josephine in front of her children, Gance creates a sentimental bourgeois family portrait in keeping with the expectations and values of a 1920s popular audience.

The rivals for Napoleon's attention and passionate ambition declare themselves as he takes his map of Italy off the window. Gance recreates the historic events of the evening of his marriage (9 March 1796, in the Second *Arrondissement*) in comic mode, as Napoleon pores over his maps, keeping everybody waiting until midnight, then in pure burlesque attempts to assume his regalia. At the town hall, he rouses the clerk from nodding off, then impatiently insists that he skip the wedding ceremony and go straight to the vows. The slapstick mood is broken by the look of bewilderment on Josephine's face, as she is overwhelmed by Napoleon's roughness and domineering manner. However, the sequence ends on an idyllic note in the marriage bed shot, where among roses strung on the gauze hangings, the lovers embrace in a long kiss which slowly fades to white, the white of prudery but also of doomed passion. Gance's striking use of tonalities in this film transcends camerawork in the tinting of the print in alternating red, white and blue washes. Their most effective use is in the contrapuntal interplay of the triple screens at the end where they form the French tricolor flag.

Napoleon's departure to head the Army of Italy came just two days after his marriage and would seem to have been arranged by Barras as a cruel trick. Gance has the general stop just as he leaves Paris to pay a visit to the empty Convention, ostensibly to meditate on the purpose of the French government before leaving on his campaign, but also to savor in retrospect the memory of his triumph as a hero before the Nation, and to accept the legacy of the Revolution. The sequence that follows has been justly hailed as a masterpiece of modernist filmmaking, as the ghosts of all the Revolutionary leaders assault Napoleon's imagination in a truly oneiric scene, a collage of history as mythological echoes of the past.

Gance overlays on the empty seats of the Convention shots of the leaders of the Revolution, focusing on Danton and Robespierre. Napoleon imagines a mandate wherein Saint-Just warns him not to betray their cause. Gance projects onto Napoleon's departure on a journey leading to Empire a different dream of a universal Republic and a unified Europe, both an eerily accurate prophecy of the economic and political negotiations at the end of the twentieth century and a betrayal of the historic realities of Napoleon's ambitions. Another rendering of the "The Marseillaise" is followed by an image equivalent to *Liberty leading the People* with the flag, an allusion to the Delacroix painting inspired by the 1830 July Revolution, another anachronism which adds however an additional historic dimension to the film.

Once en route to Italy, suffering from his separation from Josephine, Napoleon writes love letters to her every day in his carriage, along with the orders he gives to couriers on horseback. His letters to his wife are shown in his authentic unreadable scrawl (perhaps one of the reasons she supposedly never read or answered them). As the impatient general changes to his horse for greater speed, Gance pans the next shots in a dizzying crosscutting of passing trees and Napoleon galloping toward the camera (a total mystification according to the historians who claim he couldn't ride a horse).

The final sequence cuts to the wounded and starving Army of the Alps at Albenga, where Napoleon presents himself to Masséna (Philippe Rolla) and other commanders of the Italian campaign furious about this upstart and bent on ignoring him. He stares them down, even the wild-eyed Masséna, and begins to plan the campaign, giving commands to division leaders and preparing to review his troops. Gance here uses an iris out/iris in distancing the officers from the shots of the ragtag clowning troops who oppose Napoleon's discipline and authority and provide comic relief in their foolishness. A second iris out/iris in cuts to Napoleon paying his officers and contemplating a miniature of Josephine, the other object of his strategies of dominance. Gance exploits repeatedly the irony of this powerful commander filled with hopeless weakness before his wife.

Opening the grand finale sequence, the screen image begins to shrink, then shifts to the Polyvision triple screen for the reviewing of the troops. (This small central screen image in black and white shifting to a panoramic screen in colors was the forerunner of Gance's Magirama and the Cinerama movies of the 1950s.) In a panoramic shot of the entire encampment, the army has miraculously been shaped into order in one hour and is standing at attention. Napoleon's portrait occupies the center screen, as the troops cheer their new leader, echoing the populist support he found at the Convention. 11 April 1796 dawns on the triple screen, dominated by center busts of Napoleon, then depicted addressing his troops from atop the mountain, with more crosscutting between the isolated leader and the masses of troops bivouacked.

The subsequent use of panoramic mirror image shots makes the right and left screens seem to disappear into the middle. This is followed by a series of images of Napoleon giving his famous rallying speech with stirring rhetoric. Once again, film is foregrounding the power or oratory, of the word, as in *Le Retour de Martin Guerre* and *La Nuit de Varennes*. The subsequent triple screen shot is a panoramic landscape of Piedmont with a quote from Napoleon's memoirs, yet another use of text in the film. His army is mobilized in two hours, and as they march, we see the left and right mirror image screens again, with Napoleon always in the center frame, on the brink of power and glory.

Two days later, the French storm into Italy at the village of Montenotte, depicted in a triple screen battle scene. This time Napoleon is on the center screen between two cavalry shots which are not mirror images. There follow three separate battle shots, then the village panorama. Next the French flag leads mirror Napoleons galloping past his troops, followed by a triple-screen panorama of the people of Paris cheering. At Montezemolo, Napoleon is depicted on the triple screen standing against a mountain backdrop. In an equation between his ambitious visions of conquest and the art of cinematography, his eye inscribes in the sky his desires and his victories: Josephine over top of the battle, then Josephine in the center, Italy on the left and the globe on the right, creating again the equation between love and war as conquest. Then mirror Josephines flank Napoleon, showing her present power and his future dilemma. This is followed by a center shot of Napoleon between two battle scenes, then the globe in the center with Josephine superimposed, then Napoleon center, then Josephine, the globe, Napoleon and Italy alternating in musical rhythm. The last dream sequence displays images of revolution, mathematical calculations, more revolution, then the eagle in the sky, ending with "The Marseillaise" in the Coppola score, with the flag, the troops and the flame of liberty in a collage of special effects equating Napoleon with France, history and the world.

The final image, of Abel Gance's signature, is appropriate for his unique film *écriture*, as well as being indicative of his grandiose ambitions. The music continues at the end with the screen dark, duplicating the effect of a live orchestra playing in a theater as the audience leaves the hall, the strains of the stirring march which opened the film intended to prolong in the spectator's psyche the emotional state elicited by this cinema experience. The figural void invites the spectator to generate images of Napoleon's rise to master of Europe in the years following this victory which catapulted him to power. There is also a sense of the immensity of the future, of the eve or the threshold of greatness, stamping this work by a man who was just thirty-seven about a creative genius who was only twenty-seven at the time of this last scene.

Bibliography

Abel, Richard. "Charge and Countercharge: Coherence and Incoherence in Abel Gance's *Napoleon*." *Film Quarterly* 35 (1982) 2–12.

Aronson, Theo. *Napoleon and Josephine: A Love Story*. London: Murray, 1990.

Bandy, Mary Lea, ed. *Rediscovering French Film*. New York: Museum of Modern Art, 1983. 428–446.

Bonnet, Jean-Claude and Philippe Roger. *La Légende de la Révolution au XXe siècle. De Gance à Renoir*. Paris: Flammarion, 1988.

Brownlow, Kevin. *The Parade's Gone By....* New York: Alfred A. Knopf, 1969.

————. *Napoleon, Abel Gance's Classic Film*. London: Cape, 1983.

Daniel, Joseph. *Guerre et cinéma: grandes illusions et petits soldats, 1895–1971*. Paris: Armand Colin, 1972.

Darnton, Robert. *The Kiss of Lamourette*. New York: Norton, 1990.

Faure, Elie. *Napoléon*. Paris: Denoël-Gonthier, 1983.

Gance, Abel. *Prisme*. Paris: Editions Vrac, 1983.

Icart, Roger. *Abel Gance*. Toulouse: Publications de l'Institut Pédagogique National, 1960.

————. *Abel Gance*. Lausanne: L'Age d'Homme, 1984.

Kaplan, Nelly. *Napoleon*. London: British Film Institute, 1994.

King, Norman. *Abel Gance: A Politics of Spectacle*. London: British Film Institute, 1984.

————. "History and Actuality: Abel Gance's *Napoléon vu par Abel Gance* (1927)." In Susan Hayward and Ginette Vincendeau, eds. *French Film: Texts and Contexts*. New York: Routledge, 1990.

————. "Patrie et nation: fictions populistes dans le *Napoléon* d'Abel Ganz et *La Marseillaise* de Jean Renoir." *Europe* 715–716 (1988) 68–75.

Kirchberger, Joe H. *The French Revolution and Napoleon: An Eyewitness History*. New York: Facts on File, 1989.

Kramer, Steven, and James Welsh. *Abel Gance*. Boston: Twayne Publishers, 1978.

Lefèvre, Raymond. *Cinéma et Révolution*. Paris: Edilig, 1988.

Shulim, Joseph I. *Liberty, Equality, and Fraternity: Studies on the Era of the French Revolution and Napoleon*. New York: Peter Lang, 1989.

Sorlin, Pierre. *The Film in History*. Oxford: Blackwell, 1980.

Stewart, Garrett. "Leaving History: Dickens, Gance, Blanchot." *The Yale Journal of Criticism* 2:2 (1989) 145–190.

Tulard, Jean. *Le Mythe de Napoléon*. Paris: Armand Colin, 1972.

Welsh, James. *Abel Gance and the Seventh Art*. Austin: University of Texas Press, forthcoming.

————. "Abel Gance as Epic Modernist." *West Virginia University Philological Papers* 39 (1993) 121–125.

La Grande Illusion
(Grand Illusion)

directed by Jean Renoir (1937)
written by Charles Spaak

Jean Renoir's 1937 film about World War I, *La Grande Illusion*, was the first foreign film to ever be nominated for an American Academy Award, and deservedly won. This was the last great pacifist film of the period between the wars. A reconnaissance pilot, wounded twice, Renoir was present at the armistice. The script that Charles Spaak wrote for the film is based on true accounts, the title borrowed from a 1911 book on economic conflicts by Norman Angell. Essentially, this is a marginalized view of war, with almost no shots fired. Jean Gabin as Lieutenant Maréchal (a name composed of two ranks) is a man of the people, rough, but loving and heroic. Gabin wore Jean Renoir's own World War I aviator lieutenant's uniform. Maréchal is taken prisoner when shot down on a reconnaissance mission and introduced to a disarmingly cordial group at table. The POWs thrown together come from all backgrounds and races, a populist democratic conceit imposed on what was formerly a very stratified society. Like the American comedy *Stalag 17*, this film offers a society in miniature of prisoners of war in a German camp. The movie director Erich von Stroheim plays the Commandant von Rauffenstein, the aristocratic fighter pilot who is crippled and burned in a crash and becomes the "warden" of a medieval castle prison-fortress, where the primary prisoner characters wind up in maximum security. This character embodies of course the legendary Red Baron, Baron von Richthofen, but more generally all the aristocratic officers of World War I. Von Stroheim was fascinated by the character and expanded his role greatly from the sketchier version Renoir had planned. He also intimidated Renoir repeatedly, thus enacting a historic stereotype during the filming.

In the early prison sequences, we see solidarity, generosity, gaiety and vaudeville nonsense as the grab bag of prisoners of war strive simultaneously to escape and to preserve their morale. Von Rauffenstein's French counterpart, his aristocratic soul mate, played by Pierre Fresnay, is the Captain de Boeldieu, who will eventually sacrifice his life to enable his fellow prisoners to escape. Rosenthal, played by Dalio, is the mixed-blooded scion of a powerful Jewish banking family. He shares his packages of gourmet food and wine with all willingly and ultimately shares the fate of Maréchal as they escape together.

Seeing the prisoners in Folies Bergères drag singing in English "It's a Long Way to Tipperary" brings to mind a number of similar scenes from war movies filmed since then: *Das Boot* because of the song, *MASH* because of the vaudeville comedy and irreverence, among others. The soldiers' defiance of dress regulations in their outlandish transvestite outfits turns to patriotic solidarity as they sing "The Marseillaise" in response to war news. The prisoner in dance hall dress holding his wig and standing at attention is a male/female image of the French nation fighting the emasculation of defeat. The vaudeville stage entertainment interlude is repeated in parody in Renoir's 1939 *La Règle du Jeu*.

La Grande Illusion is filled with numerous forms of symbolism. There are two technical references to the German and French war production: the Gnome aircraft engine factory in Lyons employed both Maréchal and a German officer whom he meets when captured; and at the fortress, Maréchal and von Rauffenstein pun on the German machine gun named Maxim, the same as the French restaurant (Maxim's), evoking nostalgia among the officers. As in *La Nuit de Varennes*, the sense of loss of the aristocracy is intense; the common soldiers are termed the legacy of the French Revolution. When von Rauffenstein is obliged to shoot de Boeldieu and he dies, the German commandant pensively picks the only blossom from his geranium, the last flower in the castle, emblem of the flower of Europe's young leaders sacrificed, often in endless battles over a few hundred yards of ground. (In the film, the references to the four successive losses and recaptures of Douaumont echo not only the tragedies of the trenches where millions died but the long-term fate of Alsace-Lorraine, exchanged five times between France and Germany since 1800.)

The conflicts of war are portrayed as those of a series of opposing mentalities: the fun-loving French versus the *streng verboten* German disciplinarians; the duty-bound restrained and proper aristocrats (the two career officers) versus the populist, rough and vulgar common soldiers (in French grammar *vous* versus *tu*); the old guard French versus Rosenthal, the Jew born in Vienna of a Danish mother and a Polish father, proud and generous in the face of some obvious anti-Semitism. The film also abounds with confrontations demonstrating the lack of communication, linguistic and cultural, between the various races, classes, and nationalities.

When the escaped prisoners take refuge in an empty barn in the mountains and are discovered by the German farmwife Elsa, a nostalgic and lyric sequence begins in a bucolic mountain setting. The farmwife has lost her husband and brothers in battles which were considered German's great "victories" of the war; not for her. The prisoners stay on through Christmas; with Rosenthal's German, they overcome the language barrier; they build a nativity scene for the little girl Lotte. The love between Maréchal and Elsa, like the friendship between de Boeldieu and von Rauffenstein, and the love of Elle for the German soldier in *Hiroshima mon amour*, cuts across national boundaries and nationalism. Their backgrounds and common humanity, senseless suffering because of war, unite them temporarily. In all three cases, though, the love is cut short by the impossible circumstances: von

Rauffenstein is forced to shoot de Boeldieu, Maréchal and Rosenthal must push on to neutral Switzerland and freedom, Elle's lover is shot by a resistance fighter in her hometown. It is interesting that while a perfectly serious dramatic film, *La Grande Illusion* calls up scenes and images from later musical films like *South Pacific* and *The Sound of Music*, both of which also portray lyric love stories and comedy in the midst of war. And the sequence of the defiant singing of "The Marseillaise" has its echo in the similar scene in Rick's Café in *Casablanca*.

The film's lasting message is the unity of mankind, in spite of all its differences of background, race, sex, creed, in the face of the dehumanizing prison of war. And the inestimable value of the simple realities of life in the face of the surreal horrors of combat and death. The Grand Illusion is twofold: first, that the war will end quickly (it is set in 1916), and lastly, that there will never be another tragedy of that scale. It is particularly astute and poignant from the perspective of 1937, on the eve of Hitler's protracted conquest of Europe. For obvious reasons, the film was simultaneously banned in Germany, Italy and France throughout World War II, and not shown again in its entirety until 1958. As Restif de la Bretonne commented at the end of *La Nuit de Varennes*, regarding the blood bath of the French Revolution, will the Europe of 1992 make the same mistake again? Perhaps that in itself is a commentary on the pace of the changes in the world today, a world which looks very different to us than it did in 1982 or even 1989. And yet, as Resnais emphasizes in his two films on World War II, the dragon of violence—war or revolution—lies just below the surface, with one eye open. What seemed like freedom and liberation for world democracy and free trade in 1990 has in many places degenerated into infighting at the tribal and village level, to old unsettled scores of religious conflicts or territorial ambitions. It is to be hoped that the basic goodness of human beings, of the people of the world, that Renoir wanted to believe in, is not a third grand illusion.

Bibliography

Barbry, François-Régis. "Jean Renoir, maître de la réalité et de l'illusion." *Cinéma 72* 441 (May 1988) 33.

Bazin, André. *Jean Renoir*. New York: Simon & Schuster, 1973.

Bertin, Célia. *Jean Renoir: a Life in Pictures*. Baltimore: Johns Hopkins University Press, 1991.

Braudy, Leo. *Jean Renoir: The World of his Films*. New York: Columbia University Press, 1989.

Britton, C. "Semantic Structures in *La Grande Illusion*." *Film Form* I, 1 (Spring 1976) 35–51.

Daniel, Joseph. *Guerre et cinéma: grandes illusions et petits soldats, 1895–1971*. Paris: Armand Colin, 1972.

Dupuich, Jean-Jacques. "*La Grande Illusion*." *Image et Son* 265 (Nov 1972) 120–122.

Durgnat, Raymond. *Jean Renoir*. Berkeley: University of California Press, 1974.

Faulkner, Christopher. *Jean Renoir, a Guide to References and Resources*. Boston: G. K. Hall, 1979.

————. *The Social Cinema of Jean Renoir*. Princeton: Princeton University Press, 1986.

90   *La Grande Illusion*

Fronval, Georges. Interview with Jean Renoir in *Cinémonde* 436 (Feb 1937) extracted in *Image et Son* 296 (May 1975) 29.

Gauteur, Claude. "Jean Renoir de *Nana* à *La Grande Illusion*." *Image et Son* 296 (May 1975) 17–38.

Gilliatt, Penelope. *Jean Renoir: Essays, Conversations, Reviews.* New York: McGraw-Hill, 1975.

Hines, Thomas J. "War Crimes: Jean Renoir's *La Grande Illusion*." In Radcliff-Umstead, Douglas, ed. *Crime in Motion Pictures.* Kent, OH: Kent State University, 1986.

"Hommage à Jean Renoir." Special section of *Positif* 401–402 (Jul–Aug 1994) 86–98.

Koch, Carl. "*La Grande Illusion*." *CICIM* 39-40 (June 1994) 171–174.

Leprohon, Pierre. *Jean Renoir.* New York: Crown Publishers, 1971.

Lourié, Eugène. "Grand Illusions." *American Film* X, 4 (Jan–Feb 1985) 29–32, 34.

Masson, Alain. "*La Grande Illusion*." *Positif* 395 (Jan 1994) 70–72.

Pearson, Karen. "Rosenthal dans *La Grande Illusion* et La Chesnaye dans *La Règle du jeu*." *Chimères* 18:1 (1985) 41–48.

Perebinossoff, P.R. "Theatricals in Jean Renoir's *The Rules of the Game* and *Grand Illusion*." *Literature/Film Quarterly* V, 1 (Winter 1977) 50–56.

Priot, Franck. "*La Grande Illusion*: le film d'un siècle." *Archives* 70 (Feb 1997) 2–29.

Renoir, Jean. *Ma Vie et mes films.* Paris: Flammarion, 1974.

————. *My Life and My Films.* New York: Atheneum, 1974.

Serceau, Daniel. *Jean Renoir.* Paris: Edilig, 1985.

Sesonske, Alexander. *Jean Renoir: The French Films 1924–1939.* Cambridge: Harvard University Press, 1980.

Sorlin, Pierre. *The Film in History.* Oxford: Blackwell, 1980.

Strebel, Elizabeth. "Jean Renoir and the Popular Front." In Short, K.R.M., ed. *Feature Films as History.* London: Helm, 1981.

————. *French Social Cinema of the Nineteen-Thirties: A Cinematic Expression of Popular Front Consciousness.* New York: Arno, 1980.

Triggs, Jeffery Alan. "The Legacy of Babel: Language in Jean Renoir's *Grand Illusion*." *New Orleans Review* 15:2 (1988) 70–74.

Vincendeau, Ginette, and Keith Reader. *'La Vie est à nous', French Cinema of the Popular Front, 1935–1938.* London: British Film Institute, 1986.

Viry-Babel, Roger. "*La Grande Illusion* de Jean Renoir." *Cahiers de la Cinémathèque* 18–19 (Spring 1976) 37–63.

II

Literature on Film

Reconstructing
Literary Realism

Virtually from its inception, film has pursued the cinematic equation of the literary text, to the delight or more frequently the disappointment of viewers. The means of transposing literary narrative to film sound and image have been as varied as the texts of origin, from 1) completely reconceived works (*Les Liaisons dangereuses 1960*) or 2) attempts to transport word for word the printed text to the film narrative, primarily through the voice-over technique, equating reading the text out loud off camera, thus embodying and objectifying, reifying not only the subjective experience of the textual narrator but also that of the reader (*L'Etranger, Journal d'un curé de campagne*) to 3) films reconstructing textual diegesis influenced also by prior screenwriters', directors' and actors' imagings or by illustrations of the literary editions (*La Belle et la Bête, Madame Bovary*). André Bazin equated film's authenticity with its "transparency" (such an appropriate term for celluloid) and its creative voice with authorship (referring to Renoir's 1939 *La Règle du jeu*), but the question is far more complex.

Some fundamental precepts have to be addressed in establishing the equation between referential reality, text and film. The perceptual givens of lived experience include form, color, movement, sound, and perspective. As the mind makes sense of sensorial input, it creates relationships between present and absent objects, shaping and filling present experience with prior constructs. Followers of Piaget would assert that identity is a compilation of such activities. Language is an arbitrary system of signs and symbols which refer to each other and represent reality, as conceptualized by the speaker or writer. Thus through nomination, description, narration of events (with temporal and causal aspects), through functional interaction in dialogue, the speaker or writer creates a text, a coherent construct generating meaning by eliciting acoustic images in the mind of the recipient. Texts have myriad forms, from operating instructions, phonebooks, newspapers, roadsigns, ads, even clothing, to letters, diaries, essays, stories, novels, poetry (the most playful and self-sufficient use of language). The simplest tales, constituting a primitive cultural heritage, according to formalists like Propp, proffer a functioning social hierarchy of values and power, and, according to structuralists like Lévi-Strauss, recombine endlessly a limited set of positive and negative attributes. These tales are inevitably larger than life (epic) or metaphoric (fabular) and have a didactic as well as a diversionary function.

Classic literary modes include texts which presume to transcendency and rely on stereotypical or archetypal characters as emblematic of society's values, desires, phobias or taboos. Lyric or Romantic texts explore the relationship between language and the self, or between self and other, with a subjective internal focus foregrounding emotions, desires and phobias once again, within the individual, love and death, *eros* and *thanatos*. The distinction between lyric poetry or prose and autobiographic narrative can be problematic and often comes down to a pact between author and reader, not of formal or thematic considerations but of intent.

Among the first imagings of text would be cave paintings like those at Lascaux. The first imaging of performance would have been primitive theater or dance, cultural expression in a collective setting. The advent of the written text enabled reproduction of a different sort and deferred communication, but the basic relationships between text, image and social structure still prevailed. The fascination with the possible realistic representation of life through printed text or performance manifested itself rather recently in our cultural history, an outgrowth of empiricism, rationalism and scientific positivism. It did so ironically contemporaneous to Romanticism, the latter seemingly at polar odds with the ambition to document the totality of a social hierarchy. Realist texts had definite goals; they sent a message to the reader inviting identification with their diegesis, explicitly situating characters in time and place. Perhaps not coincidentally, the golden age of literary realism was also contemporaneous to the industrial revolution and the emergence of a dominant bourgeoisie. Especially in France, which had seen structures of social, political and economic dominance crumble and reform numerous times in a few short years, literary realism heralded the age of information and a faith in the surface value of material reality.

The concomitant current of Romanticism inherited from the eighteenth century pitted the individual against society in a world of longing, exile, alienation, and emptiness, the *mal du siècle* that would translate into *bovarysme* and the symbolist poets' exotic peregrinations and experiments with journeys of the mind, often aided by drugs. But it was the world of realism and naturalism that would lend itself most readily to cinematic imaging, with its emphasis on precise descriptions of the material and its social dialogical exchanges. Thus a literature often written for women, for a popular audience encountering its texts in literary magazines of the day, including works by Balzac, Flaubert, Maupassant, Zola, attracted filmmakers from the beginning. The post-World War II advent of television compounded the temptation to reify for twentieth-century audiences the world encoded in literary language.

The varied strategies of cinematic adaptation and their situational significance constitute the subject of the center section of this study, caught as it were between the historic recreations of documentary and docudrama and the self-absorbed experimental modernism of the New Wave. Thus realist (including poetic realist and neorealist) filmmaking is drawn to its literary counterpart, duplicating the totalizing coherence of its texts with a new set of strategies, a new *écriture*. Ironically, the texts generated contemporaneously to the invention of photography and the motion pictures would now be subjected to the freezing and fixing phenomena of the photographic process. The *camera obscura*, the revolving cylinder of the zoetrope or the magic lantern all found their way into literary works of the era, as characters, or objects mimetic of the imaginary descriptive processes of the text (the opening scene of Proust's *A la Recherche du Temps perdu*). Cinema would reverse this functional *mise-en-abyme* by depicting the text and acts of textual production on film, offering the spectator a signature or citation of the film's literary origin.

Any discussion of historic or literary realism in text and film eventually has to face its own reality, that is, it has to deconstruct itself; it has to delineate and define the dominant canons and models that have shaped the expectations of the reader or spectator. A printed text is no more the reality of its diegesis or enunciating narrative than the sound and light of a film or the electronic impulses of a video are equatable to the reality depicted by their images and soundtrack. And yet positing this all-too-obvious assertion in no way resolves the question of realism; it is rather the successful *illusion* of reality generated in text or film that is of interest here. It can be gauged in fact by the degree of visceral response the text or film elicits from reader or spectator: tears, laughter, fear, anxiety, etc.

Thus what concerns us foremost—and it is important to acknowledge the seminal efforts of critics like Roland Barthes and Philippe Hamon in the development of this concept—is the ensemble of illusory "effets de réel" (reality effects), to use Barthes's phrase, how the writer and filmmaker both, in very different ways, convince the recipient of the text of the reality of its diegesis. One of the impediments to popular reception of New Wave filmmaking or New Novel text has in fact been the degree of difficulty for the spectator or reader in identifying with, participating in and finding pleasure in an abstract, fragmented or subjective diegesis. The recent return to historic realism would seem to indicate a preference for the ploys and strategies that constitute the traditional canons of realism in literature and film. One wonders if this is due to a fatigue with the demands of decoding hermetic signs, an anxiety generated by abstraction and ambiguity, or a childlike desire to escape reality by identifying fully with character, plot and setting rather than contemplating the ontology of literary and film production.

In the middle between realism and abstract modernism, the popular tradition of the fantastic of science fiction has since its inception blended the realistic and prosaic with disruptive surrealistic elements. This genre with its marriage of materially realistic images and hallucinatory fantasies has fascinated and challenged readers and spectators since Mary Shelley's 1818 *Frankenstein*. A product of the industrial revolution, popular anxiety regarding man and machine, and positivist ambitions, this diegetic paradigm has been reflected in popular narrative since Verne and Maupassant, although its origins are traceable to Voltaire or Collin d'Harleville, inspired by Baron von Münchhausen. From Bram Stoker's 1897 *Dracula* to *The Invasion of the Bodysnatchers, Alien*, and *Total Recall*, readers and spectators have purged their phobias of loss of self-control, while they indulged their fantasies of power in *Star Wars, Star Trek, Batman* or *Superman.*

There is another link between realism and the two sides of modernism. The fascination with the way things work extends to metatextual considerations of the self and the processes of creative production, confirmed by the long-term success of self-reflexive autobiographic works like Fellini's *8 1/2* or Truffaut's *La Nuit américaine* (*Day for Night*), the last film treated in this work. The strategies for structuring the illusion of reality on screen can in fact best be seen in works foregrounding the process of film production. The success of Steven Soderbergh's *sex, lies and videotape* (winner of the Grand Prize at the 1989 Cannes Film Festival) and the subsequent appearance of numerous clones, in fact the development of video cameras and tapes as characters in film and television, can be attributed to the hybridization of the traditions of transparency, the process of identification with believable cinematic diegeses, and opacity, the self-mirroring strategies emphasizing the process as well as the product.

Any discussion of film adaptations of traditional literary narratives (including romantic, realist, naturalist, symbolist, psychological, stream of consciousness) must begin with an overview of the strategies for *effets de réel* in the printed text and proceed to an enumeration of the various equivalencies of effect created on film (what Bazin called years earlier "l'effet du réel"). The process of perceiving sensorial external reality in the human mind and that of identification of and with a character, plot or setting are inevitably interconnected. Memory and recognition from the reader's or spectator's lived experience are essential to the success of realist strategies. Thus proper names, streets, cities, public buildings, recognizable objects and social situations all serve as markers enabling the reader/spectator to enter a fictional diegesis. Sometimes the acoustic image generated by printed or film language is created through intertextual referentiality, hence the popularity and success of film citations, homages, remakes, the enriching effect of the subtextual function, whether informational, ironic or parodic. In foreign language films with subtitles, another layer of culturally-situated meaning is superimposed on the filmstock, often countering or betraying the original meaning of a scene, utterance or object, in an attempt to condense and transpose, this time in reverse order, image into text. Constraints on time for reading subtitles not only oblige treasonous truncating of dialogue, they sometimes prevent a literal rendering of a voice-over reading of actual text.

In both literary and filmic realist texts, markers of spatialization, temporality and consecutional logic are intrinsic to the narrative structure. Temporal markers anchor the sequence of events just as recognizable locations anchor the contextualized image. And certain effects of chronology generate the causative illusion. In fact, playing with and subverting traditional structures in ludic and subjective fashion is perhaps the single unifying characteristic of modernist, New Wave filmmaking, the topic of the last section of this study. This in turn explains why the New Novel and New Wave artists have steadfastly resisted the designation of "school." Schools imply rules; for them, rules are made to be broken.

Creating a "round" or believable character is a complex process central to the success of the literary or filmic realist illusion. The curriculum vitae does not suffice, nor does a mere physical portrayal or description. Not only does the character delineate itself through a series of interactions in time and space including change, disruption and reconstruction of coherence at the end, but the initiated reader/ spectator at the end of the twentieth century, accustomed to subjective first-person narrative, claims privileged access to the character's innermost discourse. The multiple subjective narratives of the traditional epistolary text have a modern echo in a new realism of multiple focalizations, external and internal, opposing in their polysemic ambiguity the omniscient objective narrator of Balzac or Dickens, regarded as the dominant mode of traditional realism. Postmodern realism also demands a primary psychological focus on the inner workings of the characters' psyches, including dreams, reveries and fantasies.

Two currents of thought dominated the nineteenth century and its literary production, positing ways of conceiving and structuring the real that were apparently mutually exclusive: the classic mode of essentialist mysticism and the modern materialist concepts of phenomenology, of dialectic determinism. In a sense, our contemporary perceptual and conceptual constructs (the relationship of self and reality) derive from a blending of those two currents: metaphoric equations of self and other from symbolism, plumbing the oneiric depths of the psyche from theories of the subconscious dominated by Freud and Lacan, realignment of the spatio-temporal axes of the self according to dialectic materialism (Lukàcs, Althusser, Macherey) or collective mythological notions from Lévi-Strauss or Barthes. With the postmodern dissipation of the self posited by Foucault, Deleuze, Guattari, Derrida, Baudrillard or Lyotard comes the anxiety of loss in a daunting pluralism.

The question of memory is central to both literary and cinematic realist narrative. The use of flashback insertions and digressions is critical to constructing the temporal function. Prior events lending causal credibility and temporal coherence, both senses of the word consecution, appear to fragment the chronological flow of the text but in actuality lend it the fourth dimension necessary to create the illusion of experience, in time and space, and permit identification on the part of the reader/spectator. Anamnesiac strategies are not limited to flashbacks but include framed narratives like discovered texts and second-hand tales. Conforming to the Sartrian aphorism that "nous sommes la somme de nos actes" (we are the sum of our acts), the literary or film character acquires identity through memory by means of causality and chronology. At the end of the printed or filmed text, the realist figure coalesces in a coherent finality of closure, thus satisfying the anticipation of the reader or spectator and giving meaning in retrospect to the serial sequences of the tale (open, ambiguous endings like those of De Sica's films notwithstanding).

All the above strategies and markers of realist texts have become standardized over the years to the point where the reader and spectator anticipate the dominant canons, codes and models. As we have seen in the section on historic realism, these artistic and fictional traditions infiltrate any attempt to recreate in text or film a historic event. Classic ideological realism dominates this type of artifice which proposes a more believable "realistic" reality than that of the aleatory jumble of lived experience (portraying in language or in image the multilayered unpredictable confusion of real life was a stated goal of the "hyperrealists" or surrealists). The ensemble of the strategies for restructuring the real to give it accessible coherence constitute a literary and film genre, depending on characterial interrelational stereotypes, certain styles of description, movement, and also dialogical exchanges.

In spite of these common goals, realistic effects in literature and film are generated by very different strategies, hence the inability to create on film the equivalent diegesis of certain textual passages, and the dilemma between transposition and equivalence: what camera angle, costuming, lighting, or set decor equates description, what oral dialogue equates written address, what actions or camera movement equate narrative plot constructs. One element common to both is the realistic effect of continuing intertextuality, on the order of the cycles of Balzac and Zola. In this respect, it is worth signaling the naturalist trap of "realistic" subject matter, considering as exclusive or privileging the gritty, impoverished side of life, its street dialect, its sexual and moral codes. The function of censorship has imposed on the realist impetus of cinema a restraining, diluting and distorting force, just as it attempted to control nineteenth-century texts. Intertextuality in film is also generated by character-personae created by particular actors like Charlie Chaplin and the Marx Brothers which compare in literary works to the narrator persona of a Sherlock Holmes, as well as by the real-life personae of leading actors. As the Italian neorealist directors understood, these extradiegetic identities interfere with the effects of realism on screen. An additional conundrum confronts comedy and mystery: although they may appear realistic, they depend functionally on the rupture of traditional cause and effect sequences or the undermining of classic characterial stereotypes or archetypes.

In a sense, this entire study is based on the gamut of strategies for structuring the real or subverting realist traditions, from the illusion of a totally transparent window on reality to the modernist subjective mirror of the self-reflexive voice. If indeed, however, all is illusion and the stage is a world of its own, then the distance from documentary to experimental fiction telescopes and collapses, reduced to a moral or intentional pact. In a work of fiction in text or film, there is in fact no more primary reality than the process of its own genesis.

Not only believable characters and actions but more importantly the situating of the tale all contribute to the effects of reality in both text and film. Location shooting, ambient sound effects, regional or period costumes, architecture, accents, add as much as narrative competence and consistency. It is also inevitable that in a world saturated with media images the canons of realism are evolving rapidly. Spectators have an ever greater need for authentic images in an increasingly material culture, at the same time that technological sophistication puts greater demands on writers and filmmakers alike. The imperfect acoustic image of the printed text that demands higher involvement on the part of the reader's imagination is potentially more satisfying but increasingly inaccessible to generations weaned on the media. Recently, it would seem that film has again become the reader not only of history but of historic texts, with productions like *Henry V*, *Hamlet* or *Cyrano* representing not only past events but past fictional diegeses, filtering the text of history and the history of the text through contemporary cinematic images, conforming to contemporary expectations of a society whose relationship to history has become more problematic.

Perhaps it is impossible to judge which is more realistic, the flawlessly set, costumed, lit dramatization of a particular point in time and space (with an absent objective cinematic narration), the inside-out perspective on the self of a monological musing, or the documenting of a profession, of making a film, a self-reflexive *mise-en-abyme* of cinematic creativity. In *La Nuit américaine*, Truffaut stages a Pirandellian *coup de théâtre*, as death introduces a new level of "reality" to destroy the diegetic integrity of the film set and crew, already functioning on several levels of illusion. This "real" death of an actor is but one more layer of illusion, as the person playing that actor did of course not really die. Perhaps Truffaut's intuition was correct, though, that the only true point of intersection between film and reality internal to the film is an accidental event which intrudes: bad weather, the death of a stuntman. Conversely, the point of external intersection between film and reality is the moment that Jean-Paul Sartre so resented, when the house lights come on at the end, transforming the transparent illusory world of the screen into an opaque surface.

To sort out these apparent confusions and contradictions, I propose in this section to explore a number of film adaptations of literary texts, studying first a series of classic short stories and novels and their screen adaptations (Balzac, Flaubert, Maupassant, Zola, Proust, Pagnol). I will then look at transpositions of autobiographic-style narratives by Bernanos, Thérèse, Zobel and Sartre, whose *Sartre par lui-même* (*Sartre by Himself*) raises a number of unique questions regarding the elusive equation of self, text and image. Consideration of the texts and filmed versions of plays by Molière, Pagnol and Giraudoux reveals the achievements and limitations of traditional modes of filming the stage (whereas in recent years, certain transpositions of theater and opera recreated in inherently cinematic productions demonstrate alternative constructs of meaning—*Don Giovanni, La Traviata, Carmen, Henry V, Cyrano*). I have included at the end of this section a film which demands special classification, Jean Renoir's *La Règle du jeu*. Anticipating the New Wave auteur film writing by twenty years, it reconstructs in the cinematic idiom a number of traditional literary forms, from the eighteenth and nineteenth centuries. It is an eminently theatrical film, yet Renoir's ludic rewriting of the classics produces a contemporary fable in the poetic realist mode, offering an original and intriguing contrast to his more literal adaptations (*Nana, Madame Bovary, Une Partie de Campagne*) and other directors' transposed adaptations of classic literary texts. Examples of classic fables on film, *La Belle et la Bête* (*Beauty and the Beast*) and *Peau d'âne* (*Donkey Skin*), reveal the extent to which these tales are reworkings of primitive mythologies and thus affect their audience in special ways. In all the studies, I will be looking at the relationships between textual narrative strategies for structuring the illusion of reality, their cinematic reflections, equivalents or rewritings, and ideological constructs of self and society.

Bibliography

Andrew, Dudley. "The Impact of the Novel on French Cinema of the 30s." *L'Esprit Créateur* 30:2 (1990) 3–13.

Armes, Roy. *The Ambiguous Image: Narrative Style in Modern European Cinema.* Bloomington: Indiana University Press, 1976.

―――――. *Film and Reality: An Historical Survey.* Harmondsworth: Penguin, 1974.

Auerbach, Eric. *Mimesis.* Princeton: Princeton University Press, 1953.

Aycock, Wendell, and Michael Schoenecke, eds. *Film and Literature: A Comparative Approach to Adaptation.* Lubbock: Texas Tech University Press, 1988.

Barthes, Bersani, Hamon, Riffaterre, Watt. *Littérature et réalité.* Paris: Seuil Points, 1982.

Beja, Maurice. *Film and Literature: an Introduction.* New York: Longman, 1979.

Best, Victoria, and Peter Collier, eds. *Powerful Bodies: Performance in French Cultural Studies.* Bern: Peter Lang, 1999.

Bluestone, George. *Novels into Film.* Berkeley: University of California Press, 1973.

Bordwell, David. *Narration in the Fiction Film.* Madison: University of Wisconsin Press, 1985.

Boyum, Joy. *Double Exposure: Fiction into Film.* New York: Universe Books, 1985.

Clerc, Jeanne-Marie. *Ecrivains et Cinéma: des mots aux images, des images aux mots, adaptations et ciné-romans.* Paris: Klincksieck, 1985.

Cohen, Keith. *Film and Fiction: The Dynamics of Exchange.* New Haven: Yale University Press, 1979.

Collomb, Michel, ed. *Voix et création au XXe Siècle.* Paris: Champion, 1997.

The Construction of Reality in Fiction. Poetics Today 5:2 (1984). Entire issue.

Fell, John. *Film and the Narrative Tradition.* Norman: University of Oklahoma Press, 1974.

Fleishman, Avrom. *Narrated Films: Storytelling Situations in Cinema History.* Baltimore: Johns Hopkins University Press, 1991.

Golden, Leon, ed. *Transformations in Literature and Film.* Tallahassee: University Presses of Florida, 1982.

Hokenson, Jan. "Todorov and the Existentialists." In Collins, Pearce and Rabin, eds. *The Scope of the Fantastic: Theory, Technique, Major Authors.* Westport, CT: Greenwood Press, 1985.

Jost, François. *L'Oeil-caméra: entre film et roman.* Lyons: Presses Universitaires de Lyon, 1987.

Kline, T. Jefferson, ed. "The Film and the Book." *L'Esprit Créateur* 30:2 (Summer 1990).

Leuwers, Daniel. "L'Adaptation filmée." *La Revue des Lettres Modernes* 193 (1985) 757–761.

MacLeay, Daniel. "The Word Made Flesh: Transforming French Fiction into Film." *Publications of the Missouri Philological Association* 20 (1995) 36–43.

Magazine Littéraire 354 (May 1997) entire issue.

Marcus, Millicent. *Italian Film in the Light of Neorealism.* Princeton: Princeton University Press, 1986.

Michalczyk, John. *The French Literary Filmmakers.* Cranbury, N.J.: Associated University Presses, 1980.

Naremore, James, ed. *Film Adaptation.* New Brunswick, NJ: Rutgers University Press, 2000.

Nichols, Bill. *Ideology and the Image*. Bloomington: Indiana University Press, 1981.

Prendergast, Christopher. *The Order of Mimesis*. New York: Cambridge University Press, 1986.

Recanati, François. *La Transparence et l'énonciation*. Paris: Seuil, 1979.

Richardson, Robert. *Literature and film*. Bloomington: Garland Publishing, 1969.

Ropars-Wuilleumier, Marie-Claire. *De la Littérature au cinéma*. Paris: Armand Colin, 1970.

————. *L'Ecran de la mémoire*. Paris: Seuil, 1970.

————. *Ecraniques: le film du texte*. Lille: Presses Universitaires de Lille, 1990.

————. *Le Texte divisé*. Paris: Presses Universitaires de France, 1981.

Ross, Harris. *Film as Literature: Literature as Film*. New York: Greenwood Press, 1987.

Sinyard, Neil. *Filming Literature*. New York: St. Martin's Press, 1986.

Speigel, Alan. *Fiction and the Camera Eye: Visual Consciousness and the Modern Novel*. Charlottesville: University Press of Virginia, 1976.

Taylor, Clyde. *The Mask of Art: Breaking the Aesthetic Contract—Film and Literature*. Bloomington, IN: Indiana University Press, 1998.

Wagner, Geoffrey. *The Novel and the Cinema*. Rutherford: Fairleigh Dickinson University Press, 1975.

Wolfe, Charles. "Fictional Realism: Watt and Bazin on the Pleasures of Novels and Films." *Literature/Film Quarterly* 9:1 (1981) 40–50.

Pierrette

directed by Guy Torré (1978)
nouvelle by Honoré de Balzac (1840)

The adaptation of this work to the screen for television must inevitably be viewed through the filter of Balzac's own artistic descriptive ambitions, as he referred in the *Préface* in Stendhalian fashion to the frescoes of his characterizations thus:

> Puis, en honneur de conscience, quand le dessin de la fresque littéraire où se meuvent tant de personnages sera terminé, que vous pourrez la contempler dans son entier, vous serez tout étonné de la quantité de niaiseries, de sottises, de faux jugements, pommes cuites et quelquefois crues qui aura été jetée à l'auteur pendant que son crayon courait sur la muraille, et qu'il était sur ses tréteaux (assez mal assurés), peignant, peignant, peignant.[1]

This "volonté de la totalité" (will for totality) led Balzac to avow his intent to compete with the myriad details and images of the contemporary society he observed ("faire concurrence à l'état civil"—to compete with social and political reality); yet his works are more a reworking in collage of the world around him than a simple equivalent of that world. Inevitably, the choices he made carried symbolic or metaphoric significance, and the fictional work lost the capricious arbitrary aleatory disposition of real life with all its anomalies and inconsistencies. Balzac in fact could be said to have been exercising the same sort of adaptation of the world around him as filmmakers do of literary texts. It could be said of all realist literary texts that they encode into text from their observations of reality what the filmmaker decodes back into image. Hence the interest of references to pictorial art, architecture, decorative arts, clothing. The thorough realist author serves as set decorator, costume and lighting designer, scriptwriter, and with the narrative voice, even director.

Working at the time of Daguerre's invention of photography, Balzac also declares in the *Préface* to *Pierrette* his artistic appurtenance and genealogy with his usual modesty, including himself with the prolific greats who simultaneously mastered action and reflection: Raphael, Walter Scott, Voltaire, Titian, Shakespeare, Rubens, Buffon, Lord Byron, Boccaccio, and Lesage. Balzac's paranoia regarding his critics' attacks on his ambitions and executions reveals itself in this preface, where he condemns doubly his celibate life style and his martyred role as starving artist not rewarded or appreciated by the bourgeois society of his day.

Balzac's ambitions of artistic adaptations of actual events were sometimes reined in as it were by history. An incident in the fall of 1839 was to alter radically the nature of his "delicious little story" *Pierrette*, which he had been preparing and situating all summer, having already dedicated it to Madame Hanska's twelve-year-old daughter Anna. The original story was to arouse sympathy for the innocent impoverished young orphan but to have a happy ending, wherein she married the love of her life and triumphed over her selfish, pernicious guardians (a standard format harking back to Beaumarchais, Molière and Perrault).

The Peytel affair changed all that. Like Zola sixty years later, Balzac went to the aid of an accused man whom he thought innocent. To no avail; Peytel, indicted for murdering his wife and female servant, was guillotined 28 October. A mere two days later, Balzac began to write his *Pierrette*, but now infusing it with all the malice and paranoia of the Peytel affair, the destruction of a person whom he thought an innocent victim by the evil machinations of a provincial town. Paving the way for Flaubert, Balzac executes with a vengeance his portraits of provincial evil and physical suffering, in this case in the town of Provins, nominal essence of its social identity. The semiology of Pierrette's suffering extends well beyond her physical symptoms; Balzac may well have been purging or mediating through his fictional creation his painful memories of his sister Laurence's death in 1825 at age twenty-three and of his mother's cold cruelty, which he openly stated had killed his sister and ruined him. The emotional desert of Balzac's own solitude in his early years, shipped off first to a wet nurse and then to a series of boarding schools, informs the internal focus of his characterization of Pierrette, her martyrdom and her tragic fate. The structuring of his protagonist also constituted a transposition to the female of other orphaned or imprisoned martyred literary heroes of the day, such as Fabrice del Dongo from Stendhal's *La Chartreuse de Parme* the year before.

Pierrette first appeared in serial form in February 1840 in the Liberal newspaper *Le Siècle* and finally in revised format for *La Comédie humaine*, constituting along with *Le Curé de Tours* and *La Rabouilleuse* the trilogy of *Les Célibataires*, part of *Les Scènes de la vie de Province*. Although Balzac claimed to have written *Pierrette* in a fortnight, in a frenzy of productivity, he also admitted to thirteen different drafts or rather versions of the tale, as it was evolving rapidly away from its original tonalities, under the influence of the above-mentioned Peytel affair. Written for and dedicated to a daughter he hoped to call his own, it stands as a reworking of the Cinderella paradigm, a folktale of polarized opposites of good and evil, old and young, sexual and frigid, giving and grasping, human and inhuman (Sylvie is compared to a beetle, a lobster, a hyena). It also stands as a devastating portrait of egotism, of the vanities of celibacy, of women who fear marriage and childbirth, as well as of the spiritual bond bordering on incest in the relationship portrayed between brother and sister.

The filmed version of the tale (written by Paul Savatier and filmed in Martel in Cognac) opens with a Paris street scene (presumably in October 1827 like the Balzac tale), featuring a shot of a business named "A la Sainte Cécile" (a martyred Roman virgin). Denis (Jérôme) and Sylvie Rogron (Etienne Bierry and Maris Meriko), the brother and sister proprietors of a shop called "A la Soeur de Famille," are closing up their business for good, leaving for Provins to collect a large inheritance. Denis's last, and for the spectator first, symbolic gesture is to order the cleaning up of horse manure, a prefiguration of their cover-up of first their humble origins and then their heinous crime at the end of the tale.

In a foreshadowing of Pierrette Lorrain's eventual arrival, impoverished and indebted, Denis receives a letter postage due from her, saying that she is orphaned and asking for a home. Installed in their Provins house, the Rogrons are redecorating in a gaudy, tasteless manner. Substituting for Balzacian descriptive narrative, information regarding their background is provided by two passersby, who will go on to befriend them and collaborate with them in evil. At the beginning, though, these local gossips reveal their disloyalty by condemning the Rogrons for covering up their humble origins as innkeepers' children in their desire for acceptance in the high society of Royalist Provins. The two newcomers reveal their true character with their crude, noisy conduct. Even the carpenters, the honest artisans (the class to whom Pierrette's love Jacques Brigaut belongs), are morally superior to the Rogrons. Guests at their open house declare Sylvie the ugliest woman on earth, as they comment on the room's newly fashionable ceiling molding of ovae, or eggs in Roman style, an ironic decor motif standing in opposition to Sylvie's sterile frigidity and preparing the potentially fruitful passion between Pierrette and her carpenter. A striking absence at their soirée is that of a true member of high society, the Parisian Madame Tiphaine (Lyne Chardonnet), the wife of the regional presiding judge.

The Rogrons' strolling on foot, circulating around the town, indicates that they have given up their carriage and come down to earth, and emphasizes their pedestrian mentality. Their servant Adèle (Annick Allières) is abused by the sharp tongue of Sylvie in another prefiguration of the fate of Pierrette and an echo of the fate of Peytel's maidservant. Just as the audience is given an implication of collusion and even incest between the brother and sister, the lawyer Vinet (Georges Werler) introduces himself to Rogron. And Sylvie announces to Adèle that she is demoting her to lady's maid, to make room for a cook and a butler for entertaining (who will soon be dismissed when the Rogrons are ostracized and whose place will be in a sense taken by the oppressed Pierrette). Vinet, the Colonel Gouraud (Jacques Alric) and Rogron make plans to share a subscription to the local newspaper, indicating both their avarice and their political collusion. The town's Liberals assiduously court the eligible Rogrons for their financial support of local politics and projects.

Madame Tiphaine in her salon reveals herself to be the perfect counterpart to Sylvie Rogron—a beautiful, witty and devoted mother with four daughters, in an elegant and charming home. Once again Gouraud, Vinet and Rogron are thrown together, equally hated by the local Royalists. This classic Balzacian thematic, the problem of the moneyed bourgeois attempting to buy social position or marry a noble name (a common phenomenon in nineteenth-century French society), is rendered slightly ironic by the fact that Balzac acquired a "de" for his own name in 1821 and began using it in 1830. In the film, as in Balzac's texts, almost all the characters are caricatures, a Daumier-like fresco of human foibles. Appropriately, Rogron and Vinet play a chessgame during a storm, and talk of financing a Liberal newspaper, creating a reverse *mise-en-abyme* of the original context of the story in *Le Siècle*. It is her brother's project of marriage that drives the pathologically jealous Sylvie to suggest that they adopt Pierrette instead of him having a wife and children of his own. Various elements of society are represented among the sharks who want the Rogrons' money: Vinet arranges for the visit of Bathilde de Chargeboeuf (Elizabeth Margoni), and the curé Habert is trying to marry off his sister Céleste to Rogron, as the Liberals convince him of the danger of the nobles' intent to restore to the church its property. Vinet and the Colonel both want to prevent the installation of Cousin Pierrette (Valérie Samama), scheming to marry into the family and acquire their money.

The Rogrons reveal themselves to be miserly *rogue-ogre-grognons* (as their name implies) when, upon Pierrette's arrival, they put her in an unheated bedroom and take away the candle, leaving her alone in the icy darkness. They complain about spending three hundred francs to clothe her well enough to keep up appearances. The sound of her sabots in the morning reminds us of her humble Breton origins and also prefigures the hideous beating she will receive from the insanely jealous Sylvie.

When Pierrette is received and accepted by the Tiphaines, who continue to exclude from their salon the Rogrons, the latter jealously forbid her to frequent the Tiphaine house. They are especially resentful of any signs of affection she receives from the outside, particularly of her innocent but fatal attraction for the carpenter Brigaut (Pierre-Alain Volff). On this point, Brigaut is much more important in Balzac's story, which begins with an encounter between the young lovers and flashes back to the origins of the family situation. It is their secret correspondence by "wire" in the text that dooms them and incites Sylvie to beat Pierrette's hand to get to the letter from Brigaut. This classic importance of the epistolary object as missile, as arm, as character in the literary text is reduced in the film to a portrayal of a crumpled object.

In all his works, the miseries and the unnatural life style of the celibate are vividly depicted by Balzac, who although involved with numerous women in his life married only months before his death from heart disease in 1850 and never had any legitimate children. In the *Préface* to *Pierrette*, Balzac categorizes the tale in the taxonomy of his human comedy in a hauntingly prophetic and thus ironic fashion:

> *Pierrette* est donc le second tableau où les Célibataires sont les figures principales, car, si Rogron se marie, il ne faut pas prendre son mariage comme un dénouement, il reste Rogron, il n'a pas longtemps à vivre, le mariage le tue.[2]

When the news comes that Pierrette's grandfather has died, the Rogrons make sure that they are named guardians, so they can have tyrannical control over her fate (her repentant and distraught grandmother intercedes too late to save her, as in Balzac's tale). They put her to work like a scullery maid, and give her lessons with the curé. But for her tragic end (added as noted to the original version of the tale), Pierrette is a perfect Cinderella. The curé teaches Pierrette absolute respect for her guardians, giving them the power of God. During the Rogrons' elaborate soirées, Pierrette serves wine to the guests but is denied the status of member of the family. The curé enters the greedy competition for a family connection, bringing his sister to visit, having her take his place some days, trying like others to set up a wife for Rogron in order to get to his money. The conspirators indulge in political as well as economic and social connivance, putting Vinet up for election, giving him property so he can qualify, simultaneously increasing the rent of the farmers to finance their project.

As Pierrette scrubs the floors, the text declares itself a classic fable of child abuse, as well as a tale of veiled incest. The substitution of the curé Habert's sister, ironically named Céleste (Simone Landry), as Pierrette's tutor is a double ruse, as Habert has been forbidden to enter the Rogrons' house by the Royalist bishop. Vinet and the Colonel reveal their commonness and their doubly evil ludic propensities, playing billiards at the tavern and calculating their fortunes. In a *coup de théâtre*, Vinet appears with his cousin Bathilde, a gorgeous woman garbed in symbolic scarlet (who will eventually marry Rogron, make his happiness and political fortune and then precipitate his demise). Habert's sister is thus put out of the running for the position of Rogron's wife; she will have to settle for marrying the Colonel.

Sylvie and Céleste join in abusing Pierrette together now, hypocritical old maids constantly complaining about a style of life they can hardly hope to attain, declaring themselves opposed to marriage and having children, while actually afraid of dying in childbirth. In counterpoint to their evil, Brigaut and Pierrette meet in the village and make plans to marry. It is Brigaut's courting Pierrette, his singing to her more than their exchange of love letters, that leads in the film to the fatal attack on the girl by the insane Sylvie, who first thought that Brigaut singing was the Colonel serenading her.

In a sequence which unabashedly sets up the spectator and reader, Pierrette is at last invited to an evening gathering, appropriately garbed. Balzac dwells on the transformation through embellishment of her natural grace. It isn't long before the psychotic Sylvie stages a scene and verbally abuses Pierrette in front of the guests. It is the beginning of the jealous rage that culminates in her vicious beating of the girl, wherein Pierrette's downtrodden state elicits metaphorically Sylvie's brutal stomping of her prostrate body. In Balzac's tale, Pierrette dies consumed by the infection from an abscess on her head and a gangrenous hand mutilated by Sylvie. She expires amid frustrated surgeons after many pages as a dying Romantic heroine, "un admirable chef d'oeuvre de mélancolie."[3] It is difficult not to see in her tale and especially in the descriptions of her last agony a model for Flaubert's *Madame Bovary*.

In Sylvie's ensuing public humiliation and trial for murder, Balzac has exactly inverted the original ingredients of the Peytel incident. The accused murderer Peytel (whom Balzac thought innocent and who was guillotined) has been transposed to the child victim, and the murderers now go free, thanks to Vinet's legal sophistry, basking in social glory with Bathilde's marriage to Denis and Vinet's election as a *député*. It is as though Balzac has transferred his sympathy for the accused man to the original female victims and his vengeful bitterness toward the townspeople of Bourg-en-Bresse to the villainous Liberals (conservative bourgeois capitalists) of Provins.

Into the serene elegance of the Tiphaine salon intrudes the news in Torré's film that Pierrette has died from her beating. The last irony is that because carpenters make coffins, Brigaut has to come to get her body. In both novel and film it is the young ignorant artisan's sentimental opposition to the mutilation of the body of his angel that ironically impedes the autopsy that would have undoubtedly convicted Sylvie of murder. In the next scene of the film, the *sous-préfet* (lieutenant governor) has finally come to the Rogron house, and they have achieved bliss; like Père Goriot's daughters who destroy him out of greed, the hypocritical conniving people crush the innocent (children) or anybody in their path. The final shot shows Brigaut looking through the bars of the grillwork in front of the house, bars that mark not only his exclusion from social privilege but his separation from and loss of Pierrette in death. Speaking for Balzac, he bemoans the fact that it is the criminal godless people who always triumph. Balzac's portrayal of this society condemns not only the petty, cruel and sinful conduct of the evil characters but also indicts the political machinations of the day, wherein the Liberals triumphed in the early years of the July Monarchy (which still heavily favored capitalist enterprise at the time this story was written), demonstrating that at their hands the little people, the young and the innocent were once again victims of the power structure.

Notes

1. Balzac, *Oeuvres complètes* XI (Paris: Pléiade) 391. ("Then, in honor of conscience, when the design of the literary fresco where so many characters move about is finished, and you can gaze upon it in its entirety, you will be completely astonished by the quantity of silliness, foolishness, false judgments, cooked and raw apples which will have been thrown at the author while his pencil raced over the wall, and he was on his wobbly scaffolding, painting, painting, painting." My translation.)
2. ibid., 393. ("Pierrette is thus the second painting where the Bachelors are the principle figures, for, if Rogron marries, one mustn't take his marriage as the end of the story, he remains Rogron, he hasn't long to live, marriage kills him." My translation).
3. *Pierrette* (Paris: Garnier Flammarion, 1967) 239. ("An admirable masterpiece of melancholy." My translation.)

Bibliography

Altman, Rick. "Dickens, Griffith, and Film Theory Today." *South Atlantic Quarterly* 88:2 (1989) 321–359.
Balzac, Honoré de. *Pierrette*. Paris: Garnier Flammarion, 1967.
—————. *Oeuvres complètes*. Paris: Gallimard Pléiade, III, XI.
Barberis, Pierre. *Balzac: une mythologie réaliste*. Paris: Larousse, 1971.
Bardèche, Maurice. *Balzac*. Paris: Julliard, 1980.
Baron, Anne-Marie. "Statut et fonction de l'observateur." *L'Année Balzacienne* 10 (1989) 301–316.
Barthes, Roland. *S/Z*. Paris: Seuil, 1970.
Brooks, Peter. *The Melodramatic Imagination: Balzac, Henry James, Melodrama, and the Mode of Excess*. New Haven: Yale University Press, 1976.
Esrock, Ellen. "Literature and Philosophy as Narrative Writing." In *Ideas of Order in Literature and Film*. Tallahassee: University Press of Florida, 1980.

Forest, Jean. *Les Femmes de Balzac*. Montreal: Presses de l'Université de Montréal, 1984.

Imbert, Patrick. *Sémiotique et description balzacienne*. Ottawa: Editions de l'Université d'Ottawa, 1978.

Jost, François. *L'Oeil-caméra: entre film et roman*. Lyons: Presses Universitaires de Lyon, 1987.

Lukàcs, Georg. *Balzac et le réalisme français*. Paris: Maspero, 1967.

Prendergast, Christopher. *Balzac: Fiction and Melodrama*. London: Edward Arnold, 1978.

————. *The Order of Mimesis: Balzac, Stendhal, Nerval, Flaubert*. New York: Cambridge University Press, 1986.

Vannier, Bernard. *L'Inscription du corps: pour une sémiotique du portrait balzacien*. Paris: Klincksieck, 1972.

Madame Bovary

directed by Jean Renoir (1934)
novel by Gustave Flaubert (1857)

Like Marcel Proust's *A la Recherche du Temps perdu*, Flaubert's novel of the mind has landscapes and dimensions that resist the closed imaging of filmic adaptation. The original version of *Madame Bovary*, like *La Recherche*, stretched to some three thousand pages, cut by Flaubert at the urging of his friends. And like Proust (who admired and wrote on his predecessor), Flaubert created a many-hued narrative voice, infusing his text with the ethos and pathos of Emma Bovary, ceding the narration to his protagonist in his now prototypical *style indirect libre* (free indirect style). Even more difficult to translate into image is the sustained parodic and ludic tone of the text, the onomastic puns and visual and linguistic distortions. The key sequences of the novel filtered by Emma's fantasies, phobias and desires are framed as is her existence by other voices. Flaubert situates much of his narrative from the perspective of other characters; Emma is literally surrounded by men. Her sense of impotence in this male-dominant world is exemplified by her horror when she gives birth to a daughter rather than a son.

The *incipit* liminal sequence opens in the first person plural *nous* of the schoolboys observing Charles's awkward conduct; the text closes in epilogical fashion focused on the death of the already lifeless Charles and the Dickensian fate of Emma's orphaned daughter Berthe. Hence the primary dilemma confronting any filmic adaptation, beyond that of usurping hallowed ground in the collective imagination of the readership of a great classic text, is how to translate the internal focalization from Emma's psyche into the necessarily external perspective of the camera. Because none of Flaubert's text other than direct dialogue is in the first-person singular, a subjective voice-over by Emma would have to be invented. To date, the filmmakers who have adapted *Madame Bovary* have opted instead for voice-overs from the perspective of the authorial narration, either identifying with the male novelist or creating a distance from his free indirect Emma. Vincent Minnelli in his English language 1949 version used James Mason as the figure of Flaubert as well, much as Max Ophuls enlisted Peter Ustinov for the American release of *Le Plaisir*.

None of the film versions of *Madame Bovary* made by men have Ophuls's loving gaze focused on the heroine, and none achieve either the scope of Flaubert's narrative or the transference implicit in his avowal, "Madame Bovary, c'est moi!"

None of them can say the same thing about their films. Renoir's version was the first of several equally ambitious and presumptuous attempts to rewrite in film Flaubert's tale of doom of a lyric spirit imprisoned in a provincial bourgeois world. Wrongly considered the epitome of realist narrative, this work looks both forward and back, with its Romantic Stendhalian paranoid thematic of the individual versus the collective, the alienated sensitive feminized figure trapped and destroyed by a hostile environment, and its fragmented narrative perspective and descriptions which mock the realist canons and clichés of the day. Flaubert could be said to have filtered and framed what he inherited from the Romantics, Stendhal and Balzac, and passed it on to Maupassant and Zola. In the Darwinian universe of the bourgeoisie and the industrial revolution, both the lyric character and the realist novel are endangered species. Thus the lasting relevance of Emma's tale is twofold, both as archetypal emblem and parodic mockery thereof, daunting each generation of filmmakers that reopens the impossible project. In 1972, it was a production for French television (available on video through Films for the Humanities), and in 1992, the Claude Chabrol film with Isabelle Huppert. There have been two English versions made for British television, reportedly well received. Each of the versions reflects concerns and values, sociological and artistic, of its own time and projects them on Emma. What is intriguing is the consistent inability of the actresses and directors to embody successfully the persona of Emma as imagined by Flaubert. Without the internal subjective filter of the romantic, impetuous, vain and naive schoolgirl/housewife/femme fatale, the diegesis of *Madame Bovary* collapses into trite melodrama. Destined for a female readership, *Madame Bovary* was serialized in three parts (which remain in its definitive text) in 1857, during Napoleon III's Second Empire, when most readers lent a retrospective sympathy to the plight of the frustrated small town Norman housewife of 1845 (the only date in Flaubert's text). Although conservative elements tried Flaubert for indecency and attempted to censor the work, both for Emma's illicit affairs and her suicide (decidedly the most lurid and graphically visceral sequence in the book), he was acquitted.

All the versions of *Madame Bovary* feature the requisite key scenes from Flaubert's novel. Writing his own screenplay, Renoir infuses his script with his trademark populist figures and episodic performances. He also demonstrates a realist concern for historic contextuality that Flaubert eschewed, setting the opening sequence at Emma's home, Les Berteaux, in July 1839, a date not included in the novel. More importantly are lost the opening and closing frame scenes focusing on Charles, imprisoning Emma's tale in his world. Chabrol like Renoir opens at Emma's house, with its country orchard setting and numerous bovine echoes of Charles's name and temperament. None of the filmmakers come close to achieving with visual icons Flaubert's sustained linguistic network of puns that Jonathan Culler baptizes "vealism."

Renoir's Emma is prouder, stronger and haughtier than Jennifer Jones's incarnation for Minnelli, but not as icy as Isabelle Huppert, whose calculating self-control and restrained physiognomy betray as much as belie Emma's vulnerability.

Renoir initially focuses on Valentine Tessier revealing Emma's gothic romantic spirit, delivering her opening lines to Charles (Pierre Renoir) concerning a painting of Mary Queen of Scots (historic heroine destined for tragedy). Emma's sense of elegance about riding horseback also prefigures her affair with Rodolphe (Fernand Fabre), as the horse symbolizes escape into an aristocratic, virile world. Renoir's camera work, however, maintains the populist focus, as the activities of artisans and shopkeepers literally frame Charles riding through town. More intrusive than in Flaubert's work, Charles's mother (the first Madame Bovary) serves as a power figure for Renoir, attacking his first wife regarding her debts. This second Madame Bovary is also jealous of Emma, whom Charles meets when he successfully treats her father's broken leg, setting up his presumptuous operation on Hippolyte's club foot. The first wife's sudden death not only permits Charles's courtship of Emma Rouault but prefigures his second widowhood at the end of the tale.

Renoir emphasizes Emma's thirst for life's experiences as she and Charles share a glass of liquor; her country vulgarity reveals itself more here than in Chabrol's Emma, who subdues her expression of Emma's sensual appetites. Renoir skips the wedding (elaborately detailed by Chabrol who faithfully recreates the baroque *pièce montée* of the cake); he cuts rather to a sequence of Emma picking out fabrics from Lheureux, another ironic name, the man who will precipitate her downfall. Lheureux comments on the Père Tellier (a name homaged by Maupassant) and his cough, ominously pronouncing that all excesses have their price, predicting Tellier's death. This Faustian usurer centering the tragedy in economic concerns then unctuously assures Emma not to worry about price, stating in a comment added by Renoir, "We aren't Jews."

Renoir depicts Emma as having great artistic sensitivity and ability, painting, wanting to go to Italy to the museums, the pictorial-cinematic equivalent of her passion for romantic novels in Flaubert's text. Like Maupassant's Mathilde Loisel modeled after her, Flaubert's Emma is an elegant woman with imagination literally born into and married into the wrong world. It could be said that Emma is a man trapped in a woman's body, just as the sensitive feminine reproducing side of the author is trapped in the constraints of a man's world.

Renoir's inexperienced but adoring Charles can only repulse Emma; the carriage he gives her rolls through town past herds of eponymous cows. Unwilling to repay her newfound prestige, Emma resists Charles's embrace, in perfect contrast to her later illicit carriage ride with Léon (Daniel Lecourtois). Emma's maid Félicité carries another ironic name, later given by Flaubert to the heroine of his short story *Un Coeur simple*. Charles's mother continues to create friction in his home, now by insulting Emma's reputation when she invites Monsieur Léon to a party, along with the pharmacist Homais (Max Dearly, whose role was cut to nothing when Renoir like Flaubert had to drastically shorten his original work). A shot of Emma in her bedroom isolates her from the rest of her family, just as she and other main characters are repeatedly framed in doorways or windows, converting them into family portraits, omens of future demise, fittingly accompanied by the dissonant lugubrious soundtrack by Darius Milhaud. Again ironically it is Homais, another agent of both Emma's and Charles's ruin, who describes the life in Paris where Léon is going to study, presenting the city as evil and full of pestilence, whereas it is of course the stifling ignorance of a provincial town that will prove fatal to Emma. Flaubert's life in Normandy, near Rouen, gave him the same outside perspective on Paris that he offered his heroine.

Renoir invents a meeting on the road between the Bovarys and the Marquis d'Andervilliers, so that he can invite them personally to his ball at La Vaubyessard (another Flaubert sequence imitated by Maupassant, in *La Parure*), rather than have the invitation function as a second-hand emissary of fate. Renoir cuts to the ball sequence and the waltzes, where Emma gets a dance lesson, although the film is not nearly as sensuous as Flaubert's text with its waltzing verbs. Charles is marginalized by the setting. As he gazes at the family portraits, framed emblems of death, Emma pretends not to know her own husband, enacting a profound truth in her lie.

In the first of several shifts destined to emphasize the jolting contrasts in Emma's life, Renoir cuts abruptly from the ball scene to a group of children yelling and screaming, as Emma goes to the village church seeking the help of the local curé; he proves just as insensitive to her dilemma as she is to the needs of the truly downtrodden. An equation of physical and emotional suffering is established here, as Emma's psychological and spiritual isolation and disorientation intensify. The unmaternal Emma expresses her distaste for motherhood and her dislike of Berthe. Incapable of selfless love, Emma is an egocentric dreamer suffering from the Romantics' *mal du siècle*, trapped in a syndrome which would forever be called *bovarysme*. She attempts to fill the growing void in her with all manner of material possessions, as her debts mount with Monsieur Lheureux. While fitting a dress, she knocks her daughter down in anger, infuriated by the intrusions and obligations of her flat, prosaic existence.

In Renoir's film, the operation of Hippolyte's club foot is proposed at the same time that Rodolphe Boulanger is introduced, thus linking the two fatal intrusions into the already unbalanced relationship between Emma and Charles. Renoir presents Rodolphe as do all the filmmakers as the unscrupulous but irresistible seducer that Flaubert created. He also adds another episodic date, July 1841, to the infamous central sequence of the *Comices Agricoles*, the country fair. However, Renoir needlessly destroys one of the great contrapuntal dramatic sequences of all time: Flaubert's intercutting of the intimate conversation between Emma and Rodolphe in the empty second floor room of the town hall with the boring prosaic speeches and awards in the town square below. Instead of engaging in a sensuous *discours amoureux* trembling with the anxiety of seduction, Emma and Rodolphe sit in her parlor, discussing their views on public opinion and morality versus independence and freedom of spirit, sounding more like populist propaganda than illicit libido. Renoir cuts to the presentation of the award to the old servant for fifty years of loyal service, then back to Rodolphe inviting Emma to go riding with him, destroying the rhythmic tension of Flaubert's scene. Renoir's Emma seems rather uncharacteristically preoccupied with public opinion and her reputation, resisting Rodolphe more out of conformity to collective standards of conduct than timidity due to lack of experience.

Renoir does intercut shots of the bumbling Charles operating on Hippolyte and Emma and Rodolphe horseback riding in the woods, an outing symbolic not only of sexual encounter but of her entry into equally dangerous unknown terrain. Lheureux has been instructed to give her everything she wants in anticipation of Bovary's great success and reputation, which of course will be just as bad as Emma's. Flaubert resented quack doctors and defended the good ones, as his father was a talented surgeon; the indifference he attributes to Dr. Larivière becomes a parody of the specialist in Renoir's film. Emma resists Rodolphe's first physical advances but is seduced by his language, a mimesis of the sensuous power of Flaubert's descriptions. In her interpretation of this sequence, Tessier however is inappropriately insensitive to the natural setting.

In a cut as brutal as Charles's inept butchery, Renoir uses another of the numerous shots through narrow doorways, this time of Emma holding Berthe. When Charles is ruined by the botched operation, Emma runs away from the prison of his mediocrity and his failure down to the river and to La Huchette, to Rodolphe's house, where she begs to be abducted. In her desperation to escape, Emma throws herself for the first time at Rodolphe, with as little real success as at the end. As Emma is ordering a new coat and suitcases, thinking they will run away together, we see Rodolphe through a narrow doorway writing a letter of rupture, à la Valmont. Emma is trapped by Lheureux into giving him power of attorney to abet her clandestine conduct just as Rodolphe abandons her. When she receives the letter, hidden in the basket of fruit like Cleopatra's asp, she attempts suicide, prefiguring her later successful self-destruction. And when she sees Rodolphe leaving town without her, she is physically overcome and passes out, suffocating symbolically. Renoir portrays her dressed in black, in mourning for her lost dreams, in deep depression. In all the film treatments of *Madame Bovary*, Emma's fatal syndrome manifests itself at this point. Flaubert's Emma, long the classic prototype of the bored, unsatisfied dreamer, served as model for numerous Maupassant heroines, and functions as the palimpsest of later characters like Kate Chopin's Edna and Margaret Mitchell's Scarlett. In turn, the later films reflect these variations on Emma in their incarnations of her persona.

In both Flaubert and Renoir, the next dramatic irony is the suggestion that the ailing Emma go to the opera in Rouen for distraction. Although Emma is bored by the music (appropriately *Lucia di Lammermoor*) and again suffocating, in a Stendhalian sequence the opera prepares her chance reunion with Léon, who has returned to Rouen. When Emma complains of feeling ill, Charles suggests that she stay overnight, thus unwittingly setting up another *liaison*. Renoir images his stupidity with his awkward stumbling with their drinks and the contempt he elicits from the crowd at intermission. Emma's intentions to refuse Léon dissipate during the visit to the cathedral, which their illicit desire desecrates, and she steps into the famous *fiacre jaune*, the closed taxi that becomes their first love nest. We see her tearing up her letter as they journey off into the open country, rather than through the city streets as in the novel. With the addition of this bucolic escape, Renoir strips the sequence of its original parodic vulgarity. In fact, he cuts here to another date, November 1842, and to Emma and Léon's apartment in Rouen, where the maid is appropriately named Célestine. In spite of her easy intimacy with Léon, signalled by the use of *tu* in addressing him, Emma anticipates being abandoned again, accusing Léon of being like all men. This is faithful to Flaubert's structural intent of creating vicious cycles of repetition driving Emma to her fate.

The film depicts here the blind beggar, pursued by taunting children, a carnival figure from the depths of life who is emblematic of Emma's blindness and material and emotional destitution, and who returns symbolically during the final scene of her agony. The beggar has been interpreted as a sign of venereal disease as well, and he sings a song written by Restif de la Bretonne, the notorious libertine chronicler of a society in decay.

The original thematic of the masculine-marked phallic cigars in Flaubert's text translates here into Emma smoking a cigarette, a standard image in 1930s iconography of the experienced or fallen woman. Although portrayed as a maternal lover figure in bed with Léon, whom she calls "mon petit," Emma is in a cold sweat, not only thinking of death but prefiguring her poisoning, establishing a physical and psychological equation between love and death, reinforced in French by the reference to orgasm as *la petite mort*.

The final sequences of the film begin with Lheureux announcing his foreclosure and the repossession of all Emma's worldly goods. Her offer of herself, her first true prostitution, is refused by the cynical Lheureux, who sends her to see Monsieur Guillaumin. However, confronted by Guillaumin's undisguised lechery, Emma flees, the doomed romantic incapable of giving herself to a man who repulses her.

Still unwilling to face her *huis clos*, Emma begs Léon for help, which he cannot provide. The scene of the public masked ball, which calls to mind another popular opera contemporary to Flaubert's work (Verdi's 1859 *Un Ballo in maschera*) as well as the tale of the mask in Maupassant and in Ophuls's *Le Plaisir*, contrasts in parodic echo the elegance of the initial ball at La Vaubyessard. Renoir adds a singer to complete the equation and inversion of the opera, which although elegant and refined was regarded as a world of sin until the twentieth century. Revolted by the vulgarity of the public dance hall and increasingly obsessed with morbid thoughts of her impending downfall, Emma breaks with Léon, whom she now equates with Charles as commonplace and ineffectual.

In a last attempt to forestall fate, Emma goes to Rodolphe to beg money. Still playing the perfect hypocritical gentleman, Rodolphe declares his love for Emma but won't give her the eight thousand francs (three thousand in the Chabrol) she needs, claiming that he doesn't have the money. Surrounded by Rodolphe's obvious wealth, humiliated and uncomprehending, Emma is driven even further toward her destruction; for the second time, she collapses when rejected by Rodolphe, in an inversion of her earlier sensual swooning.

The irreversible final sequence begins in the scene in which Emma obtains the key to the pharmacy storeroom from Justin and takes arsenic in front of him. Emma's thirst after her poisoning and her sense of suffocation, all her death throes in fact, are equally symptomatic of her psychic malady, as her physical agony and suffering mimic her mental anguish. True to the last, Charles doesn't have any idea what's wrong with her. As Emma is destroyed by her circumstances, the real doctors who have come to give their opinion then go off to eat with Homais, callously indifferent to Emma's tragedy. Charles, humiliated, isn't left alone; their ironic advice is that an excess of sadness can lead to extreme actions, exactly the story of Emma and a prefiguration of Charles's own imminent death, which is omitted from this film. In Renoir's film, Félicité has stayed with Emma to the end, true to her name, unlike her fate in Flaubert's text, where Emma fires her.

Renoir's film (like the others) closes with the rites of extreme unction, as Emma kisses the crucifix with the same passion she has felt for her lovers, a Mary Magdalene figure. When she hears the old blind beggar again in the street, she emits a last bitter laugh of irony which becomes a death rattle, uniting the two faces of theater, in the tragicomic mask of melodrama. Unlike the portraits throughout the film, Emma dies unframed, as Renoir, altering Flaubert, gives her the first and last words of the story. This refocusing of the tale on its titular heroine not only indicates a change from 1857 to 1934 in the social, civil and financial dependence of a woman on her husband but leaves the spectator with the unpurged agony of suffering and loss of the heroine, who is now Emma rather than Madame Bovary. Renoir may have been influenced by his own earlier depiction of another Emma, the imperious housewife of his 1932 *Boudu sauvé des eaux* (*Boudu Saved from Drowning*). Although Chabrol portrays both Hippolyte's agony and Emma's death sequence with graphic realism, he adds a hasty epilogue at the end, refocusing on the lifeless Charles, who succumbs in turn to the emptiness and psychic brutality of his world.

Bibliography

Please see the chapter on *La Marseillaise* for the general Renoir bibliography.

Ajac, Bernard. *Madame Bovary*. Paris: Flammarion, 1986.
Babuts, Nicholae."Flaubert: Meaning and Counter-Meaning." *Symposium* 40:4 (1986–1987) 247–258.
Bardèche, Maurice. *L'Oeuvre de Flaubert*. Paris: Les Sept Couleurs, 1974.
Bell, Sheila. "'Un Pauvre Diable': The Blind Beggar in *Madame Bovary*." In Gibson, Robert, ed. *Studies in French Fiction in Honour of Vivienne Milne*. London: Grant & Cutler, 1988.
Bernard, Claudie. "Monsieur Bovary." *French Forum* 10:3 (1985) 307–324.
Black, Lynette. "*Madame Bovary*: The Artist and the Ideal." *College Literature* 12:2 (1985) 176–183.

Bloom, Harold. *Gustave Flaubert's 'Madame Bovary'*. London: Chelsea, 1988.

Bluestone, George. *Novels into Film*. Berkeley: University of California Press, 1971.

Bollème, Geneviève. *La Leçon de Flaubert*. Paris: Julliard, 1964.

Brombert, Victor. *The Novels of Flaubert: A Study of Themes and Technics*. Princeton: Princeton University Press, 1966.

Collas, Ion. *'Madame Bovary', a Psychoanalytic Study*. Geneva: Droz, 1986.

Crouzet, Michel. "Ecce Homais." *Revue d'Histoire Littéraire de la France* 89:6 (1989) 980–1014.

Debray-Genette, Raymonde. *Flaubert à l'oeuvre*. Paris: Flammarion, 1980.

Doering, Bernard. *"Madame Bovary* and Flaubert's Romanticism." *College Literature* 8:1 (1981) 1–11.

Donaldson-Evans, Mary. "A Pox on Love: Diagnosing Madame Bovary's Blind Beggar." *Symposium* 44:1 (1990) 15–27.

————. "Teaching *Madame Bovary* through Film." In Porter, Laurence and Eugene Gray, eds. *Approaches to Teaching Flaubert's Madame Bovary*. New York: Modern Language Association of America, 1995.

Falconer, Graham. "Le Travail de 'débalzaciénisation' dans la rédaction de *Madame Bovary*." *La Revue des Lettres Modernes* 865–872 (1988) 123–156.

Fambrough, Preston. "The Ironies of Flaubert's Free Indirect Discourse." *West Virginia University Philological Papers* 33 (1987) 10–15.

Fleming, Bruce. "An Essay in Seduction, or The Trouble with *Bovary*." *French Review* 62:5 1989) 764–773.

Gans, Eric. *'Madame Bovary': The End of Romance*. Boston: Twayne, 1989.

Genette, Gérard. *Figures*. Paris: Seuil, 1966.

Gill, Richard. "The Soundtrack of *Madame Bovary*: Flaubert's Orchestration of Aural Imagery." *Literature/Film Quarterly* 1 (1973) 206–209.

Goodwin, Sarah. "Emma Bovary's Dance of Death." *Novel* 19:3 (1986) 197–215.

————. "Libraries, Kitsch and Gender in *Madame Bovary*." *L'Esprit Créateur* 28:1 (1988) 56–65.

Gothot-Mersch, Claudine. *La Genèse de 'Madame Bovary'*. Paris: Corti, 1966.

Guggenheim, Michel, and Henri Peyre, eds. *Women in French Literature*. Saratoga: Anma Libri, 1988.

Heller, Holly. "Emma et les fenêtres dans *Madame Bovary*." *Chimères* 19:1 (1986) 35–49.

Hill, Erica. "La Valse à la Vaubyessard: Mouvement temporel chez Flaubert." *Chimères* 15:1 (1981) 67–71.

LaCapra, Dominick. *'Madame Bovary' on Trial*. Ithaca: Cornell University Press, 1982.

Lattre, Alain de. *La Bêtise d'Emma Bovary*. Paris: Corti, 1981.

Lowe, Margaret, and Alain Raitt. *Towards the Real Flaubert: A Study of 'Madame Bovary'*. New York: Oxford University Press, 1984.

Lowrie, Joyce. "Let Them Eat Cake: The Irony of *la pièce montée* in *Madame Bovary*." *Romanic Review* 82:4 (1990) 425–437.

Lukacher, Maryline. "Flaubert's Pharmacy." *Nineteenth-Century French Studies* 14:1–2 (1985–1986) 37–50.

MacLeay, Daniel. *"Madame Bovary* on Screen." *Publications of the Missouri Philological Association* 21 (1996) 38–44.

Magny, Joël. *"Madame Bovary*." *Cahiers du Cinéma* 482 (Jul–Aug 1994) 58–59.

Mitchell, Giles. "Flaubert's Emma Bovary: Narcissism and Suicide." *American Imago* 44:2 (1987) 107–128.

Nadeau, Maurice. *Gustave Flaubert, écrivain*. Paris: Lettres Modernes, 1980.

Neefs, Jacques. *Madame Bovary*. Paris: Hachette, 1972.

————. "La Figuration réaliste." *Poétique* 16 (1973) 466–476.

Newton, George. "The Liberation of Emma Bovary." *European Studies Journal* 3:1 (1986) 9–16.

Nicholas, Brian. "How Many People Were at Madame Bovary's Wedding?" *French Studies Bulletin* 27 (1988) 4–7.

Pinzka, Lauren. "Death/Desire in *Madame Bovary*." *Iris* 3:2 (1987) 26–41.

Romazani, Vaheed. "Emma Bovary and the Free Indirect Si(g)ns of Romance." *Nineteenth Century French Studies* 15:3 (1987) 274–284.

Reynaud-Pactat, Patricia. "La Lettre de rupture de Rodolphe à Emma Bovary: L'Enonciation parle l'économie." *Nineteenth-Century French Studies* 19:1 (1990) 83–94.

Riffaterre, Michael and Barbara Johnson."Relevance of Theory/Theory of Relevance." *The Yale Journal of Criticism* 1:2 (1988) 163–178.

Rousset, Jean. *Forme et Signification*. Paris: Corti, 1966.

Sartre, Jean-Paul. *L'Idiot de la Famille*, I, II, III. Paris: Gallimard, 1972, 1975, 1978.

Schmidt, Paul. "Addiction and Madame Bovary." *Midwest Quarterly* 21:2 (1990) 153–170.

Schor, Naomi, and Henry Majewski, eds. *Flaubert and Postmodernism*. Lincoln: University of Nebraska Press, 1984.

Tondeur, Claire-Lise. "Gustave Flaubert: Le Désir, la fluidité et la dissolution." *Neophilologus* 73:4 (1989) 512–521.

Travail de Flaubert. Paris: Seuil, 1983.

VanderWolk, William. "Writing the Masculine: Gender and Creativity in *Madame Bovary*." *Romance Quarterly* 37:2 (1990) 147–156.

Vargas, Margarita. "Reality versus Illusion: A Structural Analysis of *Madame Bovary*." *Chimères* 17:2 (1984) 39–51.

Vial, André. *Le Dictionnaire de Flaubert. Le Rire d'Emma Bovary*. Paris: Nizet, 1976.

Wetherill, P. M., ed. *Flaubert: la dimension du texte*. Manchester: Manchester University Press, 1982.

Wight, Doris. "Madame Bovary's Long Tresses." *College Literature* 15:2 (1988) 180–188.

Williams, D. Anthony. "Une Chanson de Rétif et sa réécriture par Flaubert." *Revue d'Histoire Littéraire de la France* 91:2 (1991) 239–242.

Williams, John. "The Disappearing First-Person Narrator in *Madame Bovary*." *The Language Quarterly* 23:3–4 (1985) 31–32.

Williams, Michael. "The Hound of Fate in *Madame Bovary*." *College Literature* 14:1 (1987) 54–61.

Zakarian, Richard. "Flaubert's *Madame Bovary*." *Explicator* 48:1 (1989) 24–26.

Une Partie de Campagne
(*A Day in the Country*)

directed by Jean Renoir (1936—released 1946)
short story by Guy de Maupassant (1881)

Renoir worked on this film in 1935 and 1936 (assisted by Jacques Becker, Henri Cartier-Bresson and Luchino Visconti) and released it unfinished (without the planned additional location shooting) only in 1946. Along with endless bad weather, an argument with his leading lady Sylvia Bataille sent Renoir off on another project with only fifty minutes of film completed. He rejected several scripts for finishing the work, including one by Jacques Prévert, and abandoned it. Although thus unintentional, it is singularly appropriate that Renoir never completed his film of the tale Maupassant published first in *La Vie Moderne* and then at Havard in the collection with the title story *La Maison Tellier* (which figures prominently in Ophuls's 1951 *Le Plaisir* treated in the following pages of this study), for in a sense the unfinished with all its poignant sense of loss is the principal thematic of the story.

As one would expect, Renoir omitted certain details to serve his own vision, some might say to the detriment of his film "sketch." He was literally faithful to some aspects, changed others slightly and of course added a number of elements of his own invention, sometimes cleverly, sometimes gratuitously. Like Ophuls years later, Renoir takes the bait, so to speak, expanding and developing the extended Maupassant metaphor of fishing, similar to that of the hunt in *La Règle du jeu*. Although the fishing thematic has been treated by Robert Webster in an article for *French Review*, a number of key aspects of that extended symbolism remain to be explored.

Maupassant's story might have shocked as much as it attracted his contemporary audience: a family of Paris shopkeepers goes to the country for a Sunday outing. During lunch at a country inn on the banks of the Seine, the mother and daughter go off boating with two handsome young strangers. The daughter is taken to a deserted island by her *canotier*, where in the seclusion of a wooded bower, under the song of the nightingale, they make love. A year later, the oarsman returns one Sunday to his favorite haunt to find the woman with her husband lying beside her asleep; the one-time lovers declare tenderly their faithfulness to the memory of that magic encounter.

The genesis of the story's thematic would seem to turn on a homonymous association between *pêcheur* and *pécheur*, as only an accent separates fisherman from sinner (an associative mechanism generative of plot in other Maupassant tales: the *signes* of the *cygnes* in *La Confession*, or the expansion of the aphorism *un coup de collier* into *La Parure*). In any event, for Maupassant, this was not a casual risqué story. His greatest passion, as he declared in his 1890 story *Mouche* (published originally in *L'Inutile Beauté*), was the Seine. Oftentimes, there are maternal associations; almost always, sexual implications dominate. In both the story and the film, the family Dufour borrows the milkman's wagon. Thus we have in place from the first sentence and the opening sequence two maternal images, of the hearth and the milk, of a nourishing environment. In reality, Maupassant rented a room at an inn similar to this "Restaurant Poulin" at Bezons. He slept there as often as possible and spent his most cherished free hours on the river. It was in fact at Bezons that Maupassant received a year before, in May of 1880, the news of Flaubert's sudden death at his home at nearby Croisset. The 31 May setting of the story, published in April 1881, also refers to Zola's wedding day, offering thus a double allusion to loss amid the beauty of springtime.

In fact, the ambiguity of Maupassant's feelings for the outskirts of Paris, and the Seine itself, is often felt in dual descriptions of the landscape, both picturesque and corrupt. Renoir's film transposes that ambiguity into his portrayal of the Dufour family, characters who become even more *grossiers* than Maupassant portrayed them. The two women on the swing at the restaurant are excited and exciting at the same time that they are monotonous and vulgar in their movements. In the long swing sequence, the mother is hardly less vociferous than in the story, where she emits almost orgasmic squeals. And the daughter is regarded greedily by the *canotiers*, the neighborhood boys, and the camera itself, which takes a lascivious position under the swing to peek up her skirts, much as the fascinated camera registered the erotic sequence of the nearly nude girls on the swing at the victory ball in Gance's *Napoléon*. Both of these images come from dance hall shows like the Folies Bergères as well as from sensual depictions in art, including canvases by Renoir's father Auguste.

Renoir uses the popular nickname for the restaurant that transposed it from "Poulin" to "Poulain," by implication imaging the virility of the young horse. Renoir himself plays the eponymous restauranteur, who in the film serves as an enabler, along with his servant (played by the film's editor, his companion Marguerite Houllé or Huguet), setting the scene, opening the windows, furnishing food and shelter for the characters, as well as the idyllic setting and access to the river.

The blond young man who accompanies the Dufours, Henriette's future husband, has no name in the story. Renoir baptizes him Anatole (Paul Temps), and he changes the mother's name from Pétronille (whose Saint's day is 31 May) to Juliette (Jeanne Marken), in a patent allusion to the prototype of the young star-crossed lover. Renoir's adaptation also gives the second boatman a name: Rodolphe (Jacques Borel), with obvious allusions to Flaubert's *Madame Bovary* (which

Renoir had filmed two years earlier), for it is Rodolphe who goes off with the married mother for a flirtation, while Henri (Georges Saint-Saëns/Darnoux) and the daughter Henriette (Sylvia Bataille, who would later marry Jacques Lacan) fall into lovemaking and perhaps into love. Renoir has Henri make an extended speech at the restaurant about his mistrust of love and its dangers, of broken lives and illegitimate children, which speaks for Maupassant and defuses the selfish aggression of his subsequent sexual conquest of Henriette. The subtitled version of the Renoir piece opens with a dictionary definition of love, as "tenderness and affection" as well as "lovemaking," a not untypical resort to the image of text at the beginning of a film adaptation of a literary tale.

As always, Renoir popularizes and vulgarizes his characters, emphasizing their visceral reality if not vitality. Maupassant has the grandmother (Gabrielle Fontan) assiduously pursue an elusive cat; in the film, she smothers the cat in her arms continuously. Maupassant's image of her was calculated to emphasize the sensuality of the tale and the thematic of pursuit. In response to her constant deaf queries, the group replies, "On vous écrira" (we'll write you), a metatextual pun doubled in the transposition from literature to film wherein she has twice been "written."

In the film it is the future son-in-law who has a gross attack of hiccups rather than the father, thus establishing him as thoroughly revolting. The whole thematic of fishing is developed in the film by an initial image of a fisherman on the bridge (actually Renoir's son Alain) and by a long discussion between the father and Anatole regarding fishing and the carnivorous appetites of certain fish. Renoir has even changed the fish, from *goujon* (perch) to *brochet* (pike) and carp, voracious "sharks" of the river, a change that Robert Webster failed to note in his article on the fishing theme. The Parisians are also depicted as invading the outlying country-side, a transposition of Maupassant's decrying the desecration of the landscape by careless industrial development.

The cherry-red silk of the mother's dress in the story becomes a cherry tree setting for their picnic in the film. Renoir characterizes Henriette as having a special sensitivity to nature, thus setting up her entering the island bower to listen to the song of the nightingale. Maupassant makes the additional point that if the nightin-gale is singing during the day, it means that the female is hatching eggs. Henriette's speech in the film about the metamorphosis of bugs into butterflies, and her ex-tended declaration to her mother that she is full of longing, of feeling for everything, renders her vulnerable to the two-legged river shark who will prey on her and assist her metamorphosis into a sensual woman in love. Renoir has popularized the story that was told with much more restraint and style by Maupassant, emphasizing if nothing more the differences in taste and character between the popular reading public of 1881 and the moviegoers of the 1930s, and the greater constraints of language fifty years earlier.

The family has consumed a *friture de Seine* and a rabbit for lunch, both prey. Now they will become the prey of the *canotiers*, when the latter give the men fishing rods and bait to distract them while they carry off their women in their boats. There is much talk of a storm brewing, a classic film convention which Renoir has substituted for the oppressive heat of the day in Maupassant's story. In a prefiguration of the events about to unfold, the mother tries to seduce the father into taking a walk in the woods with her, reminding him of the previous year when they got lost. When the *canotiers* offer their boats and fishing rods to the family, they are appreciatively referred to as gentlemen in a dramatic irony.

In both a balletic and painterly manner, Henri's boat glides gracefully over the water, slips silently through the landscape, another preparation of the seduction scene. It is logical that Renoir would have been attracted to this particular setting for a film, as it also was a popular subject with his father Auguste, in paintings like *Le Bal à Bougival*. Because of modern development, the film was actually shot on the Loing River at Marlotte near Montigny, to approximate the rural character of the Seine in the 1880s. The costumes are quite faithful to those in the impressionist paintings of the era, when one of the most popular *guinguettes* among young people was on the nearby Ile de la Grenouillère.

In the central scene of the story, Maupassant expresses in a Flaubertian transfer the ecstasy of the lovemaking on the island in his description of the nightingale's increasingly frenetic song. For the nineteenth century, the nightingale was freighted with literary allusions and images, from its symbol of the lover in medieval poetry to the esthetic sensuality of Keats's "Ode to a Nightingale." Renoir instead images their passion with scenes of a storm on the river, giving a dark quality to the event that Maupassant did not intend. For the latter, it was rather an idyllic interval of perfection, which stood forever in the memory of the lovers in contrast to the dull prosaic nature of their daily existence. The roaring of the dam in the river is the only equivalent in the Maupassant text to the storm clouds in the film, an ominous face of nature which Renoir was forced to portray because of endless bad weather during the shooting of the film in July and August 1936.

Henriette's address in Paris was a favorite of the naturalist writers. Renoir mentions as well that she lives on rue des Martyrs in Montmartre. That is the home address of Mathilde Loisel of *La Parure*, another Maupassant heroine based on Emma Bovary, caught inexorably in endless daily drudgery with the painful memory of a fleeting idyllic adventure. It is also a street frequented in bad times by Zola's *Nana* (which Renoir had also filmed). In Maupassant's story, Henri stops by the Dufour's kitchen utensil store two months later, and it is just a year later on a hot Sunday that he returns to the enchanted grove to find Henriette with her husband. In Renoir's film, Henriette is also now married to Anatole, "Sundays are as sad as Mondays," and Anatole is sleeping beside her like a beast, but it is "many years later." There is a Proustian quality added to the story of lost love by the distance in time, and a Bergonian-Proustian final image in the film, of the river flowing on (Renoir would make a film entitled *The River* in 1950), of time passing and taking all away, as the lonely bachelor contemplates ruefully what once was. There was in this retreating lyricism equated to spatio-temporal loss an additional allusion to the ecological destruction of the area, whose development Maupassant had already decried.

Bibliography

Amengual, Barthélemy. "*Une Partie de Campagne*: un film de Guy de Maupassant et Jean Renoir." *CinémAction TV* 5 (April 1993) 36–42.

Ball, Bertrand. *Love and Nature, Unity and Doubling in the Novels of Maupassant.* New York: Peter Lang, 1988.

Barbry, François-Régis. "Jean Renoir, maître de la réalité et de l'illusion." *Cinéma 72* 441 (May 1988) 33.

Baron, Robert F. "Renoir's Neglected Masterpiece: *Une Partie de Campagne.*" *Post-Script* 3:1 (1983) 35–48.

Benoliel, Bernard. "Autour d'*Une Partie de Campagne.*" *Mensuel du Cinéma* 18 (June 1994) 66–68.

Chatman, Seymour. *Story and Discourse: Narrative Structure in Fiction and Film.* Ithaca: Cornell University Press, 1978.

————. "What Novels do that Films Can't (and Vice Versa)." *Critical Inquiry* 7 (1980) 120–130.

Comolli, Jean-Louis. "En revoyant *Une Partie de Campagne.*" *Cahiers du Cinéma* 299 (April 1979) 39–40.

Curchod, Olivier, et al. "*Partie de Campagne* de Jean Renoir." *Positif* 408 (Feb 1995) 80–95.

De Bruyn, Olivier. "*Partie de Campagne*: Jean Renoir." *Cahiers du Cinéma* Hors-série (1983) 95.

De Lauretis, Teresa. *Alice Doesn't: Feminism, Semiotics, Cinema.* Bloomington: Indiana University Press, 1984.

Donaldson-Evans, Mary. *A Woman's Revenge: the Chronology of Dispossession in Maupassant's Fiction.* Lexington: French Forum, 1986.

Faucon, P. "*Partie de Campagne.*" *Cahiers du cinéma* 482 (Jul–Aug 1994) 58–59.

Gould, Michael. "Maupassant on Film." *West Virginia University Philological Papers* 26 (1980) 7–12.

Lecarme, Jacques, and Bruno Vercier. *Maupassant miroir de la nouvelle.* St. Denis: Presses Universitaires de Vincennes, 1988.

Lerner, Michael. *Maupassant.* New York: G. Braziller, 1975.

Lesses, Glenn. "Renoir, Bazin, and Film Realism." *Purdue University Seventh Annual Conference on Film.* West Lafayette: Purdue University, 1983. 147–152.

Lethbridge, Robert. "Transpositions: Renoir, Zola, Maupassant." In Hutton, Margaret Anne, ed. *Text(e)/image.* Durham, England: University of Durham, 1999.

MacNamara, Matthew. *Style and Vision in Maupassant's Nouvelles.* New York: Peter Lang, 1986.

Magny, Joël, and Cavagnac, G. "*Partie de Campagne* deuxième! Centenaire Jean Renoir/ Ne Jetez Rien!" *Cahiers du Cinéma* 479-480 (May 1994) 120–129.

Maupassant, Guy de. *Contes et Nouvelles* I, II. Paris: Gallimard Pléiade, 1974, 1979.

Odin, Roger. "Strategie del desiderio in un' inquadratura di *Une Partie de Campagne.*" *Filmcritica* XXXIII, 325 (June 1982) 286–292.

Perez, Gilberto. "Landscape and Fiction: Jean Renoir's Country Excursion." *The Hudson Review* 42:2 (1989) 237–260.

————. "Landscape and Fiction: *A Day in the Country.*" In Naremore, James. *Film Adaptation.* New Brunswick, N.J.: Rutgers University Press, 2000.

Reboul, Yves. "*Une Partie de Campagne* ou la question de l'auteur." In Reboul, Yves, ed. *Maupassant Multiple*. Toulouse, France: Presses Universitaires du Mirail, 1995.

Webster, Robert. "Renoir's *Une Partie de Campagne*: Film as the Art of Fishing." *French Review* 64:3 (1991) 487–496.

Wegner, Hart. "The Great God Pan by the Waters of Life:Images and Symbols in Renoir's Films." *Purdue University Seventh Annual Conference on Film*. West Lafayette: Purdue University, 1983. 153–158.

Le Plaisir
(*House of Pleasure*)

directed by Max Ophuls (1951)
stories by Guy de Maupassant

Max Ophuls's work has been the subject of and subjected to multiple critical appraisals for forty years. As Paul Willemen says, a handful of terms dominate Ophuls criticism: "baroque style, camera virtuosity, rhythm, formalist, fascination, romantic, nihilist."[1] Alan Williams has signaled the form/style versus content/morality quandary. Others struggle to find a technological consistency in shots and montage. Questions of characterization and social commentary also arise. Most recently, critics like Marie-Claire Ropars-Wuilleumier have undertaken comparative studies of his filmic rewriting of literary text, in this case the Maupassant tales. Questions of the real versus the ideal as raised by Manon Meilgaard and Dolores Burdick are intriguing, but if Ophuls's own writing is a legitimate revelation of the nature of his filmmaking, they are missing the point. It is rather the desire to behold and the imperative to play the role that dominate his working ethos.

Born in Germany in 1902 as Max Oppenheimer, Ophuls took his pseudonym after World War I and became a successful theater director, marrying the actress Hilde Wall. Their son Marcel, filmmaker best known for his 1969 documentary *Le Chagrin et la pitié* and 1988 *Hôtel Terminus*, was born in 1927. Beginning a film career in Germany, Max Ophuls fled to France in 1933 and became a French citizen in 1938, working in French until forced to flee upon the German Occupation. After making several films in Hollywood, he returned to Paris to make his best-known works: *La Ronde, Le Plaisir, Madame de...* and *Lola Montes*. He died in 1957.

With a sensual flair for the esthetic and an unabashed fascination for women, Ophuls focused on them in all his films, true to his declared priority of *Die Lust am Sehen* (*The Pleasure of Seeing*). Thus decades before the feminist film theories of the gaze and the woman as object of desire, Ophuls presents a gallery of female roles where women combine seductive sensuality, mysterious vulnerability, earthy lust or even cruel egotism. In his filmmaking, Ophuls pursues his female figures with the camera, courtly, seductive or vengeful, always with an ironic touch, ranging from parody to cynicism. In the title of his autobiography, *Spiel im Dasein*, lies the key to Ophuls's work: "play being there" implies the mask, the life as theatrical persona, the eminence of artifice.

Le Plaisir, released in 1951, consists of the transposition and adaptation of three separate Maupassant stories: *La Maison Tellier* (1881), where the prostitutes' pleasure first preempts that of their clients, then enhances it at a champagne fête; *Le Modèle* (1883), where the dominance of the artist consumes and finally cripples his model; and *Le Masque* (1889), a bizarre tale of artifice and eroticism at war with the destructive realities of time and place. There is throughout the film a reworking of numerous techniques (voice-over, tracking shots) and thematics (the artist, the accidental death, the *acte désinvolte*) that Ophuls had just used in his last Hollywood film, *The Reckless Moment* (1949).

The three-part film was intended according to Willemen to have a fourth episode which was never funded, from another Maupassant tale, *La Femme de Paul*. In fact many of Ophuls's projects were abandoned for lack of funding. Williams states rather that the omitted episode was too controversial for the producers, with its tale of the husband abandoned for another woman, Paul versus Pauline. Jacques Natanson wrote the dialogues and the adaptation for *Le Plaisir*, including narrative and additions not in the original stories. Joe Hajos wrote the music, which is of considerable importance in two of the stories. The subtitled version of the film is narrated by Peter Ustinov, friend and collaborator of Ophuls, speaking in English with a French accent, usurping the original Maupassant narrative voice-over of Jean Servais. Beginning with a screen blackout, Ustinov creates a narrative frame by playing Maupassant, like the frame of Vincent Minnelli's 1949 *Madame Bovary* with James Mason (who played in *The Reckless Moment*) as Flaubert. Williams notes that the voice-over with screen blackout is in many cases incomplete, as unwary projectionists have clipped those sections from numerous copies of surviving prints. The silent solitary erotic pleasure of the text for the reader is thus transposed to that of orality and visuality in the film.

Ophuls did not film the Maupassant tales in the chronological order of their production, as he placed *Le Masque* first. His own personal thematic would have obviously drawn him to this story which opens at a carnival-like dance hall, the Palais de la Danse, in Montmartre. (The two short tales were also placed on either side of the longer *La Maison Tellier* for balance of the overall film.) The narrator of *Le Masque* proclaims that it is an old story (an intentional pun); certainly the period costumes are authentic for 1889. Like the story, the film depicts all manner of people coming together for entertainment, a *mise-en-abyme* for Ophuls of the diversionary function of film itself. The women of all social and economic classes and backgrounds display their attributes, while the men circulate like creatures of prey, ready to impose themselves on the woman they desire.

In the midst of this nightmarish surreal setting, a man named Ambroise (for the film) (Jean Galland) appears, to dance the quadrille, looking like an animated dummy or a marionette. The quadrille is an active dance like the cancan; the man keels over in the middle of the dance and is carried off the floor. He is a young handsome man with curly dark hair. As the merrymakers call for a doctor (Claude Dauphin), the gaiety of the music contrasts the anxiety generated by the lifeless figure. The doctor calls for scissors to remove Ambroise's mask, in a scene of metamorphosis revealing an old man underneath. The child is thus father of the man, and conversely the old man separates from the child mask, which then functions as a separate character. He recovers consciousness to say that he lives on the other side of Montmartre, on the rue Poissonnier in the film, the first of numerous fish images. In depicting the old man under the mask and his tragic battle against aging, just three years before his own death, Maupassant may have been expressing phobias and phantasms about his own self (he in fact attempted suicide on New Year's Day 1892 and died the following year in an insane asylum).

The doctor accompanies the old man home, carrying his head (the mask) in his hand. The spiral staircase they climb is a recurring image in the film, symbolic of the spiralling cycles of life. The man's fainting and being accompanied home by the doctor is the pretext, the frame, for the tale of revelation told by his wife Denise (Gaby Morlay). The curiosity of the doctor stands for that of the reader or spectator. The wife recounts that her husband drinks absinthe (*une verte*) to energize his aging self. Like the deadly drink that consumes as it is consumed, the wife is also consumed by bitterness, over Ambroise's infidelities. She explains that she was caught like a fish, trapped by his charm and appearance years earlier, and she has been the victim ever since of her *poissonnier* (in a Catholic culture, it is possible as well to read Christian symbolism into the fish imagery). In the film version of her framed tale, Ophuls recreates the exact dialogue from the story. Thus the story, like the old man, emerges from the mask, as the husband is textually *démasqué* by his wife. The reader/spectator's pleasure, like her suffering, comes from the revelation of his scatological conduct and its consequences.

The wife recounts that Ambroise has always been the head assistant at a prominent beauty parlor, where the primary clients were actresses and dancers, notorious for their open morality. His profession is generated in French by the expression *être coiffé(e)*—to be cheated on. Ambroise is addicted to the sadism of telling his wife about his conquests. The doctor discourses on men's need to vaunt their sexual exploits, bringing into the dialogue one of Maupassant's personal reflections. The frame narrator comments that the old man was putting on a mask to avoid old age, acting out a drama in the shadows of death. Ophuls may have been drawn to this story by a similar sense of distance from his own youthful self, having begun his career in Germany as a dashing if untalented young extra much sought by admiring female fans.

At this point, the film narrator acknowledges his identity as Maupassant (Ustinov jokes here about speaking English), as he introduces the opening frame narrative of *Le Modèle*: two men friends at the beach talking about a couple nearby, a beautiful woman in a wheelchair and the man attending her. The Maupassant figure pronounces the author's narrative discourse, his personal reflections inserted this time into the frame rather than the dialogue. As Ropars-Wuilleumier points out, there is a disconcerting lack of distinction throughout the film between the author Maupassant as historic person and the authorial narrative voice, however autobiographic, of the text.

Servais/Ustinov presents several scenes intended to illustrate the Maupassant tale within the tale, told about a friend of his by one of the men on the beach (the second-hand narrator of the tale who is also Jean Servais in the original French soundtrack). It is the story of the artist Jean Summer (Daniel Gélin), who wanted this attractive young woman, Joséphine (Simone Simon), as a model. Once again, the Maupassant character addresses the audience directly, as the narrator does his readers in the short story, about the bewitchment and hazards of sexual infatuation. This is illustrated in the film as Summer paints his model, who demonstrates from the beginning her psychological instability, threatening to kill either herself or him. In the story, this exchange comes only at the very end. Ophuls depicts the painter and his model lunching on a meal of fish, as they comment that the young and poor eat sardines while the old and rich can afford salmon. As Summer lovingly describes his model's graceful gestures, the camera explores this charming and vivacious young woman. The artist dominating his model and transforming her has a multiple metaphoric function: initially, these acts of creative reification of the subject are mimetic of literary or film production as well as art. Furthermore, this dominance of the female by the male gaze and subsequent imaging exemplifies her subordinate position in society of the time, in both text and film. Lastly, it is an esthetic rape, a violation of the integrity of the self, an act of violence conducted with the phallic *plume*/pen, the *pinceau*/brush (a colloquial term for penis), or the camera lens.

In a subsequent scene added by Natanson to the Maupassant text, the artist achieves considerable professional success. At the time of the lovers' first quarrel, the Maupassant narrator reflects on the difference between the fire of sexual passion and the harmony of temperament necessary for a lasting rapport. During an enchanted silent stroll through the woods along a river, when Joséphine comments on a fish she observes (the key symbol of entrapment again), Jean resents her intrusive babbling. The dialogue of the ensuing argument is drawn word for word from the tale. Three months later, quarrelling has become a habit, and the two are fighting all the time, having taken the bait and been trapped in their relationship. The artist depicting the model, like the camera framing the actors, becomes thus an extension of a primitive concept of entrapment of the self in the image. For Ophuls filming in 1951, the relationship has contemporary social and personal connotations.

The couple's life is marred increasingly by domestic violence, as she tries to hold the painter prisoner in their home, and the two end by breaking a mirror in anger, a classic cinematic metaphor for shattering the continuity of a situation or relationship. At this point in the film, there is an interlude where Jean loses himself in his work, then another scene at his dealer's gallery, where he has sold more paintings, inventing the need for money for a parting gift to Joséphine, whom he is about to abandon. His consumption of her image is now transposed to the deforming consumption of his work by commercial bourgeois clients, who see art as objects to be acquired and dominated, their power to consume being both the extension and the inversion of the creative artistic process.

When Jean actually leaves Joséphine and moves into a friend's apartment, the spiral staircase reappears as a metaphoric topos, now symbolic of the poverty and despair of people living on the apocryphal *sixième étage* (the seventh or top garret floor of nineteenth-century Parisian apartment buildings) and equally necessary to the dramatic ending of the tale. The placement of the artist's bed under the window is invented for the film, as a prefiguration of the climactic scene where it functions as an ironic prop.

Joséphine's journey of despair leads in the tale directly to the friend's apartment, but Ophuls has her search wildly at length for her missing lover, expanding the drama and pain of their separation and emphasizing her waiting and loneliness. Gone is Maupassant's convincing portrayal of her headstrong brashness as she returns Jean's money at once in a precipitous fit of pride. Ophuls also expands the sequence between Jean's friend and Joséphine, where he encourages her not to take the rupture so tragically, and explains that the artist is being obliged to marry someone else by his family (a classic narrative structure redolent of *La Dame aux camélias* and *La Traviata*). Assuming this to be the truth, confirmed by her lover in the text, Joséphine threatens to kill herself. With icy cynicism, Jean replies, "Go ahead and kill yourself," and gestures toward the open window. Driven beyond reason, Joséphine plunges through the window to her apparent destruction. At this point in the film, the intra-diegetic narrative intrudes again, as the Maupassant character explains to his friend that Joséphine broke both legs in her fall. This crippling disability is finally emblematic of the imprisoning and disempowering of the model by the artist's exploitation of her image. Her suicidal masochistic act is the counterpart to Jean's murderous sadistic dehumanization of her person. The narrator further explains that out of remorse Jean married the crippled Joséphine, abandoning his other pursuits and ambitions, having only his successful painting as an outlet in his prison of guilt. Thus he in turn is emotion-ally disfigured by his art. This "painterly" ending is imaged by a shot of the couple promenading along the beach in a scene that closely resembles an Eugène Boudin painting.

Maupassant's stories reflect a certain autobiographical dimension of lust, passion, and fear of the entrapments of marriage, of the distance between his artistic lyric sensibility and bourgeois responsibility. Their Normandy settings and characters are not just the product of Flaubert's and Zola's training in naturalist detailed descrip-tion and characterization; they also purge for the author innumerable unsettled scores, obsessions and haunting memories. The stories transposed to the screen thus represent initial literary reworkings of the landscape of his experience as well as of the mind.

Roy Armes in his 1985 edition of *French Cinema* and Alan Williams both comment on the fact that the Maupassant stories are treated in a different order in the original French version than in the American release. The placement of *La Maison Tellier* in the middle of the film in the original version of course creates a vastly different rhythm in the film's thematic, and at the end leaves the spectator with a negative rather than a positive image of "pleasure." It also creates the cinematic equivalent of a religious triptych.

Both *Le Masque* and *Le Modèle* ironize the title term *plaisir*, showing the dark side of both sensual and aesthetic indulgence. In the tale placed last here, *La Maison Tellier*, the tone is quite different. The narrator presents the customers arriving for an evening of pleasure at the Maison Tellier, bearing symbolically the house number 3, where Madame is held in great esteem. In this title story of one of his most important collections of tales, Maupassant presents the brothel in a positive cast. The story is set in Fécamp where Maupassant was probably born. As Ophuls's film opens, sailors and fishermen (!) are arriving at the tavern, where two women of pleasure, nicknamed disrespectfully *les pompes*, serve in the first floor bar. One is dressed in red, white and blue and called Liberty, the other is called Old Rocking Chair, but not because of her limp as in the story. Raphaële (Mila Parély) from Marseilles recalls the mysteries of the Orient, Rosa (Danielle Darrieux) drinks and sings rather than eating and singing as in the story. She has been transformed for this star-studded esthetic commercial film from the stout, stubby earthy Mediterranean physique. The film has been ethnically laundered as well; there is no longer mention of Raphaële's classic Jewish beauty.

One Saturday night, the *maison close* is literally shut, with the door locked. The play on words in French is emphasized by the travelling shot along the street and the camera peeking in the windows. The pleasures and desires of the camera are as frustrated by the barrier of the décor as those of the clients. The use of the crane is another pun, as in French *la grue* is the term for the mechanical lifting device, the camera support, and slang for a prostitute. This offers an unusual occurrence of a technical maneuver generated by a play on words in the script.

The sailors bang and shout at the barrier to their pleasure, while the bourgeois gentlemen restrain their disappointment. The English sailors don't sing "Rule Britannia" as Maupassant had them do at Turgenev's suggestion, but they are portrayed as rowdy troublemakers, an extension of their passion for the sport of boxing. There is an additional dialogue added regarding the freedom of bachelorhood versus the tragedy of solitude (the dilemma faced by many major nineteenth-century French authors: Balzac, Stendhal, Nerval, Baudelaire, Flaubert, Maupassant). The film gives the roll call of the pillars of the community as they wander idly through the streets or sit joking at the port, telling erotic tales, substituting the stimulation of narrative for lost acts. Finally their polite façade cracks and they become discontented and quarrelsome.

In explicative counterpoint, the film cuts to the train ride to Madame's brother's village for his daughter's first communion. The second-class compartment is full of *poules* (both meanings of "biddies" apply in French as well). Madame (Madeleine Renaud) is reading a newspaper discussing events in China and the possibility of war in the Pacific (a 1951 addition with nineteenth-century echoes). A peasant couple enter the compartment. The wife's original *physionomie de poule* has in the film become a meal; she now has the "face of a ham and eyes like poached eggs." The peasants are carrying a basket of live ducks. In a metaphoric equation of satisfying appetites, the whole Tellier sequence abounds in food references.

The prostitutes not only pretend but really long to be respectable; one describes the dream of having a generous husband, an image of impossible happiness. In the tale, this fantasy of a life of riches with a Vicount may have been inspired by the daydreaming of Emma Bovary or the example of Nana. A traveling salesman (classically the but of jokes and disrespect) gets on the train at Bolbec. Played by Pierre Brasseur, he has acquired the name of Julien Ledentu, offering yet another image of food and consumption, as well as a fabular palimpsest of erotic evil. There are jokes about the ducks in the basket (generated by the double meaning of *canard*). The salesman hands out garters to all the "girls," but the scabrous scene of the girls trying them on is postponed until after the departure of the peasants and supposedly occurs as the train passes through a tunnel, for prudery or for the symbolism of sexual acts. The girls and Madame reward the salesman by throwing him off the train and giving him a tongue-lashing, in an almost poignant episode of moral indignation.

The girls are met at the station by Tellier's brother, Joseph Rivet (Jean Gabin), with a horsedrawn cart. As they are introduced and loaded onto the cart, Rivet comments with obvious irony that he normally hauls just pigs. The rustic context juxtaposed with the girls' vulgar finery establishes a parodic contrast. As they drive to the farm, the narrator intrudes to wax lyric over the bucolic beauties of the countryside. It is a perfect impressionist painting; Maupassant describes the women as a bouquet of flowers in bright colors. Ophuls in fact attempted to frame the five of them together to keep the image of the bouquet. The year before Maupassant's story appeared, Zola had used virtually the identical sequence in *Nana*. Approaching the village, the girls hear the communicant children singing. It is the ceremony of their absolution, the cleansing and purifying of their souls as innocent children, in contrast to the life of sin of the prostitutes, who rediscover in this setting their own lost girlish innocence. Madame Rivet (Helena Manson) is dressed in simple country clothes. The daughter Constance (Joëlle Jany) returns from the church to meet the assembled "girls." In the film, they bring her her communion dress and fit it to her, like aunts fussing over a bride.

The narrator picks up the tale as they are bedded down for the night, in contrast of course to their professional bedding down on other nights. Rosa, who resembles more Maupasant's Raphaële, smokes cigarettes constantly, something she would not have done in 1881. In the religious silence of the night, none of the women can sleep, troubled by the silence of their souls, the spiritual anguish in them. Rosa is sleeping alone; she resists involvement with the husband, who desires her (in the tale, he attempts to rape her). She understands the interdiction of sin on a sacred occasion and within the sanctity of the home. Constance is crying, afraid to be alone. In a transforming maternal gesture, Rosa takes Constance into her bed like her mother normally does and cradles her all night. However, she is not nude, as in the story, which created erotic lesbian overtones of the type that Zola developed to extreme in *Nana*.

The pealing of the bells announces the five o'clock awakening. The narration of the description of the communicants is taken word for word from the story. All the girls are in tulle like mounds of whipped cream (more food). In the church, the six women in their city finery make an impressive entourage for the Rivet family and cause quite a stir, upsetting the normal order of seating in the pews. The hymn played in the movie is improbably the Protestant *Nearer My God To Thee*, better known to American and English audiences from the 1953 and 1958 films about the sinking of the Titanic. Then, faithful to Maupassant's story, it is followed by the *Kyrie*.

Although the prostitutes are crying, penetrated by emotion, the sermon where the priest talks of the miracle of God descending on the congregation is cut from the movie. In its place is another food scene, the family banquet in the farmyard, where Joseph Rivet gets drunk, and Julia Tellier rounds up everyone to leave on the 3:55 train. She has to chase Joseph through his house to separate him from Rosa, whom he is still pursuing. As his wife confronts him, we see the strict peasant morality which is even more confining than the bourgeois existence of the customers in Fécamp.

The return trip to the station is once again like a Monet painting. Rather than just singing, as in the tale, the girls are all picking flowers in the fields. The prostitutes are a contrast to the image of country brides in their carts covered with flowers. Jean Gabin (Rivet) beside the train elicits images for the French spectator of his earlier role as Lantier in *La Bête humaine*. But in this film he stays behind, lacking the mobility and sexual power of the engineer in the Zola novel and Renoir film. His return to the farm portrays his lonely life in the midst of natural splendor.

In the final sequence, a stroke of genius by Maupassant, all the customers show up on Sunday night, the traditional prostitutes' day off, thus like the mid-lenten ball of *Le Masque* a setting of inversion of social order. In the message sent to the fish merchant: "Your lost boat of codfish has been found" (more fish) is an allusion to the term *maquereau* for pimp and *maquerelle* for madam. The men are seen as taking the bait (*appât* in French is both bait and women's charms). The allusions to fish and fishermen give the group ritually gathered around the table the image of Christ and his apostles and the Christian ethic. The final scene of the dancing in the bar, a real party with champagne, marked by Madame's exceptional and improbable generosity, economic and personal, is seen through the *persiennes* (Venetian blinds) barriers, like a Degas painting. The last shot of the number 3 over the door, the mark of the Trinity, confirms the Christian thematic of the tale, referring implicitly to Mary Magdalene and the admonition to judge not lest one be judged.

Note

1. Paul Willemen, "The Ophuls Text: A Thesis," in *Ophuls* (London: British Film Institute, 1978) 70.

Bibliography

Allombert, Guy. *Maupassant traduit en images. Filmographie de Maupassant. Europe* (June 1969). Entire volume.

Annenkov, Georges. *Max Ophuls*. Paris: Le Terrain Vague, 1962.

Ball, Bertrand. *Love and Nature, Unity and Doubling in the Novels of Maupassant*. New York: Peter Lang, 1988.

Dizol, Jean-Marie. "Maupassant de l'écrit à l'écran." In Reboul, Yves, ed. *Maupassant Multiple*. Toulouse: Presses Universitaires du Mirail, 1995.

Donaldson-Evans, Mary. *A Woman's Revenge: the Chronology of Dispossession in Maupassant's Fiction*. Lexington: French Forum, 1986.

Lerner, Michael. *Maupassant*. New York: G. Braziller, 1975.

MacNamara, Matthew. *Style and Vision in Maupassant's Nouvelles*. New York: Peter Lang, 1986.

Meilgaard, Manon, and Dolores Burdick. "Maupassant and Ophuls: The 'Real' and the 'Ideal' in 'La Maison Tellier' (*Le Plaisir*)." *Michigan Academician* 14:1 (1981) 63–69.

Morrison, James. "Ophuls and Authorship: A Reading of the Reckless Moment." *Film Criticism* 11:3 (1987) 21–28.

Ropars-Wuilleumier, Marie-Claire. "Le Masque de Maupassant ou les enjeux d'une réécriture filmique." In Lecarme and Vercier, eds. *Maupassant miroir de la nouvelle*. St. Denis: Presses Universitaires de Vincennes, 1988.

White, Susan M. *The Cinema of Max Ophuls: Marginality, Magisterial Vision and the Figure of Women*. Dissertation Abstracts International 49:3 (1988) 362A–363A.

Willemen, Paul, ed. *Ophuls*. London: British Film Institute, 1978.

Williams, Alan Larson. "Deceit, Desire, and Film Narrative." *Ciné-Tracts* 4:1 (1981) 38–49.

―――――. *Max Ophuls and the Cinema of Desire: Style and Spectacle in Four Films, 1948–1955*. New York: Arno Press, 1980.

Gervaise

directed by René Clément (1956)
from the novel *L'Assommoir* by Emile Zola (1877)

The three films compared here adapted from Zola novels were made in the inverse order of the text production, that is, the tale of the last film, *Gervaise* (*L'Assommoir*), was written earliest of the three in the series of the twenty Rougon-Macquart novels, the equivalents of today's major film serials, whose images barely equal the richness of Zola's photographic and painterly descriptions. Both Zola's interest in photography and his contacts with his painting contemporaries can be felt on every page of his work. It is interesting to compare three different filmmakers' attempts to image on the screen the world which Zola so vividly transposed to text. Zola's preparatory comments in his preliminary notebooks for *L'Assommoir* read like a filmscript in fact. Thus the intensely cinematic quality of his sagas marks not only the finished texts but the process of their production as well.

In this literary genealogy, Nana is Gervaise's daughter. However, Jacques Lantier of *La Bête humaine* is not mentioned with either Claude or Etienne Lantier (of *Germinal*), Gervaise's two illegitimate sons born of her *liaison* with Auguste Lantier of *L'Assommoir*. Jacques was an older brother invented later by Zola, ironic considering to what extent Zola emphasizes the role of heredity in Lantier's doubly fatal destiny as an heir to alcoholics and a psychotic killer. Clément's film of *L'Assommoir* is true to the novel's original title: "The Simple Life of Gervaise Macquart," simple like Greek tragedy, a tale of destruction by an implacable destiny, reclothed in the melodrama of the nineteenth century: a working-class woman of Second Empire Paris (1860s) attempts to raise herself to a *petite-bourgeoise* shopkeeper's independence and respectability but is destroyed by two selfish alcoholic men. Clément's story of the mother Gervaise was also inevitably influenced by the previous film versions of Zola's works, particularly Renoir's and Jaque's incarnations of the persona of her daughter Nana, who is but a child in *L'Assommoir/Gervaise*.

The reader's lasting impression of this story, which made Zola famous at age thirty-six when its serialized chapters appeared in two different popular magazines, is one of a panoply of violence and destruction, of degradation and suffering at the hands of monstrous forces and a hostile nature and fate. Thus Zola achieves simultaneously the microcosm and the macrocosm, the close focus on contemporary details of the closed society of the shop, the building, the street, the *quartier*, and the mythical expansion in the primordial tale of abuse, bestiality and violence that has been reworded throughout narrative history. Above all, *L'Assommoir/Gervaise* is a tale of the subjugation of women, who are unable to escape the physical dominance of the violent men they love, in a society which has crowded generations together in subhuman housing, as they struggle with unemployment, hunger, debts, alcoholism, poor health and hygiene, in order to reproduce and survive.

Zola was accused of scandalous personal conduct for producing such texts. In fact, he led a very moral bourgeois family life until 1893, when he had an affair with his wife's laundress, with whom he had two children. Life imitated art years later. Although his novels constitute a collective outcry against the social and political injustices of his era, his most revolutionary act was his narrative style, wherein he developed Flaubert's *style indirect libre* (free indirect style) to the limit. Zola's characters not only speak in street language of the day, cluttered with vulgar popular colloquialisms, but their language as well as their opinions invade the narrative discourse. This is the triumph of naturalism, not a detached narrator, but a pluralistic narrative wherein the many voices of the characters delineated spontaneously and successively invade and usurp the text. Like Twain's Huck Finn, Zola's characters thus dominate his narrative. In contrast to Balzac's and Dickens's endless pontificating authorial narrative discourses, Zola allows himself only four or five unattributed opinions in five hundred pages of vociferous and often drunken commentary infused with the voices of the people. Like Machiavelli, who was confused with *The Prince* (really Cesare Borgia), like Laclos and Flaubert, Zola was inaccurately equated with the immoral characters he depicted. And like his predecessors, he was guilty only of bringing to the printed text a narrative immediacy whose impact can be measured in its shock effect and its durability.

A comparison of the text and film of Gervaise's tale reveals the immense challenge of adapting Zola to the screen. Intensely cinematic in their descriptive realism, his texts are also rich with images that belong only to the hallucinatory evanescent world of the imagination. It is interesting that *Gervaise* was made in black and white, under the influence of postwar neorealist films, for Zola's text is full of color and light, a constantly changing impressionist genre painting of the hours and seasons of Paris street life.

The Aurenche and Bost dialogue is more 1950s boulevard popular banter than a recreation of Zola's powerful authentic exchanges. The semantic power of the novel is diluted by dance hall humor and film noir melodrama. Appropriately, the opening scene is a crowd scene. Gervaise (Maria Schell) is at her window (the foreshadowing portrait framing the female figure trapped in her domestic environment waiting for the male), as Madame Boche inquires the whereabouts of Lantier (François Perier), who has in fact not come home all night. He is positioned in opposition, across the street with Virginie and her sister Adèle, with whom he has already been unfaithful to Gervaise. The *pathétique* of the film like that of the novel is established thus from the outset, with Gervaise and her two young sons as the victims of her illicit and unstable situation. But Clément has destroyed Zola's pluralistic narrative dynamism in favor of a lyric focus on Gervaise, who narrates parts of the film in voice-over. All of *Gervaise*, in fact, reflects the two major elements of Clément's filmmaking. At the end of World War II, he made the neorealist resistance film *La Bataille du rail* with nonprofessional actors. Then he worked with Jean Cocteau and Henri Alekan on *La Belle et la Bête*, a highly stylized and abstract fantasy. After *Le Château de verre* (like Zola's crystal locomotive) in 1950, he combined the stylized fantasy and the neorealist ambience in his 1951 *Jeux interdits* (*Forbidden Games*), working with young children in the lead roles. This combination of diegetic realism and mythical thematic made Zola a natural subject for Clément.

At the *lavoir*, the women of the quartier are literally and symbolically washing their dirty laundry. The crippled Gervaise, a laundress by profession, embodies her fate, to be crippled by her attempt to establish her own laundry, to literally and figuratively remove the stains and lead a clean life. Presented as popular and lovable, enjoying the *camaraderie* of her working class cohorts at the washhouse, Gervaise fills in background information on her life for the audience, of her eight-year *liaison* with Lantier and her recent move to Paris. When her children arrive to tell her that Lantier has left her and run off with Adèle, it is thus attributable to the evil of their new surroundings. The urban environment has prompted this sudden betrayal.

The scene of the famous washhouse brawl between Gervaise and Virginie reveals the underlying lack of solidarity among the women, who now ridicule her, in the first of two major scenes in the film of mob psychology and morality. With the battle of the buckets, the fight between the two women becomes a spectator sport, as Gervaise takes a blow from Virginie's paddle and then gives her a painful spanking. This is not just a depiction of the brutality of survival in industrial working class Paris of the Second Empire; in the film it becomes bawdy popular conduct, echoing the tone of earlier films of Zola texts, especially Renoir's *Nana* and *La Bête humaine*.

Zola frames Part II of his novel with the significant opening description of the bar called the *Assommoir du Père Colombe*, whose distilling alambic he later characterizes as an agent of destruction. Coupeau is introduced thus in his natural habitat: the corner bar. Clément's film cuts directly to Gervaise's marriage to Coupeau, whose family, the Lorilleux, will be her cross to bear. As their name implies, they work in gold and they are hideous, stingy and nasty. As the film focuses on Gervaise's disability, a club foot, it prefigures that Coupeau will be crippled too, not only by his serious accident (he is a roofer), but moreover by his subsequent unemployment and alcoholism, added to the ignorance and illiteracy that have crippled him all his life. Clément puts a blind beggar in his film, but he's a fake, an homage to René Clair and Renoir, just as Christian-Jaque puts a *fiacre* carriage in his *Nana* in tribute to Flaubert and Renoir.

In the next sequence, Gervaise enters the fabular male world of the forge to ask the blacksmith Goujet to come to her wedding. In Zola's text, she and Coupeau have been married four years and had Nana before he introduces the neighbor Goujet, who is the only heroic figure in the tale not marred by weakness. The wedding party outing sequence is remarkable, as an excursion on foot takes them to the Louvre, where they respond like ignorant children to the great works of art. Here Zola was not only using the subject matter of well-known paintings metaphorically (*The Raft of the Medusa, The Wedding of Cana, The Kermesse*); he was creating an equation between his descriptive techniques and classical artistic traditions, as well as emphasizing the cultural chasm between his characters and the museum, an alien environment. By extension, in the movie, film is specifically equated to a painting that tells a story, a narrative in images.

There are several privileged metaphoric images in the film. Clément focuses often on the shoes of these characters; Coupeau and Gervaise even have their shoes checked before leaving Lorilleux's goldshop. In the streets their shoes are always muddy, symbolic of the moral and physical slime at the roots of their lives. In addition to the images of the laundry that serve as a connecting leitmotiv throughout, the *Assommoir* and the forge are also metaphoric *topoi*.

Part IV of the novel begins a new cycle for Gervaise, of work and marriage, with her ambition to become mistress of her own shop. Just when Gervaise finds premises to rent, Coupeau has his accident, his fall foreshadowing their tragic decline. In the film, he is called down to sign the lease, indicative of the lack of civil status of women, as Gervaise can write and calculate, whereas Coupeau cannot. In Zola's text, Gervaise opposes their taking the injured Coupeau to a hospital, where the poor are mistreated, but in the film, she insists on nursing him herself in spite of the crowd's contrary advice. Her own crippled state, physical and mental, will be passed on to her husband, as if to prove that this is not a world in which women can work, own businesses, care for men, or thrive.

There are a number of significant restructurings of Zola by Clément: Etienne is apprenticed to Goujet but has not left home; Goujet's mother is already dead, and Goujet openly lends Gervaise the money to establish her shop. The shop's neglected state due to its previous abandonment prefigures Gervaise's ruin. As in the book, Coupeau never works again, incapacitated physically and morally, but here Goujet explains to Gervaise that it is fear and pride that keep him from resuming his trade or admitting his problem, perhaps in an effort to mitigate the denigration of a cripple in postwar France.

Depicting Part V of Zola's novel, the film shows Gervaise opening her shop, as Virginie turns up with a husband, the policeman Poisson (using a technique that inspired Maupassant, Zola develops extended onomastic metaphors, here situating the story near the *Barrière Poissonnière*, and on the *rue des Poissonniers*). Clément has exactly duplicated the scene where Gervaise visits Virginie, now living in her old room, where she began with Coupeau and gave birth to Nana. There are numerous cycles of absence and presence in the story, giving a recurring theme of uncertainty and entrapment. Apparently happy and oblivious to the dangers around her, Gervaise receives everyone in her shop, a metaphor for her relationship to the men she loves. After candidly revealing her situation to the rival Virginie, confirming her naive vulnerability, Gervaise reflects in the film on her impossible desires in a monological voice-over. Her hero Goujet, who entered her world the day of her wedding, a true love who arrives as a symbolic alternative to the trap closing around her, will leave her twice, like Lantier and Coupeau.

In a sequence taken from Part V of the novel, the little blonde Nana is seen playing in the gutter with the boys, prefiguring her predetermined destiny as a woman of the gutter. In the shop, in the womb-like heat and moisture, the laundresses are half undressed. Clémence particularly is figured as sexually heated. Coupeau makes a stage entrance into the boutique, lifting the sheet curtain draped across the open door. Clément builds again on Gervaise's literacy. The *lessive* gets lascivious, as the drunken Coupeau flirts openly with the girls and his wife. Coupeau has stolen Goujet's money to buy liquor; in the book Gervaise spends her savings as Coupeau drags her into financial ruin.

Gervaise takes in everybody in her easy generosity, Maman Coupeau first, then later Lantier. But it is only with Goujet (combining the names of fish *goujon/brochet*) that she finds happiness, in the dignity of true love and respect. Zola and Clément emphasize that in Gervaise's limited world, eating and providing for her family are of supreme importance. During preparations for her birthday party, Virginie tells Gervaise that Lantier is back in the *quartier*. Symbolically her goose is cooked. For *la grande bouffe*, all the guests bring flowers and plants to Gervaise, even Coupeau and his nasty family. In order to begin the feast, Gervaise, Goujet and Virginie retrieve Coupeau from *L'Assommoir du Père Colombe*. (The name of this bar is a complex metaphor, including the double meaning of *assommer*: to club, beat, overwhelm or daze and to distill cheap eau-de-vie, and the double image of the father and the holy spirit [dove], with the notable absence of the redeemer. Even Goujet as the blond bearded strongman cannot forge a redeemed destiny for Gervaise in the face of her entrapping sinful surroundings and acts.)

During the birthday party, the appalling conditions of the life of the children become more apparent, as they squabble like animals over the leftovers. Nana is depicted with her legs in the air tussling on the bed, another prefiguration of her destiny as a courtesan. In the film, it is Coupeau who brings in the old beggar Père Bru to the party, rather than Gervaise. Clément depicts the homeless Bru's lair under the stairs, where Gervaise finally dies in Zola's work. Clément recreates faithfully the minute detail of Zola's description of Gervaise's party, including the ceremony of carving the goose, with its negative connotation of Gervaise herself being carved up. The luxury of surfeit is well depicted, as an aspect of both sensuality and sexuality, with Gervaise eating like a happy animal, exchanging unambiguous looks with Goujet (in a classic sexual substitution sequence which has been exploited by numerous filmmakers, such as Richardson in *Tom Jones*). Throughout Zola's text and the film, the semantic field of consumption serves as an extended metaphor for these characters who are physically, morally and spiritually consumed by their life situation, eaten up by their downtrodden destiny.

Politics are threaded through the film as through the novel. The guests admire Poisson's skill with the knife when carving, as they talk of Cossacks and the Crimean War. The old Père Bru has lost both his sons in the war, as Clément adds to Zola's 1877 allusion to the Franco-Prussian War a second subtextual reference, to World War II, with in both cases the consequent bereavement and abandonment of the parent generation. In the film it is Goujet who is portrayed as the radical and not Lantier, as he calls for workers' retirement pensions. There is general mockery of the Emperor, and it is the conservative and ambitious policeman-officer Poisson who defends him (there is an extended implicit indictment of right-wing militarism and imperial consumption carving up the world in this sequence).

Lantier is out in the street watching the party as Gervaise sings, a frequent Zolian depiction of longing for a lost world, of sexual exclusion, and a literary metaphor later exploited at length by Proust. Clément develops the sexual attraction between Gervaise and Goujet with an embrace at the end of the party, something which never happens in the book. In opposition to the blond Gervaise and Goujet, Clément like Zola has cast Lantier and Coupeau as very similar, both dark-haired and mustachioed. Clément has Lantier sleep over on the floor after the party. Early the next morning, Etienne meaningfully steps over him on his way to work, his father become an obstacle to his and his mother's happiness, invading her world and generating anxiety.

For opening and closing the film as well as for internal transitions, Clément uses a long shot of an open zone with new high-rise buildings, to depict, as does Zola, the backdrop of the Second Empire building expansion of Paris. Clément also has Goujet lead a strike at the forge which involves Etienne. As strikes were then illegal, at an inquest Goujet is sentenced to a year in prison. Aurenche and Bost felt the need to tighten Goujet's role in Gervaise's life, as he is a typical Zola personality, the good young innocent idealist who confronts unjust adversity and who is emotionally broken by an impossible love for an unfaithful woman.

It is the return of Lantier, whom Coupeau installs in their spare room, and the subsequent renewal of the Lantier-Gervaise *liaison*, that destroys Goujet's attachment to Gervaise. Clément has invented a hospital stay for Maman Coupeau, who dies at home in the novel, in mirror compensation for the fate of Coupeau, who dies in delirium in the hospital in Zola's work. The film also stages an emotional reunion between Gervaise and Goujet, who returns from his prison stay to find her trapped between the two corrupt men who are ruining her morally and financially. As she tries to justify her situation, the film flashes back to the reprise of the affair between Gervaise and Lantier, with Gervaise's interior monologue in voice-over, as she is unable to confess the truth to Goujet. Virginie is deemed responsible for reuniting Lantier and Gervaise the evening they go to the concert hall together. Clément telescopes this sequence to that where Coupeau comes home dead drunk and vomits, soiling the marriage bed, angering Gervaise, and forcing her back into Lantier's bed, where he seduces her against her will.

In both text and film, the curious and irrepressible Nana constantly observes the adults around her. As a voyeur, like the camera and spectator, Nana has access to knowledge of her mother's true conduct, and at the end accuses her of moral laxity. In a winter setting, season of death and suffering, Gervaise hauling water from the courtyard constitutes an echo of impressionist Pissarro-style landscapes of the era. In addition, some of the bar scenes resemble certain canvases, a cinematic equivalent for Zola's descriptions, achieving Cézanne or Degas-like compositions.

In Section VIII, Zola attacks the corruption of the Second Empire through Lantier and details the contents of his library, integrating reading habits into characterization and political and sociological conditions. As if he has come from another text, Goujet offers to rescue Gervaise from her plight before her involvement with Lantier. However, their declaration of love is circumscribed by their environmental situation, part of the natural world in the novel, set in a social outing at a *guinguette* in the film, where Gervaise symbolically lets her hair down. Although she and Goujet are deeply in love, it is an unobtainable idyll, an absent intertext whose irony renders more poignant the sale of her possessions as she fails financially and morally.

Clément depicts Coupeau as a thief stealing Etienne's suitcase and the clients' sheets. Linens were still of great value even in the postwar era, and the image of the sheets being pawned recalls Italian neorealism. When Gervaise confronts Coupeau at the bar, in the counterpart sequence to the washhouse battle, the mocking crowd once again derides the misfortunes and conflicts of others. This lack of sympathy and solidarity is endemic to the plight of the people as Zola depicts them. Coupeau is shown fallen in the gutter, in French an even greater metaphor for degradation with the assonance of *égout* and *dégoût*. In the film, Gervaise abandons her last hope of escape or salvation, as she observes Etienne and Goujet leaving Paris by train, an emblem of male freedom and mobility, and an homage to *La Bête humaine* missing of course from the earlier written text of *L'Assommoir*. Gervaise again expresses her inner self in a voice-over, as she watches the departure of the only good people in her life. These voice-over monologues give Gervaise a lyric first person inner focalization and a voice which has been furthermore reclassed, lacking the colloquial speech of the streets which pervades the discourse of all Zola's characters.

Gervaise's final downfall begins with her discovery that Lantier is having an affair with Virginie, just as she loses financial control of her world, unable to meet back rent payments on the failing laundry, deserted by its employees and customers. Agent of destruction, Coupeau encourages her to give up the laundry. Gervaise cracks from grief and cedes both the shop and Lantier to Virginie, as he leaves her for the second time. At this point, the film diverges radically from the text, as Coupeau goes into delirium at home rather than in the asylum, destroys the laundry physically and is dragged off in the paddy wagon, calling for Gervaise. Zola's text maintains a much more clinical detachment in the scenes from the asylum with the doctor and attendant. In fact, Coupeau doesn't even recognize Gervaise when she visits him, thus negating her identity as his wife. In the film, Nana goes off with

Coupeau's sisters as Gervaise sits down in her empty abode and begins her final self-destruction, taking to drink.

The last sequence shows Virginie and Lantier in the shop, as a starving, filthy Nana comes begging at the door. Lantier's excessive gourmandise is subordinated to a final focus on Nana, compensating briefly the suppression of the last four sections of the novel. We simply see Nana again prefiguring her future, going to *L'Assommoir* where her mother is now a hopeless addict. Again acknowledging painting of the era, Clément portrays Gervaise in the pose of Degas's *Absinthe Drinker* and the men like Cézanne's *Cardplayers*. Nana sitting in the street puts a ribbon around her neck and in the final shot runs off to join the boys, against the backdrop of *nouveau-riche* houses where she will soon live as a courtesan, her only option with her inheritance of death and destruction. Clément eliminates from his film Zola's final scenes of extreme abuse, starvation and violent death by having Coupeau die while Nana is still very young, thus censoring images of realities so harsh they are unthinkable in the Paris of 1956, enjoying the miracle of recovery after the war, or too painful as experiences to be depicted in the morally optimistic and hypocritical climate of the day.

Bibliography

Allard, Jacques. *Zola, Le chiffre du texte: Lecture de 'L'Assommoir'*. Grenoble: Presses Universitaires de Grenoble, 1978.

Baguley, David, ed. *Critical Essays on Emile Zola*. Boston: G. K. Hall, 1986.

————. *L'Assommoir*. Cambridge: Cambridge University Press, 1992.

Barnett, Richard. "La Poétique de la désintégration zolienne." *Romance Notes* 28:2 (1987) 149–155.

Belgrand, Anne. "Espace clos, espace ouvert dans *L'Assommoir*." In Crouzet, Michel, ed. *Espaces romanesques*. Paris: Presses Universitaires de France, 1982.

Berry, Betsy. "Zola's Art of the Gutter: Aesthetic Paterns in *L'Assommoir*." *Excavatio* 6–7 (1995) 89–102.

Berta, Michel. *De l'androgynie dans les Rougon-Macquart et deux autres études sur Zola*. New York: Peter Lang, 1985.

Biard, Jean-Dominique. "Zola, *L'Assommoir* et le cimetière Marcadet." *Les Cahiers Naturalistes* 63 (1989) 205–206.

Bonnafous, Simone. "Recherches sur le lexique de *L'Assommoir*." *Les Cahiers Naturalistes* 56 (1981) 52–62.

Bonnefis, Philippe. *L'Innommable: essai sur l'oeuvre d'Emile Zola*. Paris: Société d'Edition d'Enseignement Supérieur, 1984.

Borie, Jean. *Zola et les mythes: ou, De la nausée au salut*. Paris: Seuil, 1971.

Butler, Ronnie. "Structures des récurrences dans *L'Assommoir*." *Les Cahiers Naturalistes* 57 (1983) 60–73.

Carles, Patricia. "*L'Assommoir*: Une Destructuration Impressionniste de l'espace descriptif." *Les Cahiers Naturalistes* 63 (1989) 117–126.

Cassard, Marie-Josée, et Pascale Joinville. "Le Thème de l'eau dans *L'Assommoir*." *Les Cahiers Naturalistes* 55 (1981) 63–73.

Clark, Roger. *Zola: 'L'Assommoir'*. Glasgow: University of Glasgow French and German Publications, 1990.

Cosset, Evelyne. *Les Quatre Evangiles d'Emile Zola: espace, temps, personnages*. Genève: Droz, 1990.

Cousins, Russell. "Ideology and Focalisation in *Gervaise*: The AurencheBost/René Clément Treatment." *Excavatio* 2:1 (Fall 1993) 1–10.

Deffoux, Léon-Louis. *La Publication de 'L'Assommoir'*. Paris: Société Française d'Editions Littéraires et Techniques, 1931.

Dineen, R. M. "*L'Assommoir*: Zola's 'Oeuvre de vérité.'" *New Zealand Journal of French Studies* 6:1 (1985) 39–62.

————. "A Journey through the Labyrinth: Variations on the Theme in *L'Assommoir*." *New Zealand Journal of French Studies* 20:2 (Nov 1999) 5–16.

Emile-Zola, François, ed. *Zola Photographer*. New York: Seaver Books, 1988.

Furst, Lilian R. *'L'Assommoir': A Working Woman's Life*. Boston: Twayne, 1990.

————. "A Medical Reading of Gervaise in *L'Assommoir*." *Excavatio* 1 (May 1992) 63–71.

Gallagher, Edward. "'Différent de soi-même': The Altered Self in Balzac, Flaubert and Zola." *French Studies Bulletin* 20 (1986) 9–11.

George, Ken. "The Language of Alcohol in *L'Assommoir*." *French Studies* 52:4 (Oct 1998) 437–449.

Grant, Elliott. *Emile Zola*. Boston: Twayne, 1966.

Hamon, Philippe. *Le Personnel du roman*. Genève: Droz, 1983.

Hjerpe, Cynthia. *Emile Zola: Novel to Film*. Dissertation Abstracts International 41:12 (1981) 5119A–5120A.

Knapp, Bettina. *Emile Zola*. New York: Ungar, 1980.

Kranowski, Nathan. *Paris dans les romans d'Emile Zola*. Paris: Presses Universitaires de France, 1968.

Leduc-Adine, Jean-Pierre. "*L'Assommoir*: La Terreur des ouvriers." *Littératures* 30 (Spring 1994) 61–71.

Lethbridge, Robert. "Reflections in the Margin: Politics in Zola's *L'Assommoir*." *Australian Journal of French Studies* 30:2 (1993) 222–232.

————. "A Visit to the Louvre: *L'Assommoir* Revisited." *Modern Language Review* 87:1 (Jan 1992) 41–55.

Marin, Mihaela. "La Ville structuraliste de Zola: Urbanisme et architecture textuelle dans *L'Assommoir*." *Excavatio* 13 (2000) 122–132.

Martin, Laurey. "L'Elaboration de l'espace fictif dans *L'Assommoir*." *Les Cahiers Naturalistes* 67 (1993) 83–96.

Mathy, Jean Philippe. "La Noce au musée: Le Peuple et les beaux-arts dans *L'Assommoir*." *The French Review* 67:3 (Feb 1994) 445–452.

Mickel, Emanuel. "Gervaise's Ideal and the Infrastructure of *L'Assommoir*." Ames: Iowa State University, 1987.

Minogue, Valérie. *L'Assommoir*. London: Grant & Cutler, 1991.

Mitterand, Henri. "Programme et préconstruit génétique: le dossier de *L'Assommoir*." In Hay, Louis, ed. *Essais de critique génétique*. Paris: Flammarion, 1979.

Molinari, Marthe, and François de La Brétèque. "Avatars de l'énonciation: *L'Assommoir* de Zola, filmé et novellisé." In Rousseau, Molino, and Bozzetto, eds. *Art et Littérature*. Aix-en-Provence: Université de Provence, 1988.

Moore, Mary Jane Evans. "The Spatial Dynamics of *L'Assommoir*." *Kentucky Romance Quarterly* 29:1 (1982) 3–14.

Newton, Joy. "The Decline and Fall of Gervaise Macquart." *Essays in French Literature* 16 (1979) 62–79.

Newton, Joy, and Basil Jackson. "Gervaise Macquart's Vision: A Closer Look at Zola's Use of

'Point of View' in *L'Assommoir.*" *Nineteenth-Century French Studies* 11:3–4 (1983) 313–320.

Newton, Joy, and Claude Schumacher. "La Grande Bouffe dans *L'Assommoir* et dans le cycle Gervaise." *L'Esprit Créateur* 25:4 (1985) 17–29.

Ng, Lisa. "L'Ecriture du hasard dans *Germinal* et *L'Assommoir.*" *Excavatio* 15:3–4 (2001) 22–37.

Page, H. Dwight. "Generation and Degeneration in Emile Zola's *L'Assommoir.*" *West Virginia Philological Papers* 34 (1988) 38–50.

Pierre-Gnassounou, Chantal. "Un Personnage décevant: Le Sergent de ville Poisson dans *L'Assommoir.*" *Australian Journal of French Studies* 38:3 (Sept–Dec 2001) 379–392.

Place, David. "Zola and the Working Class: The Meaning of *L'Assommoir.*" *French Studies* 28 (1974) 39–49.

Przybos, Julia. "The Aesthetics of Dirty Laundry." In Falconer and Donaldson-Evans, eds. *Kaleidoscope.* Toronto, ON: Centre d'Etudes Romantiques Joseph Sable, 1996.

Richardson, Joanna. *Zola.* New York: St. Martin's Press, 1978.

Rollins, Yvonne. "Une 'Danse macabre': *L'Assommoir* de Zola." *Nineteenth-Century French Studies* 9:3–4 (1981) 233–246.

Schehr, Lawrence. *Flaubert and Sons: Readings of Flaubert, Zola and Proust.* New York: Peter Lang, 1986.

Schor, Naomi. "Sainte-Anne: capitale du délire." *Les Cahiers Naturalistes* 52 (1978) 103–112.

——. *Zola's Crowds.* Baltimore: Johns Hopkins University Press, 1978.

Slott, Kathryn. "Narrative Tension in the Representaton of Women in Zola's *L'Assommoir* and *Nana.*" *L'Esprit Créateur* 25:4 (1985) 93–104.

Stump, Jordan. "De la répétition dans *L'Assommoir.*" *Chimères* 19:1 (1986) 19–34.

Walker, Philip. *Zola.* Boston: Routledge, 1985.

Woollen, Geoff. "Lantier versus Goujet in *L'Assommoir*: The Misuses of Literacy." *Folio* 14 (1982) 15–30.

Worth, Jeremy. "Le Grotesque et le néant: L'Enfant-adulte et l'adulte-enfant dans *L'Assommoir* et *Nana.*" *Excavatio* 15:3–4 (2001) 1–11.

Nana

directed by Christian-Jaque (1954)
novel by Emile Zola (1880)

There have been several films made from Zola's popular serialized (1879–1880) melodramatic novel about the scandalously sordid and tragic life of Gervaise's daughter Nana as an insatiable courtesan. Renoir's silent 1926 film retained the appropriate theatricality suggested not only by Nana's roles on stage but by her calculated performance in Second Empire high society. Hollywood attempted a 1934 sound version with little success. Christian-Jaque's movie is of special interest ironically because in its infidelity to the novel, symbolically appropriate for Nana, it offers a reflection of the 1950s as much as a historic portrayal of the Second Empire. Christian-Jaque also stands accused, by Dudley Andrew, of making literary adaptations (of *Boule de suif* and *La Chartreuse de Parme* as well) for "France's most ostentatious actors to dress up as their favorite characters."[1] This is especially true here of the role of Nana, exploited for and by his wife Martine Carol, who imposes on Zola's earthy heroine a glittering hollow egotist. Further evidence of this exploitation is provided by the credits, where many well-known actors and actresses of the time (including Walter Chiari, Paul Frankeur, Dario Michaelis, Dora Doll) are listed without their roles, thus foregrounding their presence at the expense of the narrative and characterial coherence of the script, emphasizing their own identities and presuming recognition on the part of the spectators.

Whereas Renoir wrote the intertitles for his film with Zola's daughter, the screenwriters Jean Ferry, Albert Valentin, Henri Jeanson (who did the dialogues) and Christian-Jaque have dismantled the structural elements of Zola's plot like pieces in a complex puzzle, resituated the characters and reordered the events to create a vastly different narrative. In spite of this reworking, certain key elements of Zola's text were inevitably retained for the film: the scenes of the theater, Nana's first apartment provided by the Jewish banker Steiner, her lovenest gone sour with her fellow actor Fontan, her gaudy palatial house provided by Muffat (Charles Boyer), the drama of the Grand Prix, Vandeuvres's suicide, Muffat's wife's infidelity, Nana's final demise. But beyond and even within these basic sequences, a great deal has been altered, with concomitant radical shifts of emphasis in both the depiction of individual characters and the social structure portrayed.

Zola's lengthy and richly detailed work is itself a gallery of impressionist paintings of an era, an extremely cinematic oeuvre in fact. It is too vast to be reduced to one film; it would be better served serialized like the original text. In several ways, *Nana* illustrates perfectly the title of this study, *The Transparent Illusion*, particularly in the scenes where her thinly veiled nude body is itself a transparent screen covering and presenting her reality, simultaneously masking and revealing her, a visceral image of the ideology of realism.

The opening scene is in an empty theater, setting the stage literally for the melodrama about to unfold and serving as an extended metaphor for Nana's life, which will end, like her ill-fated acting career, with the stage empty once again. Initially, she triumphs in *La Blonde Vénus*, lacking voice and talent but resplendent in her pale semi-nudity, infuriating her rival Rose Mignon. The comparison to *The Birth of Venus* is not a reference to the classic Renaissance painting by Botticelli but rather to an eponymous canvas by Bouguereau in 1879. Peter Brook has detailed in *Critical Inquiry* in "Storied Bodies, or Nana at Last Unveil'd" the contemporary models and pictorial equivalents of her character. In *La Blonde Vénus*, Nana also theatricalizes the thematic and mythical intertext of *L'Assommoir*, as Vénus and Vulcan are equatable to Gervaise and Goujet.

Nana takes all she can from those who present themselves before her, from prince to pauper. One of her first conquests is in fact a prince, of unnamed origin in Zola's text, which inspired the reader to supply the "key" to his identity. In this film, he has become the Prince of Sardinia, a visiting dignitary being entertained for the evening by the Comte de Muffat, who has become the Emperor Napoleon III's chamberlain, *chambellan*, an invented role alluding to his imminent drama in the other *chambre*, his love affair with Nana. It is interesting that the opening sequence in Christian-Jaque's film is not at Bordenave's brothel-theater but at Court, where we meet the Emperor and Empress (absent from the novel) and the Count and Countess Muffat in full regalia. Their daughter Estelle is presented as engaged to the officer Philippe Hugon. In Zola's account, it is Daguenet who is palmed off on Estelle at the end by Nana; Philippe Hugon and his younger brother Georges are both ruined by their passion for Nana, after she refuses them both in marriage. Georges commits suicide in despair, and Philippe is imprisoned for embezzling funds to support her.

Zola structures his text with consummate artistry. Part I is at the theater; II shows Nana's private life at home; III is an evening at the Muffats' home wherein IV is planned, a banquet at Nana's apartment, where the courtesans are served up like the elegant fare. The dynamic equilibrium of a dual world—day and night, proper and improper, overt and clandestine, city and country—continues throughout the text. Like Nana's long reflection in her mirror and her lengthy toilette before Muffat and the Prince, every episode, every character has its double, its *dessous* (underneath). The world of the theater reappears in Part V; the play, like the later production *La Petite Duchesse*, is an extended metaphor, a *mise-en-abyme* of the novel. In Section VI, Nana's country house, La Mignotte, which she desired for herself and her infant son Louiset, is next door to the Hugons' home, Les Fondettes. (The homes with their richly associative names become characters in the novel; the human characters' names are equally evocative.) When Nana and her courtesan companions set off on an excursion in carriages, they pass the Hugon household crossing a bridge on foot, a scandalous encounter embodying an economic and social inversion. The bridge, the place of passage, accentuates the gap between the two worlds and the pain generated in their confrontation. It is this sequence that resembles so closely the country outing of the prostitutes in Maupassant's *La Maison Tellier*, which appeared the following year. Given the contacts between the two at Zola's *Soirées de Médan* and the fact that Maupassant's lifelong mentor Flaubert had just died, it was inevitable that Zola's work at that time would have a strong influence on the younger writer. Any influence of prior images in the cinematic presentation of these two tales was reversed, however, as Ophuls's film appeared three years earlier.

Zola's text is alive with sensorial descriptions: the smells, the food, the light, the textures of hallways, staircases, courtyards, dressing rooms, boudoirs, dining halls. The omnipresent cats anticipate the later description of Nana as *une chatte de race* (a high-class pussy), a double-entendre epithet which complements the *cheval de race* (thoroughbred) she is later called but which leaves unsaid the implied counterpart, *chienne de race* (a world-class bitch). In Zola's text, it is Madame Laure's "soup kitchen" and not Nana's apartment that is on rue des Martyrs (the real street with the irresistibly symbolic name also used, as noted, by Maupassant in *La Parure* and *Une Partie de campagne*). Here the down and out *filles* call to mind, as did Gervaise, the Degas masterpiece *L'Absinthe*. In fact it is a Baudelairian *femme damnée* (lesbian), Satin (read Satan), who involves Nana in her most enduring love affair. Satin, pulled by Nana like herself from the gutter, reigns with the latter in her extravagant *hôtel* provided by Muffat. Zola is playing doubly on the word *hôtel*, for Nana's home is as much a public house of passage as an elegant private mansion, and it is an *autel* (altar) where both men and women worship false gods. The text is also enriched by various self-referential markers *en abyme*: Nana reading a popular vulgar novel of the day, rejecting it as too pornographic; her stage roles (Venus, the Duchess, Mélusine), and the journalist Fauchery's revealing newspaper article about her. Her own obtuse naïveté regarding these images of her lends layers of dramatic irony to the text.

It is in the transposition of description from text to film that the central paradox of cinematic adaptations is most evident. Christian-Jaque fails to find the striking comparable equivalent images for the myriad vivid details Zola furnished his avid readers. Instead of having the journalist Fauchery write a piece on Nana which is a *mise-en-abyme* of the plot and its composition as did Zola, he simply has him critique *La Blonde Vénus*. Fauchery's conquest of the Countess Sabine Muffat is given a Merteuil-Valmont-La Présidente structure in the film, as he presents Nana with a ring signalling his triumph. As will be seen later, it is rather Daguenet who is manipulated in Laclos fashion in the novel, where the *liaison* between Sabine and Fauchery counterbalances that of Muffat and Nana. The Count is doubly ruined: morally and financially by Nana, spiritually and socially by the loss of his wife, by his humiliation in his double-standard world as a *cocu* (cuckold). In addition, Christian-Jaque lacks Zola's moral and artistic subtlety; he has the priest Venot (whose name is an interesting variant on Venus, venal) following Muffat from the beginning, as the embodiment of his conscience. In the novel, Venot turns up only at the end to pick up the pieces.

The country house sequence has been cut completely from the film, thus eliminating an essential polarity in Zola, wherein the Paris corruption invades the rural innocence and beauty and destroys it, at the same time that La Mignotte represents for Nana a salvation, an escape from her sordid life, from her lavish imprisonment in a patriarchal hypocritical Paris. Her return to Paris serves as an act of surrender after an impossible interlude with Georges Hugon. It is possible that Ophuls's transposition of this segment from the Maupassant text blocked Christian-Jaque's access to the original textual description.

As with virtually all filmic adaptations of these classic nineteenth-century texts, the screenwriters and directors fail to find an equal *écriture*. Like so many of the characters in these great realist novels of a prior era, the world has changed too much. The filmmakers are caught between their own accumulated mental images as lifetime readers of such well-known texts and the inevitably frustrated search for equivalency: narrative, dialogical, iconographic, ideological. For example, Christian-Jaque expands the role of the Jewish banker Steiner, as Nana is kept by him in high style, having taken him from her rival Rose Mignon. In Zola's text, Rose instead inherits Muffat, in a reverse/revenge interlude, upon Nana's first disappearance. Nana's and Steiner's foray to his safe at the bank and their lovemaking amid the banknotes is more of a twentieth-century postwar obsession; Zola simply has Steiner serve as the symbol of the commercialization of Nana's body and the beginning of her lust for material possessions to compensate her real lack of power in the world of late nineteenth-century Paris.

Another major thematic missing from the film is the concert of references to Bismarck. Zola's novel appeared nearly a decade after the French defeat by the Prussians and can be read as an extended metaphor of Napoleon III selling out the nation with his inept leadership and irresponsible immorality. He is portrayed in this film as keeping a mistress, but it is rather the entire society that is compromised and prostituted in the Third Republic novel where the collapse of Nana's empire, like Gervaise's, equates the political situation of the day. In the France of 1954, also ten years after a war with Germany, government ministers and army officers are powerful yet vulnerable to corruption, but France is now the victor, the occupation behind her, indulging in the 1950s luxury of turning her back on politics.

In Section VII of Zola's *Nana* are back-to-back mirror images, as the Comte de Muffat learns of his wife's (mirror) infidelity with Fauchery after watching Nana perform an autoerotic dance before her mirror in perfect bestial indulgence. Muffat leaves her and prowls the streets, a cuckolded voyeur, anguishing over his wife's rendez-vous. This sequence has its best-known echo in the scene in Proust's *A la Recherche du Temps perdu* where Swann watches Odette's silhouette from in front of her house, consumed by jealousy. (As illustrated in Schlöndorff's film, Swann also becomes a self-parody by anguishing over the wrong house). When Muffat finally returns home at dawn, he encounters his wife in the hallway, as they become physical mirrors of one another.

In Section VIII, which appropriately opens on the *Fête des Rois* (Epiphany), a day of social inversion like Mardi Gras, Nana has dumped Muffat and Steiner and all her wealthy luxury to pursue with Fanton a second doomed idyll, trying to find true pure love uncluttered by materialism and commercialism. At the beginning they live out a domestic dream, as Nana shops for food and keeps house. They amuse themselves together in libertine fashion by composing love letters in response to those addressed to Nana by Georges Hugon, in the first of several echoes in Zola's text of *Les Liaisons dangereuses*. Predictably, Fanton proves to be a woman abuser, a foul misogynist who is just as bestial as the goat mask he wears in the opening play. This satyr-like character has immense sexual attraction for Nana, who masochistically professes to love him. She descends in a closed spiral to hell, ending back on the streets where she began, raided by the police in a flophouse, in spiritual and physical misery. In Christian-Jaque's film, Muffat turns up at the police station to rescue Nana and effect a reconciliation between them. Zola's narrative is more complex, as Nana escapes the raid to take refuge with Madame Lerat, her son's nanny.

In Section IX, wherein Nana returns to the theater, Zola presents a central metaphor of his text. Bordenave muses over the image of the dark house with its chandelier lowered to the ground, comparing it to a definitive departure, foreshadowing Nana's final disappearance. Her stage is already dark, as she obtains the symbolic role of the Duchess only through Muffat's influence. Her performance is expectedly a failure; she is no more capable of incarnating a duchess on stage than of exhibiting in her life the aristocratic instincts and manners the title implies. But it is in the theater, once again, that she is reunited with Muffat, who offers her the prize package she has sought for so long: an elegant house on avenue des Villiers furnished in the high neobaroque manner. This point in the text and in the film could be said to be the single moment of equilibrium in Nana's life. Soon after obtaining all from Muffat, she will enter her fatal path of destruction.

In Section X, Nana is at the summit of power and success, receiving her numerous suitors with Satin. In a sequence at dinner, however, she quarrels with the servants, demonstrating maniacal behavior that announces her ultimate collapse. Zola offers his readers here an intertextual display of his *oeuvre*, as Nana recounts her family origins, the tale of *L'Assommoir*, and the men at her table discuss the brutal murder of a woman by an alcoholic psychotic, the narrative structure in embryo of *La Bête humaine*. Zola not only expounds his determinist theories through his characters, he demonstrates them, as Nana reveals her corrupted nature by throwing a temper tantrum at the servants, breaking her birthday gifts and sending her guests away in order to have a private tryst with Satin. At the end of the chapter, they observe from their window perch a woman in rags in the street below, a Goya or Daumier-like figure of destruction which announces their fate. This haunting figure recalls the blind beggar of *Madame Bovary* and achieves the same catharsis of pity and fear for Zola's reader.

Section XI stands as one of the great society portraits of all Zola's work, as he depicts with Degas brilliance the Grand Prix race at Longchamps. Vandeuvres, who has ruined himself gambling, wagers his fortune on his filly Nana, while pretending to bet on his other horse, the favorite Lusignan (whose name announces the subtextual myth of anguish and destruction completed by Nana's stage role as the fairy Mélusine). The horse Nana's triumph is equated to that of the woman, as her bestiality is signaled again by this conjunction. The ladies of the Bois de Boulogne, the elegant courtesans who love horses and riding, will again constitute a social portrait in Proust. In this film, they echo the Cocteau-Bresson 1945 *Les Dames du Bois de Boulogne*, the tale taken from Diderot of a prostitute set up as a society match. Christian-Jaque invents a scene where Muffat and Nana go to the Bois at dawn after their first night of lovemaking to drink milk at the dairy, a society folly of the day which recalls the libertine *bergère* follies of Marie-Antoinette. Vandeuvres materializes on horseback as an intruder in this sequence. When he is ruined at the end of the Grand Prix in Zola's text, he commits suicide, prefiguring Georges Hugon's later attempt, in a manner worthy of tragic theater, incinerating himself and all his prize race horses in his stables. The film depicts the horses escaping, but Zola is unambiguous about their immolation; their screams of panic and agony are heard for miles around. Christian-Jaque and his screenwriters created a social rivalry between new and old aristocracy in extending the rivalry for Nana to Vandeuvres and Muffat (who were friends in Zola's work). Their embittered and embattled hostility leads to a duel, foiled only by the Emperor's ban. Zola's Muffat is morally superior to Vandeuvres, for he repudiates Nana and returns to his confessor when he finds her in the arms of his father-in-law, the Marquis de Chouard.

Muffat is prepared to leave Nana at the beginning of Section XII, but she preempts his breakoff by announcing a miscarriage and playing the tragic heroine. This spontaneous abortion is yet another symbol of her life, her unnatural sexuality and non-nourishing sterile existence. By the end of the section, she has recovered enough to collect in Merteuil fashion on a bargain she struck with Daguenet: having obtained Estelle for his wife, she makes love with him after his wedding ceremony. Estelle and Daguenet recall Cécile and Danceny of *Les Liaisons dangereuses*, including the assonantic echoes in their names. However, although he is manipulated by the ruthless and insatiable libertine, Daguenet is not innocent. It would be safe to say that no one in this Zola text enjoys that privileged status, except Nana's illegitimate son Louiset, who like all the others is doomed from birth.

Section XIII is the final nexus of the text, wherein the major elements of the complex plot and subplots all come to a climax. Georges attempts suicide when he discovers that Nana is also sleeping with his brother Philippe. Nana humiliates Muffat, whom she calls her *mufe*, an association from his name imaging in French *mufle* or gross beast, which translates as "skunk" (*mouffette*) in the subtitles. She betrays him with a succession of lovers whose fortunes she consumes with avidity, and reduces him to games of bestiality in her boudoir. Zola offers an extended portrait of her evil, seeking figure after figure to depict her consumption and decadence in a mystical and legendary expansion, using techniques of exaggeration popular in storytelling throughout the nineteenth century, but achieving a Baudelairian lyric dissemination of almost cosmic dimensions, comparable also to Maupassant's equally opium-inspired *fantastique*. This trimphant symphonic *coda* of Nana's melodramatic tale leads to the last tragic notes of her ultimate fate.

Nana's death in Section XIV of Zola's text, prefigured by Satin's, is redolent of the disfigurement of the Marquise de Merteuil at the end of *Les Liaisons dangereuses* as well as of the physical suffering of Emma Bovary. Flaubert wrote just weeks before his own death that Zola's last scene was "michelangelesque" and "épique." Yet it is not as mythologizing as the epic description in Section XIII of Nana's *sexe* as all-consuming and insatiable, giving her the dimension of a monstrous evil divinity, compared by recent critics to surrealist works like Magritte's painting of a female nude torso as a face. Nana's third attempt to escape the prison of her destiny and compulsions leads her to sell her possessions and leave France. She nearly succeeds, finding a wealthy Russian nobleman. Appropriately, she dies from small pox contracted from her own fatally ill son. This contagion comes symbolically from the fruit of her corrupted womb (emblematic source of the other pox, of syphillis), from a child who is portrayed throughout as sickly and marginalized, a victim child of sin, an orphan whose father is unknown and whose mother like Emma Bovary has a maternal instinct perversely misdirected to young lovers.

Nana's final damnation is prepared in Zola's perfectly constructed plot by her last theatrical appearance before her flight, as a fairy in *Mélusine*, again in opposition to Lusignan in a legendary, mythical role. Christian-Jaque keeps only her second theatrical appearance and transforms her into the follies chorus girl and singer that Rose Mignon became in the novel. So much of Zola's mythical symbolism and metaphoric structuring is destroyed in this film by transpositions that the ending is hardly surprising. When Muffat strangles Nana to death on the staircase of her lavish home, it evokes a number of earlier film noir sequences, especially Jean Gabin murdering Simone Simon at the end of *La Bête humaine*. The irony of the cinematic palimpsest thus elicited is that it represents the fatal determinist heredity foregrounded in all of Zola's work at the same time that it betrays that primary thematic in *Nana*. *Autant en emporte le cinéma.*

Note

1. Dudley Andrew, in Christopher Lyon, ed., *International Dictionary of Films and Filmmakers*, II (New York: Perigee, 1984) 93.

154   *Nana*

Bibliography

(For the general bibliography on Zola, please see the end of the chapter on *Gervaise*. Some references to Renoir's *Nana* have been included here for purposes of comparative study.)

Armbrust-Seibert, Margaret. "*Nana*: une autre source." *Cahiers Naturalistes* 73 (1999) 181–193.

Barnett, Richard. "Exorcizing the Beast: Deletions of Difference in Zola's *Nana*." *Romanische-Forschungen* 110:3 (1998) 366–378.

Beizer, Janet. "Uncovering Nana: The Courtesan's New Clothes." *L'Esprit Créateur* 25:2 (1985) 45–56.

Bergala, Alain. "*Nana*." *Cahiers du Cinéma* 482 (Jul–Aug 1994) 45–46.

Best, Janice. "Portraits d'une 'vraie fille': *Nana*, tableau, roman et mise-en-scène." *Cahiers Naturalistes* 38:66 (1992) 157–166.

Bonneau, Albert. "*Nana* et Jean Renoir." Excerpts from *Ciné-magazine* 5 (Jan 1926) in *Image et Son* 296 (May 1975) 29.

Bordeau, Catherine. "The Power of the Feminine Milieu in Zola's *Nana*." *Nineteenth-Century French Studies* 27:1–2 (Fall–Winter 1998–1999) 96–107.

Brooks, Peter. "Storied Bodies, or Nana at last Unveil'd." *Critical Inquiry* 16:1 (1989) 1–32.

Brown, Frederick. "Zola and the Making of *Nana*." *Hudson Review* 45:2 (Summer 1992) 191–217.

Chitnis, Bernice. *Reflecting on 'Nana'*. London: Routledge, 1991.

Cousins, Russell. "Revamping *Nana* as a Star Vehicle: the Christian Jaque/Martine Carol Screen Version." *Excavatio* 9 (1997) 173–182.

Duffy, John. "Diversions: the Structure of Marginality in *Nana*." *Nineteenth-Century French Studies* 27:3-4 (Spring–Summer 1999) 366–383.

———. "Les Voix de *Nana*: Refoulement et rejaillissement de la sexualité." *Excavatio* 2 (Fall 1993) 83–91.

Gauteur, Claude. "Jean Renoir de *Nana* à *La Grande Illusion*." *Image et Son* 296 (May 1975) 17–38.

Gilman, Sander. "Black Bodies, White Bodies: Toward an Iconography of Female Sexuality in Late Nineteenth-Century Art, Medecine and Literature." *Critical Inquiry* 12:1 (1985) 204–242.

Golson, Katherine. "From Theater to Cinema: Jean Renoir's Adaptation of *Nana* (1926)." *Excavatio* 13 (2000) 225–228.

Howard, Heather. "Nana mise en scène: Zola's Mythical Monster or Renoir's Stage Artist." *Excavatio* 11 (1998) 156–166.

Krell, Jonathan. "*Nana*: Still Life, Nature morte." *French Forum* 19:1 (1994) 65–79.

Krumm, Pascale. "Nana maternelle: oxymore?" *The French Review* 69:2 (1995) 217–228.

Lanskin, Jean-Michel. *Le Scénario sans amour d'une fille de joie*. Dissertation Abstracts International 50:12 (1990) 3972A–3973A.

———. "Cocottes à la ville et colombes aux champs: dichotomie spatiale dans *La Dame aux camélias* et *Nana* ou l'écologie de deux demi-mondaines." *French Literature Series* 22 (1995) 105–118.

Lowe, Romana. *The Fictional Female: Sacrificial Rituals and Spectacles of Writing in Baudelaire, Zola, and Cocteau*. New York, NY: Peter Lang, 1997.

Lundin, Jill. "Sleaze and Slime: *Humidité* and *Liquidité* in Zola's Rougon-Macquart." *Excavatio* 3 (Winter 1993) 62–73.

Mitterand, Henri. *Nana*. Paris: Folio, 1977.

Nelson, Brian. "*Nana*: Uses of the Female Body" *Australian Journal of French Studies* 38:3

(Sept–Dec 2001) 407–429.

Petit, Pierre. "Localisation structurale d'un roman de Zola: *Nana*." *New Zealand Journal of French Studies* 5:1 (1984) 19–24.

Perry, Katrina. "Containing the Scent: 'Odor di femina' in Zola's *Nana*." *Cincinnati Romance Review* 10 (1991) 158–168.

Rochecouste, Maryse. "Images catamorphes zoliennes: Deux chapitres de *Nana*." *Les Cahiers Naturalistes* 60 (1986) 105–112.

Roy-Reverzy, Eléonore. "*Nana* ou l'inexistence: d'une écriture allégorique." *Cahiers Naturalistes* 73 (1999) 167–180.

Slott, Katherine. "Narrative Tension in the Representation of Women in Zola's *L'Assommoir* and *Nana*." *L'Esprit Créateur* 25:4 (1985) 93–104.

Tintner, Adeline. "What Zola's *Nana* owes to Manet's *Nana*." *Iris* 8 (1983) 15–16.

Warren, Jill. "Zola's View of Prostitution in *Nana*." In Horn, Pierre, and Mary Beth Pringle, eds. *The Image of the Prostitute in Modern Literature*. New York: Ungar, 1984.

Worth, Jeremy. "Le Grotesque et le néant: L'Enfant-adulte et l'adulte-enfant dans *L'Assommoir* et *Nana*." *Excavatio* 15:3–4 (2001) 1–11.

La Bête humaine
(The Beast in Man)

directed by Jean Renoir (1938)
novel by Emile Zola (1890)

Emile Zola's depictions of the world of the industrial revolution and its victims perhaps reached its apex with his 1890 *La Bête humaine* (literally: the human beast), one of the last of the epic cycle of the Rougon-Macquart family novels, set in 1869–1870. Born in Paris of a naturalized Italian father and French mother in 1840, under the "bourgeois" July Monarchy of Louis-Philippe, which he would see replaced by the failed attempt of the Second Republic in 1848 and the long travesty of the Second Empire of Napoleon III, Zola observed firsthand the impact of change in the second half of the nineteenth century. His own life had its trials as well; having failed the baccalaureat, he entered journalism and soon began writing serials, the soap operas of the era. *La Bête humaine* was, like the prior novels treated in this section, serialized, in the illustrated weekly *La Vie Populaire*, from 14 November 1889 to 2 March 1890.

In many ways the most modern of Zola's works, as evidenced by the contemporary 1930s setting Renoir gave his film, *La Bête humaine* combines never-theless a number of elements integral to late nineteenth-century thought and naturalist literature: an impoverished, grimey working-class industrial setting, the power and fascination of machinery, in this case of train locomotives, and determinist theories of instinctual human drives and passions, a generation before Sigmund Freud's theory of the subconscious—theories which were in direct conflict with the dialectic materialism of Karl Marx, whose discourse foregrounds man's collective capacity to change and better his environment, his human condition.

The research for *La Bête humaine* is if anything more interesting than that written about the text. Zola consulted many different works in his naturalist drive to document his writing, however mystical or fabular it might be underneath the realistic details, driven by his passion for photography. Two major currents emerge: (1) research on trains, including a book and several newspaper reports on train crashes, and 2) research on psychotic and homicidal behavior, including court proceedings and two works from the late 1880s on criminal behavior. It is fairly certain that Zola also read the numerous accounts from August and September 1888 of the London rampage of Jack the Ripper. Zola acknowledged as well his debt to

Dostoevsky's *Crime and Punishment*, although espousing an opposing theory of crime.

Renoir's film of *La Bête humaine* combines somewhat the same double focus of Abel Gance's *Napoléon* or the Italian postwar neorealists, of a story of sexual passion and destruction set against a backdrop of historic events or collective class struggle. This work demonstrates the rapid evolution in filmmaking of the era, reflecting the influence of both Gance and Eisenstein. Renoir's choice of a contemporary setting rather than the period costumes not only gives the film the poetic realism which is synonymous with his work, it further reveals his relationship to history, his sense of contemporary social and economic problems and his leftist if not Marxist ideological leanings. Above all, it reflects his awareness of the dynamics of displacement, social, economic and geographic, in France of the 1930s, seen as well in *La Règle du jeu*. Lastly, Renoir reveals not only a childlike fascination for the machinery of locomotion but a profound sensitivity to psychic disfunction and trauma.

The idea for the film came from the producer Robert Hakim and Jean Gabin after they rejected Jean Grémillon's *Train d'enfer* (*Train of Hell*). The 1938 setting gave Renoir the opportunity to experiment with the film noir genre, inevitable in a transposition of a *roman noir*. Here there are only traces of his *gaieté parisienne* affinities; this is a different poetic realism—darker, tragic rather than melodramatic. It is intensified by the low-key naturalistic performance of the cast, especially Jean Gabin's deadpan revelation of his tragic act at the end. The tale has its own mythological and melodramatic constructs, intensified by the extended metaphor of the trains, their power and their movement. Renoir also uses music most effectively for dramatic tension and irony rather than melodrama; the song that Charles Aznavour sings at the public dance hall, "Le Petit Coeur de Ninon," is both an allusion to Zola and a *mise-en-abyme* of Séverine's tale and functions in perfect contrapuntal contrast through crosscutting to her murder.

In some ways, Renoir's relationship to this text is similar to Zola's. Shot at a historically dark moment, the film inevitably makes an allusion to the growing beast of Hitler's Reich, on the eve of World War II, just as France in 1869 was about to fall to the Prussians, weakened and divided by the collapse of Napoleon III's corrupt Second Empire. But it is the fascination with trains that transcends the three eras of the two works (1869, 1890, 1938), as Renoir did documentary naturalist research in the railroad yards like that done by Zola. With the obvious exception of the suicide leap at the end, the movie was filmed on real trains (Claude Renoir was nearly killed filming the first tunnel sequence from outside the engine). In fact the film opens and closes with reverse direction sequences, passing over the same bridge-tunnel terrain, whose effect on the audience was comparable to that of today's space wars special effects films. The train's dual journey is mimetic of the entry into the text, into the recesses of the instinctual mind, and the return from an oedipal-style discovery of identity to the subsequent inevitable self-immolation.

The real villain in the story is not Jacques Lantier (Jean Gabin), but his tragic destiny like that of a Greek classic hero, as the primitive violence which remains in modern man in spite of technology overwhelms his mental machinery, and he breaks down like his overheated train engine. The film affirms the central thematic with its initial presentation of Zola's famous assertion that Lantier was the victim of a hereditary schizophrenic disorder, a madman produced by generations of down-trodden alcoholics. Renoir maintains this foregrounding as Lantier's obsessive homicidal psychosis toward beautiful women is announced early in the film by his attack on the innocent Flore (Blanchette Brunoy), saved only by the rush of a passing train, a momentary aberration which prefigures Séverine's fate at the end. There is also a strong semiotic thematic throughout the film supporting this primary psychodrama. Tom Conley points out in the chapter on this work in *Film Hieroglyphs*, for example, the framing of Lantier in front of a sign stating *fumeurs* (smoking), which he blocks out first to *[h]umeurs* (moods) and then *meurs* (die).

Not only is Lantier's dark violence offset by moments of tenderness with Séverine, it is counterbalanced by the scenes depicting the strength, courage and energy, the *camaraderie*, of the train workers, the *cheminots*. Lantier deserts this solidarity though when he allows Cabuche (played by Jean Renoir, who often like Hitchcock took a role in his films, although rarely as central as that of Octave in *La Règle du jeu*) to be arrested for a murder he did not commit. Lantier's isolation justifies but doesn't explain Renoir's rewriting of Zola's ending of Lantier and Pecqueux (Julien Carette) fighting and dying under the runaway train filled with drunken soldiers (ironically considered too controversial for an era when France was about to be defeated by Germany, just as in 1870).

In fact, Lantier's compulsive criminal behavior is enmeshed in a world where calculated crime abounds: the rich abuse the system; people seek the help of the influential to cover up their actions; the wealthy protective godfather figure Grandmorin (Jacques Berlioz) rapes and beats young women; Roubaud (Fernand Ledoux) and his wife Séverine (Simone Simon) brutally murder Grandmorin on the train; Lantier perjures himself to save them and condemns thusly an innocent fellow worker; Lantier tries to murder Roubaud and cannot, then turns on Séverine, as his psychosis overwhelms him. Lantier's downfall is triggered by his jealousy of Séverine's control and his helpless rage when she humiliates him. The serpentine ring that Grandmorin gave Séverine at sixteen in payment for sexually abusing her is only too appropriate; she is morally and psychically poisoned and becomes an agent of evil. There is an implication that Séverine may even be Grandmorin's daughter, adding incest to sexual abuse and further explaining her own dark murderous side.

Séverine is in fact depicted as controlling from the first shot, as she overlooks the switching yard from her window and cuddles a fluffy white kitten, indifferent to the attentions of Roubaud. And it is when beaten by the angry Roubaud who has confronted her about her relationship with Grandmorin that she decides to kill him. Roubaud dies a slow painful decline rather, rebuffed by Séverine, drinking and gambling, destroyed by the woman he loved just as she destroys the other men involved with her.

The six sequences of the trains in the film add up to six symbols of the tragic drama unfolding. At the end of a run on the Le Havre (symbolic lost "haven") –Paris express, Lantier's locomotive that he has christened "Lison" (a personalized "beast") has symbolically "seized up," setting off a chain of events while "she" is being repaired. The reference to *la boîte cuite* (the cooked box) of the locomotive is at once a rather overt sexual allusion and a cerebral symbol of the severe schizo-phrenic mental disorder within Lantier. Unable to live with his killer self in the end, Lantier will jump to his death from the very same engine.

The double equation of the train locomotive with virile sexuality and the path and forces of destiny creates both male and female sexual imagery. The passages through tunnels indicate twofold penetration, into darkness, mystery and death, and a symbolic return to the womb, to the origins of identity, to the evil which haunts Lantier. In the film, the tunnel can also be equated to the dark room and theater of the moviegoing experience, of film as a journey into the oneiric zones of the individual spectator's mind, as well as the depiction of collective phobias and desires.

The naming of characters in both the text and film is intriguing and creates subtle links between objects and people. For example, Lison is the engine of the murderer Lantier, and the innocent Cabuche, when wrongly arrested for murder, tells the story of the death of Lisette in his arms, a young girl who like Séverine was the victim of Grandmorin's perversity. It would seem that Renoir had an intertextual obsession with these Zolian names, as a woman named Louison was the heroine of *La Marseillaise*, and Lisette was the name of the maid in *La Règle du jeu*.

If Balzac anticipated the invention of photography in the visual documen-tation of his descriptions, Zola the photographer paralleled that of cinematography in the detail as well as the narrative structure of his novels. The intensely cinematic nature of his works seems to anticipate the capacity of the movie camera to bring to life the sweep and saga of whole generations. Not only was he a photographer, but as noted above he prepared and researched the settings and characterizations of his novels with meticulous attention to detail, much like a modern scientist in a labora-tory. And he included all the gorey details, however sordid. Yet this writer who was called an objective naturalist was a chronicler of grandiose human passions and epic events. He not only went to great lengths, riding a train locomotive in this case, as he had gone into the mines for *Germinal*, to document his writing, he risked his life politically with *J'accuse* in 1898 and went into exile in England for defending the Jewish officer Dreyfus, wrongly accused of treason in 1894 and finally pardoned in 1906. Ironically Zola died in 1902 a victim of modern technology, as he was accidentally (?) asphyxiated by a malfunctioning chimney stove.

Renoir's treatment of Zola, including his silent version of *Nana* in 1926, offers an intriguing comparison to that of Clément and Christian-Jaque, just as *La Bête humaine* adds to the collective image of Renoir films in this study, whose similarities are striking, including casting types, male-female relationships, vaude-ville or music hall sequences, patent symbolism, populist ethos. Although Renoir may not have initially chosen to adapt this Zola novel to the screen, it is his finest tribute to that member of this father's generation of artists in Paris. And although stylistically very different from the others, *La Bête humaine* is a major piece in Renoir's own cycle of his great films of the 1930s, including *Madame Bovary*, *Une Partie de campagne*, *La Grande Illusion*, *La Marseillaise* and *La Règle du jeu*.

Bibliography

(Please see the study on *Gervaise* for the general Zola bibliography and the study on *Madame Bovary* or *La Marseillaise* for the general Renoir bibliography).

Anzalone, John. "Sound/Tracks: Zola, Renoir and *La Bête humaine.*" *French Review* 62:4 (1989) 583–590.
Baran, James. "On the Track(s) of Desire in Zola's *La Bête humaine*: Riding the Rails with Jacques Lacan." *Degré Second* 10 (1986) 31–38.
Bonneau, Renée. '*La Bête humaine*', Zola. Paris: Hatier, 1986.
Boucher, James. *The Interdiegetic and Extradiegetic Look in Renoir's 'La Bête humaine'*. Dissertation Abstracts International 44:8 (1984) 2484A.
Ciment, Michel. "Entretien avec Jean Renoir (sur *La Bête humaine*)." *Positif* 173 (Sep 1975) 15–21.
Conley, Tom. *Film Hieroglyphs: Ruptures in Classical Cinema*. Minneapolis: University of Minnesota Press, 1991.
Faulkner, Christopher. "Renoir, Technology and Affect in *La Bête humaine.*" *Persistence of Vision* 12/13 (1996) 82–101.
Gauteur, Claude. "Renoir 'auteur de films' (à propos de *La Bête humaine*)." *Ecran* 31 (Dec 1974) 30–32.
_____. "Jean Renoir." *Image et Son* 315 (Mar 1977) 19–48.
Golsan, Katherine. "'Vous allez vous user les yeux': Renoir's Framing of *La Bête humaine.*" *The French Review* 73:1 (Oct 1999) 110–120.
Hamon, Philippe. "Je veux, donc ils doivent." In Parret, Ruprecht, Coquet, eds. *Exigences et perspectives de la sémiotique*. Amsterdam: Benjamins, 1985.
Kelly, Dorothy. "Gender, Metaphor, and Machine: *La Bête humaine.*" *French Literature Series* 16 (1989) 110–122.
Lagny, Michèle. "The Fleeing Gaze: Jean Renoir's *La Bête humaine* (1938)." In Hayward, Susan, and Ginette Vincendeau, eds. *French Film: Texts and Contexts*. New York: Routledge, 1990.
Leahy, James. "*La Bête humaine.*" *Monthly Film Bulletin* LVIII, 687 (Apr 1991) 117–118.
Léonard, Martine. "Photographie et littérature: Zola, Breton, Simon: Hommage à Roland Barthes." *Etudes Françaises* 18:3 (1983) 93–108.
Possot, André. "Thèmes et fantasmes de la machine dans *La Bête humaine.*" *Les Cahiers Naturalistes* 57 (1983) 104–115.
Reboul, Yves. "Renoir devant Zola: Le Scénario de *La Bête humaine.*" In Vignes, Sylvie and Ferrieu Cantaloube, eds. *Chemins ouverts*. Toulouse: Presses Universitaires du Mirail, 1998.
Robinson, Marian. "Zola and Monet: The Poetry of the Railway." *Journal of Modern Literature* 10:1 (1983) 55–70.
Singer, Robert. "Screening Murder: Zola's *La Bête humaine* and its Cinematic Adaptations." In *Excavatio* 6–7 (1995) 11–25.
Suleiman, Susan. "L'Engagement sublime: Zola comme archétype d'un mythe culturel." *Les*

Cahiers Naturalistes 67 (1993) 11–24.

Vincendeau, Ginette. "The Beast's Beauty: Jean Gabin, Maculinity and the French Hero." In Cook, Pam and Dodd, Philip. *Women and Film: A Sight and Sound Reader.* Philadelphia, PA: Temple University Press, 1993.

Viti, Robert. "The Cave, the Clock and the Railway: Primitive and Modern Time in *La Bête humaine.*" *Nineteenth-Century French Studies* 19:1 (1990) 110–121.

Un Amour de Swann
(Swann in Love)

directed by Volker Schlöndorff (1983)
novel by Marcel Proust (1907)

Numerous projects for filming Marcel Proust's epic *A la Recherche du Temps perdu* (*Remembrance of Things Past*—a formalist "RTP" translation of the French title that deforms its original meaning, "in search of lost time") have been undertaken and some abandoned over the years, including a Visconti film, a Joseph Losey production (for which Harold Pinter wrote the screenplay, published but never filmed), and the 1999 *Le Temps retrouvé*, Raoul Ruiz's more successful film of the last sections of the novel, with Emmanuelle Béart and Marcello Mazzarella. Most recently, Chantal Ackerman has filmed *La Captive* from the segment *La Prisonnière*. Proust's three-thousand-page work, published from 1907 to 1927, stands along with James Joyce's *Ulysses* as a lighthouse of twentieth-century fiction, depicting at once the panorama of Paris prewar society and the landscape of the mind, where the coordinates of time, space, memory and imagination create a dynamic of the self unrivaled in literature. Multiple narrative voices function through the collection of novels which comprise *La Recherche*. Externalizing and concretizing, realizing, reifing the interior monologue of much of the text, especially the critical sections of the beginning and the end, seems a physical impossibility, yet the temptation is there to exploit on film the oneiric dimensions of Proustian narrative.

Nicole Stéphane, who bought the film rights to *La Recherche* in 1962, also approached Truffaut, Malle, Resnais, and Clément, as well as Losey. Peter Brook accepted in 1982, decided to limit the film to *Un amour de Swann* and then dropped the project. It was passed to Volker Schlöndorff, the German filmmaker who had transposed numerous major novels to the screen, most recently Günter Grass's *The Tin Drum*. It would be unfair to refer to this project as *Schlöndorff's Way*, as Brook had already decided to limit the film to this one section framed by *Combray* and *Noms de pays: le nom*, all of which made up the first part of *La Recherche: Du Côté de chez Swann* (*Swann's Way*). Schlöndorff, who had studied filmmaking in Paris, worked in tandem with Stéphane and Jean-Claude Carrière on the partially completed screenplay, which already had its "day-in-the-life-of" format, inspired by the temporal closure of *Le Temps retrouvé*, the final section of *La Recherche*.

Although any film production is in essence a collaborative process, this project proved to be more a competitive effort. Schlöndorff termed the perfectly constructed sets by Jacques Saulnier and Philippe Turlure and the costumes by Yvonne Sassinot de Nesle symbolic and not documentary, yet they compete with dialogues and voice-overs for the diegetic focus of the film, externalizing and reifying the floating metaphoric imagery of Proust's text. And for a period piece, the film has oddly anachronistic inconsistencies, not the least of which is the musical score by Hans-Werner Henze, whose sound track, especially the Vinteuil sonata, clashed with many a spectator's auditory imagining from prior reading. More sensitive and successful in conveying the internal-external world dichotomy of Proust's work is Sven Nykvist's cinematography. His lighting and framing of the indoor sets creates a series of tableaux genre paintings redolent of Ver Meer or the Barbizon School. Like Monet following the changing shadows and tones of light through the day, he achieves oneiric effects appropriate for a film of Proust. Only in the final sequence of Madame Swann crossing the Carousel is there the feeling of intense primary daylight, metaphorically suitable as the harsh light of reality contrasting the inner shadows of the self.

Swann's tale is a third-person framed narrative recounting events that happened when the primary narrator of *Combray* was a child (what Genette calls heterodiegetic, as opposed to autodiegetic or autobiographic narrative). For this reason, this film is classed here with fictional works and not as an autobiographic novel. However, Swann's story (integrated into the earlier *Jean Santeuil*) is not an isolated tale within a tale, but through the metonymic overlay of the personae of Swann and the narrator functions as a dual *mise-en-abyme*, of both the texts framing it in *Du Côté de chez Swann* and the global corpus of *La Recherche*.

Schlöndorff's film, with its lavish social tableaux and sensuous boudoir encounters, seems in many ways more an echo of *Nana* (Zola and Clément) than of Proust's text and its odyssey of the imagination. Saulnier and Nesle's physical encapsulation of the world of *La Recherche* constitutes a betrayal of the imaging power of the text, also like the films of Zola's work. In this regard, the film is closer to imaging the work of the realist novelist C. of *Jean Santeuil* (and relies heavily on the earlier text) than that of the impressionist painter Elstir of *La Recherche*. Numerous devoted Proust critics have howled treason in response to the screenplay assembled by Peter Brook, Marie-Hélène Estienne, Stéphane, Carrière, and Schlöndorff, with its dramatization of Proustian dialogical exchanges and voice-overs of monological musings. And this is nothing next to the travesty of the dubbing, a problem in the French version as well, as Jeremy Irons's role, although spoken in French, was postsynchronized by a native speaker.

Yet sets and dialogue are redeemed by several elements which at a deeper level are actually very faithful to Proust. First of all the admixture of *Un amour de Swann* and the image of the Proustian narrator and Proust the historic figure has a fundamental truth documented by Proust: like the pearl in the oyster in *Jean Santeuil*, the story and presence of Swann in *La Recherche* are indeed embedded in the global text as a generative seed and *fil conducteur*, as ongoing intertextual metaphor and model, like the characters in the books the narrator avidly reads. The lack of transitional sequences and continuity in Schlöndorff's film can be seen to reflect the disjunctions of the self, *les intermittences du coeur*, so central to Proust's *écriture*. For all their overstuffed elaboration, the sets float in splendid isolation, like scenarios in a dream. Although not depicting the surrealist world of the early twentieth century, the film acknowledges the surreal spatio-temporal *téléscopage* of the self in Proust in the cut where Swann steps through thirty years in crossing the threshold of the Guermantes's salon.

For every weakness one can criticize in the film, there is a counterbalancing justification or achievement. The loudest shrieking has been in response to the casting, of an Englishman and an Italian, as Swann and Odette. Yet Jeremy Irons reveals the underlying ambitions of the film to superimpose on the substantial Jewish figure of Charles Swann the frail form of Proust's shadowy autobiographic narrator, an inner if not outer reflection of the person of Proust as well. The German Schlöndorff has been accused of fascist filmmaking in this dilution of the Jewish persona. Yet the baroque nature of Proust's text and the Romantic quality of its inner focalization led contemporary critics to characterize it at its publication as the most German French novel ever written. Ornella Muti as Odette has elicited even more outrage, as she openly admitted to never having read the Proust text. Yet conversely it could be said that this illiteracy and alienation from Swann/Proust's world, her fascination as an external object, is a perfect embodiment of the distance between him and Odette and the dilemma it posed. Proust in fact states that Odette gained access to his world through her esthetic physical resemblance to an Italian Renaissance work by Botticelli, an image which is faithfully presented at the beginning of the film. And the sensual esthetic of her nudity and her voluptuous narcissism and decadence capture almost in freeze frame the suffocating sensation of impossible desire of the self and other that is so integral to the Proustian ethos.

The compacting effect of the twenty-four-hour time frame of the film (excepting the epilogical ending), beginning and ending in bed with the Proustian authorial figure, could be criticized as an absurd reduction of the psychic and physical evolution of an entire generation achieved in the totality of *La Recherche*, yet Proust not only uses the same compaction of time in *Le Temps retrouvé* but his saga closes on its beginning, offering a spiral Dantesque journey into the mind through memory and metaphor rather than a realist chronological consequential tale. That is in fact the point of *La Recherche*: the equation between the journey through the salons, theaters, restaurants and boudoirs in search of appurtenance and the ideational quest of the Swedenborgian reality behind the physical.

What seems to be missing the most in the film, as with transpositions of Zola or Joyce, is the mythical dimension Proust infused into the most prosaic details of quotidian social and sexual existence. Like those Proust muses on in the succeding *Noms de pays: le nom*, the names he gives his characters, Swann and Odette, elicit images of Tchaikovsky's ballet of love and betrayal and delineate in *La Recherche* a fantasy fable transposed into Paris society. The extended metaphor of the catleyas constitutes the epicenter of heterosexual longing and desire in the hothouse world of *La Recherche*, just as the sonata and the privileged objects (the madeleine, the spoon, the napkin, the paving stone) elicit spontaneous conjunctions with the self through involuntary memory. These epiphanies are lost, transcendent evanescent expressions of pure subjective sensorial being that escape external imaging of even the most sensitive camera work. The transposition of these levels of narrative consciousness into film would generate a Durasian scenario of sound-image disjunctions and Robbe-Grilletian I/eye camera work, a modernist cinematic abstraction in collage. This film remains to be made.

The casting, however inaccurate or irresponsible, like the sets and costumes contributes to the esthetics of the film, an equivalence of a central Proustian thematic. Alain Delon as the Baron de Charlus, Fanny Ardant as the Duchess of Guermantes, Marie-Christine Barrault as Madame Verdurin, float among other beautiful people through salons, gardens, theaters, restaurants. The interreflecting harmony between these characters and environments is more equatable to a Balzacian habitat than to Proust's labyrinthine world full of menace. Rather than accusing Schlöndorff et al of commercialization of Proust, as Phil Powrie has done, one could find in these figures, chosen for the photogenic presence that made them cinematic icons, the filmic equivalent of the dominant Proustian esthetic. Schlöndorff wanted to cast *Un amour de Swann* with unknowns but had to turn to experienced screen actors and actresses for what he called the mythical dimension he sought.

Schlöndorff's writing of Proust is in response to his reading, a substitute, as he says, like all his literary adaptations, for the primary textual revelations of the self that original screenwriting would necessitate. The evocative nature of Proustian narrative and its attention to detail, its lyric nostalgia, mask a Sadian world of cruelty, suffering, exploitation and betrayal, the more powerful for the reader who accesses those experiences through the narrative veil of distancing focalization. It is not prudery or propriety propelling Proust but the processes of transposition that occur in the recording, remembering and reordering of experience in the text. Proustian writing represents a reordering of experiential sounds and images in dialogue and description just as the filmmaker seeks the means of reordering textual imagery in a second writing. As for all the works in this section, this double decoding deforms the external real, first into the symbolic of language and then through the film set to the sound and moving image offered the spectator. It is this preemptive gesture of fixed externalizing of images that limits the polysemic rereading of the psychological narrative exploration of the mind in language and leads to the spectator's sense of having been coopted by the filmmaker. Yet Schlöndorff claims he attempted to recreate the ulterior reality of Proustian *images*, the reality behind the visible, through cinematic images, to seek inside himself experiential echoes of Proust's narrative, stating that "Le temps et les lieux, leurs amours et les nôtres se confondent, le film devient le reflet d'un monde intérieur intemporel."[1]

Access to the world of high society is problematic for Swann, Odette, and the narrator of *La Recherche*, who seeks it in himself just as his characters pursue one another in social settings. Swann's world is imaged with the credits: his *garçonnière* habitat full of books, art and a moneycase, the sum of Charles Swann's own credits. They are the bourgeois collector's substitute for a life of creativity. The framing of these objects, equated in the epilogue to his life's experience in a display case, like all of Nykvist's work creates painterly compositions similar to those of Whistler or Sargent (represented in Proust's text by the character Elstir, whose name Carrière transposes to another role). There is also a fragmenting brutality in the framing of many shots emblematic of the Proustian disjunctions and amputations of the self in society, equatable to the framing of Degas's works.

The closed world of the Proust narrative is imaged in the opening shot of the film, where the valet François opens the windows, the curtains, as the play begins as a mid-day matinée. It focuses initially on Swann's passion for Odette, as the Proustian author figure pens a declaration of love for her, a text that would be better described as a scripted manifestation of a pathological obsession. The many textual sequences of remembering in Proust, after all the principle thematic of the work, are equated with flashbacks in the film, here to the famous catleya sequence in the carriage, punctuated with Odette's breathing, creating a sensorial close-up similar to the Proustian close focus on remembered experience.

Swann has much to sacrifice to the courtesan Odette de Crécy; his lengthy *toilette* in his elegant townhouse indicates his wealth and his material vanity, reflected in the mirror of his narcissistic passion. Swann's second flashback gives Odette access to the film as it did to his life at their first meeting, the memory of which is stimulated by the Botticelli medallion of Zéphora (Zipporah, daughter of Jethro), whose likeness in the Sistine Chapel Odette conjured first in Proust. The medallion more than the portrait comes from a funerary commemorative tradition, thus overlaying on the esthetic cultural intertext a connotation of the morbidity of his passion and its eventual doom at the end of a long process of masochistic suffering similar to that experience by the Comte de Muffat under the spell of Nana.

The first of several aristocratic tableaux depicts a concert at the Guermantes (the mirror path to Swann's way). The decadence of this frozen world is conveyed by the attentions lavished on the page boys at the door by the pederast Charlus, who also sadistically torments Swann by piquing his jealousy with descriptions of Odette's activities elsewhere. Thus description and the power of the imagination are presented as destructive, text and language as weapons. Charlus, like Swann and Odette, is closer to his persona in *Jean Santeuil* than to that of the later segments of *La Recherche*. He is mainly depicted as a figure in parallel to Swann; also rejected, by the young object of his homosexual passion, he becomes an understanding aging companion to the dying Swann.

Proust's characterization of the relationship to culture and art of the aristocratic circle of the Guermantes is represented by their reverence for the Debussy-like music and their material pride in a newly acquired Titian. The power to possess and consume, essentially a bourgeois trait, pervades the film and its characters' relationships. Foremost is Swann's desire to possess Odette as another *objet d'art* in his collection, which confronts her concomitant exploitation of him as a means of access to wealth and power. In a style echoing the Renaissance, the Guermantes combine their sensibilities with indifference to human weakness, revealed in their lack of concern for their dying cousin Gilbert, a cruelty which prefigures Swann's final ostracism.

Although far too elegantly beautiful for the average reader's image of Madame Cambremer, Marie-Christine Barrault offers an appropriately vulgar self-parody of the character whose name is a pun on the "mot de Cambronne" (*merde*) uttered by the eponymous French general. In the dubbed version, her name is pronounced wrong, without the final "r." In the Guermantes's salon, the static quality of the sets, camera work and disposition of the actors is thoroughly emblematic of the static society depicted. The influence on Swann of the music prefigures his later penetration by the Vinteuil sonata, with its associative power, accessing depths of affective being like the *mémoire involontaire*. A dripping candle finally blown out becomes a phallic metaphor for Swann's passion for Odette, which he however will neither satisfy nor extinguish. He will rather go on to compromise himself socially with his attachment to her and be ostracized for marrying her. Schlöndorff creates a populist vantage point in this aristocratic world with Swann's servants, the valet François and the coachman Rémi, not just caricatures for popular humor and comic relief. Their disrespectful conduct toward Swann's follies maintains an objective correlative for the spectator, of the prosaic reality which Proust places in contrast to the power of the imagination at the service of the libido.

During the sequence at the Bagatelle Pavilion, as Charlus lunches with a young friend Aimé (the Morel character in the book), a Jewish artist whom he is courting, he characterizes Paris as a segregated anti-Semitic society. Although Schlöndorff is depicting the era of the Dreyfus affair, he has been accused of anti-Semitism for his portrayal of the Jews in the film. Odette's long-awaited appearance has emphasized for the audience Swann's denial and frustrated desire. Lavishly attired in pink, "la dame en rose" presents herself as emblem of her own sexuality, consuming "something sinful." The extent and diversity of Odette's sexuality includes lesbian prostitution, the female popular counterpart of Charlus's inversion. In counterpoint to Swann's elegant demeanor and cultured intellect, as he talks of an article he is writing on Ver Meer (the summum painter for Proust), Odette arranges a professional lesbian assignation with a mysterious woman in black. All Swann's wealth and intelligence are for naught, however, as he compulsively pursues Odette into a milieu far beneath his natural habitat. Swann's public embrace of Odette belies his private anguish over his inability to control and possess her, sexually and socially; she flaunts her body publicly to all those gazing on her in the gardens just as she exhibits herself for the audience.

Proust's tale of the anguish of Swann's impossible desire is imaged in a series of exchanges between Swann and Odette at her house, executed in counterpoint.

These dialogues are drawn for the film from *Jean Santeuil* rather than *Un amour de Swann* for the greater immediacy of the Proustian narrator's presence in the figure of Swann. Swann functions as social, sexual and esthetic voyeur, as Odette first disrobes before him in front of her *psyché* full-length mirror, aided by her maid. Caressing her own body in an echo homage to the famous sequence from *Nana*, she sets up the second half of the equation begun with her mysterious business (her lesbian assignation). Her rumored liaison with Madame Verdurin continues the allusion to Nana and her paramour Satin. Odette's open avowal of prior lesbian involvements cripples Swann emotionally, as he rages helplessly, unable to control her past, present or future sexuality. He in a sense is a spectator within the film. Odette punishes his intrusive curiosity by denying him access to her body, dressing for her evening with the Verdurins at the opera. Oblivious to the irony of her situation, Odette complains of being treated like the prostitute she is, as she takes money from Swann. Although Stéphane was adamant that the screenwriters were transcribing literally Proust's dialogues, they have rather revealed a vulnerability of his writing by unframing these exchanges from their narrated contexts. Viewed only from the outside, these characters flatten into self-parody.

The admixture of scenes transported from other segments of *A la Recherche du Temps perdu* includes Swann's visit to the brothel as sleuth, an oedipal figure maniacally pursuing blinding truth. Once again he hears lurid details of Odette's other life. At his apartment, he attempts to reintegrate her into his vision of her, gazing at the medallion and dreaming metaphorically of the catleya scene in the carriage, possessing Odette only in his mind. Like Swann's disjunctions of the self, throughout the film the biggest problem is the rhythm of transitions in the editing, which Françoise Bonnot struggled with for six months. Swann's frantic search for Odette leads him to the café opposite the opera. As he will be later in the evening, he is barred from access to her and also to the past, as he gazes through the door of the café, recalling past happiness in the midst of present suffering, another Dantesque thematic interwoven throughout Proust. The scene of the Verdurins' private dinner at a nearby restaurant poses particular problems for the filmmaker, especially Dr. Cottard's description of the surface of a contemporary painting, crudely transposed from the more subtle original. In a 1983 cultural context, the background of mannered snobbery and refinement against which the vulgarity and ignorance of the Cottards and Verdurins is played out has disappeared. The irony is lost; former self-indulgence reduces to self-parody.

When the Vinteuil sonata is played, it arouses in Swann lyric feelings for Odette. He declares his enslavement in counterpoint to her indifference, as she acts out her part in this sadomasochistic fantasy by humiliating him and leaving with her escort Forcheville. Swann's monologue of demented desire accompanies his frustrated wandering through the streets, a mythical lost soul. His plight is belittled by the mocking response of his coachman. Swann's transformation to a pathetic *fana* plays itself out in alteration with Charlus's failure to seduce Aimé. It is Charlus who makes the metatextual comment that esthetic considerations are a mask for sexual desire, a concept driving the entire structure of the film if not of Proust's text.

The Dantesque allusion is continued as Swann recalls the catleya sequence while wandering in despair. The crucial voyeur scene from Proust's text has been modified, because the camera already serves the primary function. When Swann hears the voices and sees the shadows in what he thinks is Odette's bedroom, he climbs onto the balcony and bangs on the shutter. The occupants emerging to reveal that he has the wrong house turn to farce and embarrassment the poignant passage of the silhouette at the window, omitting the metatextual metaphor for both film and fiction, and the second image of Odette frozen in profile, sign of Swann's mistaking her identity in its entirety. It is also the emblem of the novelist, characterized by Henry James as a voyeur who watches at the window of the house of fiction. The film telescopes this poignant sequence with another, as Swann gains access to Odette through a ritualistic obstacle course: the sonata, the gift of a valuable necklace, the request for "orchids" and the eviction of the rival guarding her. Driven to madness, Swann is literally trapped into marriage with Odette by his debasing lust.

The next sequence brings the twenty-four-hour time frame of the film full circle, with Swann in bed again in mid-afternoon, receiving the Baron de Charlus. Swann claims to be cured of his obsession with Odette, proving it by financing her trip to Egypt with Forcheville and the Verdurins. The irony of his blind masochism is illustrated through the intertextual implied allusion to Cleopatra destroying Anthony. His decision to marry Odette has eclipsed his reason, as he converts the woman he cannot possess into a material possession. In his paranoid fantasy, he imagines the gathered society figures in the Guermantes's salon all rising to stare at him, anticipating his social suicide.

The film's telescoping of disparate elements widely scattered throughout Proust's work is especially obvious in the epilogue segments from many years later. This visual temporal compaction is effected as Swann in grey enters the same salon of his reverie, now empty, to call on the Guermantes. The Duchess, beguiling and impeccably polite, observes his declined health and invites him to accompany them to Italy, a privileged Proustian destination. His refusal and his blunt confession that he is dying equates the narrator's frailty in *La Recherche* as much as it symbolizes the unnourishing environment of his life with Odette. In spite of or because of his suffering, he is denied access to aristocratic circles, where his wife and daughter are not received. The earlier barriers to his sexual fulfillment have been expanded into impediments to his access to desired social circles which he can no longer penetrate.

The last sequence in epilogue of the film depicts Swann and Charlus as elderly gentlemen strolling the streets of Paris, appalled by changing styles, overrun by new automobiles. Into the setting of the end of *Du Côté de chez Swann* is introduced a major element of *La Recherche*: the equation between art and life, experience and memory or imagination. The friendship between Swann and Charlus and the parallels in their situation have been constructed for the film to compensate the deviance. Proustian nostalgia is reduced to comments regarding life's ambitions and the illusions of friendship, a poignant derisive admission of the void at the end of the search. Symbolically retreating into esthetic considerations, Swann reduces his past and his accumulated affective self to *objets d'art* in a display cabinet. This "literal" transposition of Proustian dialogue is followed by a betrayal of the closing focus of *Un amour de Swann* and of *La Recherche*, substituting for male monological musings a tracking shot of Odette as Madame Swann strolling by the Arch of the Carousel, her vain and tasteless beauty untouched by time or felt experience, still an object of pursuit. The version of the sonata by Henze, in the tradition of Debussy, Wagner and Mahler, continues in the dark at the end, its dissonant chords intended to shock, surprise and captivate the contemporary audience of the 1980s. It also reinforces the thematic of the caustic discontent and painful anguish that supposedly destroyed Swann's life.

The end of Swann's tale in Proust's text telescopes time affectively, as Swann acknowledges the "decrystallization" of his passion for Odette in a liberating distancing from his past obsession: "Dire que j'ai gâché des années de ma vie, que j'ai voulu mourir, que j'ai eu mon plus grand amour, pour une femme qui ne me plaisait pas, qui n'était pas mon genre."[2] Interestingly enough, Stéphane and Schlöndorff felt that they had to go through the same delyricizing, letting go of the Proust text, in order to reformulate a work they loved, in order to achieve an *envoûtement*, to cast a spell of their own.

Notes

1. Volker Schlöndorff, "A Propos de l'adaptation d'*Un Amour de Swann*," *Bulletin de la Société des Amis de Marcel Proust et des Amis de Combray* 34 (1984) 183. ("The time and the places, their loves and ours blend, the film becomes the reflection of an atemporal inner world." My translation.)
2. Marcel Proust, *A la Recherche du Temps perdu* I (Paris: Gallimard Pléiade, 1954) 382. ("To say that I wasted years of my life, that I wanted to die, that I had my greatest love, for a woman I didn't like, who wasn't my type." My translation.)

Bibliography

Auster, Al, and Leonard Quart. "The Limits of Journalism: An Interview with Volker Schlöndorff." *Cinéaste* 12:2 (1982) 47.
Bardèche, Maurice. *Marcel Proust romancier*. Paris: Les Sept Couleurs, 1971.
Blanchot, Maurice. *Le Livre à venir*. Paris: Gallimard, 1959.
Boon, Jean-Pierre. "Concentric Patterns in *Un Amour de Swann*." *Modern Language Studies* 17:3 (Summer 1987) 62–70.
Branch, Beverly. "The Art and Fallacy of Filmic Adaptation." In Radcliffe-Umstead, ed. *National Traditions in Motion Pictures*. Kent, OH: Kent State University, 1985.
Carrière, Jean-Claude."Débusquer les gens et les choses." *L'Avant-Scène Cinéma* 321–322 (1984) 11–17.
Carter, William. "Proust Cinémathèque: Visconti, Schlöndorff and Capri's *The Basileus Quartet*."

172   *Un Amour de Swann*

Proust Research Association Newsletter 25 (1986) 39–43.

Charles, Michel. "Proust d'un côté d'autre part." *Poétique* 59 (1984) 267–282.

Chessick, Richard. "The Search for the Authentic Self in Bergson and Proust." In Charney and Reppen, eds. *Psychoanalytic Approaches to Literature and Film.* Rutherford, NJ: Fairleigh-Dickinson University Press, 1987.

Costanzo, William. "The Persistence of Proust, the Resistance of Film." *Literature/Film Quarterly* 15:3 (1987) 169–174.

Dahmani, Fatiha. *"Mort à Venise* ou *Le Temps retrouvé* au cinéma." *Bulletin Marcel Proust* 51 (2001) 125–128.

Deleuze, Gilles. *Proust et les signes.* Paris: Presses Universitaires de France, 1971.

Doubrovsky, Serge. "Faire cattleya." *Poétique* 37 (1979) 111–125.

Genette, Gérard. "Proust palimpseste." *Figures* I. Paris: Seuil, 1966.

Genette, Gérard, and Tzvetan Todorov, eds. *Recherche de Proust.* Paris: Seuil, 1980.

Graham, Mark. "The Proust Screenplay: *Temps Perdu* for Harold Pinter?" *Literature/Film Quarterly* 10:1 (1982) 38-52 and *Film Criticism* 12 (1988) 38–51.

Haas, D. *"Un amour de Swann."* Découpage intégral après montage et texte du dialogue in extenso. *L'Avant-Scène Cinéma* 321–322 (1984) 33–89.

Ifri, Pascal. *"Le Temps retrouvé* de Raoul Ruiz ou le temps perdu au cinéma." *Bulletin Marcel Proust* 50 (2000) 166-175.

Jacquemet, Marco, and Jacques Fontanille. *Autour de la petite phrase de Vinteuil: Lecture sémiotique d' 'Un Amour de Swann'.* Limoges: Presses Universitaires Limoges, 1991.

Jousset, Philippe. "L'Eloquence muette ou ce que raconte la syntaxe." *Poétique* 22:85 (Feb 1991) 87–110.

Lang, Candace. "Jean est un autre/ Je n'est personne." *French Literature Series* 12 (1985) 114–121.

Lepine, Jacques-Jude. "Swann au derniers salons où l'on cause: les Stratégies de la dissimulation dans *Un Amour de Swann.*" *Dalhousie French Studies* 35 (Summer 1996) 33–44.

Miguet, Marie. "Un Film mal aimé: *Un Amour de Swann* de V. Schlöndorff." *Bulletin de la Société des Amis de Marcel Proust et des Amis de Combray* 35 (1985) 350–362.

Milly, Jean. "La Jalousie de Swann." *Magazine Littéraire* 350 (Jan 1997) 64–66.

Moore, Gene. "The Absent Narrator of Proust's *Recherche.*" *The French Review* 57:5 (1984) 607–616.

Pasquale-Maguire, Thérèse. "Narrative Voices and Past Tenses in Novel and Film: Proust's *A la Recherche du Temps perdu* and the Pinter Screenplay." *Dissertation Abstracts International* 43: 4 (Oct 1982) 1139A–1140A.

Pauly, Rebecca. "Proust: de la bibliothèque au berceau." In *Le Berceau et la bibliothèque.* Stanford French and Italian Studies 62. Saratoga, CA: Anma Libri, 1989.

Penkert, Sybille. "Volker Schlöndorff's 'Eine Liebe von Swann'." *CICIM* 30–32 (1991) 297–306.

Powrie, Phil. "Marketing History: *Swann in Love.*" *Film Criticism* 12:3 (1988) 33–45.

————. "Sexuality in *Swann in Love.*" *French Cultural Studies* 1:3:3 (Oct 1990) 247–256.

Reyns, Christian. *"Un Amour de Swann,* ou un Cygne/Signe peut en cacher un autre." *Tropos* 22:1 (Spring 1996) 37–50.

Saraydar, Alma. *Proust disciple de Stendhal: les avant-textes d'"Un amour de Swann' dans 'Jean Santeuil'.* Paris: Lettres Modernes, 1980.

Schlöndorff, Volker. "A Propos de l'adaptation d'*Un Amour de Swann.*" *Bulletin de la Société des Amis de Marcel Proust et des Amis de Combray* 34 (1984) 178–191.

Stéphane, Nicole. "La longue marche." *L'Avant-Scène Cinéma* 321–322 (1984) 5–10.

Thomas, Chantal. "L'Allée Marcel Proust." *Poétique* 63 (1985) 301–311.

Jean de Florette

directed by Claude Berri (1986)
novel by Marcel Pagnol (1963)

Claude Berri was filming in Marrakesh, Morocco, when he chanced to read Marcel Pagnol's 1963 double novel *L'Eau des collines* (*The Water from the Hills*). Pagnol had decided to write a novel from his 1952 movie *La Manon des Sources* (*Manon of the Spring*) wherein he had adapted an old Provençal legend into a star vehicle for his beautiful blond blue-eyed wife, Jacqueline Bouvier (no relation to Jackie Onassis). What was intriguing about Pagnol's literary project was his decision to add a "prequel" section, to create another tale focusing rather on Manon's hunchback father, *Jean de Florette*. Much of the background—settings, characters, and events—of the double text comes from experiences during Pagnol's childhood vacations in the hills above La Treille, recounted in his series of *Souvenirs d'enfance* (*Memories of Childhood*), particularly *La Gloire de mon père* (*My Father's Glory*) and *Le Château de ma mère* (*My Mother's Castle*), filmed in 1991 by Yves Robert.

Paradoxically truer to the voice of *L'Eau des collines* than Pagnol's own earlier film, Berri's resulting two productions are an exquisitely painterly saga of family tragedy and betrayal, of village and farm life in the hills of Provence in the early twentieth century. Back in the 1930s, Pagnol had pioneered in developing authentic movie sets, constructing outdoor location shooting sites specific to his story line, using a local mason to build instant ruined or abandoned buildings. Like Pagnol, Berri shot on location around Pagnol's native village of Aubagne, working with the cinematographer Bruno Nuytten.

Berri's films are linguistically as well as pictorially a richly textured portrait of local color, thanks not only to the participation of many local denizens, but to an unbelievably internalized portrayal of César Soubeyran by the late Marseilles-born Yves Montand, acting for the first time with his own native Midi accent, to Daniel Auteuil's brilliant role as Ugolin, and to the incarnation of Jean and Aimée by husband and wife Gérard and Elisabeth Depardieu. The role of Jean de Florette also brought Depardieu back to his origins in a sense, as he grew up in *la France profonde* (the heartland) in a large working-class family.

Pagnol had of course presented major theatrical works in Paris which incorporated heavy Midi accents and dialectical oddities (*Marius, Fanny, César*, all performed on stage and screen). In her chapter on the trilogy in *French Film: Texts and Contexts*, Ginette Vincendeau traces the interactive evolution of the trilogy from the screen adaptation of *Marius* to the original screenplay of *César* later presented on live stage. Pagnol himself spoke Provençal back in an era when it was forbidden to speak it in school; he had a strong background in Latin as well and in fact translated Virgil professionally. There was much satiric and parodic response to Pagnol's regional comedies, whose accents and "Pagnolades" became known throughout France in the early days of sound film. In spite of the considerable success of his numerous Provençal films, many adapted from works by Jean Giono, Pagnol was still vulnerable to criticism of his incarnation of the Midi in his 1952 film of *Manon des Sources*. In fact, his wife Jacqueline was chastised for portraying Manon too much as an Antigone figure and not enough as the Provençal magic fairy Esterelle, sprite of the hills. This was somewhat ironic, considering her Nîmes upbringing and the fact that she had actually worked as a shepherdess in the Camargue as a young girl.

It was in fact a work by Emile Zola, *Naïs Micoulin*, which brought Marcel and Jacqueline Pagnol together right after World War II. Zola's tale offered central models for the thematic of *Jean de Florette* and *Manon des Sources* (the latter of which was of course first conceived as a filmscript in 1952). In *Naïs Micoulin* are the mirror images of the plot of *Jean de Florette* and *Manon des Sources*: a rich peasant family attempting to establish itself in local society (like the Soubeyrans in *L'Eau des collines*) employs a beautiful young woman, Naïs, whose father is killed while attempting to avenge her loss of honor at the hands of Frédéric, the peasants' wayward son. The story also features a hunchback character named Toine who sets traps in the hills and leads a dissolute existence with Frédéric in local bars. Zola's influence on *Jean de Florette* is acknowledged in both Pagnol's texts and Berri's film in a reference to the setting's similarity to the "Paradou de Zola."

Pagnol and his wife had two children they named Frédéric and Estelle, echoes of two dominant influences on his creative production: 1) the Provençal poet Frédéric Mistral (1830-1914) whose lyric works (including *Mireille*, made into an opera by Gounod in 1864, and *Calendal*, a sentimental tale of the Camargue) made him a heroic figure and earned him a Nobel Prize, and 2) Esterelle, the aforementioned legendary female goddess of the hills. Pagnol never adapted Mistral to stage or screen, but his works reveal myriad influences of the poet's voice, as well as those of other writers like Daudet. Another film project Pagnol never realized was entitled *Premier amour*, a sort of *Guerre du feu* (*Quest for Fire*) set in southern France.

L'Eau des collines is much more than popular entertainment; the regionalism extends to a botanical, biological and meteorological depiction of great accuracy and attention to detail. Pagnol infuses the roles of the educated characters—Jean, Manon, Bernard, the rural engineer—with his own documentation of the natural phenomena of the region. At the same time, he creates dozens of peasant and village characters with vivid superstitions and traditional wisdom and lore who are nevertheless subjected to the irony of their own ignorance. The novels are woven from a variety of tales and genres, including several intertextual allusions to Pagnol's own former works, in characters named Marius and César and a hero who is a school-teacher. In Pagnol's earlier trilogy, César is the grandfather of the child whose real father has sailed away and then returned for him. The onomastics of *L'Eau des collines* are fascinating. Other names of characters offer historic allusions to ancient Ligurean tribal lore: Clarius, Pamphile, Philoxène, Aristolène. It is not perhaps a coincidence that the tribe was conquered by the Romans, represented by Marius and César. César in fact conquers Romarins in *Jean de Florette*. In counterpart to the pagan names for the evil characters, there is a network of biblical names of the positive figures: Giuseppe (Joseph) and Battistina (Baptistine), Jean and by allusion Olivier.

Pagnol's writing and filmmaking have both been criticized over the years as too popular and simplistic; his extensive borrowing and adapting are well documented here. But the resulting texts are as much a reflection of the diversity of influences in southern France over the centuries on different cultural levels as they are a facile reworking of prior tales. And the elements of nature can be truly said to be raised to the level of primary characters, both as personalities and as dramatic functions. In a saga of the primal elements of air (wind), earth, water and fire, Pagnol includes elements of ancient Greek myth and fable, Provençal lore, witch-craft, tribal ritual and rivalry, and Mediterranean Catholicism. A study of the two texts and films reveals an intricate reworking in collage of the learned legends and experiences of Pagnol's life in Provence.

The two tales are framed, at beginning and end, by the rivalry and revealed interrelationship between two powerful families from Bastides Blanches: the Camoins and the Soubeyrans. The natural setting and the village power structure are from the beginning emblematic of the storyline: the setting is rugged, the hills steep, the "roads to heaven" difficult, the mountain spring all-important for survival and agriculture in this arid landscape. Locusts and droughts echo ancient biblical plagues; the scirocco (hot dry dusty wind) blowing out of Africa nearly kills Jean with heat stroke. The avaricious bury their gold in pots under the hearth and look after themselves; this is a Darwinian world of delicate balance. The forces of good and evil vie for the souls and lives of the inhabitants. We learn at the beginning that César Soubeyran has no heirs other than his nephew Ugolin, orphaned partly by his father's suicide, and thus marked by the family curse of madness, condemned to a role which he will act out at the end of the second film.

The structure of *L'Eau des collines* and of the Berri films is impeccable; the initial return of Ugolin prefigures Jean's arrival. The opening murder and funeral scenes both have echoes in major events. Marius Camoins, known as Pique-Bouffigue, looks out from Romarins, framed in a window, and dies, as will Jean, Ugolin, and César. Jean and Ugolin form a parallel in contrast, both pursuing rabbits, both with secret plans and ambitions, both coveting and working the land, sharing the wine, the water, the tools. Even in his hypocrisy, Ugolin is drawn to this distorted mirror of himself. But from beginning to end Manon fears and loathes

Ugolin, her higher powers of instinct reading the evil in him. Throughout the two films there are a series of voyeur scenes, where characters spy on one another unseen, like secret hidden cameras intruding into one another's lives. At the death of Pique-Bouffigue are two more prefigurations: the tall clock at Romarins is stopped for the first of three corpses in that room, and the loaded gun accompanying Pique-Bouffigue in the funeral procession, aimed backward at the cortège of villagers, announces future killings, of game and humans, as well as the revenge from beyond the grave (there is a parallel sequence in the novel of the death of Giuseppe and his reburial).

The thematic of *Jean de Florette* is based on flowers; the flowering of the tale and the characters is inscribed in their names and trades. It is possible that the whole tale was inspired by the colloquial expression *conter fleurette* meaning to court a lover. Jean's mother, the beautiful headstrong Florette Camoins, captured César's heart and broke it through an accident of fate, a letter he never received while stationed in Africa in the army, a rupture that precipitated the family split and the entire plot. Florette and César constitute an ironic tragic echo of the broken parentage of Fanny and Marius. Pagnol was himself drafted in 1914 and then discharged from the army for frail health. In another floral thematic, César's nephew Ugolin, just returned from army service, has decided to become a wholesale florist, to grow carnations which bring big money in the city markets. Carnations in French are *oeillets*, little eyes, thus making the flowers themselves metaphors for the visual function, voyeurs. In addition, Jean de Florette hides his hump under an urbane flower-patterned vest.

When Ugolin and César murder Pique-Bouffigue (who has already lost his innocence by murdering an intrusive poacher), the owner of the Romarins property, the equilibrium is destroyed and the stage is set for the unfolding tragedy. The day she inherits Romarins, Marius's sister Florette dies without receiving in her turn the letter from César asking to buy the property. Her son Jean Cadoret inherits instead, a tax collector from the city, full of ideas and lacking in experience, and comes with his family to live at Romarins. Because of his marked status of having a father from an enemy village, Crespin, and being a *citadin*, he is repudiated by the inhabitants of Bastides Blanches, who never tell him of the murderous vandalism of Ugolin and César, who stop up the spring on his property in order to starve him out. In their blind greed, the last of the Soubeyrans unknowingly capture their own relative in their trap, as they watch with sadistic satisfaction his struggle to survive against all odds.

Pagnol has inverted a number of real places and names in transposing them into his tale. He also borrowed several locales and plot elements from the works of Jean Giono, particularly *Colline* and *Regain*. When Pagnol was eight, his family bought a country property by the name of Bastide Neuve near the village of La Treille, which becomes Romarins near Bastides Blanches. When they moved in, they transported their furniture up the rough road in an open wooden cart, a sequence from *La Gloire de mon père* which becomes one of the most striking scenes in *Jean de Florette*. Pagnol spent all his summers climbing in the rocky hills above their property, exploring caves and secret springs, or down in the village watching the games of *boules*; his father was in fact the local *pétanque* champion. Joseph Pagnol was, along with his brother-in-law Jules, the model for many aspects of the character Jean Cadoret. Pagnol's tales of his childhood explorations have the tone of the *Fables* of La Fontaine, a textual source of inspiration which could be construed as the verbal equivalent (literally in French) of the fountain bringing water from the spring.

La Treille had a rocky, dusty main street lined with stucco houses, a small church, and a fountain with a copper pipe in the center of the only town square. Hunting and trapping (never called by their real name of poaching) in the hills served as sport for the local men. There were however strict unwritten rules regarding resetting traps and great pride in bagging particular rare birds (not an ecology-minded society, obviously). The grotto at Plantier was real; in fact Pagnol as a rebellious teenager threatened to leave home and live there (Plantier was Mistral's term for a hermit). The last two works in Pagnol's autobiographical tetralogy, *Le Temps des secrets* (*The Time of Secrets*) and *Le Temps des amours* (*The Time of Love*), furnished material for *Topaze* and other plays about school.

It is easy to understand how Pagnol, born at the time cinema was invented, would transpose to the screen throughout his career the elements of his adventures in the hills. The first cinema in the area was called the *Palais de Cristal* (the crystal palace) and was lined with mirrors and modern lighting, the perfect setting for reflecting the local lore and legendary tales adapted by writers like Pagnol and Jean Giono (*Colline* and *Un de Baumugnes* 1929, filmed by Pagnol in 1934 as *Angèle*, and *Regain* 1930, Pagnol film 1937). From the rowdy waterfront society of the fishermen and dockworkers of Marseilles in his early comedic melodramatic trilogy, Pagnol moved through Giono's influence to the severe, dark, suicidal Provence of the hinterlands. Other influences among local writers include the work of Justinien Baille, who was born in the village of Les Camoins in 1902 and who wrote *Le Secret du puisatier* (*The Welldigger's Secret*). The obsession with water in this arid land generates the primal thematic of all these tales; Pagnol made *La Fille du puisatier* (*The Welldigger's Daughter*) starring Josette Day in 1940.

Jean, Aimée and Manon (played by Ernestine Mauzurowna in *Jean de Florette*) represent the mythmakers, the romantics who enoble the primitive enterprise of survival on the land and ancient traditions of cultivation. There is even a metatextual comment in the film that Jean de Florette would be a nice title for a song or a comic opera. In their bucolic idyll they sing and dance, unbelieving in their growing misfortune as first the well runs dry, then a drought forces them to Herculean labors of hauling water (redolent also of Sisyphus), and finally Jean is killed while digging a new well. As he digs into the earth in search of his life source and power (like Ugolin and César revealing and then reopening the spring at Romarins, like Manon and later Bernard at the grotto spring), Jean communes on bread and wine, a last supper as he digs his own grave, a biblical allusion that will be inverted by Ugolin's "baptism" at the end, making a connection through flowers to the carnivalesque inversion of Mardi Gras.

Jean's death is prefigured by that of the Italian woodcutter Giuseppe, who lived with his wife Baptistine at the shepherd's cottage at Plantier on Jean's property. The family get their water from the spring at Plantier, and it is there that the devastated Manon, in the novel accompanied by her mother Aimée, goes to live after Jean dies. Both Jean and Giuseppe are struck down by nature, by objects falling from the sky, Giuseppe by a tree and Jean by a rock, as he is finally ensnared by the evil Soubeyrans, who have loaned him money personally against the value of his farm and enabled him to buy tools and dynamite to dig his well, abetting his failing health and alcoholism. The sequence of dynamiting the well is anchored in Pagnol's childhood adventures of preparing the guns for hunting at Bastide Neuve.

Aimée's artistic temperament is ill-suited to the rigors of country life, but she proves loyal and hardy. Manon grows up in nature, becoming very close to Baptistine after Giuseppe's death. Not only do Baptistine and Jean have marked biblical names, but when Manon gives birth to a son Jean on Christmas morning at the end of *Manon des Sources*, the tale receives its final element as a story of Christian martyrdom, of the suffering of the innocent cripple at the hands of the savage, evil, primitive villagers.

The name for Manon comes from the opera role that the soprano Aimée sang (in *Manon* by Massenet, 1884, although Puccini also wrote a *Manon Lescaut* in 1893, both based on the 1731 novel by the Abbé Prévost, in whose house in The Hague Massenet wrote his opera). However, Prévost's *Manon Lescaut* is almost an inversion of Pagnol's *Manon des Sources* (played in Berri's film by Emmanuelle Béart, who in real life was married to Daniel Auteuil). Both are lyric figures, outside society, impoverished romantic heroines, admired and loved by a handsome young suitor (the Chevalier des Grieux and Bernard). Prévost's Manon is like Ugolin obsessed by greed and dies in the desert, and Massenet's Manon is endlessly torn between suitors and fathers, whereas Pagnol's Manon is a mystical being, a goddess of the hills, of the springs, a wood and water nymph, a wild child who hunts and gathers in nature with ease and who has extraordinary powers of perception and physical strength. Pagnol wanted in fact to write the *Memoirs of Manon Lescaut* to update the Prévost work.

It is hard not to also find a reworking of Victor Hugo's 1830 classic *Notre Dame de Paris* (*The Hunchback of Notre-Dame*) in a tale of a struggling hunchback which has a good-hearted gypsy and a beautiful young woman loved by a bestial figure. There is even an echo of the author in Ugolin's name. The stunning musical thematic of the films is taken not from the *Manon* operas of either Massenet or Puccini, but from Giuseppi Verdi's 1862 *La Forza del destino* (*The Force of Destiny*), much more a reworking of *Le Cid* or *Hernani*, which Verdi also adapted into an opera. There is in this opera one thematic similarity, of the letter not delivered on the battlefield to the errant lover, the same tragic barrier that separated César and Florette. *La Forza del destino* has heavier, more ominously tragic music than either *Manon*. What is intriguing historically is the fact that not only was there also a Verdi opera featuring a cripple (*Rigoletto*), but both Puccini and Massenet abandoned projects to adapt Hugo's *Notre Dame de Paris* into opera. Massenet also wrote an opera of Cinderella, another fabular figure woven into *L'Eau des collines*. When Jean and later Manon play the theme on the harmonica, they are also alluding to the villagers in exile in *Regain*, the pariahs sent into the hills with their tongues cut out who communicated by playing harmonicas. And at some points in the score of *Jean de Florette*, as when Jean takes his produce and rabbits to market or upon his mysterious arrival at the village, there are double echoes of *Le Retour de Martin Guerre* (of the 1982 film with Gérard Depardieu and the ancient southern French legend based on a true story).

There are other literary allusions, like that to Maupassant in the tale of Aimée's necklace, which she secretly pawns as they near bankruptcy, only to discover that the emeralds are fake, and that to Daudet and Bizet in the reference to the Arlésiennes. The family also create a sustained image of the Holy Family in flight in their multiple trips with their little donkey to Plantier to get water. And when Ugolin flees rather than loan Jean his mule, Pagnol creates an inversion of the biblical palimpsest in his text.

As stated, nature dominates both tales of *L'Eau des collines*. The seasons mark the rites of passage: Jean turns up in March and dies in November. Ugolin later hangs himself from the olive tree where Manon had her swing as a child, the tree under which he and César murdered Pique-Bouffigue. And Manon is saved by the teacher hero Bernard Olivier (olive tree) at the end. The figure of Bernard is an amalgam of the experience of Pagnol and his father Joseph, who both began their careers as village schoolteachers, and of Pagnol's own childhood persona. Pagnol's first teaching job was in the village of Digne, in remote rugged country, long before his assignment to the Collège de Tarascon that served as the model of the Pension Muche in *Topaze*.

Storms, rain, wind, torrents, moonlight, hot sun are all described in detail in *L'Eau des collines*. Every bush, flower and herb figures repeatedly, as well as a dozen varieties of trees. Rock outcroppings are described by the narrator and four different characters. The nature of the water itself is analyzed, and the red silt which flows into the village storage basin. Only at the end of *Manon des Sources* do intelligent innocent characters triumph over evil ignorant locals, whom they have made to suffer deprivation in turn. In *Jean de Florette*, the suffering of Jean's plants and animals from the heat and the drought also prefigures his own sunstroke and later death.

In opposition to the purity of the water, the primary male characters all consume massive quantities of local wine, three times a day and on special occasions, and the "nonbelievers" hang around the local bar drinking pastis or pernod mixed with the springwater (substituted for the deadly absinthe outlawed in 1915, whose ceremonious consumption and noxious effects Pagnol had observed firsthand in his friend Isabelle's addicted father). There is perhaps an implicit condemnation of his own heritage in his characterization, as Pagnol's father Joseph was an avowed nonbeliever and his Uncle Jules given to drink. It was however Jules who encouraged family attendance at midnight mass in La Treille during their Christmas holidays at Bastide Neuve. The powerful negative influence of alcohol on Jean is the most poignant, prompting a slow suicide of desperation while blunting his psychic and physical pain.

The end of *Jean de Florette* is an act of dual transgression that will not go unpunished: César baptizes Ugolin "King of the Carnations" in the dead Jean's spring, in a carnivalesque parody, profaning both the church and nature simultaneously. Manon's cry of anguish as she watches Ugolin and César open the spring on her property sets the stage for her tale in the second section. She like dozens of other characters is a voyeur (sequences of spying and secrecy in these works come from Pagnol's own childhood transgressions); in fact in these moments of secrecy, nearly everybody observes someone else at some point in the tale, mimicking the function of the camera itself in recording the story. Pagnol was obviously greatly influenced in writing the two tales by the experience of filming *Manon*. It would seem that his autobiographic works, begun in 1956, were also filtered by his cinematic experience. *L'Eau des collines* thus becomes a new genre, the aftertext (before the *ciné-roman*), the novel adaptation of a prior set of images and script, which as stated above was already a collage of adaptations. The visual precision and acuity of the filmmaking experience translates itself again and again in the texts in the profusion of precise details: of nature, of food and drink, of costume, of setting, of facial expression, thus creating a multiple layering of realism, from lived experience and textual models to script to screen to aftertext, wherein one can assume Pagnol indulged in reviewing both the landscapes of his youth and his imagination. Only Ugolin's secret musings in his hypocrisy offer the equivalent of a voice-over monologue, a technique which parallels his soliloquies to nature in the text and to the dead "Monsieur Jean" who haunts him so. Ugolin is without resources to combat the pain of guilt and loss, having denied in good peasant fashion his mourning at Jean's death: "Ce n'est pas moi qui pleure; c'est mes yeux" (I'm not crying; it's only my eyes). In the second half, Ugolin and Manon suffer equally their affective deprivation, as Manon the avenging daughter echoes the roles of previous Pagnol heroines, most of whom were seduced and abandoned.

Bibliography

Bernardo, Susan. "Conspiracies of Silence in *Jean de Florette* and *Manon of the Spring*." Conference on Film, Individualism and Community. Baltimore, MD: 21 March 1992.

Bertrand, Marc, ed. *Popular Traditions and Learned Culture in France: From the Sixteenth to the Twentieth Century*. Saratoga, CA: Anma Libri, 1985.

Beylie, Claude. *Marcel Pagnol ou le cinéma en liberté*. Paris: Editions Atlas Lherminier, 1986.

Bilodeau, François. "Ci-gît Jean de Florette." *Liberté* 171 (June 1987) 62–65.

Caldicott, C. E. J. *Marcel Pagnol*. Boston: Twayne, 1977.

Calmels, Don Norbert. *Rencontres avec Marcel Pagnol: Lettres manuscrites et photographies*.

Monte Carlo: Pastorelly, 1979.

Castans, Raymond. *Il était une fois...Marcel Pagnol*. Paris: Julliard, 1986.

————. *Marcel Pagnol*. Paris: Gallimard, 1988.

————. *Marcel Pagnol m'a raconté*. Paris: Folio, 1976.

Clébert, Jean-Paul. *La Provence de Pagnol*. Aix-en-Provence: Edisud, 1986.

Coward, David, ed. *Marcel Pagnol, L'Eau des collines: Jean de Florette and Manon des Sources*. Glasgow: University of Glasgow French & German Publications, 1990.

————. *Pagnol: La Gloire de mon père and Le Château de ma mère*. London: Grant & Cutler, 1992.

Daney, Serge. "Jean de Florette." *Libération* (28 August 1986).

Faulkner, Christopher. "René Clair, Marcel Pagnol and the Social Dimension of Speech." *Screen* 35:2 (Summer 1994) 157–170.

Frodon, Jean-Michel, et Jean-Claude Loiseau. *Jean de Florette: la folle aventure du film*. Paris: Herscher/Renn Productions, 1987.

Giono, Jean. *Colline*. Paris: Grasset, 1929.

Gossett, Philip, et al. *The New Grove Masters of Italian Opera*. New York: Norton, 1983.

Higgins, Lynn. "Pagnol and the Paradox of Frenchness." In Ungar and Conley, eds. *Identity Papers: Contested Nationhood in Twentieth-Century France*. Minneapolis: University of Minnesota Press, 1996.

Jathaul, S. "La Veine romantique chez Marcel Pagnol." *Panjab University Research Bulletin (Arts)* 17:2 (Oct 1986) 99–104.

Klotz, Roger. "Le Vocabulaire et le style de Marcel Pagnol dans *Jean de Florette*." *Marseille* 150:4 (1987) 54–57.

Mugnier, F. "Sources dans *L'Eau des Collines*." *LittéRéalité* 3:1 (Spring 1991) 73–81.

Nelson, Byron. "Some Unwritten Operas by Verdi, Puccini and Massenet." *West Virginia Philological Papers* 34 (1988) 51–61.

Pagnol, Marcel. *Le Château de ma mère*. Paris: Editions de Fallois, 1988.

————. *La Gloire de mon père*. Paris: Editions de Fallois, 1988.

————. *Jean de Florette*. Paris: Editions de Fallois, 1988.

————. *Manon des Sources*. Paris: Editions de Fallois, 1988.

————. *Le Temps des amours*. Paris: Editions de Fallois, 1988.

————. *Le Temps des secrets*. Paris: Editions de Fallois, 1988.

Powrie, Phil. "Configurations of Melodrama: Nostalgia and Hysteria in *Jean de Florette* and *Manon des Sources*." *French Studies* 46:3 (July 1992) 296–305.

Rostaing, Charles. "Marcel Pagnol: Etudes de stylistique et de langue." *La France Latine* 117 (1993).

Weaver, William. *The Golden Century of Italian Opera from Rossini to Puccini*. London: Thames & Hudson, 1980.

Manon des Sources
(Manon of the Spring)

directed by Claude Berri (1986)
novel by Marcel Pagnol (1963)

The English translation of this film as *Manon of the Spring*, like that of *The Bicycle Thief*, is a real betrayal of the essential bipolar structure of the plot. Just as there is more than one bicycle and thief (in Italian *Ladri di biciclette*), there is more than one spring. There are many: the springs on the map known to all in the valley, the spring at Romarins which Ugolin and César have just reopened, known to some, the spring at Plantier where Manon and Baptistine (and in the book Aimée) pursue a life of absolute rural simplicity and tranquillity. Above all there are the various small springs that Manon alone knows about, and the secret grotto spring that she discovers in this tale. This last spring is in fact one of the main characters in *Manon des Sources*, as it gives her power over the others, almost over nature itself, and tempts her to take revenge on her enemies in an unredeemed fashion.

From the beginning of this original "sequel" to *Jean de Florette*, Pagnol makes his reader aware of the reversal of the characters' fortunes from the first volume. In spite of the apparent triumph of Ugolin, he is tortured by guilt and talks to "Monsieur Jean" day and night. His symbolic uprooting of the ancient olive grove is another act of trespass against the spirits guarding the family heritage. There are four trees left; one of them, the one with the rings for Manon's swing, will be the instrument of death for Ugolin, just as it was the site of Marius's death. The turn of fortune for César and Ugolin is also announced by the villagers, who now that the Soubeyrans have taken control of Romarins are beginning to insinuate openly their criminality. César feigns feisty indifference, but Ugolin is obviously troubled by these insults.

In Pagnol's text, Manon and Aimée are installed in surrealistic splendor in the sheepfold (*la baume*, which calls to mind *le baume*, the tree, the balm which salves wounds) with their antique furniture. The curtain giving privacy to their beds ("qui s'ouvrait comme un rideau de théâtre italien"—which opened like an Italian theater curtain) serves as a dramatic stage set for the melodrama about to unfold. In this tale, Pagnol has also woven together many traditional folk and fable elements. Giuseppe's fellow woodsmen, Enzo and Giacomo, serve as protectors and guardians of the three women. Manon tends her flock near the old *sorbier* tree (her natural family tree), piping like Pan and talking to the animals, even feeding fresh milk to a lizard in a scene bordering on a sorcerer's fantasy. The association is not arbitrary; the origin of the term sorcerer goes back to the dowser or *sourcier*, thus connecting magic power and springs as the source of life. Pagnol actually had to hire a *sourcier* to find water to supply his crew while filming *Angèle*.

Manon seems to have many magic powers. Her dream of happiness, of finding a rich husband to give her a château in her beloved hills, is answered on the next page by the arrival of Bernard Olivier (who compensates the uprooted olive trees), the twenty-five-year-old teacher who will become her husband. This volume focuses much more on the villagers than the "prequel" does, and the reader learns through village gossip about Manon's life as a shepherdess, as they refer to her as "la fille des sources" (the girl of the springs) and sing her beauty, unaware of her eventual power over them that they are thus announcing.

Ugolin becomes an *avare* (miser) worthy of Molière as he avidly counts his accumulating wealth, then acts out an imaginary intrusion by a thief who is foiled by his sign advising that all his money is at the bank. Pagnol offers, in the letters and signs from Ugolin and César, the linguistic evidence of their ignorance, with phonetic spelling that is truly original. Ugolin, transgressor that he is, goes off to the hills out of season to poach game and track Manon. In a stunningly primitive sequence, used also in Berri's film, he spies on her bathing nude in a spring, like a goddess in her virgin purity. But Manon does not rely on her innocence to protect her; twice in this story Ugolin is wounded by a rock from her slingshot, another subtextual mythological image, evoking Diana, or David and Goliath. In his crazed passion for her, Ugolin gives himself a third wound from Manon, sewing her hair ribbon into the skin of his chest in an inversion of saintly masochism. The talisman objects of Florette and Manon held by César and Ugolin have their source in Pagnol's own childhood collection of sacred objects, including a silk ribbon from Isabelle that he found on the ground under her swing. In response to the verbal wounds Manon will eventually inflict on Ugolin, he commits his final self-mutilation by hanging.

The reader of Pagnol's *Souvenirs d'enfance* is struck by the number of elements of his childhood experiences that he has transposed to his fictional texts. In a sense, one can find all the "sources" of *L'Eau des collines* in the earlier volumes, written from 1956 to 1962: the elements of nature—rocks, grasses, trees, herbs, weather; the adventure of pursuit of local game and encounters with owls, lizards, hawks, hares; the secret grottos and passages; the contemporaneous characters of Lili the peasant boy and the beautiful Isabelle from Marseilles, who are blended in amalgam in Manon; descriptions of the wells and cisterns, the shabby peasant dwellings, La Baume where Baptistin lives, the peasant family of François and Lili, or the archetypal real-life character, Mond des Parpaillouns.

Ugolin's love for Manon and his generous gifts of game are all turned against him by fate. He is in a state of permanent disgrace, carrying the moral burden for the death of her adored father. Manon reads endlessly—at one point she is depicted reading *Robinson Crusoe* lying on her stomach in the grass—and has absorbed much knowledge. In contrast, Ugolin has only one book, of popular fairy tales, including several subtexts woven into Pagnol's story: *Little Red Riding Hood*, *Beauty and the Beast*, *Cinderella*, *Ricky*, stories Pagnol's grandfather told him as a child. But Ugolin is not an empowered villain; he doesn't eat Manon as a wolf but rather fears her like a dog, howling his lust and love from a distance. And he is never transformed into a prince; like the *limbert* lizard she mesmerizes, he remains a beast and dies a beast. The fancy clothes and Boudu-like transformation effectuated at the village tailor's do nothing to break the spell protecting Manon from her primal enemy. In a black magic ceremony where he surrounds her ribbon and hair with his gold, he symbolically attempts to control and possess her, to no avail.

It is Bernard the geologist who wins her, with his clever Swiss Army knife, shy manner and learned intellect. She trades him the rabbit Ugolin has left in her trap for the knife; the progenitor patriarchal force imaged by the large breeder rabbit Jean brought to Romarins is offered to Bernard in exchange for the empowering knife, tool, weapon, phallic and castrating symbol. Bernard in the text is a prince with his own fairy godmother, Magali, the maternal protective force accepted at once by the distrustful villagers. They eventually offer Manon and Bernard total acceptance and respect, even reverence and affection, and redeem themselves from their selfish complicity by betraying and repudiating Ugolin and César. They recognize goodness and virtue in their midst and honor it. They have also been weakened by Manon's singular act of vengeance and revenge (when she blocks the hidden spring and makes the town well go dry).

From this point, Berri's film is remarkably faithful to Pagnol's text. At the time when the locusts (cicadas) emerge from their old shell, Manon overhears two villagers, Pamphile and Cabridan, discussing the true story of the spring at Romarins and learns of the Soubeyrans' greed and murderous plot (all this time she has thought they discovered the spring after her father's death). She thinks of shooting Ugolin and decides on setting fire to Romarins, where he is now living, in a purifying holocaust of revenge, a baptism of fire. Nature interferes to protect her from her own evil, and a downpour extinguishes her arson, saving her ancestral home from her enraged rebellion.

Soon after, while pursuing an errant kid, she discovers the grotto with the secret source of Bastides's town water. Like a mythical intruder in the labyrinth, as she enters the grotto she lights candles and unrolls a ball of twine. Then like Narcissus and Echo merged into one, she contemplates her reflection in the sacred secret water. Having determined that the soil in the grotto is identical to that which silts up the town basin, she returns at night to seal the spring, becoming a force of nature. Adding to the sense of mystical powers at work in Pagnol's text is Baptistine's curse on the villagers for dumping Giuseppe's bones into a pauper's common grave, a malediction which is followed by the fountain gurgling dry before their eyes. The crazed villagers rebury Giuseppe with a full mass, to no effect. They call an engineer who assesses the problem in "words a kilometer long" and manages to accomplish nothing more than to deliver a truckload of water a day. The villagers begin to suffer Jean de Florette's fate, as their crops wither and die and they are deprived of the source of life itself.

The curé's impassioned sermon about punishment for a secret crime committed by certain individuals adds spiritual and moral damnation to the social condemnation Ugolin suffers. At the gathering at the school for Bernard's birthday drink, Manon rejects the repulsive Ugolin and accuses both him and César of being her father's assassins. In this fall from grace, Ugolin's own accursed heritage overpowers his remaining force and he leaves to go take his life, a final criminal act according to the Church. In his will, he accomplishes what he could not do in real life: he restores to Manon her rightful heritage and inheritance, as well as his own hoarded treasure. As César reads the farewell letter, we see his controlling empire starting to crumble.

In the most stunning sequence in either novel, whose striking sensuality is diminished in Berri's film, Bernard convinces Manon to return to the grotto and open the spring. As he wriggles painfully through the narrow rocky opening, Pagnol compares it to a birth, which is accompanied by the water of life, but it is also a powerful image of intercourse, of a sexual return to the womb, of penetration to the sources of life itself, an act which prefigures the end of the tale when they marry and Manon gives birth to their son. Bernard respects Manon's virgin purity that night however, in spite of the full moon and their mutually intense desire. He is stained only by the blood from his penetration of the cave.

The absence of water has disrupted the social structure of the village, in a perfect parallel to its destructive power over Jean de Florette's life at Romarins. All sorts of threats are suggested against Manon and Baptistine, including a reference to the ancient pagan ritual of sacrificing a virgin beauty to appease the forces of evil plaguing the community. It is suggested that the force of the plague, like that in Thebes, must be removed by exterminating the evil members from the community. When Bernard convinces Manon to redeem herself, all these menacing primal myth images are wiped away by the return of the water during the procession of St. Dominique and the conversion of the townspeople to believers. The gentle irony of the truth only adds to the poignancy of the miracle. Pagnol's mockery of the faithful and the Church goes back to the anticlericalism in his family, in the normal school background of his teacher father, and to his own youth influenced by the Jules Ferry generation.

In another miracle, in the text Victor Périssol turns up in response to Aimée's endless letters to him which have, like Florette's letter to César, gone astray, remaining unanswered. Victor and Aimée are reunited in a love duet from the opera *Manon*, and in a melodramatic ending worthy of the tale whose descendant the novel declares itself, Victor reveals his shepherd origins at a magical banquet at Plantier, as the mother and daughter are both rescued by heroic figures whom they will marry. In Berri's film, Aimée and Victor arrive by bus together to sing their duet at Manon and Bernard's wedding. Manon poses outdoors for her portrait as the village royalty, wearing a crown of orange blossoms (appropriately stolen by the eternally poaching villagers). In perfect counterpoint, César appears at the cemetery yard next to the church to put the last of the neglected carnations on Ugolin's grave. Pagnol has saved us one last *coup de théâtre*. The aunt of the fountainmaster named Ange (the life-giving guardian angel) turns up in town as an elderly blind widow. She is named Delphine, and like the ancient Greek oracle of Delphi, she reveals a profound and devastating truth to César: Florette was madly in love with him and pregnant with his child when he went off to Africa. Although Florette married a villager in Crespin, the hunchback child she bore was a Soubeyran, Jean de Florette. After this revelation, in a primal rite of passage, of exchange of one soul for another, César dies at exactly the moment Manon gives birth to a son, at dawn on Christmas morn, as all are redeemed, evil is purged and birth triumphs over death. The baby is of course baptized Jean.

The final benediction to this extended metaphoric ritual of baptism is César's closing letter to Manon, leaving all his wealth to her, telling her the truth of her heritage, and signing himself "Your Grandfather" (an identity which has been inscribed from the beginning in his nickname: Papet). César has suffered the greatest pain of all, in the revelation of his genocide. The sealing of the spring at Romarins has metaphorically sealed off his issue, leaving him only the sterility of his godless greed. The gift of earthly material riches can never redeem for him the suffering of his spiritual paucity, but the revelation of her Soubeyran heritage gives Manon full status as a villager of Bastides Blanches and completes the reversal of the equation, as she is integrated into the community in life while César and Ugolin are exiled in death.

Bibliography

Please see also the chapter on *Jean de Florette*.

Butler, Evelyn. "Jean Giono's Provence; Marcel Pagnol's Comic Vision." *Recovering Literature* 18:2 (Spring 1992) 39–43.

Gardies, René. "Vue du village: Vision du terroir dans *Jofroi* et *Manon des Sources* de Marcel Pagnol." In Joutard and Cousin, eds. *Images de la Provence: Les Représentations icono-graphiques de la fin du Moyen Age au milieu du Xxe Siècle*. Aix-en-Provence: Université de Provence, 1992.

Hull, Stephanie. "Women and Power in the Novel and the Film: The Case of Manon Lescaut." *Romance Languages Annual* 7 (1995) 78–84.

Mugnier, F. "Sources dans *L'Eau des Collines*." *LittéRéalité* 3:1 (Spring 1991) 73–81.

Reinhardt, Olaf. "Greek and other Sources in *Manon des Sources*." *Classical and Modern Literature* 18:1 (Fall 1997) 25–36.

Rostaing, Charles. "*Manon des Sources*, film de Marcel Pagnol (1953): Etude de langue." *La France Latine* 121 (1995) 57–72.

(Auto)biography on Film: Resituating the Self

There have been numerous French autobiographical narratives, fictional as well as authentic, which have been transposed into film, including such diverse works as the 1898 *Histoire d'une âme* (*Story of a Soul*) by Sainte Thérèse de Lisieux into the 1986 film *Thérèse* by Alain Cavalier, Georges Bernanos's 1936 *Journal d'un curé de campagne* (*Diary of a Country Priest*) into Robert Bresson's eponymous film (1950), Joseph Zobel's 1950 *La Rue Cases-Nègres* (*Black Shack Alley*) into Euzhan Palcy's 1983 *Rue Cases-Nègres* (*Sugarcane Alley*). There are also *Apostrophes*-style interviews that summarize a life and work, like Astruc and Contat's 1976 *Sartre par lui-même* (*Sartre by Himself*), "documentary" footage of personal experience, and retrospective summaries of a life, less dramatized in form than the above tales of childhood and monological diary-style narratives.

Perhaps the primary consideration in establishing an equation or accomplishing a transposition between an autodiegetic (first-person autobiographic) textual narrative and comparable cinematic sounds and image, cinematic time and space, as purveyors of the experiential referential illusion, is the problem of the objectification of experience by the film lens (the *objectif*), the exteriorization and incarnation of the imaginary internal literary autobiographic persona. One of the most successful strategies, employed by numerous directors since the late 1940s (beginning with Jean-Pierre Melville's 1948 *Le Silence de la mer, The Silence of the Sea*), is the attempt to reconstruct this internal subjective autobiographic voice, to return it to the abstraction of the printed text, of the reader's imagination, through the use of the voice-over narrative. Robert Bresson's treatment of Georges Bernanos's *Journal d'un curé de campagne* stands as a landmark, even a benchmark, in French cinema (treated over the years by André Bazin and numerous other critics: Dudley Andrew, Roy Armes, Michel Estève, Ellen Feldman, Valérie Raoul, Keith Reader). It is recognized for having achieved the equivalent diverse focalization of the entity writing the diary, a narrative consciousness which in the text has a five-fold function: monological (meditation), retrospective (anecdotes from the past), conative (prayer), dialogical (reported conversations), and self-reflexive (considerations of production of the text). At one point in the film, the voice-over functions in counterpoint to the dialogue portrayed between the curé d'Ambricourt and the curé de Torcy, as the narrator's mind wanders from the topic under discussion.

Perhaps Bresson's greatest achievement was to find the equivalent cinematic markers for the relationship between the diarist's self and its inscription in the text recording prior or anticipated events and the reflections they elicit. The diarist, everyone knows, attempts to reduce the distance between lived experience and its textual recreation through the abstract encoding and mediation of signs. Some diarist authors like Gide and Colette actually wrote in front of a mirror, seeking the visceral equivalent of the image in the text, in the *Miroirs d'encre* (mirrors of ink), as Michel Beaujour depicts the written reflections of the self. Beaujour, Béatrice Didier, Gérard Genette, Eric Marty, Valérie Raoul and Jean Rousset among others have attempted to characterize the generic specificity of diarist narrative. They seem to agree that such texts float between the close-focus self-reflexive mirror of the self and the empty abstraction of a text *sans destinataire* (without a recipient) where there is no accommodation for the implied reader. There is a certain suicidal quality to the diary, as the self is transposed into a fictional character, a narrative that never closes the gap between consciousness and the word, an asymptotic folly which swallows both life and text in a narcissistic pool of ink.

The suicidal depression of Bernanos's curé and his concomitant paranoia make him a perfect persona for transposition to the screen. The doubling of his inner and outer being, so often in conflict in his self-doubting anguish, is captured by the external screen image of Claude Laydu played off against the voice-over narrative. The fragmenting effect of discrete sequences lacking narrative transitions is the cinematic evidence of what Eric Marty, writing on Gide, characterizes as the absence of Cartesian linear logic in the diary narrative. It lacks the cause and effect illusion of retrospective autobiographic narrative which structures the self like a character in a realist novel, a self which coalesces at the end as a cumulative effect of synthesizing memory. Although he is a Catholic priest, the curé wanders from one confrontation to another like an alienated existentialist hero. He is unable in both text and film to construct a coherent self, to define himself according to the meaning of his relationships and experiences. Truly a lost soul, he refuses himself internally and externally, failing both in his role as village priest and as author. Like Roland Barthes's 1975 fragmented autobiographic portrait, the curé's diary leaves to the reader the task of constructing the whole man, who in this case is incapable of confronting life in its totality until he abandons himself to death.

A more recent film, *Thérèse*, adapted by Alain Cavalier from the letters of Sainte Thérèse de Lisieux, offers a series of externalized portraits of the diarist in her Carmel. Cavalier like Bresson avoids imposing the sequential transitions common to the cinematic realist canon on her disconnected and discontinuous text, actually three separate texts conjoined posthumously by her elder sister. It is a different version of a life refused, though; it is rather her transcendent state of grace that distances Thérèse from the consequential events of lived experience. It was Thérèse in fact who uttered the curé's famous last line, "Tout est grâce," which Bernanos copied from her. Both films depict the text as object just as they incarnate the narrative voice as a character. In both, the diary too becomes a character, invaded and transformed by the drama of the narrator's struggle. And both diaries, like all autobiographic narratives, lie unfinished, as death denies textual closure of the self.

Another classic subgenre of autobiographic narrative which has been frequently transposed to the screen is that of tales of childhood. In the last few years they have come from all over the world: *My Life as a Dog, Hope and Glory, Stand by Me, Fanny and Alexander, Au Revoir, les enfants, Rue Cases-Nègres, La Gloire de mon père, Le Château de ma mère*. If we include François Truffaut's sensitive depictions of children and his own childhood, *Les Quatre Cents Coups (The 400 Blows), L'Argent de poche (Small Change), La Petite Voleuse (The Little Thief)*, a pattern emerges from these films. The problem of externalizing the self in projecting it on the screen is not as acute as it is for the subjective autobiographic narrative of the diary text, for these are retrospective tales, and the spatialization of the self in memory and imagination demands a construction of the self as character. Writers who begin life again as a textual being inevitably impose on their persona other models than their image-memories of lived experience. History intervenes and contextualizes the tale from an adult perspective. Or the adult narrative voice imposes its complexity on the child character, infusing it with intervening experiences, reversing life and shaping the adult into the child. Certain autobiographers of childhood tales manage to infuse their narrative with a Flaubertian *style indirect libre*, notably Jules Vallès with *L'Enfant*. It contrasts strongly with Nathalie Sarraute's adult perspective in her *Enfance*, where she inscribes the reverse of the diary: such a great distance separates her from her child self that the narrator and character are two different people. This impossible distance and exile is of course the stuff of Proust's *A la Recherche du Temps perdu*, wherein the voluntary memory which coherently and calculatedly reconstructs the past fails to elicit the reunion with the self offered by the flashes of involuntary memory of the madeleine, the spoon, the pavement, and the napkin. The section of *La Recherche* just treated, *Un amour de Swann*, really does not figure in this discussion, as it is a heterodiegetic framed tale isolated from *Du Côté de chez Swann*, even though it is a structural *mise-en-abyme* of the latter. It is hoped that some filmmaker will one day treat the Proustian childhood images of *Combray* and *Noms de pays: le nom*, using a screenplay like Harold Pinter's.

Joseph Zobel's reminiscences of his childhood in the black shack alley of Martinique are sensitive depictions of his anxieties, fears and dreams, and he manages to find the link between the child's voice and the grown man's narration. His verbal precocity as a child lends itself well to the sophisticated descriptive passages penned by the adult. In the film *Rue Cases-Nègres*, there are first-person voice-over passages which frame the central tale, and passages read aloud from compositions by the young José. The one that earned him the accusation of plagiarism in the film is taken directly from the Zobel text. It is the powerful sequence (quoted in full in the chapter on *Rue Cases-Nègres*) expressing Zobel's hatred for the canefields which for him were killing fields, taking first Médouze and then M'man Tine. Much of Zobel's Creole dialogue of the village children has also been recreated in the film, with all its spontaneity and vitality, but in general Palcy restructured and reworked much of the text to suit her cinematic priorities, unlike Bresson's faithful lifting intact of numerous passages of the Bernanos text.

Perhaps François Truffaut most completely exploited the cinematic medium as an expression of the self. The memorial issue of *Les Cahiers du Cinéma* bore the title *Le Roman de Truffaut* (the novel of Truffaut—both "by" and "about") for good reason. Certain of Truffaut's films are more overtly autobiographic than others, especially the Antoine Doinel series, where Jean-Pierre Léaud serves as Truffaut's surrogate persona in five films covering twenty years, three of which are discussed in the final section of this study. Léaud also creates a Balzacian illusion of the intertextual reality of his own life alongside the Doinel character. It is said that Léaud has in fact been a lost soul since Truffaut's death, having identified with him and his work for so long.

Truffaut's autobiographic cinema takes many forms. The tales of his childhood and youth, from his unhappy homelife and adolescent escapades in *Les Quatre Cents Coups*, to his early love in *Baisers volés* (*Stolen Kisses*) and married adventures and continuing pursuit of self and other in *L'Amour en fuite* (*Love on the Run*) twenty years later, all bear the novelist's stamp. This is not just the author with his distinctive personal style of cinematic writing of auteur cinema (a term coined originally in 1939 by one of Truffaut's idols, Jean Renoir). It is much more: the enshrining of the creative self as a modern-day Balzac, burning with artistic zeal and yearning for freedom of expression as much as for oneness with a woman. Truffaut like Balzac lives inside and outside his textual/cinematic diegesis, both enunciator and enunciated, narrator (director) and character. If we include Truffaut's participation in *Close Encounters of the Third Kind*, acting for fellow director Steven Spielberg, and his portrayal of the frenetic filmmaker of *La Nuit américaine* (*Day for Night*) or the morbid journalist of *La Chambre verte* (*The Green Room*, adapted in collage from three Henry James tales), his work begins to form a film autobiography even more complete than a life story or the image offered by self-reflexive films like Fellini's *8 1/2*.

The subjective nature of Truffaut's filmmaking pervades all of its generic variants, whether memories of youth restaged, transposed to the image of Jean-Pierre Léaud, or images of himself as director, writer or actor. What is intriguing in Truffaut's case is the extent to which he includes in his intertextual autobiographic persona images of himself modeled on literary antecedents (authoring like Balzac or James, reading Balzac's works and living them simultaneously) or cinematic homages, not only in his two books on Hitchcock but in his citational screenplay for Godard's *A bout de souffle* (*Breathless*) and his adaptation of both the American detective story and film in *Vivement dimanche* (*Confidentially Yours*). Truffaut retained a childlike wonder and fascination for his heroes even as a master filmmaker in his prime. It is in the total corpus of his work that he has left us his autobiography, simultaneously transparent and self-reflexive, revelatory of the man and the artist, at once awkward and sophisticated, timid and bold, always spontaneous. Like a great sketch which reveals more than the finished painting, Truffaut's films allow the spectator to observe the process as much as the product; he is everpresent in his work.

Unfortunately, on film this presence contradicts the internal focus of the autobiographic voice, converting it inevitably to biography, objectifying it literally with the camera, like the video on Sartre whose very title, *Sartre par lui-même*, is a contradiction in terms. Perhaps in the last analysis, it is rather the oneiric subjective cinematic narrative of a filmmaker like Alain Robbe-Grillet with its "I/eye" approach which offers the true cinematic equivalent of autobiographic narrative. Robbe-Grillet's films compare to his novels or his trilogy *Romanesques* (which includes the *nouvelle* (new) autobiography texts *Le Miroir qui revient, Angélique ou l'enchantement* and the novel *Les Derniers Jours de Corinthe*). His films have the same problematic fragmented time and space which constitute not a cold objective recording of the aleatory details of life but the lived expression of the artist's conscience, strategies, and more importantly, obsessions. Perhaps it is this experimental cinematic and literary corpus that best represents the self, not a retrospective illusion of causality and coherent identity, but an open polysemic creative energy constantly restructuring the self from the vast domain of recombinant signs, images and sounds, of both textual and cinematic language.

All these diverse incarnations of subjective narrative together constitute the autobiographic voice in film. But rather than the image, whose referent is the Sartrian *néant* (nothingness), the filmic text represents experience, lived and felt, inside and outside the linguistic sign and its referent. The films mentioned in this introduction are treated individually in the remaining sections of the book. A chronological study of these works can be constructed from the table of contents.

Bibliography

Abbott, H. Porter. *Diary Fiction: Writing as Action*. Ithaca: Cornell University Press, 1984.

Arana, Victoria. "'The Line down the Middle' in Autobiography: Critical Implications of the Quest for the Self." In Crook, Eugene, ed. *Fearful Symmetry: Doubles and Doubling in Literature and Film*. Tallahassee: University Press of Florida, 1982.

—————. "Metonymy and Psychological Realism in Autobiography." In James, Joann and Cloonan, William, eds. *Apocalyptic Visions Past and Present*. Tallahassee: Florida State University Press, 1988.

L'Autobiographie. *Poétique* 56 (1983). Entire issue.

L'Autoportrait. *Corps Ecrit* 5 (1983). Presses Universitaires de France.

L'Autoreprésentation: le texte et ses miroirs. *Texte* 1 (1982). Entire issue.

Beaujour, Michel. "Autobiographie et autoportrait." *Poétique* 32 (1977) 442–458.

—————. *Miroirs d'encre*. Paris: Seuil, 1980.

Le Biographique. *Poétique* 63 (1985). Entire issue.

Bourdieu, Pierre. "L'Illusion biographique." *Actes de la Recherche en Sciences Sociales* 62–63 (1986) 69–72.

Bruss, Elisabeth W. *Autobiographical Acts: The Changing Situation of a Literary Genre*. Baltimore: Johns Hopkins University Press, 1976.

Carver, Mary Heather. *Autobiography in Performance: Cinematic Representations of Women's Lives*. Dissertation Abstracts International 60:9 (March 2000).

Coe, Richard. *When the Grass was Taller: Autobiography and the Experience of Childhood*. New Haven: Yale University Press, 1984.

Dällenbach, Lucien. *Le Récit spéculaire*. Paris: Seuil, 1977.

Didier, Béatrice. *Le Journal intime*. Paris: Presses Universitaires de France, 1975.

Dubois, Philippe; Kirby, Lynne, trans. "Photography Mise-en-Film: Autobiographical (Hi)stories and Psychic Apparatuses." In Petro, Patrice. *Fugitive Images: From Photography to Video*. Bloomington: Indiana University Press, 1995.

Eakin, Paul. *Fictions in Autobiography*. Princeton: Princeton University Press, 1985.

Ecriture et altérité. Poétique 53 (1983). Entire issue.

Egan, Susanna. *Patterns of Experience in Autobiography.* Chapel Hill: University of North Carolina Press, 1984.

————. "Encounters in Camera: Autobiography as Interaction." *Modern Fiction Studies* 40:3 (Fall 1994) 593-618.

————. *Mirror Talk: Genres of Crisis in Contemporary Autobiography.* Chapel Hill: University of North Carolina Press, 1999.

Elbaz, Robert. *The Changing Nature of the Self: A Critical Study of the Autobiographic Discourse.* London: Croom Helm, 1988.

Gabara, Rachel. *Je de miroirs: French and Francophone Autobiography from Split to Screened Selves.* Dissertation Abstracts International 61:10 (April 2001).

Genette, Gérard. *Figures III.* Paris: Seuil, 1972.

Gunn, Janet. *Autobiography: Toward a Poetics of Experience.* Philadelphia: University of Pennsylvania Press, 1982.

Hutcheon, Linda. *Narcissistic Narrative: the Metafictional Paradox.* Waterloo: W. L. University Press, 1980.

Jay, Paul. *Being in the Text.* Ithaca: Cornell University Press, 1984.

Jost, François. "Le Je à la recherche de son identité." *Poétique* 24 (1975) 479–488.

Katz, John S., ed. *Autobiography: Film/Video/Photography.* Toronto: Art Gallery of Ontario, 1978.

Lavery, David. "Autobiography and Film: Introduction." *Post-Script* 6:2 (Winter 1987) 12-76.

Lejeune, Philippe. *L'Autobiographie en France.* Paris: Colin, 1971.

————. *Je est un autre.* Paris: Seuil, 1980.

————. *Le Pacte autobiographique.* Paris: Seuil, 1975.

————. "Le Pacte autobiographique (bis)." *Poétique* 56 (1983) 416–434.

————. *On Autobiography.* Minneapolis: University of Minnesota Press, 1988.

Levasseur, Audrey. "Film and Video Self-Biographies." *Biography* 23:1 (Winter 2000) 176-192.

Marty, Eric. "L'Ecriture journalière d'André Gide." *Poétique* 48 (1981) 459–478.

May, Georges. *L'Autobiographie.* Paris: Presses Universitaires de France, 1984.

Mesnil, Michel (Maurice Mourier). "Ecran d'encre." *Corps Ecrit* 12 (1985) 95–104.

Mehlman, Jeffrey. *A Structural Study of Autobiography.* Ithaca, N.Y.: Cornell University Press, 1974.

Olney, James. *Autobiography: Essays Theoretical and Critical.* Princeton: Princeton University Press, 1978.

Pauly, Rebecca M. *Le Berceau et la bibliothèque.* Stanford French and Italian Studies 62. Saratoga, CA: Anma Libri, 1989.

Pilling, John. *Autobiography and Imagination.* London: Routledge & Kegan Paul, 1981.

Prince, Gerald. *Narratology: The Form and Functioning of Narrative.* New York: Mouton, 1982.

Raoul, Valérie. *The French Fictional Journal.* Toronto: University of Toronto Press, 1980.

Renza, Louis. "The Veto of Imagination: A Theory of Autobiography." *New Literary History* 9:1 (1977) 1–26.

Ricardou, Jean. *Problèmes du nouveau roman.* Paris: Seuil, 1967.

Ricoeur, Paul. *Temps et récit* I. Paris: Seuil, 1983.

Rousset, Jean. *Narcisse romancier.* Paris: Corti, 1973.

————. "Le journal intime, texte sans destinataire?" *Poétique* 56 (1983) 435–443.

Spengemann, William. *The Forms of Autobiography: Episodes in the History of a Literary Genre.* New Haven: Yale University Press, 1980.

Ungar, Steven and Conley, Tom, eds. *Identity Papers: Contested Nationhood in Twentieth-Century France.* Minneapolis: University of Minnesota Press, 1996.

Waldman, Diane, and Walker, Janet, eds. *Feminism and Documentary.* Minneapolis: University of Minnesota Press, 1999.

Journal d'un curé de campagne
(Diary of a Country Priest)

directed by Robert Bresson (1950)
novel by Georges Bernanos (1936)

Georges Bernanos, 1888–1948, poet, playwright and novelist, represents for most critics and readers a rebellious, troubled soul, evoking the darker side of Catholicism, although he married an eponymous descendant of Jeanne d'Arc and had six children. Born in Paris, he lived a great deal of his life as an expatriot artist, on Majorca and in Brazil. His life could be summed up as a double crisis, in French a homonym: *crise de foi(e)*, a spiritual quest for salvation, for a modern humanist faith, and the long illness of the liver which finally killed him, in the midst of surgery at the American Hospital in Neuilly, on 5 July 1948.

One can only guess at the nature of his poetry, as his poems have been lost (although some of the more "poetic" or personal lyric passages of his novels and short stories invite speculation on the thematic of his actual poetic texts). In all his works, Bernanos expresses angst, pathos and irony that place him apart from the Christian humanist tradition, in many ways closer to the existentialists and their absurd universe. Bernanos's major works include *Sous le soleil de Satan* (1926), *L'Imposture* (1927), *La Joie* (1929), *Journal d'un curé de campagne* (1936), *Nouvelle Histoire de Mouchette* (1937), *Les Grands Cimetières sous la lune* (1938), *Monsieur Ouine* (1938) written in Brazil, *Lettre aux Anglais* (1942) from Rio de Janeiro, the screenplay *Dialogues des carmélites* (1949 posthumous publication in Paris), and his diary, *Les Enfants humiliés*, also published posthumously. Of the above works, a significant number have been transposed to film: *Journal d'un curé de campagne* and the short story *Mouchette*, both written on Majorca, in 1936 and 1937, were adapted by Robert Bresson in 1950 and 1967. *Sous le soleil de Satan* (*Under Satan's Sun*), originally adapted for television by Pierre Cardinal in 1970, was then directed by Maurice Pialat, who won the Golden Palm award at the 1987 Cannes Film Festival. A first attempt to film the *Dialogue des carmélites*, by Bruckberger and Agostini, occurred in 1960. The second film of *Dialogues des carmélites* (originally written as a filmscript) appeared in 1985, directed by Cardinal for Antenne 2.

Bernanos set many of his novels in the landscape of Fressin around the Pas de Calais. Before World War I, he was a monarchist activist, feeling the nobility of the people and disgusted by the self-indulgence of the bourgeoisie. After his 1917 marriage, he and his numerous family struggled financially all their life together. As Bernanos died in 1948, he uttered "A nous deux maintenant" (to the two of us now), a Christian echo of the last line of Balzac's 1834 *Le Père Goriot* and a line he had written in *Journal d'un curé de campagne*. However, Bernanos's narrative persona goes against the stereotypical nature of Balzac's characters. He follows rather the tradition of the romantic individualist of the haunted heroes of Dostoevsky. It is this element perhaps that gives his work a lasting modern quality, in spite of archaic settings and language, and which has generated the numerous reworkings on film.

In the Proust-Joyce-Svevo tradition, Bernanos loses himself in his characters, infusing the narrative voice with the subjective stream of consciousness of interior monologue. Even when engaged in dialogue, as in *Journal d'un curé de campagne*, his characters often continue their inner narrative, in counterpoint to their external ex- changes with others. All his characters are unique creatures, often priests. His narrative style is rather naturalistic, but contains a poetic of the supernatural, imbued with mystery and mysticism. His avowed goal was to "imposer au lecteur un lien passionnel avec une expérience qu'il ignore" (to force on the reader an impassioned attachment to an experience he has not had).

In *Journal d'un curé de campagne*, the work which concerns us here, there is a sort of paragrammatic distribution of Bernanos's conscience among all the characters, as in a dream. The reader encounters in succession the inner voice of the curé d'Ambricourt, the *intimiste* writer-hero, and that of the curé de Torcy, whose words are quoted directly in Ambricourt's diary. In the supernatural, oneiric tone of the diary, one finds a narrative immediacy of the fantastic, which often draws on the Bible as its literary model. At the same time, this nocturnal transfiguration is equatable as mentioned to the experience of the anguished contemporary existentialist hero: Meursault, Roquentin, Joseph K. There is as well an echo of the spiritually tormented heroes of Claudel and of the pastor's ironic narrative in André Gide's unfinished pastoral symphony of 1919, *La Symphonie pastorale* (whose ambiguous title reflects as does Bernanos's work a lonely conscience more often associated with Protestantism and Calvinism).

The tale of *Journal d'un curé de campagne* could be summed up as a struggle between good and evil for the soul of modern society. The *ennui* or *angst* of the narrator is comparable to the cancer which is devouring him and which also symbolizes the spiritual cancer destroying his parishioners. His physical and spiritual revulsion before the world, his double anguish, is most similar to that of a contemporary fictional autobiographic writing narrator, under construction since 1931: Roquentin of Sartre's *La Nausée*, finally published in 1938. Bernanos's main character is bound to the Word as a priest, but even more so as a writer. Each day he relives the experience of transpos- ing his life into text, of transcribing the social drama he observes into the theater of the imagination.

Robert Bresson's long and distinguished career as a director includes the following: *Les Anges du péché* (1943), *Les Dames du Bois de Boulogne* (1945) (Cocteau screenplay), *Journal d'un curé de campagne* (1950), *Un Condamné à mort s'est échappé* (1956), *Pickpocket* (1959), *Le Procès de Jeanne d'Arc* (1962), *Au hasard Balthazar* (1966), *Mouchette* (1967), *Une Femme douce* (1969), *Quatre Nuits d'un rêveur* (1971), *Lancelot du lac* (1974), *Le Diable probablement* (1977), *L'Argent* (1983). Bresson's affinities for Bernanos can be seen in the titles of all his films, not just the adaptations of his works. Cocteau called Bresson a poet; he is just that, with the camera and the pen. He wrote the screenplay of *Journal d'un curé de campagne* himself, after rejecting the Aurenche and Bost and Bruckberger versions as too liberal adaptations of the essence of the Bernanos text.

In the transposition of this tale to the movie screen, Bresson faced major challenges (treated by many subsequent critics, initially André Bazin). The first was how to translate the irony generated by the naïveté of the narrative voice, with its limited, innocent, childlike, simple view of the world, how to recreate with the camera lens or film soundtrack such a subjective narrative. No less important was how to find the equivalent in screen time of the temporality of the textual narrative voice, with its present tense incorporating past and future aspects. There was also the problem of the depiction of the written text (already a transposition of letters, dialogues, monologues) in the film, as object and as *récit* (tale or story).

Bresson achieved finally an extended moral dialogue, with the self and others, like Eric Rohmer in *Ma Nuit chez Maud* (*My Night at Maud's*) or Louis Malle in *My Dinner with André*. Bernanos had already expressed through his narrator the problem of the distance between consciousness and writing: "Je ne puis réussir encore à comprendre par quelle affreuse métamorphose les vies intérieures arrivent à ne donner d'elles-mêmes que cette espèce d'image schématique, indéchiffrable...."[1] Thus the distance between being and writing precedes and doubles that between the written text and the film image. And breaking up the written text are fragments, points of suspension, gaps, which mark the unspeakable. This was Bresson's most difficult challenge—to depict the unwritten: the space, the silence, the nothingness.

Inherent in the problems of transposing written diaries to the screen are certain fundamental generic constituents of the diary form that have been extensively studied.[2] Certain features which distinguish the intimist text, primarily the telescoping of the distance between the event recounted and the inscribing of that event on paper, contrast it with the retrospective focus of realist autobiographic narrative. In the diary, a textual present dominates; the writer attempts to reconcile the schizophrenic separation of the self in the narrative voice. Ironically, this results in a direct self-encounter in the mirror of the text, in narcissistic narrative, to use Linda Hutcheon's term, where the writer can drown in metatextual considerations of literary production and in self-reflexive as well as self-representational writing. Valérie Raoul applies these criteria directly to *Journal d'un curé de campagne* in her 1982 article in *Texte* 1 on the image of the priest as narcissist and his ambiguous reflections in the text.[3]

The stream-of-consciousness nature of the diary genre lends itself to metaphysical musings and can lead to a reductionary "I write, therefore I am." That "I" is not a whole entity but rather a series of fragments in a modernistic collage. Both Eric Marty and Michel Beaujour affirm that the diary's lack of retrospective denies it the linear

Cartesian causality inherent to classic narrative realism.[4] The diary records rather the arbitrary and aleatory nature of daily events. Lastly, the diary is seen by most critics as an attempt to forestall death, to reaffirm life in the daily recreation of the self on paper. All of these factors informed Bernanos's choice of the diary format.

In the mind of the curé, the drama of carnal passion, both desire and pain, is equated to the other kind of Christian passion: suffering and anguish. His dialogues with other characters and with God in prayer are filtered by the solitude and spiritual abandonment of the confessional monologue of the diary. The reader then becomes confessor and priest in turn. But the mirror of the narrator's inner conscience is tarnished. Literally, "la source est troublée" (the spring is disturbed) (153). Narcissus can't see his own real image in his text, no more than he can see his reflection in the other characters of the novel, who for him represent so many alternative destinies to his own.

Bernanos's text is rife with symbols and imagery, especially of death, but due to the inherent limitation of autobiographic narrative, it excludes the narrator's actual demise. In closure, the narration passes to the abbé Dufréty, a defrocked priest whose thus ironic spiritual curatorial function was announced in two letters at the beginning of the novel, and who describes his friend's death in a letter, a frame text added to the diary novel, wherein the narrative focus passes from the interior to the exterior.

Bresson reproduces the acts of narration with the voice-over and the acts of writing with the images of the curé writing in his diary, sequences which serve as transitions between dramatic scenes. The curé is played by Claude Laydu, chosen for his voice. Bresson's screenplay purifies the essence of the novel, enhances its central thematic of suffering and alienation. He creates a realist cinema that at certain points anticipates cinéma vérité, with the authentic ambiance of a village, the outdoor location shots, the understatement and restraint of the nonprofessional actors. There remains however the modernist component of the acts of production of the text and a double focus which exploits convention. Jean-Jacques Grunewald's music gives affective depth, and Léonce-Henry Burel's cinematography creates high contrast imagery, ironically through a technological limitation regarding the filmstock which actually contributed to the artistic success of the film. The use of nonprofessional actors (with the exception of the countess), as in the great Italian neorealist films of Rossellini and De Sica, lends a directness and simplicity to the film. Controlled absence of melodrama marks all Bresson's work; it is his auteur signature. At the end, the curé's death is frozen in eternity by a long fixed shot of an empty cross.

The spectator feels in the film the work of Bernanos as well, of the Catholic torn between mysticism and revolt, a work of anguish full of paradoxes (fantastical, realist and modernist at the same time). One feels in the cinematic writing of Bresson this same personal essence, this same psychological game of dominance played off against the main character, the same doubts, the same sense of powerlessness before one's destiny. However, in the unfolding of the film, there is a new chronology of sequences and consequences, of substitution, which creates its own order of causality, like that of the traditional linear narrative, which doesn't always express the experiential ethos of

Bernanos's diary voice.

This is antitheatrical cinema, offering a play of light and shadow, a frozen cinematic portrait, not a melodramatic tale, but simply the superimposition of sound and image (even in disjunction), wherein the dialogue, the sound, is secondary to the image, the visual. The force and the depth of the main character is not his acting ability, but rather his strength to not act, to let us intuit an order beneath his surface disorder (Gaston Bachelard: "le réel, c'est le dessous"—reality is what is underneath), his final strength before certain death which gives him grace.

Dudley Andrew, Roy Armes, André Bazin, Bert Cardullo, Michel Estève, Ellen Feldman, Valérie Raoul, and Keith Reader have all pondered the equation in *Journal d'un curé de campagne* between the original text and its role in the film.[5] I would like to reexamine here the ways in which Bresson dealt with the images and functions of the diary: the diary as object, the reification of letters and dialogues, the acts of production of text as image, the *ratures* (erasures) of *litté-rature*, the *pentimenti*, the blanks of the limits of the text, and the avatars of the diary narrative—monological commentary of theological reflection and anguish of crisis of faith in solitude; confessional dialogue, where the text becomes the father confessor as the curé seeks absolution and grace through the written word; prayer, wherein the curé addresses God directly in his text; metatextual self-reflexive considerations, where the curé writes of the problems of writing, of the difficulties inherent to his project, of the necessity of textual production of the diary as a salutory purgative enterprise.

In all these passages in the written text, the reader is privy to the innermost limits of the conscious word in the character of the curé. Yet paradoxically, the reader must, as a complex consciousness distanced from the narrator's simplicity, judge the curé and ironize his text, and thereby be excluded from the privileged closed circle of writer-reader of the diary genre. This objectification of a subjective narrative is imaged for the spectator in the film by its transpositions of both the "opaque" considerations of the acts of writing and the "transparent" recording of events and conversations. The sequences where the text becomes a pretext, where the curé recounts to the diary (which then functions itself as an implied reader) events which transpire in his daily life, are dramatized directly in the film. The retrospective narrative of the Bernanos diary, which gives a causal-sequential depth to the text and the character of the curé (a perspective usually lacking in the closed temporality of diary-writing), is omitted from the film rather than included as flashbacks, giving it the static-present quality so many critics have noted.

The direct discourse dialogue which portrays the encounters between the curé and the other principal characters—the curé de Torcy, the count, Mademoiselle Louise, Mademoiselle Chantal, Dr. Delbende, the countess, Séraphita, the Chanoine, Olivier, Dr. Laville, Dufréty and his companion—is unframed in the film, as these scenes are enacted directly. In one sequence, however, the voice-over narrative expresses the unspoken thoughts of the curé, thus returning to the monological format, in counterpoint with the dialogical situation.

The epistolary function in the curé's diary is integral to the narrative structure of the Bernanos novel, and to the dynamics of the film plot as well. Two letters from the curé to Dufréty at the beginning of the text (omitted from the film) signal the latter's role as final spiritual caretaker of the curé and prefigure in mirrored textual symmetry the final letter of the book from Dufréty, which as epilogue to the life of the priest is not truly part of his diary, yet serves as a textual benediction and crosses beyond death, the aforementioned impassable boundary of the autobiographic narrative voice. This naturally is portrayed in the film as a separate entity, as are all the letters become objects, and the voice-over passes accordingly to a different character.

The anonymous letter, identified as the textual production of Mademoiselle Louise, the count's lover, functions also as both narrative shifter and object. In the film it is found with the hymnal/missal, which offers a comparison of her handwriting in ironically spiritual notes. Thus juxtaposed, they announce her hypocrisy. Chantal's letter of hatred to her father, unopened and unread, goes into the fire, prefiguring the scene where the countess throws the medallion portrait of her dead son into the fire, in both cases a purifying fire countering the forces of evil. The countess's letter to the curé which he refuses to reveal to the chanoine or the count to save his reputation is, like Dufréty's final epistle, a benediction of grace and salvation, not to be subverted to political ends. The other important letter alluded to in the diary text remains unwritten, as the curé's pen refuses to take dictation from the chanoine, to serve an alien will.

Thus logically the varied forms of the text of the diary, descriptions, letters, conversations, all become images in the film. The battered diary with its school-boy lined pages overflows with crossed-out passages, marginal comments, ink spots, blank spaces. As a literary homage, Bresson chose a metatextual self-reflexive passage about the purpose of the diary for the opening sequence of his film. Bernanos begins with a description of the parish, exploiting the transparent function of the fictional diary. In the film, the accompanying voice-over narrative not only establishes a meditative internal focus which the viewer must share, it also creates a double identity for the text as visual object/image and spoken word, what Bert Cardullo calls "narrative trebling" in an article in *Hudson Review* 40 (1987) 127.

Bresson exploits the versatility of the voice-over; sometimes it reads the note-book, sometimes it accompanies the actual production of the text word for word, sometimes as mentioned above it represents the curé's inner thoughts during a dialogical exchange, as his mind wanders or his speech contradicts his feelings. And as oratory, as meditation, the curé's voice-over has an incantatory quality which compensates for the cutting from the film of all the scenes depicting the curé actually ministering to his parishioners. The film ends for the diary with the pen sliding off the line and the page, a jagged downward mark mimetic of the tragic fate of the diarist. Like the cheap red wine and bread he subsists on, the ink and paper of the diary become symbolic elements of the host whose transubstantiation of the body to the text is effected through the spiritual power of the word.

Notes

1. Georges Bernanos, *Journal d'un curé de campagne* (Paris: Plon, 1974) 113. ("I still cannot manage to understand by what horrid metamorphosis inner lives manage to give of themselves only a sort of obscure schematic image...." My translation.) Further references to this edition appear in parentheses after the quotes.

2. Porter Abbott, *Diary Fiction: Writing as Action* (Ithaca: Cornell University Press, 1984); Béatrice Didier, *Le Journal intime* (Paris: Presses Universitaires de France, 1975); Gérard Genette, "Le Journal, l'antijournal," *Poétique* 47 (1981) 315–322; Eric Marty, "L'Ecriture journalière d'André Gide," *Poétique* 48 (1981) 459–478; Valérie Raoul, *The French Fictional Journal* (Toronto: University of Toronto Press, 1980); Jean Rousset, "Le Journal intime: texte sans destinataire?" *Poétique* 56 (1983) 435–443. Simonet-Tenant, Françoise. *Le Journal intime*. Paris: Nathan Université 128, 2001.

3. Valérie Raoul, "Narcisse prêtre: reflets ambigus dans *Journal d'un curé de campagne*," *Texte* 1 (1982) 97–109.

4. Marty 477; Michel Beaujour, *Miroirs d'encre* (Paris: Seuil, 1980) 10.

5. Dudley Andrew, "Desperation and Meditation," in *Modern European Filmmakers and the Art of Adaptation* (New York: Ungar, 1981); Roy Armes, *French Cinema* (New York: Oxford University Press, 1985); André Bazin, *What is Cinema?* (Berkeley: University of California Press, 1967); Bert Cardullo, "Film Chronicle: Sid, Nancy and Thérèse," *Hudson Review* 40 (Spring 1987) 125–130; Michel Estève, *Bernanos et Bresson* (Paris: Lettres Modernes, 1978), *Robert Bresson* (Paris: Editions Albatros, 1983); Ellen Feldman, "Bresson's Adaptation of Bernanos' *The Diary of a Country Priest*," *West Virginia University Philological Papers* 26 (August 1980) 37–42; Tom Milne, "Angels and Ministers," *Sight and Sound* (Autumn 1987) 285–287; Valérie Raoul, see note 3; Keith Reader, "The Sacrament of Writing: Robert Bresson's *Le*[sic] *Journal d'un curé de campagne* (1951)," in Susan Hayward and Ginette Vincendeau, eds., *French Film: Texts and Contexts* (New York: Routledge, 2000) 137–146.

Bibliography

Aaraas, Hans. *Littérature et sacerdoce: Essai sur le 'Journal d'un curé de campagne' de Bernanos.* Paris: Lettres Modernes Minard, 1984.

Andrew, Dudley. "Desperation and Meditation: Bresson's *Diary of a Country Priest*." In Horton and Magretta, eds. *Modern European Filmmakers and the Art of Adaptation*. New York: Ungar, 1981.

Arnaud, Philippe. *Robert Bresson*. Paris: Editions de L'Etoile, 1986.

Baumbach, Jonathan. "On the Wings of Pain: a Meditation on Three Films by Robert Bresson." *Fiction International* 30 (1997) 62–66.

Bazin, André; Gray, Hugh (translator). "*Le* [sic] *Journal d'un curé de campagne* and the Stylistics of Robert Bresson." In Quandt, James, ed. *Robert Bresson*. Toronto, ON: Toronto International Film Festival Group, 1998.

Bernanos, Jean-Loup. *Georges Bernanos*. Paris: Plon, 1988.

Bini, Luigi. "Il Cinematografo di Robert Bresson." *Letture: Libro e Spettacolo/Mensile di Studi e Rassegne* 36:381 (1981) 729–754.

Bonnel, Roland. "Révolution et sainteté dans les *Dialogues des Carmélites*." *French Review* 64:5 (1991) 784–793.

Bresson, Robert. *Notes on Cinematography*. New York: Quartet Books, 1986.

Browne, Nick. "Film Form/Voice-Over: Bresson's *The Diary of a Country Priest.*" In Quandt, James, ed. *Robert Bresson.* Toronto, ON: Toronto International Film Festival Group, 1998.

Cameron, Ian, ed. *The Films of Robert Bresson: Collected Essays.* New York: Praeger, 1969.

Chabot, Jacques. "Passion et vocation de l'écriture." *La Revue des Lettres Modernes* 637–642 (1982) 31–58.

Comune, Antonio. "Tempo Sospeso e tempo dell'attesa nel *Journal d'un curé de campagne* di Georges Bernanos." In Bogliolo, Giovanni, ed. *Anacronie: Studi sulla nozione di tempo nel romanzo francese del Novecento.* Fasano: Schena, 1989.

La Revue des Lettres Modernes 771–776 (1986). Entire issue.

Daninos, Guy. "Le Thème de la pauvreté dans le *Journal d'un curé de campagne* de Georges Bernanos." *La Licorne* 11 (1986) 125–137.

Eades, Caroline. "Bernanos, Bresson, Pialat: Trois Visions." *Recherches et Travaux* 58 (2000) 149–157.

Estève, Michel. *Bernanos et Bresson: étude de 'Journal d'un curé de campagne' et 'Mouchette'.* Paris: Lettres Modernes, 1978.

————. *Georges Bernanos: Un Triple Itinéraire.* Paris: Minard, 1987.

————. *Robert Bresson.* Paris: Editions Albatros, 1983.

Feldman, Ellen. "Bresson's Adaptation of Bernanos' *The Diary of a Country Priest.*" *West Virginia University Philological Papers* 26 (Aug 1980) 37–42.

Gosselin, Monique, and Max Milner. *Bernanos et le monde moderne.* Lille: Presses Universitaires de Lille, 1989.

Guillaume, Jean. "Le Solitaire." *Les Lettres Romanes* 42:4 (1988) 371–381.

Hiebel, Martine. "La Fiction de Bernanos, prédication d'un secret." *La Revue des Lettres Modernes* 857–864 (1988) 191–207.

Hollander, Paul d'. "Les Personnages écrivains dans l'oeuvre de Bernanos." *La Revue des Lettres Modernes* 637–642 (1982) 95–125.

Howells, Valerie. "'Une Aventure spirituelle': Bernanos's *Journal d'un curé de campagne* as a Self-reflexive Text." *Nottingham French Studies* 40:2 (Autumn 2001) 26–36.

Kidd, Marilyn. "Les Miroirs et l'importance du reflet dans les romans de Bernanos." *La Revue des Lettres Modernes* 857–864 (1988) 143–155.

Lagadec-Sadoulet, Elisabeth. *Temps et récit dans l'oeuvre romanesque de Georges Bernanos.* Paris: Klincksieck, 1988.

Latil-Le Dantec, Mireille. "Robert Bresson: du cinéma au cinématographe." *Etudes* 387:6 (Dec 1997) 667–676.

Liscio, Lorraine. "*Journal d'un curé de campagne*: The Religious and Poetic Vocation." *Bucknell Review* 26:2 (1982) 17–30.

Lorey, Eric. "Bernanos Revisited: Nihilism and Faith at the Close of the 20th Century." *Providence* 5:3-4 (Fall–Winter 2000) 130–134.

Morris, Daniel. *From Heaven to Hell: Imagery of Earth, Air, Water and Fire in the Novels of Georges Bernanos.* New York: Peter Lang, 1989.

Nettelbeck, Colin. *Les Personnages de Bernanos.* Paris: Lettres Modernes, 1970.

O'Sharkey, Eithne. *The Role of the Priest in the Novels of Georges Bernanos.* New York: Vantage, 1983.

Palka, Keith. "From Pen and Ink to Flesh and Blood: The Curé and His Addressee in Bernanos's *Journal d'un curé de campagne.*" *Cincinnati Romance Review* 10 (1991) 146–157.

————. "On Cleaning House in Georges Bernanos's *Journal d'un curé de campagne.*" *Christianity and Literature* 49:1 (Autumn 1999) 35–47.

La Revue des Lettres Modernes 771–776 (1986). Entire issue.

Revue des Sciences Humaines 78 (July–Sept 1987). Entire issue.

Papin, Liliane. "Film et écriture du silence: De Chaplin à Duras." *Stanford French Review* 13:2–3 (1989) 211–228.

Polet, Jacques. "Bernanos à l'écran." *Les Lettres Romanes* 42:4 (1988) 443–456.

Quandt, James, ed. *Robert Bresson*. Toronto: Toronto International Film Festival Group, 1998.

Reader, Keith. "'D'où cela vient-il?' Notes on Three Films by Robert Bresson." *French Studies* 40:4 (1986) 427–442.

————. "The Sacrament of Writing: Robert Bresson's *Le* [sic] *Journal d'un curé de campagne*." In Hayward and Vincendeau, eds. *French Film: Texts and Contexts*. London: Routledge, 2000.

Renascence 41:1–2 (1988–1989). Entire issue.

Rivas, Daniel. "A propos du temps et de la création dans le *Journal d'un curé de campagne*." *Studi Francesi* 24:2(71) (May–Aug 1980) 289–294.

Scott, Malcolm. *Journal d'un curé de campagne*. London: Grant & Cutler, 1997.

Stadler, Eva Marie. "Espace acoustique et cinéma moderne: l'exemple de Robert Bresson." *Bulletin de la Société des Professeurs français en Amérique* (1986–1987) 343–352.

Vidrine, Donald. "Bernanos's *Journal d'un curé de campagne*: A Dark Night Journey." *West Virginia Philological Papers* 31 (1986) 66–71.

Thérèse

directed by Alain Cavalier (1986)
from *L'Histoire d'une âme* by Thérèse de Lisieux (1898)

Writing in *French Forum* several years ago, Michael Tobin summarized earlier critical analyses (by the late Hans Urs von Balthasar and by Guy Gaucher) regarding the influence on Georges Bernanos of the life and writings of Sainte-Thérèse de Lisieux (1873–1897). Tobin began by signalling the connection between the recorded experiences of Thérèse and the plot and characters of Bernanos's 1926 novel *Sous le soleil de Satan* (*Under Satan's Sun*). This virtually inevitable influence came from 1) her epistolary autobiography, *L'Histoire d'une âme* (*Story of a Soul*), published posthumously in 1898 by her sister Pauline (Mother Agnès), to whom many of her letters were addressed, and 2) her beatification in 1923 and canonization in 1925, which made her a mystical heroic figure when Bernanos was writing his first novel. Tobin like von Balthasar also signals the similarities between the life and concerns of Thérèse and the character of the curé d'Ambricourt, the writing narrator of Bernanos's 1936 *Journal d'un curé de campagne* (*Diary of a Country Priest*).[1]

What Tobin couldn't mention was a reversal of influences between these last two works which occurred after his article was written. In 1987, Alain Cavalier received the Jury Prize at the Cannes Film Festival for his 1986 film *Thérèse* based on her story, a film which also garnered six Césars: Best Picture, Director, Editing, Screenplay (Camille de Casabianca), Cinematography (Philippe Rousselot), and Newcomer (Catherine Mouchet as Thérèse).

Most of the reviews of Cavalier's film commented on the originality of the vignettes he used to depict the heroine's courageous search for purity and simplicity in the face of spiritual longing and physical suffering. They also all mentioned the film's similarities to the 1950 Robert Bresson adaptation of Bernanos's *Journal d'un curé de campagne*, citing the lasting influence of the classic literary and filmic images of the tormented cleric. Other influences of the Bresson film cited at the time included Bert Cardullo's comments in the *Hudson Review* on the comparative distances of Cavalier's and Bresson's cameras from their subjects and the resulting differences of identification with the characters on the part of the spectator. Cardullo felt less distance from Thérèse than from Bresson's curé, whose experience for him was offered up "primarily for our contemplation. . . less by means of long shots than by non-expressive acting, an emphasis on the physical world—on that of objects—

which sets off the ineffability or interiority of the spiritual . . . ."[2] Cardullo signaled as well the distancing effect of the transposition of the curé's diary to the screen in a process he called "narrative trebling—through the representation on screen of written pages from the curé's diary, through his voice-over of those pages, and through the depiction on screen of the actions described in them" (127). Cardullo has a very different reaction to the diary in *Thérèse*, which for him is more static and opaque than the curé's, in a film whose décor and intrigue he characterizes as "unmediated." He sees Bresson's deliberate distancing as emblematic of "the mystery of God's justice" in the curé's suffering and, I might add, his distance from himself and his parishioners. For Cardullo, the final image of Thérèse's shoes is a positive symbol of her joining Christ in heaven, opposing the empty cross in the Bresson film. As we shall see later, this distinction is based on a misunderstanding.

One of those who reviewed *Thérèse*, Tom Milne writing in *Sight and Sound*, commented on the inevitability of the Bresson film as cinematic model and the widespread use of the adjective "Bressonian . . . to describe the sense of muted beatification attendant upon the cloistered life in Alain Cavalier's *Thérèse*."[3] Like Cardullo, Milne contrasted the two protagonists, however exactly in reverse, declaring the curé spiritually superior to Thérèse, ironically supporting this response by calling *Thérèse* a "study of human vulnerability in which the calm certitudes of Bresson's 'All Is Grace' are light years away" (69). What is so ironic in Milne's use of the closing assertion of the Bresson film as a sign of its superior spiritual strength is the fact that it was, as Tobin pointed out, Thérèse who first said "All is grace" and Bernanos who copied the line from her. Both von Balthasar (an influential and controversial Swiss Catholic theologian and Claudel scholar) and Tobin affirmed the lasting and evolving influence of Thérèse's life and work on all of Bernanos's writings (culminating in his final work, the screenplay *Dialogues des Carmélites*). They feel that Bernanos through years of spiritual struggle came to better understand Thérèse's "loving acceptance" (Tobin like Milne compared Thérèse to both the curé and the heroine Blanche de la Force of *Dialogues des Carmélites*). What none of the critics mention is the difference of interpretation in the assertion "Tout est grâce" between Thérèse and the curé d'Ambricourt. Although they both reaffirm their faith in the face of physical anguish and certain death, Thérèse's utterance is a benediction, whereas the curé abandons himself in resignation to the emptiness of his world and his physical and spiritual impotence.

There are other resonances of the interwined thematic under discussion here. Bresson's first film, in 1943, *Les Anges du péché*, with a Giraudoux dialogue, was the story of a defiant and rebellious nun named Thérèse. Not only was Bernanos's *Dialogues des Carmélites* made into two films in 1960 and 1985, but Maurice Pialat's 1987 *Sous le soleil de Satan*, as stated earlier the second film adaptation of Bernanos's first novel, brought to the world's attention the story of the abbé Donissan's (Gérard Depardieu) tormented confrontation with Mouchette (Sandrine Bonnaire). All these works demonstrate a similar fascination for the drama and dilemma of spiritual and moral ambiguity.

Thus Bresson and Cavalier have continued the spiritual conjunction between Thérèse and Bernanos. And there is, in spite of opposing critical responses, an intertextual link between the four works that is at once a thematic and formal connector, confirming both an ontological and artistic continuity. Both the Bresson and Cavalier films demonstrate great respect for their textual models as they portray their characters' pursuit of "simplicity" (saintliness) against great odds. They acknowledge the bond created between these author-narrator figures in their inscription of their longing for grace. As Keith Reader says of the curé's acts of reading and writing, "They place before us a language in its materiality, with its hesitations and the instruments of its production, so that it is as though the priest were not so much capturing his agony in language as passing through language as an integral part of it."[4] Both Bernanos and Thérèse express a desire for wholeness and oneness in their textual incarnations of the self as writing narrator priest/nun. A study of the two literary diaries, one overtly autobiographical, the other a fictional subjective narrative, and of their mutual roles in the two films, helps to resolve the apparent paradox of two such different characters proclaiming the same certainty.

Between the fictional diary of the curé d'Ambricourt and the autobiographical story of Thérèse, there are striking resemblances in spite of obvious distinctions, not the least of which is the difference in the "implied reader," to use Gerald Prince's term. Whereas the curé writes only for himself, Thérèse's story is told in part to Mother Agnès, with some additional manuscripts addressed to Mother Marie, her eldest sister. Referring to Pauline as her "Dear Mother" enabled Thérèse to effectuate a substitute confidante for the real mother she lost in 1877 at the age of four. At the time, she had thrown herself into Pauline's arms, crying: "Well, as for me, it's Pauline who will be my Mamma."[5] A fourth sister, Céline, also joined the same Carmel. The holy family of Thérèse was completed for her when she ecstatically became the bride of Christ in 1890.

Her diary, like the curé's *Journal*, is a generic admixture of a number of different narrative structures. Her first manuscript (A), begun in January 1895, intermingles anecdotes of her life with affirmations of the faith, love and simplicity of the "little flower." It is a long lyric psalm interspersed with myriads of quotations from the Bible, a witnessing of God's grace, the text as testimonial to the Word. The first part of Manuscript A is divided into three periods: 1) up to her mother's death, 2) her home life with her father, 3) life in boarding school. The second section is her struggle to enter the Carmel, following the example of Pauline and Marie, and the third section is her life as a nun.

After Manuscript A come the various meditations of Manuscript B, then the resumption of the text directed in June of 1897, only months before her death, to the new prioress, Mother Marie. Just as in the curé's diary, the text ends suspended, the will to write overcome by the ravages of illness. The final agony of each is included in the text in epilogue, the curé's as a letter from Dufréty, Thérèse's appended by the editors after the accounts of Mother Agnès.

Thérèse's influence on Bernanos manifests itself in numerous forms. He also includes a great variety of other texts, copied or reported second-hand—letters, dialogues, quotes from the Bible. Both contain a large number of prayers, addressed by the curé to God and by Thérèse to Jesus, whose intimate love she constantly reaffirms. Both offer frequent self-reflexive references to acts of writing, their significance, their justification, their difficulty. For both, the pen and notebook become characters within the text. In Thérèse's case, the unwieldy pen is replaced toward the end by a tiny chewed pencil, mimetic of her bodily frailty and lengthy suffering. Both narratives embody the timidity and boldness of an ego disarming in its naïveté and lacking in ironic objective perspective. Clearly these characters are not of this world, both Christlike frail creatures marked by God, quite literally consumed by their passion, in the double sense of the word. Both approach dementia in their total self-absorption and loss of contact with reality. Thérèse's single obsession with Christ is equalled by the passion elicited in the curé by the various women he encounters: Séraphita and the countess, Mademoiselle Louise and Mademoiselle Chantal. The diarists' transposition of life into text becomes a surrogate act in their celibate state for sexual reproduction, as well as an immortalizing act which enables the self to transcend death. The spiritual power and performative function of the Word give an added dimension for both to the act of writing, making it part of their spiritual evolution.

The greatest apparent distinction in the diegeses of the two texts is the contextual situation of the narrator. Thérèse rejoices in the communion of love around her—the family, the Carmel, the spirits of all living things. On the contrary, the curé d'Ambricourt suffers an isolation of exile in the midst of his village, an anonymity signaled by his generic functional name, a solitude punctuated by visits to the villagers, the château, other curés, the two doctors, during which he is often even more spiritually isolated. The vow of silence of the Carmelites implies an equivalent isolation, but the strong communion of their souls has few parallel experiences in the curé's life: the salvation of the countess, his rescue by Séraphita, the fatherly companionship of Torcy, the unquestioning hospitality of Dufréty. It is suggested repeatedly that the curé should have been a monk, that he is incapable in his egocentric simplicity of ministering to the needs of others.

Thus Thérèse's text in its many voices offered a precedent for the various functions of the curé's *Journal* and its different types of narrative, as stated in the chapter on film and autobiography: monological (meditation), retrospective (anecdotes of his past), conative (prayer), dialogical (conversations), and self-reflexive (considerations of production of the text). And the films of these two works lead to a common conclusion, but they use quite different means to represent these religious author-narrators and their textual production.

The texts as well have some primary distinctions. As opposed to the divided narrative instance and the fictional canon of the Bernanos diary, Thérèse's is privileged by its own authenticity and polarized by its immediate implicit and explicit readers, her sisters, at whose urging she began both the sequences of 1895 and 1897. In Thérèse's writing, the epistolary form is at the same time more central to the text and more ambiguous, as a direct means of addressing her thoughts to her sisters but without the dynamic actantial functions of intrigue structured in the curé's fictional diary. Cavalier's presentation of Thérèse's diary is an extension of his portraits of her and her world—vignettes isolated in a black void like Chinese landscapes, still-life paintings, genre scenarios, a balletic stylized *mise en scène* reminiscent of Carlos Saura's trilogy *Bodas de Sangre, Carmen* and *El Amor Brujo*.

The transparence of Thérèse's narrative derives more from its grace, simplicity, innocence and enthusiasm than from the realism of its descriptions or dialogues. The codification of the self in the Christian liturgy of a soul, penetrated by the scriptures, reveals in Thérèse's text a palimpsest of the Gospel. The directness of expression, the absence of erasures or *pentimenti*, reflect the candor and purity of her being. The floating suspended isolated vignettes of Cavalier's film are perfectly mimetic of a one-dimensional spiritual world, from which ambiguity and aleatory causality are excluded. Thérèse's state of grace leads to a different drama than that of Bernanos's curé, and in the Cavalier film, instead of a narrative portrait, we have the portrait of a narrative, of a life story, as well as of its textual creation. Thérèse's candle, like the curé's lamp, shines in the surrounding darkness. Yet, as mentioned before, her contextual isolation is privileged, as opposed to the anguished solitude of the self-doubting curé. The physical similarities of their suffering (although actually dying of stomach cancer, the curé thinks he has tuberculosis) reflect the spiritual travail of these two figures, leading in the end for both to a transcendent state of grace which leaves the reader/spectator behind.

Philippe Roussselot's cinematography has the same framing and composing quality that it did in *Diva*, and the strong painterly feeling of the sets transforms the sequences into theatrical tableaux. The absence of a background musical score emphasizes the spiritual purity of Thérèse's world at the same time that it symbolizes the Carmelite vow of silence. These elements give the film the same sense of authenticity and classic timelessness that were achieved by Bresson in part through the unintentionally stern tonalities of L.-H. Burel's cinematography.

As characters in the two films, the diaries themselves have vastly different contours. That of the priest is his constant companion, his best and only intimate friend. Its tattered state shows the intensity of the experience within the priest, its blackouts like his reflect the growing sickness within, the crisis of body and soul. Almost left behind, it accompanies him at last on his final journey and sits at his bedside until his death. In Cavalier's film, Thérèse offers Pauline the gift of her pencil box, prefiguration of the greater gift to come. Her diary as a character has the same gentle yet intense luminous quality that she evinces. And it lives out its humble existence, with the chewed-up pencil consumed by symbolic passion, in a simple writing box, the monastic cell of the manuscript. In both films, the apparent simplicity of the diary-characters masks a textual metaphoric virtuosity which was successfully transposed in the totality of the film's images. And in both cases, the text, like the auteur filmmaker, participates in the film as a signature figure, a cameo-portrait of the creative source which inspired it. In the end, the binding similarity between the figures of Thérèse and the curé comes from that between Thérèse and Bernanos, between Bernanos and Bresson, between all three and Cavalier, as they struggle to portray the search for simplicity through complex textual and cinematic modes of expression.

Notes

1. Tobin, Michael. "Thérèse de Lisieux and Bernanos' First Novel," *French Forum* 10:1 (1985) 84–96. Further references are included in parentheses after the quote.
2. Bert Cardullo, "Film Chronicle: Sid, Nancy and Thérèse," *Hudson Review* 40 (Spring 1987) 127. Further references are included in parentheses after the quote.
3. Tom Milne, "Blanche: Thérèse," *Sight and Sound* 56 (Winter 1986–1987) 69. Further references are included in parentheses after the quote.
4. Keith Reader, "'D'où cela vient-il?': Notes on three films by Robert Bresson," *French Studies* 40:4 (1986) 431.
5. Thérèse Martin, *Story of a Soul: the Autobiography of St. Thérèse of Lisieux* (Washington, D.C.: Institute of Carmelite Studies, 1975); French Edition: *Histoire d'une âme: manuscrits autobiographiques* (Bar-le-duc: Editions du Cerf-Desclée de Brouwer, 1972).

Bibliography

Please see also the bibliography at the end of the chapter on *Journal d'un curé de campagne*.

Auclair, Marie. "L'Enonciation du prochain: Lecture de *L'Histoire d'une âme* de Thérèse de Lisieux." *Recherches Sémiotiques/Semiotic Inquiry* 15:3 (1995) 59–75.
Bryden, Mary. "Saints and Stereotypes: The Case of Therese of Lisieux." *Literature and Theology* 13:1 (Mar 1999) 1–16.
Cardullo, Bert. "Film Chronicle: Sid, Nancy, Thérèse." *Hudson Review* 40 (Spring 1987) 125–130.
Dorschell, Mary Frances. *Georges Bernanos' Debt to Therese of Lisieux.* Dissertation Abstracts International 54:2 (Aug 1993) 545A.
Furlong, Monica. *Thérèse of Lisieux.* New York: Pantheon Books, 1987.
Gaucher, Guy. *La Passion de Thérèse de Lisieux.* Bar-le-duc: Editions du Cerf-Desclée de Brouwer, 1973.
Martin (de Lisieux), Thérèse. *Les Derniers Entretiens.* Bar-le-duc: Editions du Cerf-Desclée de Brouwer, 1971.
———. *Histoire d'une âme: manuscrits autobiographiques.* Bar-le-duc: Editions du Cerf-Desclée de Brouwer, 1972.
———. *Story of a Soul: The Autobiography of St. Thérèse of Lisieux.* Washington, D.C.: Institute of Carmelite Studies, 1975.
Madigan, Kathleen. "St. Therese's Autobiography: The 'Ever New Hymn of Love'." *Religion and Literature* 31:2 (Summer 1999) 23–43.
Milne, Tom. "Angels and Ministers." *Sight and Sound* (Autumn 1987) 285–287.
Reader, Keith. "'D'où cela vient-il?': Notes on Three Films by Robert Bresson." *French Studies* 40:4 (1986) 427–442.
———."The Sacrament of Writing: Robert Bresson's *Le* [sic] *Journal d'un curé de campagne* (1951)." In Hayward, Susan, and Ginette Vincendeau, eds. *French Film: Texts and Contexts.* New York: Routledge, 2000.

Santa, Angels. "Thérèse de Lisieux, écrivain populaire?" In Piarotas and Millot, eds. *Ecrits et Expression Populaires*. Saint-Etienne, France: Presses Universitaires de Saint-Etienne, 1998.

Six, Jean-François. *Vie de Thérèse de Lisieux*. Paris: Seuil, 1975.

Stokes, Charlotte. "Surrealist as Religious Visionary: Max Ernst's *Rêve d'une petite fille qui voulut entrer au Carmel* (1930)." In Morse, Donald, ed. *The Fantastic in World Literature and the Arts*. Westport, CT: Greenwood Press, 1987.

Tobin, Michael. "Thérèse de Lisieux and Bernanos' First Novel." *French Forum* 10:1 (1985) 84–96.

Von Balthasar, Hans Urs. *Le Chrétien Bernanos*. Paris: Seuil, 1956.

Rue Cases-Nègres
(Sugarcane Alley)

directed by Euzhan Palcy (1983)
novel by Joseph Zobel (1950)

Euzhan Palcy, the talented black female Martinican director, studied filmmaking in Paris. She then searched for a script of a young black female facing hardships, surviving and succeeding, as she had. In the meantime, she made two extraordinary films about the rites of passage of young men in a difficult world divided by racial and economic inequities. The film that represents the French Antillean experience was adapted from Joseph Zobel's *La Rue Cases-Nègres*, an autobiographical tale of his childhood in the black shack alleys of Martinique, recounted twenty years later in France. Palcy also made in 1989 the powerful film about South Africa, *A Dry White Season*, another male narrative, by the Afrikaner novelist André Brink. For *Rue Cases-Nègres*, Palcy faithfully recreated the physical setting, social and economic conditions and affective realities of growing up poor, rural and black in the canefields and former slave cabins of colonial Martinique in the early 1930s. She focused as did Zobel on one child, José Hassam (Garry Cadenat), on his struggle for dignity, his rites of initiation, and his difficult journey through and beyond the enslaving poverty of his heritage.

A large, verdant volcanic island discovered by Columbus in 1502, Martinique was colonized by the French in 1635, given statehood in 1946 and regional status (equivalent to a province) in 1974. Its long and turbulent history informs the diegesis of *Rue Cases-Nègres*. Although often connected with Guadeloupe, the other French Antilles *département*, Martinique has a distinct character of its own. There are a number of factors at work in the shaping of what Edouard Glissant characterizes in *Caribbean Discourse* as the collective heritage of the French Antilleans, specifically of the Martinicans, and a number of false discourses or identification strategies which tempt and often mislead the Martinican seeking a self. Leading proponents of *négritude* like Frantz Fanon and Aimé Césaire (who has been mayor of Fort-de-France) encourage Martinicans to assert their independent identity and throw off the age-old yoke of white dominance. The transplanted black African who is now a French citizen consuming European products has a much better life than that depicted in Palcy's film, but is still trapped in a cultural and ideological dilemma. The school system is still alien, as are the subjects it teaches: the language, the music, the literature, the geography, the history. Still today, at the end of the twentieth century, the Martinican black faces a choice between reverting to African tradition, imitating the French, or trying to preserve the Creole language and folklore, including the musical idioms, that are truly Caribbean.

This dilemma of cultural multiplicity and conflict is depicted graphically by Zobel in his 1950 work, whose English title carries the correct literal translation *Black Shack Alley*, eliminated to soften the American release version of the film. During his decade in France, from 1946 to 1957, Zobel also wrote *Diab'là, Laghia de la mort, Les Jours immobiles, La Fête à Paris*. Since 1957, he has divided his time between his residence in Senegal and southern France, writing *Le Soleil partagé* and *Les Mains pleines d'oiseaux*. Appropriately, the wise village elder Médouze in *Rue Cases-Nègres* who preserves African tribal lore, wisdom and art was played by Senegalese actor Douta Seck.

Although Zobel collaborated on the film, writing the screenplay and even taking an adult role, Palcy made significant changes in adapting his text. José's friend and alter ego, Georges Roc, called "Jojo," the illegitimate son of the wealthy mulatto Justin Roc and a black woman, becomes Léopold, son of the aristocratic curé d'Auberville, a white Catholic priest (who of course cannot marry) and his black mistress Honorine, thus personalizing the alien presence in Martinique of the white European male dominant Catholic Church and its exploitation of the black population. In Zobel's text, the church dominates the children continually through endless catechism classes and services. Georges Roc and his mother are abandoned when Justin Roc marries another woman. In Palcy's film, the curé d'Auberville dies from a wound inflicted by a horse in a stream, adding an additional image of the distance between refined French civilization and primitive natural power and virility. In both cases, the disappearance of the father precipitates the flight and eventual destruction of Jojo/Léopold. When Léopold's dying father refuses to give him his white French family name, de Thorail, the boy suddenly feels the pain of his racial limbo, runs away from home and becomes a rebel, acting out a different response to white dominance from José's will to succeed. When Léopold later steals the paymaster's log from the sugar mill to prove the white *békés'* (overlords) unjust exploitation of the black canecutters, he is caught and suffers humiliating public punishment, establishing a polar contrast in the fate of the two boys and leaving an implicit message regarding the options of a young black male in Martinique in that era.

At one point in the film, Léopold's mother plays Josephine Baker's signature song "J'ai deux amours...mon coeur et Paris" on her phonograph. Honorine, like Baker, lives a cross-cultural linguistic and racial dilemma. Baker, the American black singer from St. Louis living in Paris, had graduated from her banana dance of the Revue Nègre and the Ziegfield Follies to such films as *La Sirène des Tropiques* (the story of a humiliated West Indian girl), *La Créole* (the Offenbach operetta with more exploitive slapstick), *Princesse Tamtam*, and *Zouzou* with Jean Gabin. A brilliant horsewoman as well as exotic sexual and social persona, Baker went on to fight with the Resistance in World War II, dedicated the Liberty Club in Casablanca in 1942, received the Legion of Honor and became a champion of orphaned black and Arab children. Thus in these two bars of a song, Palcy generates a multi-layered anticolonial intertext with a legendary black female caught between two worlds.

In Zobel's text, Stephen Roc, the schoolmaster who is José's mentor, is Justin's brother; they offer an interesting contrast in male parental support function. José's own father has abandoned him as well, and he is being raised by his pipes-moking grandmother, M'man Tine (Darling Legitimus), and initiated to wisdom and sorrow by her and Médouze, the tribal elders who transcend physical suffering through inner strength and vision. Zobel's world of the Rue Cases-Nègres, Médouze, M'man Tine and the Creole dialect is faithfully recreated in the film, with the significant exception that both José's parents are missing. In Zobel's tale, José lives at first with his grandmother in Petit Bourg, left behind when his mother goes to work in Fort-de-France. When he finally goes to live with her and attend high school, he is often left alone because he is not allowed in the white household where she is a maid, a situation which echoes the separation of black families in the days of slavery. In the film, José's mother has died, thus telescoping the old and young generations and intensifying the drama and vulnerability of the situation, leaving the past and the future face to face.

As a background to José's conforming performance in school, the black characters in *Rue Cases-Nègres*, including José, all experience humiliation and rebellion. The opening scenes of the children breaking M'man Tine's treasured porcelain bowl, getting drunk on cheap rum, setting fire to Twelve-toes's *case*, getting caught and severely beaten by their families, all echo their parents' condition. They also serve as a modern symbolic reenactment of the 1848 slave rebellion, recounted so poignantly by Médouze, as he tells José of the night when the black slaves ran down from the mountain and away from their bondage only to discover that they had nowhere to go in their insular world, so they returned to work for a pittance, economically enslaved for another century.

Historically the Africans had been enslaved on Martinique virtually since its initial colonization, with the exception of a few years during the French Revolution. Their liberation in April 1848, at the time of the Second Republic, was principally the work of Victor Schoelcher, a Paris-born abolitionist. It was an ill-considered proclamation by Louis Thomas Husson, dated 31 March, which announced de facto continuation of the blacks' slavery until they could raise funds to purchase their freedom (as though it were a commodity and not a natural state), that precipitated the futile rebellion on 21 and 22 May. Even today, the economic crisis of the canefields continues. Even though cheap labor is imported from neighboring Dominica (the young black Martinicans now refuse to work the cane), government subsidies have not been adequate to sustain the failing industry, seen as a threat by sugar beet growers in France and America.

Other sequences depicting humiliation and rebellion include José being unjustly accused of plagiarizing his composition at the *lycée* in Fort-de-France, his friend Carmen's parody of his sexual enslavement to his white female employer, José's exploitation by Madame Léonce, M'man Tine's hard labor because of José's inadequate scholarship funds, and the ticket girl Gloria at the cinema repudiating her blackness out of shame and anger after witnessing a black stealing a wallet. Gloria's internal whiteness is mirrored in the poster for Al Jolson in *The Jazz Singer* (which is interestingly enough printed "Al Johnson").

The first-person narrative voice in Zobel's work is internally focused on José's responses to his schooling with Mademoiselle Fanny (whom we see only briefly with the younger children in the film), on questions of catechism, first communion, his lack of money and clothes and his constant hunger. The narrative has far greater temporal extension, telescoped by Palcy for dramatic intensity and to establish a closer equation between screen time and narrative time. She also focuses necessarily externally and in greater breadth on the overall double standard on the island: white Catholic *békés* with great wealth versus impoverished black servants and canecutters with their African traditions, songs and voodoo. The dilemma of cultural multiplicity and conflict pervades both text and film, however. In order for José to escape the brutal labor of the canefields, he must succeed in the French imposed system, mastering the language (Creole is nòt taught in the schools) and learning the history, geography and literature of a totally alien world.

José moves in schizophrenic fashion back and forth between these conflicting cultures, symbolized by the authentic confrontation at the beginning of the film between the snake and the mongoose, which is of course also emblematic of the struggle to survive. He expresses his bitterness at the destructive force of the canefields; the sugar holds no sweetness for him. It is interesting to compare this tale to Alec Wilkinson's 1989 study *Big Sugar: Seasons in the Canefields of Florida* about the life of immigrant Jamaican canecutters in Florida today, and to the dilemma of the Haitian children working the cane in the Dominican Republic. It is not only M'Man Tine who forbids José to go into the fields; José himself cannot find the force to submit to their torture and degradation. He expresses his anger and resentment with bitter lyricism:

> . . . aucune sympathie pour les champs de cannes à sucre. En dépit de tout mon plaisir à mordiller et à sucer des bouts de canne à sucre, un champ représentait toujours à mes yeux un endroit maudit où des bourreaux qu'on ne voyait même pas condamnent des nègres, dès l'âge de huit ans, à sarcler, bêcher, sous des orages qui les flétrissent et des soleils qui dévorent comme feraient des chiens enragés; des nègres en haillons, puant la sueur et le crottin, nourris d'une poignée de farine de manioc et de deux sous de rhum de mélasse, et qui deviennent de pitoyables monstres aux yeux vitreux, aux pieds alourdis d'éléphantiasis, voués à s'abattre un soir dans un sillon et à expirer sur une planche crasseuse, à même le sol d'une cabane vide et infecte.
>
> Non, non! Je renie la splendeur du soleil et l'envoûtement des mélopées qu'on chante dans un champ de canne à sucre. Et la volupté fauve de l'amour qui consume un vigoureux muletier avec une ardente négresse

dans la profondeur d'un champ de canne à sucre. Il y a trop longtemps que j'assiste, impuissant, à la mort lente de ma grand-mère par les champs de cannes à sucre.[1]

The felt depth of this passage indicates not only the wealth of experiences that Zobel recalls in his autobiography, but his precocious command of French as a child. It gives great variety to his Flaubertian *discours indirect libre* which conveys with immediacy, intensity and authenticity the Creole dialect of the children, the joys, fears, wisdom and pain Joseph experienced when he was just José. Zobel's journey to France (this book was written at Fontainebleau) might seem to indicate an exported life of imitation, a betrayal of his Antillean heritage. Yet the text, translated into other languages, as well as this film, has brought to the attention of the world the cultural dilemma of a people, past and present.

Both novel and film recreate the diegesis of 1930s Martinique with vivid intensity. The characters are driven and limited by both social and natural environmental structures which are part of the deep history of Martinique, the island of flowers that is also an island of fire. Not only did Mont Pélée bury the town of St. Pierre in its 1902 eruption but it was St. Pierre that the rebel slaves pillaged in 1848. The background for the opening credits of the film announces and documents its period setting: a series of sepia-tinted postcards from the 1930s, several of which depict other *rues* and the dominant white colonial culture (churches, wide boulevards, ocean liners, lovely homes). The story begins in the village of Rivière Salée (Salty River), south and inland across the bay from Fort-de-France. As José recounts in an opening voice-over, it is school vacation and the canecutters' children are left to their own devices, as their parents must work the fields. When their undisciplined and unguided energy results in breaking, stealing, boozing and burning, as they spontaneously rebel against the absent authority, they are soon caught and punished, in a parody of the black adults' past and present situation. Their humor and ingenuity prevail, like that of their parents, who come home from the fields exhausted and dirty, yet sing and dance, tell tales and jokes, share rituals of voodoo initiation and rites of passage. Like the carved wood totem figure Médouze gives to José, these are traces of their African background, a primal cultural heritage transplanted to French soil, a phenomenon similar to the establishment of various excolonial subcultures in continental France in the last fifty years.

The whites on the island are the masters; the overseers, the managers, the white priest, all loom larger than life in the eyes of the young José, as he navigates a course through the awkward and humiliating events that befall him, sure in his pride and wisdom, determined and resourceful like his ailing grandmother. José's escape from slave labor through his scholastic excellence is nearly thwarted on many occasions, not the least of which is his exploitation by the black Madame Léonce. Like his girlfriend Tortilla's father, she sees José as a source of manual labor rather than a brilliant mind with an open future.

José's remarkable intelligence earns him a *Certificat d'études* and a chance to compete in a special exam for a scholarship to the Lycée Schoelcher (where Zobel

218   *Rue Cases-Nègres*

went) in Fort-de-France. He rides the riverboat *Albatros* (obviously a symbolically loaded name) with his handsome older friend Carmen, whom he is teaching to read and write. José's relationship to Carmen (who bears a woman's name) is complex but does not, as some critics have speculated, imply a homosexual experience. What is important here is the parallel between Carmen's situation as chauffeur to the wealthy white family and José's own entrapment. In the film, Carmen parodies his plight in acting out a tryst between himself and his *patronne*. In this sequence, he is appropriately reading Colette's *Chéri*, parallel *mise-en-abyme* of his emasculated status as a younger impoverished lover. José's own feminization, if it indeed exists, stems partially from his independent, alienated and lonely state as a single child who never knew his father, raised by his grandmother in his mother's absence. Old Médouze provides much heritage and wisdom but offers little as a masculine role model or sexual counsellor. José commented in his diatribe against the canefields on his aversion to the canecutters' secret sweaty copulations, which he saw as part of their entrapment. In the film, he has a strong bond of friendship but no sexual involvement with Tortilla, his female counterpart who is denied access to higher education by her father. However, the adult Zobel married and had children.

When José is granted only a token one-fourth scholarship, it creates new hardships, as he and M'man Tine must trade Rue Cases-Nègres for the city shanty-town. Their situation is perfectly emblematic of the two faces of the French secondary education system in the Caribbean, which liberates the blacks at the same time that it imprisons them in another alien system. In Zobel's book, José goes to live with his half-breed *métisse* mother in the shack in Fort-de-France, where she virtually abandons him in order to work as a maid. Her housework is transposed by Palcy to M'man Tine's taking in laundry. The double displacement generates an equation between José and his grandmother, focusing the matriarchal role on the single aging figure, in a culture where women outnumber men and pride themselves on their survival instincts.

José's triumphs in his young years are punctuated with tragedies, as he loses Médouze and then M'man Tine to death, believing with them that their souls return to Africa. After symbolically cleansing M'man Tine's feet as part of the preparatory rites for her burial, José closes the film with another voice-over narration: sure of his own future, he is returning to Fort-de-France, taking as he says his Rue Cases-Nègres with him. As he will experience the new rites of passage of the white world, he will maintain his black identity and heritage through memory, and still later, through the evocative power of the text.

There are some interesting connections between this and some of the other films in this study: Napoleon's Josephine was born on Martinique, daughter of French colonial planters. The close village and family power structures, as well as the superstitions and ritualistic conduct, recall the world of *Le Retour de Martin Guerre*, as does the power of education, memory and literacy and even the symbolic washing of the feet. But the story of the child José is a *roman d'éducation*, literally and figuratively, in the classic French sense. He belongs not with the secondary figures of children in *Le Retour de Martin Guerre, Napoléon*, or *La Bête humaine*, nor with the heroes of the books that the characters are reading in the film of *La Rue Cases-Nègres*: (Marcel Pagnol's 1928 *Topaze* and Colette's 1920 *Chéri*), but with a long-standing tradition of young heroes breaking out of the prison of their circumstances to meet the world on their own terms, against great odds—a favorite theme of nineteenth-century novelists like Balzac, transposed to the screen by François Truffaut in the Antoine Doinel films presented in the last section of this study: *Les Quatre Cents Coups, Baisers volés*, and *L'Amour en fuite*, works which together constitute not the film version of an autobiography but rather the use of film itself as the medium of expression of the auteur filmmaker's autobiographic experience and identity.

Note

1. Joseph Zobel, *La Rue Cases-Nègres* (Paris: Présence Africaine, 1974) 210–211. (". . . no attraction for the fields of sugarcane. In spite of all my pleasure in chewing and sucking the pieces of sugarcane, a field always represented to my eyes an accursed place where unseen tyrants condemned the blacks from age eight to hack and spade, under the storms which withered them and the suns which devoured them like mad dogs, blacks in rags, stinking of sweat and manure, nourished by a handful of manioc flour and two cents worth of molasses rum, and who become pitiful monsters with watery eyes and feet swollen with elephantiasis, destined to collapse some evening in a ditch and expire on a dirty wooden plank on the floor of a filthy empty shack. No, no! I repudiate the splendor of the sun and the enchantment of the hymns sung in the canefields. And the animal passion of a vigorous muledriver making love with a hot-blooded negress in the depths of a canefield. I have watched too long, powerless, the slow murder of my grandmother by the canefields." My translation.)

Bibliography

André, Jacques. *Caraibales: Etudes sur la littérature antillaise*. Paris: Editions Caribéennes, 1981.
Antoine, Régis. *Les Ecrivains français et les Antilles: des premiers Pères blancs aux surréalistes noirs*. Paris: G. P. Maisonneuve et Larose, 1978.
Burton, Julianne. "Marginal Cinemas and Mainstream Critical Theory." *Screen* (May–August 1985) 2–21.
Burton, Richard D. E. and Reno, Fred, eds. *French and West Indian: Martinique, Guadeloupe and French Guiana Today*. Charlottesville: University Press of Virginia, 1995.
César, Sylvie. *"La Rue Cases-Nègres": du Roman au Film (Etude Comparative)*. Paris: Editions L'Harmattan, 1994.
De Stefano, George. *Sugar Cane Alley. Cinéaste* 13:4 (1984) 42, 44–45.
Durham, Carolyn. "Euzhan Palcy's Feminist Filmmaking: From Romance to Realism, from Gender to Race." *Women in French Studies* 7 (1999) 155–165.
Ganim, Russell. "Saisons riches et fécondes: Education et identité africaine dans le cinéma

d'Euzhan Palcy." *Revue Francophone* 9:2 (Autumn 1994) 25–43.

Gill, June. "The Films of Euzhan Palcy: A Voice for Black History." *Quarterly Review of Film and Video* 17:4 (Nov 2000) 371–381.

Glissant, Edouard. *Caribbean Discourse*. Charlottesville: University Press of Virginia, 1990.

Haley, Marjorie, and Warner, Keith. "Joseph Zobel and Technology: From Novel to Film to Classroom." *CLAJ* 40:3 (1997) 380–391.

Herndon, Gerise. "Auto-Ethnographic Impulse in *Rue Cases-Nègres*." *Literature/Film Quarterly* 24:3 (1996) 261–266.

Hezekiah, Randolph. "Joseph Zobel: The Mechanics of Black Liberation." *Black Images* 4:3–4 (1975) 44–45.

Julien, Eileen. "La Métamorphose du réel dans *La Rue Cases-Nègres*." *French Review* 60:6 (1987) 781–787.

Kande, Sylvie. "Renunciation and Victory in *Black Shack Alley*." *Research in African Literatures* 25:2 (Summer 1994) 33–50.

————. "Renoncements et Victoires dans *La Rue Cases-Nègres* de Joseph Zobel." *Revue Francophone* 9:2 (Autumn 1994) 5–23.

Linfield, Susan. "*Sugar Cane Alley*: An Interview with Euzhan Palcy." *Cinéaste* 13:4 (1984) 43–44.

Ménil, Alain. "*Rue Cases-Nègres* ou les Antilles de l'intérieur." *Présence Africaine* 129:1 (1984) 96–110.

Monye, Laurent, and Swanson, Kenneth. "Convergences thématiques et narratives dans *La Rue Cases-Nègres* de Joseph Zobel et *L'Enfant noir* de Camara Laye." *CLAJ* 45:1 (Sept 2001) 97–113.

Parker, Gloria. *Through the Eye of a Child: Their Societies Viewed by Five Black Francophone Authors: Zobel, Ega, Laye, Dadie, and Oyono*. Dissertation Abstracts 52:4 (1991) 1353–1354.

Szeps, Christiane. "*Rue Cases-Nègres*: Literary Exile and Cinematic Kingdom." *West Virginia University Philological Papers* 41 (1995) 71–76.

Warner, Keith. "Emasculation on the Plantation: A Reading of Joseph Zobel's *La Rue Cases-Nègres*." *College Language Association Journal* 32:1 (September 1988) 38–44.

Wilkinson, Alec. *Big Sugar: Seasons in the Canefields of Florida*. New York: Alfred Knopf, 1989.

Wilson, Elizabeth. "Translating Caribbean Landscape." *Palimpsestes* 12 (2000) 15–29.

Wylie, Hal. "Joseph Zobel's Use of Negritude and Social Realism." *World Literature Today* 56:1 (1982) 61–64.

Zobel, Joséph. *Diab'là* (1946). Paris: Nouvelles Editions Latines, 1947.

————. *La Fête à Paris*. Paris: La Table Ronde, 1953.

————. *Les Jours immobiles* (1946). Liechtenstein: Kraus, 1969.

————. *Laghia de la mort*. Fort-de-France: Bezaudin, 1946.

————. *Les Mains pleines d'oiseaux*. Paris: Nouvelles Editions Latines, 1978.

————. *La Rue Cases-Nègres* (1950). Paris: Présence Africaine, 1974.

————. *Le Soleil partagé*. Paris: Présence Africaine, 1964.

Zootjens, Adrienne. "L'Apartheid, le racisme et le prix littéraire français." *Peuples Noirs, Peuples Africains* 23 (1981) 136–140.

Sartre par lui-même
(Sartre by Himself)

directed by Alexandre Astruc and Michel Contat (1976)

The autobiographic voice of Jean-Paul Sartre (1905–1980) has many modes besides the ironic self-parody of his 1964 *Les Mots* (*The Words*), whose original title of *Jean sans Terre* conveys the Sartrian sense of the alienated and dispossessed self. The first title has many literary and historic resonances: King John of England, so-called when he was stripped of his French possessions, Scott's *Ivanhoe*, Nerval's "El Desdichado," perhaps even the posthumous publication of Proust's *Jean Santeuil* in 1952, the year before Sartre began his autobiographic text. Other manifestations of his subjective voice are *La Nausée* (*Nausea*) (1938), *L'Enfance d'un chef* (*The Childhood of a Leader*) in the collection of *Le Mur* (*The Wall*) (1939), the posthumously published *Les Carnets de la drôle de guerre* (*War Diaries:Notebooks from a Phoney War, November 1939 to March 1940*), and "Autoportrait à 70 ans" (Selfportrait at 70) in *Situations* X. Juxtaposition and superimposition of these texts, and in fact all his works, generates a multi-layered portrait of the voice and the person that was Sartre, visceral, dialectic, political. Some of his most intimate affective experiences are represented in absentia in his texts, by blanks, transferences, fictional or metaphoric transpositions. His phobias, his depressions, his experiments with mescaline in the 1930s, his reaction to Simone de Beauvoir's lesbian affairs, his own involvement in numerous *liaisons* are often coded into his writings. Correlating, as does Serge Doubrovsky, *Lettres au Castor* (letters to Simone de Beauvoir), entries in the *Carnets*, and strikingly revealing passages from *L'Etre et le néant* (*Being and Nothingness*) (1943), wherein Sartre describes sexuality in impersonal (hypothetical) phenomenological terms, reveals precise details of his sexual being and involvements. Doubrovsky goes on to posit a double sexual role inversion between Sartre and Le Castor (nickname for his lifelong soulmate Beauvoir, with its allusion to the English pronunciation of her name, homonymous with the translation of *castor* (beaver), and to the French nineteenth-century literary magazine, *Le Castor*). Using this masculine gender appellation enables Sartre to concurrently feminize his affective self, a role acquired in childhood identification with his widowed mother, Anne-Marie Schweitzer, with whom he lived as his big sister and fellow boarder in her parents' apartment. Growing up, as he portrays in *Les Mots*, lighter than air, unburdened by possessions,

Jean sans Terre was never able to possess another person both sexually and emotionally, living out a paranoid alienated isolation similar to that of Stendhal's persona Henry Brulard. This "innerbiography" was never openly written and is completely omitted from this film.

Thus when this hagiographic portrayal of Sartre compiled from interviews, stills, newsreels, and some dramatized footage, directed by Alexandre Astruc and Michel Contat, appeared in 1975 (released on film and video in 1976), it generated considerable negative critical reaction, not only from his Maoist comrades of the moment, but from critics like Philippe Lejeune, who demonstrated in "L'Ordre du récit dans *Les Mots* de Sartre" in *Le Pacte autobiographique* (1975) and again in "Ça s'est fait comme ça" in *Poétique* in 1978 that Astruc and Contat had made precisely the type of enshrining portrait of man and mind that Sartre was mocking in *Les Mots*. They had made him into Simonnot, the self-important cultural icon from *Les Mots* (and echo of Swann's role in Proust's *Combray*), who generated in the young Sartre his first conscious articulation of the distinction between contingency and necessity, his depressing sense of being marginalized in life, of having no significant past or being. The original title of *La Nausée*, *Melancholia* (from Albrecht Dürer's 1512 engraving *Melencolia I* with its long history of influence on French writers, including Nerval and Baudelaire), reveals more than the cover-up of *Sartre par lui-même*, an official story masking an impossible narrative that refuses its own subjective voice. This was in fact the problem with Sartre's failed unfinished attempt at self-revelation through text from 1950, *La Reine Albemarle ou le dernier touriste* (*Queen Albemarle or the Last Tourist*), a sort of inside-outside narrative observing himself/herself traveling in Italy, a contextualizing cultural heritage and romantic topos. The title contained grammatically the same sexual ambiguity Sartre generated in the Beauvoir/Castor nomination.

Michel Contat states simply in his essay on the film in *Sartre Alive* that this filmed (auto)biography project was André Gide's fault. Contat saw Marc Allégret's 1950 *Avec André Gide* (*With André Gide*) in Switzerland in 1957 and was enchanted with the idea of an intimate conversation with a great writer. Sartre was young (fifty-two) and in good health at that time and had weathered the controversy of the postwar era and the break with Camus. The era saw a large number of young intellectual film directors pursuing cinéma vérité projects (the nonmodernist strain of the *Nouvelle Vague*). Hence documenting one of the major voices of the century as part of its literary, philosophical and political history was a natural project. But it wasn't until 1970, when Sartre emerged on the barricades to harangue about the workers at the Renault factory at Billancourt, in a news photo of great controversy in the wake of the events of 1968, that Contat thought seriously of approaching him. In 1971, Sartre accepted; the director Alexandre Astruc's simultaneous proposal was merged with Contat's, and they filmed two weekends of interviews as ground-work for a scripted biography, in February and March 1972, at Beauvoir's and Sartre's apartments in Paris. That filmscript was never fully written. Sartre was opposed to television release of the film, and backing fell through. Ironically

Giscard d'Estaing and the privatization of French television nearly derailed the Astruc/Contat project, as Marc Jullian of Antenne 2 offered Sartre a twelve-part television subjective commentary show. But fate intervened, and that production was cancelled, as Sartre's voice and vision deteriorated from the effects of an earlier stroke. Contat and Astruc also abandoned the idea of additional footage, as the change in Sartre (who had already used medication for the 1972 interviews) would destroy the continuity of the conversations they had already recorded. Thus they passed on to the world a filmic oddity, a hybrid, of a synchronic nexus of personalities gathered to praise famous men and a loosely organized diachronic parade of Sartre's experiences and works, that never coalesces.

The film would be better titled *Sartre Subject and Object*, as it is also a cross-genre collage, a "patrigraphy" as Contat dubbs it, between Sartre, Beauvoir and his followers from *Les Temps Modernes*: Jean Pouillon, André Gorz, Jacques-Laurent Bost. Claude Lanzmann was missing from the group by a chance absence from Paris. The film is less politically controversial in tone than it would have been had Marcel Ophüls's 1969 *Le Chagrin et la pitié* (*The Sorrow and the Pity*) not just been condemned by the Right. It is tempting to imagine what Sartre would have done if he had made a truly autobiographic film about himself, with a transparent subjective first-person narrative. In 1948, Astruc had coined the term *la caméra-stylo* (the camera-pen), coincidental to the development of voice-over narration, for a new style of filmmaking. And Sartre had, as Lejeune points out, been fascinated since childhood with cinema, revealed in accounts in *Les Mots* and more so in the manuscript *Feuillets pour Jean sans Terre*:

> On m'offrit un petit cinéscope. En tournant une manivelle on projetait de tout petits films. Le cinéma me devint familier: j'étais spectateur et opérateur, je voulus être auteur et metteur en scène.[1]

These lines reinforce the Sartrian dilemma articulated in *Les Mots* in the experience of childhood reading, of simultaneous separation and identification, a duality of imagination and intentionality that would later manifest itself as a conflict between commitment and disdain, fear and loathing of natural corporeal being versus an almost scientific passion for knowledge, a desire to be a major force in his era and a phobia of dispossession and death of the self in fame, in a public persona. Sartre's reaction to the film was thus predictable; in response to their closing shot of the empty desk and its unfinished manuscript, he complained, "You have already buried me at Montparnasse." Finally, given the limitations and protective self-parody of *Les Mots*, it is difficult to imagine a truly revelatory "*Sartre by Sartre*."

Although Sartre was foremost a writer/philosopher, the film opens and closes with political sequences: a 1972 conference in Brussels where he decries the *bourgeoisisation* of the intelligentsia and the impossible chasm separating his bourgeois person from his radicalized political self. Astruc and Contat fill in contextually the contemporaneous post-1968 political situation, with intercut color and sepia newsreel footage of popular resistance and demonstrations. The battle lines between the Left and the Right are drawn, as Sartre condemns Pompidou for constructing the Tower Maine-Montparnasse rather than dealing with the gulf between workers and administrators in the industrial sector. While sympathizing with the Maoists, Sartre was living his own contradiction through his last major project, *L'Idiot de la famille* (*The Family Idiot*), his biography of Flaubert depicting him as a predestined product of his bourgeois environment, which can be read as an extended self-portrait of Sartre.

After this opening political frame establishing a central dichotomy in Sartrean discourse, Contat and Astruc turn to their primary task, the Sartrian retrospective, beginning with early photos of Sartre's maternal grandparents, with whom he lived from age three to eleven. They portray that closed, old-fashioned world as Sartre did in *Les Mots*, a world of boredom that influenced both his existential dialectic and his sense of mission as a writer. Early influences on Sartre the "bookmaking machine" included his grandfather's library, where the battle for his imagination and identity was fought. Like Stendhal (his literary biography *manquée*), Sartre was acutely aware of the difference in their choice of texts; and like Stendhal, he began his authorial career by plagiarizing, by recopying articles in notebooks, since lost.

Before discussing *Les Mots*, Astruc and Contat frame the period of the text, with the move to La Rochelle. Sartre and his psychoanalytic biographers like Josette Pacaly agreed that his mother's remarriage to Joseph Mancy when he was eleven changed his whole life; he lost her, this dominant female love object whom he had possessed as a "big sister." In La Rochelle, he developed a strong sense of isolation, of paranoid alienation projected in retrospect in *Les Mots* on his earlier childhood. Stills of La Rochelle in the early century with appropriately metonymic sound effects of the war and the sea (*la guerre et la mer/e*) reflect Sartre's family battle in a household where he was expected to study math and science. Because he had always thought of this mother as his best friend, Sartre was traumatized by her new allegiance to the detested, intrusive stepfather who barred his access to her person.

The filmmakers here are guilty of excess as they use footage of the bombardments of World War I and of soldiers in the trenches, the breakup of the world as it was known, not only as a contemporary context but as an equation of the breakup of Sartre's emotional life. They also edit contextually the political world of the day with shots of Lenin and the masses in the Russian Revolution, with the suffering of the troops in the snow and repeated shots of firing squads, as Sartre claims, "I am a provincial reject of the Russian Revolution," in a blatant act of Maoist revisionism.

After the early family conflicts, the film depicts Sartre in school, further isolated by his distance from his peers, by the physical violence and hard realities of war and port life, so different from the nineteenth-century world he had inhabited with his grandfather. Astruc and Contat depict the birth of Sartre the rebel in a lie, the invention destined to impress his schoolmates of a girlfriend whom he supposedly took to a hotel. Imitating Stendhal's Henri Brulard or Rousseau, Sartre forced the maid to write a love letter that he passed around the school. This recourse to the imagination to counter unbearable reality backfired. Caught like Brulard or the

Truffaut Antoine Doinel character, he was stamped a liar and became even more of a loner, marginalized from the group by fear, isolation and violence. Further criminality led to more punishment, as Sartre's childhood is equatable to Truffaut's self-portrait in *Les Quatre Cents Coups*. Declaring their sympathy for Sartre, Astruc and Contat, working with Annie Chevallay, constructed through editing an adventure tale of the young Sartre's dramatic experiences, emphasizing that this was no ordinary childhood.

The next ingredient in the Astruc-Contat recipe of the making of Sartre the existentialist is his discovery of his ugliness, already inscribed in both *L'Enfance d'un chef* and *Les Mots*. The shock of Sartre's life was his *stade du miroir*, when he had his blond curly hair cut off, the overwhelming sense of the brutality of fate and the contingency of being, seminal elements in Sartrian dialectic, before his image in the mirror. Although claiming to have accepted his appearance without emotional scars, he revealed in *Les Mots* his deep despair as he buried his reflection under "clouds of ink," becoming a writer to mask and protect his vulnerable self from the horror of its own natural nothingness. This sense of visceral contingency and exile, the traveler without a ticket, also informed *La Reine Albemarle ou le dernier touriste*, wherein he explored the relationship of people to their bodies and the dangers inherent in privileging and sacralizing physical beauty.

The reflection in a different mirror suited him much better. Astruc and Contat include here ironically the only dramatized substitute of Sartre in the film, converting him as he did himself to a fictional character, in "la bibliothèque . . . le monde pris dans un miroir" (the library . . . the world caught in a mirror), a world of ideas where he could escape as reader the menace of concrete objects (whose images would however later invade his own writing). The classification of the world in the library gave an illusion of strength and control in ordering knowledge, an ambition Sartre later transferred to the Autodidacte of *La Nausée*. Sartre admits that it took him thirty years to get rid of the idealist heroics, the egocentric diegesis constructed from popular works like *Ponson du Terrail*. Sartre places himself in the tradition of Stendhal or Proust, escaping visceral unhappiness to seek metaphysical truth in literature, pursuing greater secrets beneath its artistic reflections of life.

Sartre confesses what we already know from reading *Les Mots*: at age fifteen he developed a neurosis about becoming more authentic by writing books, and his dreams of glory were dreams of death, of dying famous, transformed. As he explains that his literary ideology came from the past, with its antiquated positivist principles, there is a shot of a statue of Flaubert like the statue of Gustave Impétraz in *La Nausée*. Thus he believed in the immortality of fame in 1910, and his primary ambition was to externalize himself through participation in the classic literary tradition, of Balzac, Hugo, Flaubert, in spite of its inherent contradictions.

The filming of the formative influences and crucial moments in the shaping of Sartre's intellect continues with the question of his atheism, a position he adopted at the time of his mother's remarriage, another aspect of his rebellion against the bourgeois world and values of his upbringing, an equation of loss of faith and loss of the virgin mother. Other major influences on Sartre included the dominant cultural environment of the Lycée Henri IV, where he met Paul Nizan and learned about modern literature. Before Nizan, he had read Claude Ferrère, women's novels, adventure stories, and such popular literature as *La Juive du Château Trompette* and Michel Zevaco. Philippe Lejeune has indexed Sartre's childhood reading, the formation of his *être de papier* (paper being), texts of all persuasions and registers: popular hash, fairy tales, adventure stories, classics, readings complemented by his formal education. Following the prepared questionnaire based on the format of *Archives du XXe Siècle* (*Archives of the Twentieth Century*), Simone de Beauvoir asks Sartre about the influence of classical culture on him, as he talks of reading Proust, Valéry and Gide with the other students at the Ecole Normale Supérieure (rue d'Ulm).

Sartre recounts the famous incident from this era that had direct literary consequences for him. He found a notebook on the Métro (a suppository ad distributed to doctors) which had alphabetized sections for notes. In using it, he thus classified his thoughts alphabetically, the basis for the method of the Autodidacte of *La Nausée*. Astruc and Contat here attempt to bridge the gap between the person and the writing voice with a shot of a hand writing a definition of contingency: "to exist without necessity or justification or right," broaching again the question of development of elements of Sartrian dialectic. Sartre states that his concepts of the absurd, free will, freedom and responsibility, and his existential awareness, came from his loneliness at La Rochelle. He admits that he attempted early on to rewrite his life (as he is retelling it here) to compensate the loss of the loving generosity and freedom (read mother) he had enjoyed as a child.

The development of the political Sartre continues with his experience at Norm Sup, where violence, politics and morality were issues of the day. However, this was yet another privileged milieu wherein Sartre, Nizan and Maheu consciously developed *normalien* personalities: the dandy, the snob, the womanizer. Sartre's ongoing social malaise was aggravated by his comrades' jokes about his passion for Simone Jolivet, which preceded his acquaintance with the second Simone. Here Beauvoir enters the structuring tale of Sartre's development in the era she recalled in *Mémoires d'une jeune fille rangée*. Although they never planned marriage or children, preferring to produce texts instead, they planned life together and would have been willing to marry had it been necessary in order to stay together. This apparent fealty needs to be evaluated in the light of their numerous affairs and sexual experiments, which are glossed over in the film.

Instead the film shows the social context of their world, the café life of Paris of the twenties. Sartre's intellectual odyssey continues with the question of contemporary influences like Marx, Freud, or the Surrealists. The film denies rather than emphasizes their presence in his thought, accentuating rather his individuality, shifting to his *mémoire de diplôme* on *L'Imagination* in 1937, a study of sensation, perception and intentionality, published in 1940 as *L'Imaginaire*, wherein Sartre affirmed the autonomous freedom of the conscious mind (contrary to Marx, Freud and the Surrealists). The capacity of the creative imagination to conceive of non-present objects and people (a concept popularized by Piagetian psychology) would later become part of his *néant*. Sartre and his colleagues like Aron considered themselves realists rather than materialists or idealists, influenced by works like Wahl's *Vers le concret* (*Toward the Concrete*), positing that concrete reality existed, not scientific materialist or physical, but the philosophical essence of things, ontological phenomenology. Another influence in the formation of Sartre's mind and vocation as a philosopher was Bergson, with his theory of duration and enduring. The Foucaldian problem of the relationship between philosophy and language is implicit in Sartre's discussion of one of his earliest works, *La Légende de la vérité* (*The Legend of Truth*), wherein he addresses the elements of philosophical discourse that distinguish it from literature. Yet the mutual influence on Sartre's life of these two *écritures* is the crux of his intellect and of this film.

A long panning shot of all Sartre's works in the Pléiade or Edition Blanche contextualizes the body of the man in the corpus of his texts. Sartre affirms that philosophy gives unity to his *oeuvre*, as the camera carries the spectator across this impressive array of productivity, ending with a shot of the unfinished Flaubert biography, a work reflecting how far Sartre had tried to evolve from the bourgeois system of values dominant in the nineteenth century. These texts constitute a cover-up of Sartre's lyric self, revealing it in philosophical terms, a transference which also expropriates the lives of his biographical subjects: Baudelaire, Genet, Flaubert.

Politics and philosophy converge in the discussion of Sartre's stay in Berlin in 1930 and his reading of Husserl, in reaction to whose *Ideen* he wrote *La Transcendance de l'ego* (*The Transcendance of the Ego*). Accompanying Sartre's comments about the concept of voluntary consciousness he learned from Husserl, Astruc and Contat use shots of Berlin and the advent of the Third Reich. Sartre turns through the metonymic power of this concept to politics, to Hitler's rise to power. At that time, opposing the formation of the Right in France, Sartre, Nizan and Aron thought of themselves as anarchists against the bourgeoisie. Although many French intellectuals joined the Communist Party and supported the 1935–1937 Front Populaire (with leftist demonstrations commonly of half a million people, as again in 1968), Sartre and Beauvoir remained observers of the political scene, sensing confusion in the intellectual response to events and conditions in Russia.

Sartre the philosopher, writer and political figure was also Sartre the professor, a role which was reflected in his writing in the thirties and which led him to anguishing experiences, which he addresses only superficially. His dislike of traditional pedagogy occasioned feelings of revulsion and nausea (although his students, some in the room for this interview, all insisted on his excellence as a teacher). One of the great anecdotes in Sartre's career as a professor concerns the day he got drunk and took his students to the local brothel, climbed onto a prostitute's back, and then left to give the graduation address (the one in 1931 in which he declared cinema the seventh art).

These moments of indulgent energy couldn't mask Sartre's serious mental illness at the time, partially induced by experiments with mescaline. The hallucinations Sartre describes of distortion and metamorphosis were incorporated into his writing, both fictional and philosophical. Although he finally stopped out of fear of the negative effects, of chronic hallucinatory psychosis, Sartre wrote *L'Imagination* at the time of these experiments with drugs, abusing his mind in order to produce hallucinations, in a probing Rimbaldian psychological examination of the self.

The best-known revelation of the Sartrian visceral self is perhaps the experience recounted in *La Nausée* of the chestnut root, dramatized for the film with a camera eye moving through a park in Rouen, with a voice-over of the passage from the text recounting the existential illumination and subsequent dissipation of the physical setting. The undifferentiated determined being of natural objects (their *en-soi*) contrasts the order of constructs of mathematics or music whose importance is reflected in the jazz tune "Some of These Days" in the café in *La Nausée*, wherein Sartre structured his dialectic through his character Roquentin's experiences. Sartre here explains that it was a pathological intuition that led him to use Roquentin to express his philosophical convictions, that he didn't actually experience nausea himself (hiding behind the mask again, as he experienced nausea during sex). Sartre discusses the genesis of his textual nausea, avowing his transpositions of his obsessions without revealing them, as Serge Doubrovsky has since noted. Sartre explains the concept of the transfer of the *en-soi* self-sufficiency of objects that he felt to his characterization of arrogant people whom he baptized *salauds* (people who give themselves special rights in order to flee the nausea of their own nude being and are thus inauthentic). Bost here cuts in to reveal that Sartre experienced nausea and depression even in class during that period.

Sartre's response to this anguish of intuited nothingness was to seek salvation in a work of art, essentially the illusion driving Roquentin. The absence of a chapter on art in *L'Imaginaire* was later corrected. For Sartre, though, it was Flaubert who embodied the relationship between art, the self and the imagination. Taking his cue perhaps from Proust's essay on *Les Silences de Flaubert*, Sartre affirms that silence is the desire to be an *en-soi/pour-soi* man of stone who becomes a noncommunicating statue, contrasting those like himself and Beauvoir who believe in the communicative value of language, writing to engage a dialogue with the reader, the basic thesis of his 1948 *Qu'est-ce que la littérature? (What is Literature?)*.

Conjunction of Sartre's literary, political and professional selves occurred at the time of the Spanish Civil War (1936–1939), reflected in *Le Mur*, written at Laon. Sartre's first encounter with wartime *engagement* (commitment) was his sense of guilt in response to his student Bost's request for help in getting involved (the reverse of the thematic of *The Prime of Miss Jean Brodie*).

The effect on Sartre of World War II is contextualized and equated to its impact on the French nation. The nostalgic song "J'attendrai" and ambient street sounds accompany wartime images, as Hitler's haranguing visage is superimposed on the face of Paris. Historic irony infuses shots of a festival organized throughout the French world by Daladier just at the time of the Munich Pact of 1938, from which he then returned stunned and angry. Less than a year later, France was at war with Germany over the invasion of Poland in September 1939.

Sartre's initial response to France's mobilization for war (illustrated with newsreel footage and a shot of him in uniform) was ambivalent, due to his hatred of French reactionary politics and his fundamental pacifism, reflected in his 1959 *Les Séquestrés d'Altona* (*The Sequestered of Altona*). Sartre characterizes his experience in the war as one of radical change, as for the first time he lived with the people, the proletariat. Yet he lived another dichotomy in the camp, relating mainly to the priests, who were the educated intellectuals. Sent first to serve in an infirmary, then to an artists' unit, where he wrote a play, *Bariona*, Sartre claims that although placed in an elite, he nevertheless learned to respect all the soldiers as human beings, was impacted by their collective group life. He mobilized his own awareness on his return to France with the *engagement* of joining the Resistance. Unfortunately, the working structure of his cell of resistance fighters was destroyed. Sartre shifts away from discussing these experiences, recounting rather the composition of *L'Etre et le néant* and Heidegger's influence. He goes so far as to claim that his war notebooks were lost (untrue, of course; the surviving sections were published posthumously in 1983).

The invasion of the historic Sartre by the philosophical and literary continued through the war, as his dramatic political protest of the occupation, *Les Mouches* (*The Flies*), his rewriting of *Electra*, is ultimately a treatise on existential freedom. The obvious contemporary subtext of the play, the Occupation, is indicated by the directors with overlay shots of the Nazis and occupied Paris. Sartre's wartime activities also included teaching theater in a group with Jean-Louis Barrault.

A musing voice-over soliloquy by Sartre opens the second part of the film, reflecting on the moral and philosophical state of occupied France, emphasizing that it created a paradoxical new "freedom," an ongoing state of mental rebellion against Nazi horrors. Sartre equates the drama of life under threat of exile, captivity or death and conscious resistance in spite of fear to a primal myth worthy of substituting the oedipal scenario. Once again, Sartre is evading revelations of the inner self. He is also condoning passive rebellion, a concept he later rejected in a more militant radical stance. Under the Occupation, Sartre claims he achieved solidarity in solitude (resolving a dilemma that haunted Camus all his life) as a citizen of this Republic of silence and darkness.

Leaving behind the subjective soliloquy imaging the war era, the film focuses again externally on Sartre, and the interview continues, turning to the question of a dominant thematic linking the thirty texts in his *oeuvre*. He here claims that he never sought unity in his writing, although near the beginning of the interview he stated that his philosophy was the connecting link between all his works. Sartre in 1972 repudiates some of his prior thinking, changed by experience, almost guilty of *mauvaise foi*. He revises his concept of freedom, now circumstantial rather than autonomous, and historicizes the concept of contingency, seeing freedom finally as a cumulative construct of identity.

Discussing the postwar period brings up the unpleasant topic of Sartre's notoriety in an era when he was labeled an evil Communist by the Right and a Friend of America by the Left. In addition, extensive translation of his works created a broad readership that he never personally addressed (a problem he never resolves in *Qu'est-ce que la littérature?*).

Sartre acquired at this time a different kind of mask, found himself expropriated by a public persona constructed against his will, living out the existential hell of *Huis clos* (*No Exit*). He claims he collectivized and politicized his writing yet was rejected by the Left, trapped in external association with the collective polemic of the day. Yet the man who wanted to belong refused to repudiate *L'Etre et le néant* to conform to Marxist dialectic materialism, to throw away his past like Georg Lukàcs had done, declaring again that personal freedom, in the classic French Cartesian tradition of *je pense, donc je suis* (I think, therefore I am), was more important. On camera, Sartre first says "je suis, donc je pense" (I am, therefore I think), a revealing Freudian slip not convincingly countered by his affirmation that consciousness is at the base of being.

The founding of the academic journal *Les Temps Modernes* (illustrated with a cover shot of its first issue) is of course included in the film, as the editorial staff is present in the room. Sartre explains that he experienced considerable personal, political and intellectual conflict in this era, caught in the new power struggle between the Americans and the Soviets and the changed face of Communism in both camps. In spite of Europe's dependency on America, Sartre moved toward the Left.

Contat and Astruc demonstrate the right-wing paranoia of the 1950s with newsreel footage of St. Germain-des-Prés, essentially a propaganda essay about the left-wing Left Bank cult, including villains like Juliette Greco, Sartre, Beauvoir, and decrying existentialism and the Beat Generation. A sarcastic voice-over equates rock and roll with decadence, as blacks play jazz at the Café Flore. Ironically, Sartre's celebrated café work habits (acknowledged in the film with one interview done in a café) ended when he moved in with his mother after his stepfather died in 1945. Frequent public appearances were still necessary and often had unpleasant consequences. Sartre declares he especially resented the unauthorized publication of his 1946 lecture *L'Existentialisme est un humanisme* (*Existentialism is a Humanism*), a conciliatory speech he would like to forget. He and Beauvoir acquired more protective masks, hiring a secretary and resorting to hiding and secrecy, fleeing the publicity of his falling out with Camus over *L'Homme révolté* (*The Rebel*). Sartre compares the Cold War fear of annihilation to living in a trap, as he was threatened by the Russians and sure that going to America would have been intellectual suicide. *Huis clos* was in fact performed to considerable controversy in New York in 1947; surprisingly, Sartre never mentions this play, whose thematic could be said to dominate his life.

The problem of Sartre's political and philosophical uniqueness and even isolation leads him to distinguish between the transcendent dialectic of *L'Etre et le néant* and his contextually situated writing in *Le Diable et le bon dieu* (*The Devil and the Good Lord*). Sartre is obliged to acknowledge the dichotomy between Marxist and Freudian discourse in his work and attempts to sort it out, stating that his phenomenology of conscious reality is a prelude to the study of morality and freedom in *Critique de la raison dialectique* (*Critique of Dialectical Reason*) written twenty years later. He claims to treat Marxist morality of class struggle in his biography of Flaubert. Finally, he criticizes the pragmatism of the Left and admits his reluctance to commit himself politically prior to the events of 1968, an ironic avowal for a writer best known for his concept of *engagement*.

Thus 1968 represents a watershed in his thought, and explains in part his attraction to Maoism, which in retrospect seems perverse, given its anti-intellectual precepts. Sartre conceives of his developing conscience and consciousness in three stages: morality, realism and unity of politics and morality, focusing on human rights. Sartre openly admits his inability to move from the dialectic of *L'Etre et le néant* to a work on ethics. The unsaid subtext of these remarks is the unresolved lifelong tension between his ethics and dialectic.

His comments on ethics and politics are contextualized with newsreel footage of the war in Algeria, showing sweeps of the Casbah. Contat and Astruc, like Pontecorvo in *La Bataille d'Alger*, attack the Right through its own rhetoric vaunting France's contributions to Algeria, praising honor and country and the Red Berets. The question of ethics and political power continues as Sartre discusses the problem of torture in the Algerian War, Jeanson's trial, being arrested for signing the Manifest of 121, his hatred for de Gaulle and Pompidou. Astruc and Contat resort to some propaganda of their own, as the film displays official portraits of de Gaulle, Pompidou, Giscard d'Estaing, while Sartre decries them as crooks and thieves who have disfigured France by development, illustrated with shots of amorphous high-rise growth. In 1972, Sartre felt that France needed a revolution to save its society, reflecting the disillusionment of the Left after the euphoria of 1968, similar to events in the wake of the political upheavals of 1989 to 1992. Contat points out in *Sartre Alive* a rare moment of deliberate distortion of historic events by Sartre, when he accused de Gaulle of not responding to popular referenda.

The interweaving of politics and literature in Sartre's postwar work is amplified by Franz von Gerlach's closing monologue in *Les Séquestrés d'Altona*, a diatribe against modern Man, portraying him as a primal Adam, guilty, ashamed, naked, and depicting the twentieth century as a woman in labor, emphasizing the current paralyzing fear of nuclear holocaust. The significance of this piece of text in the film is its mandate for action, for taking responsibility for the collective human condition even in the face of Man's ultimate solitude. Astruc and Contat connect this stance to Sartre's concept of theater, from the ancients via Hegel, as a power struggle between ideological constructs.

At this point, the film reaches the time period of the composition of *Les Mots* (begun in 1953, reworked often and published in 1964). Thus like the film itself, *Les Mots* is contextualized as the enunciation of a *prise de conscience*, a postwar, leftist awakening revealing the folly of his bourgeois ambition of fame, authenticity, necessity through productivity. His sudden cure produced this sarcastic fable of his inauthentic life. He claims the sequel to *Les Mots* will never be published, as he is more interested in his real intellectual autobiography as portrayed in this film. The obvious irony is that just as he constructed a literary myth of the self in *Les Mots*, here he is presenting, with the collaboration of his interviewers, a political historical automyth. He avows that his writing in *Les Mots* was designed to trap the reader of this ludic farewell to literature. Sartre considered his reception of the 1956 Nobel Prize, which he refused, as emblematic of his bourgeois neurosis, a symbol of capitalist mentality and the tombstone of the writer, a dual image of the "hardness" of permanence he decries so often in his writing. Sartre situates the enduring value of his work in its reflection in the mirror of its collective critical reception. Here Beauvoir enters the picture again, as his first lifelong critic, offering simultaneous opposition and comprehension. Considering this affirmation, the absence of discussion of her own work is an obvious omission from the film.

Rather than discussing his visceral reality or affective and sexual involvements, Sartre characterizes women as oppressed, interesting and sensitive to life, agreeing with Jacques Lacan that men lack finesse and are comical. The unsaid here is the catalogue of embarrassing moments in Sartre's life. He rather acknowledges the importance of Beauvoir's intellectual companionship, preferring her conversation to philosophical discussions or debates with hard-line Marxists. Sartre restricts his attachment to Beauvoir to his concept of *engagement*, abstracting their relationship and for that matter all his interpersonal life away from their psychic and physical realities.

Returning to the political contextualization of Sartre's work and to the increasing importance of politics in his life after his farewell to literature and the past in *Les Mots*, Astruc and Contat situate Sartre against the Cuban Revolution. He claims leftist affiliation for his *Critique de la raison dialectique*, which delineates the mutual exclusion of power hierarchy and mass equality. Sartre's analysis of Cuba, which he visited in 1960, and Castro is very disjointed, as once again he evades the central paradox for him of Maoism, its pretense to support the masses while a dictatorial government represses education as fostering an elite.

Astruc and Contat reveal their own political biases in their intense depiction of the chaos in Vietnam, and in juxtaposing scenes of military brutality towards civilians with Sartre speaking at the (Bertrand) Russell War Crimes Trial, a forum for criticism of the atrocities committed that raised public consciousness and accused the USA of genocide. Shots of villagers sounding the tocsin accompany anti-American propaganda, ironic in light of the humiliating defeat of French colonialism in Vietnam in 1954 and its consequences.

Sartre attempts to outline the post-1968 changes in his own intellectual and theoretical pursuits, his shift away from the stance of the classic intellectual who specializes in the study of practical and technical knowledge based on a scientific approach. Sartre rejects the idea of scientists as intellectuals, their lack of awareness of the contradiction between the general and the specific, and the inherent injustices it fosters. The events of 1968 foregrounded the dominance of an intellectual power elite in France and forced it to abdicate authority in order to find solidarity with the rebellion. Caught again in the irreducible dilemma of Maoist rhetoric, Sartre places the intellectual in the factory, glossing or ignoring the brutalities in China and Cambodia. There is almost an implicit intellectual suicide in Sartre's desire for integration into the masses, the same kind of obsession to belong that he evinced in his youth at La Rochelle, the same dishonesty out of desperation. He tries to explain his final obsession, his fascination for Flaubert, as a sociological Marxist demonstration of bourgeois intellectualism.

Astruc and Contat and the interviewers all express an obvious desire to portray Sartre according to his current wishes, reflecting for him in their collective critical mirror the man he wants to be, taking the *enfer* (hell) of *les autres* (others) of *Huis clos* and converting it to a hagiographic paradise. The final sequences are no exception, as they depict the new activist Sartre addressing the people in the street, attempting to reintegrate himself into the mainstream, having been marginalized as an old-guard intellectual (the same dilemma that plagued him as a student). He is shown as *solidaire* of the students and the workers at the 1970 trial at Lens of factory exploitation, and decries the 1972 assassination of Pierre Overney by company guards, declaring that the French Communist Party and the government are both against the Maoists, that Fascism is back in power. There is a poignant contrast between the jazz music at Overney's funeral and the jazz theme of *La Nausée*, which Sartre said carried within it its own death. That closed aesthetic sufficiency is here transformed into a demonstration of lyric vulnerability *pour-autrui*.

At the time of the release of this film, 1976, the Maoists dissolved their organization, and Sartre was pursuing libertarian socialism, having founded the newspaper *Libération* in 1973 (today one of France's leading dailies). The ironic epilogue to Sartre's life and work was his physical blindness that prevented him from working the last two years of his life. Because he died in 1980, he did not witness France's return to the Left or the collapse of the Eastern Block totalitarian hegemony, two phenomena that would certainly have had a major impact on his philosophical and political dialectic.

There is in Astruc and Contat's alternating and overlapping of Sartre's personal narrative of his ideological journey, both literary and philosophical, and the included historic documentary footage an implicit equation between the man and the era that transcends a simple response to his compulsion to belong. Their framing of his texts, thought and person acknowledges a final desire to integrate his individual voice into the greater authenticity of the collective experiential ethos.

Note

1. Philippe Lejeune, "Les Souvenirs de lectures d'enfance de Sartre," in Claude Burgelin, ed., *Lectures de Sartre* (Lyons: Presses Universitaires de Lyon, 1986) 69–70. ("They offered me a

little movie projector. By turning the crank, you projected tiny little films. Cinema became well known to me: I was the spectator and the cameraman, I wanted to be the author and the director." My translation.)

Bibliography

Arnold, Albert James, et J.-P. Piriou. *Genèse et critique d'une autobiographie: Les Mots.* Paris: Archives des Lettres Modernes, 1973.

Aronson, Ronald, and Adrian van den Hoven, eds. *Sartre Alive.* Detroit: Wayne State University Press, 1991.

Bauer, George Howard. *Sartre and the Artist.* Chicago: University of Chicago Press, 1969.

Boak, Denis. *Sartre Les Mots.* Wolfeboro, N.H.: Grant and Cutler, 1987.

Bourdieu, Pierre. "A Propos de Sartre." *French Cultural Studies* 4:3:12 (Oct 1993) 209–211.

Brosman, Catherine. *Sartre.* Boston: Twayne, 1983.

Burgelin, Claude. "De Sartre à Flaubert ou la genèse d'un roman vrai." *Revue d'Histoire Littéraire de la France* 81: 4–5 (1981) 688–701.

————, ed. *Lectures de Sartre.* Lyons: Presses Universitaires de Lyon, 1986.

Burger, Peter. "Passé Simple: The Essay as Autobiographical Form in Jean-Paul Sartre." *MLN* 102:5 (1987) 1182–1190.

Champigny, Robert. *Sartre and Drama.* Columbia, S.C.: University of South Carolina Press, 1983.

Charme, Stuart. *Meaning and Myth in the Study of Lives: A Sartrean Perspective.* Philadelphia: University of Pennsylvania Press, 1984.

————. *Vulgarity and Authenticity: Dimensions of Otherness in the World of Jean-Paul Sartre.* Amherst: University of Massachusetts Press, 1991.

Cohen-Solal, Annie. "Camus, Sartre and the Algerian War." *Journal of European Studies* 28:1–2 (Mar–June 1998) 43–50.

————. *Sartre.* Paris: Gallimard, 1985.

Contat, Michel. "*Sartre by Himself:* An Account, an Explanation, a Defence." In Aronson, Ronald, and Adrian van den Hoven, eds. *Sartre Alive.* Detroit: Wayne State University Press, 1991.

————, and Michel Rybalka. *Les Ecrits de Sartre.* Paris: Gallimard, 1970.

————, eds. *Un Théâtre de situations.* Paris: Gallimard, 1973.

Danto, Arthur C. *Jean-Paul Sartre.* New York: Viking Press, 1975.

————. *De Sartre à Foucault: vingt ans de grands entretiens dans 'Le Nouvel Observateur'.* Paris: Hachette, 1984.

Debray, Regis. "The Book as Symbolic Object." Eric Rauth, trans. In Nunberg, Violi and Eco, eds. *The Future of the Book.* Berkeley: University of California Press, 1996.

Doubrovsky, Serge. "Sartre: retouches à un autoportrait (une autobiographie visqueuse)." In Burgelin, Claude, ed. *Lectures de Sartre.* Lyons: Presses Universitaires de Lyon, 1986.

Enthoven, Raphael. "Que reste-t-il de Sartre?" *Magazine Littéraire* 384 (Feb 2000) 64–65.

Fauconnier, Bernard. "Sartre-De Gaulle: L'Etre et le géant." *Magazine Littéraire* 384 (Feb 2000) 59–61.

Fourny, Jean-François, and Charles Minahen, eds. *Situating Sartre in Twentieth-Century Thought and Culture.* New York: St Martin's Press, 1997.

Galster, Ingrid, ed. *La Naissance du "Phénomène Sartre": Raisons d'un succès, 1938-1945.* Paris: Seuil, 2001.

Gerassi, John. *Jean-Paul Sartre: Hated Conscience of his Century.* Chicago: University of

Chicago Press, 1989.

Goldthorpe, Rhiannon. "*Les Mots*: 'Soi-même comme un autre'." *Cahiers de l'Association Internationale des Etudes Françaises* 50 (May 1998) 231–245.

Grogin, R. C. *The Bergsonian Controversy in France: 1900–1914*. Calgary: University of Calgary Press, 1988.

Haarscher, Guy. "Autobiographie: Regard de l'autre et problème de la justification chez Sartre." *French Literature Series* 12 (1985) 145–153.

Harvey, Robert. "Sartre/Cinema: Spectator/Art That is Not One." *Cinema Journal* 30:3 (1991) 43–59.

Hayman, Ronald. *Writing Against: A Biography of Sartre*. London: Weidenfeld and Nicolson, 1986.

Helbo, André. *L'Enjeu du discours: lecture de Sartre*. Brussels: Editions Complexe, 1978.

Hollier, Denis. *Politique de la prose: Jean-Paul Sartre et l'an quarante*. Paris: Gallimard, 1982.

Honigsblum, Gerald. "Sartre by Himself: Film as Biography and Autobiography." *French Review* 55:7 (1982) 123–130.

Idt, Geneviève. "L'Autoparodie dans Les Mots." *Cahiers du XXe Siècle* 6 (1976).

Issakaroff, Michel, and Jean-Claude Vilquin, eds. *Sartre et la mise en signe*. Paris: Klincksieck, 1982.

Jameson, Fredric. *Sartre: The Origins of a Style*. New Haven: Yale University Press, 1961.

————, ed. *Sartre after Sartre*. Yale French Studies 68 (1985).

Kaufmann, Dorothy. "Autobiographical Intersexts: *Les Mots* de deux enfants rangés." *L'Esprit Créateur* 29:4 (1989) 21–32.

Koch, Gertrud. "Sartre's Screen Projection of Freud." *October* 57 (Summer 1991) 3–17.

Kruks, Sonia. "Identity Politics and Dialectical Reason: Beyond an Epistemology of Provenance." In Murphy, Julien, ed. *Feminist Interpretations of Jean-Paul Sartre*. University Park, PA: Pennsylvania State University Press, 1999.

Lacapra, Dominick. *A Preface to Sartre*. Ithaca, N.Y.: Cornell University Press, 1978.

Lecarme, Jacques. "*Les Mots* de Sartre: un cas limite de l'autobiographie?" *Revue d'Histoire Littéraire de la France* 6 (1975) 1047–1061.

Lejeune, Philippe. "Ça s'est fait comme ça." *Poétique* 35 (1978) 269–304.

————. "L'Ordre du récit dans Les Mots de Sartre." In *Le Pacte autobiographique*. Paris: Seuil, 1975.

————. "Le Point final de l'autobiographie: l'Epilogue des Mots." In Duchet, Claude, and Isabelle Tournier, eds. *Genèses des fins: de Balzac à Beckett, de Michelet à Ponge*. St. Denis: Presses Universitaires de Vincennes, 1996.

————. "Les Souvenirs de lectures d'enfance de Sartre." In Burgelin, Claude, ed. *Lectures de Sartre*. Lyons: Presses Universitaires de Lyon, 1986.

Magazine Littéraire 384 (Feb 2000) entire issue.

Morita, Shuji. "Sartre dans la salle obscure." *Etudes de Langue et Littérature Françaises* 48 (Mar 1986) 102–118.

Noudelmann, François. "Entre chair et cuir: le corps selon Sartre." In *Le Corps à découvert*. Paris: STH, 1992.

————. *Sartre: L'Incarnation imaginaire*. Paris: Harmattan, 1996.

Pacaly, Josette. *Sartre au miroir*. Paris: Klincksieck, 1980.

Pauly, Rebecca M. "*Huis clos, Les Mots* et *La Nausée*: le bronze de Barbedienne et le coupe-papier." *French Review* 60:5 (1987) 626–634.

————. "Sartre et Barthes: de la chambre claire de l'imaginaire à l'émiettement du moi dans la bibliothèque." In *Le Berceau et la bibliothèque*. Saratoga: Anma Libri, 1989.

Pautrot, Jean-Louis. "Robbe-Grillet, Sartre, Duras: mer, musique, écriture." *French Review* 68:2

(Dec 1994) 274–282.

Perrett, Roy. "Autobiography and Self-deception: Conjoining Philosophy, Literature, and Cognitive Psychology." *Mosaic* 29:4 (Dec 1996) 25–40.

Polan, Dana. "Sartre and Cinema." *Post-Script* 7:1 (Fall 1987) 66–88.

Prince, Gerald. "'Dépaysement' de Sartre, ou les déboires d'un touriste." *French Review* 58:2 (1984) 255–259.

——. "Sartre Resartus." *Diacritics* 14 (Winter 1984) 2–8.

Pucciani, Oreste. "Sartre et notre culture." *Dalhousie French Studies* 54 (Spring 2001) 50–53.

Raoul, Valérie. "The Diary Novel: model and meaning in *La Nausée*." *French Review* 56:5 (1983) 703–710.

Rykner, Arnaud. "Narcisse et les mots-miroirs: Sartre, Leiris, Sarraute autobiographes." *Romanic Review* 83:1 (1992) 81–93.

Santa, Maria, introd. *Sartre. Cahiers de l'Association Internationale des Etudes Françaises* 50 (May 1998) entire issue.

Sartre, Jean-Paul. "Autoportrait à 70 ans." *Situations X*. Paris: Gallimard, 1979.

——. *Les Carnets de la drôle de guerre*. Paris: Gallimard, 1983.

——. *Le Diable et le bon dieu*. Paris: Gallimard, 1951.

——. *L'Etre et le néant*. Paris: Gallimard, 1943.

——. *L'Homme et les choses*. Paris: Seghers, 1947.

——. *Huis clos, suivi de Les Mouches*. Paris: Gallimard, 1947.

——. *L'Idiot de la famille*, I, II, III. Paris: Gallimard, 1972, 1975, 1978.

——. *L'Imaginaire*. Paris: Gallimard, 1940.

——. *Les Mots*. Paris: Gallimard, 1964.

——. *Le Mur*. Paris: Gallimard, 1939.

——. *Oeuvres romanesques*. Paris: Gallimard Pléiade, 1981.

——. *Qu'est-ce que la littérature?* Paris: Gallimard, 1948.

——. "Sartre sur Sartre." *Situations* IX. Paris: Gallimard, 1978.

——. *Le Scénario Freud*. Paris: Gallimard, 1983.

Sartre on Biography. French Review 55: 7 (1982). Entire issue.

Schroeder, William. *Sartre and his Predecessors: The Self and the Other*. Boston: Routledge, 1984.

Scriven, Michael. "Television Images of Sartre." *French Cultural Studies* 3:1 (Feb 1992) 87–92.

Siegel, Liliane. *In the Shadow of Sartre*. London: Collins, 1990.

Todd, Christopher. "Sartre flirts with the radio." In Dolamore, James. *Making Connections*. Berlin: Peter Lang, 1999.

Wall, Geoffrey. "Sartre: Scenes from a life." *Cambridge Quarterly* 29:4 (2000) 373–385.

Wilcocks, Robert ed. *Critical Essays on Jean-Paul Sartre*. Boston: G. K. Hall, 1988.

Willmott, Glenn. "Implications for a Sartrean Radical Medium: From Theatre to Cinema." *Discourse* 12:2 (1990).

Wood, Philip. *Understanding Jean-Paul Sartre*. Columbia: University of South Carolina Press, 1990.

Theater on Film:
Screening Stage and Script

Recent theoretical criticism has tended to deconstruct (through contextualization of production, performance and reception) live theater and its constituent components: the body, dialogical and monological discourse of self and other, the set (including costumes, lighting, decor, music), time, space, interaction or lack of it with the audience, situational ironies, historic ironies. Narratological concepts have also been fruitfully applied to theatrical performance: intertextual and metatextual considerations, as well as narrative structures of dialogue and didascalia. From the perspective of genre study, theater represents, as literature and as performance, a wide range, including historic or psychological realism, surrealism, modernism, the absurd, interactive or even violent staging, improvisation, or metatheatrical scripts of rehearsals. Since the Renaissance, theater has included metatextual or extra-diegetic commentary, didascalia, the play-within-the-play or *mise-en-abyme* staging, as well as extensive ludic play of exchanged roles, masks, disguises, etc. Some of the most intriguing theoretical perceptions of theater have come from semiotics, studying the signs and structures of staging the text.

Included in this study are five classically "theatrical" plays which have been filmed, chosen from a narrow band of the generic spectrum of French theater, all of which foreground stereotypical character portrayal in action and response, particularly as characters confront social, political, economic or sexual adversity. Admittedly, these filmed versions do not constitute true adaptations moving away from the physical parameters of the stage, but rather emphasize necessary transitions of focus and framing in the conversion from live performance before an audience to the "sealed" or "frozen" images recorded on film, a performance which can be repeated without variation endlessly. Thus the means of cutting, framing and presenting the staged text on screen also reveal ideological and esthetic constructs from the time of the filming. Before looking at each performance and text individually, it is helpful to consider the relationship between stage and screen in broader theoretical terms.

Theoretical considerations involved in any transposition from script to stage to screen are complex and varied. Not only are vastly different types of "writing" involved, but the distinctions between the production of theater and film are fundamental. Although both these creative processes require a group effort and a transformation from written script to live characters on a set, the fragmentary nature of film production dictates that its repetitions be of discrete parts rather than of the integral performance repeated nightly on the live stage. Perhaps the two come together in the French word for rehearsal, *répétition*, wherein incomplete parts of the play are the focus of the collaborative creative effort that stage and screen share. In spite of this one shared element in the creative process of stage and screen, most actors signal the distance for them between these two contrasting modes of performance. Often the transition is so great that the performer simply cannot function in two such disparate contexts.

The reception of live theater and canned film is equally diverse. In spite of film's capacity for imposing the reality of its illusion, the unreality of the "reel" creates an oneiric transparence that live bodies on stage cannot duplicate, no matter how surrealistic the set, costumes or script. In spite of special effects and moving performances (pun intended), the film spectator possesses the images and internalizes them very differently from the theater spectator's reception of and interaction with the live performance.

Even greater is the distance of course between the silent isolated reader of a text, not the group oral reading preparatory to performance, and the shared aural and visual reception of the stage or screen presentation, terrain which contains the line of demarcation between literature and film. Marshall McLuhan established a classic distinction in *Understanding Media* between the "cold" medium of the printed text, which demands intense positive subjective imaginary responses from the reader, and the "hot" medium of the moving picture, which fills the theater with sound and light, with preconceived, complete, full images (at once fixed and moving) that impose themselves on the senses of the spectator. Television lies somewhere in between; it has a priori de facto images which encourage a certain passivity in the viewer, but the screen is relatively small, and interruptions and distractions, including ambient lighting and other noises and objects in the immediate environment, are numerous. As TV screens get larger and sound systems more powerful, the at-home viewer is increasingly swept up passively in the illusion. And the development of video has of course bridged many of the traditionally conceived gaps between film and television. Videos and DVDs of feature films presented in virtual private home theaters are creating a new status of recipient, just as the use of video cameras has generated a new thematic of performance and documentation, contained within films like *Down and Out in Beverly Hills, sex, lies and videotape, The Big Easy, I've Heard the Mermaids Singing, Man Bites Dog, Reality Bites, Wag the Dog*. Everything from obsessive adolescent self-expression to police evidence serves as the rationale for including video production and playback as the new format of the film within the film, heir to the text in the text and the play within the play.

Here a footnote is appropriate. The films discussed in this study are all available on video or DVD, which have become increasingly popular as viewing formats in presenting cinema, due to the flexibility of editing, portability, etc. Ideally films shown on video or DVD should be presented in large format projection in a dark theater to duplicate the original effects of the filmmaker or theater performance. Even productions made originally for television which have large numbers of close-ups and special staging to accommodate the limitations of their reception lose much of their power as image and experience when viewed on a small monitor or computer screen. The newest large-format projection systems offer superior resolution of sound and image, enhancing presentation and reception.

The attraction of cinema over text since its inception and particularly since the development of sound and color is not just its sensorial novelty but the spectator's ability to experience an immediate illusion of reality. The viewer identifying with the characters on the screen is swept into the diegesis portrayed in intense ways that equal as much as they contrast the experience of the active initiated reader. Although an individual reader may experience and express more visceral emotion in the privacy of the imagination, the moviegoer's responses to tears or laughter is shared and echoed by other spectators. In text, stage and film, there is an equal capacity for catharsis in closure for the reader or spectator, but for the film cast, the fragmented nature of their performance inevitably lacks the cathartic experience of the integral performance. Harrison Ford once noted in an interview that acting on film was a challenging exploration of extending the self, but that film performance lacked catharsis due to its discrete sequential production. The collaborative collective nature of film production and reception is central to its art. In fact, film is such a collective experience that screening a film alone can be a surrealistic experience, which is often depicted as a confrontation with the self, like the end of *Cinema Paradiso*.

In contrast, the written text, encoded in black on white, is created in solitude and sent out into the world, an appeal to a potential reader to receive, revive and reinterpret the imaginary world which created the work. And not only is each reader different, but each reading of the same text is a new experience. As the Chinese proverb says, you never put your foot in the same river twice. The spectator who returns to the same movie (sometimes as many as a hundred viewings) sees new images and sounds along with remembered elements, but not in the same way that the reader recreates the text with each successive reading. Yet film also imposes the same images on successive viewings. The nonspecificity of the acoustic images generated by acts of reading makes them more vulnerable to reinterpretation through rereading. Different considerations arise with new productions of a film or play that do approximate the generative capacity of rereading the printed text. Within the realm of repetition, it is important to distinguish the generic variants between the sequel, the remake, the citation and the homage.

The totality of the theatrical performance thus stands in nearly perfect opposition to the assembling of film footage from multiple incomplete takes, recreating the play in its entirety each time before a live audience. The stage actors thus repeat integral performances while film actors prepare discrete segments of the movie, whose order is often determined by costuming, setting or the characters involved. The narrative discontinuities in such an order of production and the different order subsequently imposed in editing create a profound inherent unreality in the very structure of the experience of filmmaking. This is distinct from the playwright's or filmmaker's deliberate creation of "modernist" or surreal works that are self-reflexive and play with considerations of staging, acting, levels of reality and illusion, chronology, narrative structure. While the film flashback and discontinuities of sound and image can both be generative of oneiric or surreal effects, the reality of the illusion created on stage may be more complete for the audience observing the actors in the flesh. And yet the illusion of reality generated for the film spectator through the artifice of cutting, mixing, matting and editing is paradoxically greater.

In live theater, the acknowledged dynamic role of both performer and spectator dominates the experience, privileging the spectator as corporeal presence yet denying that recipient of performance the voyeuristic joy of the scopophiliac silently absorbing the film image in the womblike darkness of the movie theater. A live performance with its integrity and uniqueness, completeness, recreates the primitive drama of oral storytelling, never the same yet always repeated, from performance to performance and from production to production. Yet the text of a play, like the print of a film or a literary work, is duplicated endlessly and sent out into the world. Thus all three formats have their special elemental experiences, demand different responses from the spectator or reader to participate in the imaginary world depicted, at once present and nonpresent. The text creates with black print on the white page what the film creates with sound and light waves. The visceral physicality of theater sets it squarely between the other two experiences.

Yet another set of factors come to the fore with "canned theater" and the direct transposition of a staged performance onto film. We are then confronting a filmed play, a hybrid which has been accused of betraying both art forms. The filmed play has a number of texts: its original written version (which did not necessarily precede its first performance—Shakespeare, Molière), its screenplay script, and its film print. Ultimately the text of such a work is the sum of its editions and representations, staged or filmed. Film and video recordings of live theater are not only valuable complements to the study of plays as text, especially in the absence of a live performance, but they also elucidate the various factors distinguishing the reception of the three different formats involved in text, theater, and film.

Bibliography

Behar, Lisa Block de. "Les 'Cordons' dans la communication esthétique." *Degrés* 31 (Summer 1982) d1–d8.

Blau, Herbert. "Universals of Performance; or, Amortizing Play." *SubStance* 11/12:4/1 (1983) 140–161.

Brownstein, Oscar, and Darlene Daubert, eds. *Analytical Sourcebook of Concepts in Dramatic Theory*. Westport, CT: Greenwood Press, 1981.

Carlson, Marvin. "Theatre Historiography and Semiotic Analysis." *Literary Research* 11:1 (1986) 5–10.

Chambers, Ross. "Le Masque et le miroir: Vers une théorie relationnelle du théâtre." *Etudes Littéraires* 13:3 (1980) 397–412.

Elam, Keir. *The Semiotics of Theatre and Drama*. London: Methuen, 1980.

Feral, Josette, J.L. Savona and E.A. Walker, eds. "Theory of Drama and Performance." *Modern Drama* 25:1 (1982).

Helbo, André. "Approaches to Reception: Some Problems." *Assaph* C 4 (1988) 83–92.

——. *Theory of Performing Arts*. Brussels: Benjamins, 1987.

Hopkins, Patricia, and Wendell Aycock, eds. *Myths and Realities of Contemporary French Theater: Comparative Views*. Lubbock: Texas Tech University Press, 1985.

Jomaron, Jacqueline de. *Dramaturgies: Langages dramatiques*. Paris: Nizet, 1986.

MacAloon, John, ed. *Rite, Drama, Festival, Spectacle: Rehearsals toward a Theory of Cultural Performance*. Philadelphia: Institute for the Study of Human Issues, 1984.

Marinis, Marco de. "Understanding Theatre: Towards a Historical Semiotics as an Epistemology of the Theatrical Disciplines." *Les Problèmes des Genres Littéraires* 29:2/58 (1986) 5–18.

Nicolaescu, Madalina. "Theatrical Space: The Relationship Between the Fictional World, the Acting Area, and the Space of the Spectators." *Synthesis* 15 (1988) 57–62.

Poetics 13:1–2 (1984). Entire issue.

Reinhardt, Nancy. "New Directions for Feminist Criticism in Theatre and the Related Arts." *Soundings* 64:4 (1981) 361–387.

Schmid, Herta, and Aloysius Van Kesteren. *Semiotics of Drama and Theatre: New Perspectives in the Theory of Drama and Theatre*. Brussels: Benjamins, 1984.

Segre, Cesare. "Narratology and Theater." *Poetics Today* 2:3 (1981) 95–104.

Veltrusky, Jiri. "The Prague School Theory of Theater." *Poetics Today* 2:3 (1981) 225–235.

Yarrow, Ralph. "'Neutral' Consciousness in the Experience of Theater." *Mosaic* 19:3 (1986) 1–13.

Zouboff, Anne. "Diderot a parlé de cinéma." *Europe* 661 (1984) 133–142.

Le Misanthrope
(*The Misanthrope*)

directed by Pierre Dux (1985)
play by Molière (1666)

Along with *Le Tartuffe* and *Le Bourgeois Gentilhomme*, *Le Misanthrope* represents nearly the full scope of Molière's comic genius, from biting satire to grande farce and paranoid bathos. *Le Tartuffe* in particular stands as a monument to comic energy; *Le Misanthrope* represents the fine line between comedy and melodrama, satire and paranoia; *Le Bourgeois Gentilhomme* offers an outrageous parody of social graces, diversions and pageantry. In the jest (and *geste*) of Alceste, the protagonist of *Le Misanthrope*, there is so much truth that his persona becomes painful, his own antagonist, his own nemesis. The portrayal of this complex character who runs the gamut of dramatic expression from amorous acts to parody to rage is one of the supreme challenges of French theater. In his own time, Molière played his lead roles himself, sometimes inventing the play as he went, *chemin faisant*. Thus his roles are as much autobiographical or personal accounts as his plays are portraits of the era.

Born in Paris in 1622 as Jean-Baptiste Poquelin, Molière grew up in a comfortable middle-class milieu, whose foibles would serve as the subject of numerous satiric comedies destined to delight his aristocratic audiences. Molière received a good academic education, read Latin, and acquired the same type of deistic, materialistic wisdom as that evinced by his contemporary, Cyrano de Bergerac. Having failed in his first theatrical endeavors in Paris with Madeleine Béjart, badly in debt, Molière left Paris to find success in the provinces, in particular in Guyenne. By the time he returned to Paris, in 1658, he had experienced poverty, jealousy, bitterness, cynicism, as well as physical suffering from ill health.

All of his plays in some way ridicule the vanities and corruption of the day. Just as *Le Bourgeois Gentilhomme* lambasts the ambitions of the untitled rich (the French connotations of *bourgeois* as materialistic, conspicuous, competitive, vacuous), and *Le Tartuffe* attacks the cabalistic zeal of religious fanatics, so *Le Misanthrope* harpoons the fatuous pretensions of the courtiers of the petty nobility whom Molière observed in Paris drawing rooms and in the social labyrinth lavishly structured by Louis XIV at Versailles. In many of Molière's plays there are ironic reflections of the world of the court, for which and often in which they were performed, amid the agenda of banquets, concerts, card parties, hunts, outings, balls acted out by the nobility on their own stage, with great intrigue and competition for power around the person of the king.

The three plays presented here merit extended analysis not only because they are the most enduringly popular of Molière's plays, the most frequently staged and studied, but also because they all treat text and language as their central subject, thus offering both a point of departure and a *point de repère* (touchstone) in a treatment of text and film. They also present an interesting study in contrasts in terms of film adaptations of theater. *Le Misanthrope* is here adapted to the constraints of small screen viewing, video and TV formats, using extensive close-ups and a closed, four-sided set, Célimène's apartment suite. It could be said that *Le Misanthrope* is eminently adaptable to the screen because of its setting and its subject, its close focus on precious pretentions, character and caricature, love and hate. In the production distributed by Films for the Humanities, Jean Rochefort, usually known for wild slapstick performances, drips with self-pity and righteous wrath, somehow without becoming a self-parody, while Marie-Christine Barrault glows with self-indulgent sensuality and linguistic brilliance.

The staging of the play, live or filmed, is somewhat limited by the fact that the didascalia are incorporated into the text. Mingled with the alexandrines bristling with *préciosité* (affected, coded metaphoric language) are myriad comments such as "Madame, I take leave of you." In some instances, the humor invades the stage directions, as a character announces his departure but never exits, a dramatic irony which Samuel Beckett takes to the teleological level in *En Attendant Godot* (*Waiting for Godot*).

There are in this filmed version of *Le Misanthrope* some outdoor sequences shot in front of Célimène's *hôtel* (townhouse, homonymous as noted in French with *autel*, altar), which take place indoors in the stage version. There is, in addition, a somewhat gratuitous add-on ending shot of Alceste out in the street and Célimène looking down at him from behind her shutters, an attempt to visibly portray the ambiguity of their final situation, where his intransigence costs him her hand offered in marriage, the prize he has so long desired. In this case, both are imprisoned and separated by the interior/exterior dichotomy: Alceste cannot abide society and Célimène cannot relinquish it, even though spurned by her cabal.

The situation of *Le Misanthrope* had particular poignancy for Molière, for not only was he a disillusioned idealist like Alceste but he suffered great jealousy regarding the attention bestowed upon his beautiful young wife. Although the majority of his great leading roles are stereotypical or even archetypal title characters, including besides the three treated here *L'Avare* (*The Miser*), *Le Médecin malgré lui* (*The Doctor in Spite of Himself*), *Le Malade imaginaire* (*The Imaginary Invalid*), they display quirks and traits of realistic immediacy coming from Molière's own experience. In some ways, these characters are more personal than an autobiographic narrative voice, as the stage personalities speak directly in their own words, create (in dialogue and with their person as actors and actresses) stage identities of both imagination and flesh and blood.

The verve and the energy of Molière's plays, which resulted directly from his dramatic genius, have been toned down for this filmed version. Perhaps the characters are trying to restrain themselves for the camera, which in close-ups magnifies all facial expressions, or perhaps they are "modernizing" the play, letting the "serious" thematic elements through by not burying them in grande farce. Or this may be a contemporary interpretation of the essence of courtly *préciosité* and propriety, the social restraint transposed to the dramatic interpretation. The costumes and decor, the material setting of the performance, are exquisitely authentic. It is interesting to what extent here again the play refers directly to staging details, such as the green ribbons on Alceste's costume, a color coded for jealousy.

One of the most intriguing elements of *Le Misanthrope*, which takes shape literally in any staging, live or filmed, is the role of written texts on stage, echoes of the script stage of the performance. The famous sonnet sequence (Act I, Scene II), which Madame de Sévigné tells us referred to the king himself (he had written a dreadful sonnet which he read as anonymous to a courtier who criticized it), places Oronte's wretched poem center stage. Detached from its place in the written script, it recovers its original form on stage as a textual object read aloud. In the cadences of its interrupted reading and the triple commentary it elicits, the sonnet functions as a fourth character, separate from the autoapology and autocritique of its author and the contrasting responses of Alceste and Philinte. The unspoken subtext of this sequence is not just the king's sonnet; it is Molière's resentment of the popularity, success and patronage of mediocre authors in the scribbling society of his day. Rather than risking censure here, Molière is rather attempting to please the king by making exaggerated fools out of both Oronte and the excessively critical Alceste. Alceste prefers to Oronte's offering a classic Renaissance folk song, "Si le Roi m'avait donné." That song, wherein the singer values his love more than Paris and all its glory, embodies Alceste's position and anticipates the ending of the play, where Célimène refuses to leave society for a new life with the antisocial Alceste.

In the central scene of the portraits (Act II, Scene IV), Molière offers the spectator the dialogical equivalent of the *Caractères* of La Bruyère and contextualizes the latter's work as a social tradition of the day, wherein the courtiers compete in depicting one another. The sonnets and portraits constitute a satire of the decadence of poetic language since Ronsard. At the same time, Acaste offers his self-portrait in the current mode, but is deflated by the ironic reception it gets from Clitandre. There are references in the play to other plays as well: an autocitation when Alceste refers to *L'Ecole des maris* (*School for Husbands*). In the name Alceste lies a reference to a tragedy by Euripides, which would be set to music by Lully in 1674. Other characters' names are equally allusive in other ways; Arsinoé was the name of four ancient Egyptian princesses.

Text has a primary functional role in the play as well, as the three *coups de théâtre* of the play all involve letters as agents of intrigue, as principal characters. The first is the sequence where Alceste in a rage confronts Célimène with one of her love letters that Arsinoé has treacherously given him in jealous betrayal. Célimène defends herself by pointing out the lack of an addressee in the letter, ironizing its text through the context of its reception. Alceste is mollified by her clever "rewriting" of the letter, but Célimène's duplicity is irrefutably confirmed in the final scene. Before that, Alceste's departure from society and the loss of his lawsuit are announced by a nonletter, a letter forgotten by Du Bois, the servant who is literally *illettré* (illiterate) as his name also indicates. The closing epistolary sequence is that of the duet between the rivals Acaste and Clitandre, who in turn read letters of calumny from Célimène insulting themselves and destined for one another. The substitution of the subject of the letter for the recipient traps the letterwriter in the web of her slanderous behavior. It is a fitting ending to the play whose principal thematic is that of the power and abuse of language. Larry Riggs has also noted the epistolary function in *Le Misanthrope* in an article for the October 1992 *French Review*.

Bibliography

Apostolides, Jean-Marie. "Célimène et Alceste: L'Echange des mots." In Pageaux, Daniel-Henri, ed. *Le Misanthrope au théâtre*. Mugron: Jose Feijoe, 1990.

Bennett, Kenneth. "The Philanthropist and the Misanthrope: A Study in Comic Mimesis." *Theatre Research International* 6:2 (1981) 85–92.

Biet, Christian. "La Veuve et l'idéal du mari absolu: Célimène et Alceste." *Cahiers du Dix-Septième* 7:1 (Spring 1997) 215–226.

Bourbeau-Walker, Micheline. "*Le Misanthrope*, ou la comédie éclatée." In Trott, David and Nicole Boursier, eds. *The Age of Theatre in France*. Edmonton: Academic Printing and Publishing, 1988.

Cairncross, John. "Molière subversif." *Dix-Septième Siècle* 157 (1987) 403–413.

Choinski, Krzysztof. "*Le Misanthrope* de Molière: une civilisation qui s'interroge sur elle-même." *Kwartalnik-Neofilologiczny* 34:2 (1987) 155–165.

Cholakian, Patricia. "The 'Woman Question' in Molière's *Misanthrope*." *French Review* 58:4 (Mar 1985) 524–532.

Daniel, George. "The Topos of the Desert in *Le Misanthrope*." In Nelson, Charles, ed. *Studies in Language and Literature*. Richmond: Eastern Kentucky University, 1976.

Dickson, Jesse. "L'Idéologie du rire ou, comment interpréter *Le Misanthrope*." *French Review* 68:4 (Mar 1995) 594–601.

Dosmond, Simone. "Le Dénouement du *Misanthrope*: une 'Source' méconnue?" *La Licorne* 7 (1983) 25–40.

Ekstein, Nina. "The Portrait on Stage in Molière's Theater." *Romance Quarterly* 36:1 (1989) 3–14.

Ewald, François. "La Misanthropie selon Alceste." *Magazine Littéraire* 323 (July-Aug 1994) 43–44.

Finn, Thomas. "Contradictory Demands and Illusory Compliance: Women's Masks in Molière." *Women in French Studies* 8 (2000) 31-39.

Gaines, James. "Caractères, Superstition, and Paradoxes in *Le Misanthrope*." In Motte, Warren, and Prince, Gerald, eds. *Altératives*. Lexington: French Forum, 1993.

Gombay, André. "Les Déboires de la vérité: mensonges et dissimulation au XVIIe siècle."

Oeuvres & Critiques 19:1 (1994) 25–30.

Gossip, C. J. "The Initial Success of *Le Misanthrope*." *French Studies* 39:2 (1985) 143–152.

Gossman, Lionel. "Molière's Misanthrope: Melancholy and Society in the Age of the Counter-reformation." *Theatre Journal* 34:3 (1982) 323–343.

Gutwirth, Marcel. "Visages d'Alceste." *Oeuvres & Critiques* 6:1 (1981) 77–89.

Henfrey, Norman. "Towards a View of Molière's *Misanthrope*: The Sonnet Scene Reconsidered." *The Cambridge Quarterly* 18:2 (1989) 160–186.

Henry, Patrick. "Paradox in *Le Misanthrope*." *Philological Quarterly* 65:2 (1986) 187–195.

Heyndels, Ingrid. "*Le Misanthrope* dans l'intertexte philosophique de son temps." *Papers on French Seventeenth Century Literature* 16:30 (1989) 55–63.

Hope, Quentin. "Philinte's Récit in *Le Misanthrope*." *Papers on French Seventeenth Century Literature* 12:23 (1985) 511–524.

Jauss, Hans Robert. "The Paradox of the Misanthrope." *Comparative Literature* 35:4 (1983) 305–322.

Jones, Dorothy. "Love and Friendship in *Le Misanthrope*." *Romance Notes* 23:2 (1982) 164–169.

Kernen, Madeleine. "Le Role des oppositions dans *Le Misanthrope*." *Chimères* 17:2 (1984) 68–81.

Littératures Classiques 38 (Jan 2000) entire issue.

Lorimier, Renée. "Le Secret dans *Le Misanthrope* de Molière: Agrément courtois ou arme politique?" *Etudes Littéraires* 28:2 (Autumn 1995) 97–106.

Manno, Giuseppe. "Alceste et Oronte: Un Dialogue de sourds: La Politesse et la négociation de la relation interpersonnelle dans *Le Misanthrope*." *Vox Romanica* 60 (2001) 168–187.

Marsh, Rufus. "Alceste, honnête homme or faux honnête homme?" *Stanford French Review* 5:1 (1981) 21–34.

Mazouer, Charles. "*Le Misanthrope, George Dandin* et *Le Bourgeois Gentilhomme*: Trois comédies écrites pour la scène." *Littératures Classiques* 38 (Jan 2000) 139–158.

Mesnard, Jean. "*Le Misanthrope*, mise en question de l'art de plaire." In Pageaux, Daniel-Henri, ed. *Le Misanthrope au théâtre*. Mugron: Jose Feijoe, 1990.

Mishriky, Salwa. *Le Misanthrope ou la Philanthropie de l'honnête homme classique*. New York: Peter Lang, 1994.

Montbertrand, Gérard. "Hiérarchie sociale linéaire, inconvenance et despotisme dans le théâtre de Molière: Essai de 'biocritique'." *Cahiers du Dix-septième* 3:1 (1989) 33–49.

Morgan, Janet. "*Le Misanthrope* and Classical Conceptions of Character Portrayal." *The Modern Language Review* 79:2 (Apr 1984) 290–300.

Newmark, Peter. "The Integrity of the Text: The Case of Molière and *The Misanthrope*." *Franco-British Studies* 26 (Autumn 1998) 69–77.

Nykrog, Per. "Alceste and Célimène: Pulling Rabbits out of an Old Hat." In Karczewska, Kathryn, and Tom Conley, eds. *The World and its Rival: Essays on Literary Imagination in Honor of Per Nykrog*. Amsterdam: Rodopi, 1999.

Parish, Richard. "*Le Misanthrope*: Des raisonneurs aux rieurs." *French Studies* 45:1 (1991) 17–35.

Peacock, Noel. "Lessons Unheeded: The Dénouement of *Le Misanthrope*." *Nottingham French Studies* 29:1 (1990) 10–20.

———. "Verbal Costume in *Le Misanthrope*." *Seventeenth-Century French Studies* 9 (1987) 74–93.

Peters, Jeffrey. "The Rhetoric of Adornment in *Le Misanthrope*." *French Review* 75:4 (Mar 2002) 708–719.

Riggs, Larry. "Another Purloined Letter: Text, Transparency, and Transcendance in *Le Misanthrope*." *French Review* 66:1 (1992) 26–37.

————. "Context and Convergence in the Comedy of *Le Misanthrope*." *Romance Notes* 25:1 (1984) 65–69.

————. *Molière and Plurality: Decomposition of the Classicist Self.* New York: Peter Lang, 1989.

Rogers, Nathalie. "Les Structures conversationnelles dans *Le Misanthrope*." In Golopentia, Sanda, ed. *Les Propos spectacle: Etudes de pragmatique théâtrale.* New York: Peter Lang, 1996.

Schorr, James, ed. *Le Misanthrope. Studies on Voltaire and the Eighteenth Century* 248 (1986) 1–467.

Shaw, David. "Innovation and Orthodoxy: Molière as Theorist." *Seventeenth-Century French Studies* 11 (1989) 106–116.

Le Tartuffe

directed by Jacques Charon (1968)
play by Molière (1669)

The filmed stage productions of Molière's archetypal portrait plays bring seventeenth-century French theater to video format. The framing of characters' faces or groupings is critical to focusing the viewer on the nexes of the stage dynamics, which are much more apparent to the live audience spectator. Facial expressions and body language have to be toned down for the close focus of the camera; a little farce goes a long way on video. The increased impact of physiognomy on camera compensates the diminished sense of the distribution of actors on stage and overall set and lighting effects. Even in medium and wide angle long shots, the video format cannot present the figures on stage in the same perspective as they appear to the spectators. The text of the play, especially those in classical verse, is foregrounded in this format. What is virtually impossible to transfer intact to the screen is the immense comic energy generated on stage in almost all Molière plays.

Molière's incisive satirical texts entertained and impacted simultaneously the society that constituted his audience, at court and at the Palais Royal in Paris, as did the works of Beaumarchais a century later. Concepts like *préciosité* (elaborately metaphoric language) and *l'art de plaire* (the art of pleasing) are closely tied to the political, social, religious and sexual intrigues at the court of Louis XIV. The moral and ideological stance of the courtiers ranged from puritanical religious extremism to unbridled libertinage. The king's censors were intended to obstruct performances that were sexually or politically offensive, to defend the moral probity of the court. Thus they took offense to the open attack upon religious hypocrisy and greed of *Le Tartuffe*, which was condemned at its first two presentations (in 1664 and again in 1667 as *L'Imposteur*). The king himself felt the constraints of the moral counsellors and resented the *superbia* of the self-righteous; thus he approved the 1669 version of the play (wherein he figures as the element of moderation and judicious reason in the finale).

It is not just Tartuffe who threatens the family relationships in play on stage. Even more dangerous are the fanatical hypocritical members of the family, Orgon and his mother, Madame Pernelle (an abbreviation of *peronnelle*, the stereotypical character from the song of the stupid verbose woman, as well as an amalgam of *elle* and *pernicieuse*). Molière demonstrates that the morally righteous denigrate all in their presence and destroy the happiness of all in their power. Madame Pernelle lectures her maid Flipote (Denise Pezzani), her daughter-in-law Elmire (Claude Winter), Mariane's outspoken maid Dorine (Françoise Seigner), her grandchildren Mariane (Catherine Salviat) and Damis (Jean-Noël Sissia), Orgon's brother-in-law Cléante (Jacques Toja), on the virtues of Tartuffe (Robert Hirsch, who also did the sets and costumes). Orgon (played by the director Jacques Charon) has taken into his home this hypocritical religious fanatic who has usurped the rightful place of his family, including Mariane's suitor Valère (Bernard Alane). The injustice is so great that Damis has come to hate his father for his vulnerability and blindness, for letting Tartuffe become master of his house after picking him off the street. Thus Tartuffe and his sole/soul defenders, Madame Pernelle and Orgon (*orgueil* and *gorgon*— monstrous pride), are in control; the rest will attempt to release Orgon from the spell of seduction that Tartuffe has cast over him and his mother before he destroys their home and family.

This has been a popular thematic over the centuries: the unlawful (or even lawful, as in the case of the wicked stepmother or stepfather) intruder who disinherits the just and loyal family and corrupts the benighted master or mistress into betrayal in the name of goodness. René Fauchois's play on this theme, *Boudu sauvé des eaux* (*Boudu Saved From Drowning*), inspired two films: the 1932 Jean Renoir classic and Paul Mazursky's 1986 remake, *Down and Out in Beverly Hills*. Considering that Tartuffe is a mask for criminality, this play functions around the dynamic of collusion and victimization in response to the presence of an impostor like that of *Le Retour de Martin Guerre*.

In all these works, family harmony and equilibrium are destroyed by the intrusion of an outsider who seduces a principal member of the household. In *Le Tartuffe*, Madame Pernelle in her blind hypocrisy abuses her faithful and reasonable servant, thus prefiguring the conduct of Tartuffe in the ensuing scenes. The power of language is initially demonstrated by Tartuffe's inroads on the mind of Orgon, but also in the discussion of local gossip, wherein Dorine affirms that it is the self-righteous, backbiting neighbors whose conduct is the most scandalous, another clue to Tartuffe's real character. Madame Pernelle's rejection of all coquetry is inherently suspect, for at her age, even more than for Arsinoé in *Le Misanthrope*, the wiles of coquetry have for that era lost their effectiveness.

Orgon, set up as the fool and fall guy, engages Cléante and Dorine in a classic repartee with refrain, as they recount his wife Elmire's illness while he in counterpoint thinks only of Tartuffe, who is patently in disgustingly good health, gorging on their food and sleeping profoundly. When Orgon sings Tartuffe's virtues, demonstrated by his devotion in church, Cléante as Molière's spokesperson reacts with a tirade against religious fanatics. It was these passages which aroused the censors the most, as they address the audience directly with their condemnations. As in so many Molière plays, the selfish connivance of aging power figures threatens the love and happiness of innocent young people, in this case the pending marriage of Mariane and Valère ("valiant"), who adore each other and are perfectly matched.

Orgon destroys the equilibrium of his family by demanding that Mariane marry instead the repulsive Tartuffe, who obviously has plans to inherit Orgon's fortune and usurp his worldly goods in the name of piety. Mariane tries in vain to show her father that imposed arranged marriages force the child in question to in turn become a hypocrite and impostor, but to no avail. The language of the play speaks its outcome in every *réplique*; here *imposture* is followed immediately by the word *arrêté*, forecasting the arrests at the end. Dorine enters the argument against Orgon's insane decision, adding an apocryphal observation:

> Et qui donne à sa fille un homme qu'elle hait
> Est responsable au ciel des fautes qu'elle fait.
>
> (Whoever gives his daughter to a man she hates
> Is responsible to heaven for the errors she makes.
> My translation.)

The innocent characters are also capable of sophistry in response to the menace of evil among them; Dorine points out to Orgon that anger in a pious man is rather a contradiction in terms.

The whole subplot of *Le Tartuffe* is a subject close to Molière: the question of power and dominance in the family and society. Dorine protects Mariane and attacks Orgon, implying that unjust and irrational, capricious authority, paternal or political, has no place in an enlightened society. Thus *Le Tartuffe* becomes doubly subversive, as a tirade against hypocrisy and self-righteousness, against arranged marriages, paternal authoritarianism and autocracy, and by extension, all arbitrary abuse of the power and trust of loved ones or dependents. Reading the latter as subjects creates an implicit denunciation of abusive exercise of absolute political power, a dangerous implication offset by the ending.

Dorine subverts Orgon's paternal authority in encouraging Mariane to resist his abuse of power. Mariane, like the young women of *L'Ecole des Femmes* (*School for Wives*) or *L'Ecole des Maris* (*School for Husbands*), is passive at first, even threatening suicide as an alternative to life bound to Tartuffe (among the homonymies in his name are the *tarentule* or tarantula, evil spider weaving its web, and the Italian underground fungus and the eponymous layered confection, *tartufo*. The name is also an alias, affirming his imposture).

Language serves as a barrier to truth and understanding between the innocent lovers Mariane and Valère, who are comically prideful and dangerously vulnerable. Dorine restores equilibrium in suggesting they postpone her marriage to Tartuffe, but disorder is again the order when Orgon declares that the marriage should take place that very night, compounding the dramatic and comic tension. The effect of Tartuffe's long-awaited entrance with his snobbish servant Laurent is heightened when Damis hides in the closet to eavesdrop on this self-parody of masochistic penitence, presented in ironic contrast to the portrait of self-indulgence offered earlier. Tartuffe announces the coming intrigue by confessing to Dorine his lecherous weakness for women, as it is his passion for Elmire that will protect Mariane and precipitate his downfall.

Tartuffe's false prudery regarding the charms of the second sex gives way quickly to a *discours amoureux* (speech of love) when Elmire arrives; it is obvious that he has a very unpious passion for his host's wife, that he has been complaining about her visitors out of jealousy. As he paws her in vulgar gestures, stating "Je ne suis pas an ange" (I am not an angel), the spectator sees on stage not only a prototype of contemporary hypocrites, but the perfect illustration of Pascal's maxim: "Qui veut faire l'ange fait la bête" (Who wants to be an angel becomes a beast/fool). Elmire as a good mother is ready to play along to save her daughter, using her influence on Tartuffe to sway Orgon to permit Mariane to marry Valère. In a classic grande farce *geste* to which the dramatic irony has been leading and which sets up the trap unmasking Tartuffe, Damis bursts from his hiding place, confronting Tartuffe in *flagrant délit*. When Orgon stumbles on the scene, Tartuffe reverts to his mask of penitence, admitting his lustful sins, humbling himself before his host (like any good parasite).

It is at this point that the play turns doubly political, for Orgon is so taken by this deference, which flatters his pride more than the sincere treatment from his family, that he disowns his son and throws him out of his house for accusing Tartuffe of lechery. Tartuffe reacts to Orgon's hysteria by volunteering to leave instead, sure that he will be begged to stay. In all of this, there is an implication of a homosexual attraction between Orgon and Tartuffe. This play prefigures historically the usurping of the heart and soul of Louis XIV by Madame de Maintenon, Scarron's fanatically converted widow whom Louis married in 1684 and for whom he banned France's protestants.

Orgon now adds insult to injury in his fanatical plunge to self-destruction by encouraging Tartuffe to court his wife, by giving him all his worldly goods in writing, and by offering him his daughter in marriage, in comic distortion and exaggeration. It is in fact Orgon who is the villain in this play, betraying his family's love and trust and playing the vengeful puppet fool at the behest of Tartuffe, mesmerized like his mother by his duplicitous discourse.

The question of public opinion enters the scene when Cléante confronts Tartuffe regarding his iniquity and scandalous reputation. Thus, as in many Molière plays, *le tout Paris*, the collective voice, has become a character. Tartuffe's ratiocination knows no bounds, as he claims he is willing to inherit Orgon's estate to keep it from falling into evil hands, another gross irony of this grande farce. When caught in the fallacy of his argument, Tartuffe beats a retreat under the pretext of devotional duties.

Mariane begs her father not to force her to marry Tartuffe, preferring life in a convent, a destination of exile for heartbroken or disgraced women. Meanwhile Elmire decries the ironclad virgins who get irate and claw and kick at the least flirtation from a man; claiming to represent reason, declaring that a clever woman should be able to defend herself without doing battle, she lays a trap for Tartuffe, with Orgon hiding guard under the table. Her bravado about defending herself with dignity sets up the irony of her response to Tartuffe's gross sexual aggression. Tartuffe hesitates at first, suspecting a sting in Elmire's rapid about face toward him, as she entreats him with soothing kind words and invites his attentions. Then he suddenly come unhinged and assaults her, decrying God, heaven and husband simultaneously. It is the insult to Orgon's person that destroys his loyalty to Tartuffe, his wounded pride rather than rage at the religious hypocrisy or the affront to his wife. He is in fact as guilty as Tartuffe of moral turpitude. As the wife coughs and bangs the table, he sits frozen underneath the cloth, from shock rather than cowardice.

When Orgon finally throws Tartuffe out of his house, his real dilemma becomes apparent: Tartuffe is still the legal master of all he owns, even though no longer the moral master of his heart and soul. Worse yet, Orgon confided to Tartuffe the personal papers of Argas, a friend in exile, with which the traitor has also absconded. As Orgon demystified receives his family with real penitence, he urges Damis not to seek a duel with Tartuffe, a direct allusion to the royal ban on dueling. The play comes full circle as Madame Pernelle returns to the stage, incredulous as ever regarding the evil of the pious Tartuffe, denying all Orgon's allegations of betrayal and suffering, unwilling and unable to accept the painful truth Orgon has just learned.

The ironically named bailiff Monsieur Loyal (from Normandy, scene of religious scandals around 1660) arrives with a writ to seize Orgon's house and worldly goods. As Dorine leads the resistance, Loyal (Michel Duchaussoy) reminds her that women can be arrested too. Madame Pernelle is finally convinced that Tartuffe's heart is as black as his mandatory costume of *dévot*, used faithfully through the centuries in every production, an indispensable image of dual blackness. Valère returns from court to help Orgon escape, for supposedly the king has put out an arrest warrant for his person upon receiving the strongbox with Argas's incriminating papers. Valère represents the *honnête* counterpart to the vile Tartuffe, offering his future father-in-law one thousand louis to help him escape. Tartuffe bursts on stage with the king's man to arrest Orgon, but is caught in his own trap instead. In a finale paying homage to his king, rewarding him for permitting the play, Molière gives the royal officer a speech praising the king's intuitive judicious wisdom and announcing that it is rather Tartuffe who will be arrested for his misconduct. And all retire to go thank the king, who would have been in the audience for this third and finally approved version of the play. Even Argas has been forgiven, as his family had been loyal to the king during the Fronde, the 1652 failed uprising of the nobility against Louis XIII that ultimately prompted Louis XIV to entrap his aristocracy at Versailles.

Bibliography

Cloonan, William. "Tartuffe and the Game of Words." *Rivista di Letterature Moderne e Comparate* 47(4) (Oct-Dec 1994) 313-330.

Ekstein, Nina. "*Le Misanthrope* and *Tartuffe*: Two Critiques of Verbal Portraiture." *Rivista di Letterature Moderne e Comparate* 42(2) (Apr-Jun 1989) 137-152.

Faussie, Daniel. "Tartuffe and Orgon: Molière's Addictive Duo." *Tropos* 27 (Spring 2001) 55-68.

Ferreyrolles, Gérard. *Molière, Tartuffe*. Paris: Presses Universitaires de France, 1987.

Gaines, James, and Koppisch, Michael. *Approaches to Teaching Molière's Tartuffe and Other Plays*. New York: MLA, 1995.

Gethner, Perry. "The Role of Decor in French Classical Comedy." *Theatre Journal* 36(3) (Oct 1984) 383-399.

Gossip, C. J. "Elmire and Tartuffe." *French Studies Bulletin* 76 (Autumn 2000) 15-17.

Hilgar, Marie-France. "Modern and Post-Modern Interpretations of *Tartuffe*." *Theatre Journal* 34(3) (Oct 1982) 384-388.

LePage, Raymond. "Brian Bedford's *Tartuffe*: The Erotic Violence of Hypocrisy." *Theatre Journal* 34(3) (Oct 1982) 389-396.

Malachy, Thérèse. "Du droit à la folie à la folie du droit: la comédie du *Tartuffe*." *Littératures Classiques* 27 (Spring 1996) 333-337.

McBride, Robert. "L'Imposteur bipolaire." *Nottingham French Studies* 33(1) (Spring 1994) 92-100.

McKenna, Andrew. "Tartuffe, Representation and Difference." *Papers on French Seventeenth Century Literature* 16(30) (1989) 77-93.

Parish, Richard. "Tartuf(f)e ou l'imposture." *The Seventeenth Century* 6(1) (Spring 1991) 73-88.

Peacock, Noel. "'Tartuffe': Another Look." *Seventeenth-Century French Studies* 14 (1992) 177-189.

Phillips, Henry. "Molière and Tartuffe: Recimination and Reconciliation." *French Review* 62:5 (1989) 749-763.

Oeuvres & Critiques. 22:2 (1997). Entire issue.

Riggs, Larry. "Corps/performance contre texte/prétention: l'Anti-transcendantalisme de Molière." In Tobin, Ronald, ed. *Le Corps au XVIIe Siècle*. Paris: *Papers on French Seventeenth Century Literature*, 1995.

————. "Molière's 'Poststructuralism': Demolition of Transcendentalist Discourse in *Le Tartuffe*." *Symposium* 44:1 (Spring 1990) 37-57.

Sauer, Pamela. "Molière's Tartuffe." *Explicator* 60 (1) (Fall 2001) 9-12.

Serroy, Jean. "Tartuffe, ou l'autre." In Heyndels, Ralph, and Woshinsky, Barbara, eds. *L'Autre au XVIIeme Siècle*. Tubingen, Germany: Narr, 1999.

Shaw, David. "Tartuffe and the Law; Essays in French Culture and Society in Honour of Philip Thody." In Dolamore, James, ed. *Making Connections*. Berlin: Peter Lang, 1999.

Spingler, Michael. "The King's Play: Censorship and the Politics of Performance in Molière's *Tartuffe*." *Comparative Drama* 19:3 (Fall 1985) 240-257.

Tobin, Ronald. "*Tartuffe*, texte sacré." In Jomaron, Jacqueline de, ed. *Dramaturgies: Langages Dramatiques*. Paris: Nizet, 1986.

Le Bourgeois Gentilhomme

directed by Jean Meyer (1957)
play by Molière (1670)

Filming *Le Bourgeois Gentilhomme* poses more than the usual questions of registering the sounds and images of a staged performance or even of transposing the text to the open set, high-mobility format with postsynchronized sound track recently used in filming opera. Because *Le Bourgeois Gentilhomme* has performances within perform-ances (telescoped in role, mask, disguise, pageant), the relationship of the camera to the various diegetic levels within the text/performance of the play is problematic. In 1991 there appeared an entire volume of *Papers on French Seventeenth Century Literature* on the problems of staging/adapting comedy ballet. The individual articles treating pertinent aspects of this complex work are listed in the bibliography at the end of the chapter. Of particular interest is Dietmar Fricke's discussion of two controversial cinematic adaptations in the early 1980s, which he contrasts on grounds that he however fails to support. One of them, directed by Jérôme Savary for Antenne 2 and featuring Le Grand Magic Circus, is available through Films for the Humanities, without subtitles; it is a clown-act self-parody of the play, a time-warp blend of *Commedia dell'Arte*, Fellini, and Jean Genet. I have chosen, however, to discuss a well-known early black and white film of a Comédie Française production, not just to compare with the other two traditional versions of Molière plays but precisely because it foregrounds the classic staging of the work and the virtuoso exploitation of language as stage presence.

In this prose comedy ballet with music by Lully, Monsieur Jourdain, the bour-geois sheetmaker or cloth merchant, attempts to acquire through lessons from his music, dance and fencing masters, and then his philosophy master, the grace and style, the diction and *préciosité* (which he turns to parody) necessary to make him a nobleman, a *gentilhomme*. Jourdain's tailor attempts to convert his appearance as the others struggle with his performance, one of many levels of roles he assumes.

The inherent contradiction in terms of the title's oxymoron ("the middle-class aristocrat") was intended to satisfy the court of Louis XIV at Versailles and at the Palais Royal theater in Paris (which for three centuries has been the home of the Comédie Française). The fact that this text is in prose rather than verse gives rise to one of the funniest sequences of the play, wherein Monsieur Jourdain discovers to his unbridled delight that he has been speaking prose all his life. The ultimate irony of the popularity with the aristocracy of this light-hearted yet bitingly satirical entertainment was that in the course of the following century, the bourgeoisie would rise to power, threaten the aristocracy's long-standing dominance, and contribute to its downfall.

The 1957 version of *Le Bourgeois Gentilhomme* opens with frame shots of the Comédie Française's founding 1680 seal, a map of central Paris, and modern-day theatergoers entering the Palais Royal, stressing the historic continuity of this mainstay of French high culture dramatic tradition and attempting to unframe the experience of the moviegoer by encouraging identification with the theater spectators. Accompanying the orchestra playing Lully's overture are shots of the program pages turning to reveal the credits. The contemporary setting also lets us know that the subject matter of the play is as appropriate today as it was three hundred years ago, as the camera focuses with unintentional irony on the good bourgeois audience settling into their *fauteuils*. The program includes period engravings of Molière and describes the context of the play's premiere. In this version, Louis Seigner plays Monsieur Jourdain; the set decors are by Suzanne Lalique; the camerawork is by Henri Alekan (who also shot Cocteau's *La Belle et la Bête*); the production is by Maurice Hartwig, and the performance is directed by Jean Meyer. The first act opens with the musicians and employees of the *bourgeois gentilhomme* complaining of working for such a crass individual. Their consolation is their lavish financial recompense. Backbiting ceases as he enters dressed *à la turque* (not just high fashion exoticism but an overt allusion to the recent visit to Paris of the Turks and the Grand Seigneur, parodied by the ambition of Jourdain, both as Mamamouchi and in his plans for his daughter), declaring his longing to be a man of quality as he bellows for his servants. The ultra-refined ditty composed by the music master's brilliant pupil is repeatedly interrupted by Jourdain's sartorial ineptitude, as he dons and doffs his robe, reminiscent of the broken reading of the sonnet at the beginning of *Le Misanthrope*, again using one of Molière's principal comic mecanisms.

This man is obviously not at ease in his clothes or his skin; he is preordained, by the expression *dans de beaux draps* associated with his profession, to be in a perennially embarrassing situation. As the camera lingers lovingly on the painted harpsichord cover with its classic architectural scene, Monsieur Jourdain (whose name contains the vowels of his locution lesson and echoes *bonjour dédain*), of the same popular ilk as his servants, falls soundly asleep. In response to the high style *nouveau* ballad, Jourdain prefers and proffers, like Alceste before him, a song from the old Renaissance folk tradition, a song about a sheep, which of course harkens clear back to the hilarious courtroom antics of Maître Pathelin.

The first two acts are devoted to the "forming" of Monsieur Jourdain, which becomes more a battle for control of his purse strings and his social future between his various masters, ending of course with the indelible scene of his locution lesson from the master of philosophy. Jourdain's barnyard vocalizing only serves to emphasize his brutish nature. His attempted forays into the ethereal realms of the inner sanctum of taste are paried by a series of ballets, sermons, diatribes and disputes.

In the contrapuntal scene of the competition between his various masters, Jourdain manages to make *faux pas* with everyone, rendered ridiculous in all his acts: dancing, fencing, singing. Yet the people trying to teach Jourdain are also parodying themselves, the implication being that both impostors and pedants are equally excluded from the world of good taste, into which one must be born. Monsieur Jourdain's ambitions to marry his daughter Lucile above his station and his pretensions to seduction render him vulnerable to the manipulations of Dorante, who exploits him as mercilessly as Tartuffe does Orgon. The last insult will be that the object of his desire, Dorimène, who is properly horrified at his approaches, will finish by marrying Dorante, the *faux courtisan* who also exploits Jourdain financially in exchange for vague favors and influence at court, the kind of petty sycophantry that Alceste decried.

Perhaps the most effective parody of the play operates on the adage that clothes don't make the man, as Jourdain having opened as the Grand Turk now appears as a cross between Louis XIV and an ostrich at the end of Act II, victim of the greed and ambitions of his *maître tailleur*. It is to keep in mind that Jourdain's costumes in the first two acts were making fun of the competition between the king and the Grand Turk, which undoubtedly ruffled some feathers at the initial performance for the court at Chambord. In Act III, Molière exploits Jourdain's folly through the response of his servant Nicole (Molière's servants are either buffoons or clever commoners with great good sense), who reacts to his dress with a contagious *fou rire*. The camera close-ups in this "canned theater" attempt to incite riotous laughter in the movie audience as well, as they focus on the contagion spreading on stage from the wife to the lackeys. The series of close-ups mark this cinematography as influenced by, if not destined for, early television productions, like the 1956 *Topaze*.

Later in Act III, Cléonte and Covielle are summoned to the house to form the *sosie* couples, Cléonte courting Lucile, Covielle Nicole. The clever scene of the double *brouille* misunderstanding between Cléonte and Lucile, and Covielle and Nicole, creates a rapid repartee of musical dynamics. The offensive public snub of Cléonte by Lucile is finally explained: the culprit was Lucile's self-righteous religious hypocritical aunt who disproves of even eye contact between young lovers. Like Tartuffe and Arsinoé, the aunt impedes the natural course and development of true love, just as Jourdain refuses the honest and faithful Cléonte, whose sincere devotion to Lucile stands in opposition to both Jourdain's ambitions to marry Lucile into the aristocracy and to pursue Dorimène as a social prize. Further comic irony is engendered by the duplicity of Dorante, who has spent all Jourdain's money courting Dorimène on his own behalf. The three act out the pretensions and hypocrisy of social courting rituals all in the name of *bienséance*.

The banquet scene of Act IV sets the stage for Jourdain's offensive ridiculous approaches to Dorimène, at the same time that Molière enumerates through Dorante the culinary riches displayed, both as a tribute to the chefs of the day and as a theatrical mirror of the banquet during which the play would have been first performed. It would have been a clear attempt as well to please the king and acknowledge his dominion, as his consumption of food was one of the bases of his highly codified personal power structure.

After Madame Jourdain chases off Dorimène with her unabashed attack on Dorante's duplicity, Covielle turns up disguised and beguiles Jourdain by flattering his social origins, then announces that the son of the Grand Turk has come to demand Lucile's hand in marriage. Jourdain gets his second language lesson of the evening as Covielle (who has already prepared us by spouting some Picard expressions) tosses off nonsensical phrases in pretend Turkish, phrases which not only amuse by their phonetic subtexts (*caca*) but which are startlingly modern in their destruction of language and their linguistic playfulness and capriciousness. It would seem that the wine and the drinking songs had gone to everyone's head. As Jourdain is named Mamamouchi (which means roughly "good for nothing" in Turkish), he is declared a *paladin* (knight of Charlemagne), the extreme projection of his pretensions to noble heritage.

The play within the play generates its humor through the artificial Turkish phrases of Cléonte and the disparity of Covielle's interpreting (which carries an unintended irony for the spectator watching this film with subtitles in English). Jourdain clearly is out of his element and doesn't speak the language, a comic element that would have been well received by a French court that had heard more Turkish recently than it appreciated or understood. As Jourdain is ordered to prepare his daughter for her impending marriage, we see him trapped in his vanity and foolish vulnerability. The ceremony of Jourdain's induction as Mamamouchi incorporates a Mufti, Dervishes, and the Coran, all genuine Moslem elements, using the pigeon dialect Sabir spoken in Mediterranean ports. The parodic ennobling and knighting of Jourdain become Jordan includes his rejecting all other religions and forswearing shame and hypocrisy. The ceremony becomes itself a chastising purification of its very own nature, as truth, illusion and mask intermingle in the privileged realm of the stage. Confronted by his wife aghast, Jourdain speaks Italian. His only triumph is the series of respectful comments addressed to him by Dorante and Dorimène, who are initiated to the ruse and who amiably illustrate for us the ease with which the courtier of the day could invent insincere flattery to suit the occasion. Language becomes a principal character in the play throughout the fourth and fifth acts, a role which was announced in Act I by the locution lesson.

The final coup of Cléonte and Covielle is nearly foiled by Lucile's initial resistance to the forced marriage, redolent of Mariane's pleas to Orgon in the face of impending union with Tartuffe. The last game of dramatic comic irony is played out by the brash ignorance of the earthy Madame Jourdain, who has resisted for five acts the shenanigans of her household. It is her turn now to be dupe, of her own outspoken sincerity, until she is forcefully initiated to the secret and acquiesces. In a last affront to Jourdain's credulity, Dorante and Dorimène offer to feign what will actually be a true marriage ceremony, including Cléonte and Lucile, and of course Nicole and Covielle, the *truchement* (intermediary) permitting faithful interpretation of all the *turqueries* of the evening.

The play is capped by the elaborate Ballet des Nations, with participants speaking "Swiss," French, Gascon, Spanish, Italian, and even Poitevin. Thus concludes this extraordinary text, which in the guise of light entertainment and grande farce actually raises profound questions of the nature of origin and identity, national and religious affiliation. In fact, the entire text has at the same time the ability to entertain, to mock, to satirize, and to resolve the imbalance between *être* and *paraître*, between truth and illusion, if not between illusion and reality.

Bibliography

Abraham, Claude. "Molière and Ionesco—Analogies in Linguistic Iconoclasm." *Journal of the American Romanian Academy of Arts and Science* 6–7 (1985) 64–71.

Ciccone, Anthony. "Metalanguage and Knowledge in Molière's *Le Bourgeois Gentilhomme*." *Degré Second* 6 (1982) 41–64.

Fricke, Dietmar. "Deux mises en scène cinématographiques récentes du *Bourgeois Gentilhomme* de Molière: Roger Coggio, 1982; Jérôme Savary 1981/82." *Papers on French Seventeenth Century Literature* (1991) 115–122.

Gaines, James, and Koppisch, Michael. *Approaches to Teaching Molière's Tartuffe and Other Plays*. New York: MLA, 1995.

Grandvaux, Yolande. "La Réalité matérielle chez Molière." *Chimères* 14:2 (1982) 5–16.

Hall, Gaston. *Molière's 'Le Bourgeois Gentilhomme': Context and Stagecraft*. Durham, England: University of Durham, 1990.

Kapp, Volker, ed. *'Le Bourgeois Gentilhomme': Problèmes de la comédie-ballet. Papers on French Seventeenth Century Literature* (1991). Entire issue.

———. "Langage verbal et langage non-verbal dans *Le Bourgeois Gentilhomme. Papers on French Seventeenth Century Literature* (1991) 95–113.

Karro, Françoise. "La Cérémonie turque du *Bourgeois Gentilhomme*: mouvance temporelle et spirituelle de la foi." *Papers of French Seventeenth Century Literature* (1991) 35–93.

Mallet, Francine. *Molière*. Paris: Grasset, 1986.

Mazouer, Charles. "*Le Misanthrope, George Dandin* et *Le Bourgeois Gentilhomme*: Trois comédies écrites pour la scène." *Littératures Classiques* 38 (Jan 2000) 139–158.

McGowan, Margaret. "La Danse: son role multiple." *Papers of French Seventeenth Century Literature* (1991) 163–183.

Tobin, Ronald. "Fusion and Diffusion in *Le Bourgeois Gentilhomme*." *French Review* 59:2 (1985) 234–245.

Vialet, Michèle. "*Le Bourgeois Gentilhomme* en contexte: Du texte au spectacle." *Papers on French Seventeenth Century Literature* 17:32 (1990) 51–58.

Walker, Hallam. *Molière*. Boston: Twayne, 1990.

Topaze

directed by Marcel Pagnol (1951)
play by Marcel Pagnol (1928)

As we have seen in the studies on *Jean de Florette* and *Manon des Sources*, Marcel Pagnol, born in Aubagne in Provence in 1895, was an astute observer of society and chronicler of life in the Midi. For decades, he was best known for his satiric farcical comedies like *Topaze* (1928) and his Marseilles trilogy of both plays and films: *Marius* (1928/1931), *Fanny* (1930/1932) *César* (1931/ 1936). Of late, his renown has come more from *L'Eau des collines*, through Berri's films of his work, and most recently from his *Souvenirs d'enfance*, through Yves Robert's 1991 films *La Gloire de mon père* and *Le Château de ma mère*. It is in the last two volumes of his autobiographical writings, however, *Le Temps des secrets* and *Le Temps des amours*, that one finds the background, sources and key for the nature of his early theater.

Although Pagnol was long regarded as a popular boulevardier writer and filmmaker like his contemporary Sacha Guitry, his greatest successes, his regional works, contained an element of primitive mysticism that transcended the social and the comic. Perhaps for this reason, André Bazin, in discussing the differences between theatrical and cinematic language, declared Pagnol's most cinematic work to be *Manon des Sources*, and declared *Topaze* the least adaptable to the screen because of its distance from the Meridional mode. According to Bazin, the regional works adapted best to the "concrete" nature of film (location shooting, natural lighting, etc.). This judgment has unfortunately glossed the extent to which *Topaze* is indeed a Provençal work, and a product of an era. If it does not project these appurtenances, it is a tribute to Pagnol's goal of staging timeless archetypal character portrayals like those of Molière. Bazin was doubly wrong, for fabular duality of characterization and structure, and realism of setting pervade all of Pagnol's work. The original title of *Topaze* was in fact *La Belle et la Bête*.

The play was first presented on 9 October 1928 at the Théâtre des Variétés in Paris (where ironically Sacha Guitry had first tried dubbing sound onto silent film in 1915). The script of *Topaze* was first published in 1931; its single name title, although a proper name, acknowledges Molière as textual and authorial model of the play presenting the classic archetypal comic protagonist. *Topaze* satirizes most of post-World War I French society—the educators, the entrepreneurs, the aristocrats, the bourgeoisie—and ridicules oppression, hypocritical rhetoric, the false values of the right-wing conservatives of the day, social and political corruption and ambition. Thus the classroom, society and politics all become theater, a theater of mask, of the morality of surface and success, with many of Pagnol's own memories and experiences from the years 1905 to 1915 informing his script.

The first film of *Topaze* was made by Louis Gasnier in 1931, with the great comedians Louis Jouvet, Edwige Feuillère and Pierre Larquey, and is still today preferred by most critics over later remakes. Harry d'Arrast directed John Barrymore and Myrna Loy in a British version of the play adapted to film in 1933. The first of the French remakes of the film, done in 1936 by Pagnol himself, partly out of frustration over his subordinate role in the filming of his other works, notably *Marius* and *Fanny*, was a disaster. These adaptations led Pagnol to found his own film company, *Les Auteurs Associés* (*Les Films Marcel Pagnol*), and film journal, *Les Cahiers du Film*, in 1933. Other projects (filming *Merlusse* and founding his own publishing company, *Les Editions Marcel Pagnol*, the Giono films, the war) intervened, and it was not until 1951 that Pagnol directed yet another remake of *Topaze*. This time the play was transformed on film by the highly stylized personality of Fernandel as Topaze, creating a character redolent of certain Chaplin personae. The rest of the cast included Hélène Perdrière, Pagnol's wife Jacqueline Bouvier Pagnol, Marcel Vallée, Jacques Castelot, and again Pierre Larquey. The less larcenous, more comic tone illustrates the ludic element of Pagnol's creativity, on both stage and screen, as much as it reflects esthetics and values of the 1950s.

The play's autobiographical elements come from both his experiences as a student at the Lycée in Marseilles (it is dedicated to his teacher André Antoine) and his own career as a high school teacher, which led him ultimately to the Lycée Condorcet in Paris. He abandoned the profession for a successful career in the artistic and commercial world. In later years, he compared his film profits to his former measly salary at Condorcet in terms of time invested. Because Pagnol's father Joseph was first a middle school teacher, where he was awarded the *Palmes Académiques* so satirized in *Topaze*, and then, at the Ecole Normale, a reforming educator and product of the Jules Ferry generation, with its austere morality, *Topaze* could be seen as a blend of the two generations of educators. Thus, although Pagnol dropped out of the Ecole Normale Supérieure and left the profession to become immensely wealthy (a life prophesied in *Topaze*), he never lost his primary respect for good teachers. His major early works are in fact all set in schools: *Merlusse*, *Pirouettes*, *Jazz* and *Topaze*.

Topaze is also very much based on the nineteenth-century classic novel traditions like those of Dickens or Horatio Alger, where the triumph of the little man anticipates the later Chaplinesque characters. And it incorporates as primary thematic the Balzacian and Flaubertian *roman d'éducation*, wherein the naive young hero is initiated into the cruel realities of contemporary society, and despite initial moral compunctions, conforms and contorts himself in order to survive and thrive. As the work indicts the bourgeois capitalist power structure and its ability to lure people away from simpler, more honorable pursuits, Pagnol is in a sense satirizing his own career.

The first act presents the professors and directors of a boarding school revealing their *tartufferies*: hypocrisy, lasciviousness, laziness, egotism, ambition, all the while preaching a severe and rigid morality to the students (who couldn't care less) and flattering their rich parents to promote their careers. Topaze gets kicked out for the crime of honesty, for telling a pompous mother that her son deserved the zero grade he gave him. On the pretense of tutoring a student in his home, Topaze winds up involved with the corrupt trio of Suzy Courtois, Régis Castel-Bénac and Roger de Berville, a criminal threesome who reveal the degree of greed and political corruption of the power structure as they frame and trap Topaze in their machinations. But instead of remaining the passive puppet they think they have set up, Topaze gradually infiltrates their system, beats them at their own game and makes his fortune by compromising everyone, including himself, according to his own private system of immorality. As in many Pagnol works, the lie, the exaggeration, the substitution, are figures of rhetoric, enhancing both narrative and dialogue, which come from the Provençal traditions of storytelling and humor.

This hollow character who reflects for all his manipulators but who thus controls them represents a classic reverse dialectic of the master and the slave, a thematic reprised in Jerzy Kosinsky's Chaunce the Gardener in *Being There*, filmed in 1979 by Hal Ashby. Topaze's former headmaster Muche suddenly wants to marry him off to his daughter Ernestine, whom he wasn't allowed to court when a poor schoolteacher (although she found the generosity to let him correct her papers for her). And of course, they want now to award him the fabled coveted service medal which previously had evaded him, the *Palmes Académiques*. At the very end, Topaze receives a visit from Tamise, his former colleague in arms from school, and offers him a job, repeating his own earlier experience.

The 1951 film of *Topaze* is more than the fourth adaptation of the initial play, as it appeared contextually in comparable postwar circumstances. Certain aspects of the original text were modified to update it to post-World War II equivalents (prices, economic allusions), yet generally it constituted a faithful remake of the original, demonstrating the enduring significance of the work whose ambition was to emulate Molière. The play's temporal stage directions specify openly *de nos jours*, in our time. It foregrounds the refusal of oppression and false rhetoric, or corruption, and the heroism of the common man who bucks the system, as well as the vulnerability to power of even the best-intentioned characters. The film also reaffirms in its portrayal of both students and young teachers the vitality of youth, of a new generation who, as Edith Piaf's song stated, *se fout du passé*. There are those who feel that Fernandel unjustly turned Topaze into a self-parody, thus cancelling out the satiric intent of the role. Pagnol tried a fifth and final version of Topaze for a new medium, French television, in 1956, a production that cannot be judged by the same criteria as stage and screen performances and which received little critical acclaim. In fact, Pagnol's *oeuvre* has always been a source of discomfort to critics, blending brilliantly lyric or comic moments with strident social criticism and ill-considered popular melodrama or the farce of his "Pagnolades." If only by sheer volume, his productivity, which covered half of the twentieth century and included dozens of unfinished projects at his death in 1974, has made him a major figure in French literature and cinema. He also pioneered a number of cinematographic, sound and editing techniques. Other films by Pagnol include: *L'Agonie des aigles* (1933), *Le Gendre de M. Poirier* (1933), *Jofroi* (1933), *Angèle* (with Orane Demazis and Fernandel, who came from vaudeville in Marseilles, 1934), *Merlusse* (1935), *Cigalon* (1935), *César* (1936), *Regain* (1937), *La Femme du boulanger* (1938), *La Fille du puisatier* (1940), *Naïs* (1945), *La Belle Meunière* (1948), *La Manon des Sources* (1952), *Les Lettres de mon moulin* (1954), *Le Curé de Cucugnan* (1967).

Topaze, especially the opening scenes, belongs, like a number of Pagnol's other works, to a subgenre of films about children, which has been internationally rich, including, in French: Julien Duvivier's 1931 *Poil de Carotte* from the Jules Renard novel, Jean Vigo's 1933 *Zéro de conduite*, Marcel Carné's 1943 *Les Enfants du paradis*, Jean-Pierre Melville's 1950 *Les Enfants terribles* from the Cocteau novel, René Clément's 1952 *Jeux interdits*, Truffaut's 1959 *Les Quatre Cents Coups*, 1970 *L'Enfant sauvage*, 1976 *Argent de poche* and *La Petite Voleuse*, released posthumously in 1989, Diane Kurys's 1977 *Diabolo-Menthe* and 1980 *Cocktail Molotov*, Deville's 1982 *La Petite Bande*, Agnès Varda's 1986 *Sans toit ni loi*, Jean-Loup Hubert's 1987 *Le Grand Chemin*, Louis Malle's 1988 *Au Revoir, les enfants*. The cycle came full circle with Yves Robert's 1991 films of Pagnol's texts of his early childhood: *La Gloire de mon père* and *Le Château de ma mère*.

Pagnol has been attacked by numerous critics for making "théâtre de conserve" (canned theater) rather than film adaptations of plays. Filming plays in the context of their theatrical staging is one thing; trying to find a cinematic equivalent of stage space, light and language is quite another, often resulting in a treasonous betrayal of theater in the attempt (see Bazin: "Théâtre et Cinéma" in *Qu'est-ce que le cinéma?/What is Cinema?*). Yet filmed or televised theater productions have maintained their popularity, in spite of these obvious limitations, as a means of mass diffusion of performances which would otherwise have limited accessibility. Pagnol engaged André Bazin in an extended polemic by calling film a medium for creative writing (nothing like the *auteur* of *auteur* filmmaking). Bazin responded in "Le Cas Pagnol" (included only in the French Edition of *Qu'est-ce que le cinéma?* but finally translated in 1995, see bibliography) by affirming that Pagnol was not a playwright converted to filmmaking but was however one of the best "authors" of the talking cinema. Central to his analysis was an implicit criticism of Pagnol's lack of understanding of the relationship between theater and film.

Pagnol's filmed versions of his theatrical works did go beyond filming stage performances, but his real dramatic voice as a filmmaker, as Bazin said, emerged better in other works. Pagnol wanted to go beyond filming his plays; he wanted to create a new hybrid literary genre, *cinématurgie* (filmplaywriting), to reinvent the theater on the movie sound screen. Like Cocteau, he was drawn to the Six, to the music of Auric and Honegger. He took great interest in sound, in what he called sound perspective. His journal *Les Cahiers du Film* was established to create a forum for debate between film and theater, not unlike the critical territorial debate today between film and television. The journal was short-lived. Pagnol also experimented with color around 1948, but his work has more the feeling of a black and white sketch than a finished polychromatic canvas. In spite of the rather two-dimensional nature of his filmed theater (with its stylized spatio-temporal constructs), his intense interest in the nature of the relationship between theater and the cinematic medium never waned; one of his most interesting publications was his article "Cinématurgie de Paris" in *Les Cahiers du Film* (reprinted in Marcel Lapierre's 1946 *Anthologie du cinéma*).

Pagnol was enormously popular and successful with his regional literature, like Daudet, Giono, or Mark Twain. In keeping with his Provençal origins and temperament, he refused to make films during World War II in order to avoid collaborating with the Nazis. Immediately after the liberation, he founded in 1945 another production company, the *Société Nouvelle des Films Marcel Pagnol*. He was elected to the Académie Française at the same time. His financial and artistic independence led him, however, to some ill-considered projects, but he reestablished his popularity and his authorial status with *L'Eau des collines*.

As the son of a schoolteacher and a teacher himself who left to seek a different career, Pagnol gives us much more than a satiric portrait of French society in the twenties in *Topaze*. Although he never openly attempts to justify his characters, all of whom are vulnerable, he gives them here and there engaging and eminently realistic traits. This everyday realism of the little people and the petty events in their lives has an enduring value system behind it. The apparently prosaic setting actually stages primary elements of human experience: desire, pride, fear, need, embarrassment, temptation. The danger is that these models drawn from life become transformed into stereotypes rather than archetypes, that they never transcend the cardboard cutout mockup stage. And Pagnol has another very real paradox or anomaly in this play: how to reconcile the pro and the con, how to be a moralist and a satirist at the same time, how to take a moral stance and keep the comic distance necessary for the success of the play. Ultimately, the judgment occurs *a posteriori*, after the laughter has died. However, it does seem that this work never resolves its double generic nature of comedy and melodrama, that it never decides between realistic humanism and absurd farce.

If Pagnol did not achieve theatrical realism, he was recognized by Rossellini (*Roma città aperta* 1945) and De Sica (*Ladri di biciclette* 1948, *Umberto D* 1951) as having originated neorealism in 1934 with the film *Angèle*, a project which also influenced Jean Renoir's *Toni*, which Pagnol produced. The majority of his films were shot on location, outdoors, with minutely detailed sets. And it would seem that his influence continues in works like Berri's and Robert's adaptations of *L'Eau des collines* and *Souvenirs d'enfance*, all ironically more realistic than his 1952 *La Manon des Sources*, where his neorealist model of regional authenticity mingled with mythical primitive melodrama was marred unfortunately by the stylized performance of the woman for whom it was written, Jacqueline Bouvier Pagnol. Usually, though, when Pagnol is working within the diegesis of his Provençal childhood, it is hard to say whether he presents the world as he finds it or creates the world that he so convincingly presents. He openly admitted that his autobiographic *Souvenirs d'enfance* were heavily influenced by his intervening artistic creations of narrative and dialogical structuring. One element links all Pagnol's work: imbued with intense nostalgia for a lost era, values, images and dreams, he is caught like Molière in the trap of his own first profession: how to amuse and instruct at the same time. His lasting desire to disseminate his works to a popular audience is revealed in his productivity as a filmmaker, particularly in the number of times he returned to this earlier work, in successive attempts to recreate on film and through mass distribution the tremendously successful reception of the play's initial run in Paris. It would seem that Pagnol never purged in himself the moral ambiguity of his own career, returning repeatedly as it were to the road not taken, the commitment abandoned.

Bibliography

Audouard, Yvan. *Audouard raconte Pagnol*. Paris: Librairie Générale Française, 1976.
Bazin, André. "Le Cas Pagnol." In *Qu'est-ce que le cinéma?* Paris: Editions du Cerf, 1958.
————. "The Case of Marcel Pagnol." Piette and Cardullo, translators. *Literature/Film Quarterly* 23:3 (1995) 204–208.
Beylie, Claude. *Marcel Pagnol ou le cinéma en liberté*. Paris: Atlas Lherminier, 1986. Caldicott, C. E. J. *Marcel Pagnol*. Boston: Twayne, 1977.
————. "The Posthumous Publications of Marcel Pagnol." *French Studies Bulletin* 53 (Winter 1994) 11–14.
Castans, Raymond. *Il était une fois...Marcel Pagnol*. Paris: Julliard, 1986.
————. *Marcel Pagnol*. Paris: Gallimard, 1988.
————. *Marcel Pagnol m'a raconté*. Paris: Folio, 1976.
————, and André Bernard. *Les Films de Marcel Pagnol*. Paris: Julliard, 1982.
Clébert, Jean-Paul. *La Provence de Pagnol*. Aix-en-Provence: Edisud, 1986.
Delahay, Michel. "Le Saga Pagnol." *Les Cahiers du Cinéma* 213 (June 1969) 45–57.
Jathaul, S. "La Veine romantique chez Marcel Pagnol." *Panjab University Research Bulletin (Arts)* 17:2 (1986) 99–104.
Kline, P. Gounelle. *Le Théâtre de Pagnol: Personnages et thèmes dans les oeuvres de jeunesse*. New York: Peter Lang, 1986.
Michalczyk, John. "The French Academy and the Cinema: Pagnol, Cocteau, and Clair." *Stanford French Review* 5:1 (Spring 1981) 129–140.
Pagnol, Marcel. "Cinématurgie de Paris." In Lapierre, Marcel, ed. *Anthologie du cinéma*. Paris: La Nouvelle Edition, 1946.
————. "Marcel Pagnol Raconte ses débuts au cinéma." *Figaro Littéraire* (Oct 1965) 8,9.
————. "Marcel Pagnol Raconte comment est né Monsieur Topaze." *Figaro Littéraire* (Aug–Sept 1964).
————. *Le Temps des secrets*. Paris: Editions Fallois, 1988.
————. *Le Temps des amours*. Paris: Editions Fallois, 1988.
Peyrusse, Claudette. *Le Cinéma méridional*. Toulouse: Eché, 1986.
Schulman, Elie. "Marcel Pagnol et le théâtre." *L'Avant-Scène Théâtre* 775 (Oct 1985) 6–8.

La Guerre de Troie n'aura pas lieu (*Tiger at the Gates*)

directed by Raymond Rouleau (1981)
play by Jean Giraudoux (1935)

In the many currents of French theater of the twentieth century, ranging from Claudel's mysticism to Adamov's exploding absurd, certain playwrights resist clear-cut classification. Better said, they have a style and a voice entirely their own, much as the signature of certain performers stamps every role they interpret. The ironic mannerist chic of Jean Giraudoux marks all his works, whether *Amphitryon 38*, *La Guerre de Troie n'aura pas lieu*, *Judith*, *Electre*, *Ondine*, or *La Folle de Chaillot*. Yet for all their masks and linguistic arabesques shadowing the voice of the playwright, they convey obliquely a true deep-seated anguish of impotence and dispossession, as well as contemporary political allusions of primary concern.

Of particular interest here is Giraudoux's appurtenance to the group of playwrights restaging classical themes: Camus, Sartre, Cocteau, Anouilh. All staged scenarios from classical Greco-Roman antiquity, all for different reasons, admittedly. Each playwright exploited the classical model to his own ends, even decrying other adaptations, such as Sartre's critique of Giraudoux's Aristotelian essentialism (a critique which implicitly promotes his own existentialist version of ancient legends). The thread that unites these diverse "remakes" is the admixture of the classical grandeur and dimension and the popular demythifying vernacular which undermines the subject at the same time that it gives it new blood. These plays are truly both windows and mirrors, a culture acknowledging its heritage and asserting its novelty, its contemporary vitality, its need for newness, its awareness of current political imperatives. Giraudoux, wounded and decorated in World War I, with his dual German-French cultural attachments, was always a citizen of somewhere else. In spite of his upbringing in *la France profonde* in the Limousin, he was foremost a world diplomat and writer, mistrusting militarism and nationalism in any form.

Like Anouilh's *Antigone*, Cocteau's *La Machine infernale*, Camus's *Caligula*, Sartre's *Les Mouches*, Giraudoux's *Amphitryon 38*, *Judith* and *Electre* all turn to antiquity for their subjects. But with *La Guerre de Troie n'aura pas lieu* (which still awaits its literal English title of *The Trojan War Will Not Take Place*), he achieves a virtuoso medley of genres and discourses, blending tragic, satiric, comic, pastoral, and lyric in an ironic extended metaphor which finally constitutes a portrait of family, of human nature, of age-old questions of impossible union, of *hubris*, *eros* and *thanatos*. It proves itself of immediate political relevance and intuition (reflecting the Italian Fascist invasion of Ethiopia, anticipating the sell-out at Munich in November 1938 and the inexorable advance of the totalitarian Axis regimes). More generally, in 1935 it signals the balance between mentalities of *après-guerre* and *avant-guerre* periods, thus like Janus regarding the past and future simultaneously in a moment of stasis fraught with tension. It also demonstrates transcendent political wisdom, articulating an eternal truth of the balance between the individual and the collective, between fatalism, determinism and personalities in the cycles of history.

Extensively derided by uncomprehending critics, Giraudoux's distinctive voice is a blend of rhetorical formalism and a ludic element, here presenting the play as play (the French equivalent might be the *pièce* as *pièce montée*). Raymond Rouleau both staged and directed this Antenne 2 television production which updates at the same time it betrays the original Giraudoux text, emphasizing the popular vulgarity of the satire and downplaying the allegory and excesses of Giraudoux's (in)famous linguistic *préciosité* (preciousness). In this videotaped production, the play has been severely cut and edited, not always to its advantage, with the conviction that any cultural allusion or esoteric term would lose the viewing audience. Not only has the most semantically complex *préciosité* and most exotic language been cut, the longer speeches or exchanges have been spliced. Thus the tediousness and tension of awaiting the inevitable, ironized in the title, has been lost, deemed wasted on modern impatient audiences who have forgotten the closed world of war and aggression. This is in itself a commentary on the distance between Giraudoux's readers and audience and the television viewers of the 1980s. Moreover, the nude love scene between Andromache and the returning Hector has been framed by the American editors to censor their bodies, a further commentary on the different standards of censorship and attitudes toward the body in France and the United States. The play still carries however its powerful message on the relationship between individual and collective destinies and the ironies of fate and history. In addition, the hero pitted hopelessly against a hostile universe ties this play to the contemporary concept of the absurd.

Respecting the classic unities of time, place and action, the play takes place in one day in Troy, with many intratextual indications of the temporal pressures and limitations of the situation. The camera maintains the spatial claustrophobic sense of destiny and tension with tight framing of the scenes and no deep shots. Action external to the parapet set is described in second-hand narration by the characters, giving the additional sense of distance from forces governing events. Walking along the parapets of Troy with a bouquet of flowers, Andromache (Geneviève Fontanel) displays her girlish enthusiasm and naive optimism at the return from war of her husband Hector (Pierre Santini). In polar contrast, her sister-in-law Cassandra (Françoise Marie) sitting at her loom, symbolically weaving the web of fate, speaks for destiny, which she defines as an accelerated form of life, a sleeping tiger which is awakened by men full of high-sounding phrases which tempt fate. It is a beautiful day which seems to defy tragedy, a nature incompatible with death, another polarization, reflective rather of Andromache who is pregnant, bursting with renewed life. Cassandra is her foil, the disabused realist. Andromache sees a soldier patting a cat, and takes solace in this vignette, oblivious to the image of the cat as the domestic version of the tiger. Cassandra speaks with bitter irony of the cripples lying about outcast outside the gate of the city, the forgotten element of society which suffers in both war and peace. And she sees the faceless figure of war approaching in the person of Hector, the protagonist marked by fate, returning from war to make love to his wife.

Feeling in himself a powerful postwar life force to rejuvenate and reenergize his people, Hector says that he wants two thousand children (in the aftermath of the demographic decimation of World War I, this was still a primary concern in France, whose government until recently paid families to procreate). When he declares that he is going to close the gates of war, suddenly Andromache panics, full of anxiety about the recurrence of war. It is as if Schopenhauer has superseded Nietzsche, as the returning war hero's idealistic will confronts the absurd caprices of fate. He will not be able to adjust to the new rules of the game and will paradoxically destroy the very peace he vaunts.

Various members of the household blame Paris (Cassandra and Hector's brother) and Helen for Troy's fate, while they are playing *boules* with fruit that recalls Paris's choice and the myth of the golden apples. As they talk of Paris carrying off Helen in front of Menelaus, in a scene noted for its irreverent depiction of legendary figures, Giraudoux parodies Lamartine's famous aphorism of Romantic angst from "L'Isolement" in the line "Un seul être vous manque et tout est repeuplé." (A single being is lacking and all is *re*populated, instead of the original *dépeuplé*, *de*populated.)

Giraudoux undermines the mythical subtext of his play by portraying Helen as an absent *tête à vent* (airhead) of pure egotism, indifferent even to her own legendary and troublesome beauty. And the dynastic dimensions of the royal family are constantly reduced to the exchanges and squabbles of a bourgeois household, in sequences like that where Priam reproaches his son. Giraudoux's intent was to offer bourgeois audiences of the 1930s access to high culture at what he deemed the level of the *baccalauréat*. Helen is worse than vapid; she is the vain decadent figure, a *reine de village* (prom queen), under the lascivious gaze of the old men of Troy, who function as spectators within the play, as she strolls the parapets, another counterpart to Andromache. Her physical presence is countered as the ruling couple, Priam (Paul-Emile Deiber) and Hecuba (Rosy Varte), and Demokos (Claude Pieplu), the poet of Troy, characterize her as a symbol rather than an individual. Demokos (an echo of Demodokos of Homer's *Odyssey*) is ridiculed as the detested official voice spouting the dangerous warmongering rhetoric of nationalism.

When Helen (Anny Duperey) finally appears, she subverts her own legendary physical image, for she is tawdry. Her passivity is not just sloth, however. She is in sync with the forces of history and destiny, evidenced by the phenomenon of her *chromos*, images or engravings that illustrate in color for her key people and events. Helen describes herself as an instrument of destiny, not a ploy of personal passion, as she like a camera lens views the future in bright colors. The album of her *chromos* is the key image of the play, the idea of the engraving or the photograph as death (several years before Sartre's concepts in *L'Imaginaire*): fixed, frozen images of eternity, inscribed as legend. Helen's eyes are described as the lenses of the world, a metaphor ironized by the presence of the camera. Her epic force is continually reduced and undermined, however, by the crass banter on her subject, making her the face that launched a thousand quips.

The fundamental paradox of this play is the declaration of the impossibility of staging events. In illustration of the fragility of power and the capricious nature of history, a messenger arrives to report that the priests are opposed to closing the gates of war. The gates are to be closed to end war forever after a long conflict, like the optimism and almost desperate idealism at the end of World War I. Stressing the dangers of abusing the power of language, Giraudoux blames the priests and poets for war as much as anyone. The figure of Peace (Flore Bernard) is an older woman, with grey and gold in her hair, who falters in symbolic weakness. Cassandra derides noble sentiments, mocks men and their gods, their honor, abstract principles which destroy life in the name of a higher order. This is a point in Giraudoux where he parallels closely the pacifist humanist ethic of Malraux, Sartre, Camus and Saint-Exupéry, but without their idealist dialectic.

Paris (Lambert Wilson) and Helen, appropriately decadent and corrupt, self-centered and self-indulgent, are yet another accident of fate, not a conniving vengeful *Liaisons dangereuses* couple. Demokos's war song elicits extended comments regarding the appropriate nature of the national anthem, which in Troy was supposedly bucolic and pacifist, a far cry from "La Marseillaise," more a reflection of the 1930s international leftist sentiment. The characters hurl epithets at each other that are destined to insult the enemy, in an extended parody of Homer and Virgil. In a lengthy soliloquy to the dead, in counterpoint to Demokos's ravings, Hector decries the horrors of war, showing the victors as reduced to mere survivors, demythifying military heroism in a discourse far ahead of its time.

The arrival of the Greeks under Ulysses (Jean Piat), come to fetch Helen, is marked by sarcastic comments about the strangeness of their music. Giraudoux is touching on a profound truth here, of cultural alienation between different peoples and the impossibility of their reaching an understanding, regardless of the good will and willingness to compromise of their leaders, attacking provincialism, nationalism and xenophobia. Queen Hecuba declares war the lowest form of animal life, comparing it to a monkey's rear end, in graphic terms which contrast the usual witty banter. Andromache sends her daughter Polyxene (Marie-Anne Démarest) to ask Helen to leave, exploiting the innocence of children, but the girl is trapped by Helen's clever sophistry, proving that even the most noble beliefs and intentions can be coopted by the forces of destiny, can become tools of propaganda. Andromache, the romantic, wants Helen to love Paris, wants the war to emanate from great passions and high-sounding ideals, wants it to be more than vulgar conflict driven by common stupid people. From our perspective of the end of a century where almost all the noble terms have been eliminated from war, leaving the harsh realities of its horrors (or worse the abstraction of technology), Giraudoux seems strangely prophetic, if a bit detached, in his cynicism.

With the arrival of the Greeks, there are several framed narrative sequences which describe Helen and the events surrounding her capture. She undermines the mythological legend of her birth to Leda and Zeus disguised as a swan, as she gives a hilarious account of her childhood growing up surrounded by birds. The demythifying process of vulgarizing classical legend is one of Giraudoux's preferred modes. This derision carries over into the scene where Oiax (Michel Créton) taunts Hector, pitting his rough crude aggressive street character against Hector's noble pacifism, his lust against Hector's fidelity, as the two embody the inadequate resistance to the growing threat of Nazism and Fascism. When Oiax sees his own vulgarity mirrored in the language of the incensed poet Demokos, he becomes Hector's ally, as he commends his strong pride.

The central sequence begins with the Trojan group advancing ceremoniously to meet Ulysses and his entourage, the scenario of all summit negotiations, truce parlays and alliances for peace, which simultaneously demonstrates their futility. A number of secondary roles have been eliminated from this production, with the exception of Olpides (Francis Lemaire) and Abneos (René Havard), partially due to the limitations of the close focus of television, but also in response to the eighties' greater emphasis on the individual. There are fewer crowd scenes and much less sense of the vociferous populace as backdrop for the dialogue than in the original Giraudoux text, which reflected the rowdy populism of the thirties even as it condemned it.

As Ulysses interrogates Helen regarding her activities with Paris, the play within the play unfolds. Helen's whitewashed version is belied by the details of endless fornication recounted with vulgar enthusiasm by the *gabiers*, Paris's crew. In a fantasy sequence, the goddess Iris arrives with the usual garbled message from the Gods: Aphrodite says leave the lovers together or there will be war; Pallas says separate them or there will be war; Jupiter says there will be war, period. With this irreverent parody, Giraudoux is not just undermining fifth century B.C. Greek theater; he is also acknowledging comic antecedents in classical antiquity, in the works of Aristophanes, Plautus or Terence.

In their great confrontation, Hector and Ulysses compare what they weigh in the bargain, what they mutually represent and risk, what literally hangs in the balance, both a reference to Homer and an allusion to contemporary events like the talks at Stresa. In portraying the fraternal *camaraderie* and mutual respect between these two diplomats with *pleins pouvoirs* (full powers) whose ideals and lives mirror each other, Giraudoux presents an intimate view of the common bond between great men, whose privilege it is to watch war from a terrace. There is more than a little bitterness in this voice regarding the impotence of the old aristocratic diplomatic tradition in Europe (where even enemy monarchs like Kaiser Wilhelm and Queen Victoria were cousins) before the rising tide of populism, a phenomenon of the thirties as well as past revolutions where power passed from the aristocracy to the bourgeoisie to the people. This is the confraternity of the aristocracy depicted in the Renoir films of the same era. The bond between the two men constitutes a fundamental humanist cross-cultural brotherhood between political enemies, like that imaged recently in the film *Midnight Clear*. The impossible future they depict also anticipates Elle's life not lived in Marguerite Duras's *Hiroshima mon amour*.

The wise and experienced Ulysses agrees to make the gesture of good will and to try to leave with Helen. But he comments that it is a long walk back to his ship, fraught with the potential danger of assassination—both a reference to the incident which began World War I, the assassination of Archduke Ferdinand of Austria in Sarajevo, and a reiteration of his pacifist pessimism. He confesses to Hector that he is leaving because Andromache reminds him of his own wife Penelope, in an intimate confession of human vulnerability that reduces both of them from mythical heroes to lonely husbands. It establishes Ulysses-Penelope as the greek equivalent of Hector-Andromache as a loving couple (Ulysses is a much more even match with Hector than with Achilles). Both couples stand in opposition to the false lust of Paris-Helen, Oiax-Andromache, or the ultimate parody of Helen-Troilus.

Immoral lust continues its collision course with destiny when a drunken Oiax offends Andromache. Demokos, enraged at the affront, incites the people to war, and Hector kills him himself, in a potentially extremist gesture, stating that governments have the right to silence warmongers among their own people. With his last breath, Demokos names Oiax, the people kill him, and the doors of war open to reveal Helen kissing the fifteen-year-old Troilus (Jean-Philippe Puymartin). The theater of diplomacy is transformed into the theater of war. In a final ironic comment, Cassandra states that since the Trojan poet is dead, it is now up to the Greek poet to tell the tale, an obvious reference to Homer's *Odyssey* and *Iliad*, already referenced directly in a sarcastic comment from Hector to Paris. The uncertain curtain settles at this point in the play, lowering the balance on the side of history, relegating Giraudoux's fantastical alternate mythology to the wings.

The question of the *pièce à clé* (play as a key) has been addressed often in criticism of this work, as in other Giraudoux pieces. The play is also a reflection of Giraudoux's own experience in government service. Elements like Paris's very name and his badly executed abduction of Helen can be seen as an extended metaphor of the consequences of the Treaty of Versailles and the problem of reparations. This connection is strengthened by the fact that Giraudoux served from 1926 to 1934 on the commission to regulate the claims of Turkey from World War I, the country which contains the site of ancient Troy. He was named to a cabinet post in 1934 and to a ministry by Daladier just weeks before the outbreak of war.

Bibliography

Albeaux-Fernet, Michel. "Jean Giraudoux et ses héroïnes." *Nouvelle Revue des Deux Mondes* (January 1983) 104–114.

Baudin, Henri. *La Métamorphose du comique et le renouvellement littéraire du français de Jarry à Giraudoux*. Lille: Atelier National de Rep. de Thèses de l'Université de Lille, 1983.

Blanchard, Marc Eli. "The Reverse View: Greece and Greek Myths in Modern French Theater." *Modern Drama* 29:1 (1986) 41–48.

Body, Jacques. "Giraudoux et les rendez-vous de l'histoire." *Revue d'Histoire Littéraire de la France* 83: 5–6 (1983) 866–878.

————. *Jean Giraudoux, la légende et le secret*. Paris: Presses Universitaires de France, 1986.

————, and James Norwood. *Jean Giraudoux: The Legend and the Secret*. Rutherford: Fairleigh Dickinson University Press, 1991.

————. "Inédit: *La Guerre de Troie n'aura pas lieu*." *Cahiers Jean Giraudoux* 21 (1992) 211–213.

————. "Rythme et temporalité dans le théâtre de Giraudoux." *Cahiers de l'Association Internationale des Etudes Françaises* 34 (May 1982) 223–236.

————. "Les Sources grecques et françaises de *La Guerre de Troie n'aura pas lieu*." In *Humanisme contemporain*. Paris, 1968.

Boisdeffre, Pierre de. "Jean Giraudoux." *Nouvelle Revue des Deux Mondes* (February 1983) 377–396.

Brunel, Pierre. "Giraudoux et le tragique grec." *Bulletin de l'Association Guillaume Bude* 2 (1983) 198–205.

Delort, Janine. "'A la voix' ou le concept d'intonation chez Giraudoux auteur de dialogues cinématographiques." *Cahiers Jean Giraudoux* 20 (1991) 325-339.

Cohen, Robert. *Giraudoux: Three Faces of Destiny*. Chicago: University of Chicago Press, 1968.

Galand, René. "Microlecture de Giraudoux." *French Review* 60:4 (1987) 497–501.

Garguilo, René. "Giraudoux devant les portes de la guerre." *Revue d'Histoire Littéraire de la France* 83:5–6 (1983) 754–763.

Garnham, Barry. "'Real in the Unreal': Jean Giraudoux and Greek Myth." In Thomas and Le Saux, eds. *Myth and its Legacy in European Literature*. Durham, England: University of Durham Press, 1996.

Graumann, G. *La Guerre de Troie aura lieu: La Préparation de la pièce de Giraudoux*. Dissertation Abstracts International 42:1 (1981).

Hopkins, Patricia, and Wendell Aycock, eds. *Myths and Realities of Contemporary French Theater: Comparative Views*. Lubbock: Texas Tech University Press, 1985.

Lemaître, Georges. *Jean Giraudoux: the Writer and his Work*. New York: Ungar, 1971.

Lioure, Michel. "Ecriture et dramaturgie dans le théâtre de Jean Giraudoux." *Travaux de Linguistique et de Littérature* 19:2 (1981) 171–190.

Mankin, Paul. *Precious Irony: The Theatre of Jean Giraudoux*. The Hague: Mouton, 1971.

Mauron, Charles. *Le Théâtre de Giraudoux, Etude psycho-critique*. Paris: José Corti, 1971.

Pocknell, Brian. "Giraudoux's *La Guerre de Troie n'aura pas lieu* and Homer's *Iliad*: The Scales of Zeus as Dramatic Device." *Modern Drama* 24:2 (1981) 135–145.

Pomerantz, Donald. *Tragic Irony in the Theater of Jean Giraudoux*. Dissertation Abstracts International 51:8 (1991) 2765A–2766A.

Powell, Brenda. *The Metaphysical Quality of the Tragic: A Study of Sophocles, Giraudoux, and Sartre*. New York: Peter Lang, 1990.

Raimond, Michel. *Sur trois pièces de Jean Giraudoux: 'La Guerre de Troie n'aura pas lieu', 'Electre', 'Ondine'*. Paris: Nizet, 1982.

Ranger, Jean-Claude. "Nature et tragique." *Cahiers Jean Giraudoux* 20 (1991) 199–211.

Raymond, Agnès. "Giraudoux mystificateur." *Cahiers de l'Association Internationale des Etudes Françaises* 34 (May 1982) 211–221.

————. *Jean Giraudoux: The Theatre of Victory and Defeat*. Amherst: University of Massachusetts Press, 1966.

Reilly, John H. *Jean Giraudoux*. Boston: Twayne, 1978.

————. "Jean Giraudoux's Theatre: Style or Stage?" *Claudel Studies* 9:2 (1982) 40–46.

Rieuneau, Maurice. *Guerre et révolution dans le roman français de l'entre-deux guerres*. Paris: Klincksieck, 1974.

Robichez, Jacques. "L'Usage de l'allusion dans le théâtre de Giraudoux." *Cahiers de l'Association Internationale des Etudes Françaises* 34 (May 1982) 237–244.

Scheele, Elizabeth. "La Parodie de quelques principes de Machiavel dans *La Guerre de Troie n'aura pas lieu* de Jean Giraudoux." *French Studies Bulletin* 68 (Autumn 1998) 5–6.

————. "Quelques influences de Leibniz, Voltaire, du Comte de las Cases et d'Henri Barbusse sur *'La Guerre de Troie n'aura pas lieu'* de Jean Giraudoux." *Neohelicon* 24:2 (1997) 341–352.

Schuler, Marilyn. "Les Droits de la femme: Andromaque, amie de Jean Giraudoux." *Cahiers Jean Giraudoux* 18 (1989) 113–136.

Serca, Isabelle. "Argumentation et dialogue dans *La Guerre de Troie* (n')*aura* (*pas*) *lieu* (La Stratégie argumentative de justement)." *ChSigne* 5 (1995) 135–150.

Tonnet-Lacroix, Eliane. "Une Interprétation politique du mythe d'Electre: Giraudoux et la France de 1936–37." *Revue d'Histoire du Théâtre* 41:4 (1989) 357–384.

Zénon, Renée. *Le Traitement des mythes dans le théâtre de Jean Giraudoux*. Baltimore: University Presses of America, 1981.

La Règle du jeu
(The Rules of the Game)

written and directed by Jean Renoir (1939)

This last of the great French films of Renoir, an original filmscript with his own starring role, is considered by many to be his masterpiece, in spite of its flaws, not the least of which is trying to say everything in one film, including three centuries of intertextual literary, musical, and historic allusions. The film is a personal fantasy combining many diverse elements. Foremost, it represents an unmitigated indictment of the *haute bourgeoisie* (upper class) and aristocracy of France in 1939. Renoir condemns through their own actions the decadence of the aristocracy and the inanity of their effete preoccupations, in a tradition including Molière, Beaumarchais, even Proust. More immediately, he is also condemning the right-wing political elements in French society of the day, some of which were openly proNazi.

The structure of *La Règle du jeu* involves an arabesque of modern elements and citations of classic theater, particularly the contrapuntal interplay and echoes between a number of amorous couples, *sosies*, named after the character in the ancient classical play *Amphitryon*. Thus the primary host couple Robert and Christine both have alternate attachments: Robert with Geneviève and Christine with André Jurieux. André also has the affection of Jackie, to whom he is more suited, and Christine the affection of Octave, her lifelong friend and admirer. In the servants' quarters, the triangle is repeated in echo, as the poacher Marceau pursues new quarry belonging to the gamewarden Schumacher, in the form of his wife Lisette, Christine's loyal maid. This type of dynamic in echo is perhaps most readily associated with Beaumarchais's 1775 play *Le Barbier de Séville* (*The Barber of Seville*) and 1784 *Le Mariage de Figaro* (*The Insane Day or The Marriage of Figaro*), equally well known in their operatic adaptations by Rossini (1816) and Mozart (1786). In the first, Count Almaviva disguises himself and enlists the help of Figaro in order to abduct Rosina, his love, from the clutches of her evil-minded guardian, Bartolo. In the "sequel" the Count has tired of Rosina and is pursuing the maid Susanna, whom Figaro is planning to marry. The count is trapped when the two women exchange clothes and he declares his love to Rosina in his moonlit garden, thinking it is Susanna. The film abounds with references to eighteenth-century works, with its Mozart soundtrack, opening quote from Beaumarchais, antique music boxes, hunting party as a metaphor for sexual pursuit, libertine indulgences. Renoir becomes a twentieth-century Choderlos de Laclos observing the *Dangerous Liaisons* in the aristocratic society around him in his day. His character by name is associated with the Octave of Musset's 1833 Romantic comedy *Les Caprices de Marianne*, and he is referred to as a dangerous poet.

There is also in Renoir's film in filigree the long tradition of mask from the Renaissance, including the *Commedia dell'Arte* and Mardi Gras. He telescopes *en abyme* the grande farce comedy in the château, both upstairs and downstairs, and the standard diversion of the play within the play, in this case a vaudeville-style review including skits of Germans in lederhosen, Orthodox Jewish rabbis, singing skeletons, and Octave in a bear suit, all this just months after the Munich pact in November 1938 and the Anschluss. It is significant that Christine is Austrian and that Robert has German Jewish blood, descended from a certain Rosenthal in Frankfurt (an intertextual reference to his role as Rosenthal in *La Grande Illusion*). Thus this stage performance is an extended political satire like that in *La Grande Illusion* or *La Marseillaise*. It is outstaged like those of the other two films by the dramatic action involving the audience, in this case acts of violence and chaos resembling the 1930s classic situation of the characters in Agatha Christie, as well as Marivaux or Beaumarchais. The eruption of "real" violence ending in the death of an innocent "character" in the frame "play" resembles the structure of Pirandello's 1921 *Six Characters in Search of an Author* and marks *La Règle du jeu* as a modernist work, playing with multiple diegetic levels of reality and illusion.

La Règle du jeu is also a self-reflexive work, containing multiple references to the contemporary world of the arts, to music, radio, film and the artist: the broadcast interviews with André, the phonograph, talk of Christine's father Stiller (a great Austrian orchestra conductor). Further allusions to the mechanics of sound and movement in performance are embodied in Robert's collection of music boxes and the Limonaire music organ which malfunctions at the end, as well as the pianos played in two different rooms. Images of visual recording, of the camera, include the spyglass Christine uses on the hunt which becomes just that as she sees her husband kissing his mistress Geneviève (a clever symbol of the movie camera and the telephoto lens). The same hunting sequence involves live action photography of hunting wild animals during which some two hundred rabbits and birds were shot. Renoir's own role as *auteur* (the word he coined to describe this film) director is embodied in the film by Octave as observer, similar to that of Nick Carraway in F. Scott Fitzgerald's 1925 novel *The Great Gatsby*. At the mythological level, the film features a tragic legendary hero like Icarus who flies high and falls to Earth, the pilot André Jurieux who like the albatross is helpless on land.

After twenty years in oblivion due to political controversy, this film was restored in 1959 to its original edited version by Jean Gaborit and Jacques Durand and dedicated to André Bazin, the pioneer film critic of France who wrote at length on Renoir and who died in 1958. Thus it reappeared in the New Wave watershed year along with Truffaut's *Les Quatre Cents Coups*, Resnais's *Hiroshima mon amour* and Fellini's *La Dolce Vita*. The original scenario by Renoir opens with the triumphal reception of the pilot André Jurieux (Roland Toutain) at Le Bourget Airport after he has flown the Atlantic alone in twenty-three hours. Jurieux represents the aviator heroes of the era: Blériot, Lindbergh, Markham, Earhart, and of course the French author-pilot Antoine de Saint-Exupéry. His only concern is for the woman in his life, the Marquise Christine de la Cheyniest (Nora Grégor), the beautiful Austrian *ingénue* he adores. She meanwhile is occupied with vain material frivolities with her slick decadent husband Robert (Marcel Dalio) and her maid Lisette Schumacher (Paulette Dubost, who confirmed her indestructible longevity by playing the role of the grandmother in Louis Malle's 1989 *Milou en mai*). On the way out to dinner, Robert telephones his long-time mistress Geneviève de Marras (Mila Parély) to break off with her, out of respect for his wife's honesty. The consequences of their double infidelity will be played out at the houseparty at La Colinière, their country estate.

The prefigurations of major plot events are numerous and the symbolism everpresent in this film. André Jurieux, despondent over Christine's lack of love for him, attempts suicide in his car (in a very unconvincing crash sequence that Renoir reconstructed from a serious accident he had in 1927 at the same place, wherein Pierre Champagne died, and Renoir was taken to the hospital by poachers hunting nearby). Octave's nearly fatal end is prefigured twice more, when he is almost mistaken for quarry on the hunt, then trapped in his bear suit at the costume ball, as he is trapped in a role he doesn't want (a sequence echoed in the emasculating humiliation of Martin Guerre). The aristocrats laugh about the tragic fate of "Georges," a friend of theirs who accidentally shot himself in the leg on a hunting party and died within minutes. Edouard Schumacher the gamewarden (Gaston Modot) and Marceau the poacher (Julien Carette) fight over rabbits in the fields and Lisette in the château, as Schumacher repeatedly threatens to kill his rival.

Mistaken and uncertain identity, the play within the play which spills over beyond the stage into general chaos in the château, questions of proper conduct and manners mingled with outrageous behavior, all recall eighteenth-century bourgeois comedy and conjure for us today images of a Mozartian world like that portrayed in Milos Forman's film *Amadeus*. In the final sequences, the exchanging of clothing, another eighteenth-century cliché, entangles André in the escape attempt of Christine and Octave and the jealous rage of Lisette's husband Edouard. Comedy turns to double tragedy, as André dies, gunned down by Edouard, and the aristocratic characters cover up the ugly reality of the murder, lying "with class" as they have always done, resorting to conventions and manners to gloss over and excuse immoral conduct. This is the iron fist in the velvet glove; it is the decadent avoidance of reality we saw in *La Nuit de Varennes*; it is the fraternal good old boy/girl solidarity of the aristocrats in the face of outsiders, like that of de Boeldieu and von Rauffenstein in *La Grande Illusion*; it is the mask of manners of *Le Misanthrope*; it is the hunt as symbol of pursuit of woman, an object to be caught in the game of sexual conquest like Napoleon's Josephine, played out here in at least seven different styles; it is the fatal game of exchanged, assumed and mistaken identity like that of *Le Retour de Martin Guerre*.

As mentioned earlier, however, the houseparty at the château may be indifferent to the contemporary real world, but it is not completely isolated from the context of 1939. There are radios and phonographs, record flights across the Atlantic, numerous automobiles, rendez-vous by telephone, an allusion to the recently invented diphtheria vaccine, binoculars, a player piano, and two racist comments: one regarding *crimes passionnels* or crimes of passion between Poles or Italians, the other the allusion to Cheyniest's racially mixed background. Most of all, Renoir has left us an entertaining but devastating indictment of the upper crust of 1939 France, of their hypocritical decadence, which we can assume will make them victims and quarry in their turn. Clearly, the world is not a very amusing place in 1939, and in this *Dolce Vita* twenty years before Fellini's, Renoir spares no one. Sincerity may be boring, but the rules of this game are cruel and dangerous.

In this film, as with *Manon des Sources* or *Ladri di biciclette*, there is a mistranslation in the English version of the title, this time extending the singular *règle* to the plural *Rules of the Game*. What is, in fact, *the* rule of the game in French? Like the governing principle behind the match game in Resnais's *L'Année dernière à Marienbad*, it is the understanding of why the game must be played and how to control it that gives ultimate power to the *magister ludi*. Alain Resnais said this film devastated him when he saw it. The rule is also the ruler, the measure of the game, how far it can be carried, the degree of artifice and the extent of the players' conformity. It is of course the rule of the players' game, of the filmmaker pushing his art, his plot, his sets, his shots to the limit. For Renoir/Octave, it is *La Règle du je(u)*: the paragrammatic extension of the self, the ego, in the play of the ensemble of characters, as in a dream, the distribution of phobias and desires. Not surprisingly, this film was banned on its release. The rule of the game governs all performance, on stage or screen, in society, in politics: choose your costume well and never remove your mask. The reality lying beneath the surface is intolerable and uncontrollable; its portrayal in art implies surrealistic chaos.

Note: The English subtitles of this film and many critics use the characters' names La Chesnaye and Jurieu, even though they are listed in the original credits of the film as La Cheyniest and Jurieux. La Chesnaye was the name of the commander of Marie-Antoinette's guard in *La Marseillaise*.

Bibliography

Please see the chapters on *La Marseillaise* and *La Grande Illusion* for the general Renoir bibliography.

Bates, Robin. "Audiences on the Verge of a Fascist Breakdown: Male Anxieties and Late 1930s French Film." *Cinema Journal* 36:3 (Spring 1997) 25–55.
Browne, Nick. "Deflections of Desire in *The Rules of the Game*: Reflections on the theater of

history." *Quarterly Review of Film Studies* VII, 3 (Summer 1982) 251–261.

Bussot, Marguerite. "*La Règle du jeu*." *CICIM* 39-40 (Jun 1994) 179–182.

Conley, Tom. "The Laws of the Game: Jean Renoir, *La Règle du jeu*." In Denvir, John, ed. *Legal Reelism: Movies as Legal Texts*. Urbana, IL: University of Illinois Press, 1996.

Douin, Jean-Luc. "*La Règle du jeu*." *Télérama* 2313 (May 1994) 140.

Gauteur, Claude. "Jean Renoir: *La Règle du jeu*." *Positif* 257–258 (Jul-Aug 1982) 35–50.

_____. "*La Règle du jeu* et la critique en 1939." *Image et Son* 282 (Mar 1974) 49–73.

Génin, Bernard. "Renoir et la comédie humaine." *Télérama* 2331 (Sept 1994) 42–45.

Heed, Sven Ake. "Le Jeu des règles dans *La Règle du jeu*: La Dramaturgie classique et le film de Jean Renoir." In Burius, Lidman and Olsson, eds. *Nagra Hyll(nings)-centimeter*. Stockholm, Sweden: Kungliga Biblioteket, 1998.

Hines, Thomas J. "In Defense of the Past: Jean Renoir's *La Règle du jeu*." In Radcliff-Umstead, Douglas, ed. *Varieties of Filmic Expression*. Kent, OH: Kent State University, 1989.

Jehle, W. "*La Règle du jeu*." *Cinema* XXI, 4 (1975) 40–50.

Landrot, Marine. "Un monde à l'envers." *Télérama* 2313 (May 1994) 115.

Lebovics, Herman. "Open the Gates, Break Down the Barriers: the French Revolution, the Popular Front, and Jean Renoir." *Persistence of Vision* 12–13 (1996) 9–28.

Lesage, Julia. "*S/Z* and *The Rules of the Game*." *Jump Cut* 12/13 (1976) 45–51.

Levine, S.Z. "Structures of sound and image in *The Rules of the Game*." *Quarterly Review of Film Studies* VII, 3 (Summer 1982) 211–224.

Little, M. "Sound Track: *The Rules of the Game*." *Cinema Journal* XIII, 1 (Fall 1973) 35–44.

Mary, A. "L'Analyse du film." *Image et Son* 266 (Dec 1972) 3–28.

Mottet, Jean. *Les Paysages du cinéma*.

Ousselin, Edward. "'Et maintenant, mesdames et messieurs, le spectacle va commencer': L'Espace théâtral dans trois films de Jean Renoir." *Cincinnati Romance Review* 18 (1999) 90–98.

Pearson, Karen. "Rosenthal dans *La Grande Illusion* et La Chesnaye dans *La Règle du jeu*." *Chimères* 18:1 (1985) 41–48.

Perebinossoff, P.R. "Theatricals in Jean Renoir's *The Rules of the Game* and *Grand Illusion*." *Literature/Film Quarterly* V, 1 (Winter 1977) 50–56.

Petric, Vlada. "From *mise-en-scène* to *mise-en-shot*: analysis of a sequence." *Quarterly Review of Film Studies* VII, 3 (Summer 1982) 263–280.

Petrie, Graham. "Theater, film, life." *Film Comment* X, 3 (May–Jun 1974) 38–43.

Reader, Keith. "*La Règle du jeu; The Rules of the Game*." *Sight and Sound* VI, 9 (Sept 1996) 56.

_____. "Chaos, Contradiction and Order in Jean Renoir's *La Règle du jeu*." *Australian Journal of French Studies* 36:1 (Jan–Apr 1999) 26–38.

Rothman, William. "The filmmaker within the film: the role of Octave in *The Rules of the Game*." *Quarterly Review of Film Studies* VII, 3 (Summer 1982) 225–236.

Roy, Jean. "*La Règle du jeu*." *Cinéma 72* 234 (Jun 1978) 33–46.

Smith, Gavin. "A man of excess. Paul Schrader on Jean Renoir." *Sight and Sound* V, 1 (Jan 1995) 24–29.

Snyder, John. "Film and Classical Genre: Rules for Interpreting *Rules of the Game*." *Literature/Film Quarterly* 10:3 (1982) 162–179.

Vincendeau, Ginette. "The Exception and the Rule." *Sight and Sound* II, 8 (Dec 1992) 34–36.

Viry-Babel, Roger. *Jean Renoir, la règle et le jeu*. Paris: Denoël, 1986.

Warehime, Marja. "Mixing Genres, May 68 and the Ghosts of History: Louis Malle Rewrites *The Rules of the Game*." *Historical Reflections Réflexions Historiques* 24:2 (Summer 1998) 179–203.

Wiese. E. "The Shape of the Music in *The Rules of the Game*." *Quarterly Review of Film Studies* VII, 3 (Summer 1982) 199–210.

280   *La Règle du jeu*

Wood, G. A. "Game theory and *The Rules of the Game*." *Cinema Journal* XIII, 1 (Fall 1973) 25-34.

Wylie, L. "La Vérité derrière les masques." *Quarterly Review of Film Studies* VII, 3 (Summer 1982) 237–250.

Fable on Film:
Imaging Classic Myths

From the mysticism of the Middle Ages and the occult of the Renaissance to the fantasy and science fiction of the nineteenth and twentieth centuries, Western culture has been fascinated by fables of all kinds. As Russian formalist Vladimir Propp demonstrated in his 1928 *Morphology of the Folktale*, there are certain situations and functions, the primordial stockpile of myth, so to speak, which lend themselves to endless recombinant configurations. The sources of the European folktale are as varied as the modern-day mutations. One undisputed primary source is the fables of Apuleius from the second century A.D., especially the myth of Cupid and Pysche. There are in ancient Norse and Scottish mythology other legendary beasts whose iconography became interwoven with the Mediterranean sources. The modern corpus of European fairy tales also traces many of its origins to Straparola or Basile, sixteenth-century Venetian writers. Some of the most popular tales circulating in Europe in the seventeenth century were published over a twenty-year period by Charles Perrault and collected in 1697 as the *Contes de ma mère l'oie (Tales of Mother Goose)*: *Peau d'âne (Donkey Skin)*, *Les Souhaits ridicules (Ridiculous Wishes)*, *La Belle au bois dormant (Sleeping Beauty)*, *Le Petit Chaperon rouge (Little Red Riding Hood)*, *La Barbe bleue (Bluebeard)*, *Le Maître chat ou le chat botté (Puss in Boots)*, *Les Fées (The Fairies)*, *Cendrillon ou la petite pantoufle de verre (Cinderella)*, *Riquet à la houppe (Ricky Top-knot)*, and *Le Petit Poucet (Tom Thumb)*. The tales announce their archetypal stature with the definite articles of their titles, as do the plays of Molière and the *Fables* of La Fontaine. Many of these beast fables can also trace their lineage to Aesop, to the Bestiaries of the Middle Ages or to the Bible. Scattered throughout these tales are structural plot and character elements which were successfully recombined by Jeanne Le Prince de Beaumont in 1757 to create *La Belle et la Bête (Beauty and the Beast)*. Since then, there have been more than two hundred text versions of the tale of Beauty and the Beast, with dozens of different titles and styles of illustrations (perhaps the most influential by Gustave Doré in 1853), an opera, a TV series, and at least three films, creating a kaleidoscope of images. The best source of documentation of present-day versions of the illustrated tale is Betsy Hearne's book, *Beauty and the Beast: Visions and Revisions of an Old Tale*. Hearne has unearthed a taxonomy of variants and symbology in the myriad versions of the tale; she however fails to interpret the intertextual significance of elements like butterflies (implied by the Greek definition of psyche), a unicorn, or a canary named Orpheus. This is an oversight, for the corpus of a fable constitutes not just all its versions, their tellings, readings and interpretations, but also the connotative network interconnecting versions of the tale from different eras and cultures, reflecting differing ideologies, and also contextualizing the tale and its transcendent structural elements. Fable would seem to be the first genre for adaptation to film, with its strong oral tradition and myriad illustrated editions. Moreover, as the late Bruno Bettelheim pointed out, these tales are generated by certain primal needs and fears and serve as a cathartic purge, and not only in the imagination of children. Like Cocteau's "open Sesame," the magic of film and its primal power to purge phobias and desires should best serve and be served by fabular texts. This has been accomplished by studios like Disney producing animated shorts and features, but enacting fable in the flesh on film has proved more elusive. The surrealistic fantasy element defies coherent imaging or traps the filmmaker in self-indulgent silliness that betrays the power and transcendent energy of the original text(s). One of the rare examples of successful incarnation of classic fable is Jean Cocteau's 1946 *La Belle et la Bête*. It is intriguing to compare his work with other experimental adaptations of classic fable on film, particularly Jacques Demy's 1971 *Peau d'âne*. Eric Rohmer's 1978 *Perceval le Gaulois* might have served instead, but it comes from a chivalry legend tradition and therefore is literally a different genre. In the same vein, one of the most powerful fable films to date is Bertrand Tavernier's 1987 *La Passion Béatrice*, a seeringly realistic and difficult film about birth, death, jealousy, incest, murder and revenge, a fable exploring the primal subconscious, as the director states at the beginning. A closer look at Cocteau's and Demy's films and their fabular intertexts reveals to what extent they function around similar primal mythemes like the taboo of incest, thus validating Propp's structuralist contention that all fairy tales are variants of basic thematic elements.

Bibliography

Bettelheim, Bruno. *The Uses of Enchantment*. New York: Vintage Books, 1977.

Blackham, H. J. *The Fable as Literature*. London: Athlone, 1985.

Certeau, Michel de. *La Fable mystique: XVIe–XVIIe siècle*. Paris: Gallimard, 1987.

Derrida, Jacques, Brian Holmes, and Avital Ronell. "A Number of Yes." *Qui Parle* 2:2 (1988) 118-133.

Eckhardt, Caroline. "A Commonsensical Protest against Deconstruction; or How the Real Work at Last Became a Fable." *Thought* 60:238 (1985) 310–321.

Gobin, Pierre. "Fable, canevas, argument, prétexte." In Balakian, Anna, et al, eds., *Proceedings of the Xth Congress of the International Comparative Literature Association*. New York: Garland, 1985.

Hearne, Betsy. *Beauty and the Beast: Visions and Revisions of an Old Tale*. Chicago: University of Chicago Press, 1989.

Knauth, Alphonse. "Fabula Rasa: De/structuration de la fable ésopique." *Discours Social* 1:3 (1988) 317–342.

Lonsdale, Steven. "Approaches to the Beast Fable in the Liberal Arts Curriculum." *Bestia* 2 (1990) 19–29.

Martin, Louis. "The 'Aesop' Fable-Animal." In Blonsky, Marshall, ed., *On Signs*. Baltimore: Johns Hopkins University Press, 1985.

Ross, Bruce. *The Inheritance of Animal Symbols in Modern Literature and World Culture: Essays,*

Notes and Lectures. New York: Peter Lang, 1988.

Salazar, Philippe-Joseph. "Les Pouvoirs de la fable: Mythologie, littérature et tradition (1650–1725)." *Revue d'Histoire Littéraire de la France* 91:6 (1991) 878–889.

Vandendorpe, Christian. *Apprendre à lire des fables: Une Approche sémio-cognitive*. Paris: Editions du Préambule, 1989.

Vignaux, Georges. "Le Pouvoir des fables." *Sociocriticism* 3:2–6 (1987) 63–93.

Vincent, Monique. "La Fable dans *Le Mercure Galant*: un reflet de La Fontaine." *Dix-Septième Siècle* 156 (1987) 267–281.

Ziolkowski, Jan. "The Form and Spirit of the Beast Fable." *Bestia* 2 (1990) 4–18.

La Belle et la Bête
(*Beauty and the Beast*)

directed by Jean Cocteau (1946)
fable by Jeanne Le Prince de Beaumont (1757)

Jean Cocteau (1889–1963) identified his own artistic odyssey with the classical mythology of the poet, this modern Orpheus who sang of love and death like the ancient Greek figure whose lyre gave us the word lyricism. Cocteau experienced life intensely—artistically, emotionally, sexually. Although a modernist and surrealist, an unclassifiable protean genius whose work reflects the fundamental ambiguities of his life, he was elected to the traditional Académie Française in 1955. Artist, film director, playwright, novelist, short story writer, autobiographer, sculptor, screen-writer, surrealist poet, set designer for ballet, he was the long-time lover of actor Jean Marais and the intimate friend of another troubled genius, Edith Piaf. He wrote the play *Le Bel Indifférent* as a vehicle for her, and he died just hours after her passing.

His novels included *Thomas l'imposteur* (1923), *Les Enfants terribles* (1929—filmed in 1950 by Jean-Pierre Melville). His plays were *Orphée* (1926), *Antigone* (1928), *La Voix humaine* (1930), *Les Parents terribles* (1938), *La Machine infernale* (1934), *Oedipe Roi* (1949), *Bacchus* (1952), *Le Menteur, Le Bel Indifférent*. His ballets included *Phèdre* (1950) and *La Dame à la licorne* (1953). He wrote the screenplay for the 1945 Robert Bresson film, *Les Dames du Bois de Boulogne*, adapted from the hostess's tale in *Jacques le fataliste*. His films were *Sang d'un poète* (1930) made with the patronage of the Vicomte de Noailles (who also supported Luis Buñuel's scandalous surrealistic 1932 *L'Age d'or*), *La Belle et la Bête* (1946), *L'Aigle à deux têtes* (1948), *Les Parents terribles* (1949), *Orphée* (1949), and *Le Testament d'Orphée* (1960), made with the money François Truffaut earned from *Les Quatre Cents Coups* (1959).

The mythological and metaphorical trilogy including *Sang d'un poète*, *Orphée*, and *Le Testament d'Orphée* represents a long-term self-portrait of the poet covering thirty years. The sense of futurism, of modernism, of surrealism that his work leaves us is due not only to the original polymorphic works which he produced but also to the great generic variety of his creative endeavors. Above all, Cocteau's work is a voyage through the looking glass into the world of fantasy and legend, where the sexual, the surreal and the symbolic unite.

It was Jean Marais who suggested the project of a film of *La Belle et la Bête*, the fairy tale that so closely resembles its literary antecedents in Perrault's works, which Cocteau like Jeanne de Beaumont had read as a child. Her tale touched the unsettled zones of his imagination, echoed the polarizations of his sexual, artistic and physical dichotomies: good and evil, beauty and ugliness, youth and old age. Cocteau said in *Démarche d'un poète*:

> Le rôle de l'artiste sera donc de créer un organisme ayant une vie propre puisée dans la sienne, et non pas destiné à surprendre, à plaire ou à déplaire, mais à être assez actif pour exciter des sens secrets ne réagissant qu'à certains signes qui représentent la beauté pour les uns, la laideur et la difformité pour les autres.[1]

Cocteau could have filmed faithfully the original tale, but instead made numerous additions, deletions and transpositions, in his rewriting and reworking of that text, often noted by critics. In particular, the addition of Avenant (which in French means attractive), squares the plot and especially the ending. There Avenant and the Beast exchange masks, reuniting internal and external beauty and ugliness and resolving the double tension of their two dichotomies. Avenant repeats the fate of the Beast, being turned from beauty to beast because he did not believe in the powers of magic. The creation of Avenant not only offsets the Prince-Beast but also establishes a masculine equivalent of the linguistic feminine polarity of the French title: *La Belle et la Bête*. In playing the triple role, Jean Marais acts out personally the beauty/beast duality for Cocteau. The homoerotic implications of the Beast's final transformation are analyzed by Susan Hayward in her essay in *French Film: Texts and Contexts*, "Gender Politics—Cocteau's Belle is not that Bête: Jean Cocteau's *La Belle et la Bête* (1946)."

Just as Cocteau chose certain elements as agents of magic (the horse, the glove, the animated statues, the key), the original author of the tale chose the rose, the mirror, the powers of the good fairy, and the ring as central actantial symbols and characters. A comparison of the two works reveals in both cases a complex mythological thematic working through the artist that ultimately restructures the tale as primal myth.

The original fable of *La Belle et laBête* was written by an interesting woman. Jeanne-Marie Le Prince de Beaumont worked as governess to the children of the Prince of Wales and published a controversial ladies' magazine in the 1750s. Born in 1711 in Rouen, she came from a family of numerous children, including a brother who became a well-known painter, but had few financial resources of her own. Her decision to become a teacher was considered radical in her day, when most unendowed daughters wound up in a convent. A brief and unhappy marriage which produced one daughter was annulled in 1745, and Madame de Beaumont left France for England in 1748, where she stayed until 1762. She had a considerable following in her old age back in France, but had earned the contempt of both Voltaire and Frédéric Melchior Grimm, who condemned her for her pompous morality and depiction of children, declaring her ideas fit for parrots, according to Patricia Clancy in her 1982 article on Beaumont in *Studies in Voltaire and the Eighteenth Century.*[2] Certain elements of the thematic structure of Beaumont's tale can be tied to her own experiences: the merchant father who journeys to the seaport, the large number of children in the household (ironically her daughter would go on to have six children like the family in her tale), and her lesson so well learned of the dangers of bad marriages. Clancy quotes a bitter letter from Beaumont stating that she should be forgiven her divorce as her husband "could only produce victims destined for the most awful infirmities" (*SV* 196). Considering the gender of *la bête*, Beaumont could have been thinking of her own daughter or even of herself when she created the feminine dichotomy between beauty and bestiality, which is also inscribed in the polarity between Belle and her older vain ugly sisters.

The familiar and familial origins of *La Belle et la Bête* are intermingled with a number of diverse folklore antecedents, both Continental and English. The 1963 Macmillan edition of *Beauty and the Beast* speculates on the influence of British legends on the genesis of the tale, wrongly however calling it "British in origin:"

> Mme Leprince de Beaumont (1711–1780) lived in England for awhile and must have heard ghost stories there, as well as rumors of those sons of certain great families who were hidden away because of some birthmark or blemish that might frighten society and dishonor a noble name.

> Possibly one of these monsters, shut up in some Scottish castle, gave her the idea of a human beast who bears a noble heart under a frightening appearance and suffers the pangs of hopeless love.[3]

In Beaumont's tale, the Beast is lacking in beauty and also in wit (*esprit*), which could be read as a retarded, deformed animal child; he is a magic spell cast by a bad fairy, alternating between goodness, generosity and petlike devotion, and acts of violence and bestiality. The Beast remains under this spell until loved by a beautiful girl. (In Cocteau's film, he inherits a curse from his parents, who did not believe in the powers of magic.) In counter-balancing opposition to the Beast's lack of the two dominant social values of the eighteenth-century upper class, beauty and wit, Belle's two older sisters suffer their just deserts in their respective marriages to a handsome egotist and a sarcastic comic. An onomastic reading of the author's combined surnames, "the prince of the beautiful mountain," reveals further irony in the contrast between the elegant image and the ugly reality of her failed marriage to a man whom she characterized as a monster.

Beaumont's tale belongs to a thematic continuum of folklore antecedents, contemporary tales in her era and later versions like the tales collected by Wilhelm and Jacob Grimm and gothic novels like Victor Hugo's 1830 *Notre Dame de Paris* (*The Hunchback of Notre Dame*), another tale of a beauty and a beast. The numerous sources of elements of *La Belle et la Bête* in Charles Perrault's *Contes de ma mère l'oie* (*Tales of Mother Goose*) are logical, given the work's enormous popularity in her time. Belle's mistreatment by her cruel older sisters, her impoverished appearance, her household chores, her simplicity and goodness, and her subsequent transformation into a princess are all drawn directly from *Cendrillon* (*Cinderella*), as is the role of the good fairy. Even her return to the abuse and misery of her family home after her reception at the castle of the Beast/Prince could be seen as a transformation of the Cinderella scenario. The magic screen-mirror which depicts absent scenes has links to both the talking mirror of *Snow White* (published later by the Grimms) and the hall of mirrors of Perrault's *La Belle au bois dormant* (*Sleeping Beauty*), which also contains the elements of the rose and the curse of the evil fairy. And of course *Peau d'âne* (*Donkey Skin*) offers the female counterpart of the bestial disguise, as well as the incestual father-daughter relationship that must be transferred to a husband to free the girl and liberate inner beauty and nobility through love. But it is *Riquet à la houppe* (*Ricky Top-Knot*) which best embodies the double dichotomy of beauty and ugliness, brilliance and stupidity. Just as Basile's versions of *Cinderella, Sleeping Beauty* and *Ricky* served as sources for Perrault, later reworkings like Gabrielle de Villeneuve's book-length version of *Riquet* from 1740 were well known to Beaumont.

There are so many elements from Perrault's tales in collage in Madame de Beaumont's text that their similarities led to several editions of his works which included *La Belle et la Bête*, even attributed to him in error on occasion. Cocteau refers to the "Bibliothèque Rose" edition and in fact includes a number of elements in his film which are drawn from Perrault's tales. This intertextuality is particularly evident in the staircase scenes and in Belle's magic embellishments and riches. Cocteau even refers to her as Cinderella at the beginning of his diary of the making of the film.

Cocteau himself participated indirectly in a reworking of the Cinderella tale with his screenplay of *Les Dames du Bois de Boulogne*, for the plot of the framed hostess's tale in Denis Diderot's 1773 *Jacques le fataliste* concerns a common strumpet masquerading as a princess who earns the love and hand of a nobleman, thus foiling the vengeful intentions of two evil noblewomen. It is logical that Cocteau in fact did not like Diderot's story, considering it came from the camp including Madame de Beaumont's declared enemies.

Cocteau's production of *La Belle et la Bête* as his first film after the war, shot like Rossellini's *Roma città aperta* under incredibly difficult circumstances, has contextual historical and political connotations. As the prologue invites us to return to a child's version of experience and the open Sesame magic of the literary cliché "Once upon a time," it marks the film with a double nostalgia: Cocteau's desire to recapture the mysteries, at once cruel and beautiful, of a child's creative imagination, and his wish to return to the work of creative freedom and vitality which had been so crushed by World War II and the German Occupation. The film certainly stands as a parable of France during the war, with the Beast as Germany and the rose and Belle as the flower of youth sacrificed, or Vichy France as the Beast under the evil spell covering its fundamental goodness. Cocteau makes several explicit references to the state of France in 1945 in his *Diary of a Film*, in declarations such as the following:

> We are all paying now for five terrible years. "To make bad blood" isn't a mere figure of speech. For that is precisely what we all made, and it's this bad blood which now disintegrates us. Five years of hate, fear, a waking nightmare. Five years of shame and slime. We were spattered and smeared with it even to our very souls. We had to survive. Wait. It is this nervous-waiting that we are paying for dearly. In spite of all difficulties, we must catch up. Whatever the cost, France must shine again.[4]

It is also possible that Marais and Cocteau were influenced to take a sudden interest in *La Belle et la Bête* in 1945 by Antoine de Saint-Exupéry's fable of *Le Petit Prince* (*The Little Prince*), published posthumously after its author disappeared in action over Africa. The rose in the bell jar and the taming of the beast as a definition of love, as well as the ridicule of the egotistical and vain characters, the dispossession of the prince and the symbology of the serpent all serve as working metaphors and models for Cocteau's film.

Cocteau primarily chose to film *La Belle et la Bête* because it responded to his lifelong generic attraction to fable and myth. He talks of fables in one of his autobiographical texts, *Journal d'un inconnu* (*The Hand of a Stranger*):

> C'est avec la fable que le mensonge prend ses titres de noblesse...Il y a de la grandeur dans ses chimères. Sans elle...un enfant ne m'aurait pas dit avant de me conter une histoire d'animaux: *C'était du temps où les animaux parlaient encore.* (Cocteau's emphasis.)[5]

However, Cocteau affirms elsewhere that he also chose to film *La Belle et la Bête* for profound personal reasons: "I chose that particular fable because it corresponds to my personal mythology."[6] This admission compares with a second revealing statement that "the legend of Psyche is *word for word* (Cocteau's emphasis) that of *Beauty and the Beast*,"[7] an affirmation that Hayward and Hoggard both signal in the opening lines of their articles. Thus through the eighteenth-century tale, Cocteau returns to classical mythology and Apuleius's tale of Cupid and the fallen Psyche, who survives trials and tribulations to find divine love. Cocteau, Hayward and Hoggard all overlook two other Greek myths with thematic precedents for *La Belle et la Bête*: Venus in love with the deformed Vulcan, and Cephalus, the son of Hermes, whose face is metamorphosed. The reference to Psyche may have invaded Cocteau's imagination by association with the narcissism of the mirror; in French a *psyché* is a full-length looking-glass. In his 1928 work *Le Livre blanc* (*The White Paper*), Cocteau offers anonymously a confessional fantasy of his homosexuality similar to André Gide's 1920 *Si le grain ne meurt* and 1924 *Corydon*. In Cocteau's bold work are two scenes which reveal deeply-rooted personal mythemes expressed in *La Belle et la Bête*; the first involves the narrator's reaction to the revelation that his homosexual lover has a mistress: "This certainty pierced my breast like the claw of some wild animal."[8] The other is its counterpart, the homosexual lover's reaction to the narrator's engagement to his sister: he shoots himself before his *psyché*, leaving on the mirror the mark of a fatal narcissistic kiss (*LB* 73). These sequences also reflect Cocteau's ongoing attempts to transfer his own homosexuality onto his father, a talented painter who committed suicide when Cocteau was ten years old. There is a third sequence of similar significance in the book, also noted by Hayward, of the one-way mirror of the voyeur (an empowering screen-mirror like the camera lens).

As noted earlier, the double feminine of the French title *La Belle et la Bête* enabled Cocteau to access the gender of the female author and her daughter. It was also an emblem of his sexual, moral and artistic ambiguity, of the beauty and the beast (meaning in French both stupid and bestial) united in the person of the artist, as he explains:

> Art is born of the coitus between the male and female elements in all of us, elements more nearly balanced in the artist than in other men. Art is the child of a kind of incest, the lovemaking of self and self, a parthenogenesis. That is why marriage is so dangerous for an artist: it represents a pleonasm, the monster's effort toward normality.[9]

Multiple implications of the beauty-beast duality are at work in Cocteau's psyche: the beauty of the young men who attracted him versus the bestiality of his lust, the beauty of artistic creation emanating from the bestial and sometimes stupid being he felt himself to be, the beauty and bestiality of his lifelong opium addiction, and his relationship to the beautiful Jean Marais, whose roles in *La Belle et la Bête* have so many layers.

The hermaphroditic monster's self-contained incest in the above quote explains the close link in Cocteau between creativity and the Oedipus myth. *La Belle et la Bête* stands in fact between two other works which are declared adaptations of that classical legend: *La Machine infernale* of 1934 and *Oedipe Roi* of 1949. Like the multiple treatments of the Orpheus myth, including the 1926 play and the film trilogy, the theme of incest runs through all Cocteau's work, starting with his 1929 *Les Enfants terribles*.

The oedipal thematic in Beaumont's *La Belle et la Bête*, noted by such critics as Bryant and Bettelheim, figures therefore in his attraction to the tale. Numerous elements of the story mark it as a covert tale of incest: the absence of a mother, Belle's refusal of proposals of marriage, her loyalty to her father, her request of the rose (symbol of love, virgin perfection and feminine sexuality) which traps her father in a fatal gesture in the realm of the Beast. In the original fable, the father accompanies Belle to the Beast's castle and spends the night in the same bed with her before returning home. In a later sequence, Belle returns home to her ailing father and they spend a quarter of an hour in transports of rapture in bed in each other's arms—scenes involving two eighteenth-century clichés, which have however for the modern reader implications of incestuous activity. Moreover, the pairing of the father and daughter reverses the oedipal attraction of the son to the mother, thus offering an incestual mirror of Cocteau's own situation. It is therefore strange that Cocteau omitted them from the film. Perhaps the fact that the Vicomtesse de Noailles, his benefactress, used to receive him lying on a Louis XV bed defused the incestual implications of the father and daughter in bed while establishing a personal link to Beaumont's fable. The most striking sequences in the film featuring beds are those in Belle's room in the castle of the Beast, where the bed serves as metaphoric topos of their future sexual union. This elaborately draped magical bed contrasts the vertical sheets hung out to dry at Belle's house, forming a maze symbolizing the entrapments of sexual and marital relationships. Both these scenes created problems during filming: the hangings from the magic bed were stolen from the set, and it was nearly impossible to find enough intact sheets for the farmhouse maze.

A description of one of Cocteau's childhood memories reveals an interesting connection between one of the most important symbolic elements in *La Belle et la Bête*, the mirror, and Cocteau's image of his mother as a regal beauty, when "the wardrobe mirror showed me my mother, or indeed that madonna encased in velvet, choked by diamonds, beplumed with a dusky aigrette, standing tall and bristling with brilliance, like a glittering horse chestnut, distracted, torn between last-minute instructions to be good and a final glance in the mirror."[10] Cocteau's obsession with his childhood, with remaining a child, with returning to childhood, extended to his mother, whom he described as having died while still a child, thus recapturing her, as Sartre did his mother, from time and her role as wife and mother.

The underlying tensions of consuming and ferocious bestiality in the figure of the Beast, who represents a constant threat of rape and murder, echo a passage in *Journal d'un inconnu* where Cocteau affirms man's dark side:

> Mais cet espoir vient de ce que tout homme est une nuit (abrite une nuit), que le travail de l'artiste sera de mettre cette nuit en plein jour... (*JI* 15). (This hope comes from the fact that every man is a night (harbors a night in himself), that the work of the artist is to bring out this night into broad daylight. My translation.)

Cocteau goes on to say that this night is not a Freudian unidimensional id:

> Elle est une grotte aux trésors. Une audace l'ouvre et un *Sésame*. Non pas un docteur ni une névrose. Grotte dangereuse si les trésors nous font oublier le Sésame.
> C'est de cette grotte, de cette épave de luxe, de ce *salon au fond d'un lac*, que toutes les grandes âmes s'enrichirent. (*JI* 40). (Cocteau's emphasis.)
> (It is a cavern of treasures, opened by daring and a Sesame. Not a doctor or a neurosis. A dangerous cavern, if the treasures make us forget the Sesame. It is from this cavern, this luxurious wreckage, this living room at the bottom of a lake, that all great souls enrich themselves. My translation.)

In these passages can be found the origin of the sequence of the Beast drinking from the reflecting pool (a Narcissus image), the death of Avenant in his transgression of the sacred pavilion of treasure, and the union of Belle and the Prince and their heavenward flight.

Another image generative of many sequences in the film was a statue group by Gustave Doré, whose illustrations of Perrault inspired Christian Bérard's costumes. In this *objet d'art* Cocteau found yet another mythological source for the film, affirming, "This group of Perseus, Andromeda, and the dragon wouldn't be out of place in Beauty's room at the Beast's castle" (*DF* 117). In a sense, Perseus could be seen to be the masculine equivalent of Psyche, triumphing over trials and labors, to marry Andromeda and found Mycenae. And of course he rides a magic white horse. The horse of the film, *Magnifique*, which was actually a circus horse, serves as a major mode of transportation between the "real" world of Belle's family and the "fantasy" world of the castle, worlds that eventually merge. The riderless white horse carrying a mirror on his saddle comes from an old Breton legend (also used as the title thematic of Alain Robbe-Grillet's 1984 autobiographical novel, *Le Miroir qui revient*). Thus Cocteau is weaving together a number of ancient myths which are working through him in the oneiric medium of film that he renders with such surreal precision. Auric's music and Henri Alekan's photography contribute as much as the special effects to the film's impact.

Although *La Belle et la Bête* was rejected by the New Wave filmmakers and its audience appeal was questioned by the Cannes Film Festival jury, Cocteau proved to be the master storyteller and lyric, poetic, *auteur* filmmaker that he instinctively thought himself: "The rhythm of the film is one of narrative. I am telling the story...the characters don't seem to be living a life of their own, but a life that is being narrated. Perhaps that's how it should be in a fairy tale" (*DF* 38). Thus *La Belle et la Bête* becomes Cocteau's own tale, in the narrative tradition of retelling and reworking a classic thematic of folklore. He reaffirms near the end his inner compulsion to make this film, against all odds: "But this *had* (Cocteau's emphasis) to be attempted once: a poet telling a story through the medium of the camera" (*DF* 109), "la caméra poétique qui 'écrit' avec l'encre de lumière" (the poetic camera that 'writes' with the ink of light).

Dennis DeNitto, David Galef, Susan Hayward, Lynn Hoggard, Raymond McGowan, and Michael Popkin have all commented on the transpositions from the fable to the film, the "sauce" that Cocteau added to the original story.[11] Certain of these, particularly the special effects of the mirror and the statues, relate to Cocteau's work on a broader scale and emphasize the role of *La Belle et la Bête* in the larger context of the poet's lifelong reworking of his own personal myth. Cocteau reveals the intensely personal, autobiographic and almost therapeutic nature of the experience in *Diary of a Film*: "Gradually I am coaxing my myths and childhood memories back again. If only I have managed to fix them onto the screen" (*DF* 60).

The endless statues in the film, animate and inanimate, would seem to be a reworking of the ending of the Beaumont tale, where the two wicked sisters are condemned to be statufied alive, on either side of the door of Belle's new castle, eternal witnesses to her happiness. The first statues we see in the film are animal statues ornamenting the formal garden (actually part of the château that was used as the Beast's castle); the first animated statues are the special effects of the live arms holding candelabra and pouring wine, as well as the smoking faces of the caryatids on either side of the Beast's hearth. There is a surrealistic and paranoid dismemberment in these faces and arms emerging from pedestals and walls, emanating from nothingness. This surreal world is carried back to Belle's house when she materializes through the wall wearing the magic glove and where the gorgons on either side of the fireplace suddenly come to life, directly after Avenant's remark to Ludovic, "I can't wait to see how your sisters will look."

The statue sequences culminate of course in the revenge of the goddess of chastity when Diana returns Avenant's opening arrow to him. His symbolic invasion of the sisters' room with his arrow at the beginning of the film prefigures his bodily invasion of the sacred pavilion, an architectural metaphoric rape, signaled by the stolen key and luminous keyhole, which is resisted by the power of chastity, by Diana the huntress, female pursuer of *la bête*.

Naomi Greene offers an intriguing psychoanalytic critique of Cocteau's *oeuvre*, using a Gilles Deleuze approach, characterizing it as a homosexual masochistic discourse which enhances the role of the mother and annihilates the father, elements that fit Cocteau's biography better than the fable, which is rather an incestual mirror of Cocteau's own oedipal compulsions. For this reason, perhaps, Greene mentions the film only briefly, as an illustraton of the dangerous yet necessary sexual journey into the realm of the surreal. Obviously this is an oversight, as the film contains endless examples of the "Deadly Statues" she analyzes in other films, of the female figure in the mirror, of the static camera fixing and fixating on a series of privileged images, of the realistic embodiment of the dreamworld, of the objectification of being.[12]

Both the mirror and the statues *copy* organic life, frame it, freeze it, objectify it, deform it. One of Belle's older sisters sees not her reflection in the magic mirror but a monkey, a creature associated with man's bestial origins and also a mimic, a live parodic mirror image. The connections between the complex symbolism of the mirror and that of the statues in *La Belle et la Bête* is clarified in Cocteau's quote in *Diary of a Film* of a line from his earlier *Sang d'un poète*, when the statue says: "You have written that you walked through a mirror and you didn't believe it" (*DF* 69). It is also elucidated by his musings before the mirror in *Diary of a Film*, where he contrasts the hideousness of his infected face, his own beast mask, with the beauty of the work he is creating: "The movie screen is the true mirror reflecting the flesh and blood of my dreams" (*DF* 69).

Whereas the film and the filmmaking process mirror the filmmaker's psyche, the magic mirror in the film also serves as a screen, depicting non-present scenes, becoming a *mise-en-abyme* of the transparent function of film itself, just as the screen-mirror in the fairy tale stands for the magical power of illustrations and the printed text. With the last image of the dying Beast, the mirror cracks, signaling the end of the film and of the separation and the alterity of beauty and beast. This is the cracked mirror from the old French legend (from the province next to where Madame de Beaumont grew up), of the magic white horse which returns riderless.

Cocteau's film is filled with tricks and camera angles which constitute a very self-conscious poetic style of filmmaking. One of the most striking sequences in the film is when the Beast carries the fainted Belle in his arms up the stairs, conjuring multiple intertextual images for the initiated moviegoer. The rays of light penetrating the cage next to the staircase are a central symbol of the film, not only an homage to expressionist films of the era, but a metaphor of the illumination of the prison of bestiality by the liberating light of love. Cocteau reveals the power of cinematic images for him for expressing his own ideology in *Démarche d'un poète*:

> Le cinématographe est encore une manière de graphisme. Par son entremise nous parvenons à écrire en images, à procurer à une idéologie qui nous est propre, puissance de fait. *DP* 47.

> (The cinema is another means of writing. By its mediation, we manage to write in images, to procure for our ideology the power of fact. My translation.)

A comparison of elements of Beaumont's *La Belle et la Bête* and the Cocteau film reveals the extent of restructuring done by Cocteau, who could be said to have rewritten the fable from within himself.

Beaumont	Cocteau
three daughters, three sons	three daughters, one son
no suitor present for Belle	Avenant always present
father lost in snowstorm	wind and blowing leaves
father takes treasure chest	Belle takes treasure chest
father accompanies Belle to castle	father stays behind
father ruined by speculation	ruined by son's gambling
Belle dines at nine p.m.	dines at seven p.m.
Belle transported by ring	by white horse, glove, key
Belle sees scenes in dreams, mirror	in mirror only
magic book serves Belle	invisible servants
treasure chest disappears	necklace turns to rope
Belle's sisters marry unhappily	do not marry
Beast is stupid	Beast is ferocious
Belle waits all day for Beast	Belle rushes to garden
sisters become statues at end	statues throughout film
no one exchanged for Belle	Avenant dies in pavilion
Belle's family brought to castle	Belle flies off with Prince
all transported to magic kingdom	disappear into clouds

An earlier version of this chapter appeared as an article, *"Beauty and the Beast: from Fable to Film,"* in *Literature/Film Quarterly* 17:2 (1989) 84–90.

Notes

1. Jean Cocteau, *Démarche d'un poète* (Munich: F. Bruckmann, 1953) 29. ("The role of the artist is thus to create an organism having a life of its own drawn from his life, and not destined to surprise, to please or displease, but to be active enough to arouse secret meanings, reacting only to certain signs which represent beauty for some, ugliness and deformity for others." My translation.) Subsequent references to this work follow the quote in parentheses with *DP*.
2. Patricia Clancy, "A French writer and educator in England: mme Le Prince de Beaumont," *Studies in Voltaire and the Eighteenth Century* 201 (1982) 195. Subsequent references to this work follow the quote in parentheses with *SV*.
3. Mme Le Prince de Beaumont, *Beauty and the Beast* (New York: Macmillan, 1963) 35. There is also a Norse legend of three gods who kill a deer and then must bring a beautiful woman to the house of an evil giant disguised as a rapacious eagle before they can consume the deer.
4. Cocteau, *Beauty and the Beast: Diary of a Film* (New York: Dover Publications, 1972) 57. Subsequent references to this work follow the quote in parentheses with *DF*.
5. Cocteau, *Journal d'un inconnu* (Paris: Grasset, 1953) 141–142. ("It is with the fable that the lie takes on its nobility...there is greatness in its illusions. Without fables...a child wouldn't have said to me, before telling me a story about animals: 'It was the time when animals still talked to each other.'" My translation.) Subsequent references to this work follow the quote in parentheses with *JI*.
6. George Amberg, *Beauty and the Beast: Diary of a Film*, introduction, viii.
7. Cocteau, *Past Tense* (New York: Harcourt Brace Jovanovich, 1987) 175.
8. Cocteau, *Le Livre Blanc* (London: Peter Owen, 1969) 59.
9. Robert Phelps, *Professional Secrets* (New York: Farrar, Strauss & Giroux, 1970) 295.
10. Phelps, 22.
11. See Bibliography.
12. See Bibliography.

Bibliography

Armstrong, Christine. "Et si l'introduction à l'analyse narrative nous était contée par *La Belle et La Bête.*" *The French Review* 70: 5 (Apr 1997) 658–667.
Ashton, Dore, et al. *Jean Cocteau and the French Scene.* New York: Abbeville Press, 1984. *La Belle et la Bête. L'Avant-Scène Cinéma* 138–139 (1973). Filmscript.
Berg, Walter. "Archaïsme et utopie: Cocteau et son art nouveau du cinématographe." *Recherches et Travaux* 52 (1997) 203–216.
Bettelheim, Bruno. *The Uses of Enchantment.* New York: Vintage Books, 1977.
Bory, Jean-Louis. "C comme Cocteau, c comme cinéma." *Cahiers Jean Cocteau* 3 (1968) 17–24.
Brosse, Jacques. *Cocteau.* Paris: Gallimard, 1970.
Bryant, Sylvia. "Re-Constructing Oedipus through *Beauty and the Beast.*" *Criticism* 31:4 (1989) 439–453.

Bucknell Review 41:1 (1997) entire issue on Cocteau.

Charensol, Georges. "Jean Cocteau et le cinématographe." *Cahiers Jean Cocteau* 3 (1968) 9–16.

Clancy, Patricia. "A French Writer and educator in England: mme Le Prince de Beaumont." *Studies in Voltaire and the Eighteenth Century* 201 (1982) 195–208.

Cocteau, Jean. *Beauty and the Beast: Diary of a Film.* New York: Dover Publications, 1972.

———. *Démarche d'un poète.* Munich: F. Bruckmann, 1953.

———. *La Difficulté d'être.* Paris: Paul Morihien, 1947.

———. *Journal d'un inconnu.* Paris: Grasset, 1953.

———. *Le Livre Blanc.* London: Peter Owen, 1969.

———. *Past Tense.* New York: Harcourt Brace Jovanovich, 1987.

———. *Portraits-Souvenir.* Paris: Grasset, 1935.

Crowson, Lydia. *The Esthetic of Jean Cocteau.* Hanover: University Press of New England, 1978.

DeNitto, Dennis. "Jean Cocteau's *Beauty and the Beast.*" *American Imago* 33:2 (1976) 123–154.

Fischlin, Daniel. "Queer Margins: Cocteau, *La Belle et la Bête*, and the Jewish Differend." *Textual Practice* 12:1 (Spring 1998) 69–88.

Galand, René. "Cocteau's Sexual Equation." In Stamboian, Marks, and Howard, eds. *Homosexualities and French Literature: Cultural Contexts/Critical Texts.* Ithaca, NY: Cornell University Press, 1979.

Galef, David. "A sense of Magic: Reality and Illusion in Cocteau's *Beauty and the Beast.*" *Literature/Film Quarterly* 12:2 (1984) 96–106.

Gilson, René. *Jean Cocteau.* New York: Crown Publishing, 1969.

———. *Jean Cocteau, cinéaste.* Paris: Lherminier, 1988.

Greene, Naomi. "Deadly Statues: Eros in the films of Jean Cocteau." *French Review* 61:6 (1988) 890–898.

———. "Jean Cocteau: A Cinema of Baroque Unease." *Bucknell Review* 41:1 (1997) 130–147.

Hains, Maryellen. "*Beauty and the Beast:* 20th Century Romance?" *Merveilles & Contes* 3: (1989) 75–83.

Hammond, Robert. "The Authenticity of the Filmscript: Cocteau's *Beauty and the Beast. Style* 9 (1975) 514–518.

———. *Cocteau Reflects for me/I Reflect for him.* New York: O'Flaherty & Co.

Harvey, Stephen. "The Mask in the Mirror: the Movies of Jean Cocteau." In Peters and Delvaille, eds. *Jean Cocteau and the French Scene.* New York: Abbeyville Press, 1984.

Hayward, Susan. "Gender Politics—Cocteau's Belle is not that Bête: Jean Cocteau's *La Belle et la Bête* (1946)." In Hayward, Susan, and Ginette Vincendeau, eds. *French Film: Texts and Contexts.* London: Routledge, 2000.

Hearne, Betsy. "Beauty and the Beast: Visions and Revisions of an Old Tale, 1950–1985." *The Lion and the Unicorn* 12:2 (1988) 74–111.

———. *Beauty and the Beast: Visions and Revisions of an Old Tale.* Chicago: University of Chicago Press, 1989.

Hoggard, Lynn. "Writing with the Ink of Light: Jean Cocteau's *Beauty and the Beast.*" In Aycock and Schoenecke, eds. *Film and Literature: A Comparative Approach to Adaptation.* Lubbock: Texas Tech University Press, 1988.

Hubert, Judd. "A Reactionary Feminist Novelist: Gabrielle de Villeneuve". *L'Esprit Créateur* 29:3 (1989) 65–75.

Keller, Marjorie. *The Untutored Eye: Childhood in the Films of Cocteau, Cornell and Brakhage.* Rutherford: Fairleigh Dickinson University Press, 1986.

Knapp, Bettina. *Jean Cocteau.* Boston: Twayne, 1989.

Langlois, Henri. "Jean Cocteau et le cinéma." *Cahiers Jean Cocteau* 3 (1968) 25–32.

LePrince de Beaumont, Marie-Jeanne. *Beauty and the Beast.* New York: Macmillan, 1963.

Levitt, Annette. "The Cinematic Magic of Jean Cocteau." *Bucknell Review* 41:1 (1997) 42–56.

MacLeay, Daniel. "Vision and Re-vision: The Restoration of Films by Jean Cocteau and Alain Resnais." *Publications of the Missouri Philological Association* 25 (2000) 107–112.

McGowan, Raymond. "Jean Cocteau and *Beauty and the Beast.*" *New Orleans Review* 8:1 (1981) 106–108.

Michalczyk, John. "The French Academy and the Cinema: Pagnol, Cocteau, and Clair." *Stanford French Review* 5:1 (Spring 1981) 129–140.

Mourier, Maurice. "Quelques aspects de la poétique cinématographique de Cocteau." *Oeuvres et Critiques* 22:1 (1997) 152–161.

Peters, Arthur et al. *Jean Cocteau and His World: An Illustrated Biography.* New York: Vendome Press, 1986.

Phelps, Robert. *Professional Secrets.* New York: Farrar, Strauss & Giroux, 1970.

Philippe, Jean-Claude. *Jean Cocteau.* Paris: Seghers, 1989.

Popkin, Michael. "Cocteau's *Beauty and the Beast*: the Poet as Monster." *Literature/Film Quarterly* 10:2 (1982) 100–109.

Propp, Vladimir. *Morphology of the Folktale.* Bloomington: Indiana University Press, 1958.

Salazar, Philippe-Joseph. "Les Pouvoirs de la fable: Mythologie, Littérature et tradition (1650–1725)." *Revue d'Histoire Littéraire de la France* 91:6 (1991) 878–889.

Sprigge, Elizabeth, and Jean-Jacques Kihm. *Jean Cocteau, the Man and the Mirror.* New York: Coward-McCann, 1968.

Steegmuller, Francis. *Cocteau: a Biography.* Boston: David R. Godine, 1986 (reprint of Little, Brown 1970 edition).

Steinberg, Victoria. *The Primitive Mirror and the Films of Jean Cocteau.* Dissertation Abstracts International (Sept 1994) 588A.

Peau d'âne
(Donkey Skin)

directed by Jacques Demy (1971)
fable by Charles Perrault (1697)

Appropriately, *Peau d'âne* opens the modern edition of Charles Perrault's 1697 *Contes de ma mère l'oie* (*Tales of Mother Goose*), as it was one of his earlier tales (they often appeared in *Le Mercure Galant*), and it contains numerous elements common to one or more of the others (see introduction to this section). Sources and analogues for these tales have themselves become legend, as critics have attempted to retrace the constituent thematics to their origins in sixteenth-century Venetian works like Basile's *Pentamerone*, Straparola's *Piacevoli Notti*, or even the *chansons de geste* or *fabliaux* of the Middle Ages. Pursuit of other sources for beasts with character like La Fontaine's leads back to Aesop and Greek mythology, to Cephalus (who is mentioned in *Peau d'âne*) and to the classical thematic of metamorphosis and transfiguration.

In the end, one must concede the impossibility of pinpointing origins, confronted with the multiplicity of variants, versions and hybrids circulating in oral folk tradition through the centuries. These oral tales often served as maternal cautionary narration and hence could be said to embody primordial feminist canons. What is intriguing and pertinent is the recurrent recombinant thematic which, in the broader perspective of the fable as a genre in occidental culture, could be deemed obsessive or compulsive. In his *Preface* to the current Livre de Poche Edition of Perrault's *Contes*, the late Bruno Bettelheim emphasized the preeminence of certain primal themes, primary among them that of incest as a taboo. In primitive cultures, the interdiction of sibling or offspring marriages was intended to create economic liaisons between families and villages. Exceptions included ruling dynasties which attempted to limit access to their power through closed blood lines; from the Egyptians to the Spaniards, these genealogical presumptions ended in disaster.

Tales of unknowing incest like the oedipal myth lead to tragedy just as those of covert or overt infraction. Bernard Tavernier's 1987 film *La Passion Béatrice* depicts the brutal deflowering of an innocent virgin beauty by her own mad father. This tale is not unlike Stendhal's *Béatrice Cenci*, his 1831 tragedy adapted from a sixteenth-century Italian tale, that is, a source not far from Basile and Straparola. In all the oedipal legends, transgressions of the primary taboo contaminate the innocent and lead to acts of violence, revenge, murder or mutilation. Perrault's tale mitigates the impact with a happy ending, a morality lesson, and also with its language, as it is one of the Perrault *Contes* originally written in verse.

A number of key ingredients in classic fairy tales point to sources in numerology and the occult in the Middle Ages as well as a reworking of numerous biblical elements. The predominance of the number three is pervasive in many tales. Here the princess requests three successive dresses from her father to forestall his demand of her in marriage after her mother's death. Guided by her fairy godmother, she demands literally the sky, the moon and the sun, or as we would say, the sun, the moon and the stars. Extravagant charges and mandates are an intrinsic functional thematic in fairy tales. The unusual twist in Perrault's tale is the magic donkey which produces gold for manure, like the goose that laid the golden eggs. The daughter's request for the hide of the donkey is a mimesis of her own duality, as she hides her golden beauty under the foul skin and escapes, travestied.

Just as one could find echoes of the Catholic trinity in all the three-part episodes in these tales, Peau d'âne's exile contains an echo of the suffering and penitence of penniless wandering medieval mystics. in hairshirts. In a broader context, the transformation of this beauty into a beast (and not just any beast but the beast of burden that carried the Holy Family on their flight) can be read as an extended metaphor of the evil effects of unholy desire and unions, which reduce even the wealthiest and most elevated, blessed souls to foul bestiality. To continue the symbolism, the proper union (in this case with the wandering prince) reveals the true beauty beneath the humble disguise, just as in the ending of the later *La Belle et la Bête* (*Beauty and the Beast*), where Belle releases the prince from his prison by declaring her love for him and forsaking her controlling father.

Further connections are at work in Jacques Demy's film, which features Catherine Deneuve as the princess, Jean Marais (Cocteau's 1946 Beast) as her father, Delphine Seyrig as the fairy godmother, and Micheline Presle, Jacques Perrin, Fernand Ledoux and Sacha Pitoëff. As with numerous films adapted from printed texts, Demy's work opens with a bookshelf and the book of tales seen as an object, as a source narrator-character so to speak. As expected, the film ends with the same tome closing. The voice-over narration by Jean Servais (Ophuls's narrator in *Le Plaisir*) is not from the original poetry version of the tale but from the 1781 prose adaptation. However, its poetic origins are acknowledged early in the film in a scene where the father reads to the daughter from the poetry of the future, more precisely, "L'Amour" from *Le Guetteur mélancolique* by Guillaume Apollinaire and in a literary if not filmic citation, "Les Muses" from Cocteau's *L'Ode à Picasso.* (The other book in the film is the parodic counterpart to the volume of poetry: the princess's cookbook from which she prepares the cake requested by the prince.) The second-hand reference to modernism and surrealism also announces the nature of Demy's interpretation of this classic tale. His characters move back and forth between fantasy and realism with dizzying agility. The natural elements of the birds and the deer in the forest are also undermined by both fantasy and humor. The deer is revealed to be the fairy godmother's pet, the princess's pet parrot parodies her love songs, and the prince's parents give a Ball of the Cats and the Birds.

Demy's film is rife with citations and references to other texts, to other films. Along with the numerous allusions to sets and scenes from Cocteau's *La Belle et la Bête*, *Peau d'âne* with its comic opera score by Michel Legrand is virtually the sequel to Demy's 1964 *Les Parapluies de Cherbourg*, which launched Deneuve's career. However, here the songs are not linked by recitative to form a coherent musical entity, a true film-opera. Rather they intrude in parodic and even discordant fashion and are more redolent of characters' bursting unpredictably into song in Hollywood musicals. The comic characterization of the fairy godmother as a flighty starlet defuses the dramatic intent of the original tale, which is acknowledged only rarely, as in the foreboding music at the beginning.

The artifice and artificiality of the sets are but one aspect of the surreal modernist veneer that distances the film from the more serious original tone of the text, from the drama of the fable as recreated in a film like *La Passion Béatrice*. Color is used in mood washes: the king's household is entirely in blue, with blue faces, a blue piano, a blue parrot. The fairy godmother before her mirror switches her costume on a whim from yellow to pink in a capricious use of her magic power. The prince's world is colored red—his clothes, horses, his entire household and the princesses who present themselves. Scattered through the film are light-hearted anachronisms intended as humor: when the queen dies, she is carried out into the snow in a plastic or glass bubble; the fairy godmother mentions that her magic is fading, her "batteries" are running down; the princess has a cookbook; and in the *coup de théâtre* ending, the king and the fairy godmother arrive for the prince and princess's wedding in a helicopter, telescoping centuries, like the ending of *La Nuit de Varennes* ten years later. Part of the playful anachronistic character of Demy's film can be attributed to his early work as assistant to the animator Paul Grimault. Demy made one more fairy tale film after *Peau d'âne*, (*Le Joueur de flûte—The Pied Piper of Hamlin*), but never found his own creative voice in this genre.

Peau d'âne systematically undermines itself and its generic fable origins by exaggeration and deformation of its models. Jean Marais as the king both echoes and parodies his performance as the Beast in the Cocteau film. Catherine Deneuve leaping through the woods in slow motion becomes a parody of Josette Day's entrance into the castle of the Beast. The numerous deer both statufied and live echo the deer in the Cocteau film, symbols of the victims of the Beast. There are even statues with real eyes in another obvious Cocteau citation. Other important imitations of Cocteau include the identical magic mirror, the broken mirror, the use of the mirror as a movie screen to depict non-present events, the transporting of bodies by magic. Even if Demy had wanted to give a faithful portrayal of the original fable, he would have been contaminated inevitably by Cocteau's earlier work. But the parodic nature of his frequent citations makes his homage fundamentally ambiguous. The process of doubling in the film (reflections in mirrors and ponds, the parrot repeating the songs) is eminently narcissistic and ultimately gratuitous. And Demy's film marks itself frequently as a product of the years following the late-sixties social revolution. The prince and princess offer themselves an extended idyllic fantasy, wherein they gorge on rich food, quaff wine, smoke a pipe, laze along in a boat, caper like children on a hillside, go walking at night, in short do everything forbidden, combining classic fairy tale images of transgression and contemporary allusions to social and sexual liberation. The capricious satiric and irreverent mode of the film and its audacious use of color, song and fantasy connect it as much to a work like the 1968 George Dunning *Yellow Submarine* as to other fairy tale films or classic illustrated versions of the texts of the tales.

Thus Demy has created a film that is as much a hybrid as the princess in her donkey skin. Her magic treasure chest and wand, her ability to appear and disappear, to garb herself at will, her escape from the palace in slow motion past the statues, her flight in a carriage which becomes a cart full of straw, all call up prior images of other tales, editions, and films, just as do the people who are all motionless, statufied, as she enters the farmyard, or the woman spitting toads. Taken from *Les Fées* (*The Fairies*, another Mother Goose tale), the toads are evil words from the mouth of woman, as opposed to pearls of wisdom. As the princess gazes into the pond (a natural mirror) in the woods, the initiated spectator sees Cocteau's Beast gazing into his pond, as well as an echo of the classic myth of Narcissus. The prince's encounter in the woods with the surrealistic talking rose elicits images of the roses in the Beast's garden, at the same time that it acknowledges the rose as a symbol of woman, of her beauty, of her sexuality (both mouth and genitals in this case), and yet parodies the whole tradition, including Disney animations.

The discussion at the table in the farmyard between the prince and his courtiers regarding whether or not to believe in fairy tales recalls the opening message from Cocteau in *La Belle et la bête*, the original curse on the Beast because his parents didn't believe in magic, and the fate of Avenant who sneers at the magic pavilion in the Beast's garden and dies therein. The magic invisible shield surrounding the princess's cottage in the woods is as much an image from Star Trek as it is a classic symbol of the protective power of virtue and virginity. When the prince is pining for his secret love and demands a cake from her, Demy undercuts the dramatic potential of the symbolism—of the nourishing gesture, of the traditional Twelfth Night cake with the toy or bean in one slice which makes the recipient king or queen for a day—by having the prince wolf down the cake and choke on the ring. The scene of the princess preparing the cake has been similarly undermined by the dual images singing from the cookbook and the magic of the chick hatching from the egg. Even the fabulous emerald ring of the original tale, an obvious talisman of power, has become a dainty pearl and ruby ring. It still retains however its perfect symbolism of the power of the covenant of a blessed marriage union, in contrast to the ugliness of incest or of arranged marriages (all the portraits and princesses presented to both the king and the prince are horribly repulsive).

In an interesting historic allusion, Demy has the minister (who is an incredible malaprop) announce each aristocratic pretender who comes to try the ring, in a mockery of traditional nobility—a Goya-like parade of young, old, ugly, thin, fat women. And in a historic tour de force, he names the dominant aristocratic families of the court of Louis XIV, of the original context of the tale. The Marquise Marie de Rabutin-Chantal is better known as Madame de Sévigné (who died in 1696, two years after the original publication of *Peau d'âne*). In the same scene, the *coup de théâtre* of Peau d'âne emerging from her donkey skin to reveal a royal princess garbed in gold and diamonds is undermined by the courtiers fainting from the smell of her disguise. The final *coup* of the arrival of the king by helicopter is as much a parody as a citation of the ending of Cocteau's film, where the prince and princess fly off into the sky in a Molière-like *pièce-à-machine* ending. The final parade of kings from far-off lands, with elephants and camels, makes reference to the aristocratic pursuit of collecting or hunting exotic animals and also to the Bible, to the Three Kings paying homage to the Christ child.

In sum, Demy has freely mixed a variety of film and literary genres, blending classic fable, history, science fiction and fantasy, using costumes, sets and masks to create a carnivalesque mood, which could be said to be a cinematic homage to Fellini. However, in the last analysis, one wonders if Demy himself believed, like Cocteau, in the power of magic, of the open Sesame of the imagination, in this case, of the oneiric power of film itself to generate meaningful symbols and images of primal fears and desires in all of us, something that the classic fables do so well.

Bibliography

Barchilon, Jacques, and Peter Flinders. *Charles Perrault*. Boston: Twayne, 1981.

Bareau, Michel, et al. *Les Contes de Perrault/La Contestation et ses limites/Furetière*. Paris: Papers on French Seventeenth Century Literature, 1987.

Belmont, Nicole. "De Hestia à *Peau d'âne*: Le Destin de Cendrillon." *Cahiers de Littérature Orale* 25 (1989) 11–31.

Berl, Emmanuel. "Celui qui a conté *Peau d'âne*." *Preuves* 2 (1969) 55–59.

Bettelheim, Bruno. *The Uses of Enchantment*. New York: Vintage Books, 1977.

Demorris, René. "Du littéraire au littéral dans *Peau d'âne* de Perrault." *Revue des Sciences Humaines* 1 (1977) 261–268.

Desveaux, Emmanuel, and Maleuvre, Jean-Yves. "Hélène reconquise ou la 'canonisation de *Peau d'âne*; en hommage à Claude Lévi-Strauss." In Vielle, Swiggers and Jucquois, eds. *Comparatisme, mythologies, langages*. Louvain-la-Neuve: Peeters, 1994.

Flahault, François. *L'Interprétation des contes*. Paris: Denoël, 1987.

Franko, Marc. "Deux métamorphoses de Perrault." *Corps Ecrit* 26 (June 1988) 123–129.

Fumaroli, Marc. "Les Enchantements de l'éloquence: 'Les Fées' de Charles Perrault ou de la littérature." In Fumaroli, Marc, ed. *Le Statut de la littérature: Mélanges offerts à Paul Bénichou*. Genève: Droz, 1982.

Jacques Demy. Cinéma (July/August 1981). Special issue.

Logan, J. L. "For a New Critical Biography of Charles Perrault." *French Forum* 8:2 (1983) 162–180.

Loskoutoff, Yvan. "La Surenchère enfantine dans les *Contes* de Perrault." *Dix-Septième Siècle* 153 (1986) 343–350.

304   *Peau d'âne*

Malarte, Claire-Lise. "La Fortune des contes de Perrault au vingtième siècle." *Papers on French Seventeenth Century Literature* 11:21 (1984) 633–641.

Marin, Louis, Béatrice Marie, and Richard Macksey. "La Cuisine des fées; or The Culinary Sign in the Tales of Perrault." *Genre* 16:4 (1983) 477–492.

Marx, Jacques. "Perrault et le sommeil de la raison." *Cahiers Internationaux de Symbolisme* 40–41 (1980) 83–92.

McGlathery, James. *Fairy Tale Romance: the Grimms, Basile, and Perrault.* Urbana: University of Illinois Press, 1991.

Morgan, Jeanne. *Perrault's Morals for Moderns.* New York: Peter Lang, 1985.

———. "Structural Precedents of Perrault's *Contes.*" *French Studies Bulletin* 5 (Winter 1982–1983) 3–6.

Nykrog, Per. "'*Peau de chagrin*'—'*Peau d'âne*'." *L'Année Balzacienne* 14 (1993) 77–79.

Perrault, Charles. *Contes.* Paris: Librarie Générale Française, 1987.

———. *Memoirs of My Life.* Columbia: University of Missouri Press, 1989.

Petrie, G. "Jacques Demy." *Film Comment* 7:4 (Winter 1971–1972) 46–53.

Propp, Vladimir. *Morphology of the Folktale.* Bloomington: Indiana University Press, 1958.

Reseigh, Jayne. "Preciosity and Structure in Perrault's *Contes.*" *French Studies Bulletin* 7 (Summer 1983) 5–6.

Rigolot, François. "Les Songes du savoir de la 'Belle endormie' à la 'Belle au bois dormant'." *Littérature* 58 (May 1985) 91–106.

Saintyves, Pierre. *Les 'Contes' de Perrault: En Marge de la légende dorée, les reliques et les images légendaires.* Paris: Laffont, 1987.

Strick, P. "Demy Calls the Tune." *Sight and Sound* 40:4 (Autumn 1971) 187.

Todorov, Tzvetan. *Introduction à la littérature fantastique.* Paris: Seuil Points, 1970.

Vessely, Thomas. "In Defense of Useless Enchantment: Bettelheim's Appraisal of the Fairy Tales of Perrault." In Collins, Robert, and Howard Pearce III, eds. *The Scope of the Fantastic: Culture, Biography, Themes, Children's Literature.* Westport, CT: Greenwood Press, 1985.

Zarucchi, Jeanne Morgan. "Imprisonment and Liberation in Perrault's *Contes.*" *Publications of the Missouri Philological Association* 13 (1988) 57–62.

———. "Lucre and Seduction in Perrault's *Contes.*" *Chimères* 19:1 (1986) 69–80.

III

Film on Film

The New Wave:
Reflections in a Broken Mirror

The term *Nouvelle Vague* was coined in 1958 by Françoise Giroud, in an article for *L'Express*, to describe the large group of new young filmmakers who burst on the Paris scene in the late 1950s and who constituted an explosion of experimental talent working against the limitations of commercialized "bourgeois" filmmaking and conservative artistic and political constraints of the era. Ironically, at the same time, directors like Godard and Truffaut acknowledged their debt to and their love of classic Hollywood cinema. Weaned on the Cinémathèque, Truffaut claims he had to learn to follow a story, that at first he saw only movement and rhythm. The inter-textuality of their citations and homages to Hollywood is not a contradiction, but part of the self-conscious filmmaking of the group. Heavily criticized for their hollow formalism, they acknowledged many influences while seeking a new freedom of expression.

The official debut of the New Wave as a major force in French filmmaking was at the Cannes Film Festival in 1959, with three films which created an upheaval in French cinema: François Truffaut's *Les Quatre Cents Coups* (*The 400 Blows*), Alain Resnais's *Hiroshima mon amour* and Marcel Camus's *Orfeu Negro* (*Black Orpheus*), followed the next year by Jean-Luc Godard's *A bout de souffle* (*Breathless*). During this same period, Fellini made *La Dolce Vita* (1959) and Antonioni *L'Avventura* (1960), both also turning points which marked the demise of neorealism and the arrival of a new cinematographic and cinematic poetry, a subjective, self-conscious, narcissistic and self-reflexive voice.

These new filmmakers tried most of all to avoid stereotypes, for they shared the belief that perception of reality, if it exists at all, changes radically from point to point in time and space. The end of cinematic if not celluloid transparency had come. In McLuhanesque terms, the medium had become the message, and a new cinematic poetic was born, which harkened back to surrealism but which was less dominated by the visual and the sensational, which still had a narrative voice, but a voice no longer dependably coherent, consecutive, or logical, a new style of filmmaking that was deliberately and consciously amateurish, what Robert Bena-youn called "rough-draft cinema,"[1] countering the positivist belief in the surface of reality, literally pursuing filmmaking as a creative game. Traditional plot structure and images of realist filmmaking follow the canonic logic I outlined in "Recon-structing Literary Realism," and they attempt to compensate for the visceral anxiety of dislocation in the spectator occasioned by the passing of so many images, 84,600 an hour. Modernist film emphasizes that *angst* by denying closure and continuity and foregrounding ambiguity, fragmentation, and frustrated desire.

The New Wave was not a school (just as the New Novelists defied theoretic coherence in their collective canon, as indicated by Robbe-Grillet's essays in *Pour un nouveau roman* and the Cerisy conferences). Moreover, there were more than thirty different filmmakers in this group, mostly young talents, along with several long-established well-known directors in whose work they found affinities and resemblances to admire if not imitate. The names on the list vary from critic to critic; most agree on the following: Alexandre Astruc, Jacques Baratier, Robert Benayoun, Charles Bitsch, Philippe de Broca, Marcel Camus, Claude Chabrol, Jacques Demy, Jacques Doniol-Valcroze, Louis Félix, Georges Franju, Jean-Luc Godard, Louis Malle, Chris Marker, Edouard Molinaro, Jean-Daniel Pollet, Jacques Rivette, Eric Rohmer, Jean Rouch, Jacques Rozier, François Truffaut, Roger Vadim, Agnès Varda, Raymond Vogel, a dozen of whom stand as major filmmakers of the last half of the century. Alain Resnais, Alain Robbe-Grillet and Marguerite Duras, while not of the group, stand as masters of New Wave filmmaking, taking the *ennui* and *angst* of the era to the level of art.

One of the principal uniting forces of the movement was the *Cahiers du Cinéma*, titled in 1949 but actually founded in 1947 by Bazin and Astruc with the name *La Revue du Cinéma*. Astruc wrote the opening manifesto with his 1948 article on *La Caméra-stylo*, although the term *auteur* came as mentioned from a comment by Jean Renoir on *La Règle du jeu*. Astruc called for cinema to "break free from the tyranny of what is visual, from the image for its own sake, from the immediate and concrete demands of the narrative, to become a means of writing just as flexible and subtle as written language."[2]

Other contributors included Chabrol, Doniol-Valcroze, Godard, Rivette, Rohmer, Truffaut, who stand as the critical voices of the New Wave. Chabrol, Rohmer and Truffaut all wrote on Alfred Hitchcock, whose innovative and irreverent film noir antics were one of the leading influences on them. These new directors were also the artistic heirs of Luis Buñuel, Jean Cocteau, and some of Max Ophuls's work, of the evolution of the avant-garde since the beginning of the century, of the esthetics of modernism. Blending this influence with a certain poetic realism, most of them avoided the dangers of an equation between individualism and abstraction, seeking a less structured formalism that got them accused of anarchy and irresponsibility.

Of the filmmakers who have left the greatest impact, some will be more appreciated by certain generations and schools of critical theory than others; each will find his or her paradigmatic echoes in time. Although the New Wave was not equatable to the New Novel, there is a definite conjunction of purpose, as film's reflection of textual narrative renders it vulnerable to the direct influence of contemporary events in literature, in this case the fragmenting of time and space in the name of the primary unifying force of subjective narrative consciousness. Dramas of the individual set off against the backdrop of collective dilemmas were no longer politically motivated. In their attempt to create a hybrid of modernism and neorealism, the former political filmmakers found themselves suddenly in the trap of the new *politique des auteurs*.

Auteur filmmakers, identifiable by their very distinctive film narrative or film writing, paradoxically eschew adaptations of major literary works, preferring B-grade plots that leave more room for cinematic improvisation, for first-person expression. Most auteur New Wave filmmakers play with textual sources and citations in order to construct original scripts, sometimes creating directly in the medium, writing the script day by day or working without any written text. Truffaut and Godard's mock-citational *A bout de souffle* is enough of a parodic pastiche to constitute a rebellion against its literary and filmic models. Truffaut's filmmaking explores the relationship of text and film in all its myriad ramifications, experimenting with literary sources and images, autobiographic filmmaking, citational homage films and self-reflexive films about the collective creative process of cinematic art. The memorial issue to Truffaut of *Les Cahiers du Cinéma* in 1984 was entitled appropriately *Le Roman de Truffaut*.

The paradox of auteur filmmaking is of course the fact that the individual creative voice or stamp of the director necessarily expresses itself in the context of the collective technical solidarity of the collaborative effort of film production. Truffaut like other New Wave *cinéastes* attempted to resolve this disparity by working again and again with the same cast, like a repertory theater troupe: Jean-Pierre Léaud, Jeanne Moreau, Catherine Deneuve, Gérard Depardieu, Fanny Ardant, and crew: Suzanne Schiffman, Nestor Almendros, Georges Delerue.

Sometimes New Wave film seemed to be working against the very processes of its own production, with the inevitable and unfortunate result that suddenly a bad film, a badly made film, became desirable. The fear of commercialization, of form itself, of the apparent causal logic of coherent narrative, created senseless films, which sought a false freedom in their lack of formal constraints and considerations. Although *auteur* risked becoming synonymous with the negative meaning of *amateur* rather than that of opposition to commercialism, this quality epitomized the intense need for personal freedom and style of the 1960s; and New Wave auteur cinema, like the political Left, was dynamized, polarized and politicized by the events of 1968, from demonstrations for Henri Langlois at the Cinémathèque to shutting down the Cannes Film Festival. After 1968, these filmmakers had to make conscious decisions regarding their relationship to political and social issues. Truffaut depicts his directorial persona in his 1973 *La Nuit américaine* as obsessed with resisting politicization of his filmmaking.

Perhaps it was more than anything else their pervasive fear of thematic coherence that prevented these directors from serving politics, as they remembered the dangers of traditional rhetoric which pretends to give the audience the truth just as it distorts it. For truth is often not very realistic. Weaned on documentary and neorealism, Truffaut and others sought a cinematic expression of trivial incidents which would closely approximate the absurd aleatory nature of experience. Their search for authenticity of expression led some to postures of angry, self-indulgent adolescence, others to seek the lost magic of childhood, as explorations of cinematic subjective reality led them into the self, to the spatio-temporal coordinates of memory and imagination.

These New Wave films of deliberate confusion, mixed up, ideologically shallow or unsound, refuted doctrinaire postwar humanism as much as bourgeois commercialism. Rejecting all high-sounding ideals, even their own, these directors gave their films an anti-political, clandestine, arbitrary, capricious tone, in their apparent indifference to or mockery of social, political and economic concerns of the day. In spite of the leftist leanings of many of these filmmakers, they were unwilling to subordinate their filmmaking to the doxis of the Left, preferring satire, parody or personal lyricism. They chose to force audiences to rethink their stereotypes and expectations in more original ways, as Truffaut said, "with the intention of premeditated assault."[3]

Some of the seminal films from this group include Franju's *Hôtel des Invalides* (1951), Varda's *La Pointe courte* (1956), Vadim's *Et Dieu créa la femmme* (1956), Astruc's *Une Vie* (1957) and *La Proie pour l'ombre* (1961), Camus's *Mort en fraude* (1957) and *Orfeu Negro* (1959), Rouch's ethnographic cinéma vérité, Baratier's Algerian films and contemporary Arab legends, Marker's *Lettre de Sibérie* (1958), Chabrol's *Le Beau Serge* (1958) and *Les Cousins* (1959), Resnais's *Hiroshima mon amour* (1959) and *L'Année dernière à Marienbad* (1961), Godard's *A bout de souffle* (1960), Malle's *Zazie dans le métro* (1960).

The New Wave was reshaped in 1968 by the political realities of the social revolution for a new order, which temporarily refocused creative cinematic consciousness on the immediate considerations of social, political and economic conflict. The deception of the failure of that revolution during the 1970s and its redefinition within the power structure of the 1980s redirected many filmmakers away from their own original revolutionary stance, yet they continue to seek new ways of engaging their spectators in their creative illusions, whether of historic or exotic diegeses or the recognizable reality of their own experience.

In this study, I have chosen to explore the relationship between New Novel and New Wave in the collaboration of Duras and Resnais on *Hiroshima mon amour* and Robbe-Grillet and Resnais on *L'Année dernière à Marienbad*, major examples of the genre *ciné-roman*. I will look at another collaboration, of Truffaut and Godard, in *A bout de souffle* and at Truffaut's later B-movie citational pastiche, *Vivement dimanche*. I have included Carrière and Buñuel's *Le Charme discret de la bourgeoisie* as an example of ludic sabotage of coherent satire. Lastly, I would like to compare three of Truffaut's "autobiographical" Antoine Doinel films: *Les Quatre Cents Coups, Baisers volés* and *L'Amour en fuite*, and end with his mirror-film, *La Nuit américaine*, a demonstration of self-representational filmmaking affirming the primacy of illusion in the cinema.

Notes

1. Peter Graham, *The New Wave* (New York: Doubleday, 1968) 163.
2. Graham, 18.
3. Graham, 98.

Bibliography

Armes, Roy. *The Ambiguous Image: Narrative Style in Modern European Cinema*. London: British Film Institute, 1976.

Brode, Raymond, Freddy Buache, and Jean Curtelin. *Nouvelle Vague*. Lyons: Serdoc, 1962.

Buache, Freddy. *Le Cinéma français des années 60*. Paris: Hatier, 1987.

—————. *Le Cinéma français des années 70*. Paris: 5 Continents/Hatier, 1990.

Ciclier, Jacques. *Nouvelle Vague?* Paris: Editions du Cerf, 1961.

Château, D., A. Gardies, and François Jost, eds. *Cinémas de la modernité*. Paris: Klincksieck, 1981.

Collet, Jean. *Le Cinéma en question*. Paris: Editions du Cerf, 1972.

Douin, Jean-Luc, ed. *La Nouvelle Vague 25 ans après*. Paris: Editions du Cerf, 1983.

Downing, David B. and Susan Bazargan, eds., *Image and Ideology in Modern/Postmodern Discourse*. Albany: State University of New York Press, 1991.

Durgnat, Raymond. *Nouvelle Vague, The First Decade*. Loughton: Motion Publications, 1963.

Graham, Peter. *The New Wave*. New York: Doubleday, 1968.

Hayward, Susan, and Ginette Vincendeau, eds. *French Film: Texts and Contexts*. New York: Routledge, 2000.

Higgins, Lynn. *New Novel, New Wave, New Politics: Fiction and the Representation of History in Postwar France*. Lincoln: University of Nebraska Press, 1996.

Kline, T. Jefferson. *Screening the Text: Intertextuality in New Wave French Cinema*. Baltimore: Johns Hopkins University Press, 1992.

Monaco, James. *The New Wave*. New York: Oxford University Press, 1976.

Murcia, Claude. *Nouveau roman/nouveau cinéma*. Paris: Nathan, 1998.

Prédal, René. *Le Cinéma français contemporain*. Paris: Editions du Cerf, 1984.

Santandreu, Patricia de. "Le Phénomène Nouvelle Vague." *Journal Français d'Amérique* (8–21 September 1989).

Speigel, Alan. *Fiction and the Camera Eye: Visual Consciousness in Film and the Modern Novel*. Charlottesville: University Press of Virginia Press, 1976.

Stam, Robert. *Reflexivity in Film and Literature*. New York: Columbia University Press, 1992.

Hiroshima mon amour

directed by Alain Resnais (1959)
ciné-roman by Marguerite Duras

This revolutionary work, nominated for an Academy Award, has disturbed its spectators for almost half a century since its appearance at the Cannes Film Festival in the watershed year of 1959, year one in a new era of filmmaking. Narrative summary of its deceptively simple plot does not begin to describe the film: Elle, a French actress (Emmanuelle Riva) making an antiwar film in Hiroshima, falls in love with Lui, a Japanese architect (Eiji Okada) she meets in a bar. Their passion reawakens in her buried memories of her traumatic love affair with an occupying German soldier (Bernard Fresson) in her home town of Nevers during World War II and her ensuing humiliation and madness. Her two love affairs years apart with Axis power citizens prove equally impossible. The impact of the film is rather in the understated dialogue, the lyricism of its soliloquies, the striking contrapuntal interplay of sound and image, the dual diegesis interwoven in filigree, the visceral close-ups, the haunting musical score, the proliferation of signs and icons, the layers of meaning that resist closure, the disjunction of time and space.

It is significant that the title of this film has never been translated to "Hiroshima My Love;" it has thus become a symbol for the spectator of its French-Japanese dichotomy (or perhaps Americans could not accept the implicit equation between the bomb and love, parodied in Kubrick's 1964 *Dr. Strangelove or How I Learned to Stop Worrying and Love the Bomb*). It is equally interesting how many critics refer to the title as *Hiroshima, mon amour*, including a treasonous comma that places love in aposition and destroys the equation blending body and history, time and space, love and death.

Many New Wave directors were weaned on documentary and neorealist docudrama-style filmmaking. The apparent anomalies and surface paradoxes between the pact of transparency of the documentary and the experimental opaque nature of New Wave film are resolved in some cases through underlying thematics or structural similarities. Perhaps the most obvious case is the resemblance (which I discuss in my introduction on "History on Film" and in an article in *French Cultural Studies*) between *Nuit et brouillard* and *Hiroshima mon amour*, made three years later.

After Resnais finished *Nuit et brouillard*, he was asked to make a documentary on the atomic bomb. He abandoned the project in frustration, stating that he was trapped in the format of the earlier film, repeating its structure. He had done some editing in

1956 for Agnès Varda on *La Pointe courte*, an intellectual conversation between lovers set against the poverty of the old port of Sète on the Mediterranean. Thus Resnais and Marguerite Duras both created the contrapuntal rhythm of the script for *Hiroshima mon amour*, characterized by Lynn Higgins as the encounter of *caméra-stylo* and *écriture filmique*, of Elle's two affairs, alternating between the horrors of war and the destructive force of love, between present anguishing desire and former passion, loss and madness. The hallucinatory *mélopée* or litany, of the sound track as well, leads to an ending as ambiguous as the film; Resnais himself never made a decision about the fate of the lovers after the end of the film text.

The traces in *Hiroshima mon amour* of his original documentary project include opening authentic footage from 1945 of the aftermath of the firestorm and radiation, and the film within the film, where Elle plays a Red Cross nurse in a pacifist demonstration against all war, reflecting contemporary political events in Japan as well as Europe. Her personal love stories are made possible by the conjunction of individuals due to historic events and serve as a metaphor for that history: France caught in the middle between the political and military Axis of Germany and Japan. These chance encounters crossing national and racial boundaries engender passions vulnerable to loss, destruction, vaporization, like that from the bomb.

Like the two "theaters" of World War II, this is a dual theater of agony, of holocaust, where the main characters serve simultaneously as actors and spectators. Mimetic of its thematic, the film combines two parallel narratives alternating between Nevers and Hiroshima. The Japanese sequences were shot first, in August and September of 1958, the exteriors in Hiroshima (whose dynamic reconstructed skyline and flashing neon signs contrast so effectively the opening shots of devastation) and the interiors in Tokyo. Working with cinematographer Michio Takahashi and accompanied only by the scriptgirl Sylvette Baudret, Resnais could not communicate with the Japanese crew (appropriate irony), so they used Cocteau's 1949 film *Orphée* to illustrate their needs and wishes: camera angles, lighting, sets, direction. Okada spoke no French and memorized his part like an opera singer (thus his comment about how good his French is is doubly ironic). The French part of the film was then shot in Nevers in December (the seasonal metaphor of a dead past love), by cinematographer Sacha Vierny, who filmed the frame color segments of *Nuit et brouillard*. Henri Colpi, Resnais's editor for that film and for the later *L'Année dernière à Marienbad*, recombined the two sets of footage into Duras's contrapuntal screenplay. Artistic continuity resulted from daily collaboration between Resnais, Duras and Gérard Jarlot, and from the linking effects of voice-overs and the dual thematic of Giovanni Fusco's haunting soundtrack, punctuated by Georges Delerue's lyric waltz for the café sequence (Delerue was also the music director for *Nuit et brouillard*). This waltz is equatable to the Chopin piece heard on shipboard by the autobiographical heroine of Duras's *L'Amant* (*The Lover*), a novel published in 1984 but which recounts events from her adolescence, filmed in 1991 by Jean-Jacques Annaud. She would return to this thematic in 1991 with *L'Amant de la Chine du Nord*, written in response to Annaud's film, which displeased her.

When Resnais turned to Duras for a screenplay, they created a hybrid embodying her past personal lyric loss and his sense of the fragmentation of reality by the horrors of war and the holocaust. Duras translated the atomization and devastation of the nuclear firestorm into a segmented modernist narrative of two seeringly destructive passions, connecting the burning flesh of the holocaust to that of passionate desire, the opening image of the film. From her own bicultural background, she wove the tragic account of a woman doubly *désaxée*, twice driven mad by impossible love. The Axis is literally and figuratively broken into a crosscut montage, particularly effective near the end of the film, and dissipated in time and space, as the transparent illusion of reality is replaced with new temporal and visual rhythms challenging the spectator's perceptions.

Duras's integration of the two stories turns not only on her adolescent love affair with a Chinese transposed into *L'Amant* but on another coincidence revealed in her 1985 diary narrative *La Douleur* ("suffering" translated as *The War*). In *Hiroshima mon amour*, Elle recounts in flashback that she left her prison of madness and bicycled to Paris to freedom and a new life on 6 August 1945, the day that Hiroshima was bombed. Duras herself, after awaiting so long the repatriation of her real-life deported husband, then turned around and left him for good that same date, a rupture that generated for her a second connection between the atomic explosion and the deforming effect of human passion. Born and raised in Indochina, outside of Saigon, Duras lived personally the intense passion and impossible anguish of the type of cross-cultural interracial affair depicted in *Hiroshima mon amour*, an experience which also has echoes in *Un Barrage contre le Pacifique* (*The Sea Wall*) and *La Maladie de la Mort* (*The Malady of Death*). The deadly interplay between love and death, between *eros* and *thanatos*, is reflected at the beginning and the end of the script in the litanous phrase: "Tu me tues, tu me déformes jusqu'à la laideur." (You kill me, you deform me into ugliness.) Duras conceived her screenplay of *Hiroshima mon amour* with a quadripartite thematic of the body, oblivion, Nevers and the river, and in five parts or acts; this is true film-theater, not the canned theater of filmed productions of stage performances, but the use of the cinematic medium and all its signifiers to stage a dramatic encounter in discrete segments. The first section depicting the lovers' nude bodies covered in ashes, like the victims of the bombing, and then in sweat, the equation of the heat of two passions, is accompanied by a battle of the wills. Elle affirms, "J'ai tout vu à Hiroshima" (I saw everything in Hiroshima), with her determination to document past events in present screen images (the landscape of the holocaust, the charred bodies and twisted steel in the museum, the tortured skin and hair and long slow suffering in the hospital, so redolent of the concentration camps of *Nuit et brouillard*). Lui denies the possibility of re-presenting history: "Tu n'as rien vu à Hiroshima!" (You saw nothing in Hiroshima!). Elle expresses the will to remember, to participate as a compassionate observer or spectator in this historic horror, exploring the surviving evidence of the holocaust as preparation for her framed film role. As with any film within the film, the scenes of the antinuclear demonstrators and Elle in her Red Cross nurse's uniform constitute a *mise-en-abyme* of the frame narrative, in this case not just a documentary about Hiroshima, but a 1950s militant political antiwar film intruding into a dual love story, affirming the impossible distance in time and space between nations, between eras, between lovers. *Hiroshima mon amour* is thus doubly a product of its own era, as a political film with its own contemporary intertext, like Algeria for *Nuit et brouillard*, here the Cold War obsessive fear of nuclear extinction in the midst of prosperous reconstruction. The militancy of the young Japanese was generated by the irradiation of the twenty-three crew members of the fishing boat *Lucky Dragon 5* by the hydrogen bomb test in 1954 on Bikini Atoll. As a result, the *hibakusha*, the survivors of the A-bomb explosions, were officially acknowledged for the first time in a decade. Thus reconstruction of repressed past horrors functions in this film in several contexts. Ultimately, Lui's negation of Elle's will to remember, to document, affirms the impossible access to suffering of that magnitude, as well as the impassable barrier between past and present, memory and oblivion, film and spectator, text and reader. It is the distance affirmed two centuries earlier by Diderot in *Jacques le fataliste*, as the implied reader challenges the narrator: "Vous n'y étiez pas; il ne s'agit pas de vous."[1]

In the second segment, the lovers in bed recount framed narratives to one another of their life stories, seeking past knowledge like the documentarist. The strength of Elle and her testimony, as witness in the hospital and museum, as nurse in the framed film, as past and present lover, is reinforced by her onomastic equation with Nevers, her home town in France. Lui, the Japanese architect whose parents were incinerated by the bomb, is equated with Hiroshima. Their representation by two systems of nomination is interconnected; both the disjunctive pronouns Lui and Elle and the place names Hiroshima and Nevers are disjoined, separated, isolated in the syntagmatic space of the film. The barriers between them are manifest in the central sequence where Elle in uniform enacts her film role. The crowd scene shots of militant demonstrators marching, threatening to separate the lovers, contrast their prior intimacy.

In the subsequent café sequence, Lui serves as a catalyst of transference, first arousing Elle's passion, then eliciting the tale of her impossible first love with the occupying German soldier, a tale which first enters the frame narrative in a three-and-a-half-second flashback shot of his dead body, a Proustian experience of involuntary memory like that of the madeleine, triggered by the sleeping Lui's quivering hand, as the past momentarily invades the bed she shares with her present lover. The will to remember and document struggles doubly with the inevitable distance between past and present, East and West, but it is most daunted by the distance between the experiential and narrated layers of the self. Lui attempts to bridge this distance at the café through grammatical empathy, substituting himself out of compassion, curiosity, perhaps jealousy, for her dead German lover (shot by a Resistance sniper as the two attempted to escape to Bavaria in 1944), using the first person to interact with Elle and elicit a therapeutic confession of a past agony walled up inside her. To paraphrase the end of *Combray*, "Tout Nevers est sorti, ville et jardins, comme des fleurs japonaises, de son verre de bière." (All Nevers appeared, town and gardens, like Japanese flowers, in her glass of beer.) In French, this is possibly triggered in the script by the homonym *bière* meaning both the drink and the funeral bier.

All of Duras's work echoes intertextually the thematic of *Hiroshima mon amour*, of phobias of loss and dissipation of the self, silence and absence, social and familial disjunction, the dominance of the mother (the film refers to both her repressive parental role and her incarceration near Nevers for madness). In *Hiroshima mon amour*, it is of course transferred to the daughter figure, who is walled alone in a white gown, head shaved, in the basement of her home, and who mutilates her own body bloodying her hands clawing the walls. The female voice-over echoes the male voice-over of Michel Bouquet in *Nuit et brouillard*, and her gestures recall the claw marks on the plaster ceilings of the gas chambers, just as the close-up of Elle and Lui nude together in the shower alludes to the deadly showers of both Auschwitz and atomic rain. This female figure called Nevers, suffering the past and present political and affective disjunction of the self, is at once intimately autobiographical and metaphorically emblematic of national identity.

The fifth and final "act" develops all the themes of the film while nevertheless refusing closure. Elle returns to her hotel room and in her soliloquy before the mirror evokes the impossible future of her lost past ("Nous irons en Bavière"—We will go to Bavaria), while standing above the flowing water so symbolic for Duras of the irreversible passage of time. The sequence at the café *Casablanca*, with its English language exchanges and mention of America, is both an homage to Michael Curtiz's 1942 film of lovers united then separated by war and an allusion to postwar relations between the U.S. and Japan. At the train station, the old Japanese lady represents the traditional culture that separates the lovers physically and linguistically. As Elle continues her journey down the street, Lui cannot leave her ("impossible de te quitter") and yet cannot reach her (another virtual future unfulfilled: "Il viendra vers moi"—He will come toward me). In the final hotel room encounter, Lui and Elle are resorbed into their respective landscapes, as he becomes "Hiroshima" and she "Nevers en France." For the speaker of English, this closing utterance carries both a lasting protest message against nuclear devastation in Europe and an assertion of the impossibility of their continuing affair or future reunion (they are both "happily" married to someone else).

Thus *Hiroshima mon amour* abandons the traditional documentary evidence of death and destruction, in favor of human passion, of a personalization, a personification, of historic roles. And the chance encounter between Elle and Lui, due to her assignment to work on the antiwar film in Japan, leads through their consuming passion to a reconstruction of images of the holocaust of Hiroshima, the city now reconstructed on the wide island of its name, on the delta of the Ota river, washed by the tides, a river once burned dry and lifeless by the bomb. The French counterpart to the Japanese river is of course the Loire flowing through Nevers, the deceptively peaceful scenic Loire, which, like the past and like the passion of the body, is unnavigable, due to its sand bars, barriers deposited over time.

The Durasian conceptualization of the flow of the river is beyond lyric. The turbulence and currents carry away experience on the waters of time, less a Proustian or Bergsonian duration or inner conjunction of psychic time than an implacable force which denies the human dimension. This force which carries away youth and love also obliterates the memory of past horrors, an oblivion simultaneously feared and desired.

This passing of time is marked in *Hiroshima mon amour* by numerous shots of clocks and watches (which all stopped when the bomb exploded) and by Elle's steadily approaching necessary departure. Echoing that of the victims of the camps and the bomb, the slow personal suffering of Elle, whose future has no place for her past or her present, connects the Shoah of *Nuit et brouillard* to the holocaust of *Hiroshima mon amour*.

Both the Shoah, the systematic extermination of a people, and the holocaust, the sacrificial consumption by firestorm, have haunted the voices of our era, particularly the *fin-de-siècle, fin-de-millénaire* period obsessed with images of apocalypse. The union of death, desire and madness, central thematic of the works of Duras, is also central to the dialectic of theorists like Gilles Deleuze, Michel Foucault, René Girard, Félix Guattari, and Paul Ricoeur. The deconstruction of the self, of the subject, reenacts at the level of the individual conscience the massive barbaric violence of Shoah and holocaust. Jean Baudrillard and Michel Serres also transpose the Durasian equation of libido and destruction into dialectic. Faced with the impossibility of possessing the self or the other in the self, the Durasian character retreats into amnesia. Thus the original four themes of the body, oblivion, Nevers and the river are but one. Duras and Serres both affirm this inevitable flow of being, born on turbulent eddies, leading the self inexorably to its predictable end.

In the face of the dissemination and dissipation of the self in time and madness, in the circular hell of the self-destructive and self-reflexive libido posited by Baudrillard, Deleuze, Duras, Girard, Guattari, and Lacan, survival in an apocalyptic society is probably, as Marc Bensimon would suggest, best attained in art, in the symbolic evocation of the self in a creative project, where one can reaffirm being. To quote the closing comment of Bensimon's essay, "Apocalypse Now or in the Magic Hole?" in *Modernism: Challenges and Perspectives*, "The artists apprehends both himself and the Real in the circular instant, eternal return of a same, identical and different, where past and future meet in a jolt, where the sacred, the natural, the material, the real, folds back into itself but also is raised in the noon sun, winged Word."[2]

Thus it is in the text, script or film that the impetus toward destruction and oblivion is countered, through the reproduction of the self in the eternal present of the symbolic. And re-presenting through language and image of past passion leaves a lyric legacy of primal preoccupations with love and death to be endlessly re-experienced by the reader or spectator. Thus the "message," urgent as it is, at the end of *Hiroshima mon amour*, "Nevers en France," is much more than a cry against nuclear destruction on French soil. It is the affirmation of the impossibility of conjunction of self and other and, at the same time, the renewed resituating of the self in a socio-historic context.

A history irony that demonstrates the continuity of Resnais's work is the fact that both *Nuit et brouillard* and *Hiroshima mon amour* elicited much resistance from government officials when submitted to the Cannes Film Festival. They in fact were both shown outside the competition for fear of offending the very people whose actions they addressed. For Resnais was condemning not only inhuman acts but those who obliterate the memory and knowledge of such acts by censorship, denial or repression.

This chapter first appeared as an article in the October 1992 issue of *French Cultural Studies*, published in England by Alpha Academic.

Notes

1. Denis Diderot, *Jacques le fataliste* (Paris: Garnier Flammarion) 110, quoted in François Jost, *L'Oeil-caméra* (Lyons: Presses Universitaires de Lyon, 1987) 11.

2. Marc Bensimon, "Apocalypse Now or in the Magic Hole?" in Monique Chefdor, Ricardo Quinones and Albert Wachtel, eds., *Modernism: Challenges and Perspectives* (Chicago: University of Illinois Press, 1986) 300.

Bibliography

Alleins, Marguerite. *Marguerite Duras: Médium du réel.* Paris: L'Age d'Homme, 1984.

Armes, Roy. *The Cinema of Alain Resnais.* New York: Barnes, 1968.

Bajomée, Danielle, and Ralph Heyndels. *Ecrire dit-elle: Imaginaires de Marguerite Duras.* Brussels: Editions de l'Université de Bruxelles, 1985.

Baker, Deborah. "Memory, Love, and Inaccessibility in *Hiroshima mon amour.*" In Ricouart, Janine, and Anne-Marie Alonzo, eds. *Marguerite Duras Lives On.* Lanham, MD: University Press of America, 1998.

Benayoun, Robert. *Alain Resnais: arpenteur de l'imaginaire.* Paris: Stock, 1980.

Borgomano, Madeleine. *L'Ecriture filmique de Marguerite Duras.* Paris: Albatros, 1985.

Bounoure, Gaston. *Alain Resnais.* Paris: Seghers, 1962.

Brée, Germaine. "Autogynography." *The Southern Review* 22:2 (1986) 223–230.

Brown, William and Selena Mustaphalli. "Anamnesis in *The Dead* and *Hiroshima mon amour*: the Loss of First Loves." *West Virginia University Philological Papers* 47 (2001) 56–62.

Burch, Noël. "A Conversation with Alain Resnais." *Film Quarterly* 13:3 (1960) 27–29.

Cardullo, Bert. "The Symbolism of *Hiroshima*, [sic] *mon amour.*" *Film Criticism* 8:2 (1984) 39–44.

Clerc, Jeanne-Marie. "Marguerite Duras, collaboratrice d'A. Resnais, et le rapport des images et des mots dans les 'textes hybrides'." *Revue des Sciences Humaines* 73:202–2 (1986) 103–116.

Cohen, Keith. "Pleasures of Voicing: Oral Intermittences in Two Films by Alain Resnais." *L'Esprit Créateur* 30:2 (1990) 58–67.

Colpi, Henri. "Editing *Hiroshima mon amour.*" *Sight and Sound* 29 (1959–1960) 14–16.

———. "Musique d'*Hiroshima.*" *Les Cahiers du Cinéma* 18 (1960) 1–14.

Crawshaw, Robert, and Karin Tusting. "Approaching the Text: A Methodological Framework for Text Analysis." In Crawshaw and Tusting, eds. *Exploring French Text Analysis: Interpretations of National Identity.* London: Routledge, 2000.

Duras, Marguerite. *L'Amant.* Paris: Editions de Minuit, 1984.

———. *Hiroshima mon amour.* Paris: Gallimard, 1960. New York: Grove Press, 1961.

———. *The Lover.* New York: Pantheon, 1985.

———. *L'Amant de la Chine du Nord.* Paris: Gallimard 1991.

Etienne, Marie-France. "L'Oubli et la répétition: *Hiroshima mon amour.*" *Romanic Review* 78:4 (1987) 508–514.

Glassman, D. "The Feminine Subject Written as History Writer in *Hiroshima mon amour.*" *Enclitic*

5:1 (1981) 43–53.

Guers-Villate, Yvonne. "From *Hiroshima mon amour* to *India Song*: A Novelist's Cinematic Production." *West Virginia University Philological Papers* 26 (Aug 1980) 60–65.

Hachiya, Michihiko. *Hiroshima Diary*. Chapel Hill: University of North Carolina Press, 1955.

Hanet, Kari. "Does the Camera Lie? Notes on *Hiroshima mon amour*." *Screen* 14 (1973) 59–66.

Harvey, Stella, and Kate Ince, eds. *Duras, femme du siècle*. Amsterdam: Rodopi, 2001.

Hershey, John. *Hiroshima*. New York: Knopf, 1985.

Higgins, Lynn. "Durasian (Pre)Occupations." *L'Esprit Créateur* 30:2 (1990) 47–57.

Jackson, Earl, Jr. "Desire at Cross-(Cultural) Purposes: *Hiroshima*, [sic] *mon amour* and *Merry Christmas, Mr. Lawrence*." *Positions* 2:1 (Spring 1994) 133–174.

Knudsen, Britta Timm. "Hiroshima Blues." *(Pre)publications* 105 (Mar 1987) 28–39.

Kriedl, John Francis. *Alain Resnais*. Boston: Twayne, 1977.

Lane, Nancy. "The Subject in/of History: *Hiroshima mon amour*." In Simons, John, ed. *Literature and Film in the Historical Dimension*. Gainesville: University Press of Florida, 1994.

Long-Innes, Chesca. "'Hiroshima mon amour': A Barthesian Reading." *South African Theatre Journal* 5:2 (Sept 1991) 80–91.

Luchting, Wolfgang. "*Hiroshima*, [sic] *mon amour*, Time, and Proust." *Journal of Aesthetics and Art Criticism* 21 (1962–1963) 300–309.

Macaskill, Brian. "Figuring Rupture." In Downing, David, and Susan Bazargan, eds. *Image and Ideology in Modern/Postmodern Discourse*. Albany: State University Press of New York, 1991.

Marguerite Duras. Les Cahiers du Cinéma 312 (1980). Entire issue.

Medhurst, Martin. "*Hiroshima mon amour*: From Iconography to Rhetoric." *The Quarterly Journal of Speech* 68:4 (1982) 345–370.

Mercken-Spaas, Godelieve. "Destruction and Reconstruction in *Hiroshima*, [sic] *mon amour*." *Literature/Film Quarterly* 8:4 (1980) 244–250.

Michalczyk, John. "Alain Resnais: Literary Origins from *Hiroshima* to *Providence*." *Literature/Film Quarterly* 7:1 (1979) 16–25.

Monaco, James. *Alain Resnais: The Role of Imagination*. New York: Oxford University Press, 1978.

Moses, John. "Vision Denied in *Night and Fog* and *Hiroshima mon amour*." *Literature/Film Quarterly* 15:3 (1987) 159–163.

Murphy, Carol. "New Narrative Regions: The Role of Desire in the Films and Novels of Marguerite Duras." *Literature/Film Quarterly* 12:2 (1984) 122–128.

Oms, Marcel. *Alain Resnais*. Paris: Rivages/Cinéma, 1988.

Pauly, Rebecca. "From Shoah to Holocaust: Image and Ideology in Alain Resnais's *Night and Fog* and *Hiroshima mon amour*." *French Cultural Studies* 3 (1992) 253–261.

Pingaud, Bernard, ed. *Alain Resnais*. Lyons: Serdoc, 1961.

Prédal, René. *Alain Resnais*. Paris: Lettres Modernes, 1968.

Raskin, Richard. "Alain Resnais: *Hiroshima mon amour*" and "Bibliographie." *(Pre)publications* 105 (Mar 1987) 3–55.

Ravar, Raymond, ed. *"Tu n'as rien vu à Hiroshima!"*. Brussels: Institut de Sociologie, 1962.

Reinton, Ragnhild Evang. "Hiroshima mon amour." *Vagant* 1 (1990) 6–12.

Ropars-Wuilleumier, Marie-Claire, and Kimball Lockhart. "Film Reader of the Text." *Diacritics* 15:1 (Spring 1985) 18–30.

Ropars-Wuilleumier, Marie-Claire. "How History Begets Meaning: Alain Resnais's *Hiroshima mon amour* (1959)." In Hayward, Susan, and Ginette Vincendeau, eds. *French Film: Texts and Contexts*. New York: Routledge, 2000.

Rosello, Mireille. "Amertume: L'Eau chez Marguerite Duras." *Romanic Review* 78:4 (1987) 515–524.

Roud, Richard, ed. *Cinema, A Critical Dictionary* 2. New York: Viking, 1980.

Schulman, Peter. "Vercors et Duras: L'Occupation des silences." *New Zealand Journal of French*

Studies 19:1 (May 1998) 14–25.

Shoos, Diane. *Speaking the Subject: The Films of Marguerite Duras and Alain Resnais.* Dissertation Abstracts International 47:7 (1987) 2347A–2348A.

Stanbrook, Alan. "The Time and Space of Alain Resnais." *Films and Filming* 10 (1964) 35–38.

Steinberg, Rafael. *Postscript from Hiroshima.* New York: Random House, 1966.

Sweet, Freddy. *The Film Narratives of Alain Resnais.* Ann Arbor: UMI Research Press, 1981.

Théry, Chantal. "Marguerite Duras: La Mémoire étoilée ou l'intime de l'éternité." *Francofonia* 7:12 (1987) 21–33.

Tison-Braun, Micheline, and Michael Bishop. *Marguerite Duras.* Paris: Rodopi, 1985.

Ward, John. *Alain Resnais or the Theme of Time.* New York: Doubleday, 1968.

Williams, James, and Janet Sayers, eds. *Revisioning Duras: Film, Race, Sex.* Liverpool: Liverpool University Press, 2000.

Williams, Linda. "*Hiroshima* and *Marienbad*: Metaphor and Metonymy." *Screen* 17:1 (1976) 34–39.

Willis, Sharon. *Marguerite Duras: Writing on the Body.* Urbana: University of Illinois Press, 1987.

Wilson, Emma. "'Duras mon amour': Identité et mensonge." *Dalhousie French Studies* 50 (Spring 2000) 7–15.

L'Année dernière à Marienbad
(Last Year at Marienbad)

directed by Alain Resnais (1961)
ciné-roman by Alain Robbe-Grillet

The two Alain R.s, both born in 1922, met in 1960 in attempting to create a truly new cinematic and cinematographic language. Resnais had just finished *Hiroshima mon amour*; Robbe-Grillet had just written the screenplay for *L'Immortelle*, his first film that he would direct in Turkey while Resnais made *L'Année dernière à Marienbad* in Germany and Paris. Critics refer to their idea of co-signing the film and the closeness of their cooperation, but recent interviews and comments indicate to what extent their collaboration was a compromise between Robbe-Grillet's attempt to persuade Resnais to accept his finished shooting script, which would preempt his creative adaptation of the customary screenplay format, and Resnais's determination to impose his own vision on numerous elements of Robbe-Grillet's work, specifically eliminating the rape scene. Yet the film has a deeper coherence than these divergences would indicate. When Henri Colpi finished editing the endless footage given him by Resnais into the final version, it was very nearly Robbe-Grillet's original *ciné-roman*. Thus this work so apparently open, polysemic and ambiguous has its own unifying yet complex structure.

Looking at both Resnais's and Robbe-Grillet's production over the years, it is easy to interpret *L'Année dernière à Marienbad* as the meeting point of their respective theories of radical modernism—New Novel, New Wave—of the calculated, mathematic fragmenting of the traditional coordinates of time and space informing cinematic or literary realism. The absence of chronology, of certainty, the game of chance, of substitution, the rhetoric of persuasion, the air of mystery and cruelty, all mark this film, with its self-reflexive *mise-en-abyme* engravings of its own sets (château and garden) and theatrical presentation of its own plot, as a point of no return in cerebral abstract cinema.

In the ensemble of Robbe-Grillet's *oeuvre* can be found (in the titles alone) an extended reworking of the obsessional mythology of the self, always in evolution. From *Boris, un régicide*, written in 1949 but published in 1978, and his now classic *nouveaux romans* of the 1950s, *Les Gommes*, *Le Voyeur*, *La Jalousie* and *Dans le labyrinthe*, Robbe-Grillet ventured into experimental filmmaking with *L'Immortelle*, *L'Année dernière à Marienbad*, *Trans-Europ-Express*, *L'Homme qui ment*, *L'Eden et après*, *N a pris les dés*, *Glissements progressifs du plaisir*, *Le Jeu avec le feu*, *Piège à fourrure*, *La Belle Captive*, and *Un bruit qui rend fou*. After a series of novels pursuing the topology of the self in the landscape of the imagination, in recent years he has focused on the project of an autobiographical trilogy, *Romanesques*, including *Le Miroir qui revient*, *Angélique ou l'enchantement* and the final volume published as a novel, *Les Derniers Jours de Corinthe*, a narratological injoke, as the autobiographer cannot textualize his own death, passing rather into a literary transposition of the self as a character of fiction.

Cinema and text are closely interwoven, if not interchangeable, in Robbe-Grillet's work, linked as stated by persistent elements of narrative fragmentation of setting, intrigue and chronology, and by an air of mystery, of absence, by acts of perverse cruelty mingled with playful games, by an intertwined obsessional thematic of personal mythology and cultural legend. The surrealistic uncertainty of his universe carries its own powerful message: form is its own content, nothing is certain, the only truth is in fiction, and ambiguity is the only absolute. In addition, as Marie-Claire Ropars-Wuilleumier has indicated, the transformational procedures from text to film and film to text are quite different. The relationship between the eye and the object is much more problematic in literary narrative than the necessary framing I/Eye of the camera of filmic presentation. This greater ambiguity of textually elicited image was signalled and preferred by both Sartre and Barthes in their discussions of the phenomenology of image.

Critical discourse and its rational strategies are thwarted by the deliberate abstraction and ambiguity of *L'Année dernière à Marienbad* (whose title is a trap); hence the inexhaustible attraction of the film (and all Resnais's and Robbe-Grillet's *oeuvres*). The primary achievement of the film is its destruction of the traditional continuities of cinematic narrative and its substitution of a new structure. The logical sequence of scenes is fragmented by repeated substitutions with variation, like jazz idioms, changing costumes, sets, characters and dialogue in a kaleidoscopic aleatory recombinant mode. Even the spectator's trust in the optics of the camera is threatened. Recalling the experimental films of Méliès in 1900, Resnais and Robbe-Grillet change the positioning of the actors, the set, the lighting (shadows appear and disappear at will), the costumes, the sound track, in a cinematic baroque arabesque.

The elements of magic mark the film generically as a fable, a legend, a myth. Resnais and Robbe-Grillet exploit to the fullest the oneiric quality of film. The entire film is a ludic experiment, a game of mirrors, of illusions and allusions. At the beginning, the camera-eye of Sacha Vierny's cinematography enters the château in order to linger before an engraving of the same château, a miniature model of the set and thus of the opening sequence of the film itself. It then enters the château's theater to watch the end of a play entitled *Rosmer* (interpreted as an intertextual allusion to Ibsen, but actually an arbitrarily selected name) where the actors in the film become spectators applauding the ending of their own drama about to unfold. And the camera will return to this same theater for a concert later in the film, a concert whose performance is never heard on the soundtrack, where disjunction of sound and image is the order of the day.

The choice of sets for *Marienbad* was significant; Resnais used different castles in Germany (Marienbad is a spa in Czechoslovakia): Schleissheim for the park and facade, Nymphenburg and Paris studio sets for the interiors, thus blending interior and exterior in collage. There is a haunting echo in these German castle sets where the characters are marked only by initials, of Robbe-Grillet's experience recounted in *Le Miroir qui revient*, of working in a tank factory in Nuremberg named M.A.N., during which sojourn he attended concerts in a baroque church, fabricated steel chess pieces and lived a surreal experience "faite de légèreté, d'absence et de suspens, de n'être qu'un touriste."[1]

During the initial guided tour of the set, with its haunting voice-over, the camera follows the descriptive adventure of the decorative molding and panelling, passes through mirrored hallways, up and down massive staircases, in and out of salons, bars, bedrooms, all to the obsessive persistent musical score for organ by Francis Seyrig. This film of the absurd becomes a theater of the absurd which assaults the spectator, as the obsessively voyeuristic and insatiably curious camera pursues its elusive subject. Marie-Claire Ropars-Wuilleumier's description of Robbe-Grillet's novels applies to the effect of the Robbe-Grilletian décor on the spectator: "La gravure, le dessin, le tableau, mais aussi bien le décor, la scène, la fenêtre ou la cité marquent la règle topologique qui permet d'affronter le fantôme du regard. Et le miroir lui-même offrirait la protection de son cadre s'il ne reconduisait, sous forme de dédoublement, l'extradition de l'oeil qui se réfléchit dans la vue, et par là cède au regard venu de la vue même."[2]

L'Année dernière à Marienbad is the depiction of a series of mental processes, a film which has both fascinated and enraged its spectators since its release. Under the guise of pure objectivity of the camera, Resnais and Robbe-Grillet made a film of pure imagination. The frozen characters, like the statues in the garden, offer themselves to the spectator and to each other without passion or feeling. Their dehumanized detachment generates a dream mood, where Cartesian logic is banished in favor of a new set of absolutes, where objects appear, disappear and change without narrative continuity, without cause and effect. The dominant mode of lethargic boredom and ambiguous frustration cancels all traditional pacts between the filmmaker and the spectator. Most of all, the film willfully defies resolution. Whether or not A (Delphine Seyrig) and X (Giorgio Albertazzi) actually met last year at Marienbad is not only not verifiable, it is irrelevant. Film becomes a pure rhetoric of persuasion of its own presence, the inverse of documentary. The characters remain designated only by initials, as in a filmscript. A's intertextual model is the heroine of *La Jalousie*, referred to only as A...; a contemporary intertext is offered by the characters of L and N in *L'Immortelle* and their *lit mortel*. Since Robbe-Grillet states in *Le Miroir qui revient* that "revenants et fantasmes, dans *L'Année dernière à Marienbad*, envahissent de facon trop visible l'écran,"[3] it is perhaps significant that his father held an engineering degree called "A. et M." (pronounced "azéhème") and established a factory that made cardboard packaging for dolls.[4]

Like the phantoms they are called, these haunting intertexts and experiential antecedents merely float as ghosts in the film's diegesis of uncertainty. Moreover, whether or not M (Sacha Pitoëff) is A's husband (M for "mari," A for "adultère absente" or Angélique?), whether or not she was raped last year by X (mark of illiteracy, of anti-text, of mystery, or of a topological phenomenon), whether or not A murdered X or X died accidentally, whether or not A and X actually leave together (in a Cinderella allusion, at midnight) is simply not the point. The point is rather that the spectator will never have verifiable evidence to solve this mystery thriller, to affirm one of its proffered endings as valid, for the fundamental truth of film and fiction is its primal illusion. As Robbe-Grillet stated in *Le Miroir qui revient*, "Les personnages de roman, ou ceux des films, sont aussi des sortes de fantômes . . . les héros, si visiblement sortis du royaume des ombres, qui peuplent *Marienbad* . . . à leurs airs absents, dépaysés, en trop dans le monde . . . comme s'ils tentaient désespérément d'accéder à une existence charnelle, qui leur est refusée . . . ou bien d'entraîner dans leur quête impossible l'*autre*, tous les autres, y compris l'innocent lecteur [spectateur]."[5]

The game of remembering and forgetting, of memory and oblivion, that taunted the spectator of *Hiroshima mon amour* is here reduced to a game of chance (called nim or pim), played by M and X throughout the film, with cards and matches, and then by A as she lays out the photographs (mirror duplicates) from "last year" on the floor of her bedroom in the pattern of the game. The documenting function of photography is thus questioned, reduced to an idle ludic activity, as the photo images are like the film rearranged in mysterious geometric patterns. And this apparent game of chance which in reality incorporates a complex system of mathematical formulae enables the *magister ludi* to win every time. Thus X, like the spectator, is trapped in defeat by his own lack of understanding of the rules of the game. The prominence of the game in the castle setting with aristocratic characters generates a sustained homage to Renoir's *La Règle du jeu*, a film that Alain Resnais confessed impacted him tremendously when he first saw it (a film which was rereleased in 1959).

Speculations on past and future temporal aspects are subordinated to and dominated by the only temporal cinematic absolute, the present of the film on the screen. Questions of space and displacement are rendered irrelevant by the passage of the reel before the projector and the sound waves from the speakers. Thus *L'Année dernière à Marienbad*, representing an eternal elsewhere in time and space, a perfect present absence, stands as the ultimate deconstruction of the essence of film art. Any apparent meaning left represents a transparency generated inadvertently by this perfectly opaque work, which projects its structural functional process as its primary thematic. The systematic refusal of cause-effect realism and sequential plotting forces the spectator to read the film as a series of arranged signs whose postulated correlations are constantly negated on the level of reality and affirmed on the level of play. The spectator's attempt to impose meaning on the film is simply an admission of cinematic and artistic naïveté, or cowardice, the inability to shirk inculcated responses to traditional realist canons, to comprehend this new disposition of filmic text and acknowledge it as a totally original creative construct.

The primary ambiguity of the film's title signals a double irony, in time (*l'année dernière*—last year) and space (*à Marienbad*—at Marienbad). The name Marienbad introduces a fictional intertextual space as well, from the Argentine short story, *La Invencion de Morel* by Bioy Casares (contemporary of Borges and of Cortàzar, who provided the intertext if not the idea for Antonioni's *Blow-Up*). In his chapter on the film in *Screening the Text*, Jeff Kline posits an intriguing originary if coincidental scenario for the film's setting: Jacques Lacan was to have presented his thesis on the Mirror Stage for the first time at a conference at Marienbad in 1937. Because his speech was interrupted, it never appeared in the papers of the conference, thus creating a fundamental absence and uncertainty in a discourse of the structure of identity.

Unfortunately, this intriguing coincidence had no influence on Robbe-Grillet's screenplay/*ciné-roman*, any more than Kafka's visit to the Marienbad spa, yet the dreamlike uncertainty functions at many levels. The multiple layers of ambiguous meaning in the title create a nominal imbalance reflected in the frozen water and mirrors throughout the film, announced in the term "dark mirrors" in the opening exploratory sequence with voice-over. Delphine Seyrig in white feathers, a mythical swan gliding on absent ponds, trapped in a dream, elicits intertexts of her own, specifically the image of Ginger Rogers dancing with Fred Astaire in the Hollywood classic *Top Hat*, which has in its narrative plot line the same fundamental ambiguity of prior acquaintance between the man and the woman and their final elopement together. Other mythical intertexts specifically cited by Resnais include *Sleeping Beauty* and the legend of the envoy of Death who comes to get his victim a year later.

The emotional detachment of the characters and their frozen tableaux is a carefully calculated symbol of their distance from reality, of their disorientation in the world of oneiric imagination, dreams telescoped within dreams, with no beginning and no end, without the boundaries in realistic sequences of Buñuel's embedded surrealistic dream tales. Moreover, in this film, there is no movement backward or forward, in spite of apparent flashbacks; there are only substitutions of a succession of present moments distinct from one another, discrete, which resist the coherence of consecution, creating a planar film text. Resnais and Robbe-Grillet have captured the ontological essence of cinema, beyond linear narration, an oneiric montage of the mind, as Keith Cohen would call it. Yet there is in the sequence of shots in the film a solid narrative structure which unfolds inexorably, almost mechanically, with a perfect modernist formalism of its own, in spite of Allen Thiher's rejection of the term for this film in *The Cinematic Muse*. Roy Armes sees an entropic movement toward closure in the series of choices never coopted by the filmmakers, an inevitability of the final sequences. I see the film rather as a selection of visual and aural patternings that succede one another in jazz or fugue-like fashion, leading arbitrarily to their own end, having, as Sartre said of the jazz theme in *La Nausée*, a sufficient time of their own, not subject to the contingencies of being, or in this case, imitations thereof in art.

The statue group in the garden, an object distinguished like the film itself by the precision of its form and the ambiguity of its identity, generates a narrative in response to the camera's close examination, as the characters invent its past and significance (a depiction of Charles III), playing the same game of hermeneutics the spectators are engaged in. Appropriately and ironically, it was the only object in any of the sets other than A's costumes which was actually made for the movie. Thus the statue is like its narrative a reified illusion; it has no story outside the film, like the characters themselves.

The triangular game of nim which serves as the leitmotiv of the film, which is so apparently aleatory and which is in reality based on specific calculations, offers a model of both the film's structure and its modernist thematic. In the game of its forms, in the rhythm of its images, one can discern a tension between activity, animation, and freezing, petrification, which stands as its own monument to a fundamental truth of real life: the tension between melancholia and creativity, between desire and repulsion, between love and death.

One of the major points of divergence, as noted, between Robbe-Grillet and Resnais was over A's rape scene, intended by Robbe-Grillet, whose works are full of violent crimes, to have graphic aggression, cut by Resnais who preferred the mythical dreamlike symbolic sequence. In her feathered peignoir, A is transformed as she submits to the approach of X in her mirrored bedroom, reversing the male-female roles of the mythical coupling of Leda and the swan, vulnerable yet sensual in her airy, graceful movements. Later in the film, she appears in the garden in the inversion of her previous attire, a black feathered cape. In French, the equation between pen and feather in *plume* offers thus the metaphor of the text, of writing, in black and white, both on film and on the printed page. A is also the return of the mythical-historical figure of Angélique of Robbe-Grillet's autobiographical writing.

The characters in the film seem troubled themselves by the open ambiguity of their story. Like the real-life spectators, they spend their time trying to explain what is happening around them, what has happened before, as they watch twice the play *Rosmer*. The source of the title seems appropriately ambiguous: although seen as an allusion to another theatrical house, Ibsen's *Rosmersholm* (Delphine Seyrig was playing in an Ibsen work in New York when Resnais contacted her about doing the film), it also generates echoes of Eric Rohmer and combines two morphemes representing obsessional themes in both the Ibsen play and Robbe-Grillet's work: *la rose*, the virgin, and *la mère*, the mother.) The triple suicide of the *ménage à trois* in the play equates the fate of the actors we are watching, as well as the death of the traditional film character as we know it. Jeff Kline in *Screening the Text* connects the film to Freudian theories of sexuality based on sexual abuse and incest, using the Ibsen play as a model for the structure of *L'Année dernière à Marienbad* and the struggle for persuasion and dominance between Robbe-Grillet and Resnais. The influence of these constituent elements on the film is persuasive, but it is clouded by the fact that they are in essence primordial and thus inform endless numbers of narrative structures. In fact, the recent American film *Rambling Rose* is another tale of the servant girl hoping to wed the master of the house, driven by the victimizing experience of incest at the hands of her father. The name Rosmer was actually that of Leon Trotsky's lawyer, chosen arbitrarily by the set decorator for the playbill he designed, a perfect reflection of the aleatory nature of modernist New Wave filmmaking.

Regardless of the extent of conscious or unconscious structuring of primal myths in this work, Resnais's and Robbe-Grillet's film is indeed a masterful game between perception or memory and repression or doubt. If the film manages to convey any meaning in the classic sense of the term, it is once again the rejection of the rational scientific positivism driving traditional realist narrative, and the affirmation that each individual perceives and conceptualizes reality differently, reflecting contemporary philosophical pluralism.

This fragmentation of reality is evoked in the film by "flash" sequences of eight images (one-third of a second in length) scattered through the film, by the large number of different shots in the film (336) and by its dramatic sequences of rupture: the rape, the broken glass, the gunshots, the broken balustrade, the broken shoe. This discourse, in the form of discordant and disconnected images, is the film equivalent of the absent "I/Eye" narrator in a novel like *La Jalousie* (translated as *Jealousy*, halving the ambiguous French term also referring to the pattern of light and shadow created by the louvered window or Venetian blind, which opens and closes like the human eye or camera shutter). Moreover, the absence of a specific narrative point of view forces the spectator to construct his own meaning from all these images, from all these "necessary" and not humanly "contingent" objects, which together offer no explanation of present or absent time and place.

The lack of synchronization between the soundtrack and the images in the film is an extension of the contrapuntal play or disjunction between sound and image in *Hiroshima mon amour* and a harbinger of future experimentation, such as the work of Marguerite Duras in films like *Le Camion* (*The Truck*). The scene in the shooting gallery adds to the atmosphere of rupture, of mystery and of danger, offers a cinematic homage to the detective story and film noir, and continues Robbe-Grillet's prior use of classic murder mystery elements in his novels. The plot of the *polar* (*roman policier*—detective novel), with its holes and lack of consequential logic, is the popular culture equivalent, like science fiction, of the New Novel, of the inexplicable in the world and the psyche which unsettles both the reader and the spectator.

The film's lack of closure, generated by its offer of three hypothetical premises as endings never chosen, is its final statement of its own diegetic uncertainty. It is tempting to read into the final scenes an exploded Cinderella myth, as A and X flee the castle at midnight, or as A breaks her shoe in the garden. Then again, Georges Sadoul compares the mythological, fabular nature of the figure of A to

Eurydice, thus including the film in the corpus of reworkings of the Orpheus legend. The labyrinthine nature of the film and sets, itself a citation of Robbe-Grillet's 1959 *Dans le labyrinthe*, evokes other mythical tales of impossible journeys into the netherworld of passion or death and the problematic return of the protagonist.

Thus the final and only truth of this untrustworthy, unverifiable film is its perfect artifice, the essential reality of the creative imagination. It is also a confession of the pure pleasure of exercising this creativity, of playing the game of filmmaking. Roy Armes has delineated the extent of the complexity of the film's mirror structure and symmetrical patterning, an underlying formalism so well imaged by the décor of the interiors, the geometry of the gardens and the mathematical constructs of the nim game. As Resnais said, quoting knowingly or not an old German saying, "Pourquoi faire simple quand on peut faire compliqué?" (Why make it simple when you can make it complicated?).

Notes

1. Alain Robbe-Grillet, *Le Miroir qui revient* (Paris: Editions de Minuit, 1984) 146. ("made of lightness, of absence and of suspense, of being only a tourist." My translation.)

2. Marie-Claire Ropars-Wuilleumier, "Les deux yeux de la chouette. Note sur l'intervalle du cinéma et de la littérature chez Alain Robbe-Grillet," *L'Esprit Créateur* 30:2 (1990) 45. ("The engraving, the drawing, the painting, but also the decor, the set, the window or the city mark the topological rule(r) which permits confrontation with the phantom of the gaze. And the mirror itself would offer the protection of its frame if it didn't bring about, in the form of doubling, the extradition of the eye that reflects itself in the scene, and thus bows to the gaze emanating from sight itself." My translation.)

3. *Miroir* 69. ("revenants and phantoms, in *Last Year at Marienbad*, invade the screen in too obvious a manner." My translation.)

4. *Miroir* 51.

5. *Miroir* 21. ("Characters in novels or films are also kinds of phantoms, heroes so obviously come from the realm of shadows that people *Marienbad*, with their absent, lost, awkward air, as if they were desperately trying to acquire a carnal existence which is denied them or to drag into their quest for the impossible the other, all the others, including the innocent reader [spectator]." My translation.)

Bibliography

Allemand, R.M., and Alain Goulet. *Imaginaire, écritures, lectures de Robbe-Grillet*. Lion-sur-mer: Editions Arcane-Beaunieux, 1991.

———. *Alain Robbe-Grillet*. Paris: Seuil, 1997.

Alter, Jean. *La Vision du monde d'Alain Robbe-Grillet: structures et significations*. Genève: Droz, 1966.

Armes, Roy. *The Cinema of Alain Resnais*. New York: Barnes, 1968.

———. *The Films of Alain Robbe-Grillet*. Amsterdam: John Benjamins, 1981.

———. "Robbe-Grillet, Ricardou and *Last Year at Marienbad*." *Quarterly Review of Film Studies* 5:1 (1980) 1–17.

Beltzer, Thomas. "*Last Year at Marienbad*: An Intertextual Meditation." *Senses of Cinema* 10 (Nov 2000) online.

Blumenberg, Richard. *Manipulation of Time and Space in the Novels of Alain Robbe-Grillet and the Films of Alain Resnais*. Athens, OH: Doctoral Dissertation, Ohio University, 1990.

Brochier, Jean-Jacques. *Alain Robbe-Grillet*. Lyons: La Manufacture, 1985.

Brunius, Jacques. "Every Year in Marienbad." In Bellone, Julius, ed. *The Renaissance of the Film*. New York: Macmillan, 1970.

Caldwell, Roy, Jr. "The Robbe-Grillet Game." *French Review* 65:4 (1992) 547–556.

Château, Dominique, and François Jost. *Nouveau cinéma, nouvelle sémiologie: Essai d'analyse des films d'Alain Robbe-Grillet*. Paris: Union Générale d'Editions, 1979.

Cohen, Keith. *Film and Fiction: the Dynamics of Exchange*. New Haven: Yale University Press, 1979.

—————. "Pleasures of Voicing: Oral Intermittences in Two Films by Alain Resnais." *L'Esprit Créateur* 30:2 (1990) 58–67.

De Ley, Herbert. "The Name of the Game: Applying Game Theory in Literature." *SubStance* 17:1 (1988) 33–46.

Dittmar, Linda. "Structures of Metaphor in Robbe-Grillet's *Last Year at Marienbad*." *Boundary* :3 (1968) 215–221.

Estève, Michel, ed. *Alain Resnais et Alain Robbe-Grillet: Evolution d'une écriture*. Paris: Lettres Modernes, 1974.

Ferua, Pietro. "Marienbad." *Spectrum* 1:3 (1977).

Fletcher, John. *Alain Robbe-Grillet*. New York: Methuen, 1983.

Fragola, Anthony, and Roch Smith. *The Erotic Dream Machine: Interviews with Alain Robbe-Grillet on his Films*. Carbondale: Southern Illinois University Press, 1992.

Gardies, André. *Le Cinéma de Robbe-Grillet: essai sémiocritique*. Paris: Editions Albatros, 1983.

Guppy, Shusha. "Alain Robbe-Grillet: the Art of Fiction." *Paris Review* (Spring 1986) 43–76.

Higgins, Lynn. "Screen/Memory: Rape and Its Alibis in *Last Year at Marienbad*." In Higgins and Silver, eds. *Rape and Representation*. New York: Columbia University Press, 1991.

Jaffé-Freem, Elly. *Alain Robbe-Grillet et la peinture cubiste*. Amsterdam: J. M. Meulenhoff, 1966.

Kaiser, Grant, Majewski, Henry, and Lewis Kamm, eds. *Fiction, Form, Experience: The French Novel from Natualism to the Present*. Montreal: France-Québec, 1976.

Kawin, Bruce. *Mindscreen*. Princeton: Princeton University Press, 1978.

Kirsch, Walter, Jr. "Marienbad Revisited: A Feast for the Senses." *Creative Screenwriting* 3:1 (Summer 1996) 26–30.

Kline, T. Jefferson. *Screening the Text: Intertextuality in New Wave French Cinema*. Baltimore: Johns Hopkins University Press, 1992.

Kriedl, John Francis. *Alain Resnais*. Boston: Twayne, 1977.

Leki, Ilona. *Alain Robbe-Grillet*. Boston: Twayne, 1983.

Mathieu-Kerns, Lyliane. "Black and White as a Symbolic Device: An Approach to Varda's *Cleo from Five to Seven* and Resnais' *Last Year at Marienbad*." In Radcliff-Umstead, Douglas, ed. *Holding the Vision: Essays on Film*. Kent: Kent State University, 1983.

McGlynn, Paul. "*Last Year at Marienbad*: The Aesthetics of 'Perhaps'." *University of Windsor Review* 16:1 (1981) 5–12.

Miller, Lynn. "The Subjective Camera and Staging Psychological Fiction." *Literature in Performance* 2:2 (1982) 35–42.

Monaco, James. *Alain Resnais*. New York: Oxford, 1979.

Morrissette, Bruce. "Games and Game Structures in Robbe-Grillet." *Yale French Studies* 41 (1968) 159–167.

————. *Novel and Film: Essays in Two Genres.* Chicago: University of Chicago Press, 1985.

Nelson, Roy Jay. *Causality and Narrative in French Fiction from Zola to Robbe-Grillet.* Columbus: Ohio State University Press, 1990.

Nerlich, Michael. *Apollon et Dionysos ou la science incertaine des signes: Montaigne, Stendhal, Robbe-Grillet.* Marburg: Hitzeroth, 1989.

Pfeiffer, Jean. "Marienbad et l'être du personnage romanesque." *Obliques* 16–17 (1978) 147–150.

Pingaud, Bernard, ed. *Alain Resnais.* Lyons: Serdoc, 1961.

Prédal, René. *Alain Resnais.* Paris: Lettres Modernes, 1968.

Ramsay, Raylene. *Robbe-Grillet and Modernity. Science, Sexuality and Subversion.* Gainesville: University of Florida Press, 1992.

Ricardou, Jean, ed. *Colloque Robbe-Grillet: Analyse, Théorie.* Paris: Union Générale d'Editions, 1976.

————. *Le Nouveau Roman.* Paris: Seuil, 1973.

Robbe-Grillet, Alain. *L'Année dernière à Marienbad.* Paris: Editions de Minuit, 1961.

————. *Last Year at Marienbad.* New York: Grove, 1962.

————. *Pour un nouveau roman.* Paris: Editions de Minuit, 1963.

Ropars-Wuilleumier, Marie-Claire. *Ecraniques: le film du texte.* Lille: Presses Universitaires de Lille, 1990.

————. "Les deux yeux de la chouette. Note sur l'intervalle du cinéma et de la littérature chez Alain Robbe-Grillet." *L'Esprit Créateur* 30:2 (1990) 38–46.

Shoos, Diane. "Sexual Difference and Enunciation: Resnais's *Last Year at Marienbad.*" *Literature and Psychology* 34:4 (1988) 1–15.

Sipala, Carminella. "*L'Année dernière à Marienbad*: Tempo e racconto." In Bogliolo, Giovanni, ed. *Anacronie: Studi sulla nozione di tempo nel romanzo francese del Novecento.* Fasano: Schena, 1989.

Smith, Roch. "The Image as Generative Narrator in *L'Année dernière à Marienbad* and *L'Immortelle.*" *New Novel Review* 3:2 (Spring 1996) 25–37.

————. *Understanding Robbe-Grillet.* Columbia: University of South Carolina Press, 2000.

Stoltzfus, Ben. *Alain Robbe-Grillet: Life, Work, and Criticism.* Fredericton, N.B.: York Press, 1987.

————. *Alain Robbe-Grillet: The Body of the Text.* Rutherford, N.J.: Fairleigh Dickinson University Press, 1985.

Sweet, Freddy. *The Film Narratives of Alain Resnais.* Ann Arbor: UMI Research Press, 1981.

Szanto, George. *Narrative Consciousness: Structure and Perception in the Fiction of Kafka, Beckett, and Robbe-Grillet.* Austin: University of Texas Press, 1972.

Thiher, Allen. *The Cinematic Muse: Critical Studies in the History of French Cinema.* Columbia: University of Missouri Press, 1979.

Thomas, François. *L'Atelier d'Alain Resnais.* Paris: Flammarion, 1989.

Tomasulo, Frank. "The Intentionality of Consciousness: Subjectivity in Resnais's *Last Year at Marienbad.*" *Post-Script* 7:2 (1988) 58–71.

Van Wert, William. *The Film Career of Alain Robbe-Grillet.* Boston: G. K. Hall, 1977.

————. *The Theory and Practice of the Ciné-Roman.* Blooomington: Indiana University Press, 1975.

Virmaux, Alain and Odette. *Un Genre nouveau: le ciné-roman.* Paris: Edilig, 1982.

Williams, Linda. "*Hiroshima* and *Marienbad*: Metaphor and Metonymy." *Screen* 17:1 (1976) 34–39.

Willoquet-Maricondi, Paula. "*L'Année dernière à Marienbad* and *Cet Obscur Objet du Désir*: The Interpretive Quest." *Romance Languages Annual* 5 (1993) 129–135.

A bout de souffle (Breathless)

directed by Jean-Luc Godard (1960)
screenplay by François Truffaut

In more than four decades as a filmmaker, Jean-Luc Godard, the *enfant terrible* of the *Nouvelle Vague*, has blended an array of literary, political and cinematic allusions into strikingly original, irreverent and often rebellious scenarios. Godard exploits the two-dimensional surface space of the screen as a modernist, using extravagant graphics, icons whose form creates a dynamic tension with the message. *A bout de souffle*, Godard's cynical tribute to Hollywood written with Truffaut, is a citational parodic collage of intertextual literary and filmic allusions, full of homages and injokes.

Born Paris in 1930, Godard returned from Switzerland after the war and evolved at the center of New Wave filmmaking and criticism, contributing his articles, energy and intellect to the *Gazette du Cinéma* and the *Cahiers du Cinéma* until 1959. He collaborated throughout the fifties with Jacques Rivette, Eric Rohmer, François Truffaut, in many short-subject films, first as an actor. After his sudden fame with *A bout de souffle*, he went on to make the censored anticolonial film on Algeria, *Le Petit Soldat*, and *Une Femme est une femme*. A series of collaborative efforts mark his work during the sixties: *La Paresse* (one of the *Sept Péchés capitaux* films, the others by Demy, Chabrol, Molinaro, Vadim, Broca, Dhomme), *Le Nouveau Monde* (the episode *Rogopag*, along with films by Rossellini, Pasolini, Gregoretti), *Les Carabiniers* with Rossellini, *Le Mépris* with Carlo Ponti, *Le Grand Escroc* (one episode of *Les Plus Belles Escroqueries du monde*, the other parts by Chabrol, Polanski, Gregoretti, Horikawa), *Montparnasse et Levallois* (one episode of *Paris vu par—*, the other parts by Chabrol, Douchet, Pollet, Rohmer, Rouch). Then followed his signature films: *Alphaville, Pierrot le Fou, Masculin féminin* (two stories by Maupassant), *Made in USA, Deux ou trois choses que je sais d'elle*, the episodic *Anticipation* and *L'Aller et retour, Weekend, Vent d'Est, Sauve qui peut, Prénom Carmen, Je vous salue Marie*. Godard's work evinces lasting internal collaboration as well, creating a repertory crew in film after film: music by Michel Legrand, cinematography by Raoul Coutard, and Jean-Paul Belmondo and Anna Karina in lead roles. Since the mid 1980s, Godard has pursued a number of projects, including the 1993 *Hélas pour moi*, a pseudoautobiography

JLG/JLG autoportrait de décembre (1995) and numerous segments of *Histoire(s) du cinéma*. Most recently, after a film on the millenium, he offered *Eloge de l'amour* with an expected film-within-the-film mirror and duality. Considered one of the world's greatest (living) filmmakers, Godard continues to explore and exploit the possibilities of cinema.

Godard the revolutionary breaks down traditional roles, barriers and expectations in a Pirandellian manner. Godard the angry activist subverts all topics he touches, not to a personal militant dialectic but to his cerebral capacity to dismantle; gangsters, prostitutes, all the crimes and horrors imaginable, populate a Brechtian godless world where characters wander in an abandoned, disjointed, dematerialized, fragmented universe. Godard has been criticized for his abstraction, his art for art's sake, for selling out to experimental narcissism, but that experimentation and his lucidity in depicting the absurdity of modern reality constitute a search for pure freedom in devising constantly changing forms of expression. His exploration of the limits of cinematic form reflects a consciousness if not conscience in crisis, an amoral nihilism. Godard's films combine a highly original surrealistic montage and diegesis and numerous homages and citations of other texts and films, demonstrating his vast culture and exacting great effort from the spectator.

Godard could be said to be an insightful observer of the aleatory anguish of life. Almost all the relationships between his characters are destructive. Although he explores questions of leftist politics, of commitment, of artistic freedom, his messages are always somehow ambiguous. The Godard of *A bout de souffle* is at the point of departure for forty years of experimentation and exploration of cinematic art. The strain of nihilism in Godard's work, of the angry modernist, goes counter to the creativity of filmmaking, constitutes the triple meaning of the end of *Weekend*, "Fin de cinéma:" the end of this film, the goal of filmmaking and the end of cinema as we know it. Godard's films unsettle and challenge his spectators, countering their expectations and habitual rhythms, fragmenting the reassuring linear coherence of traditional narrative, and denying closure. The positive force of Godard's work is the virtuosity of his ludic disposition of the constituents of cinema, whether sound, image, movement, lighting, musical score, characterization, in sum, his fearless and calculated disregard for cinematic tradition that simultaneously displays intense interest in and commitment to its creative process.

Truffaut's script for *A bout de souffle* was not his first collaboration with Godard on film; they produced a film in 1958 with characters designated only as Lui and Elle, a pronomination repeated the following year by Resnais in *Hiroshima mon amour*. The contemporaneous influence of these filmmakers on one another cannot be overestimated. The intertextual continuity of their own work is equally important; *A bout de souffle* has many elements repeated by Truffaut in *Vivement dimanche*, his other experimental film noir citation at the end of his career. Together the two films reveal the extent and nature of his evolution as a filmmaker.

A bout de souffle begins in the aural mode, with a jazz soundtrack and a black screen, already an allusion to American expatriot music in France. The film has been called a remake of Howard Hawks's 1932 *Scarface* (with Paul Muni, George Raft and Boris Karloff, considered the finest gangster film to come out of Hollywood). Both films were remade in 1983, the same year that Truffaut's nostalgic *Vivement dimanche* appeared. Woven into the citational frame of *A bout de souffle* are countless other allusions and homages, namely to Humphrey Bogart and Raoul Walsh, joined by the implicit reference at the end of the film to *High Sierra*. The opening shot of Michel Poiccard (Jean-Paul Belmondo) hiding behind a newspaper, and slowly lowering the image of the female figure on the side of the paper facing the camera along with the paper, establishes two ideas reworked throughout the film: the role of the printed texts in communicating information, and his relationship to women, betrayer and betrayed. He begins by stealing an American registered and tagged Oldsmobile, dumping his female accomplice, and splitting solo. The tough guy love-em and leave-em image of the *voyou salaud* (nasty bad guy) is continually parodied by Poiccard's baby face, his bad timing, bad luck and cowardice. He comes across more as a splendid, lazy, self-indulgent adolescent, a heroic figure of the counterculture of the ensuing decade.

Poiccard's illicit journey through a classic French landscape mocks the American presence in the film and in France, as well as naive images of France in American films. The Oldsmobile penetrating the landscape like an invasion draws the spectator down the road into the text of the film. Dangling his comically oversized phallic cigarette, Michel breaks up this *locus amoenus* by deliberately alienating and distancing the audience he has just abducted, shouting into the camera, "If you don't like the sea, the mountains, the big cities, get stuffed!" ("Allez vous faire foutre!"). In his second act as a tough guy, he rejects two female hitch-hikers, then in a nihilistic *acte gratuit* aimlessly fires a revolver he finds in the glove compartment, firing off a soliloquy to match. Pursued by motorcycle cops for speeding, he takes off the hot wires, kills a cop, and flees on foot across a field (initiating his role as quarry and prefiguring the final scene). Truffaut has created a breathless character fleeing the fascistic forces of his world, blending Antoine Doinel and stereotypical Hollywood gangsters.

Godard constantly undermines the heroism and heroics of his simulated gangster, trivializing his moves and motives. Belmondo's narcissistic character (with his mirror Cs in the center of his last name, omitted by the critic Dennis Turner) is a distorted parodic pathetic reflection of Bogie, reduced to an echo, as evidenced by the iris out after he stands down his alter image in the Bogart poster. His *minable* (miserable) existence involves trips in and out of hotel rooms, cafés, apartments, several car thefts, a murder and his own violent death. But this is not Al Capone; it is rather an antihero of the post-Beat-generation modernists, alienated, adrift, gratuitous. Godard and Truffaut parody the criminality of their own profession in a conversation between Poiccard and one of his molls, where she talks of working as a scriptgirl in television, and Poiccard claims he was once an assistant film director.

The ludic aleatory nature of Godard's pursuit of his intertextual referentiality, in essence mannerist filmmaking, is embodied in Poiccard's itinerary. Like Godard, he is also fleeing, running from imprisonment, from the past. The film combines arbitrarily characters with names of many nationalities in its cultural self-consciousness. Poiccard entering American Express to ask for M. Tolmatchoff images Cold War France caught between the U.S. and the Soviets. The Italian names and destination of the film are more than fragmented echoes of Capone's mafia in *Scarface*; they also offer an implicit homage to Italian filmmaking, to the *amateur* quality of neorealism.

Jean Seberg's role as Patricia Franchini has become a cinematic icon. Like Godard taking inspiration from his models and then asserting his identity, the film first depicts her selling the Paris edition of *The Herald Tribune* and then shows a French girl hawking the *Cahiers du Cinéma*, the theoretical heartbeat of the New Wave. Begging Patricia to go to Italy with him, Poiccard explains that he is in danger. When he finds no horoscope in her paper for him, he reads it as an omen that he has no future, a nihilist parody but also a comment on a particular style of French filmmaking. The attraction to America is embodied in Poiccard's attempts to seduce and abduct Patricia. Accompanying the jazz soundtrack is an ad for Jeff Chandler and Jack Palance in *Vivre dangereusement jusqu'au bout* (to live danger-ously to the end), a summary of the plot of *A bout de souffle* and another allusion to the numbers of commercial American films shown in Paris as part of the Marshall Plan, on the Champs-Elysées during the 1950s.

The oneiric quality of the arbitrary violence erupting in Godard's films is especially well illustrated by the next shot, where suddenly a man is hit by a car. Michel who began the film hiding behind a newspaper is now reflected in it, as he is in the Bogart poster, in an article wherein the other motorcycle cop has identified him as his partner's killer, stating that he is already condemned to die (for previous crimes, but also as an existential hero). Michel will never make contact with his true self, only his reflection in the glass covering the poster for Humphrey Bogart in *Plus dure sera la chute* (*The Harder They Fall*).

When Michel finally reaches Tolmatchoff, they joke about "mieux rouillé que dérouillé" (better bored than beat up, a pun on better red than dead), one of many inside gags and puns, none of which the outsider American Patricia understands. In a call to a certain Antonio Berruti about money he is owed, Michel gives the phone number as *nonante-neuf huitante-quatre*, a nod to Godard's Swiss French upbring-ing in Lausanne. Godard makes another playful reference to his own origins when Poiccard decries to Patricia the exaggerated reputation of Swedish women, stating that the prettiest girls come from Lausanne and Geneva. Poiccard's name is a mask like the film; his "real" name is an homage to the Hollywood cinematographer Laszlo Kovacs. Raoul Coutard's cinematography is central to the significance of this self-conscious film, with its slow iris out after the Poiccard-Bogart encounter and expressionistic contrastive lighting. Many shots white out, a cinematic homage that is also an emblem of both intensity and nothingness, prefiguring death.

The long sequence of Michel and Patricia in her bedroom contains a series of reflective idioms: the grimaces they imitate, their cigarettes, the pornography magazine and their sexuality, Patricia's reflection in the mirror as she announces her pregnancy (a visceral reflection in itself), Michel's comments on the reflection in Patricia's eyes which stimulates his desire, the Picasso of Romeo and Juliet, the Renoir portrait, the Matisse above the bed. They are added to this gallery of portraits, frozen in their indecisiveness. There is an implicit homage to Jean Renoir when Patricia focuses on Michel through the rolled Renoir poster, imitating the telescope or the camera lens (just after she discovers his passport in the name of Laszlo Kovacs).

The scene also abounds with gestures of mock violence: Michel's stranglehold on Patricia, her slaps, their insults, Michel's contention that he could have been a great boxer (an allusion to Marlon Brando in *On the Waterfront* and by extension through the setting to *Streetcar Named Desire*). These gestures constitute a *mise-en-abyme* of the film, with its "real" violence which is also artificial and gratuitous.

The realistic minute details of their conversation in this closed environment stand in contrast to the techniques of commercial film melodrama, with its very different semiosis of *ennui* and *angst*. The claustrophobic setting and paralysis recall the diegesis of Beckett's *En Attendant Godot* (*Waiting for Godot*). The disjointed conversation also recalls the other Lui and Elle, from the previous year, in Resnais's *Hiroshima mon amour*. Their affective impasse and the barriers of incommunicability determining their loneliness are classic themes of the era, united in the quote from William Faulkner's *The Wild Palms*: "between grief and nothing I will take grief." The nihilist Michel, predicting his own fate, choses nothingness, calling grief a compromise.

The counterpoint between them stamps the whole film, with its tragicomic contrasts. They are also set off against the series of cultural intertexts, of the references to films, novels (real and invented: *The Wild Palms*, Dylan Thomas's *Portrait of the Artist as a Young Dog*, *Candida*), paintings, and against contemporary political events, the radio program on de Gaulle and his later motorcade down the Champs-Elysées. None of these references has meaning for the film; they stand as images, as icons, unintegrated in the primary nihilist diegetic.

Further parody of Hollywood and commercial filmmaking is achieved by a cut from a close-up of Michel and Patricia kissing to shots of the Louvre and Notre Dame, icons of bourgeois romances set in Paris. The shots of landmarks also echo Truffaut's signature use of the Eiffel Tower in *Les Quatre Cents Coups* the year before. Another car theft involves an American icon of the day, a Thunderbird convertible, symbol of power, mobility and luxury. Traversing the landscape of Paris, worrying about his survival, Poiccard is now reflected on the cover of *France Soir* as his fame grows. When he is recognized by a journalist, the camera irising out announces his imminent extinction.

An equation is made between filmmaking and auteur textual authorship during the interview sequence with the imaginary filmmaker, Parvulesco (played by the director Jean-Pierre Melville), who like the journalist Patricia has been writing a novel, entitled *Candida*. Continuing Truffaut's image, the Raoul Walsh persona digresses on women, love, Rainer Maria Rilke, comparing American and French women, acknowledging the dominance of men, money and power. Questions comparing love and eroticism lead to a reference to Cocteau's *Testament d'Orphée*, which Truffaut was financing at the time. Parvulesco declares his hatred of nine-teenth-century Romantic music, Brahms and Chopin, another rejection of cultural dominance, coupled ironically with his confession of his own ambition to become part of the canon. Anticipating the relationship between women and the camera in years to come, Patricia stares down the camera with her gaze (an existential metaphor for power and control of identity and the female returning the dominant male gaze).

Although Michel turns the car over to a junkyard as planned, he receives no money, thus failing to grasp women, money or power throughout the film. His failures are more than a parody of the value system of commercial bourgeois filmmaking; they represent a rejection of the entire right-wing social structure. As he and Patricia cross Paris in a taxi, Michel complains of the new buildings ruining the city, echoing a major leftist criticism of the French government's capitalist devel-opment, also heard in *Sartre par lui-même*. Disempowered as a passenger, Poiccard now tells the taxi driver how to drive, then escapes through the window to pursue Berruti, and again, on a bet from Patricia, to childishly lift a girl's skirt. They go underground literally, walking through a tunnel passage to the Champs-Elysées, where the background is de Gaulle's motorcade. Their covert passage is emblematic of the undercurrent of rebellion in Paris intellectuals of the day.

A major dramatic irony is established when Patricia expresses admiration for a girl Michel describes who remained loyal to her lover after discovering the truth about him, just before Patricia betrays Michel to the police. Trapped by the cops at the office of *The Herald Tribune*, she is forced to cooperate with them when they threaten to take away her work permit and passport. In a sequence repeated in Truffaut's *Baisers volés*, Michel follows the cop who is tailing Patricia, who, to the strains of "The Marseillaise," escapes into a movie theater to an American movie, then joins Michel at a western. The counterpoint in this scene is redolent of the fair scene in Flaubert's *Madame Bovary*, with their embraces and quotes of Aragon and Apollinaire set off against the soundtrack of the western.

They are again reflected in the press, in an article revealing that Michel is already married, against the backdrop of another tourist cliché: the Place de la Concorde at night. What Truffaut and Godard try but fail to achieve in their parodies is the French equivalent of the Hollywood mythology of America.

The next car stolen in this episodic series of repetitions is a Cadillac Eldorado convertible. Godard here puts his graffiti signature on the film with a lighted moving sign announcing that Michel's arrest is imminent. In a sequence of sexual exploita-tion, Berruti and another crook, Karl Zumback, are running a porn extorsion sting, and Patricia drops her American boyfriend, anticipating her final betrayal of Michel and announcing Godard's artistic intentions, apparent in the the later *Pierrot le fou*. Michel hides at the apartment of a photographer's model, another woman before the camera, who goes out for the evening with just a bikini under a trenchcoat, a setup that Truffaut used again in *Vivement dimanche*. More dominant cultural icons in counterpoint include a Mozart clarinet concerto and the cover of Maurice Sachs's *Abracadabra* with Lenin's phrase "Nous sommes tous des morts en permission," (we're all dead men on leave), a multiple allusion to the magic of cinematic writing and text and Marxist political dialectic. Both Marie-Claire Ropars-Wuilleumier and Jeff Kline have written extensively on the significance of this title with its ABCs of cinema.

Patricia now turns on Michel and betrays him, as the travelling camera follows her closing in, circling around her victim while they continue a sustained contrapuntal dialogic on love. Now refusing to continue running like a *salaud* and a *lâche* (coward), Michel assumes his heroic suicidal confrontational stance, refusing money or escape, and going to meet his destiny in a classic Hollywood *High Noon* showdown ending. He is trapped not by his love for Patricia but by Godard and Truffaut's experimental script, wherein they have combined in ludic chaos parodies of the clichés of American gangster and western melodramas.

Once outdoors, Michel is shot and stumbles down the rue Campagne-Première, as Patricia pursues him unscathed and invulnerable. Fatally wounded, Michel dances down the street to a jazz theme of death. After he falls, he makes three grimaces at her, utters the condemning "Tu es vraiment dégueulasse" (you really stink) and dies, closing his own eyes with his left hand, in a parody of the death of Roy Earle (Humphrey Bogart) at the end of Raoul Walsh's *High Sierra* (1941). Patricia's query to the camera, "What does that mean?" echoes Ida Lupino's ending question, "What does it mean when a man crashes out?" All the play in this film with artistic models and influences indicates Truffaut's and Godard's childlike fascination, authority anxiety and rebellious tendencies. If Michel's last utterance is an acknowledgement of Hollywood's achievements and influence, it is also a rejection of American commercialism, just as Patricia's uncomprehending confusion is a stab at American cultural naïveté. What Godard and Truffaut have destroyed is the same thing lost in Jim McBride's disastrous cross-cultural remake of *Breathless*: the primary significance of the film for its makers and its audience. Just as the ethos of the American West has no meaning for the French, the legend of Al Capone is reduced to nominal fragments (Franchini, Berruti) and the desire to escape to Italy. It is not until 1992 that the escapist film declares its own generic identity, with the epilogue of Gabriele Salvatores's *Mediterraneo*: "This film is dedicated to all those who are running away."

Bibliography

Andrew, Dudley. "Au début du souffle: le culte et la culture d'*A bout de souffle*." *Revue Belge du Cinéma* (1986) 11–21.

———, ed. *Breathless*. New Brunswick: Rutgers University Press, 1987.

Aumont, Jacques. "Godard: The View and the Voice." *Discourse* 7 (1985) 42–65.

Barr, Charles, and Ian Cameron, eds. *The Films of Jean-Luc Godard.* New York: Praeger, 1970.

Bergale, Alain, ed. *Jean-Luc Godard par Jean-Luc Godard.* Paris: Editions de l'Etoile, 1985.

Brown, Royal, ed. *Focus on Godard.* Englewood Cliffs, N.J.: Prentice Hall, 1971.

Busto, Daniel, and Jean-Marie Touratier. *Jean Luc Godard: télévision/écritures.* Paris: Galilée, 1979.

Dawson, Jonathan. "*A bout de souffle.*" *Senses of Cinema* 19 (Mar–Apr 2002) online.

Dixon, Wheeler. *The Films of Jean-Luc Godard.* Albany, NY: State University of New York Press, 1997.

Falkenberg, Pamela. "'Hollywood' and the 'Art cinema' as a Bipolar Modeling System: *A bout de souffle* and *Breathless.*" *Wide Angle* 7:3 (1985) 44–53.

Flambard-Weisbart, Véronique. "La Relation ambivalente à l'autre dans *A bout de souffle* de Jean-Luc Godard." *Romance Languages Annual* 7 (1995) 56–59.

Fontanille, Jacques. *Sémiotique du visible: des mondes de lumière.* Paris: Presses Universitaires de France, 1995.

Jean-Luc Godard: au-delà du récit. Etudes cinématographiques 57–61 (1967). Entire issue.

Kline, T. Jefferson. "The ABC's of Godard's Quotations: *A bout de souffle* with *Pierrot le fou.*" In *Screening the Text: Intertextuality in New Wave French Cinema.* Baltimore: Johns Hopkins University Press, 1992. 184–221.

Lefèvre, Raymond. *Jean-Luc Godard.* Paris: Edilig, 1983.

Lesage, Julia. *Jean-Luc Godard: A Guide to References and Resources.* Boston: G. K. Hall, 1979.

Lev, Peter. "Godard's 'Cruel Muse'." *Literature/Film Quarterly* 26:1 (1998) 76–78.

MacBean, James Roy. *Film and Revolution.* Bloomington: Indiana University Press, 1975.

MacCabe, Colin, Mick Eaton and Laura Mulvey. *Godard: Images, Sounds, Politics.* Bloomington: Indiana University Press, 1980.

Marie, Michel. "'It really makes you sick!': Jean-Luc Godard's *A bout de souffle* (1959)." In Hayward, Susan, and Ginette Vincendeau, eds. *French Film: Texts and Contexts.* New York: Routledge, 2000.

Milne, Tom, and Jean Narboni. *Godard on Godard: Critical Writings by Jean-Luc Godard.* New York: Da Capo, 1986.

Mussman, Toby, ed. *Jean-Luc Godard: A Critical Anthology.* New York: Dutton, 1968.

On the Films of Jean-Luc Godard. Wide Angle 1:3 (1976).

Prédal, René, ed. *Le Cinéma selon Godard. CinémAction* 52 (1989).

Radcliff-Umstead, Douglas. "France and America: The Fatal Affair in Godard's *Breathless.*" In Radcliff-Umstead, Douglas, ed. *Sex and Love in Motion Pictures.* Kent, OH: Kent State University, 1984.

————. "The Color of Violence." In *Crime in Motion Pictures.* Kent, OH: Kent State University, 1986.

Raskin, Richard. "Five Explanations for the Jump Cuts in Godard's *Breathless.*" *pov* 6 (Dec1998) 141–153.

Ropars-Wuilleumier, Marie-Claire. "La Forme et le fond ou les avatars du récit." In *L'Ecran de la mémoire.* Paris: Seuil, 1970.

————. "The Graphic in Film Writing: *A bout de souffle* or the Erratic Alphabet." *Enclitic* 5–6:1–2 (1981–1982) 147–161.

————. "L'Instance graphique dans l'écriture du film: *A bout de souffle,* ou l'alphabet erratique." *Littérature* 46 (1982) 59–81.

Roud, Richard. *Jean-Luc Godard.* London: Thames & Hudson, 1970.

Selous, Trista. "Death of a Hero, Birth of a Cinema: Or, Who or What is *A bout de souffle?*" *Esprit Créateur* 35:4 (Winter 1995) 18–27.

Smith, Steve. "Godard and film noir: A Reading of *A bout de souffle.*" *Nottingham French Studies* 32:1 (Spring 1993) 65–73.

Temple, Michael. "The Nutty Professor: Teaching Film with Jean-Luc Godard." *Screen* 40:3 (Autumn, 1999) 323–330.

Thomson, David. "That Breathless Moment." *Sight and Sound* 10:7 (Jul 2000) 28–31.

Turner, Dennis. "*Breathless*: Mirror Stage of the Nouvelle Vague." *SubStance* 12:4/41 (1983) 50–63.

Wills, David. "The French Remark: *Breathless* and Cinematic Citationality." In Horton, McDougal, and Braudy. *Play it Again, Sam: Retakes on Remakes.* Berkeley, CA: University of California Press, 1998.

Vivement dimanche
(*Confidentially Yours*)

directed by François Truffaut (1983)
from *The Long Saturday Night* by Charles Williams

Much has been said about the role of his unhappy childhood in shaping the life and career of François Truffaut (1932–1984), *auteur* "novelist" screenwriter and filmmaker of the New Wave. Certainly much of his cinematic creativity, beginning with the landmark 1959 *Les Quatre Cents Coups* and echoed in the later *Argent de poche* and the unfinished *La Petite Voleuse*, which he called the "female *400 Blows*," was generated by his experience. Truffaut fled his alienated adolescence into the movies, hanging around the Parisian *ciné-clubs* of the late 1940s. Meeting André Bazin literally changed his life, as he was freed from jail for debts, and later from the army, through Bazin's efforts. Truffaut became editor of the critical journal *Arts* before collaborating with Godard, Rivette and Rohmer on the *Cahiers du Cinéma*. His début as a movie critic gained him instant notoriety; he lambasted bourgeois commercial cinema and became the premier spokesperson of the *Nouvelle Vague*. He made two experimental shorts, *Une Visite* et *Les Mistons*, before the 1959 *Les Quatre Cents Coups* (Grand Prix, Cannes Film Festival) catapulted him to international acclaim. From then until his death he made about a film a year: *Tirez sur le pianiste* (*Shoot the Piano Player*), *Jules et Jim* (*Jules and Jim*), *L'Amour à vingt ans* (*Love at 20*), *La Peau Douce* (*Soft Skin*), *Fahrenheit 451*, *La Mariée était en noir* (*The Bride Wore Black*), *Baisers volés* (*Stolen Kisses*), *La Sirène du Mississippi* (*Mississippi Mermaid*), *L'Enfant sauvage* (*The Wild Child*), *Domicile conjugal* (*Bed and Board*), *Les Deux Anglaises et le continent* (*Two English Girls*), *Une Belle Fille comme moi* (*Such a Georgeous Kid Like Me*), *La Nuit américaine* (*Day for Night*), *L'Histoire d'Adèle H.* (*The Story of Adèle H.*), *L'Argent de poche* (*Small Change*), *L'Homme qui aimait les femmes* (*The Man Who Loved Women*), *La Chambre verte* (*The Green Room*), *L'Amour en fuite* (*Love on the Run*), *Le Dernier Métro* (*The Last Metro*), *La Femme d'à côté* (*The Woman Next Door*), *Vivement dimanche* (*Confidentially Yours*), *La Petite Voleuse* (*The Little Thief*, finished by Claude Miller).

Analyzing Truffaut's *oeuvre*, his cinematic novel, involves recreating his life as filmmaker, actor, critic, screenwriter, a life of, by, and for the movies. Among his most autobiographical works are the five Antoine Doinel films, studies of three of which follow. However, all his films constitute such immediate personal expression of his creative identity, with infinite screen transpositions of personal desires, fears and obsessions, that his work as a whole constitutes a quarter century of intertextual autobiographic portrayal, like that of his idol Jean Cocteau. In his acting career, Truffaut incarnated the gamut of his own professional virtuosity, playing a journalist, a doctor, a writer, a technical advisor, a filmmaker. His *oeuvre* also offers an intertextuality with the illusion of reality that recalls Balzac, Truffaut's favorite writer, whose texts are depicted in the Doinel films. As with other filmmakers studied here, the books that characters read in movies are, unless satiric symbols, inevitably artistic models of the films themselves.

The confusion between the illusion of reality and the reality of illusion in Truffaut's films derives from the real-life intensity of his imagination, which was so volatile that he preferred to work from an open text, without a finished polished script. The script thus became the sketch, the draft, which Truffaut reworked into the final edited film text. Often he and Suzanne Schiffman, his scriptgirl for almost all his films, were the only people who knew where a film was headed. Frequently, the film's dialogue was in Truffaut's head. He preferred to shoot outdoors, on location, in authentic settings, without artifice (hence the irony of the title of *La Nuit américaine*), but at the same time he idolized filmmakers like Hitchcock, Renoir, Resnais, and his films are loaded with homages to their works, as well as references to his own previous work. This self-reflexive intertextual quality of his films gives them an artistic opacity that is often belied by his conventional filmmaking techniques and their illusion of realistic transparency. Truffaut espoused Resnais's goal of making simplicity complicated.

Truffaut's fascination with Hitchcock produced not only critical books on his work but infuses many of his films, in particular his last completed film, *Vivement dimanche*, a collage of homages to American film noir gangster films of the thirties, forties and fifties. *Vivement dimanche*, while ostensibly a film adaptation of *The Long Saturday Night*, actually uses Williams's potboiler as a point of departure, as much of the original text proved unfilmable. Truffaut had already used this technique in *Tirez sur le pianiste* in adapting David Goodis's gangster novel to the screen, imposing formal constraints on his work which he compared to those of a Perrault fairy tale.

The leading roles of the boss-secretary couple become detectives in spite of themselves, who resist each other and spar constantly, recall several classic matches in Hollywood cinema: Bogart-Bacall, Myrna Loy-William Powell (the Thin Man series), Tracey-Hepburn, couples who have also inspired American remakes and derivatives, such as *Absence of Malice* (Field-Newman) and *Legal Eagles* (Redford-Winger), even *Superman*. Truffaut's return to black and white, while a necessary part of his homage, also enabled him and Nestor Almendros to create intimate effects of light and shadow which constitute an extension of the nuances of *grisaille* in many of their color films. He also returns to the original black and white of *Les Quatre Cents Coups*, that he later historicized in faux documentary framed sepia sequences in *L'Amour en fuite*.

In more than one way, Truffaut could be considered to be the Woody Allen of French cinema, full of complexes, a film addict, a revolutionary filmmaker of protean genius, comic, delicate and crazy at the same time, always focused on the individual, even in a group, on the solitude beneath all the attempts to establish contact with the other, attracted successively by all the actresses he directed, and finally drawn to depicting his personal identity and the experience of filmmaking. For both these filmmakers, but especially for Truffaut, originality and virtuosity mark their entire opus, a strange admixture of technical expertise and ingenuous lyricism.

Truffaut embodies the term *"auteur"* filmmaker in several ways: first, in the originality of his production, which, in spite of its thematic variety, always carries his distinctive mark; secondly, because of his original film writing, especially *"la politique des auteurs;"* and lastly, because of the everpresent images in his film of literature, of writing, of writers, of texts. In fact, he planned to make thirty films and then spend the rest of his life writing. His untimely death from an inoperable brain tumor extinguished a luminous spirit at the height of its creative powers.

With *Vivement dimanche* Truffaut returned to black and white with the nostalgic project of filming an American detective story, Charles Williams's *The Long Saturday Night*. In spite of Truffaut's lifelong attachment to classic literary and film artists (Balzac, James, Renoir, Hitchcock), he expressed sympathetic interest in and respect for the lives and work of popular culture writers and filmmakers. The fact that Charles Williams committed suicide and died an unknown added to Truffaut's sympathy for his source. However, the structure of Williams's book forced Truffaut to invent the entire center section of the film. In so doing, he turned to other models as well, generating a collage of detective-story filmmaking. Jean-Louis Trintignant, working for the first time with Truffaut, plays the real estate agent Julien Vercel, the older boss of the vivacious secretary Barbara Becker, played by Truffaut's wife Fanny Ardant, whose role in *La Femme d'à côté* inspired Truffaut to make a film noir spoof.

The plot is a classic: Vercel is framed for a double murder, first his wife's lover Massoulier and then his wife, Marie-Christine. He must lie low literally in their underground office while Barbara tracks down the real killer. Truffaut assembles his film family again: Nestor Almendros, Georges Delerue, Suzanne Schiffman, Jean Aurel. The outsider non-professional investigator or the innocent accused and his feisty sidekick belong as I mentioned to a classic Hollywood film tradition. In this case, they work first against and then with both a private detective (Lablache) and the police (Santelli). The identity of the killer is properly concealed by a clever series of false leads, suspects and shady characters.

The opening shot of Fanny Ardant walking down the street behind the credits is accompanied by a lilting melodious theme song by Delerue. The first sequence of the film is shot in a marsh where Vercel is also shooting, duckhunting with a shotgun. Interspersed are film shots and gunshots of two other hunters. We see only the lower half of the body of the third man as he shoots the second hunter point blank in the face. As Vercel walks out past the dead hunter's abandoned Porsche 911, he stops to close the door and turn off the lights.

The film cuts back to Barbara Becker walking down the street, pursued by a handsome blond man whom she fends off with a light touch. At the office, Vercel's shrewish wife calls to demand that Barbara withdraw money for her and send it to Room 813 (mistakenly transcribed as 183 in one set of subtitles) at the Hotel Garibaldi in Nice. Barbara is perplexed by the fact that she hears trumpets in the background, which she tells Vercel, who proceeds to fire her for talking rudely to his wife. At this point, the police commissioner Santelli and detective Jambrau burst in to question Vercel about the murder of the hunter Massoulier, whose brother Claude is a priest.

In one of several narrative inconsistencies in the film, Barbara leaves the office putting on her suit jacket but already has it belted in the next shot. These moments so characteristic of New Wave filmmaking actually add to the effectiveness of the film, creating doubt and uncertainty in the mind of the spectator. The film was also shot not only in black and white but largely in the dark, with a lot of expressionist spot lighting.

At this point, Vercel receives the first of several anonymous phone calls accusing him of killing Massoulier. As if to agree, the lighting, camera angles and music all turn sinister. The suspicion of Vercel's guilt continues until the *dénouement*, even beyond all reasonable doubt and character definition. Truffaut adds other film noir touches, such as the iron gate across the front of the office and a shot of the phone ringing in the dark. He also uses forties-style typewriters and phones and costumes for effect, even though the film is obviously shot in the 1980s (cars, etc.). A second anonymous phone call castigates Vercel's wife, who has supposedly had lots of lovers and even stolen their wedding silver.

A major subplot is introduced by a cut to a play within the film, an amateur production of a ridiculous medieval farce, starring both Barbara and her exhusband Bertrand. The play is not thematically a *mise-en-abyme* of the movie itself, but rather the comic interval style of *divertissement* which Renoir so often used. And it sets up the sequence of Barbara in costume playing detective in Vercel's trenchcoat, a clever literal layering of her assumed roles.

As Vercel's wife returns home attired in a leopard coat and carrying a leather suitcase, again pure forties style, she is observed by a man with his right arm in a sling, who is ostensibly walking his dog, but who spies in voyeur fashion through the window on Vercel and his wife arguing, transferring to his character the role of the camera. The wife admits that Massoulier was her lover, but declares that she no longer has feelings for him. In her old style armchair is an interesting anachronism, a patchwork pillow which should stand for antique but which was actually the latest chic in France in 1983. As a furious Vercel proposes divorce, his wife tries to seduce him. She runs upstairs to hide when the doorbell rings, inadvertently leaving her suitcase in the front hall as a clue. The next sequence of Vercel being interrogated at the police station is the first of three scenes set there, actually shot in a kitchen, giving an antiseptic look to the set. Vercel is told that Massoulier was shot by number six cartridges, which supposedly only Vercel in town used (the film is set in Hyères). He is accompanied by his lawyer, Maître Clément. Vercel has been accused in yet another anonymous phone call, all from a woman. These calls stand in counterpoint to the series of anonymous phone calls which the real killer makes to the Lablache detective agency.

In the second of many comic sequences spoofing the film itself, an Albanian political refugee interrupts Vercel's interrogation, wanting asylum. We also learn that Bertrand is a news photographer for *Le Provençal*; he turns up repeatedly as another characterization of filmmaking. As Clément drives Vercel home, he discourages him from filing for divorce under the circumstances and then drops him off, all in the same Volvo stationwagon that was parked next to Massoulier's Porsche if you are paying attention.

Back at the theater, as Barbara is waiting to go on, Vercel comes to find her. In an ironic amusing cut, the actors repeat Barbara's entrance cue while she drives away with him. As they arrive at the office, there is another moment of uncertainty in the filming, as you can see bright sunshine through the rain machine effects, a technical inconsistency typical of New Wave filmmaking which also harkens back to early Hollywood films. Once again the office is dark. Vercel is headed for Nice to find someone, announcing that his wife has been murdered at their house (hence by transposition for Truffaut a murdered mother figure), and that he lied to his lawyer, saying that she had not returned home. Truffaut repeats the scene of Vercel returning to the house with Clément, this time finishing the sequence (a technique used often), as he finds the house ransacked and his wife dead, her body seen first in a mirror. She has been shot in the head, sometime between seven and midnight.

At the office, when Vercel falls asleep from exhaustion, Barbara decides to go to Nice in his place. She takes his wallet and gun, puts his overcoat on over her costume, then repents and leaves the gun on a shelf. She drives to Nice in his Renault stationwagon in the pouring rain, with lyric sad music, and leaves the car at the airport police station, taking a taxi into town. On the picture of Vercel and his wife is her former business address, 57 rue des Entrepreneurs, for the beauty salon. What Barbara finds is a red light district with a tough nightclub, L'Ange Rouge, Truffaut's cinematic tribute to the von Sternberg classic *L'Ange bleu* (*The Blue Angel*). Building suspense, the taxi driver explains that the club is run by Louison, a terrifying character. As Barbara checks into the hotel, there is even a sinister poetic type in the elevator, in full evening dress, with a bra sticking out of his pocket. This is another of many comic touches which play with the generic parameters of film noir.

The maid is cleaning 813 where Madame Vercel spent the previous night. When a prostitute from across the hall distracts the maid by asking to borrow her costume, Barbara finds a note that says "Mon Amour / Le Capitaine." Not only does the strange man from the elevator prowl down the hall, but another unidentified man forces his way into the room while Barbara is asleep. When she tears off part of his coat in a struggle, she finds the name of the Lablache private detective agency in his wallet. As Marie-Christine's dead body is dramatically carried from the Vercel home, Barbara, still in Nice, bursts in on Lablache, who explains that his client dealt by phone and remained anonymous. As Barbara waits for her bus back to Marseilles, she hears trumpets and over the fence sees the horses Mon Amour and Le Capitaine in a race. She calls Lablache with the information, from the same phone booth Madame Vercel used at the beginning of the film. Thus Barbara is not only in Vercel's clothes, but having slept in his wife's (hotel) bed, she usurps another function, of the phone caller, all prefiguring her final image as Vercel's wife.

Exploiting the unexpected, Truffaut has Barbara collect a resounding slap from Vercel on her return to the office. She accuses him of being the killer, and he plays along. Bertrand reappears, taking pictures of their agency and accusing her of sleeping with Vercel, another prefiguration of subsequent events. After some small talk about coffee, Vercel and Barbara finally become conspirators working together, as they both get on the phone, to listen to the same anonymous woman. A mysterious stranger wearing hiking boots comes into the office inquiring about a château for a summer camp; he is in fact Massoulier's brother. We learn that Vercel's wife was using an alias, that she was in fact a prostitute named Josiane Kerbel, running a beauty parlor as a front. In another comic touch, Vercel reveals his vulnerability to women as he admires the legs of the women passing on the sidewalk, becoming in turn a voyeur through the ground-level window of his office.

Finally dressed normally, Barbara pays a visit to the lawyer Clément. She overhears and sees a hysterical client complaining about a scandal, to which Clément replies, "Life is not a novel." Barbara is grabbed by the cop Santelli as she is leaving Clément's office. During her interrogation at the police station occurs the gag of the broken faucet. After another heated exchange with Vercel, Barbara calls the Cinéma Eden (the name is a tribute to Duras's *Un Barrage contre le Pacifique*, hence Paula Delbèque becomes another murdered mother figure), which is playing Kubrick's *Paths of Glory* (another Truffaut tribute), and together they recognize the voice as that of the anonymous woman caller. When she gets to the theater, Barbara realizes that the woman is Clément's hysterical client. The camera lingers on a poster for the film *Le Convoi de la peur*, an allusion to the 1977 American remake of Clouzot's *Le Salaire de la peur?* Truffaut admired Clouzot and his confrontational cinema. Barbara recognizes the man at the cinema as the same from the Ange Rouge in Nice, and follows him as he escorts the woman home, then enters another Ange Rouge brothel nightclub. In another light touch, when a john approaches her on the street and asks "C'est combien?," she replies with the time. Barbara calls from a payphone to explain the setup to Vercel. Pay phones are key characters in the film, especially in the final sequence. And all these phone calls give Truffaut a chance to summarize the events for the spectator. It is also a fidelity to Williams's text which is all second-hand hearsay, phone calls and telexes. As the cinema woman meets the mystery man, he gives her a key and she enters an apartment building. Barbara copies the names from the building directory.

In a reprise of the amateur theater production rehearsal sequence, Bertand complains to Barbara that his girlfriend has left him because she realized that he was still in love with Barbara. They have found a stand in for Barbara who is awful, a parody of a parody. Barbara sneaks out, stealing Bertrand's company car, and returns to Vercel with the information that the cinema cashier is named Paula Delbèque. As she leaves to pursue this trail, Vercel stows away in the back seat of the newspaper's Citroën. We learn that Paula was also Massoulier's mistress, and Vercel goes off to search her apartment for clues. When the mystery man enters the same building, Barbara follows, and she and Vercel subdue him in a struggle in the apartment. In fact, she knocks him out with a statue of the Eiffel Tower, the signature symbol in all of Truffaut's Paris films. She calls the police to the apartment and when the car won't start, grabs Vercel and kisses him in a doorway to conceal his identity, because she "saw it in a movie." This leads to a lyric interlude above the city where they gaze out over the lights and muse over the impact of death, as Vercel says in a metatextual and for Truffaut autobiographical monologue that death from illness is real, but being murdered is like fiction, an abstraction. They are dwarfed by the mass of humanity stretching out below, and Julien gives Barbara an embrace.

The next day, Barbara attends Massoulier's funeral, where Paula angrily removes the Ange Rouge flowers from the coffin. The mystery man is revealed to be Massoulier's brother Claude, who says the mass. After a comic sequence of a blonde bimbo applying for Barbara's job, Barbara gets an anonymous letter telling her to mind her own business. Having worked out that the theater is a front for the ugly prostitution gambling ring of the Ange Rouge (a mimesis of the duplicity of the film itself), the intrepid Barbara goes off to play a whore, with a slit black skirt and her sweater knotted up. She gets herself escorted to Louison, where the everpresent Bertrand is taking publicity photos, become a symbol of the camera recording events which are edited into the film narrative. Intimidated by the fact that Louison is the curly burly villain, Barbara escapes to the ladies' room. She and we can't see the man who enters, struggles with Louison for some letters, and murders him with a knife. Louison dying tells Barbara to warn Paula. When Barbara returns to Clément's office still dressed as a whore, she sees the sign for Marie-Christine's beauty salon next door and finally cracks open literally the mystery, as his bookcase revolves between the two offices.

Barbara is too late to save Paula, who enters the movie theater, where the sounds of the film cover her screams when she is knifed to death. Because the police are closing in, Vercel plans to run off to Clément's house, at which point Barbara confesses her love for him, and they spend the night together in the office. Commenting that being in love makes you feel like an idiot, echoing the aphorism from *L'Amour en fuite*, Barbara gives the title line of the film, saying she can't wait for Sunday, when they will supposedly escape. Vercel thinks he has been betrayed when the cops burst in to arrest him and thank Barbara for her cooperation.

In the final sequence at the police station, we learn that Vercel's wife was already married, to a Belgian trainer, and that when he landed in jail, she ran off with another man who died on the highway, a sordid story. Clément is undone by Barbara's announcement that she has the envelope someone typed and used to send instructions to Lablache. As Clément leaves to phone Lablache one last time, Barbara reveals her discovery in Clément's office, and Truffaut runs the sequence again, this time to its completion, using again the cumulative flashback technique. Clément out at the phone booth, unable to bribe Lablache, confesses that he had a fatal weakness for women, whom he felt were magic (the answer to Alphonse's query in *La Nuit américaine*). He says there will be another dead body and shoots himself as the cops close in.

The film cuts with sharp contrast to its final very positive sequence, a choir of children singing, two rings on a plate, and Barbara, very pregnant, being married to Vercel by Massoulier's brother, officiating over the life cycle rites of passage. Bertrand is there taking photos, documenting events as does the movie camera, while the children play soccer with his lens shade. The closing credits of the film, in narrative form, reveal that the restaurant next to the Ange Rouge was named after the makeup girl, Thi Loan Nguyen. This is Truffaut's last joyful message before his illness, radiating love and creative delight, a far more fitting closure for his life's work than the bitter *La Petite Voleuse*. Closure for this study is not with citation and homage in collage, however, but with the cinematic mirror of *La Nuit américaine*, starring the filmmaker and depicting the production crew on location, layering levels of reality and illusion in the gestation and birth of a film.

Bibliography

Allen, Don. *Finally Truffaut*. New York: Beaufort Books, 1985.
Anzalone, John. "Heroes and Villains, or Truffaut and the Literary Pre/Text." *The French Review* 72, 1 (Oct 1998) 48–57.
Bonnafous, Eli. *François Truffaut*. Lausanne: L'Age d'Homme, 1981.
Cahoreau, Gilles. *François Truffaut, 1932–1984*. Paris: Julliard, 1989.
Collet, Jean. *François Truffaut*. Paris: Lherminier, 1985.
Dalmais, Hervé. *Truffaut*. Paris: Rivages/Cinéma, 1987.
De Baecque, Antoine, and Toubiana, Serge. *François Truffaut*. Paris: Gallimard, 1996.
Desjardins, Aline. *Aline Desjardins s'entretient avec François Truffaut*. Paris: Ramsay, 1987.
Dixon, Wheeler, and Ruth Hoffman. "The Early Film Criticism of François Truffaut." *New Orleans Review* 16:1 (1989) 5–32.
Dixon, Wheeler. "François Truffaut, a life in Film." *Films in Review* 36:6–7 (1985) 331–336; 36: 8–9 (1985) 413–417.
Fanne, Dominique. *L'Univers de François Truffaut*. Paris: Editions du Cerf, 1972.
Gillain, Anne. *Le Cinéma selon François Truffaut*. Paris: Flammarion, 1988.
————. *François Truffaut: Le Secret perdu*. Paris: Hatier, 1991.
Guérif, François. *François Truffaut*. Paris: Edilig, 1988.
Hedges, Inez. "Form and Meaning in the French Film, III: Identification." *French Review* 56:2 (1982) 207–217.

Holmes, Diana, and Ingram, Robert. *François Truffaut*. Manchester, England: Manchester University Press, 1998.

Insdorf, Annette. *François Truffaut*. Boston: Twayne, 1978.

——. *François Truffaut*. New York: Simon & Schuster, 1989.

Julian, Robert. "Truffaut's Notes." *Partisan Review* 57:3 (1990) 407–413.

Le Berre, Carole. *François Truffaut*. Paris: *Cahiers du Cinéma*, 1993.

Rabourdin, Dominique, ed. *Truffaut par Truffaut*. Paris: Editions du Chêne, 1985.

——. *Truffaut by Truffaut*. New York: Abrams, 1987.

Ronder, Paul. "François Truffaut—an Interview." *Film Quarterly* (Fall 1963) 3–13.

Le Roman de François Truffaut. Les Cahiers du Cinéma 366 (December 1984). Special issue.

Simon, John. "François Truffaut: Saved by the Cinema." *The New Criterion* 9:1 (1990) 35–43.

Smith, Alan K. "Incorporating Images in Film: Truffaut and Emblems of Death." *Mosaic* 32:2 (Jun 1999) 107–122.

Thiher, Allen. *The Cinematic Muse: Critical Studies in the History of French Cinema*. Columbia: University of Missouri Press, 1979.

Tinazzi, Giorgio. "François Truffaut." *Belfagor* 38:1 (1983) 49–63.

——. "François Truffaut tra parola e immagine." *Problemi* 103 (Sep–Dec 1995) 228–233.

Truffaut, François. *Les Aventures d'Antoine Doinel*. Paris: Mercure de France, 1970.

——. *Correspondance*. Paris: Hatier, 1988.

——. *Les Films de ma vie*. Paris: Poche, Champs Contre-Champs, 1984.

——. *The Films in My Life*. New York: Simon & Schuster, 1978.

——. *Hitchcock*. New York: Simon & Schuster, 1967.

——. *Le Plaisir des yeux*. Paris: Cahiers du Cinéma, 1987.

Le Charme discret de la bourgeoisie
(The Discreet Charm of the Bourgeoisie)

directed by Luis Buñuel (1972)
screenplay by Buñuel and Jean-Claude Carrière

The complex relationship between modernism and the cinema has intrigued many critics, like Marc Bensimon, François Jost and Youssef Ishaghpour. One of the best illustrations of modernity in film is the work of Luis Buñuel, whose creative life spanned half a century, a major part of the history of French cinema (1926–1976). Although all film texts could be said to be oneiric, few films better illustrate cinema's capacity to exploit dream sequences than Buñuel's, from *Un Chien andalou* (*An Andalusian Dog*) to *Cet Obscur Objet du désir* (*That Obscure Object of Desire*). However, it is *Le Charme discret de la bourgeoisie* that best combines the techniques of realism and fantasy, moving back and forth between deceivingly realistic sequences in the classic bourgeois narrative canon and spontaneous intrusions of mystery, horror, parody, fantasy, satire and black humor. The film's surrealist technique is best symbolized by the reference Florence makes to her "complexe d'Euclide," not just an idle pun on the *complexe d'Oedipe* of the dream sequences recounted by soldiers, but rather a metatextual comment on the careful mathematical structure of the film, of symbols, repetitions, and narrative framing *en abyme* (in abyss) that is the essence of Buñuel's cinematic craftsmanship.

With his send-up of nearly every aspect of French and international hypocrisy and corruption, Buñuel also torpedoes bourgeois filmmaking in this surrealistic tour de force. The pretensions of wealthy suburbanite industrialists, of diplomats, of terrorists, the injustices of Latin American dictatorships, corruption in the diplomatic corps, petty militarism in a peacetime army, deep-seated evil in the Catholic Church, self-indulgence of adolescents, drug-running, arms sales, police brutality—Buñuel rips the masks off everyone, to reveal the hideously deformed nightmare visage beneath the surface. Like the images in a Dali painting, society is not just disfigured but even dismembered in this merciless portrayal.

Buñuel in a sense evolved with surrealism from its beginnings. Born in Aragon in 1900, with the century, he died in 1983, the old lion of avant-garde cinema. He was a close friend of Salvador Dali and Garcia Lorca at the University of Madrid in the early 1920s. In 1926, he went to Paris and collaborated with Dali on two surrealist films which created a social and political scandal and thus were the joy of their makers: *Un Chien andalou* and *L'Age d'or*, like Cocteau's *Sang d'un poète* sponsored by the Vicomte and Vicomtesse de Noailles. Buñuel, like Dali a revolutionary nonconformist and leader of the surrealist movement, left us a corpus crisscrossed with an intertextual obsessive thematic.

Buñuel belonged to the New Wave long before it existed, supporting the politics of the auteurs who favored films reflecting the director's personal cinematic writing over the commercial collective politics of big studio productions. Subversive, atheist, surrealist, often condemned or exiled, he waded through the absurdities of the twentieth century with a profound sense of humor—clever, black and mocking—and with the clear, logical vision of a Cartesian mind. Buñuel lived and worked in Spain, France, the United States and Mexico. Although a naturalized citizen of Mexico, Buñuel's cosmopolitan creative virtuosity marked him rather as a citizen of the Western world.

Buñuel's best-known works include: *Un Chien andalou*, which opens with the razor blade cutting the eyeball; *L'Age d'or*, made with Dali and the German expressionist painter Max Ernst, a film censored and banned as anti-Semitic; *Tierra sin pan* or *Las Hurdes* (*Land Without Bread*), banned as too revolutionary; *Los Olvidados*; *Nazarin*, a Mexican film about Christ which resembles Pasolini's *Il Vangelo secondo Matteo*, both with the figure of Christ surrounded by peasants in rags; *Viridiana*, filmed in Spain, banned and burned in public; *El ángel exterminador* (*The Exterminating Angel*), made in Mexico, a return to surrealist atheism, leftist and subversive; and the final French films written with Jean-Claude Carrière: *Le Journal d'une femme de chambre*, with Jeanne Moreau, *Belle de jour*, with Catherine Deneuve, and the tetralogy *La Voie lactée* (*The Milky Way*), *Le Charme discret de la bourgeoisie*, *Le Fantôme de la liberté* (*The Fantasm of Liberty*), *Cet Obscur Objet du désir*.

Buñuel never lost his energy, his iconographic dynamism. His is a baroque cinema—activist, lucid, comic, ironic, violent, capricious, picaresque. His films can be divided into two camps: 1) films of pure surrealism (but paradoxically without a lot of self-conscious camerawork like high-speed or slow motion, exotic shadows, double exposures, rather with the implacable and accusing lucidity found in certain surrealist paintings) and 2) the more readable films, with an adventuresome leading role (à la *Don Quixote*), fanciful narration, subtle invasions and disruptions of cinematic space and time by obscure powers of the dream world.

The title of *Le Charme discret de la bourgeoisie* is full of dual meanings and ambiguities: "charme"—social graces or magic spell; "discreet"—sober, restrained, but also hidden and mysterious, and "discrete," as in linguistics, in discontinuous parts, broken, fragmented. In this film, the concrete, the utopian, the erotic and the comic play a contrapuntal game, in a complex arabesque. Yet this irrational world is depicted with the hard logic of a rigorous thematic construction. Moreover, there are numerous parodies and homages in this work: the six characters in search of a plot (Pirandello), the merciless terrorists and cover-ups (Godard), bourgeois eroticism (Truffaut), other Buñuel films (this film is nearly a thematic inversion of *El ángel exterminador*). All of France before and after the ill-fated social revolution of 1968 finds itself mocked and ridiculed. The elegant aristocratic detachment of the early surrealist society combines with a cold-blooded attack on human weaknesses, reflecting at once the vulnerability and the cynicism of the 1970s. And the series of social events (dinners, lunches, cocktail parties) *interrupti* indicates a more serious break-up of French social structures, an angry indictment of all power structures abused in France and on the chessboard of the world.

Buñuel revealed in his conversations with Jean-Claude Carrière, *Mon Dernier Soupir* (*My Last Sigh*—whose French title is but one letter away from "my last supper"), "When I ask myself what surrealism really was, I still answer that it was a revolutionary, poetic and *moral* movement."[1] As in the structure of Buñuel's films, the apparent surface fragmentation and discontinuity, the planar function of surrealist art, masks a deep coherence of the new surrealist morality: "We had other criteria: we exalted passion, mystification, black humor, the insult, and the call of the abyss."[2] Gustave Flaubert defined a bourgeois as "anybody who thinks lowly." As with Flaubert, both poetic and moral questions are at play for Buñuel. The call of the *abîme* is also formalistic, as Buñuel incorporates sequences *en abyme* in his work, both plumbing the deeper layers of the psyche and echoing the structure of the film in miniature.

The conjunction of surrealist and Communist rhetoric in the desire to overthrow the old corrupt order and the vision of a liberated new society led Breton and others in the 1920s and 1930s to Moscow, only to return dismayed, their hopes betrayed. The Communist defense of the Spanish Republican cause against Franco attracted Buñuel to his native Spain; sent to America and trapped there in exile by their defeat, he pursued an unintentionally surrealistic activity helping Frank Capra and editing Nazi war propaganda, including Riefenstahl's *Triumph of the Will*, into what could be called the U. S. Army remake. Denounced by his lifelong friend Dali as a leftist atheist, Buñuel went to Mexico in 1947. He returned to his adopted Paris in the 1960s and 1970s, after years of filming elsewhere, in Spain and mainly in Mexico. They had been years of conflict; the student revolutions in Mexico had resulted in numerous violent clashes at the University of Mexico which had left hundreds and even thousands dead. Political events of the sixties and seventies all over the world were creating daily surrealistic scenarios of extremism: brutality, torture, corruption, on the part of both the Left and the Right. Although Buñuel decries the military Right in Latin America, one of the most extreme movements was the anti-intellectual, anti-patrician leftist populism embodied first by Mao's Red Guard and later by the Cambodian Khmer Rouge.

Le Charme discret de la bourgeoisie appeared at the apex of Mao Tse-Tung's Cultural Revolution, which lasted from 1966 to 1976. Mao's sayings, distributed in the little red book, were waved and quoted by a generation of populist extremists, who committed incredible atrocities in their zeal to rid China of its traditional society and power structure. In his 1988 book on traveling through China by train, *Riding the Iron Rooster*, Paul Theroux quotes a number of Mao's *Selected*

Thoughts, including poems and songs. Mao's favorite song could be the thematic of *Le Charme discret de la bourgeoisie*:

> A revolution is not a dinner party,
> Or writing an essay, or painting a picture, or doing embroidery:
> It cannot be so refined, so leisurely and gentle,
> So temperate, kind, courteous, restrained and magnanimous.

(Theroux notes that Mao affirmed these to be the virtues advocated by Confucius, whose writings, as the dominant traditional ethic, represented the system of values to be overthrown.) The song continues:

> A revolution is an insurrection
> An act of violence by which one class overthrows another.[3]

Buñuel's film deftly dismantles the niceties of life, turning the cracks in the façade of social manners into epistemological rifts, depicted though a series of surrealistic sequences where the surface gives way to reveal the monsters beneath. But rather than promote the cause of the Left, Buñuel steps back, with his ironic and aristocratic perspective on historic and political events, and demystifies all the conflicting optics of the pro- and antagonists, leaving the viewer with a sense of the hopeless frailty of reality, of the vulnerability of all ambitions, a *vanitas, vanitas, omnia est vanitas* world wherein the only reality is a telescoping illusion of oneiric scenarios, foregrounding phobias and desires, and whose diegetic displacement is a journey to nowhere.

I would like to retrace this journey to tally the victims of Buñuel's merciless cynical wit and to explore the dream world beneath the façade to ascertain whether Buñuel's stated morality of surrealism asserts itself or if the film is just, as so many critics have felt, a spontaneous and somewhat decadent exercise in comic filmmaking. Carlos Fuentes, in his 1973 *New York Times Magazine* review, and later Michael Wood, in a 1982 article in *American Film*, both referred to the film using the title "The Discreet Charm of Luis Buñuel." However they and Gwynne Edwards, in her 1982 book *The Discreet Art of Luis Buñuel*, all translate *discret* as "discreet," accentuating the suave surface hiding the underlying events, rather than "discrete," emphasizing the fragmented structure.

Buñuel's Six Characters in Search of a Meal (an obvious metaphor for bourgeois consumption and mannered social rituals already noted by the critics) include Raphael Acosta (Fernando Rey), the Ambassador to France from the Republic of Miranda (the non-existent Latin nation which constitutes a compendium of corruption, whose name means utopia in Spanish, which calls up intertextual allusions from Shakespeare to Beckett and historic references to Pancho Villa's defeat of the Miranda empire in Mexico), the businessman François Thévenot (Paul Frankeur), his dazzling blond *valiumée* wife Simone (a languishing Delphine Seyrig), her teenage sister Florence (played with obvious relish by Bulle Ogier, who adlibbed most of her role), and the primary hosts, entrepreneur Henri Sénéchal (Jean-Pierre Cassel) and his wife Alice (Stéphane Audran, who is the perfect willowy brunette counterpart to Seyrig's decorative yet indecorous blond).

Behind the opening credits, Buñuel places a classic cliché of film narrative: car traffic at night, the perfect mimesis of film—light and sound projected into darkness—opening the journey of the plot. Four elegantly attired guests alight from the chauffeured black Cadillac limousine and enter a lovely suburban home. The spectator is now Buñuel's mouse; the hostess is in pyjamas, gracious but perplexed; she was expecting her guests the following night. The *malentendu*, like the mistaken identity scenario, is a classic sign of danger, the initial rent in the fabric of the logical, consequential, comfortable, predictable reality of the bourgeoisie, whose correct mannered conduct is broken by a magic spell, hence the untranslatable dual meaning of the French *charme discret*.

Undaunted by the absence of their host, the four guests carry off the hostess to a nearby inn ominously named *L'Auberge de la Sabretache*, the mark of the saber prefiguring the death within. In the first of seven death sequences, five of which are embedded dream tales, the dinner group finds the auberge empty and the staff mourning the newly deceased owner in the back room. Death has broken the banal surface of life, silenced the mindless menu chatter and postponed the bourgeois socializing to another time. Throughout the film, Buñuel intertwines classic cinematic realism, polished filmmaking, perfect clarity and color, meticulous attention to detail, traditional camera angles and sequences of shots, with the *dessous*, the other reality underneath: death, destruction, corruption, revolution, drugs, and the complex machinations of phobia and desire.

Thévenot and Sénéchal turn up at the Ambassador's office the next day and are planning a luncheon, when their conversation is interrupted as the Ambassador fires at one of three toy mechanical dogs displayed on the sidewalk below by a mysterious dark young woman. This calls to mind another Mao aphorism, his reference to his enemies as "running dogs." When the girl flees to a waiting car, the subplot of terrorist assassination attempts is introduced, another threat to the surface control of bourgeois reality.

As the three men discuss their illicit drug deals with great anxiety, the noise of passing traffic (the other kind) is the first of a series of interferences symbolizing power play cover-ups of corruption in high places and leaving the spectator as confused as the characters. It almost masks the reference to the United States Ambassador's abuse of diplomatic immunity and his drug dealing and the news that four ambassadors have been arrested for drug trafficking, prefiguring their own later dream sequence arrest. They are all delighted with the purity of their drug, forty kilos of cocaine, in ironic contrast to the impurity of their morality. The three also note they are planning to convert their profits to German marks, another political allusion, to illicit practices of laundering money abroad, and also to the continuing presence of Nazism in Latin America.

The second planned meal is again at the Sénéchals' house, but the host couple's spontaneous lust interferes, as they dash off into the bushes in order not to be overheard. The sequence of their *coitus interruptus*, the first of two, baptizes the film as a *prandium interruptum* (a term I prefer to another critic's neologism of *coeatus interruptus*), as the characters' attempts to satisfy their desires are continually thwarted and frustrated. The question of class consciousness is introduced in this sequence as well, as the supposedly refined bourgeois demonstrate their martini ritual, testing it maliciously on the chauffeur, who of course fails by quaffing it off in one gulp. Confused and frightened by the news of their hosts' disappearance, they drop their masks, gulp their own martinis and race for the car. Throughout the film, Florence demonstrates her excessive fondness and intolerance for alcohol as her dominant trait of character, or lack of it, as she is both nauseous and nauseating (*dégueulasse*).

The sudden arrival of the bishop Monseigneur Dufour (Julien Bertheau) at the Sénéchals' in their absence may be triggered in the script by the other meaning of the absence of the host, of another missed consumption, of the deconsecration of religious ritual by hypocrisy and sin. When the worker-bishop returns to the house dressed as their gardener, clothes make the man, and he is rudely dismissed by the Sénéchals, who have just crept out of the garden on all fours like Adam and Eve expelled from Paradise. Only when the bishop resumes his official garb do they receive him and pay him tribute, giving him the job he seeks, at full union wages. The connection between his obsession with gardening and the arsenic poisoning of his parents is revealed in a later sequence.

At this point occurs the first of three signature sequences in the film, of the six characters walking down a country road to nowhere, emblematic of the plot leading to nowhere, refusing bourgeois narrative coherence, and of the failure, of the breakup into discrete parts, of middle class society. In the other recapitulations of this sequence, the six are first returning, then walking back down the same road again, on their disjointed and pointless journey.

The tea salon sequence reinforces the unreliability of reality, its frailty, as the waiter explains they are out of everything but water, and Florence is revolted by the sexually suggestive fingering of the cellist. Once again, in a *prandium interruptum*, their narrative is usurped by a stranger, this time a soldier who recounts his unhappy childhood in a perfectly oedipal dream sequence, in which he avenges his dead mother and her lover, his real father, by poisoning his authoritarian official father with arsenic. This second and graphic depiction of death is enhanced by a change in lighting and filmstock and the use of color filters. In the three dream sequences framed as narrative tales, the oneiric diegesis of Buñuel's cinematic world is a perfect antireality, dark and foreboding. The two telescoped dreams, however, are disarmingly realistic and unframed at the beginning, deliberately trapping the viewer. The dreams are linked by their focus on sexuality, paternity, and violence, and the fact that only men dream in the film.

Simone Thévenot rushes off to an assignation with the Ambassador, already anticipated by his fingering her neck surreptitiously at the Sénéchals'. Then in a tantalizingly ambiguous sequence, she refuses to disrobe with the lights on, stating that she is not yet healed. Noting that she no longer has any marks on her hands, the Ambassador then takes an unidentified pill. The arrival of her husband (the classic French gag: "*ciel, mon mari*") is the second *coitus interruptus*, another appetite discomfited by fate. She stays but a minute to see his nonexistent collection of *sourciques* and then dutifully follows her husband to his waiting chauffeured Jaguar.

When the Ambassador observes the arrival of the girl terrorist assassin, he pulls a revolver from the soup tureen, a gesture inspired in French by the expression *dans la soupe*, in trouble, and of course another example of violence hidden beneath stylish elegance. Jason Weiss's 1983 interview in *Cinéaste* with Buñuel's co-screenwriter Jean-Claude Carrière emphasizes this open-ended technique even in its title, "The Power to Imagine." The conversation between the Ambassador and the assassin, who is quoting Mao, is drowned out by the noise of a siren in the street, just as any hope of entente between the Left and the Right is precluded by violence. She repulses his lascivious attentions but fails to assassinate him. As he orders her out with debonaire sang-froid, he signals his henchmen to abduct her.

At the next dinner party at the Sénéchals', the bishop-gardener tries repeatedly to place Miranda, and Florence mocks the International Feminist Movement as one more meaningless institution, attacking their diamond-shaped logo as trite symbolism, standing for "Fasciste, Communiste, Le Christ est notre maître, Victoire." (Interestingly and ironically, this diamond losenge as symbol of woman comes from Arab Africa.) There is mention of dirt or blood beneath Florence's fingernails, another mysterious allusion which the astute spectator is tempted to connect to the marks on Simone. This meal is interrupted by the arrival of the army for maneuvers. Expected the next day, just as were the original dinner guests, the soldiers settle in to dine *à l'improviste*. Their socializing includes smoking a joint, offering Florence another occasion to demonstrate her self-indulgent enthusiasm. Their discussion of the use of drugs and alcohol by French and American soldiers gives the hypocritical Thévenot a chance to condemn drugs, as the bourgeoisie and the church accommodate the military.

This dinner is in turn interrupted by news of the arrival of the "enemy." Before they go off to their weekend warrior games, a young sergeant recounts a dream of death, which scenario takes over the film. His dream has a haunting resemblance to the lieutenant's earlier tale. The physical resemblance between characters in these sequences creates an ambiguity that Buñuel later foregrounds in the double female role in *Cet Obscur Objet du désir*. In this dream, the bell tolls for the characters who are of course all dead, smell of earth and disappear mysteriously. The final female character is another dead mother who haunts her son (this was a dream experienced by Buñuel). Like Lazarus, whom the bishop mentions, Buñuel's characters return from the dead to haunt the living, ghostly ancestral revenants who appear in surreal fashion to remind us that life's only enduring reality is death. Bruce Babington and Peter Evans offer an interesting concordance between elements of dreams in Buñuel and antecedents in Freud, Breton and Sade in their 1985 article in *Critical Quarterly*, "The Life of the Interior: Dreams in the films of Luis Buñuel."

The colonel's invitation to dinner at his house generates a new sequence, as the scene shifts obediently to the street address he gives them. Once the guests are inside, they discover that the hosts are again absent; Sénéchal playfully places the hat of Napoleon on the bishop's head, a comic historical allusion to the conspiracies of church and state and simultaneously a literary allusion to Stendhal's *Le Rouge et le noir* (*The Red and the Black*). As the dinner guests settle in, they gradually come unglued, as they first discover that the alcohol is fake and the chickens are rubber stage props, and then reel in horror as the curtain rises and they are the unprepared and unsuspecting characters in a play. Like Pirandello's six intruders, they have usurped the stage without a role. The prompter gives them lines from *Don Juan Tenorio*, a popular Spanish play written by José Zorrilla in 1844, "Et pour montrer votre valeur, vous avez invité â dîner le spectre du commandeur. Pour lui faire croire qu'il avait assisté à ce banquet, vous l'avez endormi avec un narcotique." (To show your bravery, you invited the commander's ghost to dinner. To make us believe he attended this feast, you drugged us with a narcotic.) Booed by the audience, they flee, in the cinematic nightmare sequence of fear of failure. The spectator learns it was just Sénéchal's dream, as he and his wife go at once to the general's house for his reception, embarrassed to arrive so late. This time it is Florence who is trying on Napoleon's hat.

The spectator here is genuinely trapped, for we are expecting a realistic sequence after a dream sequence, and the initial moments are clear and logical. Thus when the insults about Latin America start flying in the face of the Ambassador, who denies the presence of such things in Miranda—comments about guerillas, student massacres, extreme poverty, government, judicial and police corruption, numerous murders—we are slowly horrified then spellbound as the colonel and the Ambassador exchange insults, a slap and finally gunfire. Buñuel has had his way with us, and he then shows us Thévenot waking up to say, "J'ai rêvé...ou plutôt j'ai rêvé que Sénéchal a rêvé..." (I dreamed...or rather I dreamed that Sénéchal dreamed...), thus announcing the embedding and telescoping of one dream sequence within another in a display of narrative virtuosity. Babington and Evans point out that this is a revenge wish fulfillment dream for the cuckolded Thévenot.

The surrealistic nature of the film is again signaled by a second sequence of the six characters strolling down the country road to nowhere, with jet noise in the background, this time carrying branches and headed in the opposite direction from before. This scene constitutes not only allusions to the conflict of pacifism and arms dealing, but cinematic homage to the *Nouvelle Vague*, especially Godard, and Italian auteur filmmakers like Fellini and Antonioni, as much as it serves as Buñuel's own signature within the frame of this pictorial creation.

The next meal sequence is lunch at the Sénéchals'. This time the gardener-bishop is suggesting planting hydrangeas on both sides of the driveway from the gate to the front door, the plant symbolic of death whose flowers dry rather than wilting. In another class-conscious sequence, a poor old woman turns up in a cart to ask for a priest to give last rites to an old gardener about to die. As the bishop accompanies her to the farm, she openly states accusingly, "Je déteste Jésus Christ" (I hate Jesus Christ). The bishop dismisses her in an implied indictment of the social irresponsibility of the Church, in his unredeemed haste to encounter the gardener whose confession he hears. It is of course the murder of his own parents he is told, as he stares at himself as a young boy in a bedside photo. The gardener-bishop becomes in turn another gardener-assassin as he takes a shotgun and blows away the feeble dying murderer, avenging his parents' death.

Returning to the luncheon sequence, the menu is announced, whetting our constantly foiled appetites. Just as the meal is under way and the Ambassador is inviting everyone to Miranda, the police arrive and take way the lot, under arrest. We see them in their jail cell, indignant, complaining and threatening the inspector. Reality cracks again and the myth of 14 June (and not 14 July as Gwynne Edwards states in *The Discreet Art of Luis Buñuel*), of the annual return of the Bloody Brigadier, another revenant, takes over the film. We see him torturing a young student who is receiving intensely painful shocks while wired to an electrified piano. Even the cockroaches (the French symbol of depression: *le cafard*) leap overboard. We are rescued from this nightmare as the police commissioner awakens in his office from his dream. This time the Minister of the Interior is calling to tell him to release the prisoners; once again his reasons are drowned out by hostile cover-up noises, in this case of fighter jets, a second indictment of French arms sales overseas. The police commissioner's explanation to the detective is also drowned out, by the sounds of the typewriter. The whole affair is hushed up.

Yet another dinner is begun at the Sénéchals'. The guests arrive late, and the hostess sends them straight to the table, complaining that her *gigot* (leg of lamb) is going to be overcooked. Jeff Kline sees in this menu another satiric pun, an allusion to and declaration of affinity with the theater of the absurd, with the implied title *En attendant gigot* a variation of Beckett's *En attendant Godot* (*Waiting for Godot*). There are in fact numerous elements in this film which echo such works as Ionesco's *La Cantatrice chauve* (*The Bald Soprano*): the temporal dislocation, the absurd bourgeois couples, the tallcase clock, the surrealistc tales which interrupt the frame narrative, the ending erupting in violence but going nowhere. In Ionesco can be found precise intertextual models for the guests coming to dinner when nothing has been prepared, the intrusive stranger who tells his story, the series of unexpected visitors at the door, the omnipresent maid, the search for more chairs. In Jean Genet's *Le Balcon* (*The Balcony*) can be found antecedents for the role and costuming of the bishop, Napoleon, and the police chief.

This time at table, conversational surface reality is invaded as the guests question the maid Inès about her boyfriend. She reveals that she has been abandoned as too old, confessing that she is in fact fifty-two. Someone then questions the Ambassador about ex-Nazis hiding in Miranda (an amalgam of Argentina, Colombia, Peru, Mexico, Guatemala). Florence gives Raphael's horoscope and exhorts him to develop a personal morality, in another improvisation which adds to the encroaching surrealistic ambiance. This time the dinner party is definitively disbanded by the arrival of the cartel competition, drug-dealing Mafia thugs from Marseilles, who gun down all present with their Uzis, finishing off the table setting and the Ambassador, as he greedily reaches up from under the table to sneak a slice of lamb. Then, once again, the dreamer, this time Raphael, awakens and, deciding that he really is alive, goes to the kitchen to raid the refrigerator for, naturally, some cold roast meat. All this *basse cuisine* is in French perfectly symbolic of the decline and fall of social mores and conduct, of the thin veil of hypocrisy barely masking the gross appetites and cowardly fears of the ruling class, the upper class French bourgeoisie of industrial, diplomatic and inherited wealth.

In the closing sequence, the six characters wend their way back down the road to nowhere, to the sound of the jets, in the open discursive space of modernistic narrative which destroys the linear causality of the dominant bourgeois realist canon. In his own way, Buñuel has contrived to integrate historic and political realities into a lyric subjective discontinuous film text, successfully expressing a coherent dialectic in an apparently capricious montage of realistic and illusionary sequences, unmasking the surrealistic immorality of contemporary society by using the elements of surrealist revolutionary poetics and morality as he defined them: passion, mystification, black humor, the insult and the call of the abyss.

There is a sustained homage to this classic film in Louis Malle's 1989 *Milou en mai* (*May Fools*), also written by Jean-Claude Carrière, with the group gathered for meals, the presence of death, the spontaneous sexuality, the political events as background. Other critics have read *Milou en mai* more as a reworking of Jean Renoir's *La Règle du jeu* (particularly because of the presence of Pauline Dubost as the grandmother, who was Lisette in *La Règle du jeu*); thus it constitutes an intriguing double homage, with its preoccupied landed gentry deaf to the events of May 1968.

This chapter also appeared as an article in *Literature/Film Quarterly* 22:4 (1994) 232–237.

Notes

1. Luis Buñuel, *My Last Sigh* (New York: Knopf, 1983) 109. (Buñuel's emphasis).
2. *My Last Sigh*, 107.
3. Paul Theroux, *Riding the Iron Rooster* (New York: Ivy Books, 1988) 259.

Bibliography

Aranda, Francisco. *Buñuel: A Critical Biography*. New York: Da Capo Press, 1976.
Babington, Bruce, and Peter Evans. "The Life of the Interior: Dreams in the Films of Luis Buñuel." *Critical Quarterly* 27:4 (1985) 5–20.

Bini, Luigi. "Il Cinema di Luis Buñuel, 'ateo per grazia di Dio'." *Letture: Libro e Spettacolo* 38:393 (January 1983) 3–32.

Borau, Jose Luis. "Laughs with Buñuel." In Kinder, Marsha, ed. *Luis Buñuel's 'The Discreet Charm of the Bourgeoisie'*. Cambridge, England: Cambridge University Press, 1999.

Buñuel, Luis. *My Last Sigh*. New York: Knopf, 1983.

Conrad, R. "I am not a producer! Working with Buñuel: a Conversation with Serge Silberman." *Film Quarterly* 33:1 (1979) 3–11.

Durgnat, Raymond. "*The Discreet Charm of the Bourgeoisie*." *Film Comment* 11 (1975) 52–59.

————. *Luis Buñuel*. Berkeley: University of California Press, 1974.

————. "Defetishizing Buñuel." *Cineaste* 23:4 (1998) 4–7.

Edwards, Gwynne. *The Discreet Art of Luis Buñuel*. Boston: Marion Boyars, 1982.

Flasher, John, and Douglas Radcliff-Umstead. "The Derisive Humor of Luis Buñuel." *Perspectives on Contemporary Literature* 7 (1981) 7–17.

Fuentes, Carlos. "The Discreet Charm of Luis Buñuel." *New York Times Magazine* (11 March 1973) 27–29.

Fuentes, Victor. "The Discreet Charm of the Postmodern: Negotiating the Great Divide with the Ultimate Modernist, Luis Buñuel." In Kinder, Marsha, ed. *Luis Buñuel's 'The Discreet Charm of the Bourgeoisie'*. Cambridge, England: Cambridge University Press, 1999.

Gantrel, Martine. "La Gastronomie française au cinéma entre 1970 et 1990." *The French Review* 75:4 (Mar 2002) 697–706.

Gaston, Karen Carmean. "Luis Buñuel's Use of Metaphysical Conceits." *New Orleans Review* 9:2 (1982) 40–44.

Higginbotham, Virginia. *Luis Buñuel*. Boston: Marion Boyars (Twayne), 1979.

————. "Convictions & Contradictions of Luis Buñuel: *Mon Dernier Soupir*." *Post-script* 6:2 (Winter 1987) 63–73.

————. "Feminism and Buñuel: Points of Contact." *RLA: Romance Languages Annual* 1 (1989) 464–467.

Kinder, Marsha, ed. *Luis Buñuel's 'The Discreet Charm of the Bourgeoisie'*. Cambridge, England: Cambridge University Press, 1999.

Mellen, Joan. *The World of Luis Buñuel: Essays in Criticism*. New York: Oxford University Press, 1978.

Mora-Catlett, Juan Roberto. "Buñuel the Realist: Variations of a Dream." In Kinder Marsha, ed. *Luis Buñuel's 'The Discreet Charm of the Bourgeoisie'*. Cambridge, England: Cambridge University Press, 1999.

Olney, Ian. "Repetition (With Difference) and Ludic Deferral in the Later Films of Luis Buñuel." *Quarterly Review of Film and Video* 18:1 (Jan 2001) 71–82.

Pauly, Rebecca. "A Revolution is not a Dinner Party: The Discrete Charm of Buñuel's Bourgeoisie." *Literature/Film Quarterly* 22:4 (1994) 232–237.

Rafael, George. "The Discreet Charm of Luis Buñuel." *Cineaste* 25:2 (2000) 32–33.

Rechy, John. "How Marilyn Monroe Profoundly Influenced *The Discreet Charm of the Bourgeoisie*." In Kinder, Marsha, ed. *Luis Buñuel's 'The Discreet Charm of the Bourgeoisie'*. Cambridge, England: Cambridge University Press, 1999.

Rees, Margaret, ed. *Luis Buñuel: A Symposium*. Leeds: Trinity & All Saints' College, 1983.

Rubenstein, Elliot. "Buñuel's World, or the World and Buñuel." *Philosophy and Literature* 2:2 (1978) 237–248.

Sanchez-Vidal, Augustin. "A Cultural Background to *The Discreet Charm of the Bourgeoisie*." In Kinder, Marsha, ed. *Luis Buñuel's 'The Discreet Charm of the Bourgeoisie'*. Cambridge, England: Cambridge University Press, 1999.

Sandro, Paul. "The Management of Destiny in Narrative Form." *Ciné-Tracts* 4:1 (1982) 50–56.

————. *Diversions of Pleasure: Luis Buñuel and the Crises of Desire*. Columbus: Ohio State University Press, 1987.

Stam, Robert. "Hitchcock and Buñuel: Desire and the Law." *Studies in the Literary Imagination* 16:1 (Spring 1983) 7–27.

Velasquez, E. and J. Ignacio. "Buñuel vs. Buñuel: La Pluma y la camara." *Insula* 38: 440–441 (1983) 27.

Virmaux, Alain and Odette. *Les Surréalistes et le cinéma*. Paris: Seghers, 1976.

Weiss, Jason. "The Power to Imagine: An Interview with Jean-Claude Carrière." *Cinéaste* 13:1 (1983) 6–11.

Williams, Linda. "The Critical Grasp: Buñuelian Cinema and Its Critics." *Dada/Surrealism* 15 (1986) 199–206.

————. *Figures of Desire: a Theory and Analysis of Surrealist Film*. Urbana: University of Illinois Press, 1981.

Wood, Michael. "The Corruption of Accidents: Buñuel's *That Obscure Object of Desire* (1977)." In Horton, Andrew, and Joan Magretta, eds. *Modern European Filmmakers and the Art of Adaptation*. New York: Ungar, 1981.

————. "The Discreet Charm of Luis Buñuel." *American Film* 7 (1982) 34–39.

————. "'God Never Dies': Buñuel and Catholicism." *Renaissance and Modern Studies* 36 (1993) 93–121.

Les Quatre Cents Coups
(The 400 Blows)

written and directed by François Truffaut (1959)

The title of *Les Quatre Cents Coups* comes from the colloquial expression *faire les quatre cents coups*, to raise hell, and thus implies both the giving and receiving of blows, as well as marking Truffaut's debut as creative hell-raiser. The idea for the film came from several sources: a French television show called *Si c'était vous* (*If It Were You*) about parent-child relationships, *Germania anno zero* (*Germany Year Zero*) by Roberto Rossellini, and Jean Vigo's *Zéro de conduite* (*Zero for Conduct*), also homaged in *La Nuit américaine*. Truffault based his film entirely on real-life experiences, although not entirely autobiographical. The film's protagonist is a stronger personality and less *révolté* than Truffaut himself, mainly due to the choice of Jean-Pierre Léaud as his surrogate persona. Léaud gave the role a quality of his own which made it diverge necessarily from Truffaut's remembered self at age eleven. This latitude came from Truffaut's belief like Renoir's that the actor as a person was more important than the persona of the character. The person showing through the role could be said to constitute another facet of "the transparent illusion" in the relationship between cinema and reality. Other transpositions throughout the film are in some ways more revealing than the truth of lived experience, as they represent a conscious choice of a metaphorical substitute expression of self and other.

Avowing distaste for documentary filmmaking and having abandoned the idea of a documentary about adolescence, Truffaut unwittingly documented, observed and recorded faithfully the drama of growing up absurd, his understated realism the polar opposite of melodramatic documentary and newsreel footage of the day. Truffaut was concerned about the reception of his film as a creative artistic product more than its political or social place in France of the day. He need not have worried; not only was the film a sensation at the Cannes Film Festival in 1959, with its gritty comic blend of fantasy and neorealism, but like Fellini's *La Dolce Vita* released the same year, it struck a deep chord in the collective psyche of its spectators. Jean Renoir commented that the film was a portrait of France at that moment in time.

This film began the chronicle of an affective odyssey covering twenty years of this character, a Balzacian or Zolian cycle, as Léaud successively portrayed

Antoine Doinel in *Antoine and Colette*, one of the five episodes of *L'Amour à vingt ans* (other directors included documentarists Marcel Ophüls and Andrzej Wadja), *Baisers volés, Domicile conjugal* and *L'Amour en fuite*. This extended lyric film writing compares to the Orpheus trilogy of Jean Cocteau which covered thirty years. Appropriately, Truffaut financed, as mentioned, Cocteau's last film, *Le Testament d'Orphée*, with the profits from *Les Quatre Cents Coups*. Truffaut acknowledged his debt to Cocteau's vision in his choice of the apartment he rented for filming interiors, rooms which evoked Cocteau's sets from films like *Les Parents terribles* or *Les Enfants terribles*. Cocteau had also played the role of Bellon in the 1950 film *Colette*, about one of Truffaut's major film-text-writer-persona homage characters.

Truffaut had nothing but praise for the acting skills of the children in the film; marveling at their natural style and instinct for realism, he gave them no set lines, unlike the adults in the cast. He encouraged dramatization of certain scenes by suggesting childlike moods and feelings they might portray. Perhaps the greatest lasting achievement in his career as director will be his work with children on screen, acknowledging their lyric spontaneity, their naïveté, their solitude and insecurity, their need for love, their rebellion against constraints, embodying the child in himself and all his spectators. Not only Léaud but his foil Patrick Auffay, playing René Bigey, turned in legendary performances enabling spectator identification with the protagonists pitted against the system: outwitting parents, avoiding school, surviving economically, fearing and experiencing arrest, losing their minds.

The roles of the parents are critical to the success of the film and the portrayal of the family. Truffaut thought Claire Maurier was too stylized and staged as the mother, but a more natural actress would have seemed less distant and mysterious, thus closing the gap between mother and son and destroying the sustained sense of alienation, desperation and impossible longing of the film. The fact that Truffaut changed the famous excuse Antoine invents, to explain his truancy, from his father's capture by the Nazis to his mother's death is revelatory of the fantasms at work beneath the script. The two fathers, Albert Rémy as Doinel and Georges Flamant as Bigey, are appropriately unaware, preoccupied and antipathetic.

Jean Constantin's music sets a surrealistic yet light-hearted carnival mood from the beginning, interspersed later with bittersweet melancholy pieces. Henri Decaë's cinematography was critical to the success of the enterprise. They rented a CinemaScope (Dyaliscope) lens, as Truffaut explained, to give broader context to many of the scenes, added realism and dimension. The film was shot in black and white rather than color not just to save money but to allow for improvisation, to avoid too careful planning of shots and sequences (ironic considering the aleatory nature of the color film *Baisers volés*). Truffaut's amateur improvisational style of filmmaking created for him an alternate reality on the set and on the screen and gave him access to a new-found personal freedom after years of constraints in family, school, juvenile detention, the army, an asylum. This deeply felt need for autonomy drives the theory of auteur filmmaking that he posited and explains his opposition to political filmmaking, yet another commitment and constraint, just as it informed his personal commitment to his alternate film family.

Fortuitous situations during filming included the pigeons in the frame as the boys steal the typewriter (they were filming on the Champs-Elysées). Other outdoor shots in the streets and the metro were achieved with brown-bag cinematography, keeping the camera under wraps to avoid self-conscious crowd responses. This economized on extras, just as eliminating studio time and well-known stars cut costs. Cameo appearances by Jeanne Moreau (who would star in *Jules et Jim* two years later) and Jean-Claude Brialy thus stand out as a parody of star-system films. Truffaut was virulently and outspokenly opposed to the *"cinéma de papa"* and Hollywood-style commercial filmmaking. The exception as stated elsewhere was his reverence for Renoir and Hitchcock. His presence in his own films as cameo, actor, director, writer is thus not just autobiographical but citational. Truffaut worked with other young filmmakers at this point, notably Philippe de Broca, whose long successful career, predicted by Truffaut, included the 1966 *King of Hearts*.

The original title of the film was *La Fugue d'Antoine*, alluding both to running away from home and the complex structure in five parts of the musical fugue: exposition, development, entertainment, constraints, ending. Fugue is also the term for a form of schizophrenia where the psyche escapes its primary referentiality to begin a new existence completely divorced from its former identity, a complete repression of the past. This abandoned title gives continuity to the cyclic nature of the Antoine Doinel films, closing twenty years later with *L'Amour en fuite*, meaning both intradiegetic flight and the vanishing point of cinematic perspective. Appropriately, this final film closes with a sequence from *Les Quatre Cents Coups*. Truffaut intended to open the latter film with a liminal *fugue*, a capricious flight by Antoine and René to see the Eiffel Tower, in a taxi driven by an Algerian who couldn't find the access to it (ironically a prophetic political metaphor). The only shots retained were the opening travelling which speeds to a pan (anticipating the later zoetrope effect) of the Paris skyline from street level, of the Palais de Chaillot and the tower. The landmark became as noted the signature emblem of all Truffaut's Paris films. As the camera explores the Eiffel Tower's base, the structure (built for the 1889 Centennial of the French Revolution) also becomes a metaphor of the hierarchy of power in society and of complex entanglements, and of upheaval, including the well-engineered machinations of the *gamins* that will follow. A Freudian interpretation would see in it a phallic symbol regarding access to one's own masculinity and virility, as well as filmmaking as a creative sexual act (the camera being designated as phallic instrument or substitute, like the writer's pen). The film is dedicated to André Bazin, Truffaut's cinematic father and mentor, who rescued him from an army asylum in Germany and employed him, helping him find freedom and a new life in the world of the cinema. Bazin died the night before Truffaut began shooting the film.

The film opens as text, with Doinel writing in class, then receiving punishment in response to the first of his own four hundred pranks, a reprimand for coloring on a pin-up calendar. Setting the stage for a rebellion, the authoritarian schoolmaster leaves Antoine alone in class during recess, whereupon he signs his identity in another text, in graffiti on the classroom wall. He goads the teacher even as he cleans it off. In the schoolyard, we hear background conversation between the teachers about Madame and Monsieur le Directeur. The twelve-year-old Doinel is wearing a black turtleneck, which will become his trademark, as well as the "school uniform" of Truffaut and other New Wave filmmakers.

In counterpoint to Doinel's rebellious use of language, Truffaut depicts a struggling young boy covering his notebook with ink-stained scribbles, a hyperactive messy child unable to comply with his assigned task. Doinel and his classmates are manifestly ingenious troublemakers, not failures in the system. In a historically ironic comment, the teacher despairs of what French society will be like in ten years (1953 in the film, but for the filmmakers 1968, when the spirit of rebellion expressed in this film exploded on a national scale).

In the second setting of conflict, his small apartment home, Doinel verifies the safety of his cache of money, indicating his status as economically independent miscreant. Truffaut at that age skipped school often and spent his lunch money on movie tickets if he couldn't sneak in for free. The film recreates events from 1943, during the German Occupation, but Truffaut never signals the political background of the era, giving the film much more of a timeless quality, focusing the rebelliousness on the solitude of the individual only child, in spite of his schoolmates' roles.

The sequence where Antoine sits at his mother's dressing table carries multiple significance: it is the image of makeup and reflection emblematic of the actor preparing his role, and his curious desire to play his mother's part, including the narcissism of the looking glass, to know her, to penetrate the lies and masks which dominate his life. It is also the feminization of the male by the creative reproduction of the self in the screen mirror, in character, in cinematic imagery and writing.

Antoine echoes Cinderella in his life as a downtrodden and abused child; his dutiful attempt to set the table and start his homework is interrupted by the arrival of his cold and self-centered mother, who reprimands him for having forgotten to buy flour, in another of his blows. Offering a contrasting role reversal, his father is kinder and more childlike. The next hint that Antoine has pulled off many previous *coups* is his use of an expensive Mont Blanc pen, which he has obviously stolen. Against the backdrop of his parents' arguing, Antoine takes out the garbage, to the sound of babies crying at the bottom of their dirty stairwell. This is one of several shots documenting Antoine's prosaic existence that Truffaut felt succeeded because of the CinemaScope format, extending stylistically the visual images and avoiding claustrophobic close framing which would counter the desired lyricism.

The next morning, Antoine gets the first of many brutal awakenings, roused from his sleeping bag to find he is late for school. Here begins the series of *vagabondages* of truancy and flight, as his friend René convinces him to attend *l'école buissonnière*, to play hooky with him. Naturally, they first go to the movies to see *The White Slave*, then cross the street against the traffic (privileged urban emblem of nonconformist rebellion), play the pin ball machines, and finally ride the gravitron at the carnival. As the floor of the spinning cylinder falls away, Antoine is pinned against the wall, depicted from many angles, held only by centrifugal force. The gravitron has been compared to the zoetrope precursor of cinema by Annette Insdorf and Daniel Towner. Not only is there also a perfect metaphor for the spinning madness of life in the distortion of the high speed superpan of the experience, which leaves Antoine so disoriented, but this disorientation is concretized directly when the boys then see his mother Gilberte (an allusion to Proust) with another man. Both mother and son are committing crimes of irresponsible truancy. The next blow is a betrayal by a schoolmate who sees them pick up their schoolcases and tells on Antoine to his father.

Doinel's first attempt at writing is an imposture, a fake letter of excuse which he copies so literally that he signs René's name. When his mother doesn't come home for dinner, his father reveals his cuckolded emasculated state by symbolically donning her apron. It is clear that he will never stand up to his wife. There is poignant dramatic irony in the father's lecture to his son about taking initiative and his defense of Doinel's mother, in the first of two comments in the film affirming that women are exploited at the office. Confronted with his father's defense of his mother, Antoine is empowered by his secret knowledge of her activities.

Although it is Balzac (another unhappy son abused by a cold-hearted mother) that he will enshrine, Antoine has other literary models, in Stendhal and Flaubert, or in Maupassant's *Pierre et Jean* and *La Parure*, both tales of young misery, poverty and jealousy. And the echoes of classic fables in this film are not surprising, considering Truffaut's admiration for Cocteau. Antoine overhears his mother threatening to put him in boarding school or a convent. The autobiographic elements of this rejection return later in Truffaut's characterization of women and the number of insecure male characters he creates who are obsessed with them, seeking passion, possession, tenderness, or respect.

Antoine's audacious *acte gratuit* of inventing his mother's death is not just a vindictive desire to see her dead, as the father thinks, but the revelation that she has died for him as a mother, between her cruelty and her infidelity. When his humiliated father slaps him in front of the class, the literal blow prefigures more to come and marks the end of his family life, as his parents' abusive conduct and constant fighting push him to run away from home. Truffaut commented to Anne Gillain that the success of Léaud's potentially melodramatic announcement of his break with his family was inspired by Jean Gabin's deadpan confession at the end of *La Bête humaine*: "Eh bien! voilà, je ne la reverrai plus. Je l'ai tuée, tu sais...il faudra continuer à travailler...." (Well, that's it, I'll never see her again. I killed her, you know...I'll have to go on working...). Truffaut added that it is this sort of influence that most profoundly affects filmmakers in their work, these models of delivery at critical points in a film.[1]

This new vagabond stage of Doinel's life is marked by alternate sequences of street slang and bravado and by a profound *pathétique* as he wanders sad, lonely and pensive before storefronts stating *Joyeux Noël* and prowls the streets at night, stealing milk to survive, gulping it down under an ad for a ski resort. Truffaut's parents met at a ski resort; they were avid rock climbers and left him alone every weekend to pursue their sport. This thematic is repeated in *Baisers volés* when Doinel is abandoned to work as a night clerk in the Hotel Alsina (Alpina) in Montmartre, while Christine is away on a ski vacation. The milk is contextually a loaded symbol as well, as it was so extensively promoted as nourishment for children in postwar France. Truffaut returns to this metaphor in his last screenplay, *La Petite Voleuse.*

In an abrupt about-face, Antoine's capricious mother interrupts his English class to take him back home, where she attempts to win him over in complicity with bribes, telling him of her unhappy childhood, where she ran off with a lover and wrote all her secrets in a diary, then trying to bribe him to do well at school, an offer which will have disastrous consequences as she in turn corrupts her son. With a typical New Wave lack of continuity and a neorealist desire to balance the individual against the collective, Truffaut interrupts the intrigue with the grande farce sequence of the kids ducking out of a group fitness walk through the streets. By the time the teacher has lost all but two students, the moviegoer realizes the significance of the image on the screen: an entire generation is about to rebel against the repressive treatment of the fifties and seek its own path. During this walk, as Tom Conley points out, there flashes a graffito on a wall by Giraudoux, the rallying-point patriarch of the *politique des auteurs*, who stated, "Il n'y a pas d'oeuvres, il n'y a que des auteurs" (There are no works, there are only authors).

As Truffaut depicts Doinel at home reading Balzac while smoking a cigarette, both the voice-over and close-ups of the text give us the ending of *La Recherche de l'absolu* (*The Search for the Absolute*, an 1834 novel in the *Etudes philosophiques* of *La Comédie humaine*, whose title alone conjures images not just of Balzacian heroes but of the Rimbaldian *voyant/voyou/vagabond*). Doinel copies this final passage with its "Eureka" of self-discovery in class from memory (Truffaut in fact skipped school to read Balzac in the public library). The flame of inspiration is lit in the shrine Antoine has created to his literary hero, but his actions backfire, as he sets fire to the house. At his guilty mother's urging, he is not punished but goes with his parents to the Gaumont Palace to see *Paris nous appartient*, a movie whose title echoes the much-quoted ending of another Balzac novel, *Le Père Goriot*: "A nous deux maintenant." Thus the character Antoine not only transposes Truffaldian adolescence but equates his experiences to those of romantic heroes like Stendhal's Julien Sorel and Balzac's Louis Lambert or Eugène de Rastignac. The evening at the movies is a stolen night of family happiness under the magic influence of the cinema, an evening of gaiety, of nourishment, an interlude of normalcy before the explosion of his world.

When Antoine is expelled from school for plagiarizing Balzac, René defends him, also gets expelled by the furious teacher, and then takes him to his house, where he hides him with the cats and a horse statue, stealing money from his drunken loveless mother to provide for them. In the dinner sequence with his father, René provides a few *coups* of his own, stealing food for his friend and resetting the clock to get rid of his father, whose prime obsession is socializing at his club. It is a cruel Dickensian Balzacian adult world that Truffaut depicts. In defiance of those forces, the two adolescent vagabonds set off on an adventure, full of brio and sass, accompanied by light-hearted music. In one of the few examples of Truffaut's lack of cinematic experience, rather than of deliberate disregard of narrative causality and continuity, he chains shots of totally different weather in quick succession.

The long nighttime shot depicts the two friends going to the *ciné-club* (Truffaut actually went to jail for unpaid debts run up in operating his own *ciné-club*), then stealing a poster pinup and an alarm clock, which goes off in Antoine's pocket. A stroll in the park leads to the sequence of the guignol puppet show, where it is apparent to what extent Truffaut adores children and directs them brilliantly, as he intercuts shots of *Little Red Riding Hood* and the symphony of expression of the children's faces. Antoine and René are writing their own contemporary version of a classic fairy tale in the tradition of children in trouble or in danger; they even talk of pawning René's father's valuable puppet collection. In the subsequent sequence which will land Antoine in jail, it is clear that no traditional fable is capable of depicting or purging these adolescents' fears and longings. They are more appropriately heirs to American cinematic and literary rebels like Huck Finn or *Rebel Without a Cause*, or to the ethos of the wilderness sagas and their outlaws.

René and Antoine now adventure into adult criminal activities, as Antoine sneaks into his father's office and steals a typewriter (first drawing, then reading, now textual printed production as acts of rebellious defiance). Truffaut came full circle with this thematic, from this first film about juvenile delinquents to his last script, *La Petite Voleuse*. As Antoine and René carry the heavy typewriter across Paris, we and they begin to realize the impossible burden of the life they are choosing (symbolically to steal fiction from life). For the spectator of thirty years later, there are echoes in contemporary images of young teenagers delivering drugs and stolen goods to protect adult criminals.

Petty crime becomes a life of crime when Antoine's parents repudiate him definitively and he is dragged into the penal system, before children's court, to the department of correction, and handed over to the authorities, in a sequence based on Truffaut's own arrest and incarceration. Doinel is locked up with prostitutes and pederasts beneath a sign for rat exterminating. A shot of Antoine's face behind the grill shows the barrier to freedom and to the future that society has placed before him. When he is taken away in the paddy wagon, he prays and clutches the bars in the back, crying in sincere self-pity and fear as they roll past houses of corruption. The backlit image of the officer in the doorway of the prison works the audience with its film noir ominous surrealistic shadowing.

Antoine sits alone in a filthy cell, spitting out foul coffee, rolling a cigarette, and then has mug shots taken, antiportraits in profile, the freezing photograph that anticipates the final frame. A new explanation for Antoine's conduct is offered when the mother tells the judge that he is not his father's son, an avowal prefigured by the practice question in English pronunciation class, "Where is the father?" Once again, Truffaut abruptly shifts the intrigue to a different setting; although not opposed to classic sequential editing of cinematic narrative realism, he eschews canonical narrative transitions in cutting to Antoine at an observation center for delinquent minors. The inmates exchange their tales of misconduct in between scenes of militaristic regimentation. Two guards return with a runaway who has been caught, as three little girls are shown abandoned in an outdoor cage redolent indeed of classic fairy-tale children's woes and also of contemporary (1943) wartime images of prisoners and camps. This shot has often been misinterpreted, as it was intended to depict the warden's daughters being protected from the inmates; even understood correctly, it conveys yet another image of the confining restraints of an autocratic patriarchal society and the impossibility of freedom for children. Once again Antoine, whose hunger for food equals that for life, gets in trouble for not conforming, this time for eating his bread too soon, and collects the hardest physical blow of the film, as he is resoundingly slapped by a guard.

In a remarkable sequence, Antoine faces the camera and recounts to the resident "spychologist" his life's story, depicting the abuse suffered by an unwanted child, explaining with frightening objectivity his illegitimacy and his robbing his grandmother, who had prevented his abortion. The countershots of the psychiatrist were never filmed, creating a syncopated monologue. His mother's cruelty and his father's cowardice become archetypal as he generates the narrative of his own fable. In keeping with the injustice of the justice system, they refuse entry to his friend René, but allow his mother to come to tell him that his parents are cutting him out of their lives for good because of a letter of betrayal he wrote to his father. The power of written text permeates this film with its strong literary echoes of the confessional autobiographic narrative of Rousseau and Stendhal and its implicit citation of epistolary fiction.

After a final series of *coups*, this time in a soccer scrimmage, Antoine escapes and runs through the woods, then down a road along a fence row past cows and farms, toward "La Seine, son embouchure, la mer" (The Seine, its mouth, the sea). Written beneath these lines is the frustrated longing of the rejected child to have "le sein de la mère dans sa bouche," his mother's breast in his mouth. This longest shot of the film, a tracking shot, conveys the determination of his desperate flight for freedom, backed in ironic counterpoint by ambient sounds of bird calls and a bucolic setting. By the end of this now classic sequence, Antoine has run clear to the beach, to the sea. He covers the last meters across the wide tidal sands and runs into the water, in a symbolic reunion with "la mer/mère." The famous final freeze frame, duplicated many times since in imitation or homage by other filmmakers, captures the self-portrait of this adolescent experiencing a painful rite of passage, a disarmingly ingenuous depiction of the emotional scarring which would mark all of Truffaut's work.

Note

1. Anne Gillain, *Le Cinéma selon François Truffaut* (Paris: Flammarion, 1988) 101.

Bibliography

Please see the chapter on *Vivement dimanche* for the general Truffaut bibliography.

Colville Georgiana. "Children Being Filmed by Truffaut." *French Review* 63:3 (1990) 444–451.
Conley, Tom. "Tirez Sur le *PP*." *L'Esprit Créateur* 30:2 (1990) 26–37.
Conomos, John. "Truffaut's *The 400 Blows*, or the Sea, Antoine, the Sea." *Senses of Cinema* 6 (May 2000) (online journal Victoria Australia).
Dixon, Wheeler. "François Truffaut, a Life in Film." *Films in Review* 36:6–7 (1985) 331–336; 36:8–9 (1985) 413–417.
Gillain, Anne. *Le Cinéma selon François Truffaut*. Paris: Flammarion, 1988. 87–107.
———. *François Truffaut: Le Secret perdu*. Paris: Hatier, 1991.
———. "The Little Robber Boy as Master Narrator." *Wide Angle* 7:1–2 (1985) 107–117.
———. "The Script of Delinquency: François Truffaut's *Les 400 Coups* (1959)." In Hayward, Susan, and Ginette Vincendeau, eds. *French Film: Texts and Contexts*. New York: Routledge, 2000.
Harcourt, Peter. "Mad Love and a Sense of Play: 'Reading' the Early Films of François Truffaut." *Mosaic* 16:1–2 (1983) 113–124.
Lopez, Anna. "An Elegant Spiral: Truffaut's *The 400 Blows*." *Wide Angle* 7:1–2 (1985) 144–148.
Nelson, Roy Jay. "The Rotor: Elements of Paradigmatic Structure in Truffaut's *The 400 Blows*." *Wide Angle* 7:1–2 (1985) 137–143.
Neupert, Richard. "The Musical Score as Closure Device in *The 400 Blows*." *Film Criticism* 14:1 (1989) 26–32.
Raskin, Richard. "A Note on Closure in Truffaut's *Les 400 Coups*." *A Danish Journal of Film Studies* 2 (Dec 1996) 95–100.
Sievers, Heiko. "'Ici souffrit le pauvre Antoine Doinel': Ein Graffito François Truffauts als Paradigma seiner 'biographie imaginaire'." *Lendemains* 13:50 (1988) 101–108.
Towner, Daniel. "Antoine Doinel in the Zoetrope." *Literature/Film Quarterly* 18:4 (1990) 230–235.
Turner, Dennis. "Made in U.S.A.: The American Child in Truffaut's *400 Blows*." *Literature/Film Quarterly* 12:2 (1984) 75–85.
Walz, Eugene. "Antoine's First and Final Adventure." *Mosaic* 16:1–2 (1983) 139–143.

Baisers volés
(*Stolen Kisses*)

written and directed by François Truffaut (1968)

The second Antoine Doinel film was an episode of the 1964 *L'Amour à vingt ans*, chronicling the love between Antoine and Colette. *Baisers volés*, made a decade after *Les Quatre Cents Coups*, continues the saga of Doinel/Léaud/Truffaut with variations; this time Léaud injects more of himself into the Doinel persona, who confronts life awkwardly in a series of attempts to find a profession and a true love. Not wanting to be too autobiographical, Truffaut portrays Doinel as a detective, a variation on his own background as a journalist. Truffaut has compared this film to a Balzac novel depicting a *début dans la vie* and to Flaubert's *L'Education sentimentale*, at the same time that he has confessed his anxiety about the loose structure and improvisational nature of the work. This latter technique of Truffaut connects all his work to that of Pirandello through the title of his play *Tonight We Improvise*. It is a cinematic equivalent of a *roman d'initiation*, but in a comic mode, an open text which invites the spectator to write into it.

Truffaut's use of technicolor brings this work out of the dream realm of *Les Quatre Cents Coups*, giving it greater realism and spontaneity, continuing more the tone of *L'Amour à vingt ans*. Like all Truffaut films, *Baisers volés* is self-reflexive and self-conscious cinema. Its opening shot of the Musée du Cinéma and its dedication to Henri Langlois and his Cinémathèque uses film for a rare militancy, as Langlois had just been fired from his post as curator, creating a storm of protest among the contemporary New Wave directors. To a certain extent, the rough edges of the film are due to Truffaut's exceptional preoccupation during the shooting with the politics of the Cinémathèque's direction.

Truffaut sought out intelligent, experienced actors from repertory theater to handle the unpredictability of the script: Delphine Seyrig as Fabienne Tabard, chosen for her stunning image in *L'Année dernière à Marienbad*, Claude Jade as Christine Darbon, whose family name was stolen from cast member François Darbon, Michel Lonsdale as Monsieur Tabard, Harry Max as Monsieur Henry, Daniel Ceccaldi as Christine's father, Monsieur Darbon, and André Falcon. Collaborating with Truffaut on the screenplay and dialogue were Claude de Givray and Bernard Revon. Antoine Duhamel's music and Charles Trenet's 1942 song "Que reste-t-il de nos amours?" with its title lyrics mark the film as a nostalgic retrospective, with a nonspecific temporal dislocation. All the credits are displayed in front of the grill gate on the Cinémathèque announcing RELACHE (an opening ironic commentary on the controversy as well as an acknowledgement of its importance in forming Truffaut artistically and technically). Technical council was provided by a detective agency and research by Givray and Revon; Truffaut's fascination with Hitchcock and the film noir are readily apparent, although his improvisational directing style contrasts Hitchcock's known mania for advance preparation.

The film opens with a shot of the skyline of Paris and the Eiffel Tower, the signature frame of the Doinel films. This time the perspective is higher, looking down at the buildings, to a small grilled window, mimesis of the film screen as well as of episodes of imprisonment and confinement in Truffaut's prior films and his own past. Doinel still in the army sits in a cell reading Balzac's *Le Lys dans la vallée* (*The Lily in the Valley*), the 1835 epistolary novel of impossible love. The camera glimpses the commander, who is overhead making rude comments comparing mine and bomb defusion to handling women. Doinel, who enlisted and served three years, is being dismissed as unfit for military service (incarnating Truffaut's painful experience), having been AWOL everywhere. He is also the rebellious hero of 1968 (the film was shot before the events of May). He has been denied an honorable discharge by General de Gaulle, who represents the hated bourgeois and military power structure. Doinel is indifferent to the doors closed to him in the future by his stigma, like the doors in the film which will symbolically close to shut out both the characters and the spectators.

Doinel generates echoes of *Les Quatre Cents Coups* as he runs through the city traffic to a whorehouse, where, as in the earlier film, prostitutes are being picked up by the police. Incurably romantic, Doinel drops the first prostitute in disgust over her controlling demands that she remain clothed and he not kiss her on the mouth, then returns upstairs with a more accommodating type. Establishing a refrain that will become the title of the last Doinel film, Antoine then returns to his room, dashing frenetically through the obstacles of Paris traffic. After examining a book and a toy train, he walks across his bed and opens the window to gaze at the Sacré Coeur, counterpart to the initial emblem of the Eiffel Tower, nominal sign of a love story.

Arriving at his girlfriend Christine's elegant house, he is greeted by her parents, whose indulgent hospitality contrasts his own abandonment. When he confesses to her father that he has received a permanent discharge for instability of character, the father says that the army is like the theater, a marvelous anachronism. Antoine's odyssey into the world of employment begins when Christine's father gets him a job as a night clerk at the Hotel Alsina in Montmartre. Christine is away on vacation skiing because her conservatory is closed, but not for vacation; the school has a new dean whom the students are boycotting in protest and in sympathy with the former dean, a transposition of the Langlois-Barbin issue at the Cinémathèque. On the job at the hotel, Doinel once again reads Balzac, this time the 1831 *La Peau de chagrin* (*The Skin of Sorrow*), a fabular tale of the hero Raphael's Faustian pact and his love for the maternal Pauline, who in the end acquires vampire powers. Truffaut's ambition to record life's prosaic lyricism on film, which competes in his psyche in importance with life itself, draws him to writers like Balzac and Henry James. Moreover, it is legitimate to read all these textual references hermeneutically, as emblematic of the meaning of Truffaut's filmmaking, or as textual models of character or intrigue.

As an initial indication of her nourishing support of Antoine, Christine knocks at the window with a gift of vitamins for him from her parents. As she and Antoine chat, they frame a train poster for *wagons-lits* (pullman cars—beds on the run) hanging behind them. The Darbons' patronage of Antoine continues when he is invited to dinner at their home. Their hospitality to outsiders, their protection, their help in finding a job, constitute a tribute to André Bazin's crucial role as Truffaut's mentor and savior.

Two suspicious men enter the Hotel Alsina while Doinel is taking out the trash, supposedly looking for a Madame Collin who is to catch the train for London with them. Doinel's naïveté is obvious as he opens her room for them to find the woman in bed with another man (the plot segment announced by the poster combining beds and trains). This situation has been set up by a private detective with her husband in order to obtain evidence of her infidelity, an obsessive thematic Truffaut used fifteen years later in *Vivement dimanche*. In all cases, it is a tranference of Truffaut's anguish over his mother's infidelity to his father and his fantasy of tracking down and even murdering the offending lover. The hotel owner Shapiro is furious, and predictably Doinel is fired for letting the private detective in to trap his client's unfaithful wife in a police raid. Doinel in this film develops a persona as an innocent maladroit, a Chaplineseque classic character type, while the film gently mocks the improbable sequences of American B-grade film noir.

Doinel advances from guard dog to bloodhound when illogically the detective offers him a job. He thus becomes a snoop, a voyeur like the cameraman or the hero of a *polar* or a *Nouveau Roman* like Robbe-Grillet's *Le Voyeur*. Doinel's ineptitude on his first assignment, to follow a suspicious woman in black, leads her to report him to a police officer, and he is chased off her trail. This entire sequence echoes the extended parodic homage of *A bout de souffle*.

In a rare *truc*, Truffaut initiates the next sequence in reduced format, in the left corner of the screen, a film within a film on *noir*, then expands to a full-screen shot. Christine carrying a violin case is being followed by a mysterious man (Serge Rousseau), a continuation of the camera arbitrarily following the girl with the violin case in *Tirez sur le pianiste*. When she arrives home to find her father and Doinel waiting, they mention that her mother is absent because of a train strike, another intrusive allusion to political unrest and another improvisation on the jazz-like thematic of trains. It is jokingly suggested that Doinel might become a portrait painter, writer, taxi driver, poet, beggar, in a satiric taxonomy of professions, arts and employment options. Doinel confesses that he has joined Blady's agency and is now shadowing, searching and investigating. The hero as detective identifies with detective heroes of Hollywood and represents the means of investigation of the filmmaker, of others and the self, the private eye/I. Antoine is clearly seen as a man who loves women as he kisses Christine in the wine cellar (overcoming her resistance, contrasting the prostitute who said, "I don't kiss customers on the mouth"). This sequence is included in flashback in *L'Amour en fuite*.

The use of the detective agency theme enables Truffaut to include a veritable catalogue of oddities in the cases they have, the harassment case of a boss who is trying to frame his clerk for shoplifting because he's in love with her, or the client whose male lover has vanished, a classic schizoid villain with one bare hand and one gloved in black (reminiscent of the brilliant antics of Peter Sellers in *Dr. Strangelove* but also emblematic of sexual ambiguity).

A series of vignettes depict Doinel trying the tricks of the trade in attempting to gain access to clients. He faces the same barrier in his own life, entering Christine's house just as she escapes by the cellar door. His boss is seen kissing the secretary, adding to the list of stolen kisses: of the woman in the hotel, the prostitutes, Christine. Truffaut cuts from Doinel and his boss commiserating about women with confessions of Doinel's difficulties and ineptitude to a shot depicting him with a very tall blond girl, another cameo used in flashback in *L'Amour en fuite*. The boss tells Doinel of making love with his cousin after his grandfather's funeral, asserting that "Making love is a way of compensating after a death, of proving that you still exist."

Another comic case is illustrated as Doinel tells Christine about a nurse caring for twins whose mother became suspicious of her actions. It turned out the nurse was abandoning the babies to a concierge and going off to do a striptease act, combining in her person the two polar female functions of *la maman* and *la putain*, imaging the fascination and the ambiguity of women for Truffaut in this tragicomic film of fear, longing and loss.

Doinel takes Christine to a show at a club, where we see performing the magician who left the man with the black glove. It is a Felliniesque vaudeville clown act, with the magician doing rope tricks, a Renoir-like variety show within the script. Doinel leaves to track the magician, but predictably loses him as he enters a building, the quintessential evasion of the magician escape artist. As Doinel has a chance encounter with his former love Colette, now married with a baby, the first strains of the film's nostalgic theme song are heard. In another reference to the current political climate of activism and unrest, Christine has just been to a demonstration rally. Doinel reports to his agency that the magician entered the post office and never came back out (using his obvious professional ability to disappear).This whole sequence is repeated by Eric Rohmer in *La Femme de l'aviateur* (*The Aviator's Wife*).

Michel Lonsdale as Monsieur Tabard is the next client presented, coming to the firm to complain about his employee problems at his busy shoe store (by implication a *casse-pieds*). Tabard is a classic paranoid narcissist, wanting to see himself through others. He is also a racist, an archetypal hypocritical bourgeois. He complains about the insolence of both his wife and his salesgirls, demonstrating his obvious need to dominate women. Antoine's attempts to go undercover as an operative at the shoe store are truly Chaplinesque, as he is hired as a stockboy, after struggling hopelessly to wrap a package. Doinel's failure to *emballer* (which also means enchant) is reinforced with the endshot freeze frame from *Les Quatre Cents Coups*. In a sequence unintentionally ironized by the events of May 1968 after the filming, Doinel runs into a rebellious female friend on the street who is writing plays for television. Tabard's negative persona is reinforced during Doinel's lunch with the salesgirls, who refer to their boss as "the dinosaur." In an inversion of men abusing female employees, the virago female manager of the store inveighs against Doinel when he cannot locate a pair of Louis XV-style shoes. As he takes refuge up a ladder, the doorbell rings. When he descends and walks under another ladder to investigate, it is suddenly dark outside, a temporal hiatus typical of New Wave narrative inconsistency, of the spontaneous amateurish tone of Truffaut's "family-style" filmmaking which gives his films a certain parodic surrealistic quality, at the same time that it reaffirms his primary motive as a director, that of a true *amateur*, filmmaker by personal obsession more than by profession.

Delphine Seyrig's first appearance as Fabienne Tabard shows her speaking Russian to a friend on the phone. Doinel falls for her of course, and we see him practicing Russian at home, with a record set that says *Cours d'anglais* (English Course), yet another comic inconsistency. As a lady customer leaves the store with twins in horrid clown masks, Christine comes in, still followed by the mysterious stranger we have seen from the beginning of the film, the counterpart to all the private detectives, to Doinel, to Félix in *Le Lys dans la vallée*. Madame Tabard overhears the girls talking about Doinel's infatuation for her. Doinel at home before the mirror practices naming first Fabienne Tabard and then Christine Darbon with Antoine Doinel, seeking through the performative force of nomination to strengthen his identity or create a bond between him and one of the women, to choose between them. As he and Tabard enter Tabard's apartment, their reflections are distorted in the mirror. While he has supper with Fabienne and his boss, they speak of Oleg and Natasha, in a spoof of KGB spy novels. Tabard explains that the only way to learn a foreign language is in bed. His open defense of Hitler announces his fascism, an implicit attack on the Right in France, which was challenged by the events of 1968. Doinel is intimidated by the beauty of Madame Tabard and runs from the apartment in panic, back to the shoe store. Fabienne follows him, and soon the detective tailing her is reporting that she has a lover. At Blady's agency, the man with the glove goes berserk when he learns that his homosexual lover has married, and they have to forceably eject him from the office. This parody of the private sleuth will be polished to the level of homage in *Vivement dimanche*.

Doinel goes home to find a gift of the neckties the detective has reported purchased by Fabienne. Following Balzac's epistolary model, Doinel attempts to reach Madame Tabard by composing nineteen letters, finally resorting to an open comparison with Félix de Vandenesse and his love for Madame de Mortsauf in *Le Lys dans la vallée*. Truffaut's camera follows the pipes as a special delivery letter is sent by pneumatic service under the streets of Paris, the modern counterpart to the spatio-temporal distancing of nineteenth-century correspondence. Doinel has to leave his post at the shoe store, as he has become hopelessly embroiled with Fabienne, risking a love affair with this older married woman, finding that the suspect he sought is now himself.

This futile attempt to escape is thwarted when she presents herself to him at his bedside the next morning to make love with him, comparing their relationship to that of Félix and Madame de Mortsauf, stating that Mortsauf died from not sharing her love, gazing on Doinel in bed as a love object, marvelling at the uniqueness of individuals. She then proposes a contract to make love with him one single time and separate forever. This entire sequence can be read as a Truffaldian oedipal fantasy of possession of the forbidden and rejecting mother. At this point Christine comes to Antoine's apartment to find the door locked and leaves, perplexed, still followed by the mysterious gentleman. Another employee of Blady's now reports Fabienne's visit to Doinel, who is thus trapped, like the secretary still pursued by the boss. Yet another detective in the midst of a phone call dies suddenly of a heart attack. After his funeral, Doinel remembering his boss's story seeks out a prostitute to reaffirm life in the face of death. These are yet more disconnected elements that will coalesce in coherent fashion fifteen years later in *Vivement dimanche*.

In the final sequence, Christine is home watching television as her parents leave for the weekend. Having deliberately broken the television set, she calls the TV repair company SOS in a ploy to get Doinel to the house. He arrives to crash the truck into her father's car. As the lovers abandon the television, a prowling private eye camera follows their tracks up the stairs to look in one room—it's empty—then finds them asleep together, like a detective documenting their liaison.

As Christine and Doinel are having breakfast, they send notes back and forth, another epistolary love exchange, kept secret from the audience. We understand the content as Doinel slips a bottle opener over her ring finger; it has been a declaration of love and intent. Doinel and Christine are strolling happily in the park when the mysterious stranger again approaches Christine and declares his undying fidelity to her, stating that he plans to follow her forever—the romantic Dantesque or Keatsian cliché of eternal futile pursuit, elevating the thematic to a classic dimension. Accompanying her disbelieving response is the song "Que reste-t-il de nos amours?" Truffaut presents a comic yet painful portrait of the vicissitudes of a young man's heart, counterbalanced by the impossible fidelity of an older man's longing, images of Truffaut past and present. The stranger following Christine is also an echo of the Faust contract of Balzac's *La Peau de chagrin*, thus leaving the spectator with an open ending that undermines the pursuit of the other throughout the film.

Bibliography

Please see the *Vivement dimanche* chapter for the general Truffaut bibliography.

Gillain, Anne. *Le Cinéma selon François Truffaut*. Paris: Flammarion, 1988. 193–205.

————. *François Truffaut: Le Secret perdu*. Paris: Hatier, 1991.

Insdorf, Annette. *François Truffaut*. Boston: Twayne, 1978.

————. *François Truffaut*. New York: Simon & Schuster, 1989.

L'Amour en fuite
(Love on the Run)

written and directed by François Truffaut (1979)

Like Jean Cocteau's *Testament d'Orphée* completing a trilogy covering thirty years, *L'Amour en fuite* represents the final film of the Antoine Doinel cycle, a cinematic autobiographic production covering twenty years. In fact, all of Truffaut's cinematic *oeuvre*, from 1955 until his death in 1984, could be said to be an extended autobiography of the filmmaker, reflected in a variety of characters as well as embodied in his own filmmaking persona. Even a film like *Vivement dimanche* which reflects his lifelong fascination with classic film noir could be deemed a critical or citational autobiography, as it harkens back to his work with Godard twenty-five years earlier. Truffaut thus presents his many facets: avid filmgoer of the *ciné-clubs* and Cinémathèque, film critic hailing his predecessors of choice and skewering the others, Balzacian novelist of the *Nouvelle Vague*, filmmaker on the set, offering multiple images of a career and a creative imagination that coalesce in the complex intertextuality of his life's work, as critic, scriptwriter, actor, director, lyric poet of the oneiric adventure of the cinema.

The opening shot of *L'Amour en fuite* images its titular thematic, love on the run, as Doinel embraces his lover Sabine and announces his new program of chastity. Love is on the run in numerous ways in the film: Doinel is running away from commitment; his marriage has crumbled; he dashes about at a frenetic pace; he pursues his past in flashbacks and in a *fugue* that will lead to the mirror of a Gidian *acte gratuit* when he spontaneously boards a departing train. The significance of the title is doubled by the fact that in French, *la fuite* can mean flight, escape, leakage, loss (affective loss due to temporal erosion) or point of view, the vanishing perspective of images captured by the cinematographer, in this case again Nestor Almendros. This is one of Truffaut's most intriguing original filmscripts, for which he had the collaboration of both Marie-France Pisier (whose writing includes the novel *Le Bal du gouverneur*) and Suzanne Schiffman. Behind the opening credits is a scene of morning lovemaking between the reluctant Antoine and his current paramour Sabine (played by Dorothée), on the floor of her room with the lights off and the shades drawn, the artificially darkened world of desire equatable to that of the cinema. The lineage of intertextuality in Truffaut's work is evident, as Sabine is the name of Jules's and Catherine's daughter from *Jules et Jim*, like Alphonse in *La*

Nuit américaine a child of the cinema. The film's appurtenance to the classic Parisian genre is signaled by its theme song by Alain Souchon, which returns at the end. The rest of the soundtrack background music is by Georges Delerue.

Antoine this particular morning is heading home without breakfast. Sabine wants him to move in and stop rushing off, proving her loyalty by giving him all nineteen volumes of the diary of Paul Léautaud, a textual *mise-en-abyme* and nominal origin of the multiple volume diary of Léaud playing Antoine. The frustrated oedipal nature of Doinel's obsession with women is signaled by his avowal that he wanted to make love to his mother, an attraction initially acknowledged in *Les Quatre Cents Coups*. The future of the relationship between Antoine and Sabine includes plans for a shared vacation and a rendez-vous to attend a friend's housewarming that night. Doinel is then shown literally on the run, as he dashes from her apartment to return home to shave and dress before work. His projects are shattered by a telephone call from the past, as his wife phones to remind him of their appointment for their divorce settlement that morning, as well as his obligation to take his son to the train that evening.

Now accommodating past obligations in present scenarios, the frustrated script begins again, as Doinel dashes off to find Sabine at work in the Barnerias record store to explain that he cannot go out with her. During their subsequent taxi ride, Christine and Antoine reminisce about their years together, illustrated with flashbacks. In a self-reflexive commentary on his modernist style of realism, Truffaut brings up the question of *vraisemblance* (verisimilitude), a primary concern of New Wave filmmaking, in a series of retrospective sequences. Doinel remembers their wedding date, 26 February, the day of St. Nestor, a comic allusion to Almendros and the power of the cinema to depict, as the film flashes back to their fights and breakup, then to more tender scenes: their nuttiness in reading pornographic comments into articles in the newspaper while lying in bed.

Time is both telescoped and fragmented in these scenes, as the film returns to the narrative present, and Christine Doinel goes first into the judge's chambers, while Antoine flashes back to the first two sequences in the wine cellar (refilmed from *Baisers volés*, thus recalled internally in the diegesis of the frame film rather than quoted cinematically in the original; one problem of including original flashback footage was the CinemaScope format of the earlier films). As Doinel then enters the judge's chambers, there are sociological comments about the new divorce law (Truffaut divorced his wife of twenty years). The second sequence of the Doinels embracing in the wine cellar is intercut with their divorce proceedings, and the very specific terms of custody and alimony. Doinel, whose imagination, like the editing and the film itself, is always on the run, is thinking of his wife in bed with him years earlier because of the female judge's eyeglasses. Looking out the window, he sees a wedding party running to a waiting Mercedes, a cliché contrast of rites of passage. The Doinels are interviewed by the press, as they are the first couple to divorce under the new no-fault law. Their lawyer then greets his colleague Colette (Marie-France Pisier), Doinel's first love, and they comment that Doinel's divorce is a momentous occasion. Truffaut intended Pisier's role to be that of a psychoanalyst, to whom Léaud would recount his past in flashbacks (continuing the format from *Les Quatre Cents Coups*), but their prior affair preempted professionally this arrangement. The allusion to literature through Colette prompts a cut to Antoine on the run again, to his office, a printing press where he works as a copy editor. We learn that Doinel is caught in an emotional trap, that he has a fatal fascination for elegant bourgeois women, parodied in the flashback from *Baisers volés* of the very tall blond girl walking with him.

The film's literarity is reinforced in the next sequence where Colette is in the Barnerias bookstore, looking for Antoine Doinel's novel and for a tale by Dalloz about mad murderers, the *mise-en-abyme* of the subplot of her next case, just as Doinel's book, *Les Salades de l'amour* (*Love Lettuce*), textualizes and intertextualizes the film's primary intrigue. Colette is infatuated with Xavier Barnerias, the bookseller. The mention of Doinel's autobiographic work elicits a cut to a sequence from his cinematic childhood in *Les Quatre Cents Coups*.

At the Gare de Lyon, Antoine puts his son Alphonse on a train for music camp, as Colette leaves for Aix-en-Provence to research the genocide case she has been asked to take. Antoine calls Sabine on the phone and hangs up on her after a high-strung exchange of reproaches. The train station is of course a place of rites of passage, a nexus of arrivals, departures, encounters, a Truffaldian thematic in filigree, and a symbol of the entry into the story line, depicted by Colette carrying Doinel's autobiography as she boards her train. Doinel mimetically leaps into the text of his past as he jumps on her train. As Colette (Doinel has been reading the eponymous novelist) begins to read his book, which is also her tale as part of his past (from *L'Amour à vingt ans*), the film illustrates the text with the scene of their encounter at a Salle Pleyel concert. The film has an extensive musical thematic, as Doinel's wife, son and former lover Liliane all play the violin (*violon d'Ingres?*), and he met Sabine in the record store where she works. Music is not only a sister art, it is the aural equivalent of the printed images of the literary text and the audible half of the sound and image essence of film. It is thematically evocative and significant in all the Doinel films. Here its role in the film's structure is implicated by the triple meaning of *fugue*: interwoven melodies, spontaneous flight, schizoid doubling.

Colette reads from Doinel's book one of Truffaut's more intimate observations, that self-destructive behavior indicates someone who is in love. As Colette reads Doinel, the mirror of him reading Colette, the film flashes back to them dining with her parents years earlier, an echo also of the scenes with Christine and her parents in *Baisers volés* and *Domicile conjugal*. In an act of textual production, Colette responds to Antoine by letter, hurting him with her lack of emotional involvement. Their versions of the tale conflict as he reinvents the past in his book, having her move in with her family across the street from him; she corrects the story, showing rather that he moved in across from her to pursue her. In a sequence from the period of *Domicile conjugal*, Antoine decides to marry Christine Darbon

(Claude Jade), whom he calls Peggy Sage, because she salves his ego. When he later encounters Christine entering the office of a gynecologist and then sees a poster of a baby in the Métro, Doinel finally understands that his wife is pregnant, in a perfect metonymic sequence, where juxtaposed signs convey associated meaning.

Colette wants the mysterious stranger waiting for her in the dining car to be Xavier, but it is merely Doinel, a Sartrian traveler without a ticket, a classic alienated character, contingent, absurd, in search of himself. As Doinel tries to distance himself from his textual autobiographic past, Colette recalls her version of what really happened, showing that his autobiography is full of lies, that he was living in the shadow of her family. Doinel claims that his characters are amalgams of real people, relating that he was married five years earlier and then separated because reconstructing his childhood memories made him irritable and drove him and his wife into contention. Truffaut uses scenes from previous Doinel films and flashbacks within the present film to weave an arabesque of images, wherein memory and imagination are indistinguishably intertwined, a fundamental truth of all text, literary or cinematic. He achieves a Proustian conjunction of the self in this spatio-temporal depth.

Doinel questions the motives for writing, affirming that it is not art if it is just to settle old scores, thus initially repudiating the therapeutic function of autobiographical writing. As Doinel discusses his new girlfriend Sabine, it becomes apparent that he and Christine are still in love, but that he forced on her the roles of daughter, mother and sister without acknowledging her as a wife. Liliane (Dani) is introduced as a character in the novel of their life. Both Antoine and Colette are seen as spies, embodying the voyeur function of the camera, reader and spectator. Christine tells Antoine that Liliane writes children's books, and in a comic intertextual allusion, claims that the two of them did the costumes for Rohmer's 1978 *Perceval le Gaulois*. Antoine finds himself marginalized by his wife's friendship with Liliane and fantasizes a lesbian rivalry because he was reading Colette at this time. At their country house, the two women are presented tap dancing together.

In a dramatic return to the frame film present, the lawyer Colette saves a little boy playing with the outer door of the train, a complex gesture counterbalancing her later revelation about her daughter and her defense of the child murderer, and prefiguring Antoine's subsequent leap from the train. Colette maneuvers Antoine into her train compartment as a lecherous gorilla type eyes her. Doinel then introduces a supposed fictional work he is struggling with: *Le Manuscrit trouvé par une sale gosse* (manuscript found by a rotten girl). Its intrigue interweaves elements from the autobiographic text and the frame film sequences. The scenario depicts the hero Doinel eavesdropping (the aural voyeur) on a conversation in a phone booth, with an overlay of illustrating images and narration. The hero reconstructs the torn photograph left by the caller and tracks down the girl in the picture, an homage to Hollywood fiction and to the hermeneutic function of all filmgoing.

Antoine confesses that this adventure led him back into the trap of the same unhappy relationship with Sabine, that only meeting new people interests him. In a sequence depicting her female vulnerability, Colette gets a proposition from the gorilla next door, Antoine falls off the luggage rack onto her professional robes, and she feels doubly victimized, attacking Antoine's adolescent egotism. Antoine inadvertently drops the torn picture of Sabine, at Colette's feet, connecting textual fiction and image once again, as he pulls the emergency brake and jumps from the train in a capricious *fuite*, escaping physically and emotionally from his story's primary diegesis.

The film cuts to a conversation between Antoine and Sabine where he discovers that he has lost the photo of her, thus preventing the integration of his fiction and his life, his past and his present, a gap imaged by the window separating the two as they break off their relationship. She throws his letters back at him in another rupture of textual communication, a reversal of the epistolary function. Meanwhile the picture of Sabine, fragmented image in collage, is tucked into the pages of his autobiographic book that Colette is reading. In another self-reflexive mirror inversion, Colette the character in his book is reading his book in the film while he is again depicted reading Colette, in a tour de force game of exterior and interior, narrative frame and framed diegesis, enunciation and enunciated.

In another rupture in the narrative, the film cuts to the printing press, with galleys for a book about the time de Gaulle disappeared for a day, 30 May 1968, resituating the historic political perspective of the film, as the secret manuscript is locked in the safe. In another collapsing of past and present, text and image, a mysterious man spying on Antoine in the office, talking through the glass window, turns out to be his mother's lover Lucien, who tells him about her, her rebellious nature, that she was an anarchist, against everything. Lucien recounts that he was friends with Antoine's father before he died, that he then read aloud to his mother as she lost her sight. Truffaut intercuts pictures of Doinel reading Balzac in secret from *Les Quatre Cents Coups* and the sequence of Antoine playing hooky and, in complicity of illicit conduct, seeing his mother Gilberte kissing Lucien in the street. Doinel's memories from film five to film one establish the Balzacian intertextuality giving the illusion of lived experience to artistic expression, reaffirming Truffaut's assertion that he did not exist outside the cinema. The subsequent sequence inserts the scene from *Les Quatre Cents Coups* where he lies to the head of school about his truancy by saying that his mother has died. We see Antoine in his black turtle-neck as his parents come to take him home and deliver two of his blows. In response to Lucien's query regarding Antoine's absence from his mother's funeral, Truffaut screens the scene from *Baisers volés* where Doinel is in military prison in Germany and doesn't have the money to get home. This entire sequence acquired an extra external dimension of poignancy, loss and affective imprisonment from the death of Truffaut's mother in 1971, after completion of the prior Doinel film in 1970.

In a *coup de théâtre* prepared by the lie and the absence of the earlier films, Lucien reveals to Antoine in the diegetic present of the frame film that his mother is buried in Montmartre, next to Marguerite Gautier, the model for the heroine of

Dumas's *La Dame aux camélias*. She is thus in turn equated to a historic real model for a classic fictional character. Learning that Antoine has never been to his mother's grave, Lucien takes him there, telling him the rest of his own life story. The picture on the tomb of Gilberte Doinel, the ultimate lost love, can be equated to the torn portrait of the broken love, Sabine, in the capturing of the living subject as dead fictional object by the camera lens. Doinel's mother's tombstone is engraved like the textual (auto)biographic page with the dates of her life.

Antoine is portrayed next in another act of textual production, writing to Sabine to tell her about meeting Lucien and recalling the incident from *Les Quatre Cents Coups* when he was questioned by the psychologist at the reform school. Truffaut also includes here the scene where Gilberte, returning home from a tryst, steps over her sleeping son. The film then screens the scene where Antoine tells his "spycologist" of his attempts at sexual initiation. The camera returns to the letter of the frame film, as Antoine continues his confessional narrative with the sequence from *Baisers volés* where he feels he must prove himself with all the women he sees, in response to his sense of rejection and betrayal as a result of his mother's conduct. As he is penning this letter in *L'Amour en fuite*, he tears it up and talks of having his character die in his novel, a metatextual self-reflexive narrative ambition to textualize the impossible, to image one's own death, in this case a transposition of a suicidal urge.

The frame film shifts to Colette in Aix gathering information about the child murderer, reintroducing the subplot. Due to the murderer's attempted suicide in prison and a postponement of the trial, Colette returns to Paris for a week. She rushes to Xavier for solace, then looks at the photo of Sabine with Xavier's last name, Barnerias, thinking they are married. Indulging her and our imagination, the film shows Xavier meeting Sabine at the movies, as they confide to each other their imminent mutual ruptures with Antoine and Colette. Crying over the movie they are watching, Sabine repeats Antoine's earlier refusal to use a kleenex, as the frame film cuts to Colette learning that in fact Sabine and Xavier are brother and sister.

Opening the final sequence, Doinel's past loves Christine and Colette both seek out Sabine and in her absence finish by confiding in each other. Feeling guilty about having hurt Antoine, Colette tells Christine about their rupture, when she introduced Albert to him at her parents' house. Christine in turn fills in another gap in this tale of intertextual loose ends, recalling ironically first the arguments between Liliane and Antoine, then the shock of finding them in bed together, their own subsequent separation, and Antoine's short-lived cohabitation with Liliane. Truffaut here creates a ruse, with a composite fake flashback using their dispute in the courtyard from *La Nuit américaine* (where the same actors play different roles) and new footage of Christine watching from a window above.

The next flashback is the scene from *Baisers volés* of Antoine running into Colette and Albert with their baby. Colette continues, narrating the traumatic sequence where her daughter Julie was killed by a car in the street, concluding with the irony that she is going to defend a man who killed his own three-year-old child.

In a therapeutic moment of self-knowledge achieved through film narrative, Colette realizes that she indeed loves Xavier and goes off to tell him, giving Christine the torn picture of Sabine to deliver to Antoine. When he receives it, he realizes that he is trying to put the pieces of his life together in the form of a woman he loves, just as the film editor creates in collage the composite image of a fragmented character and Truffaut combines the intertextual fragments of the many Doinel films.

As the happy endings begin, Colette is at the bookstore embracing Xavier and lowering the blind (curtain) on their story. Sabine and Antoine are still arguing, reconnecting the plot to the opening scene, as Sabine accuses Antoine of using his unhappy childhood to avoid commitment with a woman. As Antoine tells the telephone booth story and we again see the man shouting at Sabine over the phone, his "novel" becomes yet another episode in his frame film life. Antoine tells of his dogged detective pursuit of Sabine's identity, a grail-like quest, and that he has concealed his feelings all his life out of fear of getting hurt. As a pair of lovers enter the store and request Alain Souchon's latest song, which is of course the title song of the film, Sabine and Antoine embrace, as do the couple, hidden in the listening booth. Truffaut intercuts the scene of Antoine from *Les Quatre Cents Coups* in the luna park gravitron, the essence of film as the equivalent of the Zoetrope cylinder, precursor of moving pictures. The camera of the frame film then begins to pan in 360 degrees, in a cinematographic self-reflexive homage, as the film ends on a reaffirmation of the dizzying craziness of life.

Bibliography

Please see the chapter on *Vivement dimanche* for the general Truffaut bibliography.

Gillain, Anne. *Le Cinéma selon François Truffaut*. Paris: Flammarion, 1988. 379–387.
————. *François Truffaut: Le Secret perdu*. Paris: Hatier, 1991.
Insdorf, Annette. *François Truffaut*. New York: Simon & Schuster, 1989.

La Nuit américaine
(Day for Night)

written and directed by François Truffaut (1973)

Truffaut wrote, directed and starred in this mirror-film, like Fellini's 1963 *8 1/2* or 1972 *Roma*, as well as many other recent films, a self-reflexive and self-representational film about filmmaking, about transitions between the person, the professional, the role, between layers of reality and illusion. Although its subject gives *La Nuit américaine* the look of a production documentary, Truffaut mistrusted documentary filmmaking, preferring to make instead, as aptly signaled by the title, a detailed depiction of the artifice of filmmaking, using all the tricks of illusion and allusion which it simultaneously reveals and portrays. Although not autobiographic in the true sense of authentic subjective retrospective narrative, the film generates an autobiographic effect in casting Truffaut as a film director and foregrounding the passion and anxiety of film production, the pressures and joys experienced by everyone on a film crew. The French title embodies a multiple significance that is lost in the English; not only is the daylight filter a technique of illusion enabling night shot effects in broad daylight, but it came from America, whose influence Truffaut always felt and which he acknowledges on several occasions in the film. The title has also been interpreted as marking the end of the great star-system Hollywood-style filmmaking (referenced in remarks about the early career of Alexandre and Séverine and the present condition of Julie Baker), but it is rather the magic of the dark movie theater, the night of film noir gangster black and white, that it represents in Truffaut's retrospective imagination. Appropriately, in a mirror tribute, the film received an Oscar.

The frame film and the film within the film were both made in Nice, where daytime outdoor location shots and evening studio sequences created a counterpoint between the scattering of the crew on paths of adventure diurnally and their recentering at nightfall, comparable to the interdiegetic rhythm of the classic American western, a similarity noted by Wayne Douglass in his article demonstrating the film's debt to Howard Hawks. James Card finds just as many correlations between *La Nuit américaine* and Kelly and Donen's 1952 *Singin' in the Rain*. Truffaut's many interviews acknowledging his childlike passion for film and filmmaking reaffirm, however, his two primary models: Hitchcock and Renoir. Not only was Truffaut actually referring to Renoir's *La Marseillaise* in his comment about the daily rhythms of dissemination and regroupment, but it was Hitchcock who first suggested to Truffaut in the early 1960s the idea of a film about filmmaking.

Truffaut was in Nice editing *Les Deux Anglaises et le continent* (*Two English Girls*) when he chanced on the abandoned set at the Victorine Studios from the movie of the Giraudoux play *La Folle de Chaillot* (*The Madwoman of Chaillot*). It was the set he would use for the film within the film, *Je vous présente Paméla* (*I Want you to Meet Pamela*), whose anodine plot makes a Chaplinesque parody of the film crew's melodramatic involvement in the project. The film presents yet another variant of the intertextual persona of Jean-Pierre Léaud, who also starred in *Les Deux Anglaises et le continent*: the temperamental Alphonse (the name as mentioned of Antoine Doinel's baby in the 1970 film *Domicile conjugal*). It is also said that Truffaut had the idea for *La Nuit américaine* from his sense of the mutual invasion of the actor's life and role, the cross-contamination of life and art, of reality and illusion, during the making of *Les Deux Anglaises* (in the film *Paméla*, she supposedly met her husband in England in circumstances referred to in the earlier film). Truffaut lived the oscillation between reality and illusion throughout his career, falling in love with his leading ladies and infusing autobiographic subjectivity into all his filmscripts in one fashion or another.

The interplay of life and artifice is perhaps more pervasive in film than on stage, as actors go in and out of costume and character on a daily basis for shooting discrete sequences, as they surrealize themselves in multiple takes, bad takes, mistakes. Furthermore, for Truffaut, who grew up nourished by the illusory reality of the silver screen, the filmmaker's art and the process of film production were as important and "real" a reality as that of real life (having substituted for the dreary anguish of his own youth on many occasions). They prove to be mutually generative and reflective, achieving paradoxically in this metacinematic self-reflexive work Truffaut's stated goal that the spectator be spellbound by the illusion of reality, escape into the film's diegesis as into the imagination when reading great literature.

The relationships between Jacqueline Bisset as the high-strung star Julie Baker, Jean-Pierre Aumont as the leading man Alexandre, Truffaut as the filmmaker Ferrand, Jean-Pierre Léaud as the moody Alphonse, Dani as his girlfriend Liliane (a role reprised in flashback in *L'Amour en fuite*), the Italian Valentina Cortese as Séverine, and Nathalie Baye as Joelle the script girl, reveal the vulnerable nature of the creative actor or actress's affective life, on and off camera. They and other members of the cast elicit intertextual images of their roles in other Truffaut films and of other actors Truffaut used, such as Pierre Lachenay or Julie Christie. The central illusion of transparency in the film is our supposed privileged inside look at Truffaut playing his professional self as the director, mirror image of himself like the name Ferrand.

The onomastics of Truffaldian characters indicate an almost obsessive anagrammatic reworking of a name central to Truffaut's real and creative angst, that of his mother, Janine de Montferrand. Not only do his male and female characters have names beginning with J, but they have the double mirror letters of both Truffaut and Montferrand and assonantic rhymes of her first and family names: Antoine Doinel, Julien Davenne, Julien Vercel, Joelle, Julie (also in *La Mariée était en noir* and the name of Colette's daughter, whose tragic death is shown in flashback in *L'Amour en fuite*), Bertrand Morane, Jules, Jim, etc. Characters echoing the last syllable of his mother's given name include Séverine, Christine, Jardine, Prévine, Delphine, Martine, Catherine, Sabine. A psychoanalytic approach discerns in Truffaut's creative production of cinema's oneiric imagery an attempt to recuperate this primal loss of a mother's love through recourse to alternate models in text and film.

Accompanying the credits at the beginning, the orchestra is heard tuning up and then performing, with the voice-over instructions of the conductor. The filmstock is photographed off-center to display the soundtrack print visually on screen. Georges Delerue wrote the music for the film; he at one point plays the ball theme for *Paméla* over the phone from Paris (a musical autocitation of the love theme from *Les Deux Anglaises et le continent*). The film is dedicated to Dorothy and Lilian Gish, the grandes dames of Hollywood cinema, shown in a monochrome still from the silent era. The first sequence depicts Léaud/Alphonse emerging from the Métro in his *vie de chien*, surrounded by people walking their dogs, a parody of a cliché Paris street scene. He walks up to Aumont/Alexandre playing his father and slaps him soundly, an act of aggression altered and amplified in the closing scene where he shoots him in the back. This opening sequence is not framed, thus the surprise impact of the "cut!" from the director, of the diegetic shift to the set decorator, the script girls and the lighting. The 1991 American film *Postcards from the Edge* opened in the same manner, blending the drama of the film and of life in the film industry. There are numerous examples of films which trap the audience in order to shock spectators with such a rupture, perhaps reflecting the affective dislocation inherent in filmmaking.

For a publicity shot, the announcer facing the camera presents the film, whose very title is an introduction, *Je vous présente Paméla*. Pamela, however, is still in Hollywood. Jacqueline Bisset's part is intensified by the fact that she has both the role of Julie and the title role in *Paméla*, alluding simultaneously to the eighteenth-century literary heroines Julie and Pamela, who struggle with virtue and passion in the eponymous novels by Rousseau and Richardson. All the other participants have but one named role, as actors in the frame film. They are anonymous in *Paméla*, marked only by their interrelationships, setting up Julie/Pamela's titular dominance and primary intertextual resonance. Truffaut also characterized Jacqueline/Julie/Pamela as an amalgam of the four English actresses he had worked with.

The producer Bertrand (Jean Champion) refuses to be interviewed, stating that he is not part of the show, a dramatic irony considering his role in the frame film. Although based on a true story, the plot of the film they are making reads like a soap opera; it is the frame film that demonstrates Truffaut's fascination with cinéma vérité, realism and naturalism. Some of the accusations of amateurism in New Wave cinematography and directing have come in response to shortened antidramatic takes intended to duplicate life's aleatory jumble. This structure makes these films difficult to discuss coherently, as that demands yet another reordering of their myriad disparate elements. In *Paméla*, Alexandre plays Alphonse's father and the husband of Séverine, an actress once madly in love with him. Her name is an homage to the female protagonist of Renoir's *La Bête humaine*. Meanwhile in *Paméla*, the father falls in love with his new English daughter-in-law. The story is presented as a classic bourgeois melodrama, wherein the father and daughter-in-law run away together (an allusion to *La Peau Douce—Soft Skin*), and everyone meets his destiny, a thematic repeated with variations in the frame film.

As the cast and crew repeat the first take, a long shot of the outdoor set gives the filmmaking frame diegesis its own sweeping melodrama, a classic cliché of Hollywood sagas. The requisite complementary aspect of fraternity around the camp fire is represented by the interior shots and by the crew's accommodations at the Hotel Atlantic in Nice, where the makeup girl Odile (Nike Arrighi) and Joelle amicably exchange rooms, preferring each other's bath and shower, prefiguring their later sharing of Bernard (Bernard Menez). Ferrand in the hall examines a vase which he appropriates for a prop (an allusion to vases as "characters" in earlier films and to film stealing from real life), then contemplates photos of Julie, commenting on her resemblance to her actress mother, on her sad and sensuous appeal. Ferrand's interest in Julie and her mother mirrors the *Paméla* plot, where Julie's role is infatuated with father and son. The film emphasizes the pressures on children, families and lovers of actors and the emotional hardships filmmaking generates in their off-screen lives. Alphonse creates the first of these affective "real-life" intrusions by bringing Liliane along to work as an assistant to Joelle.

In an ambiguous admixture of illusion and autobiographic truth, Truffaut gives his persona director Ferrand a hearing aid (supposedly needed because of a war wound, a heroic experience contrasting Truffaut's own anguishing military service). Truffaut had considered an artificial voice-box for Ferrand as a symbolic communicative disability, but it proved too expensive to simulate, and Truffaut did admit to a real-life hearing loss from participating in artillery maneuvers in the army. As a variation on the technical artifice of the film's title, one of the technicians presents for approval a candlestick with a hidden light in the back to illuminate the face of the person holding it (later used by Julie in nineteenth-century costume, reinforcing the literary intertextuality of her role). Liliane accuses Alphonse of being a womanizer when he gazes at the hotel maid, an accusation ironized by her later playing around with every man on the set and running off with the stuntman, a body-double parody of Pamela planning to run off with her father-in-law (who will be replaced by a body double at the end). Liliane and Alphonse, rearranging their hotel room, continue arguing, revealing their obvious incompatibility (she prefers cozy restaurants; he is a cinephile, racing off to the movies on three different occasions in the film, representing Truffaut's own addiction). In spite of this tension, Alphonse madly if insincerely proposes marriage to Liliane.

In the first of several voice-overs, Ferrand compares filmmaking to a stagecoach trip to the far west (itself a cinematic cliché and a reference to John Ford's 1939 classic), because you don't know if you will finish the trip, designating the frame film as a classic adventure story. The realism of the film is enhanced by details of Ferrand's professional responsibilities, defining the job of director: choosing cars for a chase scene, musing over a role, making technical decisions. The temporal parameters of the film diegesis are established by a constraint imposed on Ferrand: the American backers want to hold to a seven-week shooting schedule, to finish by 31 October, giving him just thirty-five days to complete the film. This time frame is played off against the internal temporal structure of *Paméla* and the film's actual running time of 115 minutes, creating temporal layering. Truffaut adds more effects of (meta)cinematic realism, as Ferrand checks a wig for Julie and chooses a gun for Alphonse to shoot Alexandre. This sequence establishes a dramatic irony, as they will have to use a double for Alexandre, because he dies in the frame film before they film the scene where he is shot in *Paméla*.

When the crew assembles in the projection room for screening rushes (becoming mirror role spectators viewing the film within the film), they discover that the lab in Paris has destroyed the opening scene that we saw, which will have to be done over. Séverine and Alexandre are missing from the screening. Someone is always late or missing from the set, giving the frame film a screwball comedy flavor. These absences also embody the lyric sense of loss and incompleteness found in all Truffaut's work. The next rush screened depicts Alphonse and Séverine discussing the fact that his father and wife have run off to Paris together. Séverine offers to go away with Alphonse in a mother/son *fugue*, but he has already decided instead to kill them. While watching the rushes, Alphonse mouths his lines, creating a conjunction between his levels of identity, giving him a triple persona of actor, role and spectator, layered on the intertextual palimpsest of Léaud and his other roles. As Liliane casually shares a joint of marijuana with the man sitting next to her, Alphonse possessively caresses her thigh, a gesture he will repeat one morning, futile attempts to maintain his grip on their relationship. The entire film is a series of variations on the thematic of the tenuousness of control, artistic, technical, affective, of both life and career.

An aging, depressed Séverine, who is losing her memory because of excessive drinking, suffers repeated humiliation during a scene with Alexandre, doubled intertextually by their former love affair. Prefiguring the performance of the high-strung Julie, Séverine goes to pieces on the set, unstrung by opening the wrong door to exit the set, by her wig which she removes. When she forgets all her lines, she explains that she used to work with Fellini, who had his cast recite numbers on camera and postsynchronize the dialogue. When Séverine is rebuffed and forced to say her lines on camera, she breaks down completely. Truffaut uses a black-out from stage right, first leaving just Alexandre and Séverine in his comforting embrace, then closing to black. Annette Insdorf reads this moment as paternal protection of the cast and an illustration of the understated restraint that Truffaut used in all his films when depicting sexual encounters. The fade can also be read as the cinematographic metaphor of the faded film star.

These melodramatic scenes in the film are balanced by moments of warm humor and spontaneity: the kitten who can't act, Joelle and Bernard at the stream, Julie comforting Alphonse. Throughout the film there are invasions and inversions of the double diegesis, as when Julie betrays her older husband Dr. Michael Nelson (David Markham) with Alphonse, the reverse of the *Paméla* plot. There are numerous sexual liaisons, marriages planned and broken, pregnancies and adoptions, all manner of family rituals among the crew during the filming of *Paméla*, which we of course never see in its chronological sequence or entirety. This *Nouvelle Vague* structure is not just an effect of modernism but a working reality of the filmmaking profession.

A specific reference to the New Wave style of filmmaking is the agent who represents the German porn star sisters, Greta and Diana Goerring (an implicit accusation of pornography as fascist), accosting Ferrand and asking him why he never makes a political or erotic film. The apolitical or subjectively veiled political nature of much of the New Wave filmmaking was altered by the events of May 1968, when directors like Truffaut and Godard shut down the Cannes Film Festival, but the political voice of their filmmaking remains a thematic in filigree, never foregrounded or didactic at the expense of personal cinematic creative expression. In this film, the transparent function and illusion give way to a poetic function referring either to the process of its own production or to other films and filmmakers.

In the first of three refrain dream sequences, Ferrand is asleep in bed, dreaming the German's query, "Why do you not make a political film, an erotic film?" The dream, of a little boy with a cane running anxiously along a sidewalk to a locked movie theater, is repeated as a fragment before shown in its entirety the third time, where the boy steals stills of *Citizen Kane*, an obvious homage to the film Truffaut said changed both cinema and his life forever. He used this cumulative flashback technique again a decade later in *Vivement dimanche*. The oneiric image is equatable to traumatic experiences in Truffaut's troubled childhood. It likens him to the hero of *Citizen Kane* as well, the little boy neglected and unloved who grew up to become rich and famous but never found family integrity, a lack which Truffaut compensated in his film family, a repertory-style admixture of ongoing talents including Suzanne Schiffman, Nestor Almendros, Claude Miller, Georges Delerue, Marcel Berbert, Monique Dury, as well as the actors and actresses.

The hyperrealistic discontinuity of *La Nuit américaine* is enhanced by the presence on the set of various outsiders and strangers, including a policeman who is allowed to watch the filming (and who, of course, like everyone on camera except some technical crew members, is yet another actor in Truffaut's film). Another intruder adding to the effect of reality on the set is the unit manager Gaston's wife (Zenaïde Rossi), who sits in a chair knitting and hounding her husband, a perfect *emmerdeuse* who eventually shouts vituperations at the entire crew, decrying filmmaking. Liliane and Alphonse are arguing again, in the shot Truffaut used in flashback in *L'Amour en fuite*. Ferrand faces yet another problem: the blonde actress Stacey (the father's secretary in *Paméla*), played by Alexandra Stewart (whose English stage name is an implicit reference to *Les Deux Anglaises* and Truffaut's ongoing passion for English actresses), is three months pregnant. She cannot continue filming scenes in a bathing suit for two more months. After some debate, her role is cut short, as the actress's "real life" invades and thwarts the fictitious world they are attempting to construct. She is present in all the final scenes of the frame film, however, very pregnant, emblematic of the arduous processes of gestation and production of a film.

Many writers have noted the sequence where Ferrand receives a package of books in the mail, monographs paying homage thus not only to the directors Lubitsch, Godard, Rossellini, Hawks, Bresson, Dreyer, Hitchcock, Buñuel, and Bergman, but also to cinema studies and critics and to his own film criticism (as in *A bout de souffle*), with the inclusion of the cinema journal *Travelling*. Truffaut singles out Howard Hawks as the only American-born director, although others in the group worked in Hollywood, thus making him the primary figure of homage. The title of this film, as stated, in itself acknowledges the profound influence on all the New Wave directors, in their early days at the Cinémathèque, of the work of Ford, Hawks, Fuller and Aldrich, among others.

In this poignant film of multiple arrivals and departures, numerous shots of jet planes signal the uprooted and temporary nature of the film crew's existence. Julie Baker's arrival stands out, as it completes the film family. She is subjected to a lot of big-star hype at a press conference, where rude reporters push her to admit her breakdown, noting the resemblance between her own life and the movie scenario, emphasizing thus not only its status artistically as a *mise-en-abyme* but the problem of typecasting faced by all actors and actresses.

The first scene Julie plays with Alphonse is their arrival at his parents' place and her meeting his father and mother, duplicating the actors' arrival on location. In the frame film, she then chats with Alexandre, who knows her mother. Julie comments on the kaleidoscopic nature of filmmaking, the fragmentation of life in shooting, and the boredom of the empty moments between takes on the set, which her mother hated so. Later Ferrand counters this in a tribute to the world of and on film. In an ironic foreshadowing of his death in the frame film, Alexandre talks with Ferrand about the number of times he has been killed off in films, prefiguring and enhancing the *effet de réel* when he "dies." Although obviously Jean-Pierre Aumont didn't really die, the tragedy (prefigured in *Paméla* by the stunt scene staging Pamela's car accident) served as a tribute to Françoise Dorléac (Catherine Deneuve's older sister, who played Nicole in *La Peau douce*), who was killed in a car crash on the way to the Nice airport in 1967. In more moments of displacement, Julie kisses her doctor husband goodbye as a passenger jet passes overhead, and Stacey takes her leave, while the filmstock itself journeys through time and space, as miles of film pass through the movieola viewing machine.

The effect of the intrusion of "reality" onto the film set, the bungalow where the father gets Pamela into bed, continues, as a crew member Georges requests several days leave because his mother has just died. The illusion of the real-life melodrama of the cast and crew is enhanced by the scene where Bernard is driven to the edge by his reluctant feline and Joelle humiliates him by finding a stand-in cat who performs perfectly. The cat is one of three body doubles in *Paméla*. *La Nuit américaine* includes a tribute to stuntpeople, as evidenced in the director's concern for their safety during takes and the reverse viewing of the sequences of the staged car crash, which restores to wholeness the splintered elements of the scene, a reconstruction impossible in real-life tragedies.

In another leitmotiv refrain, Alphonse repeatedly queries the other men on the set if they think women are magical, one of Truffaut's own lifelong fascinations, along with cinema. Accompanying Dr. Nelson to the airport, Alexandre gives his credo as an actor, affirming the vulnerability of the profession, the constant close contact with others, the demand to express love in many roles. Alexandre faces his own personal affective crisis as he greets Christian at the airport, his young male companion whom he hopes to adopt, an allusion to Jean Cocteau, whose name is seen later in the film. The imprint of a role on the actor's public persona is great enough that Jean-Pierre Aumont was reluctant to portray this aspect of the Alexandre role.

Ferrand and Joelle duplicate Truffaut and Schiffman's improvisational style of filmmaking, working all night on the script, written and rewritten on a daily basis, sometimes borrowing lines from the cast's experiences in the frame film, interweaving primary and secondary diegetic elements, thieving and adapting at will from "real-life" events and encounters. Julie also discusses the life of an actress, working fourteen hours a day, spending three hours on makeup. She is depicted on several occasions rehearsing her lines, given to her daily; this constant rewriting and improvisation tested any Truffaut cast and added a second dimension of heroism to his leading roles.

Ferrand affirms that any subject is worthy of filming, acknowledging Truffaut's New Wave postmodern naturalism. Joelle and Ferrand discuss the psychological structure of *Paméla*, commenting that Julie understands the film perfectly. In another comic segment, two crew members play along with a cinema trivia quiz show on television, with great success, identifying two films of Jeanne Moreau, who serves as a multiple intertext in the film, for it was she who capriciously demanded the "country butter" on the set of Joseph Losey's *Eva* and who first suggested for Truffaut the interdiegetic intrusions of *La Nuit américaine*, when a technician came on the set to scratch her back during the filming of *Jules et Jim*. Moreau's emotional state while making that film is also referenced in the adaptation of dialogue for *Paméla* from Julie's situation.

Another special effect repeated in *Vivement dimanche* uses fake rain for the kitchen scene, seen through the camera's cross hairs viewfinder, as Pamela recites the lines Julie has contributed from her experience in the frame film. Dreaming again that night, Ferrand transfers the thievery of the script (Julie's line "Let's leave like thieves in the night") to the sequence of the boy running down the street, carrying the cane that announces the homonymous homage to come. The term day for night is extended thus symbolically in the film to refer both to the cycles of adventure and encampment of classic westerns and to the interplay of levels of the self between waking and dreaming.

The next day Ferrand has to reprimand Alphonse for becoming increasingly difficult and self-indulgent. In a voice-over statement of faith, the director states that at the beginning he wants a beautiful film, that half way through he just wants the film completed, and in the second half he hopes to correct the mistakes of the first half. These confessional soliloquies constitute the most autobiographical sequences of the film. Finally the film project achieves dominion over the vicissitudes of their lives. Ferrand's skill as a craftsman is demonstrated by his attention to detail in placing Julie's hands, in setting the angle of her profile, of adjusting Alphonse's slap or caress. Further cinematographic tricks are revealed in the car scenes with one camera mounted on a truck towing the car and the other on the trunk. The massive equipment required includes booms and travellings.

At the requisite final cast party, hosted by the leading man Alexandre, he announces that he is planning to adopt his protégé Christian. His exotic life style is echoed in the game the children of the crew are playing, with cards representing various roles. The arrival of the heman Mark Spencer, the stuntman from London, brings up the language issue; there is a lot of English and Italian in the film, and translated dialogical exchanges abound, reflecting the international character of filmmaking. The film family is an international mini society, with social issues of responsibility, loyalty, work ethic, etc. Often the cast of this adult crew act much like the children in Truffaut's films of youth.

As the crew leave the hotel (move 'em out) for a day's shooting, Julie and Alphonse remain behind, framed by their bedroom windows, prefiguring their coming involvement and mirroring their exchange in *Paméla*. Heading for location, Ferrand drives his BMW 2002 convertible down the rue Jean Vigo, an homage to the director of *Zéro de conduite* whose first film was entitled *A Propos de Nice*, past numerous arrow-signs pointing the way to *Paméla*. In a mad scene of spontaneity, Joelle seduces Bernard, who has stopped to fix a flat tire for her, a scene which sets up the *coup de théâtre* when Liliane and Mark run off to London together. The melodrama of the frame film begins to overshadow the filming of *Paméla*, as Liliane says she is sick of Alphonse and his dependency. While they try in vain to assemble the complete cast and crew for a photo, Julie reveals to Alphonse that Liliane has left him and sets off the first stage of the final chain reaction.

The obsession with the impossible family motivates the cut to Ferrand's third dream sequence, which includes a cinema marquis, and the same boy with the cane (a secondary homage to Charlie Chaplin's ubiquitous prop). The cumulative flashback now continues, to show him taking the stills of *Citizen Kane* and running away, with, as Annette Insdorf observes, stolen films rather than stolen kisses. Back on the set, it seems as though Alphonse's love life is a failure in both films. The screening of new rushes elicits multiple responses from the cast and crew as spectators, generating a self-parody sequence.

At the hotel, Joelle, elegantly dressed for the evening, finds Alphonse pouting in his room and Bernard in bed with Odile. The spontaneous sexual involvements and numerous infidelities in the frame film not only offer reflections and variations of the primary actions of *Paméla*, but they mark *La Nuit américaine* as very much a product of an era, at the same time that they allude to sexual entanglements in classic French literature, also echoed in a film quoted by Joelle, *La Règle du jeu*.

At the dinner before her departure, Séverine tells the story of an Italian actor breaking character in the midst of Hamlet's soliloquy, a *mise-en-abyme* of her problems in the film, as the group invites a stranger to join them. Séverine waxes sentimental and nostalgic about the end of the film, when the group with all its love has to disband. As they are heading off to bed, Alphonse emerges at last from his room and asks for money to go to a brothel. Ferrand attempts to calm Alphonse, who is threatening to leave the film, saying that there is more harmony in films than life, that films keep going on, like trains, that the only sure happiness is in the work of creating films, which have no traffic jams, no dead spots, that they have their work to get them through the bad times in their lives. Alphonse has decided to walk off the film because he is too upset to work, indulging in real masochism, simultaneously loving and hating Liliane. Looking for magic, he thinks life is more important than the cinema, in contrast to Ferrand/Truffaut.

When the snooping camera voyeur invades Julie's room to find it empty, it becomes apparent that she has slept with Alphonse; *Paméla* has this time invaded the frame film. Joelle has been at the airport all night, retrieving the ball costumes which La Joie mistakenly sent back to Paris, obtaining the necessary masks for cinema to work its magic. Alphonse has decided to run away with Julie and calls her husband to confess their infidelity, thus mirroring the love triangle of *Paméla*. When Dr. Nelson calls her on the phone, Julie collapses with grief and guilt, then practically delirious asks for a bowl of country butter, which occasions a *supercherie*, as none can be found in Nice. In this surreal indulgent escapist ambiance, Alexandre tells of an Austrian actress who had a rainmaking machine installed at her Los Angeles home. Alphonse is finally located after a mad chase, at the go-cart track, working off steam, reverting to childhood, displaying the flip side of the Doinel persona, an egotistical, self-indulgent *enfant terrible*. Explaining to Ferrand that her husband left his wife of twenty years to marry her, a real-life *Paméla*, Julie has now decided to leave the acting profession and live a life of solitude to assuage her guilt over allowing her film crew life to invade her private life and marriage, lines Ferrand shamelessly borrows for his film.

In a sequence where the crew kills time by recording background effects of applause and conversation, Dr. Nelson reappears, meriting a freeze frame, to forgive and comfort Julie, as a healing father figure. Alphonse, dressed in his Romantic nineteenth-century costume for the *masque* in the film within the film, avows that he too is giving up filmmaking. Like Sartre's *adieu* to literature in *Les Mots*, this autobiographical self-reflexive film attempts to find its own metatextual closure. As events on the set have intruded into the fictional diegesis of his film, Ferrrand has rewritten the script accordingly. Accompanied by the ball theme song, in a lyric nineteenth-century candlelit setting, Julie and Pamela merge as heroines of the two films, as the husband and wife in *Paméla* have now slept together in the frame film, and they are using lines from their lives. Then the frame film overwhelms *Paméla* when it is announced that Alexandre has been killed in a car accident.

Ferrand's final voice-over recounts Alexandre's funeral and mourns the end of the star-system era of cinema, noting that Alexandre was killed by his generosity, another tribute to classic Hollywood films. The *Paméla* film must be further rewritten, to accommodate Alexandre's death. A double is found, as fake snow in the form of soapsuds is sprayed over the scene, and the final sequence is completed. The snow scene recalls numerous sweltering winter shots, but refers in an insider's allusion to the filming of Eisenstein's *Alexander Nevsky*. Alphonse has received an offer to play a role in a film in Japan mentioned earlier, the French first love of a Japanese girl, a literary adaptation which is a reverse echo of *Hiroshima mon amour* and an allusion to Doinel's affair with Kyoko in *Domicile conjugal*. Julie and her husband are leaving for a medical conference in Australia.

Like the postscripts added to recent docudramas, all the characters are accounted for: Alphonse is taking a vacation, Odile and another crew member are getting married. Walter the photographer is thanked and complimented. Ferrand and Alphonse are too upset about Alexandre's death to make any statement to the press, but Bernard is happy to oblige with some mindless verbiage. As the cast and crew split up to go their separate ways, the film production literally deconstructs itself. There are cameo inserts of the real cast in their various frame film roles, a gallery of portraits inserted in a long shot of the set, linking the layers of identity of the person, the professional, the performer, the mask. Apparently, on the set of *La Nuit américaine*, there were times when various aspects of making this film intruded and interacted with the film crew roles, when actors playing assistant cameramen or propmen actually worked in those capacities for the real life film crew, who after all were there unacknowledged throughout the film and who like Truffaut himself occasionally assumed roles on the set before the camera, thus creating a fourth line of demarcation between reality and illusion, adding a last level of irony to this Pirandellian creation.

Bibliography

Please see the *Vivement dimanche* chapter for the general Truffaut bibliography.

Card, James. "'More than Meets the Eye' in *Singin' in the Rain* and *Day for Night*." *Literature/Film Quarterly* 12:2 (1984) 87–95.

Crittenden, Roger. *La Nuit américaine (Day for Night)*. London, England: British Film Institute, 1998.

De Baecque, Antoine, and Toubiana, Serge. *François Truffaut*. Paris: Gallimard, 1996.

Douglass, Wayne. "Homage to Howard Hawks: François Truffaut's *Day for Night*." *Literature/Film Quarterly* 8:2 (1980) 71–77.

Gillain, Anne. *Le Cinéma selon François Truffaut*. Paris: Flammarion, 1988. 297–308.

———. *François Truffaut: Le Secret perdu*. Paris: Hatier, 1991.

Insdorf, Annette. *François Truffaut*. Boston: Twayne, 1978.

———. *François Truffaut*. New York: Simon & Schuster, 1989.

Klein, Michael. "*Day for Night*: A Truffaut Retrospective on Women and the Rhetoric of Film." *Film Heritage* 9:3 (1974) 21–26.

Maillet, Dominique. "Interview avec François Truffaut." *Cinématographe* 3 (1973) 14–18.

Truffaut, François. *Day for Night*. Translated by Sam Flores. New York: Grove Press, 1975.

———. *La Nuit américaine et le Journal de tournage de Fahrenheit 451*. Paris: Seghers, 1974.

Conclusion

The forty films studied in this volume represent sixty years of filmmaking in France, from Gance's 1927 *Napoléon* to Berri's 1986 *Jean de Florette* and *Manon des Sources*. It is worth noting that six of the French language films included here were made by foreign directors: Pontecorvo, Wajda, Scola, Ophuls, Schlöndorff, and Buñuel. Thus together they constitute a composite and cosmopolitan collage of images and ideologies, and range generically from onsite documentary footage of the ravages of war and the pathos of repatriation to transpositional adaptations of literary texts, oneiric fantasies of the imagination, and finally mirror images of the processes of filmmaking.

Although films as generically disparate as Resnais's documentary *Nuit et brouillard* and New Wave modernist *Hiroshima mon amour* both consist of a fiction film incorporating archival footage, and an interwoven virtuoso montage, and both treat the battle between memory and oblivion central to all filmmaking, as well as the frustration over the impossible distance from the past, they are separated by the disparity in their purpose, by their pact with the audience.

The true documentary film expresses an ideology, a morality, of authenticity, attempting to achieve cinematic transparency in its portrayal of real experience. However, since all cinematic images are illusory and the only true transparency is of the celluloid filmstock, all styles of filmmaking are vulnerable to exploitation and subversion, to political propagandizing, to artistic ludic manipulation in parody or pastiche. The examples of historic realism in this study demonstrate well the different perspectives and motives shaping the work of filmmakers like Vigne, Scola, Gance, Renoir, or Wadja, their portrayal of a distant diegesis. Their relationship to history is marked by the collective paradigm of their own era as well as their personal ideological constructs. Thus the historic film is always doubly so: window on the past, mirror of the moment of production. In the last analysis, all documentary and historic filmmaking is a framing, reordering and reproducing of reality that transforms and necessarily deforms it in the process.

Because the only true intertextual reality of a fictional creation is another fiction, film has pursued infinite transpositions of literary text to the screen. Film criticism has established hermeneutic equivalencies to literary theory in semiotics, narratology, historicism, deconstruction, cultural studies. Suffice it to say that the variables of restructuring text on film are nearly as endless as those of literary textual structure and function. I have offered a variety of textual genres and their film adaptations to illustrate the distinctions and challenges they pose, as cinematic versions create new genres, distorting and transforming the structures, functions and parameters of the literary text, just as they substitute complete closed images for the ambiguity of language and the open referentiality of the reader's imagination.

The illusion of historic or intertextual transparent referentiality is missing in modernist films, where self-reflexive and self-representational modes are foregrounded in Pirandellian games of reality and illusion. Time and space and causal chronology are acknowledged as illusory, as fragmented images and disjunctions of sound and image affirm the profound self-knowledge of New Wave filmmaking: the primary message of their cinema is in its ambiguity and abstraction, in the oneiric illusion of sound and light projected in the dark. An acknowledged relativism marks works of postmodern realism, reflecting the self-conscious disbelief of both *cinéaste* and spectator. After a century of filmmaking, the process itself of this collaborative art has been foregrounded once again, as it was in the beginning, not with the naive childlike fascination of the Lumière brothers or Méliès, but with a postmodern honesty of self-revelation and a desire to expose the techniques and artifices that have created so many convincing, even potentially destructive illusions of reality.

Questions of violence and audience response to controversial films depicting particular cultural dynamics leave filmmaking open to criticism, as viewers wonder whether the response-ability of the audience is the responsibility of the filmmaker, or if the director's right to express ideology through image is inalienable and a necessary freedom enabling artistic expression.

In recent Derridian studies deconstructing film writing, like earlier works positing a philosophy of language as an opaque system, analysts like Deleuze and Ropars-Wuilleumier have brought critical film theory to a level of detailed abstraction, redefining the constituent elements of film sound and image, movement and time, written and oral text, beyond semiotics and narratology. At this point, image and ideology constitute meaning, with in French the triple definition of *sens* as "meaning," "direction," and "feeling," emblematic not only of the existential process of being as becoming but, in the cinema, of the moving nature of film itself. Film cannot ever be completely objective or transparent, offer a univocal message, whatever the ambitions of the director. The metaphoric nature of images carries inevitably a secondary connotation, which can even overwhelm the primary level of meaning. The framing and fragmenting of experience in the process of filmmaking also create a necessary polysemic complexity, in a collaborative art which depicts above all the collective subconscious of a cultural heritage and its mythologies. The images of these ideologies await interpretation, decoding, by the spectator, student or critic, and integration into nascent ideologies forming in the context of their reception.

Bibliography

Film Theory

Allen, Richard. *Projecting Illusion: Film Spectatorship and the Impression of Reality.* Cambridge: Cambridge University Press, 1997.

Andrew Dudley. *Concepts in Film Theory.* New York: Oxford University Press, 1984.

————. "Historical Critique and History as Criticism." *Camera Obscura* 18 (September 1988) 127–135.

————. "The 'Three Ages' of Cinema Studies and the Age to Come." *PMLA* 115:3 (May 2000) 341–351.

Armes, Roy. *The Ambiguous Image: Narrative Style in Modern European Cinema.* Bloomington: Indiana University Press, 1976.

————. *Film and Reality: An Historical Survey.* Harmondsworth: Penguin, 1974.

Augst, Bertrand. "The Order of (Cinematographic) Discourse." *Discourse* 1 (Fall 1979) 39–57.

Aumont, Jacques. *L'Oeil interminable: cinéma et peinture.* Paris: Seguier, 1989.

————, and Michel Marie. *L'Analyse des films.* Paris: Nathan, 1988.

————, Alain Bergala, Michel Marie, and Marc Vernet. *L'Esthétique du film.* Paris: Nathan, 1983.

Baudrillard, Jean. *The Evil Demon of Images.* Sydney: Power Institute Publications, 1988.

Baudry, Jean-Louis. *L'Effet cinéma.* Paris: Albatros, 1978.

Beja, Maurice. *Film and Literature.* New York: Longman, 1979.

Bellour, Raymond. *L'Analyse du film.* Paris: Albatros, 1979.

Bergala, Alain. *Initiation à la sémiologie du récit en images.* Paris: Les Cahiers de L'Audio-Visuel, 1979.

Birò, Yvette. *Profane Mythology.* Bloomington: Indiana University Press, 1982.

Blanchard, Gérard. *Images de la musique au cinéma.* Paris: Edilig, 1984.

Bonitzer, Pascal. *Le Champ aveugle: essais sur le cinéma.* Paris: Gallimard, 1982.

Booth, Wayne. "Is There an 'Implied' Author in Every Film?" *College Literature* 29:2 (Spring 2002) 124–131.

Bordwell, David. *Film Art: An Introduction.* New York: Knopf, 1986.

————. *Making Meaning: Inference and Rhetoric in the Interpretation of Cinema.* Cambridge: Harvard University Press, 1989.

————. *Narration in the Fiction Film.* Madison: University of Wisconsin Press, 1989.

————, and Noel Carroll, eds. *Post-Theory: Reconstructing Film Studies*. Madison: University of Wisconsin Press, 1996.

Boyd, David. *Film and the Interpretive Process*. New York: Peter Lang, 1989.

Branigan, Edward. *Point of View in the Cinema: A Theory of Narration and Subjectivity in Classical Film*. New York: Mouton, 1984.

Braudy, Leo. *The Spoken Seen: Film and the Romantic Imagination*. Baltimore: Johns Hopkins University Press, 1975.

————. *The World in a Frame*. Garden City: Anchor Doubleday, 1977.

————, and Marshall Cohen, eds. *Film Theory and Criticism: Introductory Readings*. New York: Oxford University Press, 1999.

Browne, Nick. *The Rhetoric of Filmic Narration*. Ann Arbor: UMI Research Press, 1982.

————. *"Cahiers du Cinéma 1969–1972: The Politics of Representation."*

Brunette, Peter. "Toward a Deconstructive Theory of Film." *Studies in the Literary Imagination* 19:1 (Spring 1986) 55–71.

————, and David Wills. *Screen/Play: Derrida and Film Theory*. Princeton: Princeton University Press, 1989.

Burch, Noël. *Theory of Film Practice*. Princeton: Princeton University Press, 1981.

Bywater, Tim, and Thomas Sobchack. *An Introduction to Film Criticism: Major Critical Approaches to Narrative Film*. New York: Longman, 1989.

Cadbury, William. *Film Criticism: A Counter Theory*. Ames: Iowa State University Press, 1982.

Cardullo, Bert. *Indelible Images: New Perspectives on Classic Films*. Lanham, MD: University Press of America, 1987.

Carroll, Noel. *Mystifying Movies: Fads & Fallacies in Contemporary Film Theory*. New York: Columbia University Press, 1988.

————. *Theorizing the Moving Image*. Cambridge: Cambridge University Press, 1996.

Casetti, Francesco. *D'un regard l'autre: le film et son spectateur*. Lyon: Presses Universitaires de Lyon, 1990.

Cavell, Stanley. *The World Viewed: Reflections on the Ontology of Film*. Cambridge: Harvard University Press, 1979.

Chatman, Seymour. *Story and Discourse: Narrative Structure in Fiction and Film*. Ithaca: Cornell University Press, 1978.

————. "What Novels Can Do that Films Can't (and Vice Versa)." *Critical Inquiry* 7 (1980) 120–130.

Chion, Michel. *La Parole au cinéma: La Toile trouée*. Paris: Editions de L'Etoile, 1988.

————. *Le Son au cinéma*. Paris: Editions de L'Etoile, 1985.

————. *La Voix au cinéma*. Paris: Editions de L'Etoile, 1982.

Cohen, Keith. *Film and Fiction*. New Haven: Yale University Press, 1979.

Conley, Tom. *Film Hieroglyphs: Ruptures in Classical Cinema*. Minneapolis: University of Minnesota Press, 1991.

Costanzo, William. *Reading the Movies: Twelve Great Films on Video and How to Teach Them*. Urbana: National Council of Teachers of English, 1992.

Cozyris, George A. *Christian Metz and the Reality of Film*. New York: Arno Press, 1980.

Deivert, Bruce. "Shots in Cyberspace: Film Research on the Internet." *Cinema Journal* 35:1 (Fall 1995) 103–124.

Deleuze, Gilles. *Cinéma 1. L'Image-Mouvement*. Paris: Editions de Minuit, 1983.

————. *Cinéma 2. L'Image-Temps*. Paris: Editions de Minuit, 1985.

Devereaux, Leslie, and Roger Hillman, eds. *Fields of Vision: Essays in Film Studies, Visual Anthropology, and Photography*. Berkeley: University of California Press, 1995.

Durgnat, Raymond. *Eros in the Cinema*. London: Calder & Boyars, 1966.

Eberwein, Robert. *A Viewer's Guide to Film Theory and Criticism*. Metuchen, NJ: Scarecrow Press, 1979.

Ellis, John. *Visible Fictions: Cinema: Televison: Video*. Boston: Routledge & Kegan Paul, 1982.

Estève, Michel. *Cinéma et condition humaine*. Paris: Editions Albatros, 1978.

Fischer, Lucy. *Shot/Countershot: Film Tradition and Women's Cinema*. Princeton: Princeton University Press, 1989.

Focillon, Henri. *The Life of Forms in Art*. New York: Wittenborn, Schultz, 1948.

Frick, Thomas. "Ghost Texts: Film about Writing/Writing About Film." *The Kenyon Review* 4:4 (Fall 1982) 99–112.

Galloway, Alex and Jason Middleton, eds. *Film Studies and Postmodern Theory*. *Polygraph* 13 (2001).

Gaudreault, André, and François Jost. *Le Récit cinématographique*. Paris: Nathan-Université, 1990.

Gauthier, Guy. *Initiation à la sémiologie de l'image*. Paris: Cahiers de L'Audio-Visuel, 1979.

————. *Vingt leçons sur l'image et le sens*. Paris: Edilig, 1982.

Gentile, Mary. *Film Feminisms: Theory and Practice*. Westport, CT: Greenwood Press, 1985.

Gledhill, Chistine and Linda Williams, eds. *Reinventing Film Studies*. New York: Oxford University Press, 2001.

Grant, Barry. *Film Genre: Theory and Criticism*. Metuchen: Scarecrow Press, 1977.

————, ed. *Film Genre Reader*. Austin: University of Texas Press, 1986.

Gunning, Tom. "Film History and Film Analysis: The Individual Film in the Course of Time." *Wide Angle* 12:3 (July 1990) 4–19.

Heath, Stephen. *Questions of Cinema*. Bloomington: Indiana University Press, 1986.

Hebdige, Dick. *Hiding in the Light: On Images and Things*. London: Routledge, 1989.

Hedges, Inez. *Breaking the Frame: Film Language and the Experience of Limits*. Bloomington: Indiana University Press, 1991.

Henderson, Brian. *A Critique of Film Theory*. New York: Dutton, 1980.

Higson, Andrew, and Richard Maltby, eds. *"Film Europe" and "Film America":*

Cinema, Commerce and Cultural Exchange 1920-1939. Exeter: University of Exeter Press, 1999.

Hill, Gibson, Dyer, Kaplan, and Willemen, eds. *The Oxford Guide to Film Studies.* New York: Oxford University Press, 1998.

Houston, Beverle, and Marsha Kinder. *Self and Cinema.* Pleasantville, N.Y.: Redgrave Publishing Company, 1980.

Hurt, James, ed. *Focus on Film and Theater.* Englewood Cliffs, N.J.: Prentice Hall, 1974.

Ishaghpour, Youssef. *Cinéma contemporain: de ce côté du miroir.* Paris: Editions de la Différence, 1986.

Jameson, Fredric. "On Magic Realism in Film." *Critical Inquiry* 12 (Winter 1986) 301–325.

————. *Signatures of the Visible.* New York: Routledge, 1990.

Jarvie, I. C. *Philosophy of the Film: Epistemology, Ontology, Aesthetics.* New York: Routledge & Kegan Paul, 1987.

Jost, François. *Cinéma de la modernité: films, théories.* Paris: Klincksieck, 1982.

————. *L'Oeil-caméra: entre film et roman.* Lyon: Presses Universitaires de Lyon, 1987.

Klinge, Peter and Sandra. *Evolution of Film Styles.* Lanham, MD: University Press of America, 1983.

Kavanagh, Thomas P., ed. *The Limits of Theory.* Stanford: Stanford University Press, 1989.

Kolker, Robert P. *The Altering Eye: Contemporary International Cinema.* New York: Oxford University Press, 1983.

Lagny, Michèle; Ropars, Marie-Claire; and Sorlin, Pierre, eds. *Esthétique plurielle.* Saint-Denis: Presses Universitaires de Vincennes, 1996.

————. *Hors Cadre* 7 (Winter 1988-1989) Entire issue.

————. *Hors Cadre* 8 (Spring 1990) Entire issue.

Lauretis, Teresa de. *Alice Doesn't: Feminism, Semiotics, Cinema.* Bloomington: Indiana University Press, 1984.

Leutrat, Jean-Louis. *Kaléidoscope: analyses de films.* Lyons: Presses Universitaires de Lyon, 1988.

Lev, Peter. *The Euro-American Cinema.* Austin: University of Texas Press, 1993.

Lotman, Jurij. *Semiotics of Cinema.* Ann Arbor: University of Michigan Press, 1976.

Lyon, Christopher, ed. *Directors/Filmmakers. The International Dictionary of Films and Filmmakers,* Vol. II. New York: Macmillan, 1984.

Maillot, Pierre. *L'Ecriture cinématographique.* Paris: Méridiens Klincksieck, 1989.

Marie, Michel, and Marc Vernet, eds. *Christian Metz et la théorie du cinéma.* Paris: Méridiens Klincksieck, 1990.

Mast, Gerald, and Marshall Cohen. *Film Theory and Criticism: Introductory Readings.* New York: Oxford University Press, 1985.

Matich, Rosemary I. *Functional Criticism: Cinematic Space/Time Theory and Phenomenology.* Dissertation Abstracts International 51:1 (July 1990) 11A.

Metz, Christian. *Film Language: A Semiotics of the Cinema*. New York: Oxford University Press, 1974.

———. *Language and the Cinema*. The Hague: Mouton, 1974.

———. *The Imaginary Signifier*. Bloomington: Indiana University Press, 1982.

Mitry, Jean. *La Sémiologie en question*. Paris: Editions du Cerf, 1987.

Monaco, Paul. *Ribbons in Time: Movies and Society since 1945*. Bloomington: Indiana University Press, 1987.

Neale, Steve. *Cinema and Technology: Image, Sound, Colour*. Bloomington: Indiana University Press, 1985.

———. *Genre*. New York: Zoetrope, 1980.

Nichols, Bill. *Ideology and the Image*. Bloomington: Indiana University Press, 1981.

———, ed. *Movies and Methods*. Berkeley: University of California Press, 1976.

———, ed. *Movies and Methods* II. Berkeley: University of California Press, 1985.

———. *Representing Reality*. Bloomington: Indiana University Press, 1991.

O'Connor, John. *Image as Artifact*. Malabar, FL: Krieger Publishing, 1990.

Oumano, Ellen. *Film Forum*. New York: St. Martin's Press, 1985.

Palmer, R. Barton, ed. *The Cinematic Text: Methods and Approaches*. New York: AMS, 1989.

Pelletier, François. *Imaginaires du cinématographe*. Paris: Librairie des Méridiens, 1983.

Peterson, Sidney. *The Dark of the Screen*. New York: Anthology Film Archives: New York University Press, 1980.

Philippe, Jean-Claude. *Le Roman du cinéma, I: 1928–1938*. Paris: Fayard, 1985.

Polan, Dana. *The Political Language of Film and the Avant-Garde*. Ann Arbor: UMI Research Press, 1985.

Richardson, Robert. *Literature and Film*. Bloomington: Garland Publishing, 1969.

Rodowick, David. *The Crisis of Political Modernism: Criticism and Ideology on Contemporary Film Theory*. Urbana: University of Illinois Press, 1988.

———. *The Difficulty of Difference: Psychoanalysis, Sexual Difference, and Film Theory*. New York: Routledge, 1991.

Ropars-Wuilleumier, Marie-Claire. *De la Littérature au cinéma*. Paris: Armand Colin, 1970.

———. *L'Ecran de la mémoire*. Paris: Seuil, 1970.

———. *Ecraniques: le film du texte*. Lille: Presses Universitaires de Lille, 1990.

———. *L'Idée d'image*. Paris: Presses Universitaires de Vincennes, 1995.

———. *Le Texte divisé*. Paris: Presses Universitaires de France, 1981.

———, and Dana Polan. "The Cinema, Reader of Gilles Deleuze." *Camera Obscura* 18 (September 1988) 120–126. Reprinted in Boundas and Olkowski, *Gilles Deleuze and the Theater of Philosophy*. New York: Routledge, 1994.

———, and Pierre Sorlin, eds. *Art(s) et fiction*. Saint-Denis: Presses Universitaires de Vincennes, 1997.

Ross, Harris. *Film as Literature: Literature as Film*. New York: Greenwood Press, 1987.

Rothman, William. *Documentary Film Classics*. Cambridge: Cambridge University Press, 1997.

Salvaggio, Jerry L. *A Theory of Film Language*. New York: Arno Press, 1980.

Schefer, Jean-Louis. *L'Homme ordinaire du cinéma*. Paris: Gallimard, 1980.

————. *Scénographie d'un tableau*. Paris: Seuil, 1969.

Short, K.L.M., ed. *Feature Films as History*. London: Helm, 1981.

Siska, William Charles. *Modernism in the Narrative Cinema: The Art Film as a Genre*. New York: Arno Press, 1980.

Slater, Thomas J. "Considering the Active Viewer: The Basis for Seeing Film's Liberating Impact on Language." *Style* 23:4 (Winter 1989) 545–565.

Sloan, Kay. *The Loud Silents: Origins of the Social Problem Film*. Urbana: University of Illinois Press, 1988.

Sorlin, Pierre. *European Cinemas, European Societies, 1939–1990*. London: Routledge, 1991.

————. *The Film in History*. Oxford: Blackwell, 1980.

Snyder, Stephen. *The Transparent I: Self/Subject in European Cinema*. New York: Peter Lang, 1994.

Stam, Robert. *Reflexivity in Film and Literature: From Don Quixote to Jean-Luc Godard*. New York: Columbia University Press, 1992.

Tinkcom, Matthew, and Amy Villarejo, eds. *Keyframes: Popular Cinema and Cultural Studies*. London: Routledge, 2001.

Turim, Maureen. *Abstraction in Avant-Garde Cinema*. Ann Arbor: UMI Research Press, 1985.

————. *Flashbacks in Films: Memory and History*. New York: Routledge, 1989.

Virilio, Paul. *Guerre et cinéma* I: *logistique de la perception*. Paris: Editions de L'Etoile, 1984.

Weiss, Allen S. *Subject Construction and Spectatorial Identification: A Revision of Contemporary Film Theory*. Dissertation Abstracts International 51:2 (August 1990) 321A.

Wilson, George M. *Narration in Light: Studies in Cinematic Point of View*. Baltimore: Johns Hopkins University Press, 1988.

Winston, Douglas. *The Screenplay as Literature*. Rutherford: Fairleigh Dickinson University Press, 1973.

Wollen, Peter. *Signs and Meaning in the Cinema*. Bloomington: Indiana University Press, 1973.

Wyver, John. *The Moving Image: An International History of Film, Television and Video*. New York: Blackwell, 1989.

French Film

Abel, Richard. *French Cinema: The First Wave, 1915–1929*. Princeton: Princeton University Press, 1984.

———. *French Film Theory and Criticism: A History/Anthology 1907–1939*. Princeton: Princeton University Press, 1988.

Agel, Henri. *Miroirs de l'insolite dans le cinéma français*. Paris: Editions du Cerf, 1958.

Andrew, Dudley. *André Bazin*. New York: Columbia University Press, 1978.

Armes, Roy. *French Cinema*. New York: Oxford University Press, 1985.

Bandy, Mary Lea, ed. *Rediscovering French Film*. New York: Museum of Modern Art, and Boston: Little, Brown, 1983.

Bazin, André. *Le Cinéma français de la libération à la Nouvelle Vague (1945–1958)*. Paris: Editions de L'Etoile, 1983.

———. *Qu'est-ce que le cinéma?* I, II, III. Paris: Editions du Cerf, 1958–1962.

———. *What is Cinema?* Berkeley: University of California Press, 1967.

Bordwell, David. *French Impressionist Cinema: Film Culture, Film Theory, and Film Style*. New York: Arno Press, 1980.

Buache, Freddy. *Le Cinéma français des années 60*. Paris: Hatier, 1987.

———. *Le Cinéma français des années 70*. Paris: Hatier, 1990.

Buss, Robin. *The French Through Their Films*. New York: Ungar, 1988.

Daniel, Joseph. *Guerre et cinéma: grandes illusions et petits soldats, 1895–1971*. Paris: A. Colin, 1972.

Douin, Jean-Luc, ed. *La Nouvelle Vague 25 ans après*. Paris: Editions du Cerf, 1983.

Ehrlich, Evelyn. *Cinema of Paradox: French Filmmaking Under the German Occupation*. New York: Columbia University Press, 1985.

Faulkner, Christopher. "Teaching French National Cinema." *Cinema Journal* 38:4 (Summer 1999) 102-108.

Flitterman-Lewis, Sandy. *To Desire Differently: Feminism and the French Cinema*. Urbana: University of Illinois Press, 1990.

Forbes, Jill, and Michael Kelly, eds. *French Cultural Studies: An Introduction*. New York: Oxford University Press, 1995.

Garrity, Henry. *Film in the French Classroom*. Cambridge, MA: Polyglot Productions, 1987.

Harvey, Sylvia. *May '68 and Film Culture*. London: British Film Institute, 1980.

Hayward, Susan and Ginette Vincendeau, eds. *French Film: Texts and Contexts*. New York: Routledge, 2000.

Hedges, Inez. "Form and Meaning in French Film, I: Time and Space," *French Review* 54:1 (1980) 27–36.

———. "Form and Meaning in French Film, II: Point of View," *French Review* 54:2 (1980) 288–298.

————. "Form and Meaning in French Film, III: Identification," *French Review* 56:2 (1982) 207–217.

————. "Form and Meaning in French Film, IV: Language." *French Review* 58:2 (1984) 223–235.

Hillier, Jim, ed. *Cahiers du cinéma: New Wave, New Cinema, Reevaluating Hollywood.* Cambridge: Harvard University Press, 1986.

Issari, Mohammad Ali, and Doris Paul. *What is Cinéma Vérité?* Metuchen: Scarecrow Press, 1979.

Jeancolas, Jean-Pierre. *15 Ans d'années trente.* Paris: Stock Cinéma, 1983.

Jeanne, René, and Charles Ford. *Histoire encyclopédique du cinéma,* Vols. I, IV, V. Paris: Laffont, SEDE, 1947–1962.

Kline, T. Jefferson. *Screening the Text: Intertextuality in New Wave French Cinema.* Baltimore: Johns Hopkins University Press, 1992.

Lagny, Michèle, Marie-Claire Ropars, and Pierre Sorlin. *Générique des années trente.* Saint-Denis: Presses Universitaires de Vincennes, 1986.

Lherminier, Pierre. *Cinéma pleine page.* Paris: Lherminier, 1985.

Lowry, Edward. *The Filmology Movement and Film Study in France.* Ann Arbor: UMI Research Press, 1985.

Mesnil, Michel (Maurice Mourier). *Le Parfum de la salle en noir.* Paris: Presses Universitaires de France, 1985.

Michalczyk, John J. *The French Literary Filmmakers.* Cranbury, N.J.: Associated University Presses, 1980.

Monaco, Paul. *Cinema & Society: France and Germany during the Twenties.* New York: Elsevier, 1976.

Passek, Jean-Loup, ed. *Dictionnaire du cinéma français.* Paris: Larousse, 1987.

————. *D'un cinéma l'autre: notes sur le cinéma français des années cinquante.* Paris: Centre Georges Pompidou, 1988.

Pinsker, Sanford and Jack Fischel. *Literature, the Arts, and the Holocaust.* Greenwood, FL: Penkeville Press, 1987.

Prédal, René. *Le Cinéma français contemporain.* Paris: Editions du Cerf, 1984.

Radcliff-Umstead, Douglas. *National Traditions in Motion Pictures.* Kent, OH: Kent State University, 1985.

Reader, Keith. *Cultures on Celluloid.* New York: Quartet Books, 1981.

————, and Ginette Vincendeau. *La Vie est à nous: French Cinema of the Popular Front, 1935–1938.* London: British Film Institute, 1986.

————, ed. "100 Years of French Cinema." *French Cultural Studies* 7:3:21 (Oct 1996) entire issue.

Roud, Richard. *A Passion for Films: Henri Langlois and the Cinémathèque française.* New York: Viking Press, 1983.

Rouyer, Philippe. *Initiation au cinéma.* Paris: Edilig, 1990.

Russell, Sharon. *Semiotics and Lighting: a Study of Six Modern French Cameramen.* Ann Arbor: UMI Research Press, 1981.

Sadoul, Georges. *Le Cinéma français.* Paris: Flammarion, 1962.

————. *Dictionary of Films*. Berkeley: University of California Press, 1972.

Spiegel, Alan. *Fiction and the Camera Eye: Visual Consciousness in Film and the Modern Novel*. Charlottesville: University Press of Virginia, 1976.

Schwartzwald, Robert. "Passages/Home: Paris as Crossroads." *Esprit Créateur* 41:3 (Fall 2001) 172–190.

Thiher, Allen. *The Cinematic Muse: Critical Studies in the History of French Cinema*. Columbia: University of Missouri Press, 1979.

Torok, Jean-Paul. *Le Ciné-roman: un genre nouveau*. Paris: Edilig.

————. *Le Scénario: histoire, théorie, pratique*. Paris: Editions Henri Veyrier, 1988.

Virmaux, Alain and Odette. *Les Surréalistes et le cinéma*. Paris: Seghers, 1976.

Williams, Alan Larson. *Republic of Images: A History of French Filmmaking*. Cambridge: Harvard University Press, 1992.

Zimmer, Christian. *Cinéma et politique*. Paris: Seghers, 1974.

————. *Le Retour de la fiction*. Paris: Editions du Cerf, 1984.

Appendix:
Film Journals

Afterimage
American Film
Apertures
L'Avant-Scène Cinéma
Ça Cinéma
Les Cahiers de la Cinémathèque
Les Cahiers du Cinéma
Camera Obscura
CICIM (Centre d'Information Cinématographique de l'Institut Français de Munich)
Cinéaste
Ciné-Critique
Cinéma
Cinéma d'Aujourd'hui
Cinéma de France
Cinema Journal
Cinéma Politique
Cinéma '83
CinémAction
Cinématographe
Cinémonde
Cinéthique
Cinétracts
L'Ecran Fantastique
Etudes Cinématographiques
Film Comment
Film Criticism
Film Quarterly
Films and Filming
Films in Review
Framework
French Cultural Studies
The French Review
French Studies

Grand Angle
Hors Cadre
Hudson Review
Image et son
Iris
Journal of Film Studies
Journal of Popular Film and Television
Libération
Literature and Film
Literature/Film Quarterly
The Monthly Film Bulletin
Mosaic
New Orleans Review
October
PMLA
Positif
Post-Script
Première
Quarterly Review of Film Studies / of Film and Video
Revue Belge du Cinéma
La Revue du Cinéma/Image et Son/Ecran
Screen
Sound and Light
Télé-Ciné-Vidéo
Variety
Vertigo
Visions
West Virginia University Philological Papers
Wide Angle

Appendix:
Literature/Film and Film Conferences

Kent State University Annual Conference on Film

Literature/Film Association Annual Conferences

Ohio University Film Conference

Purdue University Conference

Screen Studies Conference

Society For Cinema Studies Conference

Tallahassee Comparative Literature & Film Conference

West Virginia Annual Colloquium On Literature & Film

Note: Many additional French conferences have film sessions. These include:

American Association of Teachers of French Conferences

Modern Language Association Conferences

Nineteenth-Century French Studies Conference

Twentieth-Century French Studies Conference

Appendix:
Glossary of Film Terminology

French-English

une animation	a cartoon, an animated film
un appareil photographique	a camera
en arrière plan	in the background
auteur, caméra-stylo, ciné-roman	dominant style of director/scriptwriter
la bande sonore	the soundtrack
une caméra	a movie camera
un cadreur, une cadreuse	a cameraperson who frames
le caractère	a person's character
un cascadeur	a stuntman, stuntwoman
un/une cinéaste	a filmmaker, director
le cinéma muet	silent movies (1895)
le cinématographe	full name formerly of le cinéma
la cinématographie	cinematography
un comédien, une comédienne	an actor/actress
les costumes	costumes
en couleur	color
un court-métrage	a short
le décor	the set
le dénouement	the ending
au deuxième plan	in the middle ground
(un) documentaire	documentary
l'écran	the screen
un élément à échelle réduite	miniature element
un élément grandeur nature	life-size element
l'équipe	the crew
les extérieurs	outdoor shots
faire passer/présenter un film	to show it
le film	the movie
film noir	expressionistic high-contrast thriller
les films sonores	sound movies (1927)

un flash-back	scene out of chronology
flou(e)	out of focus
un fondu	fade out/in (dissolve)
la fréquentation	attendance
le générique	the credits
un gros plan	a close-up
la grue	the camera boom
interpréter, jouer	to play a role, a part
les interprètes	the actors and actresses
un long-métrage	a feature-length film
la lumière	light
le maquillage	makeup
le metteur-en-scène	set director
la mise au point	focus (precise)
la mise-en-scène	the staging, sets
le montage	editing
montage entrecoupé, rapide	crosscutting, montage
un moyen-métrage	a medium-length film
la narration, le récit	the storyline
le noir	the dark
en noir et blanc	black and white
un objectif	a lens
l'ombre	shadow
un opérateur, une opératrice	a cameraperson who films
une optique	a point of view
la pellicule	the film (celluloid)
un personnage	a character (fictional)
le personnel	the cast
un/une photographe	cinematographer
sur place	on location
un plan	a shot, coherent ensemble of visual images
un plan américain	three-quarter figures
un plan général	a long shot, landscape
un plan moyen	a medium-length shot
un plan panoramique	a pan
un plan rapproché	a detail shot
en plein air	outdoors
de premier ordre	first run
au premier plan	in the foreground
principal	primary, leading
la production	the backers (financial)
le projecteur	the projector

la projection	the projection
un réalisateur, une réalisatrice	a director
le rôle	the part
les salles de cinéma	movie theaters
le scénariste	the scriptwriter
le scénario	the script
la séance	the show (time)
secondaire	small, bit
une séquence	a series of shots, a coherent visual or narrative unit, a cinematic or syntactic entity
une société de production	a movie company
le son	sound (noun)
sonore	sound (adjective)
les sous-titres	the subtitles
le spectacle	the show
en studio	soundstage shots
un studio	a studio, a studio set
la (post)synchronisation	dubbing
un téléobjectif	a telephoto lens
un tour de manivelle	a crank of the camera
le tournage	the making of a movie
tourner un film	to make a movie
un (chariot de) travelling	a moving camera (travelling shot)
le truquage/trucage	special effects
une vedette	a star
une voix off	voice-over narration
une vue	a frame
un zoom	a change of framing distance

English-French

an actor/actress	un comédien, une comédienne
the actors and actresses	les interprètes
attendance	la fréquentation
the backers (financial)	la production
in the background	en arrière plan
black and white	en noir et blanc
a camera	un appareil photographique
a cameraperson who films	un opérateur, une opératrice
a cameraperson who frames	un cadreur, une cadreuse
the camera boom	la grue

a cartoon, an animated film	une animation
the cast	le personnel
a change of framing distance	un zoom
a character (fictional)	un personnage
the cinema	le cinéma(tographe)
cinematographer	un/une photographe
cinematography	la cinématographie
a close-up	un gros plan
color	en couleur
costumes	les costumes
a crank of the camera	un tour de manivelle
the credits	le générique
the crew	l'équipe
crosscutting, montage	montage entrecoupé, rapide
the dark	le noir
a detail shot	un plan rapproché
a director	un réalisateur, une réalisatrice
documentary	(un) documentaire
dubbing	la (post)synchronisation
editing	le montage
the ending	le dénouement
expressionistic high-contrast thriller	film noir
fade out/in (dissolve)	un fondu
a feature-length film	un long-métrage
the film (celluloid)	la pellicule
a filmmaker, director	un/une cinéaste
first run	de premier ordre
a flashback (scene from the past)	un flash-back
focus (precise)	la mise au point
in the foreground	au premier plan
a frame	une vue
a lens	un objectif
life-size element	un élément grandeur nature
light	la lumière
on location	sur place
a long shot, landscape	un plan général
makeup	le maquillage
to make a movie	tourner un film
the making of a movie	le tournage
a medium-length film	un moyen métrage
a medium length shot	un plan moyen
in the middle ground	au deuxième plan

miniature element	un élément à échelle réduite
the movie	le film
a movie camera	une caméra
a movie company	une société de production
movie theaters	les salles de cinéma
a moving camera (travelling shot)	un (chariot de) travelling
out of focus	flou(e)
outdoors	en plein air
outdoor shots	les extérieurs
a pan	un plan panoramique
the part	le rôle
a person's character	le caractère
to play a role, a part	interpréter, jouer
a point of view	une optique
primary, leading (role)	principal
the projection	la projection
the projector	le projecteur
the screen	l'écran
the script	le scénario
the scriptwriter	le scénariste
a sequence series of shots, narrative entity	une séquence
the set	le décor
the set director	le metteur-en-scène
shadow	l'ombre
a short	un court-métrage
a shot (ensemble of visual images)	un plan
the show	le spectacle
the show (time)	la séance
to show a film	faire passer/présenter un film
silent movies (1895)	le cinéma muet
small, bit part	rôle secondaire
sound (adjective)	sonore
sound (noun)	le son
sound movies (1927)	les films sonores
soundstage shots	en studio
the soundtrack	la bande sonore
special effects	le truquage/trucage
the staging, sets	la mise-en-scène
a star	une vedette
the storyline	la narration, le récit
a studio, a studio set	un studio
a stuntman/woman	un cascadeur

the subtitles	les sous-titres
a telephoto lens	un téléobjectif
three-quarter figures	un plan américain
dominant style of director/scriptwriter	auteur, caméra-stylo, ciné-roman
voice-over narration	une voix off